CHRYSLER

Chrysler

THE LIFE *and* TIMES
of an AUTOMOTIVE GENIUS

Vincent Curcio

OXFORD
UNIVERSITY PRESS
2000

OXFORD

UNIVERSITY PRESS

Oxford   New York

Athens   Auckland   Bangkok   Bogotá   Buenos Aires   Calcutta
Cape Town   Chennai   Dar es Salaam   Delhi   Florence   Hong Kong   Istanbul
Karachi   Kuala Lumpur   Madrid   Melbourne   Mexico City   Mumbai
Nairobi   Paris   São Paulo   Singapore   Taipei   Tokyo   Toronto   Warsaw

and associated companies in
Berlin   Ibadan

Copyright © 2000 by Vincent Curcio

Published by Oxford University Press, Inc.
198 Madison Avenue, New York, New York 10016

Oxford is a registered trademark of Oxford University Press

Library of Congress Cataloging-in-Publication Data
Curcio, Vincent
Chrysler: the life and times of an automotive genius / Vincent Curcio.
p.   cm.   Includes biographical references and index.
ISBN 0-19-507896-9
1. Chrysler, Walter P. (Walter Percy), 1909–   2. Chrysler Corporation—History.
3. Automobile industry and trade—United States—History.
I. Title: Life and times of an automotive genius.
II. Title.
HD9710.U52   C453   2000
338.7'6292'092—dc21   [B]   00-021335

Book design by Adam B. Bohannon

2 4 6 8 9 7 5 3 1
Printed in the United States of America
on acid-free paper

This book is dedicated to

Pierre Sorlin

Who encouraged me to write a book
of larger social scope and deeper background
than I had previously attempted

Contents

Preface

Walter Chrysler lived three lives: mechanical master of the railroads, automobile manufacturer, and tycoon. Although he built a world-famous skyscraper at the height of Manhattan's ascent to the pinnacle of world power, he was born in the shadow of the Cheyenne and Lakota, and the raids of Dull Knife on the Kansas prairie. He mastered the rail industry just as it was reaching its zenith as America's premier mode of transport. However, such was the pace of change during his lifetime, from 1875 to 1940, that he also had the opportunity to move into the automobile business as it began its rise to a position of dominance in American transportation. The chance came to him after years on the railroads, where he learned to make the nuts and bolts of mechanical engineering race along his pulses. When the automobile came into his line of vision, he climbed aboard without hesitation and rode it to glory as far as any man of his time. But this self-educated working man, the son of an immigrant, not only succeeded at creating enormous projects in his lifetime, he also understood the future implications of such achievements.

Locomotion was his enterprise. Like Henry Ford, he improved its forms and means of production at a pace so rapid that as a direct result new conditions of social intercourse, with their attendant blandishments and problems, were being created faster than most people could comprehend them. He saw this situation as an opportunity deserving of all one's energy and intelligence. Meet the challenge, he believed, and both individuals and society in general could not fail to progress. Fail to meet it and, as he discovered, the world would leave itself open to all manner of social ills. His triumph was that in good times and bad he was to show himself a victor in almost any struggle that life and time put forth.

This book is the story of how Walter P. Chrysler accomplished so much in the span of sixty-five years.

Introduction

History is what survives. Memories and documents, buildings and roads, images and ceremonies, artifacts, tree rings, furniture, clothes, corpses, and fossils—all are caught in a web of meaning and interpretation, which is our understanding of the past. But much of that understanding contains great gaps because of the inadequacy or disappearance of these raw materials of history. And so, much of what we think of as history is a matter of educated assumption at best; at worst, wild surmise. A dedicated biographer tries with all his strength to achieve the first and avoid, even abjure, the second, in hopes of writing a real approximation of his subject's true life.

Sixty years ago Walter P. Chrysler was considered by many to be among the most admired and respected business executives in America, second only to Henry Ford. But Chrysler's personal traces, unlike Ford's, are few, and amazingly fragile.

In Ellis, Kansas, a woman named Anne Hedge ran the Chrysler Boyhood Home Museum for many years, succeeding Kitty Dale, its first curator. With little money, but boundless civic pride in Walter Chrysler's life there, she kept track of his family's things, and all the local stories about them, and knew where local records could be found. Many in the town of Ellis care about him, but in the end that one committed eighty-year-old lady on the western plains of Kansas made an enormous difference to the preservation of his story.

In Trinidad, Colorado, Judge Dean C. Mabry, a hearty western man of parts if ever there was one, turned out to be that special person who mattered. He loved his town, he loved the railroads that ran through it every which way to the four points of the compass, and in a very warm and personal way he loved the fact that Walter Chrysler lived an important part of his life in Trinidad and never forgot it. A big man with superb carriage, silver-white hair, and merry blue eyes, Judge Mabry strode through town in his white Stetson, white suit, and polished brown boots pointing out every spot that had anything to do with Chrysler and often conjuring up the past with vivid word pictures if the land had been altered or buildings destroyed. Many people in Trinidad cared about Walter Chrysler too, but most were either dead or had moved away. Judge Mabry was just one man, but without him much would be lost, buried, or unrecoverable.

In Chestertown, Maryland, there was Chrysler's great-grandson, Frank B. Rhodes, Jr., grandson of Bernice Chrysler Garbisch and the family historian. Affable, enthusiastic, and at forty-one the image of Walter Chrysler, he has an appreciation and love of his family's story that is almost painfully touching in its intensity. In his home and in a musty old barn where he makes superb reproductions of antique furniture (Chrysler would have been proud to see one of his descendants working with his hands), Frank Rhodes has saved a wonderful, eclectic collection of Chrysleriana. On the day that Pokety Farm, first Chrysler's and then the Garbisch's Maryland homestead, was being auctioned off, Frank Rhodes realized that many family treasures were headed for the dumpster. He simply backed up a truck and carted them away. If he hadn't, many parts of Walter Chrysler's life would simply have disappeared without a trace.

Walter Chrysler, Jr. left his personal effects, which contained many mementos of his father, to his nephew, Jack Chrysler, Jr. Though a rip-snorting Western outdoorsman and world-class jet pilot, he nevertheless treated this legacy with tender respect, and thus preserved important parts of Walter Chrysler's story.

Barbara Fronczak runs an extremely busy tiny band of devoted researchers at the Chrysler Information Resources Center of the Chrysler Historical Foundation in Highland Park, Michigan. With former Chrysler president Robert Lutz's permission, she turned herself inside out making every photograph, every file, and every frame of microfilm on Walter Chrysler at Chrysler Historical available for this book. Her enthusiasm for this project was almost palpable. But in the vastness of this then seventy-year-old $60 billion corporation, all the information on Walter Chrysler could fit into a space four-foot-square. And in Chrysler's fiscal crisis of the early 1980s, almost all of it was sold and carted away.

In Rancho Mirage, California, Fred Zeder and Fred Breer, scions of two of the members of Mr. Chrysler's all-important engineering team of Zeder, Skelton, and Breer, were most generous with their recollections and papers.

In Flint, Michigan, Professor Richard Scharchburg of the General Motors Institute opened both his files and his superb scholar's mind to this project.

The National Automobile History Collection at the Detroit Public Library and the New York Public Library were invaluable in helping to uncover the public, but now often obscure, record on Walter Chrysler.

But for such a man as this, there was less, less, less, than one would ever imagine. And what records there were depended on the ministrations of these few, disparate, and in some cases unlikely people. In terms of physical artifacts, fifty-nine years after Walter Chrysler's death there remain a ring and a drinking glass, a toy bank, a silver cornet, a band uniform, a shaving set, a manicure set, a few railroad passes and club membership cards, a tie bar, some golf tees, a half-filled bottle of his brandy, a papier-mâché clown mask of his face, a bar pin with his signature written out in gold letters, his famous set of handmade tools, and little else. Words and pictures, too, of course, but everything in all the places together would fit into the smallest space in a ministorage warehouse.

Yes, there is the gigantic Chrysler Corporation, now part of Daimler-Chrysler, which was the achievement he pioneered car by car and dollar by dollar; at Chrysler headquarters in Auburn Hills, Michigan, his words are carved in granite, his bust is cast in bronze, and his portrait in oils is hung. The Chrysler Building, perhaps the finest and certainly the most famous example of Art Deco architecture in the world, stands in New York City because he built it; its lobby contains a bronze plaque commemorating his work. But his person, and his traces, long ago disappeared from these things. His works remain thriving and intact, still speaking his name to glory. But when one thinks of the man, Shelley's Ozymandias comes to mind, in this sense: after a number of years fewer than those that he lived, around his living memory "the lone and level sands stretch far away."

An automobile historian named Menno Duerksen, for decades familiar to the readers of Cars & Parts magazine for his fine articles, led me to my interest in Walter Chrysler. In the 1970s and 1980s I read his informative—inspirational even—pieces on Chrysler, and each time I finished one I told myself I must visit the New York Public Library to read the books about him. When I finally did go in 1989, I found that there weren't any. No famous scholars, no popular biographers—no one had done his story.

But with a little more searching I discovered that Walter Chrysler himself, in collaboration with Boyden Sparkes, had turned out a slim volume of personal memoirs called *Life of an American Workman* in 1937. I went to a special collections room at the library and with white-gloved hands sat and read it in a privately printed edition, bound in gilt-lettered red leather.

That book convinced me to write this one. From page after page there emerged a man so vibrantly alive that he might as well have been standing before me. Smart and unpretentious, modest and proud, tough and sentimental, nostalgic and hopeful, he was above all a clear-eyed observer of his own existence, writing so that you saw it exactly as he did. It made the hair stand up on the back of my neck.

But in the end it was simply a memoir, not a full biography, mostly dealing with his early years and trailing off later. Since no one else had addressed the task of writing a full biography, I decided that I would. I am not a professional historian, and previously have written only one biography. Clearly I am writing this biography because I admire Walter Chrysler, though I am not a hagiographer. I have approached his work seriously, and I hope without pretension. You will see that there is also a great deal of automobile history because I think it is impossible to understand the man and his achievements without knowing the context in which he worked.

Perhaps my book can be no more than a gesture to this great man. But I have tried to make it with an eye unclouded and a mind unclenched.

The book begins with Chrysler's crucial formative years with the railroads. They prepared him for the rest of his life in automobiles and no serious biography would be complete without the full story of those years.

CHRYSLER

PART ONE

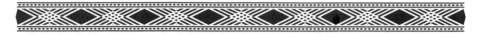

The Early Years

1

The Land from Which Walter Chrysler Sprang

O Pioneers

A hundred and twenty million years ago, before time began, the entire middle of what is now the United States of America was covered by the vast Niobrara Sea. For aeons flying reptiles swept over it and swimming ones dwelt in its waters. But eventually this sea dried up and a huge chalky plain developed in the remains of its basin. The name Niobrara now is attached to a small river wending its way east from Wyoming through Nebraska and into the Missouri River. But the alkaline alluvial plains remain, stretching eastward for hundreds of miles from the Rocky Mountains to the Mississippi River.

At the very heart of this area is Kansas, named for the Kansa Indians. Coronado was the first European known to visit it, searching for the supposed wealth of the cities of Quivira, described to him by an Indian guide named the Turk. Travelling there in 1541, he discovered only a few small Indian villages in what is now central Kansas. It was not until 1706 that another white man, a Spaniard named Ulibarri, went there again. For the most part it was left to the Indians and the buffalo until it became a United States possession through the Louisiana Purchase in 1803.

Three years later Zebulon Pike was sent by General James Wilkinson to explore the headwaters of the rivers west of St. Louis; after crossing through Kansas to the Rocky Mountains and Santa Fe, he made this observation: "As the vast plains are incapable of cultivation, they will prove of great benefit to the United States, not only in restricting its population to certain limits and thus keeping the Union intact, but also providing a barrier against invasion from that quarter." Fourteen years later Steven Long, after a two-year exploratory tour of the region, reached similar conclusions. The result was that for decades thereafter everyone thought of this area as the Great American Desert; every schoolchild saw it described thus in his geography textbook. But this was not true, though it took a vast social upheaval to make this evident.

Mari Sandoz, in *Cheyenne Autumn*, her haunting tale of the last struggles of the Cheyenne against the implacable onrush of white settlement in their ancestral lands, tells us that "in the 1830s and the 1840s the buffalo indians were considered the most romantic of peoples, drawing visitors from everywhere. Such men as Prince Paul of Werttemberg, Prince Maximillian, Sir William Drummond Stewart, Catlin, Parkman, and hundreds of others came to ride in the surrounds, to eat roast hump ribs, to study and become one with this Great Red Hunter. But that was before the white man wanted these Indian lands. The discovery of gold and the rise of political and economic unrest over much of the civilized world, with millions of men hungry for a new start, changed that." Indeed it did.

People came to the great wilderness west of the Missouri River to escape the miseries of the present and to seek some happy unfettered future they were sure they would encounter at the end of their journey. In the east there were financial panics, like the one of 1837, that ruined the hopes of thousands and led to great urban despair. Diseases, such as cholera which spread north from New Orleans, decimated large urban population centers and caused widespread panic that drove many to seek faraway homes. Famine and enormous political and social actions throughout Europe in the 1840s forced millions to seek new lives in new places. But Kansas was not a destination to these people. It was considered a terrifying wasteland to be gotten through to reach whatever lure awaited them at journey's end. As it turned out, it was the journeying to other places itself that caused the settlement of Kansas.

The U.S. government's criterion for considering an area "settled" was a population of 2 citizens per square mile. In 1850 that meant that west of the Missouri the only settled areas were sections of California and Texas, small parts of Wasington and Oregon, and the land surrounding Santa Fe and Salt Lake City. Everywhere else was essentially void of population, at least as far as the white man was concerned. It was just around this time that huge migrations of people across such areas began to take place.

Beginning in 1844, the adherents of the Church of Jesus Christ of Latter Day Saints began their three-year odyssey from Illinois to Utah following the assassination of their founder, Joseph Smith, in a mob action at Carthage, Illinois. Their new leader, Brigham Young, said he would know the right spot for their next location when he saw it, and that spot turned out to be one of the most inhospitable ever settled by pioneers. It is today Salt Lake City, situated in the Great Basin of the United States. It came into being at 9:30 A.M. on July 23, 1847, founded by 143 men, three women, and two boys. It was so blisteringly hot that the sun had baked the earth into rock that broke iron-tipped plows, but the small band of Mormons persevered, and 1,800 more Saints arrived shortly thereafter, with 13,000 more joining them soon after that. And they just kept coming. Most of these people came by route of the Mormon trail through Iowa and Nebraska, but this hooked up with the Oregon Trail which partly went through Kansas, and so many began their journeys from this area.

Another important destination point at this time was Santa Fe, then a fairly large and prosperous town in the southwest. The Santa Fe Trail through central and southern Kansas was the old way it could be reached from the east. In the 1850s various partnerships began forming for the purpose of shipping freight to Santa Fe along this trail, the most notable ones involving William H. Russell, who was to figure greatly in the setting up of transportation routes through Kansas.

These became necessary and profitable when gold was discovered in the western part of Kansas Territory, which was established in 1854 and stretched to the Rocky Mountains, where gold was found in the South Platte River. The trouble was that all existing routes ran north of the goldfields, very frustrating to the great number of people who needed to get there in 1858. The obvious thing was to run a line farther south. Russell, who was partnered in the great freighting firm of Russell, Waddell and Majors, fulfilled this need with a new partner, John S. Jones, forming the Leavenworth and Pike's Peak Express Company.

It was quite a large undertaking. Horace Greeley, who took his first trip to Denver on this line in December 1859, described it thus: "Such acres of wagons! Such pyramids of axletrees! Such herds of oxen! Such regiments of drivers and other employees! No one who does not now see can realize how vast a business this is, nor how immense are its outlays as well as its income. I presume that this great firm has at this hour two millions of dollars invested in stock, mainly in oxen, mules and wagons."

This trip was not on the Kansas route, however. A mail delivery contract between St. Joseph and Salt Lake City was bought out by the firm, and so the Kansas route was replaced by one along the Platte River in Nebraska in July 1859. However, a great hue and cry went up in newspapers in the Kansas Territory for a direct route through the center of Kansas to the goldfields. Most thought the best way would be along the Smoky Hill River, since it was properly situated and ran the length of the territory.

But a ghastly situation involving the three Blue brothers earned the route the appelation "the Starvation Trail" in 1859. These men got lost, ran out of provisions, and as they and a companion died off one by one, the survivors resorted to cannibalism. Only one brother, Daniel, survived, and his tale put the hex on the trail. The next year a route was laid out, but the start of the Civil War, shortly after Kansas became a state on January 29, 1861, preoccupied everyone and left consideration of new routes to the goldfields far from everyone's minds.

Immediately upon the war's end, David Butterfield looked at the Smoky Hill maps laid out in 1860 and decided that this would indeed be a perfect route through Kansas to the west, and by the summer of 1865, his Butterfield Overland Despatch was in operation, advertising service "to all points in Colorado, Utah, New Mexico, Arizona, Buffalo and Montana Territories and the State of Nevada. . . . Time to Denver 8 days." Internal company documents show a distance of 592 miles from Atchison to Denver—116 miles with no listed stops from Atchison to Fort Riley and thirty-nine stops from Fort Riley to Denver. The number and location of the stops changed. Some prospered, others were abandoned, but these fragile spots, and a few military forts which preceded them, became the basis for the permanent settlement of Kansas. What was true of the stage stops of the Butterfield Overland Express continued to be true a few years later in the case of the railroad towns, which were constantly inaugurated at the end of track on the Kansas (later the Union) Pacific.

So people came to Kansas for various reasons having to do with transporation across it. Many continued on, but some stopped and stayed, and eventually settlement of the territory became permanent. Advertising helped, land grants helped, the railroads helped, the army helped, good farmland helped, pioneering relatives helped, greed helped, and Manifest Destiny helped. But there was one beleaguered, savage, desperate enemy who came to fall into the pit of despair and annihilation by the time this piece of history was over: the Buffalo Indian of the plains. In twenty-five years his culture, his timeless way of life, had all but vanished. He was packed up, shoved off, moved on, or simply killed.

Henry Chrysler, the father of Walter P. Chrysler, arrived in Wyandotte, Kansas, in 1858 at the age of eight or nine, and together with his family lived through every bit of social upheaval the next twenty-five years would bring. Walter Chrysler himself was a child of this time and place and, as we shall see, a true son of the pioneers.

2

The Background
of the Chrysler Family

Whence

It was in Germany that the Chrysler family saga started, and it was from there that they took off along a great winding route to Kansas in the New World. The Chryslers went through almost as many moves and changes of place as their name went through changes of spelling.

Kreussler, Kreusler, Krausler, Kriesler, Kruisler, Krislor, Krisler, Kreyselaer, Kruyselaar, Krysler, Greyselaer, Gresler, Gressler, Greissler, Greisler, Greysler, Criselar, Crissler, Chrisler, Crysler, Chrysler: These are some of the most popular ways in which different branches of this four-hundred-year-old family spelled its name. It is no wonder that the orthography is so varied. According to H. Crysler Hilliker, an American who wrote a family genealogy and donated a copy to the Ontario Provincial Archives, there are some five million descendants of the progenitors of the North American segment of this family alone. Its directly traceable European roots go back 150 years before any of them set foot on the North American continent for the first time.

The family is very well, one might even say exhaustively, documented. The original impulse for this came from Walter Chrysler himself. In 1921 John North Willys, for whose company he then worked, asked him for information on his family background. From this almost casual request Chrysler and his children began genealogical research that continued for almost forty years. Mr. Chrysler was curious to know about ancestors somewhat further back than the plainsmen and nineteenth-century Canadians he either knew himself or heard his parents speak of. In the late 1920s and the 1930s his children, enormously rich for that time, entertained great social ambitions and continued these investigations for possible historical connections that could propel them into the institutions of high, not just café, society. As the Dodge Brothers' wives had discovered many years before in

The Chrysler family crest. (*Courtesy Frank B. Rhodes*)

Detroit, money alone was not enough to gain important social position, if that was what was wanted. No matter how much money you had, society was not easily willing to forget that thirty years earlier your father had been a grease-stained railroad mechanic. But if you could show that your family helped settle the Hudson River Valley almost two hundred years before, fought in the Revolution (even if sometimes on the British side), and possibly had grand aristocratic, even royal forebears, that could make a big difference.

So the research went on, culminating about 1959 in a huge gold-tooled leather-bound volume, with endpapers of cerise watermarked silk and containing hundreds of oversized gold bordered pages detailing family history. In it every primary and collateral family line is traced, with research backing up each statement. Beautiful photographs of the major nineteenth- and twentieth-century family members are faced with vellum, as are full-color copies of all the family crests connected with the Chryslers, complete with the descriptions of every figure and color contained therein.

Most wondrous of all, there are embossed color charts detailing Chrysler genealogical descent from Scottish and Saxon kings, beginning with Cedric of Briton (traced to his landing there in 495) and continuing through such notables as Edward I, Aethelred the Unready, and Henry II of England; Duncan I and Malcolm I, II, and III of Scotland; and the doges of Venice, beginning with St. Pietro Orseolo I, whose reign began in 976, and whose branch eventually connected with Emperors Henry III and IV of the Holy Roman Empire. The genealogy also listed as ancestors several Viking rulers of Norway, Denmark, and Sweden, including Harold Haarfaare, Harold III, Harold IV, Olaf III (the Pacific), and Magnus II of Norway; Gorm, Sweyn, and Harold Bluetooth of Denmark; Edmond and Erik II of Uppsala; Vsevold I and Vladimir II, grand dukes of Kiev; and perhaps best of all, both Clovis and Charlemagne! This amazing volume was dedicated to, and its enormous cost was subsidized by, Mr. Chrysler's daughters, Thelma and Bernice.

Mr. Chrysler himself might have been a bit skeptical of some of its airier historical flights back through time. He was once heard to remark, after getting a rather stiff bill for genealogical research, "If you pay enough money, they can relate you to Jesus Christ!" But certainly this volume, and Hilliker's separate and independent work, provide invaluable information on the family's history and peregrinations in the last 435 years, which for all practical purposes comprises its existence.

❧   ❧   ❧

The River Lahn rises in the cellar of a house built high in the Rothaar Mountains in Germany. It flows east, south, and southwest and finally enters the Rhine between the towns of Oberlahnstein and Niederlahnstein. Its winding valley, sometimes narrow and steep, sometimes broad and undulating, divides into two nearly equal parts the territory of Nassau, which was until the nineteenth century an independent and sovereign duchy of Germany. The Lahnthal, as this area is known, is most famous as the birthplace of Baron von Stein and the favorite resort of Goethe, and is also the location of the venerable universities of Giessen and Marburg and the cathedrals of Limburg and Wetzlar.

Haunted, romantic ruins line the banks of the Lahn. The castle of Lahneck, where the last Knight Templar is said to have died a hero's death, the twelfth-century church of St. John of Jerusalem, and the ancient abbey of Arnstein all arose in medieval times, when German culture centered around the Rhine and its tributaries and reflected the civilization of the Romans who had early discovered the healing effects of the waters of the famous Bad Ems. The annals of the Lahn extend as far into antiquity as 54 B.C., when Teutonic tribesmen contended for its possession.

The first recorded verifiable ancestor of the Chrysler family was Johann William Kreussler, who was born about 1560 and died prior to 1621. He was chief magistrate or mayor of Niederhadamar, a little town north of

Limburg-on-the-Lahn. The family bore a coat of arms, which can today be seen on the tombstone of Friedrich Kreussler in the Johannis Cemetery at Jena. It is described thus: *Arms:* Argent, Three roses gules, quiquefoliated, stalked and leaved vert, growing separately from a mound vert; *Crest:* the charge of the shield. Judging from the Kreusslers' position in the community and the families with which they intermarried, this was a family of position and influence. The church books of the Lahn Valley are so incomplete that no one knows if the family was Catholic or Protestant.

Johann William's son was Hans (Johann) Caspar Kreussler, who became chief magistrate or mayor of Niederneisen-on-the-Aar. This man and his family lived in terrible times, for he found himself right in the middle of the most awful scourge of the age, the Thirty Years' War. Fleeing with his family from his home, he took refuge in the fortified town of Dietz, only to encounter the plague then sweeping through Germany, Holland, and England. He died at Dietz on June 12, 1635, and in August his wife, Catherina, followed him after watching three of her children also die of the plague.

Their son Hans (Johann) Friedrich Kreussler, probably very young in 1635, somehow miraculously survived the plague, and was most likely raised by his much older brother (possibly half brother) Hans Daniel, Land-hauptmann of the county of Nassau-Dietz. He eventually became chief magistrate of Flacht-on-the-Aar, where he had twelve children by two wives before he died on September 26, 1685. It was the eighth of those children who was to bring the family to America.

This was Johann Philipp Kreussler, born at Niederneisen and baptized at Flacht-on-the-Aar on January 26, 1679. The period in which he was born, following the conclusion of the Thirty Years' War in 1648, was not a good one for this part of Germany. Crops and buildings had been completely destroyed, and many people were destitute. A protracted period of increasingly worsening weather across Europe did not help matters. The years around 1710 recorded the worst European weather in the last five hundred years, and destitution led to desperate measures.

In 1708 some fifty people of the Lower Palatinate, called Palatines, petitioned the British government to transport them to the American colonies. Knowing that the Palatines were industrious and would make desirable citizens, the British government in 1709 granted their petition, and these people became known as the First Settlement of the Palatines in America. Johann Philipp Kreussler and his wife, Anna Catherina, were among those who decided to go. They and their sons Johann George and Johannes seem first to have gone to Holland, then to England, where they joined the rest of the emigrants aboard ships cruising the English coastline for four months, awaiting favorable weather and their convoy of three warships of the royal navy.

Finally, in the spring of 1710, they set sail from Plymouth across the

Atlantic. The winter of 1710 was the single worst since the fourteenth century, and this voyage of the First Settlement of the Palatines, lasting over six months in toto, was one of the most awful ever recorded. Of the 3,200 souls who departed England, about 470 died along the way. After untold hardships, at last they reached the port of New Amsterdam (New York) in June 1710.

Most of the Palatines arrived without any means of support and were placed by the authorities in two camps, the East Camp and the West Camp, on either side of the Hudson River about a hundred miles north of New Amsterdam. The Kreusslers, however, along with about 360 others, remained in New Amsterdam during the winter of 1710–11, implying that they had the means to support themselves. In 1711 or 1712 they removed to the West Camp, where they seemed to stay for some time. By 1733, when his daughter Anna Catherina was married, Johann Phillipp's wife had died and he was living at Kiskatom at the foot of the Catskill Mountains.

According to the agreement with the Crown, it was understood that each Palatine immigrant was entitled to forty acres of land and five pounds in money, clothes, utensils, tools, and other necessities, in addition to his transportation. But by the spring of 1711, nearly two years after the Palatines had left Germany, most of the promises had not been fulfilled. As a result, some of them decided to rely on the promise of government assistance no longer and made deals with the Indians along the Schoharie River, moving there with their families. In that area they found some of the most fertile soil in all of New York State. Though records are a bit sketchy at this period, it appears that Johann Phillipp and one of his sons, Johann Hieronymus, born at the West Camp on March 6, 1713, moved to the area sometime after June 1737, settling on a large tract of land at Breakabeen near Fultonham in the township of Fulton, where their name is still preserved in the geographical name Crysler's Hook.

The sons of Johann Hieronymus were fiercely loyal to the Crown during the Revolution, when "Crysler's Raids," led by William, John, Philip, and Adam, were the terror of the countryside. According to the *History of Schoharie County and Border Wars*, at the beginning of the war of the Revolution all four of them removed to Canada and took up arms against the colonies; at one point William even burned down the Dutch church across from the graveyard at Schoharie, reportedly because of a grudge he held against some of its members.

Another of Johann Philipp's sons, Johannes, born in the Lahnthal in 1703 and known by the surname Kreisler or Greisler, in turn sired a boy named Heinrich, born and baptized in 1739 at Theerbol in Greene County. During the Revolutionary War Heinrich served as a private in Captain Isaac Vosburgh's company of the Eighth Regiment of the Albany County Militia, also known as the First Claverack Battalion. Later on he too went to Canada, serving in the Indian department and settling along with his cousins on what is now Niagara-on-the-Lake, where all of them are listed as "old settlers" by 1787. In the Revolution Philip and John had served in the King's Royal Regiment at Fort Stanwix, whereas Adam and William served as lieutenant and private, respectively, in the feared "Butler's Rangers" of Fort Niagara.

Life was not easy for these immigrants to Canada. They had few belongings, as almost everything they had was confiscated before they left the United States. It is recorded that when Adam Crysler arrived with his family at Niagara in 1781, he possessed six wineglasses, six ebony-handled knives and forks, seven yards of black taffeta, a pair of silver shoe buckles, three yards of lace, and a nightcap.

The main problem was shelter. Their first buildings were log cabins seldom exceeding 15 by 20 feet. Roofs were generally thick slabs of timber, and doors were openings covered with skins. Chimneys and fireplaces usually dominated one end of these cabins.

Food was plentiful, however. The Niagara River and Lake Ontario were filled with salmon, giant sturgeon, and other fish, and the woods provided deer, bear, porcupine, duck, and wild turkey.

The settlers proceeded to clear the land with primitive tools, burning the timber they felled to create as much potash as possible from the hardwood ashes, since this was a good source of cash income. Their first crop was maize, planted around the stumps of the big trees. Later, when seed was available, they planted wheat, oats, barley, and other grains. As time went on, stumps rotted, were burned, or were pulled from the ground. Before long sawmills and gristmills were built, making life easier. After 1800 more land was freed of trees and made available for cultivation, and mixed farming developed. Wheat, potatoes, and corn became the main crops, and herds of cows were plentiful.

John Graves Simcoe, Upper Canada's first lieutenant governor, was in charge of distribution of lands to Loyalist troops who had fought in the Revolution. Henry Chrysler was included in a supplementary list of the "Return of Loyalist and Disbanded Troops" compiled by the Hon. William Hamilton, supervisor of the western District of Niagara, and so was entitled to a grant of 200 acres. After removing to lands back of Burlington Bay, along with his son Henry Junior, he requested his lands on that spot. He was granted his wish, for by 1797 Henry Junior had joined two lots he had inherited from his father to his own lot in Ancaster Township there.

Governor Simcoe also figured prominently in the life of another of Henry Senior's sons, William, born in 1777. In 1792 he was one in a party of surveyors who mapped out a boundary of East Flamborough Township near Niagara, and when he declined to accompany his father to the lands back of Burlington Bay, he applied to Governor Simcoe for his own lands in

Niagara, despite the fact that he was only seventeen years old. When his petition was refused, he resigned himself to applying for lands opposite his father's and brother's along Dundas Street, the great road Simcoe laid out across the Niagara Peninsula from Burlington Bay to the River Thames. He obtained the grant in 1794, receiving a Crown deed in confirmation in 1797.

The Chrysler family lands were in a protected section known as the Old Landing Place and lay in a little valley along a stream that widens to become the inlet at the head of Burlington Bay. The land here was very beautiful. Coote's Paradise, a marsh abounding in wildfowl and tortoises, stretched along its borders. From the back of his farm William Chrysler could see a cataract of water ninety feet high and, a mile or so to the east, a promontory known as Sydenham Mountain. The area was prosperous, with numerous mills along its streams and a market featuring a lively trade in Indian furs and western produce.

Nevertheless, though he kept the farm until 1816, sometime after 1800 William Chrysler received a land grant in Kent County near Dolsen's, a thriving little pioneer town named after the United Empire Loyalist family that founded it. In 1820 he and his sons James and Henry moved a few miles farther up the Thames River to the site of Governor Simcoe's wartime navy yard. He erected a log cabin and became the first permanent settler of what is now Chatham, Ontario. The family cleared land around the cabin, planted tobacco, and raised 2,000 pounds of it in 1822, a success that had a bearing on the development of the tobacco industry in Kent and Essex Counties, which subsequently became one of the most important agricultural centers in Canada. The money earned from that first crop induced William Chrysler to build a new home on King Street, and there in 1826 his younger son, James, established the first private school in Chatham. But it was in the elder son, Henry, great-grandfather of Walter P. Chrysler, that the first real glimmerings of the future industrialist could be seen. Born in 1799, he was too young to serve in the War of 1812, and so he flung his energies into the auxiliary service and became a blacksmith and toolmaker, the first recorded in the family.

This Henry married significantly. His wife was Martha Dolsen, descendant of Teunis Van Dalsen, the first white male born in New Amsterdam after it was ceded to the British. (When the family removed to Kent County in Ontario it dropped the aristocratic "Van" and changed the spelling to Dolsen.) It appears that Henry and Martha were married in 1820 or so, just as the family moved to Chatham. Henry was a leading citizen of Chatham, serving as superintendent of schools, chief of the Board of Health, and dispenser of charities. They were the parents of eight children, the third of whom was John Matthew, born in Chatham in 1829. He was the grandfather of Walter Chrysler.

Henry Smyth, a onetime mayor of Chatham who knew John Matthew, described him as a very handsome man, and noted that all the members of his family, especially the women, were particularly fine-looking. As a boy, he undoubtedly apprenticed in his father's blacksmith shop, since he bought out the business from him in 1847, when he was only eighteen years old. He sold the business in 1853, and by 1854 documents list him as "merchant," amending to "hardware merchant" in 1855 and 1856.

John Matthew Chrysler was married twice, first to Hannah Lundy, of unknown family background, who may have died in childbirth bearing her third child, Sarah. His second wife, Isabella Clapperton, bore him four daughters, all in the United States.

The second child of his first wife was Henry Chrysler, born September 17, probably 1850, at Chatham, Ontario. He was the father of Walter P. Chrysler.

It appears that soon after the death of his mother, Martha, in late 1857 John Matthew Chrysler decided to pull up stakes and emigrate to the United States. He remained in Chatham to witness the marriage of his sister Theresa to Robert Blythe on January 14, 1858, but shortly thereafter left Canada with his family, reappearing at journey's end in Wyandotte, Kansas.

And so this family, which had spent the first 150 years of its recorded history in a small area of Europe, transported themselves over and over again for the next 150 years, remaking themselves in the images of the customs, the politics, and the occupations of they lands through which they passed. Moving through space and moving through time (which Tennessee Williams called "the longest distance between two places"), the Kreusslers of the Lahnthal became the Chryslers of Kansas. Traits of their Germanic origins dwelt in each of them, like templates in the mind: intelligence, industry, thrift, endurance, arrogance, choler, sentiment, vision. What had become equally imbedded was something new, non-European. This was the spirit of the pioneer, which was the essence of being American, and in some ways still is, even today. Mobility is at the heart of pioneering, whether physical, social, political, economic, or cultural, and that is the one thing Americans have, or conceive of themselves as having, in abundance. For the Chryslers, every kind of mobility they had began with movement through space. Until Kansas, all their traveling was done by means of the only motive power available to mankind from before the dawn of history to the middle of the nineteenth century: wind, water current, and animal and human locomotion. All of them had severe limitations. But now rails were being laid for machines to move people and things by no living or natural force, and in less than seventy years even railroad transportation, constricted by timetables and the very rails that defined it, would be superseded as the major means of ground transportation, leaving right of way as the only restriction to travel. Introduced to this revolution in travel by his father, Walter Chrysler was to learn everything there was to know about transport by rail and apply it diligently, incrementally, to individual self-propelled motor transportation. In so doing, he was at the heart of a process that changed the material circumstances of mankind more than any other in history. When it was completed, for the first time the physical being of man was free, existentially free, to change his life through uncircumscribed movement to any place of his choosing. Walter Chrysler did not initiate this process, nor was he its great disseminator. That was Henry Ford. But he did a great deal to bring the fruits of the transportation revolution to all Americans. By the time he was finished, he probably knew more about how it was done than anyone who ever lived. Walter Chrysler's life was all about the development of motive power; in the end, he was a true genius who had been through and understood it all.

3

Kansas, the Plains Indians, the Stage Coach, and the Coming of the Railroad

Whither

Kansas in 1858 was not just Kansas but "Bleeding Kansas," due to the seven years of conflict that followed the passage of the Kansas-Nebraska Act of 1854. Through this act both areas became territories of the United States, and both were to choose whether they would enter the Union as slave or free states. It was assumed that Nebraska would be free, but the situation in Kansas was not so straightforward. Through the Missouri Compromise, its neighbor Missouri was the only slaveholding state permitted north of 36 degrees 30 minutes north latitude, and its slaveholding neighbors to the south expected it to exercise its influence on sparsely settled Kansas to get it to join the Union as a slave state.

Despite the Missouri Compromise, slaves did exist in Kansas. After 1830, when treaties were established to remove the Indians to reservations, some few whites, possibly eight hundred in all by 1854, lived on these lands, and slaves were among them. But the new settlers who began pouring into Kansas after 1854 were decidedly antislavery, and brought no slaves with them. Therefore they had nothing to lose if the new state were to be free. Slaveholding Missourians were in a much different position. If they moved to Kansas and it became free, they would lose all the slaves they held as property, which could be a considerable economic loss. Therefore the Missourians resorted to intimidation, election fraud, military intervention, and other outrages to push their position, mostly to its detriment. The passions of the nation on both sides of the issue were aroused to the boiling point, particularly following the sack of Lawrence, Kansas in May 1856, after which a band of men led by the fanatical abolitionist John Brown murdered and mutilated five proslavery men on Pottawatomie Creek. This led Governor Geary to take action to stop the dreadful events then devastating eastern

Kansas. Before he could, however, two hundred people had been killed and the press had labeled the territory "Bleeding Kansas."

The protracted struggle over which type of constitution, slave or free, would be adopted continued until 1861. To their everlasting credit, Kansans repudiated the pro-slavery Lecompton Constitution, supported by President Buchanan, on August 21, 1858, by a vote of 11,300 to 1,788, despite the promise of millions of acres of public land should it have been accepted. On October 4, 1859, Kansans ratified the anti-slavery Wyandotte Constitution, and it was under this constitution that it was admitted to the Union as a free state on January 29, 1861.

Among the 107,206 souls living in Kansas in 1860, according to that year's census, were the Chryslers, who witnessed these monumental events, a clear precursor of the Civil War, which began less than three months after Kansas achieved statehood.

In 1858, when the Chryslers moved there, Wyandotte City, Kansas, was a small town not far from the Missouri River that would one day, along with several other similar places, be absorbed into what is now Kansas City. Once the family reached Wyandotte, John Matthew started a farm and also ran a general store; his son Henry worked with him in both enterprises.

As it did for millions, the Civil War held an irresistible appeal for young Henry. God knows living in Kansas gave him an up-close understanding of what it was all about. He was desperate to get involved, but his father opposed this, due to his tender age. Nevertheless, he ran away to Armourdale, Kansas, and there he enlisted in the Union Army on March 12, 1863. On May 2 he was mustered into Company I, Twelfth Regiment, Kansas Volunteer Infantry, under Captain Joseph T. Gordon. He was "promoted musician" at a later date, probably following the death of George Hanford of Wyandotte, musician of Company I, also mustered in on May 2, 1863, and accidentally killed at Fort Smith, Arkansas, on September 5, 1864. For certain Henry was a drummer boy, and drummed for his regiment until the end of the war, despite his father's vigorous attempts to get him out of the army. It is notable that Edward O'Hare of Wyandotte was mustered into Company A of the Twelfth Regiment on September 25, 1862, and served until discharged for disability at Fort Smith, Arkansas, also on September 5, 1864. O'Hare was probably Henry's stepuncle on his father's side, and likely stirred his enthusiasm for entering the war. In any case, Henry was a hardy youth and escaped the war uninjured, though years later he used to regale his eager children with stories of war hardships, such as tales of hunger and sleeping in rain or snow with only a blanket to shield him from the elements.

He was discharged from service at Little Rock, Arkansas, on June 30, 1865. Later he received a medal for his service, which remains in the family as one of its proudest possessions.

By this time John Matthew had become an alderman of Wyandotte City, and young Henry returned to work in his father's businesses at the conclusion of the war. This state of affairs was not to last very long, however, as John Matthew died in March 1866 at Chesapeake, Missouri, at the early age of thirty-seven. His widow, Isabella, decided to return to Chatham with her daughters, but Henry remained in the Kansas City area, where he went to work for the Kansas Pacific Railroad.

Both the prolonged slavery struggle and the nation's preoccupation with the Civil War had retarded the growth of settlement in Kansas, but soon after this the plains began filling up from all directions. Some of the people who came were disappointed gold seekers from the Rockies, some were farmers leaving the increasingly crowded Mississippi River valley, some were easterners wanting a fresh start in life, and some were European immigrants lured by the promise of free land.

Several factors induced these various groups to come to the plains. The most important was the Homestead Act of 1862, passed while the Civil War was raging. Under it, a man could stake a claim to unoccupied public land by living on it and cultivating it for five years. Congress limited these claims to 160 acres each to favor the establishment of small independent farms, rather than huge spreads resembling southern plantations that would require slave or tenant labor to work them. No one seemed to take into account that this dry, harsh land could barely support a single family on 160-acre plots, and the people rushed in. Six months after the act was passed, settlers claimed 224,500 acres in Kansas and Nebraska.

In Europe the call went out for settlers in pamphlets and posters printed and distributed by the millions in languages including Swedish, German, Dutch, Norwegian, Danish, English, French, and many more. Locals in these countries were hired by the railroads to boost the settlement campaigns. "Land for the Landless!" and "Homes for the Homeless!" were familiar poster slogans. Among the poor of Europe and those made desperate by war, civil strife, and other varieties of human extremity, such offers struck a deep and resounding chord. The response was enormous, especially when the first arrivals wrote back home to persuade family and friends to join them in America. So many Germans moved to Kansas and Nebraska in the 1860s and 1870s that one tribe of Kansas Indians spoke German, rather than English, as a second language.

Then there was the railroad, when it was finally built. Vast uninhabited areas bordered its tracks, which it realized it needed to fill up to create business in passengers and freight. It had been given large tracts along its right-of-way, and began selling land off to settlers at $2.50 an acre. The railroad land offices began distributing enormous amounts of advertising that depicted the prairies and plains as the next thing to paradise. Railroad salesmen frequently cited the words of William Gilpin, who had traveled across the grasslands many times, beginning as early as 1843. In his words, the region was a "vast amphitheater," its face lifted "towards heaven to receive and fuse harmoniously whatever enters its rim. The PLAINS are not *deserts*, but the OPPOSITE, and the cardinal basis of the future empire." Such a sentiment was yet another phrasing of the doctrine of Manifest Destiny, first proclaimed by James L. O'Sullivan, editor of the July–August 1845 issue of *United States Magazine and Democratic Review*, in which he stated that it is "our manifest destiny to overspread the continent alloted by Providence for the free development of our multiplying millions." The term became a catchword implying divine approval of the territorial expansion of the young nation.

When the new settlers arrived, however, there was much to deal with and overcome. The climate, for one, which could freeze you or broil you, drown you in flash floods or burn you out. It provided temperatures as low as forty below zero in winter, accompanied by sudden blizzards so fierce that a man could lose his way and freeze to death between his house and his barn. In summer there were parching droughts that led to prairie fires that burned all in their path, alternating with freak hailstorms severe enough to kill men and cattle. In the period from June 19, 1859, until November 1860 there was not a single decent rainfall. The entire area was cracked and desiccated, with some people rendered so destitute that they were "living on acorns and clothed in bark," according to U.S. Representative Marcus J. Parrott.

As if the weather weren't enough to contend with, suddenly in 1874 there appeared out of nowhere a plague of locusts of almost biblical proportions. They flew eastward from the Rockies by the billions, consuming every plant in their path, covering the ground in moving layers as much as six inches deep, the combined weight of their bodies so great that they snapped the limbs off cottonwood trees. After three years they disappeared just as suddenly as they came, leaving only the ghastly memory of devastation in their wake.

Then there was the land itself. Once beyond the rather lush river lowlands of the eastern part of Kansas, one found the real prairies, vast arid stretches of land, desolate of any form of vegetable life but endless seas of waving grass, over it moaning the incessant and ceaseless wind, which drove many a lonely settler mad.

But of all problems the settlers faced, none was so harsh and intractable as the Buffalo Indians of the plains. Since forever the plains were their ancestral lands, and they considered that any member of the tribes now alive, or who had ever lived or ever would live, was in a divine circle of harmony with nature. They respected every bison's curl, every blade of grass, every feather from a bird, because it was part of the oneness of being they perceived as the ground of all existence. And this place of existence, the plains, was theirs. To pluck them from it was to leave them deracinated creatures dangling in nothingness, their circle of life shattered and disappeared forever. Despite smiles, gifts, treaties, and entreaties to the contrary, that was exactly what the white man planned to do, and the Indians recognized it early—as soon as the Kansas-Nebraska Act was passed, in fact. They knew they would have no place in the Kansas inhabited by the white man's railroads, cities, and farms. Indeed, as Mari Sandoz tells us, "suddenly the romantic Red Hunter was a dirty, treacherous, bloodthirsty savage standing in the way of progress, in the way of manifest destiny. By 1864, with the nation at war ostensibly to free the black man from slavery, the public had been prepared to accept a policy of extermination for the red." Not even Lincoln, the Emancipator, objected. It is certainly a matter of interesting speculation to consider what our opinion of Lincoln would be if he had lived and had to deal with the mounting Indian problem.

No matter what we think of the Indians' position, it is incontrovertible that their resistance to the white man was fierce. Partly it was defense, partly it was a scare tactic, partly it was revenge, but nevertheless, what the Indians did to the travelers and settlers provoked horror and terror in the white man's heart. After some of the ghastly mutilations and agonizing deaths inflicted even on noncombatant women and children, it is not hard to see how whites came to look upon these Indians with hatred as bloodthirsty savages. What sympathy might have attached to the displacement of the Indians declined with each fresh hell related in the merciless slaughter of some little band of travelers in prairie schooners on the plains or camped out at a forlorn way station.

Arthur Pound contends in *The Turning Wheel* that it was inevitable that the red man should lose out to the white man in the struggle for America because of a basic fact of technology: Indians never developed and used the wheel. "At one time or another the American aborigines had used the other five primary machines: the lever, wedge, screw, pulley, and the inclined plane. With these the Mayas of Yucatan and Guatemala and the Incas of Peru had built massive edifices. But there is no evidence that the red man ever had command of the wheel. In the meantime, through the centuries of recorded time and before, the Asiatics, Europeans, and the Egyptians had not only evolved wheeled carts and chariots, but also they had made so many efficient combinations of the wheel with the other five primary machines that they had evolved the compass to to guide them to America, domestic tools of many sorts, the well-ground sword blade, and the musket which spat fire. The conquerors had inherited a superior technology as well as superior form of carriage on land and sea. Hence the aborigines gave way. One reason—and perhaps the root reason—for the failure of the aboriginal inhabitants effectively to occupy and defend North America may well have been their failure to master the wheel."

It was certainly the inevitable, unstoppable turning wheel that defeated them and effectively drove them out of Kansas after twenty-five years of bitter struggle. The process started when ever larger numbers of people wanted to get across Kansas to the Rockies and beyond. Initially they did it by stagecoach.

The first real travel on the Butterfield Overland Despatch began on June 24, 1865, hard on the heels of the party that had just completed surveying its route. This inaugural commercial train carried seventy-five tons of freight, and thus was typical in size of the usual ox-team train, which ordinarily consisted of about twenty-five large wagons carrying around three tons each, pulled by six pair of yoked oxen. With spares, there were about 330 head of cattle and four or five mules for herding and riding. Since there were no established way stations on the trail then, there could be no exchange of animals along the route, so the animals that started the trip had to pull for the entire trip across the plains, making for slower passage than would otherwise have been the case. To give an idea of how expensive an enterprise this was, we need only note that a good yoke of oxen cost $160 to $170 in Atchison at that time, so it cost $1,000 just to provide animals for one wagon alone. Considering that fifty years later, in the inflated money of 1915, two Model T Ford touring cars could be bought for this price, we can see how costly it was to operate this business at that time. Freight costs of 22.5 cents a pound were probably neither a bargain nor exorbitant.

The first stagecoach rolled over the line in September of that year. With Colonel Butterfield aboard, it left Atchison on September 11, 1865, arriving without serious incident at Denver on September 23. The citizens turned out to greet Butterfield en masse, with Mayor Clark and other distinguished citizens escorting him through the streets in a carriage preceded by the First Colorado Band, inspiring all with lively and patriotic airs. When Butterfield appeared on the veranda of the Planters House, he was greeted by a huge salvo of cheers.

The one-way fare was $175, not counting meals. Fried ham, bacon, and buffalo hump were the staple meats, along with fresh eggs, chicken, vegetables, butter, cream, and coffee on the eastern end. The choice of food diminished considerably as one traveled west, and the price of a meal went up from fifty cents in the East to a dollar in the West. As to sweets, one driver said, "It's dried apple pies from Genesis to Revelations."

When another passenger complained about the dirty food, he was told by the stationmaster, "I was taught a long time ago that we must eat a peck of dirt in our lifetime." The traveler shot back, "I am aware of that, sir, but I don't like to eat mine all at once."

Travel along the route wasn't too bad up to Fort Ellsworth, approximately in the middle of present-day Kansas, but after that it was much more difficult until important new stops such as Fort Hays were established or smaller ones were strengthened. Some spots were heartbreakingly forlorn, none more so than Grady's Station, on the north bank of the Big Sandy. Bayard Taylor, a *New York Tribune* reporter who traveled the Butterfield Overland Despatch in June 1866, noted, "At Grady's Station there was but one man, a lonely troglodyte, burrowing in the bank like a cliff swallow."

As soon as the Indians realized that the stage line was to go directly through their most prized hunting grounds, trouble began. They canceled the fall buffalo hunt to deal with the usurpers on their land. On October 2, 1865, thirty Indians attacked a stagecoach near Monument Station, close to present-day Wakeeny. Reports of other attacks ensued, and the army decided to establish a new fort, Fort Fletcher, in the vicinity of what is now Fort Hays, on October 11, 1865. Such military establishments were manned by battle-hardened Civil War veterans who were confident that they knew all there was to know about war tactics, and assumed the battle with the Indians would be brief. But the Indians had war methods the soldiers had never encountered—the Indians would strike and be gone before the soldiers could even organize pursuit—and the conflict turned out to be a fifteen-year battle that spread through all the western states.

The Indian problem caused huge financial difficulties for the Butterfield Overland Despatch, and in the spring of 1866 it was bought out at a bargain rate by Ben Holladay, who had the mail contract on the Platte River and needed to counter competition from a new Wells Fargo line from Missouri to Salt Lake City. During the rest of 1866 new stations were established and the military forts were much better equipped and stocked for future problems.

The Indians were preparing themselves, too, and all through the winter of 1866–67 they warned of a coming all-out spring assault along the entire frontier to drive the white men from their hunting grounds. General Winfield Scott Hancock, accompanied by the Seventh Cavalry under George Custer, tried to arrange a meeting with the great chiefs to avoid the coming conflict, but the Indians, when they saw his huge force, were sure that they were to be annihilated, ran from the meeting site, and launched a preemptive strike at Lookout Station, which they completely destroyed. It was the beginning of a war that would last until 1869.

Perhaps the worst of it was in the single, tumultuous month of June, 1867. There was Indian trouble at Fort Wallace, and then suddenly on the night of June 5th, a torrential prairie thunderstorm inundated the entire area around Fort Hays to the east, nearly sweeping away everything in its path. Indians then attacked everywhere from this area west to Fort Wallace. The culmination was an attack on the 26th in which 300 Cheyennes under the famous Chief Roman Nose attacked Fort Wallace in a fierce battle. In July, 1867, *Harper's Weekly* reported this of the incident: "The Indians committed unheard of atrocities. A powerful warrior was sent to pick up the bugler, Charles Clark, who had been pierced by three arrows, and strip him as he rode along; after taking off all his clothing, he mashed the head to a jelly with his tomahawk, and threw the body under his horse's feet. The body of Sergeant Frederick Wyllyams was also fearfully mutilated. His scalp was taken, two balls pierced his brain, and his right brow was cut open with a hatchet. His nose was severed and his throat gashed. His body was opened and his heart laid bare. The legs were cut to the bone, and the arms hacked with knives." Each of these wounds, though they seemed erratic and demonic, were actually marks of the tribe of the Indian that inflicted them. Calculated expressions of tribal rage, in other words, intended in Indian belief to identically cripple the spirits of the slain men in the afterlife. To the readers of *Harper's Weekly*, and the citizens of Kansas, they were nothing other than an abomination. They were also typical, and they continued. Many a soldier's feelings towards the Indian were frozen into stone hatred the first time he found the remains of one of his comrades who had been viciously mutilated or roasted alive over an open fire.

On March 2, 1868, none other than General Phil Sheridan, famed for his leadership in the Civil War, took command of the vast Department of the Missouri, which had control over the whole Indian territory, and he began to make a difference. He was given a force of only 2,600 men to command. Eighteen hundred of them were occupied protecting forts, stage lines, and workers for the new railroad line now moving its way across the state. There were just eight hundred men to fight the plains warriors, not at all a sufficient number, so he turned to volunteers, to be organized by George A. Forsythe, whom he gave the rank of brevet colonel. He also reinstated General Custer, who had run into difficulties. Winter campaigns were instituted for the first time, which, though hard on his own men, were far more devastating for the less well equipped Indians, who had always used the brutal winter to recover from the depradations of war. The battles and skirmishes continued unabated, from attacks on small outposts and farms to grand pitched battles such as Arickaree Creek, where the magnificent chief Roman Nose finally met his doom.

By 1870, however, an event of truly great significance occurred. The stage lines, which had really initiated all this trouble, ceased to exist. On August 18, 1870, the Kansas Pacific, which began building near the Missouri line on September 7, 1863, and stalled out for a long while near Sheridan in the middle of the state in 1868, finally reached Denver. As it went westward, the eastern terminal of the Butterfield Overland Despatch moved farther and farther west. On the day the railroad was completed, the B.O.D. ceased operation altogether, supplanted entirely by the newer technology of the "iron horse." Something about the iron horse and the steel rails on which it rode gave the settlement of the plains a permanent reality that the stage lines never quite could. The Indians feared it, and knew in their hearts that nothing they possessed could stand up against it or match it for strength and endurance. It was there, and couldn't be run off or scared off. The white civilization, and all it represented, had built it to bring more white civilization along with it. Powerful forces stood behind every mile of it, determined, by a long list of ignominious methods, to force the red man off all the territory that surrounded it.

Was there a treaty with the Indians? Well then, don't abide by its provisions or tear it up completely. Were the Indians on agreed reservation land? Well then, starve them out and force them to move to some new Godforsaken land that no white man would want. Did they survive on the buffalo? Well then, put a bounty on buffalo hides and empty the plains of them. Did you need to put an official face of concern on your treatment of the Indians? Well then, create Indian agencies, give them big appropriations, have them run by nonentities with no supervision and provide ample opportunities for most of the monies and supplies to be stolen, or replaced with damaged, rotten, or inferior goods. And above all, justify this by relentlessly portraying the Indians in their worst light, as lying, bloodthirsty savages, enemies of everything good Christian American civilization stood for.

In fact, what was needed was the end of the red man's way of life, so that it could be replaced with the white man's way of life on the same ground; because of the extensive resource requirements of each, they could not really coexist. The red men were essentially survivors of the stone age, who had seen the white man's technology and social structure and rejected it. They did not feel any God-given mandate to "improve" themselves and conquer the wilderness around them. They did not cultivate the land, instead living off the buffalo and what grew wild around them. The notion of the land belonging to anyone but the entire people, specifically Indians, was utterly alien to them. In contrast, the white men came to the plains with a long tradition of working soil in carefully measured and clearly owned plots, so for them the Indians' use of these huge lands solely for hunting was a terrible waste. They believed that God had sent them there to end that waste, and saw the Indians who stood in their way as no more than brutal, subhuman savages, whose mystical culture was nonsensical and contemptible. "I suppose they must be exterminated," said General Sherman of the Sioux and Cheyenne in a letter to his brother. Roman Nose knew it, and died resisting it for the sake of his people.

Dull Knife, the great Cheyenne chief who figured slightly in the life of Walter Chrysler, knew it, too. In December 1878 he sat in council with Red Cloud and army men at Fort Robinson, where he and his people were being held captive because they would not go south, to the Indian Territory, rather than north, where they belonged. After listening to commands and importunings, Mari Sandoz tells us that he arose and said the following: "We bowed to the will of the Great Father and we went far into the south where he told us to go. There we found that a Cheyenne cannot live. We belong here. . . . I am here on my own ground and I will never go back."

And indeed he did not. In the bitter depths of the winter of early 1879, he led his people to break out of Fort Robinson, and after much privation and loss of life, they regained their ancestral homelands in the Yellowstone country. At that late date it was no more than a gesture, albeit a heroic one, and in fact very few of the people actually survived the breakout and journey. It was the last great action of Indian resistance.

In the end General Sheridan, who had thought the Indians so inferior and did so much to destroy them utterly, summed up their wild and fierce resistance best: "We took away their country, broke up their mode of living, their habits of life, introduced disease and decay among them, and it was for this and against this that they made war. Could anyone expect less?"

4

The Birth of Walter Chrysler;
How Financial Corruption Built
the Railroads; What Texas Cattle
Meant to Kansas

> Men don't ride the rails; the rails ride men.
> —*Walden*, Henry David Thoreau

The transcontinental railroad began on July 1, 1862, when President Lincoln signed the Pacific Railway Act, authorizing two lines, the Union Pacific and the Central Pacific, to build a line linking the Missouri River with the West Coast. The Union Pacific was to build westward from the 100th meridian, at Fort Kearny, Nebraska, and the Central Pacific was to build eastward from the Pacific Coast. They were to meet at the California-Nevada state line. However, that left the territory from the Missouri River to the 100th meridian without any building authorization.

Everyone had known the railroads were coming though. As early as 1861 the Territorial Legislature of Kansas had chartered no fewer than fifty-one railroads, but the bulk of these had no tracks or even grades. After the Pacific Railroad Act was passed, there followed a great race between the Union Pacific, out of Omaha, and what billed itself as the Union Pacific, Eastern Division, out of Kansas City, to reap the financial rewards of reaching the 100th meridian first. The Union Pacific, Eastern Division, which later became the Kansas Pacific line, began when a railroad foreman named H. H. Sawyer drove a stake in the ground near the Kansas-Missouri border on September 7, 1863. Nearby stood a post with Slavery printed on the Missouri side and Liberty on the Kansas side.

Though people felt quite sure that this southern line, under Samuel Hallett, would get to Fort Kearny first due to better management and superior preparation, it didn't turn out that way. A series of problems, from financial wrangles, lack of materials, and bad weather to the murder of Hallett by a disgruntled former employee, delayed progress of the line. After about fifteen months it became apparent that the Omaha line would reach its goal before the one in Kansas, and a new plan was hatched to save the situation. This was to continue the Kansas line westward along the Smoky Hill Trail to Denver. Such a line would be 134 miles closer to Denver than the northern route, and would go up a fertile valley no other line would come near. President Andrew Johnson gave life to the new project by accepting the first forty miles of the line on October 30, 1865. The folowing July he signed a bill authorizing the railroad to proceed up the Smoky Hill and on to Denver. This was clearly a great thing for the future of Kansas.

Sometime before his father's death and his stepmother's return to Canada, Henry Chrysler (who was universally known as Hank) returned to Armourdale, Kansas, where he had enlisted in the Civil War. He went to work on the Kansas Pacific, which would later be known as the Union Pacific. According to a Kansas newspaper article of May 22, 1908, Hank Chrysler's first job as a railroad fireman was on the *Delaware*, the second engine built for the Union Pacific. His run was from Kansas City to Lawrence, then the western end of the line. When the line was extended westward from Lawrence, sometime in November 1865, Hank Chrysler was promoted to engineer, and ran the first trains in to Wamego and Junction City, which was reached on November 1, 1866. At first the engines of these trains were wood-burning, but when the railroad bought its first coal-burning locomotive, it was Hank Chrysler who was chosen to run it. According to his son Walter, he was the best locomotive engineer on the division, famous from one end of the Union Pacific to the other.

The trains Hank Chrysler's engine hauled at that time supplied the construction gangs that laid the first rails across the state. According to Keith Wheeler, author of *The Railroaders*, "The actual laying of tracks. . . . . . . began when lightweight carts, each drawn by a horse along the newest section of track, were positioned beside a stockpile containing all the supplies the track gang would need for the coming day. Six-man crews hastily piled each of the little carts with 16 rails plus the proper number of spikes, bolts and rail couplings called fishplates. Then, in series, the carts would be hauled by running horses to the very end of the last pair of rails spiked down.

"The bed of each cart was equipped with rollers, and the rails were removed faster than they had left the flatcar. They were pulled off in pairs, five men to a rail. Now came the men with the notched wooden gauge, spacing each pair of rails precisely four feet eight and one half inches apart—and the spike men would begin swinging their mauls. Meanwhile the cart would have been unceremoniously dumped off the tracks to make way for the next one coming up on the run. Then back it would go for a new burden of rails."

(Curiously, fewer than fifty years later various aspects of this process—bringing the work to the men, and having it proceed along a centralized track—would figure importantly in Walter Chrysler's attempts to set up a progressive system of production, first at ALCO locomotive works and then at Buick. Surely from boyhood he would have heard tales of this method of work from his father.)

Every sixty miles or so, as this work progressed, towns would be created by the railroad, most to be abandoned as the road pushed forward. The train would roll into the designated spot on newly laid rails and all hands would dismount, setting up tent buildings as lodgings, stores, mess halls, saloons, whorehouses, and whatever else the workers required, a good deal of it dissolute and debauched; it was not for nothing these places gave birth to the phrase "hell on wheels." One long-lasting tough town, Sheridan, had six bodies in its graveyard, Boot Hill (the first one ever so named), before it was a week old, and twenty more shortly thereafter; not a one took up residence in his "underground bungalow" due to death from natural causes. Even temporary exceptions to the general lack of moral tone were worthy of note. *The Junction City Weekly Union* of June 13, 1868 reported: "Monument, the new town started last week on the U.P. Railway, already contains a population of five hundred souls, and up to twelve o'clock last night not a man had been shot or hung in that city, which speaks volumes for the moral worth of its citizens." These towns exploded with activity for a while, and most expired like mayflys when the railroad moved on. But a few, for whatever reasons, hung on and survived, even prospered. Among the towns that figured in Walter Chrysler's life, Laramie and Cheyenne, in Wyoming, and Ellis, in Kansas, were end-of-rail tent cities that made it.

Hank Chrysler did not continue with the work trains all the way out to Denver. After a while he began making regular runs, first as far as Junction City and later west over the plains. His runs were not easy in these early days. In addition to the depradations of bad weather, which could cause grade or bridge washouts or harm to equipment, the trains were sometimes stopped by huge herds of migrating buffalo, or attacked by marauding Indians and bandits. Perhaps his worst scare happened one day when his engine went dead on the plains. The crew suddenly saw a party of men approaching them at great speed. Fearing Indian attack, the crew went into the caboose with the only weapon at hand, an old shotgun, and prepared to defend themselves as best they could. Before any shots were fired, they saw with great relief that the approaching horsemen were a troop of United States soldiers who had come to protect the train from attack by the Indians. Others were not so lucky. Twenty years later, when he would take young Walter for rides on his regular run to Junction City, Hank would point out the graves of men he knew in the cemetery by the little station in Victoria. "Indians got 'em," he would deadpan to the impressed boy. Out on the plains he pointed to the graves of still more men he knew. But Hank was lucky, because neither Indians nor bandits ever wrecked his train, and though he was in three crashes, he was never seriously hurt.

◆   ◆   ◆

In 1871 the twenty-year-old Hank Chrysler decided to take a wife. On April 2 of that year he married Anna Maria Breymann at Pleasant View Farm, near Kansas City, Missouri. The ceremony was performed by the Reverend George W. Scott of the Baptist Church.

The Breymann, or Breydemann, family dates back almost as far as the Chrysler family. Its origins were to be found in Germany also, at Gebhard-shagen, a small village near Salder, in the district of Wolfenbuttel, Braun-schweig. There the death of one Henning Breydemann was recorded in 1614. Many learned men, a famous sculptor, and several army and navy men are recorded in the family archives. This family certainly was a distin-guished one, for it had a coat of arms, described thus: *Arms*—Or, a savage girdled and crowned with garlands, holding in his sinister hand a fir tree, the dexter resting at his side, all proper, a bordure gules. *Crest*—The savage issuant, holding the tree of the shield.

With one exception (Adolph Ludwig Breymann, who came to America for a time in the nineteenth century before returning to Germany), the Breymann family stayed in the Braunschweig–Hanover area until Anna Ma-ria's father, Wilhelm Georg Carl Breymann, emigrated to the United States sometime prior to 1840, when he would have been twenty-three years old. He lived first at Rocheport, Missouri, in the center of the state, where he married Zeralda Jane Simmons, daughter of Pinckney Simmons and Eliza-beth Berry-Thomas Simmons on February 9, 1840. They were to have ten children. Some years after the wedding, he and his family removed to Pleas-ant View Farm, about a hundred miles to the west.

Before October 1865 he had engaged in "the new business, the hotel." Further occupations can be known through his correspondence. An 1879 letter was addressed to him at "Mr. William Breymann & Co., Commission Merchants, Clay Center, Kansas," located about thirty miles northwest of Junction City. In March 1884 he was the manager of the Dispatch Hotel Stables at the same location. By September 1885 his address was "Wm. Breymann & Sons, Chemical Laboratory, Ellis, Ellis County, Kansas," where the Henry Chrysler family had then been residing for six years.

Anna Maria was born in Missouri, probably on September 29, 1852, though some sources list the date as 1853. She was a large, quite hand-some, and strong woman, with a well-developed sense of morality and prac-ticality and a will of iron. A life of good hard work as a Kansas frontier housewife and mother who earned extra money on the side selling milk and eggs from her backyard turned the pretty young thing Hank had married into a sturdy, formidable woman by the time Walter Chrysler was old enough to know her. He was her image, almost exact; his Ellis neighbors all agreed that "Walt takes after his mama." Years later, he would remark that he could sometimes seem to see her eyes looking at him from the face of one of his grandchildren. "Sometimes, in a mirror, I catch a fleeting trace of her in my own eyes," he said.

After their marriage, Henry and Anna Maria set up housekeeping in Wamego, Kansas, which stands by a large bend of the Kansas River. The house in which Henry and his bride resided showed that their financial circumstances were above those of most of the families who were their neighbors, for it was made out of wood. Most people in Kansas in those days were "sodbusters," people who had made their homes of strips of the one building material readily available, prairie sod. Sometimes these dwellings were dug out of the sides of little depressions in the landscape and thatched over with sod; these houses were surprisingly strong and snug, able to withstand the freezing Kansas winters very well. Sometimes they were freestanding, even large and elaborate, but these leaked horribly or collapsed in the driving rainstorms that often bedeviled the landscape, so they frequently needed to be redone. In any case, if you built a sod house, it meant that you could only afford to use material that was free.

Not the Chryslers. Their house, which still stands today in a run-down section of Wamego south of the railroad tracks, was small but comfortable for the time and place. The original section, where they lived, consisted of a single story divided into two rooms fronted by a porch supported by several wooden columns. It was modest, but it was a good little place for the family to take hold, especially as Hank often made runs from Wamego to points east and west.

The first child born to them there was Edward Ernst Chrysler, who came into the world on January 3, 1872. Walter Chrysler was a big man for his time, 6 feet tall and about 190 pounds, but his older brother dwarfed him completely. He was much taller and weighed considerably more than Walter, and in family photos he resembles a giant.

Next came a family tragedy. Harry Gilbert Chrysler was born at Wamego on September 13, 1873, but survived little more than a year, dying on October 24, 1874. No one knows today what happened to him, but such infant deaths were common in those days when medicine was scarce in such places and medical knowledge was even scarcer. Many families had more than one child die early in life, and this was one reason why pioneer families were frequently so large; with just one child or two, a husband and wife could easily wind up childless.

The winter of 1874–75 was a particularly brutal one in Kansas, and through it all, as Hank battled the elements in his locomotive, Anna Maria, known to all now as Mary, carried her third child to term. As spring was breaking, Walter Percy Chrysler was born at Wamego on April 2, 1875, the fourth anniversary of his parents' wedding. Since Harry had died during this pregnancy, baby Walter must have been a great consolation to his parents, an expression of hope for the future of this little family.

The 1870s were very bad times for the United States. On September 19, 1873, the Credit Mobilier scandal caused a financial collapse on Wall Street that sent the nation into a five-year depression, the worst the country had ever known until that time. It had been caused by the unscrupulous robber barons who ran the railroads' affairs.

The building of the transcontinental railroad clearly called for more capital than was ever put into any single enterprise in the history of high finance. Collis P. Huntington of Sacramento and Dr. Thomas C. Durant of New York City were responsible for raising the money required for the construction of the Central Pacific and Union Pacific Railroads, respectively. With the nation distracted by the Civil War and few people understanding the ultimate value of these businesses, they were having a hard time raising any money. By dreaming up clever financial instruments and through fraudulent dealings with the government, these men were able to create and attract capital to their ventures, Huntington doing so in collaboration with Governor Leland Stanford of California, Mark Hopkins, a forty-niner who had come west from Michigan by the Oregon Trail, and Charles Crocker, a 265-pound dry-goods storekeeper who started out as the son of a saloon keeper in Troy, New York. In the beginning, Durant performed his machinations alone.

These men had no trouble seeing themselves as preordained to do anything necessary to achieve the result of seeing their railroads built. They seemed cosmically in tune with Herbert Spencer, who borrowed freely from the recently published theories of Charles Darwin to create what became known as the doctrine of Social Darwinism, which held that "the pursuit of wealth by a spirited few was the major process by which a civilization perfected itself," according to Keith Wheeler. "This view of life . . . made avarice a virtue, or at worst a heroic excess; it dismissed traditional business ethics as a tame, inadequate approach to life's great contest. Fierce, unrelenting competition, Spencer preached, was the only mechanism that fulfilled the harsh terms of natural selection."

Anything necessary was exactly what Huntington and Durant did. They begged, they borrowed dizzying sums, they bribed to the hilt, and finally with the creation of Credit Mobilier ("Moveable Loan" in French) in 1863, named after a respected French firm, and the unwitting help of Abraham Lincoln, the cash poured in and the railroads were built—but at a cost that would stagger the nation.

What happened was this. Frustrated by the lack of actual building,

President Lincoln, who had been a great supporter of the transcontinental railroad, determined to do what he could to get it moving. A few weeks before his assassination, he called into his office Oakes Ames, a sixty-year-old millionaire congressman from Massachusetts who wore about him an aura of unimpeachable integrity. He asked Ames to take charge of the building of the troubled Union Pacific. Ames agreed, and he and his brother Oliver put in a million dollars. Within a few weeks, their Boston associates and friends put in another million and a half.

The trouble was that the brothers put this money not into the Union Pacific but into Credit Mobilier, which turned out to be one of the great money-grabbing bonanzas of the century. Credit Mobilier was a company formed to do the actual building of the railroad, a common practice of railroad promoters in the East. As the directors of the railroad were also the directors of the construction company, the costs of construction included a profit (usually not extravagant) for its investors, in order to bring in investment capital to build the railroad. But such a situation was open to the possibility of wild abuses, as the construction company could pad its actual costs to the limits of its ability to collect these bloated sums. That is what Durant had done when building the Mississippi and Missouri railroad a few years before this. By 1864 Credit Mobilier was charging the Union Pacific $50,000 per mile for construction that was actually costing only $30,000, which caused honest chief engineer Peter Dey to resign in favor of the famous General Grenville Dodge of the Union Army, later to become the mainstay of the Union Pacific. Dodge was slow to catch on to the financial manipulations involved but eventually got fully into the swing of things. In the end, investors in the Credit Mobilier made a profit of $20 million by creating a railroad worth just half of its total capitalization of $110 million.

By 1865 Credit Mobilier directors had sold shares to a few "selected" investors and declared a 100 percent dividend. In the west, the "Big Four" directors of the Central Pacific were doing the same thing through the establishment of the Contract and Finance Company, whose president was Charles Crocker. East or West, by now it was clear that fortunes could be made by building railroads for the sake of building railroads, without a thought given to operating them. This led to a mad scramble of western railroad promotions by the time 1867 arrived. Congressional land grants alone made such ventures enormously profitable. By 1872 Congress had given away land grants totaling 116 million acres, twice the area of Utah, to railroad promoters, even though only one line had actually been built from the Mississippi to the Pacific. It was all accomplished through congressional bribery on a monumental scale. Huntington alone was spending $200,000 to $500,000 at each session of Congress, and rumors of bribery extended to future presidential candidate James G. Blaine, future president

James A. Garfield, Vice President Schuyler Colfax, and even President Ulysses S. Grant himself.

The whole business finally began to unravel in a gigantic scandal in the summer of 1872. Oakes Ames and Dr. Durant got into a bitter feud, and Ames fired Durant. Durant fought back hard, and the whole affair wound up in court, forcing Congress to investigate. When it did, the workings of the entire shoddy business came to light. The sanctimonious Ames, who claimed he was only fulfilling the mandate given him by the martyred Lincoln, sat in the witness chair for a year, seemingly oblivious to any wrongdoing on his part. But a scapegoat was needed, and he was it. Congress censured him, and he returned to Massachusetts, where he shortly died of a stroke. Durant had sold out years earlier and walked away safely from the whole mess, retiring to live quietly in the Catskills.

Huntington, Hopkins, Stanford, and Crocker also came out of it unscathed. When Huntington was called before Congress, his memory of the affairs of his company became quite spotty, considering he was the financial genius behind the Central Pacific. And then there was the unfortunate fire a month before, which had gutted company headquarters and destroyed all the records. Though Congress found that he and the others had made at least $63 million, held most of the $100 million in Central Pacific capital stock, and controlled 9 million acres of land the government had granted the Central Pacific, Congress could not prove any crime and did not hand up any indictments. The congressional committee did not even bother to call the other three C.P. principals.

What sent the country into a tailspin was caused by yet another flimsy railroad enterprise, this one run by New York financier Jay Cooke. His methods were run of the mill for railroad barons; in the government bribery department, he managed to reach not only the aforementioned suspects Colfax and Grant, to whose 1872 reelection campaign he gave millions, but even another future president, Rutherford B. Hayes, a new one on the list. In 1873 a consortium led by J. P. Morgan and Company set out to destroy him. Morgan spread rumors about Cooke's credit, preventing him from obtaining a vital $300 million loan he needed to complete his line, a rickety financial contraption called Perham's People's Pacific Railroad, which Congress, in yet another moment of reckless abandon, had given a charter and 47 million acres of land (after original proprietor Josiah Perham went broke, Cooke had picked up the road for 15 cents on the dollar). When the loan didn't come through, the financial panic known as Black Friday ensued on September 19, 1873, and the country was effectively knocked on its economic ear for the next half decade.

Buckets of cold water were thrown on the western railroad business. But as Charles Francis Adams, grandson of John Quincy Adams and a future president of the Union Pacific, clearly saw, "The simple truth was that through its energetic railroad development, the country was producing real wealth as no country ever produced it before. Behind all the artificial inflation which so clearly foreshadowed a catastrophe, there was also going on a production that exceeded all experience." With all the talk about a transcontinental railroad, it was only when Congress made it possible for sophisticated thieving financiers to bilk the public out of untold millions that the job actually got done. When the battered public regained its footing, it found out that though it had been robbed, it eventually got its money's worth.

Through all this time of corruption and mounting scandal the Union Pacific line was busy and prosperous. The reason was Texas cattle. They were in high demand in eastern markets, but there was no efficient way for Texas ranchers to get them to market. Texas had no railroads, so the only way to bring them east was by driving them over the land. But that was problematic, too, because Missouri and the farmlands of eastern Kansas wouldn't let them on their lands, due to fear of diseases spreading locally from tick-infested Texas cattle. Joseph G. McCoy, partner in a family livestock shipping business in Springfield, Illinois, came up with the solution. He noted that the line of prohibition ran through an area near Junction City, Kansas, and realized that cattle could be shipped from this point without breaking the law. But Junction City, and Solomon City and Salina farther west, wanted no part of stockyards and cowboys, so in 1867 McCoy settled on a ratty little town called Abilene on Mud Creek. On September 5 of that year the first cattle shipment left Abilene for the East, and the era of the cow towns of Kansas had begun. Thirty-five thousand head were shipped out by the end of the season, almost all on the Hannibal and St. Joseph line, due to the initial shortsightedness of Union Pacific officials. Eventually, however, the Union Pacific made a great deal of money from the cattle-shipping business.

The spring of 1868 produced the beginning of a long nightmare for formerly sleepy, respectable little Abilene. Trains from the East disgorged every kind of disreputable person imaginable, people who had come to cater to, and fleece, the wild, hardworking cowboys on their way up from Texas. Carpenters began building a section north of the tracks called Texas Abilene from huge piles of construction materials dumped out of the trains. By July, when the gamblers, whores, and saloon keepers had established lively trades among the cowboys, the *Topeka Commonwealth* noted, "At this writing, Hell is now in session in Abilene." By 1869 it had earned the sobriquet "Godless Abilene" in eastern papers. In 1870 the respectable elements in town determined to clean it up, first by hiring Tom Smith as marshal, and then, after he was murdered, Wild Bill Hickcock, former marshal of Hays, in 1871. He tamed the town that year, which would prove to be Abilene's greatest, and last, year of prosperity as a cow town. By now, farmers were plowing

THE BIRTH OF WALTER CHRYSLER

up the grass and fencing out the cattle here. Besides, the town of Ellsworth, sixty miles west and, with twelve-hundred citizens, much larger than Abilene, was closer to the Texas ranges and nowhere near hostile farmers, so after this it became the major shipping point for cattle. Some hundred-thousand head were waiting to be shipped out of Ellsworth as early as July 1872.

Ellsworth was just as rough a town as Abilene, even though it was bigger and established longer. The usual gunfights hadn't started in the spring of 1872, but this item from the *Ellsworth Reporter* of May 16th of that year gives an idea of typical goings on: "The other morning we witnessed the marshal and assistant arguing a point with a woman. The point in dispute seemed to be the proper way to go to the cooler. The marshal insisted on her walking and she insisted on being carried. As is always the way, the woman came out victorious. Drunk was no name for it."

The town fathers were determined not to have the lawless situation in Abilene repeat itself in Ellsworth, but the usual situations developed by the time twenty-two-hundred cattle were grazing in the environs by midsummer, causing a reporter to remark, familiarly, "Hell is still in session in Ellsworth."

Its season of prosperity and trouble would all be over by the end of 1873, however. In late September the financial panic caused the market for beef to dry up, and cowmen who had not already sold their herds couldn't give them away. The climate had been exceptionally dry, and ranchers moved a lot of cattle west from Ellsworth to find forage. Then the drought caused terrifying dust storms that blighted the entire state. Ranchers went bankrupt and railroads went into receivership, and a hundred miles to the south, Wichita, on the Santa Fe line, began building stockyards and shipping pens, as Dodge City, the last of the great cow towns, was also to do shortly. In 1874, an even drier year, only fourteen thousand cattle were shipped from Ellsworth.

Though the cattle industry remained an important one in Kansas, it was really only an evolutionary step along the way to permanent settlement. Most important, the buffalo had to be gotten rid of to make the Indians back off and disappear from the land. Buffalo hides sold for about $3.50 each, and hunters killed untold millions of these animals between 1868 and 1881, when the herds were finally exterminated. Just the bones alone brought in $8 a ton, each of which was made up from the skeletons of a hundred buffalo. More than $2.5 million worth of bones, representing the carcasses of thirty-one million buffalo, were harvested from the Kansas prairies alone. When the prairies were emptied of the buffalo and the Indians who depended on them, the cowmen, and then the farmers, moved in.

In the center of the state the city of Hays, which established itself around Fort Hays, became a cow town whose history in that trade lasted much longer than Abilene's or Ellsworth's because it was much farther west. After the farmers closed down Ellsworth as a shipping point, Hays would have been the next likely railhead for cattle, but because of the establishment of Witchita and Dodge City to the south as shipping points, it never became more than a way station. Fifteen miles to the west of Hays another little town was started on the Union Pacific, a town that figures greatly in the story of Walter P. Chrysler. This is Ellis, where he was destined to spend all of his formative years.

5

Ellis, Kansas: The Cradle of Walter Chrysler's Life

The emigration's bound to come
and to greet them we will try
Big pig, little pig, root, hog or die
—A. O. McGrew

The wild and wicked border town of Ellis, Kansas, was born at the end-of-track on July 1,1870, when a train pulled in from Ellsworth with section men, equipment, and small buildings that were to be transplanted to a new division the Union Pacific had decided to place there. The main reason was water. Big Creek, which runs through Ellis, provided this scarcest of plains elements in something like abundance for this part of the world. In 1870 the buffalo were all-pervasive on the prairies of western Kansas, and no tree or blade of grass grew that was not eaten or trampled by them, or withered by lack of water. For town civilization to flourish here, water was essential. When the Union Pacific men saw the greenery by the banks of the creek, they knew the needs of people, livestock, cultivation, and locomotives could all be satisfied in this place. The company decided to build the very first roundhouse west of Hays here, and gave signals that it would be maintained as a permanent, important settlement. Ellis never had to fight to establish its footing.

The town was named for First Lieutenant George Ellis, who had joined Company I of the Twelfth Kansas Infantry at Leavenworth on November 3, 1862, and was killed in battle at Jenkin's Ferry in August 1863. This was the same infantry company to which Hank Chrysler belonged, and though they never met, it is interesting to note that his family was to live so long in a town named for his comrade in arms.

Henry H. Metcalf was appointed the first postmaster of the town on July 27, 1870. It was listed as having a population of 150, located 302 miles from the "state line" at Wyandotte.

On August 10, 1870, Mrs. H. W. Smith, affectionately known as Mother Smith, became the first woman to set foot in town. She came to run a big boardinghouse, not yet erected when she arrived. All the town dwellings were either tents or railroad boxcars at that point, and Mother Smith and her seven children lived in Boxcar Row like any tough railroad man until the boardinghouse was built. Later that year Mrs. Dan Moore opened a private school for the few children who had then come to Ellis, and she continued to run it the following year.

Shortly after the railroad men had settled in and begun establishing the Union Pacific's facilities, merchants, doctors, homesteaders, cowboys, tradesmen, and buffalo hunters started to arrive. Of course, in their wake came the usual assortment of bartenders, gamblers, and fancy ladies, along with wanted men shifting along the railroad. Overnight a real town sprang up, with dugout homes on Big Creek, the boxcar buildings, tents out over the prairies, and several small houses built by the Union Pacific and shipped into town. The very first permanent building was a blacksmith shop, erected on Edwards Street (now West 9th Street). By the end of 1870 the Union Pacific had a roundhouse with fourteen stalls servicing locomotives. It was a big, clangorous place employing lots of men. The huge furnaces billowing steam through its smokestacks made it look like a steamboat afloat on the prairies.

In these early days there was lots of land grabbing and claim jumping, and men were mysteriously found shot dead, as there was little regard for law. Both good and bad men died with their boots on. Organized religion did not appear until the First Congregational Church was established on May 30, 1873. Previously, the very first sermon in town was preached by S. D. Storr, superintendent, standing on a dry-goods box at the corner of the Kansas House, otherwise used mostly as a whorehouse.

During the winter of 1871–72 what was to become one of the most famous hotels in western Kansas, the Ellis House, was built at trackside, as a combination hotel, restaurant, and depot. Its dining-room service was celebrated from the Missouri River to the Rocky Mountains. The hotel's advertisement, posted in the lobbies of nearly all hotels between Missouri and Denver, read: "ALL KANSAS PACIFIC RAILWAY TRAINS TAKE MEALS AT THE ELLIS HOUSE—John H. Edwards, Proprietor. This house is centrally located between the Missouri River and Denver in the middle of the great Buffalo Range, and is the only headquarters for buffalo hunters on the line of the Kansas Pacific Railway. All its appointments are first class. Reliable guides and hunters are always at hand to accompany hunting parties. Buffalo humps, tongues and hams furnished to order." One day early in its history, when he didn't like the way things were going at Ellis House, Buffalo Bill Cody, an occasional guide in the area, "managed" Ellis House for six hours to straighten out a few "misunderstandings."

As can be seen from the above, buffalo figured importantly in the beginnings of Ellis. The bounty on their hides had been established for only a couple of years, and they were still plentiful when the town came into existence. Buffalo hunts were widepread, and nearby Hays was a well-known center for such activity.

It is hard to imagine the abundance of the buffalo from our perspective today, but they were a fearfully majestic presence for plains settlers in the early 1870s. Maxine Bradbury in *Profiles of Ellis III*, recalls: "I have read. . . .that early settlers travelling through the Great Plains would occasionally hear throughout the day a hum and drone, as though a distant thunderstorm was approaching, only to behold a huge mass of buffalo coming towards them. One can only imagine the emotion which must have swept through the wagon trains as they travelled, for buffalo could, with little provocation, stampede, and a buffalo stampede took all in its path to destruction." Even standing still they were awesome. "The black mass was alive. Acres of buffalo—miles of buffalo—millions of buffalo," said Zane Grey.

Jennie Smith Martin, a daughter of Mother Smith, remembered their vivid presence at Ellis: "Buffalo over the plains were almost a moving mass. They had three bedding places around Ellis. . . . The herds would come in after dark for water (at Big Creek), then go back and lie down on the ground all night. In the morning at daylight, they would begin to get up, a few at a time, and move off, grazing. Some would be out of sight before the others started. The men would go out and shoot a few, which frightened them and they did not come so close, but for years we could see them grazing in every direction." As time went on, bounties made the plains a killing field for the buffalo here as elsewhere, and the herds were decimated and disappeared. John Begler, a photo historian of old Ellis, said that in those days his pioneer family was one of those who made a living from collecting the buffalo bones left behind by the hunts, selling them for fertilizer.

The buffalo declined precipitously after 1874, and in their place came the Texas longhorn cattle. Because of its exceptional railroad facilities, Ellis had a large, if somewhat brief, part in the Texas cattle trade during the years when so many were being driven north to be shipped east to market. It seems that the Kansas Legislature, responding to the pleas of farmers who wanted tick-infested Texas cattle kept away from their domestic herds, passed an act creating a "dead line" beyond which no Texas cow was to be driven. The line drawn across the state left only two towns on railroads outside the zone—Dodge City and Ellis. The former already was a prosperous cowtown, but now Ellis also found a place in the cattle bonanza.

With the buffalo out of the picture, the Texas longhorns, called "Calico Cows" due to their motley array of colors, foraged and fattened on the plains. Very different from the beef cattle of today, these were hardy, lean creatures with legs built for long, elastic strides and quick travel, perfect for droving up from Texas to the railheads of Kansas. Over a million head were shipped from Dodge City and Ellis between 1876 and 1879. However, in the summer of 1878, interest in driving cattle to Ellis dried up, and Dodge City regained its position as undisputed "queen of the cow towns" for as long as such places remained important. Hence the famous phrase, "Abilene the first, Ellsworth the meanest, and Dodge City the last." As for Ellis, all in all the Union Pacific kept the cattle business booming there for about five years.

Of course, with the cattle business came the cowboys, and with them the inevitable dens of iniquity and lawlessness they engendered. Cowpunchers who frequented Ellis at the end of their cattle drives branded it a wild, tough town. The saloons and dance halls along the main sin strip, Edwards Street, never closed, and the cowboys loved it. According to Kitty Dale, Ellis historian and the first curator of the Chrysler Boyhood Home: "In the '70s ability with a gun was the measure of a man's success. Along Edwards Street, full of whiskey and the devil, cowboys would whoop it up, riding their horses out of the streets and onto the plankboard sidewalks, shooting out a few glass storefronts and lassoing lampposts and hitching rails." Harry Buskirk, who clerked at Tom Daly's store, which shared a building with Tom Daly's saloon on Jefferson Street, had it rough. Cowboys used the furniture in the saloon as shooting targets, and the walls and ceilings were riddled with bullets. Since he lived over the saloon, he had a piece of thick steel laid under his bed to prevent being accidentally shot as he slept. Despite all this, Kitty Dale noted that the cowboys were "never less than perfectly polite to ladies."

Among the somewhat shadier ladies to be found at Ellis was a notorious madam named Ida May, who first showed up as a pioneer prostitute at Hays in 1869, though her stay there was brief. In April 1878 she rented the notorious Western Hotel on Edwards Street and opened her own brothel. She made a bundle from the free-spending cowboys that summer, but in late September some of the wild ones broke into her house, destroying windows, furniture, and everything else they could lay their hands on. The September 28 Hays City Sentinel sadly opined, "The 'Western House' in Ellis has been deserted by its frail inmates."

The cowboys were determined to have a good time in Ellis, and the citizens were just as determined to keep the peace, so clashes inevitably developed. Lawmen there were kept plenty busy, but one of them, "Texas Jack" Moody, a cowboy who walked both sides of the legal fence, contributed mightily to the wild reputation of early Ellis and its surroundings. At various times he was either a marshal or sheriff's deputy, committing assault (armed or otherwise), and sometimes he was both. After three months of Moody's shenanigans, the Hays City Sentinel carried this item on June 8, 1878: "Deputy Sheriff Moody, by accident, received a 'thirty-two' pistol ball in his teeth. Jack bit it close and passed it around into his cheek, where, at last account, it still lingered. He says he is not to be killed by powder and ball, and there's no use shooting at him any more."

A man named Pat Hickey early on built Hickey's Corner, a ramshackle collection of buildings that housed some of the town's first businesses. Hickey himself was known as the town's "curbstone banker," and his Hickey's Stone Barn and Livery Stable was the site of the town's first court, of the kangaroo variety.

Where there are people, either permanent or transient, businesses spring up, and they did in Ellis, too. Hickey's Corner on Edwards Street housed Ramsey's Barber Shop, M. M. Fuller's law office, the Ellis Print Shop, and later A. I. Cromb's candy and notions store. Next to it were Tom Daly's store and saloon; the post office building; the Griffin and Holman Drug Store (which dispensed more entertaining drinkables than drugs); John Geyer's property, partitioned into a saloon and Forker's meat market; G. G. Lee's building, divided into a tin shop and saloon on one side and Mrs. Keyser's bakery shop on the other; the firm of Kelly and Omerod; the express office (where a $20,000 payroll disappeared one day; later the express office became a cowboy supply store and then a doctor's office); and finally at the end, the infamous Western Hotel. All of this on one principal street, by the mid-1870s.

In 1874 Mennonite immigrants from the Crimea introduced a new kind of wheat to the plains. It was quite hardy, capable of withstanding the extremes of heat and cold found in that part of the country, and it quickly became a popular crop. By 1876 there were population increases around Ellis due to the wheat farming that homesteaders and settlers were bringing with them. Many of these people were migrants from the East who disembarked from the Union Pacific trains and established little settlements near Ellis. Earlier, in 1872, the first group to come was the Syracuse Colony, followed by the Ohio Colony and the Illinois Colony. Germans, Swedes, Russians, Frenchmen, and Austrians all came to Ellis, later establishing separate colonies of their compatriots around the town. (To this day the numerous immigrants from the town of Bukovina in Austria support a lively society in Ellis.) These immigrants all maintained their quaint national customs and dress, and spoke in their native languages. To deal with the tribulations of their strange new lives, they also needed the solace of their own faith, which meant among other things that in 1876 a Catholic priest, the Reverend Adolph Wibbert of Salina, began saying mass on the third Saturday of each month in the township hall. Eventually the individuality of each little hamlet of foreigners was recognized with nicknames like "Little Moscow" or "Humbogen."

There was also the "Colored Exodus," which came from Kentucky and Tennessee; some destitute families among them remained in Ellis, but others, many barefoot, trekked forty miles to establish their own promised land in the colony of Nicodemus, where they established their spreads on homestead land near the banks of the Solomon River.

All through this early period Ellis was a frontier town, and throughout the 1870s that meant danger of various kinds, from weather to cowboys and gunslingers. Of all the terrors menacing the early settlers, however, none was worse than the fear of Indians. Partly it was because they seemed utterly different from the white man, their ways mysterious and little known. They kept themselves hidden, and when they appeared it often meant trouble. Famous and terrible incidents that occurred around Ellis in the 1870s kept the townspeople constantly vigilant throughout the decade.

The first happened in September 1872. Ellis residents Dick Jordon and his brother George, both buffalo hunters, decided to go on a hunt with their hired Swedish boy. Dick's wife, Mary, a daughter of Mother Smith, was depressed over the loss of her four-month-old baby and went along with them, as she had done before. Since buffalo hunts took weeks, no one expected to hear from them for some time. The return of the Jordons' Newfoundland, Queenie, three weeks later didn't alarm anyone because she had been sent home before for chasing buffalo. But a few weeks later a man came to Buffalo Station with the news that on Walnut Creek, some twenty or twenty-five miles south of the Smoky Hill River, he had come upon a wagon with some sacks bearing the name R. Jordon, and a body lying nearby. Fort Hays, contacted by telegram, sent a sergeant and ten privates to the scene, guided by the hunter who had discovered the scene. A grisly sight awaited them. Dick Jordon and the Swedish boy, Fred Nonnan, were found scalped; later, George Jordon was also found scalped some distance away. Of Mary Jordon, only her apron and sunbonnet, which was buried with her husband, were ever found. Since the Interior Department considered the Indians subdued and friendly by this point, the army could do nothing. But the residents of Ellis felt an ominous chill that never left them whenever moccasin prints were discovered in the dirt outside of town. For years mothers used this tale to frighten wandering, careless children, and it always sent them running home whenever they realized they had strayed too far from home.

Two years later, in September 1874, newspaper articles and army bulletins reassured people that the Smoky Hill Valley was settled, and with the red men gone to the reservations, Indian raids were a thing of the past. This attitude was pervasive and everyone relaxed their vigilance. This led to one of the worst massacres western Kansas had ever seen.

The German family of Georgia, John and Lydia, their six daughters and one son, decided in 1866 to leave their home in the Blue Ridge Mountains, which had been devastated by guerillas in the Civil War. It took them four years to accumulate the money to outfit a wagon and oxteam. In 1870 they set out for Colorado, proceeding very slowly, stopping to make money for the journey wherever they could. On August 15, 1874, they left Missouri on the last leg of their journey. At Ellis, they were encouraged to go south on the old B.O.D. trail, as there was not enough water or grass for the animals if they followed the railroad tracks. Besides, they were told, the Indians would be no danger. They set out towards the west on the Smoky, as advised. On the morning of September 11th, a party of seventeen warriors led by Kicking Horse attacked the family and murdered John, Lydia, daughters Rebecca and Julia, and son Stephen. Four other daughters, Catherine, 17, Sophia, 12, Juliana, 7, and Nancy Adelaide, 5, were taken off by the Indians. Shortly thereafter the two younger girls were abandoned on the prairie, but somehow survived and were recovered in November. After protracted negotiations, the two older girls, half starved like the Indians, were handed over at the Cheyenne Agency on February 26, 1875. The incident was widely publicized, and aroused great national sympathy for the four orphaned girls.

Aside from one more important Cheyenne disturbance almost four years later that figures in Walter Chrysler's life, this really was the end of the Indian troubles of western Kansas. Human beings relate peculiarly to tragedy, however. Not only the event but the ghost of the event lives long in us, shivering in our souls. No one then living in Ellis ever forgot these dreadful deeds, and new arrivals like the Chryslers in 1879, assumed knowledge of them like garments never to be discarded.

So this was the place to which Hank Chrysler's family migrated when young Walter was about three years old. They had moved to Brookfield when he was one and a half in late 1876, and resided there in a handsome building made of native sandstone, topped by an attractive mansard roof. Though the house was small, it was expensive-looking for that time and place. Then, when Hank Chrysler was assigned the run from Junction City to Ellis that became his for the next twenty-seven years, the family settled in the town at the end of his run. And this is where the story of Walter P. Chrysler really begins.

6

Boyhood in Ellis

Little fishes in a brook
Papa catch 'em on a hook
Mama fry 'em in a pan
Baby eat 'em like a man

"I am a machinist. Trained from my boyhood to penetrate the workings of machines, I find myself now excited by the thought of exploring my own mechanism, for it is in keeping with my character that I should seek to discover what makes me, this man I am, tick and go. I always want to know how things work. Had I been Aladdin, I am certain that after just one wish or two, I'd have taken that old lamp apart to see if I could make another, better lamp."

In 1936 Walter Chrysler began working on a memoir, in collaboration with C. Boyden Sparkes, which was eventually called *Life of an American Workman*. It was serialized in the *Saturday Evening Post* in 1937, and printed up in book form in a limited edition of five hundred copies, given as gifts to family, friends, and major libraries in the United States. What is quoted above is the opening not of this book, but of the original manuscript, when it was to be called *Taking the Lamp Apart*. Jack Chrysler, Jr., a grandson of Walter Chrysler, has preserved this manuscript. As always with manuscripts, there are things in it that are closer to fresh memories and original impressions than the final polished version, and particularly since Chrysler was a man of such clear, vivid expression, it is especially illuminating to have his first thoughts available to us.

Young Walt's very first memory, from when he was five years old, involved a lamp, an adventure, and a promise. The little barefoot boy, in gingham shirt and denim pants attached to it with buttons, was nagging his mama for a slice of sugar bread as he played at her feet. She, with a German fairy-story fancifulness that might have been appreciated by Walt Disney (many of whose family also came from the environs of Ellis) focused on an old brass lamp on a shelf, using it to help the child understand his own needs and those of others. "You must go to the store," she told him.

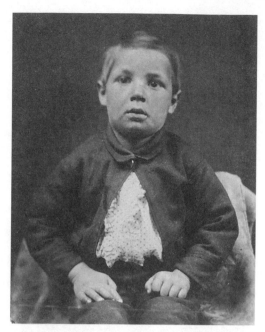

The earliest known photograph of Walter Chrysler, age three. (*Courtesy Frank B. Rhodes*)

"The lamp is empty and therefore hungry—just like you," she told him. "We must give his wick a big drink or he will sulk and keep us in darkness tonight. You take this can and get some coal oil." Off he went, with a piece of blackened potato on the spout of his hungry oil can friend, toward the railroad tracks and the stores.

Suddenly he saw a young boy racing over the tracks toward him at full speed. "Indians! Indians are coming!" he yelled. Still clutching the oil can, Walt turned tail and ran home, "clearing buffalo grass at just about the height of a prairie chicken when it flies for fresh cover." Yipping a warning to his mother, he clattered down the stairs to the cyclone cellar, where "my memory of that occurrence ends as abruptly as a picture that is torn across."

Another memory, probably of the same event, was of sitting in the dust on the second floor of the Ellis House amid frightened ladies in shawls and sunbonnets and men making savage gestures of bravado with rifles, axes, and whiffletrees. The Indians didn't get him then or ever, despite recurrent scares. Late in the decade it was the famous Dull Knife who caused the fear. When Walt was three and a half, little more than two years after Custer's Last Stand at Little Bighorn, Dull Knife and a band of Northern Cheyennes, whose people were dying from the unaccustomed climate of the Southern

Walter Chrysler, age eight. (*Courtesy Walter P. Chrysler Boyhood Home*)

Cheyenne territory where they had been domiciled since 1876, broke out of Fort Reno in a desperate attempt to reach the northern territory of the Sioux. In their flight they laid waste all the settlers' homes in their path, killing 20 in Decatur County and 11 in Rawlins County. The Indians murdered every man they could find for 15 miles along Beaver and Sappa Creeks; coming upon one schoolhouse, they killed all the bigger boys. Captured in northwestern Nebraska, they broke out once again, this time from Fort Robinson, on January 9th, 1879. But now Dull Knife was just about the only one to escape to the Sioux, and the last great Indian raid on the plains was over.

Around places like Ellis, though, rumors of trouble and raids persisted for years, fanned by the flames of gossip told over steaming mugs of coffee in settlers' kitchens. After all, Dull Knife had escaped and lived as a free man until his death in 1883, and in those circumstances anything was possible. Why, in the '70s, according to John F. Taylor, another Ellisite, George Kinney, had actually picked up Dull Knife's ration ticket on the plains and carried it in his pocket during the chase given after the old chief's last raid. Many thought that more than likely he would be seen

Miss Cartwright's music class. Della Forker is at the extreme left, last row, and Miss Cartwright is seated to her left. Walter Chrysler is seated dead center, second row. (*Courtesy Walter P. Chrysler Boyhood Home*)

again, seeking some bloody vengeance on the town. He never was. That age was past.

❖   ❖   ❖

The Chryslers' first house in Ellis was one of three the railroad owned. It was a small adobe-covered place situated on a little knoll at what is now the corner of Washington and Eleventh Streets. It was very plain, as railroad cottages always were, and not well put together. Sometimes, when they got out of bed in the pitch black of winter mornings, the family had to scamper through several inches of snow that had drifted in at night through the cracks around the badly fitting windows. For years the kitchen fire was the only source of heat the family knew in winter, and each day, with her amazing energy, Walt's mother woke up the family before sunrise with the clangor of iron lids on her cookstove.

That kitchen stove was fired with coal, not buffalo or cow chips, because this was a railroad family, privileged to buy coal from the company. Despite its plainness, the house did have a few amenities. There was a little porch, and in addition there were two bedrooms besides the main room where the family cooked, ate, and spent most of its time. Looking back on his early years, Walter's image of his father always had him with a paintbrush or a hammer or a saw in his hand, trying to make a better life for his family. "A railroad shanty? Oh, no. It was Hank Chrysler's home, a house to swell my mother's heart with pride as she showed it off to neighbors who still were living half buried in the prairie earth in houses built of sod."

A little girl entered the household on December 17, 1883, when Irene Chrysler was born to Mary and Hank. She must have been a great consolation to mama, for at last she had a little female companionship in a household of noisy energetic men.

Meals were big and hearty for this hardworking family. Walt was often sent out early to the butcher for a great big hunk of gristly maroon and blue buffalo rump. It was plentiful and cheap, and the closest to beef anybody in Ellis came until the early 1880s. Mama simmered it overnight in a huge iron pot and served it the next day as the delicious foundation for a huge Kansas breakfast, followed by Buffalo steak, potatoes, and pancakes. Sometimes there was hominy to build a dyke for a lake of gravy. They owed every grain of that to Mama. She not only cooked it but grew and processed the corn herself. "There was no task she ever dodged for lack of strength or skill or willingness," wrote Walt.

She was also no softy. Mama ruled the roost with an iron hand, and in that hand she held a good strong hairbrush with which she exercised her authority. "We two boys. . . . were a pair of fighting, chore-dodging cubs, unruly and frequently in need of taming." When they neglected their chores, "or when we disobeyed her slightest order, our mother spanked us." She continued to do so until he was seventeen, once jarring all the bristles loose from the brush. Big as he became, he never doubted his mother's ability to "improve" his moral outlook and intentions toward his responsibilities.

In this and in all things her instincts and feelings were reflective of her Germanic background. She had a Teutonic sense of thrift about the household, knitting or sewing every garment the family wore. When Walt finally was old enough to need long pants, she took an old pair of Hank's, turned them upside down and inside out, recut them to Walt's measure, and made him a pair he was proud to wear.

She spoke German to her children when their father was not around. It was gibberish to Hank, but the children understood it. "Now I have forgotten almost all my German, but this I do remember: in her tenderest moods, my mother's words came boiling out of her in German," Walt wrote.

Hank was the softy. His skin had been turned to leather by the Kansas sun and wind and blizzards, but it was wrapped around a tender heart. He never laid a hand on his sons in anger, instead reasoning with them to get obedience. The children respected and loved him, and were fiercely proud of him, too. "My mother's pumpkin pies were famous out in Ellis, but Henry Chrysler was known, I guess, from end to end of the Union Pacific."

In the mornings Walt would walk beside his papa, lugging along his dinner pail as he left the house. A big six-shooter sagged below his father's coat, "with a black butt of a size to fill his fist. When I was ten, the handle of that weapon hung on my father just at the level of my stubbly, home-cut hair, above my eager eyes." Even that late, in the mid-1880s, dangers lurked along the railroad, and earlier experiences had taught Hank Chrysler that a locomotive engineer had to be prepared for any emergency. The gun certainly lent credence to any tales of menace along the tracks that he told his adventure-hungry sons.

Very occasionally he would get a permit for Walt to ride with him up in the cab all the way to Brookville. They would see the blue-coated soldiers at Fort Hays, and Hank would give the boy chills as he pointed out the sites of Indian ambushes that had occurred beside the tracks. They would take in the atmosphere of Brookville for a few hours, but the biggest thrill came during the night run home, when Hank made the engine roar across the land in a fast-paced drama of fire and muscle. Sometimes Walt got to put his hands on top of his father's big greasy fingers as he pulled the cotton bell cord; sometimes he even got to pull the whistle cord all by himself, sending a low hooting moan out through the blackness of the prairie night. "It was a perfect experience to ride in the midst of that fire-and-water mir-acle and to know that to the boss of it, my father, I was more important than his engine. The old engine was just our slave. Climbing down, at the end of our run, to the cinders of the right of way in Ellis, the part of me most tired would be my face, and it was tired from grinning in my hours of ecstasy."

Mama's unfailing law was that the boys must not be out alone after dark, and if they were, they could be sure they would encounter her for-bidding figure, hairbrush in one hand, as they came through the back door. However, despite this foreknowledge of doom, sometimes Walt and Ed would hop the evening train to Hays, riding the baggage car to adventure along the tracks. "On certain nights the excitement was worth the fee."

But not everything that interested the young boy was adventure on the railroad. Making music was always a merry part of Walter Chrysler's life, and this interest began at his father's instigation. When Walt was twelve or so, the veterans of the GAR (Grand Army of the Republic) chose and or-ganized ten boys into a drum corps so they could march with the men in their Memorial Day parade. Walt was one of the chosen ones, and Hank drilled and taught them all, drawing on the experience of his three years' service as a drummer boy in the Civil War. They learned to drum as he had, one twenty time at first, then as they improved, faster. "I stamped around that hall behind my father until he fixed into my blood the rhythm of the beat for marching men. It seems as if I hear his voice and see the dust rise from the floor as he marked the time with his big foot and called out, 'one step, one step, one step.'" Hank bought his son "a snare drum that was good enough to take to war, and he taught me how to stand as soldiers do. The drilling of those days fixed on me, I suppose for life, the habit of putting my feet at right angles, heels together, with my hands at my side." Indeed, through all the years of his fame, even fifty years later, this was Walt's almost invariable stance in pictures, unchanged from his 1890s poses with the Union Pacific band.

This was just the beginning of his musical education, however, as Mama thought a working knowledge of something more elevated than a drum was required for her son. So once a week he was sent off to Miss Cartwright's classes to learn to play the piano, one of three boys in town so enjoined. He learned to play, but mainly he remembered that whenever his attention wandered, he fixated on "17 round buttons arranged in a series of extraordinary curves over the promontories in the front of Miss Cartwright's basque." What kept him going, however, was neither the piano nor the basque, but an extraordinarily pretty girl in the class named Della Forker, who one day would become the mainstay of his life.

Later on, Walt learned the B-flat clarinet, tootling and tweeting on the thing until his mouth got sore, and the tuba, which he took up after his brother Ed's instrument turned green from neglect. To the end of his days, if it hooted or tweetled, if you could bang it or plunk on it, Walter Chrysler could play it, and play it well. Through the decades untold foot-tapping, jiggly fun came from his music, wherever he was. There are hilarious films from the 1930s showing his swanky kids being serenaded by a string orchestra as they bathed in the waters of Palm Beach, while nearby, Walt is tinkling out some piece of razzmatazz on an old upright. Wherever Walt Chrysler was making music was the place to be if you wanted to have a good time.

Besides music, the other thing Walt played was marbles. Walt was the local champion, good enough to play, and win from, the men. That was how he kept himself in marbles, since his mother would never have allowed him to spend money on anything so frivolous.

He got something else besides marbles from those men—a thorough knowledge of bad words. His salty railroad man's vocabulary stuck with him for the rest of his life, and he became famous for it.

Like all Ellis boys then, he was a scrappy little hellion. He had to be. There were often four or five fights in the fifteen minutes of school recess, and if you fought back hard against your attackers, you didn't have to do battle as often. Those who couldn't do it led a dog's life, and some ran away.

Ellis was a rough town in those times. On days when the cowboys or the railroad men were paid off, the saloons were set like traps, and all hell broke loose. People cowered in their homes as half the town got shot up by bands of thirsty, carousing men bent on the devil and destruction. Considering the raw quality of the liquor at the time, some of these people were literally crazed with drink during these episodes, oblivious to their actions until they had slept off the effects of their benders.

In these circumstances, neither nature nor nurture made Walt a docile boy. When he came home from the Methodist church on Sundays, his mother made him take off his good clothes. "Probably with the clothes I stripped off something of the spirit," he said.

If he wanted to make a few nickels for candy or other things, he worked for the money just like everybody else in town. His first moneymaking notion came from an advertisement in one of the many catalogs and magazines passed around among neighbors in Ellis as a means of keeping up with the latest in the world outside. Walt decided to be an agent for calling cards, and his mother was his first customer, choosing a design of chaste clasped hands cuffed in lace, decorated with forget-me-nots and roses that hid the caller's name. When the cards arrived and were passed around, all the ladies wanted cards of their own, and the boom was on. Samples at the ready, enterprising young Walt cleaned up.

When that pond was fished out, he began peddling silverware from an elegant-looking sample case lined in red plush and white satinette that practically sold the silver all by itself. The housewives were desperate to have it, and every payday many would buy a box of nine assorted knives, forks, and spoons, until they had a dozen of each.

Though Walt was very satisfied with the results of his businesses, Mama had a milk business of her own with her three cows, and she needed help. A bit of hairbrush persuasion convinced Walt to give up other financial pursuits to join his mother in this enterprise. Ed was supposed to help out, too, but as he got older he slacked off and beat up his brother if he didn't do all the work. Frequently using some of the colorful vocabulary he had picked up from the railroad men, Walt mucked out the stable, forked down the hay, and milked the cows.

He also had to sell the milk and cream, and that's where the money part came in. Every evening he dragged a big open tin can full of milk from house to house, where he measured out each customer's share with a tin quart cup he carried along. Orders for cream meant extra trips. He had about twenty customers in all. Nobody paid for anything until payday, so he had a small account book he pulled out of his hip pocket at every stop to keep his records straight. He collected on payday at the rate of 5 cents a quart. For his labors, Mama paid him one cent a quart.

Much later on, when he became a works manager and later a manufacturer, he would keep small but precisely detailed cost books in his jacket pocket all the time so that he always knew where he was with manufacturing expenses; it was a habit he learned early.

❧   ❧   ❧

Ellis grew in population and the trappings of civilization pretty fast. Soon the railroad town gained a real bank and a butcher that sold real beef. Next thing people knew, there was a coal yard and a lumberyard, a second general store, and an independent post office not part of any store. The Methodist Episcopal congregation was organized in 1878 with Dr. A. Caruthers as minister. Tom Daly donated materials for a building, and at a cost of $1,200 free from debt, the church was dedicated on January 25, 1880. In 1882 the town went all out and constructed a fine two-story stone school building with an elaborate ornamental tower. All classes were given here, and the basement housed the GAR hall. A Masonic lodge was chartered on February 15, 1887, with eighteen members. At last, as evidence of its growth and stability, Ellis was incorporated as a Third-Class City on January 30, 1888. George Johnson was its first mayor.

The growing prosperity did not pass by the Chryslers, and in 1889 Hank Chrysler built his family a new home, much bigger than the old one, at 104 West 10th Street. It had two stories, a shingled roof, a nice porch with a dormer window above it, and a picket fence around the yard. He planted lilac bushes, still there today, in a corner of the front yard, and maples that grew large enough to shade the property. It also had something very progressive for Ellis then: a windmill, so that the house could have running water. This occasioned a bathtub, for which a special room was built next to the kitchen. He built the tub out of sheets of copper enclosed in a sheath of tongue-and-groove boards. It was the marvel, and envy, of all the neighbors.

Sam Beverly, a childhood friend, had one clear memory of that house. He used to stay over in Ed and Walt's upstairs bedroom from time to time. It was quite comfy enough for three boys to bed down, only they didn't stay bedded down very long. The old iron bed with its pieced coverlet was placed by the window, but only two heads at a time could bob at the opening to see and hear the trains go hooting out of town, so big fights ensued, with Walt usually the loser. Every time a boy stayed the night, there was a pillow fight that did not end until Walt, the smallest boy, got so mad he tore off half the other boys' nightclothes and chased them with a baseball bat. Walt got teased at home, teased at school, and later teased in the shops. It maddened him, but it certainly toughened him up.

This is the house now known as the Walter P. Chrysler Boyhood Home, dedicated as a museum in a ceremony attended by Chrysler chairman K. T. Keller and other company officials on August 27, 1955, and maintained as such to this day by the City of Ellis. In 1994 Jack Chrysler and Frank Rhodes, Jr., Walter Chrysler's grandson and great-grandson respectively, added a fine small museum dedicated to Chrysler's life in a building behind the Boyhood Home.

In 1889 Walt turned fourteen and began to grow in body and interests. Hank gave him a double-barreled Remington shotgun, cut down in the railroad shops to fit him. Of course, he loaded his own shells the same as everyone else did. He was a good shot, and at Christmas he received a dozen brass shells from his father, which was a very nice present. Still his parents weren't overly generous, and he had to keep an eye out for moneymaking opportunities. At sixteen he took a summer job as a delivery boy for Henderson the grocer, relieving that man from doing the job himself. For $10 a month, he worked from 6 A.M. to 10:30 P.M.

The next year, when he had finished high school, he went back to work for Henderson, now earning $14 a month. But he did not like the money or the prospects, and quit to learn about machinery. This made Ed, a Union Pacific apprentice, sore, because he thought one machinist in the family was enough. "Why don't you be a boilermaker?" he'd yell at Walt, who would yell back just as loudly, "I don't want to be a boilermaker!"

Hank was on Ed's side, but not because he wanted Walt to be a boilermaker. He wanted his son to be the first in the family to get a college education. One of the prosperous merchants in town was going to send his son to Quincy College at Quincy, Illinois, and wanted Hank to send Walt, too, so his son wouldn't get lonely. But Walt liked that other boy even less than he liked the idea of college, and put up a big struggle. After being nagged to distraction, Hank put down his foot and refused to give the necessary approval for Walt to become an apprentice at the Union Pacific machine shop.

Walt had not been an ideal student by any means. Lanny Frost, the longtime schoolmistress at Ellis, did not have an easy time filling his head with "jogafy," "pomes," "rithmatic," and moral lessons from the ubiquitous McGuffey Readers. Though he spoke as if he had graduated from high school, evidence seems to indicate that he did not. The first class graduated from the high school in 1892, and according to Anna Maude Leisenring, one of its three members, Walter Chrysler was not among them. She claimed that he had dropped out to learn the machinist's trade at the Union Pacific shops before the term ended. In addition to Leisenring's statement, the high school has never come up with any record of his actually having graduated. He was certainly hot-tempered and headstrong, so what actually did happen at that time would be consistent with the turn of events she described.

Walt got mad as hell at his father when Hank refused to allow him to become an apprentice, so he went down to the shops and got hired as a sweeper. For 10 cents an hour, ten hours a day, he swept the greasy planks of the shops as they had never been swept before, and did all the other jobs a janitor was supposed to do. He carried miles of alkali-caked boiler flues, 16 feet long and 150 pounds each, to the sheds where they were cleaned up. No matter how hard the work was, he loved it. At the shops he could see the mechanics work on the mysteries of the locomotives' exposed engines, and he envied them their knowledge and labor. He was allowed to bring any tool from home and grind it on the big shop grindstone, and this too made him feel closer to being part of the mechanics' lives.

Cocky and stubborn, he stuck it out for six months, at the end of which he confronted the master mechanic, Edgar Easterbrook, later his brother's father-in-law. Easterbrook knew Walt worked hard, didn't bellyache, and was liked by the men, so he took it upon himself to persuade Hank to give his son permission to become an apprentice. He succeeded, and Walt began his four-year term as a machine-shop appentice with the Union Pacific. His starting pay was 5.5 cents an hour, a little over half what he had earned as a sweeper. But at last he had the chance to become what he wanted to be in life. He was in ecstasy, as only a seventeen-year-old can be.

7

Going to Work at the Union Pacific Roundhouse

Where is my April of old?
Frank Loesser
Spring Will Be A Little Late This Year

In 1936, when he was over sixty, Walter Chrysler kept a special memento of his father on his desk high up in the tower of the Chrysler Building. It was his big glass-covered silvery steam gauge, upon which his life, and so many others, had depended through the years. This was Hank Chrysler's dearest implement, tested constantly for accuracy. For Walter Chrysler it had become a talisman of his own young manhood, and the life he formed from it.

"Gazing upon its face, obliged no longer now to register demonic pressures, it sometimes seems to me as if I can hear my father's engine whistle blowing to me faintly on the wind from far out of Ellis on the Kansas prairie horizon. What I hear, of course, is just a shrillness in the traffic noises rising from the street; yet it works a miracle! I can almost see the bustling at the little Ellis station platform at the moment his engine pulled the night train from Junction City into Ellis. It was his engine; his in a way that a trooper's horse is his, an extension of his power and intelligence, to defend, to brag about and love.

"Sometimes the vision takes another form and the engine, venting cautious chuff, chuff, chuffs, is nosing through a roundhouse door and I am down below the level of its wheels, working in a roundhouse pit with a sooty face and my arms grease-blackened, all my muscles hard and lean and young. Many times I have wished I really could hear again my father's engine whistle as I used to hear it just before it reached the Big Creek bridge. Well, music works a trick for my memory, too; a band marching up Fifth Avenue may send a bit of melody, just a bar or two, that touches things within my mind. It sets me thinking of a time when I was a machine-trade apprentice in the railroad shops, when I played a tuba in the band, played

The Ellis Nine, 1889. Walter Chrysler is in the back row, second from the right. (*Courtesy Walter P. Chrysler Boyhood Home*)

second base on the baseball team, and walked, on Sunday afternoons, with Della Forker to the Big Creek bridge."

To have become a Union Pacific apprentice was to live on one of life's dizzying peaks, as it seemed to him then. He thought of himself as "a cadet of that vast loom for weaving the Western half of the continent into the nation. Not merely the U.P. but railroading, the entire art as we then knew it, held my imagination in focus." He had passed the stiff apprentice examination and was proud of it, as many others didn't make the grade. Now he was ready for what he saw as his life's work, and all the other things that he folded into it.

❧   ❧   ❧

One of the things he dearly loved in those apprentice days was baseball. A team had been formed among the boys in Ellis by the mid-1880s, and Walt got caught up in this new craze, just like so many other kids across the country. He was good at it too, a sought-after and admired player. On June 8, 1894, the *Ellis Review* published a picture of all the players on the team. A lean and taut Walt is squinting at the camera from the back row. Ed McDonald wrote verses for each of the players on the team. This is Walt's:

The Union Pacific Band, Ellis, Kansas, c. 1894. Walter Chrysler, holding cornet, is in the center. (*Courtesy Walter P. Chrysler Boyhood Home*)

Walt Chrysler he is on the team
   At running he is smart;
He could catch a streak of lightning
   Unless it got a start.

Wherever he went on the railroads he played baseball, and if there wasn't any around, he got it organized. Decades later, when he was a great auto magnate, he could be seen with sleeves rolled up and bat at the ready in company-sponsored games at places such as Belle Isle in Detroit. "Hi, I'm Walt," he'd say, with a big smile and his hand extended.

And then there was his music. Any time the Union Pacific Band played at Ellis, it could turn the dullest day into a time of excitement and fun. Walt was part of it from the beginning, swelling with pride from the cheers of the folks lined up along the wooden arcade in front of the shops. Among the band's nineteen members, Walt played the snare drum, Ed played the tuba, their friend Joe McMahon played the slide trombone, and Walt's friend Charlie Keagy played the bass drum. After Walt took over Ed's forgotten tuba, he became so proficient at it that he invested in a noble silver-plated one with a burnished golden bell, imported from Kansas City. He learned other instruments besides the drum and tuba to serenade the ladies, but of the latter instrument he remarked, "You could play a solo on the tuba, but you were likely to be the only one who cared for it." In later years, in

Walter Chrysler, left, and other young sports of Ellis. (*Courtesy Walter P. Chrysler Boyhood Home*)

moments of triumph or stress, he would take any brass instrument at hand and blat out the tuba part from *The William Tell Overture*—surely a unique way to express bursting emotion.

The Union Pacific band was formally organized in 1890, and from the beginning it was a big hit, playing and winning band contests even in distant cities. From Topeka to Denver it was known as the best band on anybody's railroad. Ed Pearson, who led it, won first-place honors and a gold medal over eighteen other contestants in a solo cornet contest; he was the only cornetist in western Kansas who could triple-tongue his instrument, and he made quite a show as he marched at the head of parades in the streets of towns they visited. They won contests as far away as Salt Lake City, and when they won $100 in the second-class (without reed instruments) category in Denver in 1896, the *Denver Post* said: "It was a second-class band, but its music was first class."

For "state occasions" the band wore blue trousers with their jackets; otherwise they usually wore just overalls with the coats. Walt's band jacket hangs today on a hook attached to a closet door at the Boyhood Home. It is dark scarlet, with black piping around the collar, and scalloping down the front forming maroon clovers looped around with gold. Gold-and-green striped epaulets piped with gold braid adorn the shoulders, completing an altogether handsome and impressive uniform top.

Walter Chrysler at eighteen with two of the belles of Ellis. (*Courtesy Walter P. Chrysler Boyhood Home*)

Walt remembered other less formal times when "our uniforms were simply overalls and caps with long bills, so that when we marched, with red bandannas around our necks, we looked like locomotive engineers. One year, in our overalls and wearing big sunflowers, we band fellows rode, on railroad passes, to Kansas City and marched in the Priests of Pallas parade, an annual festival; *Creole Belles*, it seems to me, was what we played best that year."

According to Kitty Dale, one Hays old-timer remembered sticking very close to Walt whenever the Union Pacific band came to that city because Walt gave twenty-five-cent tips to kids who held his music in nighttime parades; the other players just gave out nickels and dimes. This same man recalled that Walt was considered the "bon vivant, or Beau Brummel, of Ellis. He just about had his choice of the prettiest girls in Hays. But Hays equaled the score with the late George Philip. George had his pick of the comeliest girls in Ellis. That's the way the score stood as one remembers hearing the back fence conversation."

Walt Chrysler always knew how to have fun in a robust, hearty way. Music and jokes and sports and dancing were the thing, and he plunged into all of them with gusto, pulling everyone along with him into a good time. And nothing could make a good time better than a pretty girl. But this was Ellis, and if you wanted to take up with any of the decent daughters of the town, you kept your high spirits in check. Whiskey, cigarettes, card playing, and "bad women" were frowned upon, and woe to the young blade who had a reputation for a close association with any of these works of the devil. Nevertheless, the Ellis boys indulged in such things (except in the case of the bad women, where it was only conversation) in an underground fashion—literally underground, for the Union Pacific shop boys had a hideout below the floor where they partook of such things in secret by the light of a single candle stuck in a bottle. Walt had a particular reason to make sure these things would not be evident: Della Forker.

Della's family had been among the leading lights of Ellis since their arrival in the spring of 1872. George Forker raised livestock and ran a meat market, the first in Ellis to sell the beef that was being shipped to eastern markets from the area. He opened pens, a slaughterhouse, and a rendering plant next to his market. An additional interest of his was Thoroughbred horses, which he raised and raced. From all of this he did very well financially. His family lived in the nicest house in town, and the Forker women were always beautifully dressed in the latest fashions. Mr. Forker himself was very elegantly attired, and was often photographed in a handsome sulky behind one of his beautiful horses. His wife was the former Sarah Catherine Weese, whom he had married in 1867 in Pennsylvania, where they both were born.

Della herself was one of the great belles of Ellis, a petite creature with dark mysterious eyes set in creamy porcelain cheeks framed by rivers of lush auburn hair. From her earliest days men found her enchanting, and her personality was so pleasant that all the girls were happy to be in her inner circle of friends. She rode, she ice-skated, she played piano, she had all the accomplishments a young girl growing up in Ellis could want. There are pictures of young Walt and her in Miss Cartwright's music classes when they were both very young. He looks a bit solemn, but she is a pretty little dreamboat, and you can easily see why he kept up his lessons.

They were sweethearts from the beginning, even before they knew what that meant. Walt writes that even when he was young and full of wanderlust of various kinds, "I showed a wisdom far beyond my years when I obeyed the inner promptings that told me the world did not contain a girl to match my Della."

Events were not kind to Della in the period following her childhood. Her long-suffering mother died in early 1893, when Della was not quite seventeen, and two years later her sister-in-law Minnie died also. The next year her brother John, and later her father, moved to Cheyenne Wells to start a new business and life. Della stayed on at Ellis with relatives because that

Della Forker and her Ellis girlfriends. (*Courtesy Walter P. Chrysler Boyhood Home*)

was where her home and her heart were. It was also where she waited for Walt.

It was quite a wait, through his Union Pacific apprenticeship and subsequent wanderjahren, which both of them knew he had to live through if he was ever to settle down. She was a woman of extraordinary single-mindedness and strength of character when it came to him. With her beauty and position, she could have taken her pick of the beaux of Ellis, as her closest friends did. But she saw something in the little roundhouse sweeper, something she could not deny herself or live without.

What he saw in her was self-evident. "Della Forker and I were waltzing in the G.A.R. Hall on a Saturday night. Her olive tinted young throat was soft in a wrapping of velvet; just at the level of my mouth was her dark hair that waved back from her forehead into a Psyche knot. We were engaged; we had music aplenty in our hearts, and it was no concern of ours what sort of squeaky tune the other couples heard. Of course, for an ordinary dance our crowd could not afford to import a four piece orchestra from Junction City; we took our music raw out of a piano thumped by a thin colored girl, and a violin that was squeezed and maltreated by a lanky fiddler." Nothing else mattered as long as he had the joy, never withheld, of holding this beautiful woman in his arms and in his heart.

Still, the most exciting part of his youth was centered on what went on in the roundhouse of the Union Pacific at Ellis. He worked very hard at his job, but there was something extra about Walt that set him apart from even the brightest of the other boys. For one thing, he had an unquenchably curious mind. He learned quickly from the older men, retaining everything.

The Union Pacific Roundhouse at Ellis in the 1890s. (*Courtesy Walter P. Chrysler Boyhood Home*)

One of the ways he satisfied his thirst for knowledge was through reading. Among the magazines he got in Ellis was *Scientific American,* which probably did more to spread the new culture of science among young men throughout the United States than any other single instrument. The latest machines, diagrams, and theories were published here each month, and boys and men from Syracuse to Kokomo to Sacramento got the same information all at once, allowing new mechanical and scientific ideas to be known and put into practice simultaneously across America. It didn't matter how isolated your community might be; *Scientific American* brought you the news. People have often wondered how the automobile seemed to spring to life spontaneously at diverse places in the United States at more or less the same time, apparently without its various inventors having the least knowledge of each other's experimental work. This magazine was one of the main reasons. It published schematics and descriptions of Gottfried Daimler's internal-combustion vehicle almost as soon as it was revealed to the public in 1885; thereafter all sorts of information relating to self-propelled vehicles of this type was made available here, as it had been previously with steam vehicles and stationary gasoline engines. Men read it in all sorts of places, and went to work on some sort of car without a clue that others were doing exactly the same thing. This was not understood until sometime later, which is why there were so many disputes over who was the Zeus from whose forehead the Athena of the American automobile had sprung in its pristine state. The truth was that this Zeus was hydra-headed.

Walter P. Chrysler's original toolbox, containing tools he made himself in the early 1890s. (*Courtesy DaimlerChrysler Corporate Historical Collection*)

Walt devoured every issue of the magazine. Among its most popular features was a question-and-answer column, whose editor Walt worried on more than one occasion with his queries. He was sure that "in that editorial office, whoever received the questions from subscribers must have thought that Walter P. Chrysler was the pen name of a dozen youths, at least half of whom were crazy." They answered a lot of his inquiries, though, climaxing in the notable issue of November 5, 1892, when they answered five at once, on subjects ranging from the composition of Harden fire-extinguishing hand grenades to whether there are any two acids which, when mixed together, will cause an explosion. (The answer to that was a terse yes.)

Another thing that set Walt apart from other boys was the quality of the things he made. The most important were his tools. In those days a workman was expected to furnish his own, and "the unfailing sign of a skilled workman was the chest of tools he brought to any job. With good reason, he prized them above anything he owned. A good workman was likely to mistrust any tool whose metal had not been tempered by himself." Walt made his own for that reason, and another: He couldn't afford to buy any.

First he made a little pair of calipers that could measure a four-inch diameter, then other tools as he needed them. One day he was amazed by a catalog picture of a depth gauge, which he had never seen before. Around the shop they used a wire, fingernail, and ruler homemade system that, with luck, might be accurate to one-sixteenth of an inch. With the catalog picture as a model, he made his own depth gauge accurate to one-thirty-second of an inch, and after this he could make a plug for a hole in a piece of metal that was right the first time, eliminating the need for chipping and filing, and thus saving time. This was the sort of incremental step toward standardization of machines and labor that would stick with him for the rest of his life and be of vast importance in his future work as an automobile production man. Finally, after he had made a pair of granddaddy calipers with legs almost as long as his arms, he got up the nerve to ask to be allowed to work on the first lathe, where the locomotive piston rods were turned, and succeeded there, as he had at every other task. An old carpenter in the shop with a practiced eye had watched Walt make his tools, and in a workman's gesture of admiration made him a box to keep them safe from the nightshift men who had a habit of permanently "borrowing" any that they found lying around. By the time it was finished, Walt had marked all his tools with the initials "W. P. C." etched in acid, as he had learned from an article in *Scientific American.* Today that box of tools stands in a display case on a platform in the two billion-dollar Chrysler Technology Center in Auburn Hills, Michigan.

To the delight of the whole town, Walt made a 28-inch model of the engine his father drove. There were no blueprints then, so he had to lay out the proportions by himself, then took a solid piece of iron and started to form the locomotive with drill, chip, and file. "A sculptor trying to release in marble some shape of beauty that is captive in his mind can give no more loving care and craftsmanship to what he does than was done by me as I created that locomotive model. Of course, that engine had to live within my mind so real, so complete that it seemed to have three dimensions there. That, so it seems to me, is what the fault is when someone fails to learn from books. My fingers were like an intake valve through which my mental reservoir was being filled; of course, my eyes and ears were helping in the process, but what I learned with my fingers and my eyes together I seem never to forget." When it was done, he laid track down in his backyard and invited all to see it run. "When its tiny whistle blew, you should have seen my father's mustache widen with his grin of pride."

Most importantly, a crusty, grease-stained old mechanic named Arthur Darling took a liking to Walt. He was the best mechanic they had, much better educated than anyone else in the shop, a whiz at math with a knowledge of other roads and types of locomotives no one in Ellis had ever seen. He was the first to teach Walt how to handle steel, and myriad other things as well. One piece of advice Walt never forgot was this: "When you start a valve job always take your own port marks! No matter if someone says he has taken them already; you take your own port marks and you won't go wrong."

When other men tried to pry something loose from his storehouse of knowledge, Darling was usually unhelpful and surly, but not with Walt, to whom he seemed eager to impart his mechanical wisdom. The basis of this friendship lay in the fact that Darling was a drunk, and liked to get away at nights from the vital and onerous task of setting valves on locomotives. Men who could do this job were few, hard to get, and of great importance to the line, for the pulling power of a locomotive depends on the setting of its valves. One night Darling decided to set off on a spree and leave his apprentice, Walt, alone to get this job done. Walt certainly did not want to see this extraordinary man get sacked, so he worked through the night with checkups every three hours from the sozzled but still attentive Darling, and in the morning the job was finished, and finished right. In the months that followed Walt did almost all of Darling's valve-setting work, covering up for the old man and in the process getting valve-setting experience that far exceeded many journeymen's. When Darling said he was a great young mechanic, Walt agreed with him, inside.

Young Walt could do a lot with metal and machinery, but he was still far from being able to handle himself. One day another young fellow named McGrath slopped him with a slimy rag soaked in greasy waste water. After the boy ran away, Walt grabbed another dripping, filthy rag and lay in wait for him to come through a door. When it opened, Walt unexpectedly took his heated revenge on the general foreman, Gus Neubert, who fired him on the spot. After several days of living in what he thought was hell, but turned out to be purgatory, Mr. Easterbrook called him back and allowed as how he might get his job back if he apologized to Neubert. Walt begged pardon and cried, after which Neubert dressed him down for half an hour, out of earshot of the other men. Walt got his job back—"When you see a retriever frisking in the ecstasy that comes when you get out your gun, you will know just how I felt when I went back to work"—and began to learn valuable lessons in self-control. These lessons didn't come easily or quickly to him, but it was essential that he learn them before he could become the master of the fates of tens of thousands of working men, which was to be his destiny. You cannot master other men if you cannot master yourself. Over much time, and through many painful experiences, he finally brought his temper and pride under control, learning to keep his anger in check except on those rare, fine days when it did him some good. Without it he never would have left railroad operations for manufacturing, never would have left Buick and Willys-Overland to seek the opportunities that ultimately made him one of the greatest car manufacturers and perhaps the paradigm industrialist of his age. But that was a long, long way off from the Union

Pacific shops at Ellis, and bright and promising though he might be, he was still a very rough cob.

Around Ellis, he had plenty of reasons to think very highly of himself. Long before the Union Pacific trains were equipped with air brakes, he had taken it upon himself to find out how these contraptions worked by writing to the Westinghouse Company, which had invented them. Naturally, when the Union Pacific decided to use air brakes, he got the job of fitting them on the division locomotives. He was making 15 cents an hour then, in the last year of his apprenticeship, but he picked up some extra cash examining firemen who wanted to be promoted to be engineers; he did this on a little car rigged up with the air brake equipment.

Next came steam heat for the trains, and then electric signals. Of course, Walt had studied these things as well, long before the line decided to use them, and so when the time came, he got those installation jobs, too.

But by now he was thinking, "Gosh, here I am already twenty-two and still in Ellis. What the hell do I want to stay around here for? With what I know, I could get a job in China!" Besides, there was Della; it was fine to be engaged to her, but how could he marry her on $1.50 a day? Both young people were agreed that there were better chances almost anywhere outside of Ellis. And after all, in addition to gaining experience at other shops on other lines, "You couldn't hell around in Ellis. If the gang even had a keg of beer out at the ball field, every mother knew it and spoke her mind." Especially at that time, as Ellis had just elected an all-female slate of public officials to run the town, and these women were determined to clean up the remnants of sin that still existed in its environs. No doubt about it, Walt wanted out.

Surprisingly, it was Gus Neubert, who, having long forgotten the wet-rag incident, proved to be Walt's ticket out of Ellis. By now he had left the Union Pacific and taken a more important position with the Atchison, Topeka, and Santa Fe. After Walt wrote to him asking for his help, he wrote back offering him a job at the Santa Fe shops at Wellington, Kansas. Just hop on a train and see a Mr. Sherwood there, Neubert said, and that was all there was to it.

Mama cried and reminded him that not all cooking was like hers before she pleaded with papa to talk some sense into him. Papa warned him that a man can start out to be a bum by wandering. Why leave Ellis, where everybody knew and liked him and he was soon to get a journeyman's wages? He urged Walt to stay and settle down.

But Walt went off to Mr. Easterbrook and quit, with all thanks for what had been done for him at the Union Pacific during his apprenticeship. Hurt and astonished, the smile with which Easterbrook had greeted Walt faded like a light blown out. But the young man was determined, and said goodbye to his mentor for what would turn out to be the last time. The following

August 20th, Easterbrook, the father-in-law of his brother Ed, was shot dead outside the Ellis House by a disgruntled former Union Pacific employee named William Leach who had mistakenly believed that Easterbrook had fired him.

Soon thereafter, with Mama's well-stocked food basket in his hand, he boarded a coach for the day-long ride to Wellington, down in Sumner County, on the border of Indian country. He had given himself the chance to be a man away from home.

8

Working on the Railroad

> When I am in a new city, before I have found companions . . .
> *The Glass Menagerie*
> Tennessee Williams

Wellington, Kansas, was a division point on the Santa Fe line, another dry, dusty town in the western part of the state. But it was a good deal bigger than Ellis, and for young Walt it was a world beyond what he had known until now, because it was a world of self-sufficiency and freedom. But he carried something else there besides his suitcase and his lunch pail: a very large chip on his shoulder. In his youth it might as well have been a boulder that often threatened to crush his career. It got knocked off many times, at Wellington and elsewhere, but he always managed to replace it, until gradually he learned to remove it when necessary himself, by slipping it into his pocket, or overnight, into a drawer until he could find the tools to knock off some of its edges, unless it was one of those rare occasions when hurling it into the teeth of opposition or adversity was just what was needed to clear his path to new horizons of accomplishment. But it was a long time before he could master its uses in that way.

Mr. Sherwood, a middle-aged Englishman with curtain whiskers, was the division master mechanic at Wellington, and the man young Walt had to see to get his job. He faced him in a bright room where he was seated behind a battered old oak roll-top desk, its bottom drawer scuffed bare by shoes. Asked his age, Walt said he was twenty-three, which indeed he would be, in another ten months. Could he set valves? "Good enough for Mr. Neubert," came the reply. Could he lay out shoes and wedges? Affirmative. But Sherwood was not impressed. Some of his old hands couldn't do these jobs, much less this lanky youth. So he laid it out flat. He had a journeyman's job available. Journeyman's pay was 27.5 cents an hour for the best, 25 cents for the next best, and 22.5 cents for lathe hands looking to learn more about their trade at the Wellington shops. Walt would have to work for two weeks to determine his rate of pay. The young man agreed, then added, "But if I don't get the top pay, I don't want the job." Now Sherwood was

Walter Chrysler, center, in front of Union Pacific locomotive at Ellis, early 1890s. (*Courtesy Walter P. Chrysler Boyhood Home*)

impressed, and told Walt that he was a cheeky young fellow. "No," Walt declared. "I'm just a good mechanic." Concealing a smile, Sherwood passed him off to Bill Hart, the general foreman.

Walt's self-confidence rubbed Bill Hart the wrong way, so the foreman gave him valves to set on a brand-new type of locomotive that the Santa Fe had just acquired. Walt didn't know a damn thing about this rig, but he set to anyway in the tried-and-true manner he had been taught by old Darling, taking his own port marks. Hart said this was not necessary, as he had taken them just the day before, but Walt insisted; Hart glared and bawled him out, then strode away. After he left, one of the apprentices told Walt that Hart had been unable to set these valves the previous day, and put Walt on the job to rawhide him. "Yeah?" Walt replied with a smirk, and started out.

As he worked he found a few unfamiliar items to learn about in the cab, but when he looked at the reverse lever, he struck pay dirt. The quadrant slot was missing a plug designed to prevent the lever from being opened too wide. He replaced it, grinning broadly. One look at the valves told him they were all right, and he had the drive wheels off the rollers in jig time. He was in Hart's face looking for another job in a preposterously short time. Blustering, Hart told him he wouldn't have a job if the engine didn't pull

Walter P. Chrysler, second from left, outside the Santa Fe Roundhouse in Wellington, Kansas, 1897. (*Courtesy Walter P. Chrysler Boyhood Home*)

as it should. "Hook her to a string of cars—she'll take 'em away!" Walt called out confidently. And she did. Sherwood chuckled as Walt told him about the missing plug, information he had refused to give Hart. Walt was put on air brakes right away and got the top rate of pay. But skill and money weren't all, and his insolent attitude continued to dog him.

For this small-town boy, Wellington was a big city, filled with exciting things to do, at least at first. But soon a pall fell over his new life. Walking two miles to work from a hotel, eating his noontime meal of dried-out sandwiches and soggy apple pie from a lunch pail, having no friends—these were not scenes from a life he knew or liked. He was lonesome as could be, heartsore for Mama's cooking and the Ellis he loved. But things would soon look up.

One day as he sat on a railroad tie outside the roundhouse, elbows on knees, hands limply hanging between them and eyes downcast, he saw a pair of enormous feet. As he looked up, he saw that they were the pedal extremities of an enormous boilermaker named Prince, at several inches over 6 feet by far the biggest fellow in the shops. But Prince was a boiler-maker with a tender heart. "Do you want a cigarette, Chrysler?" he asked. Walt was completely broke, without even a nickel for cigarette makings until payday, so Prince's proffered smoke was tastier than heavenly manna. He breathed out that first delicious drag and broke into a big grin as he twisted his face up and around to gaze into Prince's. They were pals now, rough, tough guys chasing around all over Wellington in their idle hours, full of laughs and adventures.

Walt's good luck continued. Another day in the shops a sympathetic old blacksmith heard him moaning about his shabby hotel and invited him to board with him and his wife in their vacant room. Only $12 a month, including meals. They were nice people, and my, could the missus cook! Well, maybe it wasn't as fine as Mama's cooking, but life was beginning to seem almost good, especially since the bosses at the shop really liked his work and were giving him all the best jobs.

One day the circus came to town, not much of a circus, but it offered a free parade, and Walt and a dozen of the boys wanted to see it. When Walt asked the foreman for the time off, Hart blew up and waved his arms about like Don Quixote's windmill. Walt told the boys; they all got sore and decided to show Hart a thing or two. "Our dignity, which I have discovered, is a lot more important than any other human factor, had been wounded," recalled Walt years later. So they cleaned up and walked off to see the parade.

It was tawdry and second-rate, but none of it could match the crumminess that Walt felt inside as he sat on a curbstone and realized the importance of what he had done. It wasn't Bill Hart he had deserted, but the railroad, a thing of human guts and brains and vast clangorous precision that depended on him as much as it depended on all the men who made it go. What if all the men deserted it to go to a circus? He was mortified, and slunk back to face a grim-faced Sherwood.

This man was no Bill Hart. No yelling, no bluster. His simplicity was devastating. In all his years of railroading, he had never seen anything like this, he said. He could fire them all, of course, and they knew it, but what would be the point? "I am simply going to hope that never so long as you call yourselves railroad men will any of you do a thing like this again." They were ready to cry, and Walt apologized for all of them. Sherwood shook his head and walked away. As for Walt, he would never desert his duty again.

After a while though, the siren call of Ellis drew him back home. He missed his parents, and of course he could be with Della, too, with whom he corresponded faithfully during his absence. When his friend Frank Merrill was made master mechanic at Ellis and offered Walt the job of night mechanic at 30 cents an hour, he grabbed the chance to go home; on his return, he was treated to "the finest meal any prodigal ever ate."

It was a good job, but still, after a few months restlessness began to chafe. After Wellington, Ellis seemed smaller than ever. If he wanted to become a master mechanic, a dream he confided only to Della, Walt needed to go to a bigger place to get experience. Mama cried softly into her apron whenever he complained, because she knew what was coming.

Finally the day came when he quit and took a job in the Colorado and Southern shops at Denver. He boarded the train with a suitcase, a lunch his mother had packed, and his burnished silver tuba stuffed into an imitation leather case, which he used as a pillow on the twelve-hour journey.

But he hated Denver, a wild and reckless town filled with fierce, dissipated-looking men and all manner of evil things his parents had warned him about. After two weeks, he quit.

Next came Cheyenne, Wyoming. A Union Pacific conductor he met knew Hank and deadheaded Walt's tuba and suitcase up to Cheyenne, though the man was fearful of being caught if he did the same for Walt. So Walt simply found an open boxcar in the freight yard and hopped in, joining the half dozen frowzy men already inside, and that's the way he traveled.

Cheyenne, Rawlins, and Laramie (two other Wyoming towns that Walt would work in) were typical railroad cities of that time and place. They grew up from hardscrabble beginnings on the alkaline plains of eastern Wyoming. Beginning as desolate collections of tents and shacks in the 1860s, they got railroad passenger service and were chartered as towns in the latter part of that decade. They fought off the Sioux in 1874, got telephone service and distributed high school diplomas in 1878, got electric light service and built stone depots and opera houses in the 1880s (Lillie Langtry sang at Laramie in 1883 and 1884), and celebrated statehood at a grand ball in Cheyenne in 1890. By the time Walt Chrysler showed up the late nineties, these were stable and prosperous communities.

Whenever he could, Walt joined the band in any of these towns. The tuba was his calling card. At the first band practice he met all the young folks of the town; he cut quite a figure, for in addition to his musical skills, he danced pretty well, too. Laramie had one of the best bands, and there he hooked up with Joe McMahon, an old machinist friend of his from Ellis who played a mean trombone.

He didn't stay anywhere too long, however. He learned plenty in the shops from every good mechanic; he learned about shop practices; he learned about the workings of a variety of engines. And he learned about men, including himself. But he was impatient. If the shop foreman didn't appreciate him or dressed him down, he'd pack his bag, forward his tuba, and go off to the next shop town. He loved the freedom, adventure, and lack of responsibility. He spent his money as fast as he made it, sometimes faster. After all, he was homesick, and that was one way to get over the blues. But even though he always found work, in the late 1890s America was recovering from half a decade of tough times, especially on the railroads, and Walt had plenty of hard knocks along the way during these years of wandering.

WORKING ON THE RAILROAD

For a very long time railroads had been the symbols of explosive growth in the United States, much as the biotechnology and computer industries are today. The railroads had opened up vast deserted stretches of the country, and towns, farms, and businesses sprang up wherever tracks were laid, resettling enormous numbers of people along their routes. After periods of boom and bust for the railroads in the 1860s, '70s and '80s, an unquiet period followed by disaster settled over them in the early '90s. Among a few mighty others, The Union Pacific had been built up by General Grenville M. Dodge, a commander of the Union Army in the Civil War. Military men mostly built the railroads, which is why they were run in a military manner. He left the U.P. soon after it was completed. Jay Gould then ran it, saving it from bankruptcy during the Credit Mobilier scandal of 1873. Gould built it up, but later left to found the Missouri Pacific after tiring of the "Gordian Knot" and its relationship with the federal government. Charles Francis Adams, neither an astute financier nor an efficient manager, took it over in 1884. He was friendly with Dodge however, and looked to him for advice. One result is that the U.P. bought out the Denver and Fort Worth line, in which Dodge had a large financial interest as the original builder. Things were not going as well as they should by the early '90s, at which time Gould came back to the Union Pacific and tried hard to shore it up. But he died in December 1892, shortly before the United States fell into the worst and most tenacious depression it had ever experienced. Within 15 months Sidney Dillon and Frederick L. Ames, who together with Gould were the most dominant figures on the Board of Directors, followed him in death. Just when the company needed a strong leader the most, there was no one to run it.

The World's Fair Columbian Exposition in Chicago was the great event of 1893, a marvel of pavilions, lakes, and exhibitions celebrating the four hundredth anniversary of Columbus's arrival in the New World. In Chrysler's effects there is a ticket to the fair dated October 10, 1893, along with photos and a card tribute. This was just three weeks before the festive closing celebration of the exposition, whose gaiety masked the misery of fast-spreading hard times.

Two hundred thousand people were already unemployed in the country, their ranks swollen by drifters and vagrants. In October 1893 the Union Pacific went into receivership. A $2 million profit in 1892 turned into a $2.6 million loss in 1893. Gross earnings were off 17 percent from 1892, and in 1894 they were to fall 16 percent further. Red ink and erratic earnings were to continue for two more years. The receivership was a mess, with all branches of the line getting separate receivers, so it was tough to put the line back together again in 1894. The line had 7,691 miles of track in

October 1893, which shrank to 4,537 miles by the summer of 1895. From September 1892 to September 1893 6,238 employees lost their jobs, and some shops cut back to thirty-five-hour weeks; the backup of repairs caused by these drastic measures caused the line to go back to forty-eight-hour weeks by October 1893, just to stay in business. In the end the Union Pacific was sold out of receivership at a freight depot in Omaha in November 1897. As things turned out, E. H. Harriman restored it to more than its former glory after this, at what was the beginning of an extraordinary new business boom.

But back in 1893, the Union Pacific was not alone in its miseries. By year's end 583 banks and nearly 10,000 businesses had failed. In Colorado thirty thousand men were unemployed in the smelters; textile factories in New England and steel mills in Pennsylvania were shuttered. But nothing shook the public like the railroad failures. The Richmond Terminal, a rickety holding company of southern railroads, failed in 1892. In May 1893 the Philadelphia and Reading failed, followed later in the year by the Erie, the Northern Pacific, and the Atchison, Topeka and Santa Fe, in addition to the Union Pacific. All told, these five lines controlled 21,000 miles of track, and their collapse had enormous effects. Foreigners repatriated their gold, and western banks called on eastern ones to bail them out. Farmers had great harvests but couldn't give away their produce and grains, and freighting rates fell off precipitously.

The whole thing dragged on for four years; nobody knew why it had occurred or what it meant, or whether it would be temporary or permanent. A populist movement sprang up in the West, its adherents believing that Wall Street crooks and Shylocks had caused the whole thing. Political convulsions came from raging debates on this subject. William Jennings Bryan challenged monied interests at the 1896 Democratic Party Convention by proclaiming, "You shall not crucify mankind upon a cross of gold!" But Bryan and the cheap-money silver interests lost out, and all the stirring about didn't bring relief until the business cycle played itself out. However, the political views of many were altered, in some cases permanently, by this episode in our national life. Henry Ford, who came from a Michigan agrarian background, was one of those so affected.

It was in this world that Walter Chrysler was seeking his destiny among the railroad towns in the vast middle of the country. Sometimes as he traveled on the railroads he identified himself as a Union Pacific engineer's son and was allowed to travel in the caboose. But often the train crews were punctilious about extra riders; if they weren't, they could be fired. When the engine stopped to take on water, they'd take their brake sticks and hunt through the train for anyone hitching a ride. Then they'd try to pull out and leave the freeloaders behind. If they succeeded, a little band of castaways would form by the water tower. They were usually a disparate group.

Some were machinists or boilermakers; some were other kinds of roving workingmen; some were shady-looking characters with battered faces and scars; and some were just ragged vagrants. But they were all in same situation, and an instant camaraderie developed until the next train came along. They'd rustle up some wood for a bonfire, and anyone who had some tobacco shared it with his newfound mates. Conversation was usually lively, but if it flagged, you took out your penknife and carved your initials on the water tank post. Walt always carved an arrow underneath his, so anyone following on the line would know the direction he was headed. Years later, when he looked back with nostalgia on his youth, he used to say that he would like to visit those towers again, to see how many still had his intials and arrows in place.

It could be pretty tough traveling when the weather was cold, however, and often he didn't have enough food. But this gave rise to one of his proudest memories of that time and place: the kind of people he met there. "No one had to go empty in the west. If you got to a water tank and were put off by the train crew, you would walk to town, a mile or so away, and if you had no money, you would go to a back door and say that you were hungry. In my life my mother must have fed thousands out our way. Any time you knocked at a back door out West and explained that you were on the move, looking for work, you got something to eat; maybe just bread and butter, maybe a few slices of cold meat. No one ever felt a need to blush in those days for eating such a meal. When you had eaten and rolled a cigarette, you could feel a happy glow inside at the thought of the swell job you might get in the next town." Forty years later, at the end of the Great Depression, when he asked, "Does anyone suppose I don't know what it means to look for work?" the question was merely rhetorical. Alone among the major figures who built the automobile business, he had experienced firsthand every aspect of an industrial worker's life, not excluding cold, hunger, penury, and a vagabond existence when the work ran out. He was strictly a blue-collar mechanic for the first thirty years of his life, with one brief exception. His identification with the working man was to remain with him always, and when times got really hard in the early 1930s he absented himself from the felicity of the good life he had earned, working as hard as he ever had to keep his company together. He had respect for workingmen as his equals, and when hunger bit in their stomachs, he felt it. The lessons of youth are the lessons of a lifetime.

Wherever he went, the tuba preceded (or sometimes followed) him. "There was not a lot of music in that instrument, but somehow I always enjoyed the big noise that I valved out of it; it seemed especially grand when any band I was a part of played the overture to *William Tell*." Eventually, though, he lost it. After six weeks in Ogden, Utah, boredom hit him again and the boxcar traveler was off to Pocatello, Idaho, a prosperous town with the second busiest roundhouse on the Union Pacific. As soon as he got there he wished he hadn't come. The wind blew incessantly, throwing up gravel right into his face. After two weeks he couldn't stand it anymore and rode a string of empty boxcars into Salt Lake City. When he hopped off, he realized that he had forgotten to arrange for the tuba to be sent down, and that was the end of it. Today there are two instruments in a glass case at the Chrysler Boyhood Home in Ellis: a brass trombone with floral etching on its side, and a silver cornet from Carl Fischer in New York, embellished all over with flowers, leaves, and butterflies. But the old tuba was never seen again.

Sam Smith, an old friend from Ellis, now the roundhouse foreman at the Salt Lake shop of the Denver & Rio Grande Western Railroad, got Walt a job there. Walt liked Sam and he liked the shop, and things worked out well for him there; Sam arranged for him to get 30 cents an hour. He liked Salt Lake City, too. At the lakeshore Saltair Pavilion he found companions and fun dancing and swimming. It was here, too, that he finally came to a major decision to change his life. "I was often dreadfully lonesome. Every time I saw a railroad train moving eastward I wished myself aboard it. Every time I heard a locomotive mournfully whistling 'who, who-oo-oo, who-oo-oo-who.' I knew the answer to my lonesomeness: Della Forker." The year was 1900, and the new century was to open up a vital new chapter in the life of Walter Chrysler.

◨ 9 ◩

Getting Married,
and the First Big Break

At Last

Walt and Della had been engaged in 1896, but thoughts of marriage were completely out of the question then. No matter how much they loved each other, how could they marry on his wages of $1.50 a day?

Throughout their youth, Della had always listened to Walt's dreams of the future with sympathy and understanding, and when he left Ellis she was the only one who realized it was a necessary thing for him to do. He wanted to marry her, but he wanted to do it the right way, providing a good life for this beautiful girl who had been raised in a genteel manner in one of the best families in town. And he had ambition, too, even if at the time it was no more than the desire to become a master mechanic on the Union Pacific. After all, this was a railroad town, and that would mean a man had gone pretty far. He knew he had to get out of Ellis to learn what he needed to make himself a success. Back of it all, though, was the itch to leave what he had always known, see what there was in the great world, and measure himself against other men. He had to square his shoulders and push forward against life. Young as Della was, she knew these desires could not be thwarted if Walt was to lead a happy life, and so she made an extraordinary leap of faith. She gave him his freedom with both hands open, believing that the way to really bind him to her was to be willing to let him go for as long as he needed. "We exchanged letters faithfully. She never wavered during that time when I was a wandering mechanic; she knew why I was roving, knew that she was completely interwoven with my ambitions."

It wasn't easy for either of them. When he was down in the dumps, he would reread her letters and breathe in their faint perfume. Motherless and living with relatives in Ellis, she had to endure the derision of the other ladies of the town. After all, to be single in your mid-twenties in those days

Walter and Della Chrysler immediately after their wedding on June 7, 1901, in Ellis, Kansas (*Courtesy Walter P. Chrysler Boyhood Home*)

meant you were likely to end up an old maid, no matter how beautiful you might be. An article in the *Kansas City Star* in April, 1919 titled "And The Other Girls Said She Picked A Lemon" spelled out what Della was up against. As far as everybody else in Ellis was concerned, Della was waiting around forever for a floor sweeper and mechanic, somebody far below her social standing. Walt was doing very well, but Della was considered "the champion lemon picker east of the California state line." Still, she didn't care what other people thought, and when he was ready for marriage, so was she.

Walt was circumspect about a number of things in his memoirs, as he wrote in a much more reticent age than our own. Railroad men like him were tough and strong in the way they lived. Strong language, strong drink, good smokes, hearty meals, and now and then a roundhouse punch were the things that buttressed the life of backbreaking labor that most of them took in confident stride. What about women? Walt never said, but it's safe to assume that one of the reasons he wanted freedom was that he wanted to escape the prying eyes of the mothers and other "good women" of Ellis.

Ed, Irene, and Walter Chrysler. (*Courtesy Frank B. Rhodes*)

Railroad towns, give or take, had their share of deviltry, and the lures of
"fast women" were among them. He speaks of saloons and the cries of
raucous women in the rooms above them, and though his background went
with him, he was probably not impervious to the blandishments these places
offered to a boy with a pocketful of cash and a ready smile on Saturday
night. Walt was young and curious then, and the blood ran high. He most
likely took comfort in, and the edge off youthful excitement with, some
pretty fancy female companionship when he was banging around on the
rails. After all, the wages went somewhere, and he was so often broke. Such
things were not unexpected. But in time the appeal wore off and the homesick blues got worse; home more and more began to mean not Ellis but
Della.

Walt worked and saved the best he could for more than a year in Salt
Lake City. He bought a derby hat and a fine suit of fancy clothes for the
wedding he now eagerly anticipated, and still he went on saving. At last he
was able to write to Della and tell her he was coming home and that she
should pick the day for the ceremony. He said he had enough money for
expenses plus a bit more to tide them over until the next payday. The Denver
and Rio Grande Western gave him a pass to Denver (with the return for
"W. P. Chrysler and wife"), but no matter how long he had worked for the
Union Pacific, he was on his own for the fare for the rest of the way back
to Ellis. So in Denver he bought the first railroad ticket of his life.

Walt and Della were married at last at the Methodist Church in Ellis on

June 7, 1901, just down the street from the Chrysler family home. The Reverend J. F. Johnson presided, and since Della's mother had died, it was a quiet wedding with just the two families and a Mrs. Cooper from Salina present. Della wore a dress of white organdy embroidered with roses, very popular at the time. Later that day they had their picture taken, Walt in his new suit and bowler hat tilted back, Della in a starched white blouse with leg-o'-mutton sleeves and a huge hat trimmed with enormous flowers and a big ostrich plume curving over the top. They look taut and tense, staring solemnly down at the pages of a small book, probably containing the text of their wedding ceremony. At midnight they left for Denver on the train, stopping at Cheyenne Wells to stay over with Della's father and brother John, who had moved there after her mother died. After that it was on to Salt Lake City, where the rest of their lives was about to begin at last.

Della remains a bit of a mystery. From the minute Walt became a public figure, he praised her constantly and extravagantly, never losing an opportunity to point out that he could not have become the success he did without her unwavering, uncritical support. Surely he was sincere, but there is something almost studied in all of this, as if he were a king reporting the value of his consort to the populace. Her preferences and interests, her habits and opinions, her aspirations for her own life and her children's lives—these things are never mentioned by Walt, either in his book or anywhere else. Nor does she ever speak of these things in her own voice in any forum. Curiously, aside from pictures, her descendants seem to have saved little of her, and have scant understanding of her life. To be sure, this was not unusual for women of the time, even wealthy, highly placed ones, though, for instance, we know a good deal more about Clara Ford than Della Chrysler. Sometimes we know her indirectly, however, and we can be sure that she was indeed the mainstay of his life no matter what his physical and moral peregrinations might at times have been. A certain wry detachment from the "great man" seems to have been hers and that helped to keep him focused on the basics of what his life was all about. We may hear her opinions only by echo sometimes, but we hear them nevertheless.

They began life in Salt Lake City with the $60 Walt had saved. He was earning 30 cents an hour, or $3 for a ten-hour day, grabbing overtime whenever he could. That summer they lived in a little rented house, moving in the fall to a row of terraced flats they had watched going up. Their attractive new residence was located on Carter Terrace. Walt bought $170 worth of furniture on time to furnish the place, and at last their housekeeping was set up.

Now Walt was more fired up than ever. From another Ellis boy, Bill Kirkpatrick, who had apprenticed at Salt Lake City, he got the idea to take a correspondence course in electrical engineering from the International Correspondence Schools. He was to continue to study with them for a number of years on a variety of subjects in his slow and utterly precise way. Eventually the school claimed him as its most famous and successful student.

He was enterprising too. With two Union Pacific co-workers, he rented a barn, and after work the three men labored there repairing machinery to earn extra cash. After a while they managed to save up enough money to start a small foundry, which continued to operate and pay Chrysler dividends long after he had left Salt Lake City.

In the autumn of 1901 Walt had the first big lucky break of his career. Salt Lake City was, of course, a Mormon center, having been founded by Brigham Young in 1847 as a new home for his people after they had been driven from Missouri. Twice each year Mormons tithed, or paid one-tenth of their income, to the church. Tithing time was a festival period, with thousands of Mormons moving about to bring a tenth of anything they had produced to church officials. It was a very busy time for the Denver and Rio Grande Western, as they had to haul both an enormous number of passengers and huge amounts of freight. A special train, the Tintic Branch, was put on to bring people from the Wasatch Mountains who wished to pay their tithes in Salt Lake City. Because the line was short of motive power, the same engine had to take a 3 P.M. train out to Denver.

As Walt was taking some work off the register book, he saw John Hickey, the master mechanic, come tearing into the roundhouse waving a telegram at the roundhouse foreman, Sam Smith. Hickey was normally a smooth, unflappable sort who always came to work in a cutaway and striped pants, but he was flapping a good deal just then. It seemed that no. 46, the Tintic special, had blown out a back cylinder head and was crippled. Since it was the only engine available that could pull the train to Denver, Hickey was in a hell of a spot. When Smith said Walt was the one who could tackle the problem, Hickey sputtered, "Crissler! [which was what he called Walt] Can you put a back cylinder head on number forty-six and have her ready for the through trip?" Cautious for once in his life, Walt answered carefully, "If anybody can, I can." They set him to work.

He chose two helpers and laid his tools beside the roundhouse pit where the job was to be done. Next he went to the machine shop and loaded a new back cylinder head, wrist pins, bolts, studs, and other items into a hand truck and brought it to the pit. Then Walt and the helpers went to the coal chute where the locomotive would first pause when she arrived.

Since she was working on only one side when she rolled in, he began stripping off nuts and crossheads with his wrench from the idle side as he walked along beside her. When the fire dropped out of the engine he nearly scorched his shins, but he and his helpers paid no attention and kept going as fast as they could. Walt first touched her at 12:10 P.M., and two hours and forty minutes later he yelled to Smith, "You can take her away, she's ready." The train pulled out on time.

Hickey, who seemed to be praying to his watch, came over to Walt full of admiration; he had been sure the train would be at least an hour and a half late. The men's wages were fixed, so he couldn't give Walt a raise, even though he wanted to, so he gave him the rest of the day off.

It was three o'clock. Walt sat by the side of the pit, ate to the bottom of the dinner pail that Smith had been thoughtful enough to get from Della, and smoked his cigarette to the stub. Then he walked around for fifteen minutes and went back to work. "I felt grand; I wasn't going to sacrifice a minute of my feeling of triumph."

A few months later, in February 1902, Hickey called him in and said, "Walter [he was no longer "Crissler"], do you think you can hold down the job of foreman over in the roundhouse?" After he was assured that his friend Smith would be moving on to a better job, he accepted.

Now he was foreman over ninety men. He had an office, really just a hole in the wall with a dinky little roll-top desk and a telephone, but it was his first ever. He was management now, an enormous step. The union made him give up his card, because his new job was considered to put him on the company side. (Actually, he got a withdrawal card, just in case he ever lost his job and needed work.)

This boost couldn't have come at a better time for him because of another big event that happened that month. On February 13 his first child, Thelma Irene, was born.

This whole time would have been perfect if only, shortly after he started in his new position, he hadn't contrived to make John Hickey madder than hell.

◨ 10 ◪

Putting a Lid on It,
and the Go-Ahead Signal

Great fleas have little fleas upon their backs to bite 'em,
And little fleas have lesser fleas, and so ad infinitum
And the great fleas themselves, in turn, have greater fleas to go on;
While these have greater still, and greater still, and so on.
A Budget of Paradoxes
Augustus De Morgan

The voice of Hickey's clerk gargling over the phone froze Walt to the marrow. Like a drowning man, he saw his life flash by in a second, because he had anticipated doom summoning him from that quarter for some time, and now it suddenly was.

A few days earlier Hickey had written Walt a sharp note for some mistake he had made, and as usual, Walt's anger flared up and he immediately sent an equally prickly note back to his boss. The only surprise was that it took Hickey so long to send for him. Now he was finally being called on the carpet. (Literally; the cubbyhole office of a man like Walt was covered with an oilcloth mat to catch any drippings from the grease-stained mechanics who came and went there; but Mr. Hickey, the boss of thousands over the whole railroad, had a much bigger and finer office. He had a carpet, just the thing to lend gravity to the proceedings he was about to hold.)

Hickey had a right to be mad. He had fairly rebuked Walt in the first place, and he should never have received Walt's stinging reply. But Walt needed his job now. He was a married man with a child, and his $90 a month was what kept the family going. There would be no hopping into a boxcar to solve his problems now. He wasn't going to whimper, so he squared his shoulders and clenched his teeth as he stood outside the boss' door. But when he opened it and stepped into the room, he was sure that all was lost. Not only did what happened inside catch young Walter Chrysler completely off guard, it taught him a lesson that would stand him in good stead for the rest of his life.

Hickey greeted him and spent time chatting on about some new locomotive drawings until he was sure that Walt was completely relaxed. Then he praised him for his courage and good, hard work. He pointed out that when he had made him roundhouse foreman he made him responsible for men as well as machines.

Walt knew Hickey was getting to the heart of the matter. Had he yelled at him, Walt would have gotten his back up and yelled even louder. But Hickey was kind and gentle, and that made Walt determined to listen to him. "He knew plenty about human beings," Walt wrote later. "There isn't a one of us who won't listen carefully to a sermon that begins with praise of our work or something else that we take pride in. You can bet I listened that day."

Hickey continued mining his positive vein, bringing up an incident with new Baldwin cross-compound locomotive engines the line had taken on. Walt had practically lived with the Baldwin man when he came out to Salt Lake City to set up these engines, and whenever one of them was disabled, Walt was the only one who could fix it. Many was the time he was hauled out of bed by the call boy in the middle of the night to do such a job. (He generally fixed it in an hour, which was very quick; too quick for the night man, who would make him put in for 10 hours overtime and then send him home to bed, so he could get a full day's pay the next day. Did Hickey know about this little scheme? Was that why he was bringing it up? Was this going to add to his woes?)

If Mr. Hickey knew about this little bit of dishonesty, that was not his purpose in discussing those Baldwin locomotives.

After telling Walt he had a future he shouldn't throw away on hurt feelings, he got to the point. "Now and then I get a letter that makes me boil with rage. You know what I do?" Mr. Hickey pulled out Walt's letter from a small drawer beneath the pigeonholes deep inside his desk. Walt blushed scarlet with shame. Hickey explained that he put such letters in that drawer for three or four days until he was sure he was calm; then he took them out and read them over.

He never read the letter out loud, to Walt's immense relief. Then he said: "If you had put my letter in a drawer until you cooled off, Walt, you'd have dealt with it much more soundly; you would have been fair to me and fair to yourself. Don't you see? Now, boy, you remember what I've told you."

Walt apologized on the spot. "Words of contrition poured out of me the way potatoes do when you spill the barrel."

From that day forward Walter Chrysler never answered a letter when he was in a fury. He might lose his temper with someone face-to-face, but never again on paper. No matter if a letter brought his blood to an absolute boil, he would put it in his bottom desk drawer until he cooled off. He would always think of Hickey as one of his best teachers, a man whose wise counsel helped him to curb a temper that could easily have sidetracked or derailed him in life.

Early in the spring of 1903 Walt received a telegram from Trinidad, Colorado. H. C. Van Buskirk, superintendent of motive power of the Colorado & Southern, which ran from Denver to Texline, Texas, where it linked up with the Fort Worth & Denver City, was offering him a job. At a wage of $15 more a month than he was now earning, Walt could become general foreman of the Colorado & Southern's shops at Trinidad. But who was this Van Buskirk, and how did he know about Walt? In a terrific quandary, he went off to sort it out with Hickey.

Hickey allowed as how he knew the man, and speculated that Van Buskirk had heard somewhere that Walt was a hustler and a good mechanic, the kind of man he needed for a tough job.

Then he expanded on his own background for a while: apprentice, machinist, locomotive engineer, foreman, and at last master mechanic of the Sheboygan & Fond du Lac Railroad in 1873. He pointed out to Walt that the next step after the general foremanship he was now being offered was master mechanic. Walt sputtered that the estimable Mr. Hickey had been to college, unlike himself. But Hickey said an education could be obtained without college, and urged Walt to continue on with his correspondence courses. "You'll learn faster and better than most fellows, because you are getting it through your fingers and your eyes, instead of through your ears."

He hated to lose someone like Walt, but he had an excellent general foreman who Hickey expected would keep the job until he died or got fired. Of course, Walt could keep his present job, but Hickey advised: "Take the job! It's a great opportunity for you. You're learning how to swing authority while you're young. . . . I should regret to see you let a fine opportunity slide by just because you are comfortable in a job that you have mastered. Don't be afraid of your future."

When Walt protested that he had a wife and baby to consider, Hickey urged him to talk it over with Della. "Let me know. And good luck!" he said. Then, with a magnificent railroadman's gesture, "he waved his arm widely, as conductors do when they hold a lantern in their hand and signal to the engineer to go ahead."

Della said simply, "Dad, you are the one to say. I won't fret or worry, whatever comes. Certainly we could use that money." That was it, then. They were on their way.

11

Trinidad: The First Major Responsibility

Sweet Water from a Deep Well

If you were approaching Trinidad, Colorado, in 1904 you would behold a monumental bluff that dominated the town in a way that the then-unheard-of Cecil B. DeMille would have been proud to devise. You would head toward this tall sandstone glory from the side by railroad, then curve around it and gaze up to see the word *TRINIDAD* literally emblazoned on top of the bluff in huge letters illuminated by thousands of light bulbs. This was one of the first electric signs to appear after electricity became known in that part of the world, and it was a great attraction for the town. To this day it is a stunning, unexpected sight in the rugged mountains of southeastern Colorado, and most likely it was the first sight Walter Chrysler saw when entering the town.

Trinidad began about 1596 as a rudimentary Spanish winter camp settlement, eventually used by Frenchmen and others. It might have been named for the Blessed Trinity, though local legend says it was named by a man who threatened to shoot anyone who disputed calling it after his daughter, Trinity. The town was incorporated in 1869, making it the second oldest incorporated town in Colorado. The Santa Fe Trail ran through Trinidad, and by 1903 its zigzag path had turned into the town's main street, making it part of a general broadway to California. Nearby ran the Rio de los Animos Perdidos, named for the early Spanish settlers killed by Indians or floods and buried without benefit of clergy.

Trinidad was a wild railroad town, like all the others. It had a red-light district with over five hundred girls, so many that there was even a madams' association that built a rest home for disabled prostitutes, once run by the fabled Jeannetta Kremchek and her colorful sidekicks L. B. Cutler, an ex-gunslinger known for screaming wildly as he plugged his victims, and Leo "the Decorator" Meyer, a fancy man who furnished the home with items he salvaged from a string of brothels that had closed in other towns. The Colorado & Southern actually ran its own whorehouse near the railroad tracks, so the boys didn't have to waste any time getting back to work. Bat Masterson was a marshal here, and Wyatt Earp ran a gambling hall; he spent more time here than in Dodge. Doc Holliday came to Trinidad with Earp after the gunfight at the O.K. Corral in Tombstone, Arizona. At one point there was an arrest warrant out for Holliday on a gun charge, which was mistaken; actually, he had stabbed somebody. Of course, there were saloons everywhere, and generally speaking, everyone in the vice trades did a land-office business.

Carrie Nation went through town, trying to clean up the saloons with her hatchet. The only time she ever failed was at Claris's Place in Trinidad. Nation hired a band to lead her to the local hotel, where she was stopping prior to giving a speech at the Western Theater the following day. Then she set out down the main street. After wrecking Aiellio's saloon with her hatchet, she proceeded to Claris's Place, where she was greeted at the door by Claris herself. With a voice sharper than Nation's hatchet, Claris told her, "You can give your speech and distribute your literature, but if you swing that hatchet I'll throw you out on your ass. After I wipe up the floor with your ass." Nation fumed, but she left. On the next street over, at John's, the proprietor got into a fistfight with her, making himself a local hero. "Here's a go for Mr. Aiellio!" he roared as he threw her a roundhouse punch. When she marched over to McGonagle's, the saloon keeper there stood petrified with his arms spread out across the doorway, yelling, "Keep her out! She'll God damn well ruin me!" Her reign of terror finally ended, Carrie Nation returned to the hotel, gave her speech to a packed and respectful house the next day, and left town. Everybody breathed a big sigh of relief and headed for the nearest gin mill.

Carrie Nation would have had no trouble finding a band for hire here, for there were plenty of them, mostly staffed by musicians originally from places such as the lower Balkans, Italy, and Greece. Though they played primarily at funerals, madams hired them to tout the arrival of their new girls, labor groups and companies used them in parades, and the occasional visiting celebrity, including Carrie Nation, employed them to trumpet the importance of an appearance in town. Eventually the concatenation of brassy concerts became too much for everyone to bear, and the City Council banned the bands for all but funerary purposes. Unfortunately, they overlooked the fact that this ban included the Salvation Army, which gave concerts in the streets every Wednesday and Saturday. But a law was a law, and since the Salvation Army wouldn't comply, the city had them arrested and thrown in jail. After a couple more arrests, the Army sued the city for false arrest and imprisonment, under the grounds that the free expression of their religion was being impaired. The Army won big damages, and the case was appealed all the way to the Supreme Court, which agreed that parades were an established part of the Salvation Army's religious practice. The Army told the city to keep its money, that all they wanted to do was establish the principle of their religious freedom. The city paid $1, and the parades continued into the 1950s.

Religion was established and had its place here, but Saturday night in Trinidad remained quite an experience until the Depression hit in the 1930s. However, the best expression of this dynamic, vigorous town came on New Year's Eve. At the stroke of midnight, every bell rang and every whistle blew, each with its distinct sound—church bells and fire sirens, locomotive and plant whistles, blowing the lid off Trinidad and yelling up to Kingdom Come.

Trinidad had its share of desperadoes. The infamous Black Jack Gang struck the town four times, on September 3, 1897, July 11 and August 16, 1899, and November 18, 1902. This last time was their undoing. According to the *Denver Times* on the following day, five men held up a train at Twin Mountain, about ten miles south of Trinidad, looking for the railroad payroll. They jumped on to the tender from a height near the water tower and got the engineer to stop the train. Then they uncoupled all the cars in back of the baggage car, and since no one would open the safe, they tried unsuccessfully to dynamite the express car where the safe was kept by placing a bomb underneath it. By now the old conductor found an opening and started shooting. One man was killed and one injured, and three got away, without any loot.

According to local Judge Dean C. Mabry, the three escapees were soon captured, including the gang leader Tom Ketchum (his brother Sam was the man wounded by the conductor). Since train robbery was a capital offense, Tom Ketchum was tried and dutifully hanged by order of Judge O. T. Clark. They hanged him so high they jerked his head clean off. The irony in all of this was that there was no payroll car on the train, and even if they had succeeded in blasting open the safe, they still would have gotten nothing, for by 1902 everyone was paid in cheques.

The town was never bigger than it was in the early twentieth century, when Walter Chrysler arrived. The Union Depot, a $100,000 building constructed of native sandstone and brick, was erected jointly by the Denver & Rio Grande Western and the Missouri Pacific in 1890. Nine new stalls were added to the roundhouse at that time, as were extensive repair shops. By the time Chrysler got there, three different lines had railheads at Trinidad: the Colorado & Southern, the Denver & Rio Grande Western, and the Santa Fe. Around Trinidad there were some thirty small coal-mining towns with at least a thousand people each. The Colorado & Southern had the greatest number of spurs running throughout the mountains to many of these towns, but the Santa Fe had major coal lines, too. Some of the spurs carried loads for 10,000 to 15,000 people. Trinidad was the headquarters for the whole area, filled with merchants and buildings providing the services, legal and otherwise, that the small mining towns lacked. The buildings included service plants of various kinds connected with the different types of raw materials and products shipped out from the rail yards. Marshaling yards for all the coal in the area were located here.

Though passengers were transported through Trinidad, freight took precedence. In addition to coal, cattle and processed beef were shipped from here; both Swift and Armour had stockyards and packing plants in the area. Lettuce and peas were grown locally and rushed to market. Celery from Pueblo and even some beets raced away from Trinidad, in competition with California produce. Because of this the locomotives were never allowed to get cold.

All these things are gone now. In those days Trinidad was the foremost business town in Colorado, but everything it dealt in has been replaced. What used to be transported by rail is now trucked. Coal is long gone as a major fuel source. Railroads use oil and diesel fuel; power plants use oil, gas, and atomic energy; steel mills use electric furnaces; and copper mills use gas. The vegetables once raised here no longer have to be grown in such remote areas. By the 1930s much of the trackage in the area had been ripped up and many of the buildings razed, and by the 1950s the railroad yards were gone, too. Trinidad today is beautiful still, but rather somnolent compared to its glory days. But it does have one absolutely up-to-the-minute claim to fame: for the last 35 years it has been the world capital for the performance of transsexual operations, due to the efforts of a pioneeering local physician.

But from the 1880s through the 1920s prosperity was rife, and the streets of Trinidad were filled with hardworking people of every kind. Inevitably, since most of them were workers employed by huge corporations, a good deal of labor trouble was added into the mix. Mine strikes began in the 1880s with the Western Federation of Miners under Wild Bill Heywood, followed by the Industrial Workers of the World under Joe Hill and, eventually, the United Mine Workers under John L. Lewis. Damon Runyon, who was born in Pueblo, Colorado, came to Trinidad as a correspondent covering labor strife, and wrote several stories here, including "The Taming of the Wolf" and "The Defense of Strikeville"; in his fiction, he always called the town Trinity. The railroads had their share of labor trouble, too. In fact, just before Chrysler's arrival in town, a big strike against the Colorado & Southern by machinists, boilermakers, blacksmiths, and helpers was amicably settled, according to the *Denver Times* of March 12, 1903. It was not uncommon for goon squads from the various companies to mill around strike locations. To the question, "You company or union?" the smart, wary reply was, "You first."

⬧   ⬧   ⬧

Walter Chrysler at first came alone and stayed with the family of a highly respected foreman for the Santa Fe named Harlo J. Bennett. The coal mining town Walter encountered here made quite an impression on him. Years later he recalled: "When I see mascara on the fringes of a woman's eyes today I am amused, because I am invariably reminded of Trinidad's coal miners on the loose to spend their pay. They were rough fellows who washed themselves in buckets, basins, troughs or not at all. But whether they had washed or not, they were never quite free from the black dust of their jobs when they lined up at the bars of Trinidad. Those were cheap saloons. In front of each one rough speaking idlers clustered. Oh, there were fine staunch people in the town, but they did not hang around saloons. Any time you walked along a portion of that street in 1903, you were apt to see a silk hatted gambler on his way to work upstairs above some saloon. By night you did not have to listen hard to hear the mechanical pianos, the rattle of poker chips and the screeching laughs of women who likewise worked above saloons. Nearly always there would be a few cowboys around, their fantastically big spurs making music against the sawdust floors wherever they stepped. There were plenty of Mexicans too; by daylight there were sure to be a few slumbering on their bare feet, upright against an alley wall, their faces muffled in bright scarves, zerapes. That was a bleak and scary place into which to bring a sweet young Kansas woman and her baby girl."

Nevertheless, after a month he sent for his family and rented a shabby one-story four-room house for $12 a month. It was right on the old Santa Fe Trail at 1108 North Linden Avenue, near the Colorado & Southern yards, which adjoined the Santa Fe yards; only an irrigation ditch separated them. It was important for him to live close by the yards in case the call boy had to notify him of some looming crisis. That could happen at any time. They bought a stove for the house but were still wretched with the winter cold. The warmer months were much more pleasant. The house had a narrow front porch, and in the summer the little family could sit there and enjoy the star-filled nighttime sky mixed up in a crazy quilt pattern with the black snow-capped mountains. Out front there was a small yard enclosed by a picket fence where Thelma toddled about safely, and in back Della grew a kitchen garden in an effort to save money on food. As usual, she made do with the circumstances her husband handed her.

All kinds of buildings were clustered around the two-story brick headquarters in the yards. There were houses and boardinghouses, some of brick but mostly wooden ones, a few quite large; the inevitable whorehouses; stockyards and packing plants; an icehouse; two huge smelters; and the roundhouse, with coal chutes slanted down inside. Day and night the yards were filled with the movements of steaming, clanking locomotives and squealing freight and passenger cars. It was here that Walt spent most of his time.

His new job as general foreman meant that for the first time in his career Walt was out of overalls, and he intended to keep it that way. "What I would wear to work was the oldest suit I had; it was worn and spotted, but it was good enough to distinguish me as one who worked entirely with his head." For a mechanical man on the railroad this was an enormous step forward, for it meant that he was valued no longer for his brawn but for his ability to direct the physical labors of others. It also made visible the fact that he had bridged the yawning gap between management and labor. From now on he was known as the "old man," a term of respect that had nothing to do with age and everything to do with the sway his new position gave him. It meant he was the boss. Anyone who had such a job automatically received this sobriquet, and in Walter Chrysler's case it remained with him for the rest of his life, in all the plants that bore his name. But it was here in Trinidad he gained this moniker (along with another one of shorter duration, "Bull of the Woods," which may have been related to his membership in a fraternal organization called the Woodmen of the World).

He worked under the division master mechanic, a sixty-five-year-old man named H. Geigoldt, who was "a dignified, quiet speaking gentleman more than six feet tall. He was slender, wore a big moustache that fully masked his mouth, but did not hide a wedge shaped adam's apple that pranced about each time he spoke. As if to compensate for all that movement, he had learned to chew tobacco so unobtrusively that it was always a surprise when he spurted juice." Walt became quite fond of Geigoldt. However, he was physically not vigorous, which made Walt's work much harder than it would have been otherwise.

Walt had complete charge of locomotives, both repairing and overhauling, which in the latter case meant he rebuilt them totally. According to his friend Harlo Bennett, he planned and built a water-powered hydraulic lift for locomotives, which remained in use for many years. He also was responsible for keeping the freight cars in good shape, and even built some new ones. There was a great deal to be done, because the shops were rundown when he arrived, and this was reflected in the state of both the general equipment and the motive power.

For the next twenty-one months he worked like a demon, bolting meals, not sleeping enough, and thinking of little else but his job. He was later to say that this was the only time in his life that he allowed himself to become physically run down. According to Judge Mabry, some in town said that he had a bit of a breakdown during this period, due to all the overwork. It paid off handsomely in the end, though. By the beginning of 1905 both the roundhouse and the shops were in much better condition than Chrysler had found them, and he had located a first-rate man to establish there as roundhouse foreman, eliminating any worries in that department.

One day, after a walk through the shops, Van Buskirk, the superintendent, offered him the job of division master mechanic. Though he was ready to leap at the chance, Walter was worried about the possible fate of old Geigoldt; reassured that Geigoldt would be moved up to a division out of Denver, Walt eagerly accepted the new job. Hand outstretched, Geigoldt was the first to congratulate him.

Still under thirty, he was now the "old man" to a thousand men—engine crews, shop men, car men, roundhouse men—over several hundred miles of track. Van Buskirk charged him with nothing less than turning the Colorado & Southern into a first-rate line. That meant a 24-hour-a-day responsibility for one thing: no lateness, ever. "Responsibility, I was learning, is something that weighs more heavily than iron," he later said.

Still, it was an enormous boost to be so young and have such an important job, and the $140 a month he would now earn wasn't bad, either. The raise meant the family could move to somewhat better quarters in a house at 337 East Topeka Street, located on a height very near a survey marker on the Santa Fe Trail. This house had a nice view of soft mountains and a mesa in the distance, and provided a pleasanter atmosphere for Della.

Fortunately for Walt, his new job brought new chances to prove his abilities, this time under the auspices of George Cotter, a Trinidad friend who was appointed division superintendent there at the same time Walt arrived to become general foreman. Rosy-cheeked, blue-eyed, and handsome, Cotter had the build of a light heavyweight and a winning way with men. He liked Walt because he was a hustler, and Cotter began coming to the shops to hang around the engines, a love they both shared. Walt idolized him in a way. Though less than two years older than Walt, he was much more highly placed. Walt was sure Cotter's college background gave him the sophistication, cultured speech, and natural ease that allowed him to be taken seriously enough to be given a high position on the administrative side of the railroad at such a young age. But Walt had fooled himself. Years later he discovered that Cotter, from a railroad family like himself (his brother William later became president of both the Pere Marquette Railroad and the Cincinnati, Hamilton and Dayton Railway), had left school at fourteen to become a railroad telegraph messenger, then an operator and afterward, like his brother, a train dispatcher, chief dispatcher, train master, and at last division superintendent. It was railroading itself that had been George Cotter's college, and had given him his polish.

What Cotter gave Walt was opportunity. One day he came to Walt in a dither about alkali, a big problem on most western railroads. The roadmaster could hardly keep the well out beyond the watershed working at all, and what came up was loaded with dissolved alkali. Walt knew what that meant; his first job had been knocking alkali out of huge boiler tubes at the Ellis shops, and here the problem was much worse. Cotter knew there was sweet water below the watershed, but he couldn't reach it with any ordinary pump. Solving this problem would put an end to the biggest problem they had. Did Walt have any ideas?

"George, have you ever heard of a submerged well?" Walt inquired, repeating "submerged" as if to suggest that everyone knew about this. Actually, Walt knew about this from one of the magazine articles he had read so voraciously years before, though he never told Cotter where he got his information. The principle involved an air compressor and a steam boiler to run it. A pipe runs into a casing the way a straw is submerged in a glass of soda, only instead of sucking, you blow and air pushes the water up into the casing.

Cotter was enthusiastic and asked, "Will you do it for me?" Walt said "Sure." In reality, he had never even seen one of these things, but he wasn't going to let that stop him.

He set out to get estimates on the job to get to the water, which they knew was about 600 feet down. The cost was $9,500, a lot of money in those days. But Cotter got the funds, and Walt was told to supervise the job.

He drilled down 600 feet and cased to about four-fifths of that. A 75-foot length of pipe with three-quarter-inch holes for blowing air was attached to the bottom of the pipe; a concrete foundation was built; and steam boiler and compressor were installed.

Things were going well and the job was within a week of completion when a telegram from Cotter arrived saying he would come down to join Walt for the completion of the project. Being with his friend was always fun for Walt, and he looked forward to Cotter's arrival—until he showed up in a private car attended by a staff of roadmasters, bridge construction superintendents, and others, including division officers. Still just a small-town Kansas boy, Walt was very nervous about how to act around all this railroad brass.

First thing, Cotter invited Walt to lunch in the private car. He demurred that he was too busy, and already had a packed lunch. Twice more that first day Cotter invited Walt to the car, but he always came up with an excuse for not going—he was too dirty, or needed some sleep. The truth was that he had never before been in a private car and had no idea how to conduct himself there.

The next day at noon Cotter grabbed Walt by one arm and a huge Irish roadmaster grabbed him by the other; the two of them swept him off to lunch, like it or not. As they boosted him aboard the private car in his dirty, greasy clothes, he felt "as nervous and excited as if they were trying to shove me down my well."

They sat him before a spotless white tablecloth that was a rebuke to his filthy well driller's outfit. Not to mention the rebukes he felt from the rolling eyeballs of the colored waiters, who were the first he had ever encountered. But it got worse.

On the plate in front of him a waiter placed two long skinny steaming objects wrapped in cornhusks and tied with string at each end. They were tamales, of course, but for all of Walt's familiarity with them, they might as well have been rocks from the moon. "I was as alert as a prairie chicken trying to select the moment to abandon cover and fly up in a hunter's face," he said. Casting glances to the other men for clues about how to deal with these items, he found no help. Cotter was gesticulating in the midst of a disquisition about Fort Worth, and the roadmaster was ever so slowly preening his moustache. Well, Walt didn't have the luxury of time, so he had at it with his knife and fork, slashing off an end of one of the damned things and tried like hell to eat it.

The lot of them at the table were a bunch of Irish tricksters, and after watching him saw and munch away on the cornhusks for some time, they couldn't stand it any longer and burst into howls of laughter; merry tears rolled down Cotter's cheeks. Abashed, Walt managed the rest of the meal without further disaster, no thought but escape on his mind. Knowing Walt's hot temper to be the instant reflex of a sensitive nature, Cotter didn't let him leave until he was sure he was not wounded by the laughter.

All afternoon on the rig he ate himself up over his social ignorance. "I began to get my wife's slant on certain aspects of living. She had never nagged me once, but I knew that back in Ellis, where all the girls went in heavily for refinement, she had eaten at a table somewhat differently served than when she had just me to feed. Table manners? The appetite a machinist brings home when the noon whistle blows was never meant to suffer any kind of waiting. Put food on the table and let a man eat is manners when he is ravenous from working hard and has to get back to a job before another whistle blows.

"Yet I realized, after that first experience in a private car, that there were a lot of things in the world besides machinery and men. I went back to eat with George that night and for the balance of the week I ate all my meals there, including the one which was in celebration of the completion of the submerged well." To his credit, he wasn't mulish and sullen over this incident. He knew the acquistion of social grace was a challenge, a new kind of knowledge to learn and master, and he faced it like an eager student who realizes it will lead him into worlds unknown.

"The well worked right from the start, because the hydraulic calculations had been sound. To get good sweet water out of it, all that was required was to turn a valve." As Chrysler turned that valve the first time, with Cotter and his crowd looking on, water spurted 40 feet into the air. As advertised, it was sweet water, without any trace of alkali.

Shortly after this Cotter got a better-paying job with much more authority as general superintendent on the Fort Worth and Denver City, which joined up with the Colorado & Southern at Texline, Texas, continuing on to Fort Worth and Dallas. Before he left, he offered Walt a job with him, working on a big shop problem he was to inherit. "You see how you like it first, George," was Walt's reply.

As always, Chrysler made many friends while at Trinidad. He attended the Methodist church, and like just about all the other men in town, he was an active Mason, having been admitted as a 32nd-Degree Master of the Royal Secret, according to a certificate dated December 15, 1900, when he was living in Salt Lake City. He was also a member of Isis Temple of the Ancient Arabic Order of Nobles of the Mystic Shrine, belonging to the consistory at Salina, Kansas. Of course, most of his friends were mechanical men of one sort or another, and he formed close, long-lasting ties with them. Many were hired by Chrysler years later in his auto business, or were called upon by him to test out new gadgets for Chrysler Corporation cars. (If an item turned out to be a success, Chrysler would always send a car out to say thanks.) Virtually all were motor-mad and eventually wound up in the car or airplane business. One of the Vorhees brothers became a Chrysler executive, and Orville Amidon, Donald Eicher, and Jack Starkes were taken on by Chrysler as engineers. There was Roy DeRouen, an expert machinist, whom Walt, calling on his old skills, helped to make several scale-model locomotives. DeRouen was a master at this, and made whole model trains. Olly Knecht was a first-rate machinist and designer. Wilber Davis was a battery expert. Wendell Day and Duke Guigliano owned garages, and Mr. Steinbaugh worked at the Studebaker garage. Bill Orth became a Hudson man. Clarence Crabtree sold Nashes and Packards. Fred Turri and his brother were race car drivers who had a circuit here. Chrysler later hired them for a Pike's Peak climb and sent out mechanical innovations for them to test. George Heap sent several inventions on to Chrysler, and to the War Department in World War II. A Mr. Van Brudenbock was sent an electrical system, a carburetor, a fuel pump, and motor mounts by Chrysler. (In the 1930s one of these men got carried away with what he thought was his contribution to Floating Power engine mounts and sued the company, unsuccessfully.)

He was well acquainted, too, with Agnes Smedley, who lived in Trinidad at the same time as he did. She lifted herself up by her bootstraps to become an internationally famous correspondent for the *Manchester Guardian* and the *Frankfurter Zeitung*. Though she claimed she never joined the Communist Party, she certainly was a sympathizer, accompanying Mao Zedong on the Long March; later he said he never could have succeeded without the people she brought to his cause. (She also taught him how to dance.) In the 1930s she used her acquaintance with Chrysler to approach him for support for a project in China that would establish schools there to bring children out of poverty, train them to become machinists, and eventually hire them for plants she would set up. Henry Ford had already pledged money to her, but he never paid it. Walter Chrysler flat out said "no," because by the mid '30s he was disenchanted with any of the sort of radical social notions she espoused. She tried to play off the two men against one another, but it didn't work. (Many later blamed her for her communistic leanings. Eventually Senator Joseph McCarthy got after her and all who had anything to do with her. He sent investigators to Ford Motor because of old Henry's pledge, and to Chrysler too, because of her request. He even sent investigators to Trinidad. But she survived, and in the end wound up the only American woman buried in the National Cemetery of Heroes in Peking.)

And then there was Harlo U. Bennett. He was the son of Harlo J. Bennett, with whom Chrysler boarded when he first came to Trinidad. Ten years younger than Walt, he had been born in Green Bay, Wisconsin, and moved about a lot with his family, as was common for railroaders then. He became a Colorado & Southern machinist's apprentice in 1900 and got his card in 1904. He and Walt were good friends, palling around and playing the inevitable baseball together. (During one game with a rowdy bunch from Texline somebody pulled a knife on Walt, and Harlo conked him out with a well-placed fastball.) They were also involved in the sport, peculiar to the area, of chasing coyotes with specially trained greyhounds and horses. After Walt left town, Harlo was fired from the Colorado & Southern in a lockout, and began selling Willys-Overland cars; when Chrysler began selling his own cars, Harlo signed up the Bennett Motor Company as a dealer immediately. Most everybody in Trinidad drove Chrysler cars because they liked the man, and because, no matter what happened, he never forgot them. They also remembered that in the big mining strikes in the area, which culminated in the Ludlow Massacre of 1913, the railroads, especially the Colorado & Southern, always supported the strikers, and Walt Chrysler was the biggest supporter of all. If trains were bringing in troopers or scabs, they just didn't run.

In 1929 Walter Chrysler returned to Trinidad to show the first new Dodges he brought out after buying that company. Judge Mabry, then a boy, remembers meeting him at that time. "He seemed to me to be a big man with a big, semigruff voice and colorful language, very friendly, who went all over town shaking hands with everyone he met." One of the men he greeted was the owner of the Radford Foundry, a big outfit which had supplied many of the items Chrysler needed in his Trinidad days. Since Radford was also a close friend of John D. Rockefeller, he arranged for Mr. Rockefeller to come to Trinidad in his private railroad car at that time, and there he introduced the two men.

But the best thing that happened during this visit was the night in the speakeasy. To celebrate, Walt went with Harlo U. Bennett and his wife to a booze joint in El Morro, outside of town; though it was Prohibition, nobody paid any attention to the small jazzy speaks in the countryside. There was a hot little band, and Walt sat in, strumming the ukelele, which he said he had never played before, and a mandolin. It was smoky and noisy as hell in there, and everybody was good and liquored up. Now, Mrs. Bennett was an active socialite and quite a charmer, though usually more than a bit on the reserved side. But not this night. In the heat of the good time she climbed up on a table and, dancing to the ever wilder shouts of the crowd, did an almost complete strip; it was mighty drunk out that night. The next day, the society section of the *Denver Post* had a picture of her over an article titled, "Women Who Lead in Trinidad." People talked about it for years.

❖   ❖   ❖

Three months after George Cotter left Trinidad in 1904, he wired Chrysler from Fort Worth to meet up with him in Childress, Texas, a little village south of the Red River, near the southwest corner of Oklahoma, about three hundred miles from Trinidad. Chrysler said that when they met, Cotter explained that the shops at nearby Clarendon had burned down the previous week, and he wanted to build new ones at Childress, a much better strategic location. Here he could have a longer division and save a lot in operating costs. Walt could build the shops any way he wanted, and then run them as master mechanic. Though he was excited by the chance to design and build shops with a free hand, he would still have to talk to Della. "All right. Tell her you get twenty dollars more a month," was Cotter's lure. Walt told Cotter he wanted to come, but as they talked, he noticed all the red clay on their shoes and pants, which was nothing compared to the red stuff on Cotter's face. He thought he'd better take a walk around and see what this place was like.

Childress was then just a little village and the most godforsaken dusty place you could imagine. Walt could find just one house for rent, a four-room unpainted box without a single convenience, stuck in the middle of an 8-acre cornfield. The only water nearby came from a sulfurous well, "a spa in embryo," as Walt called it. That meant water would have to be hauled in from elsewhere. The farmer who owned the house was willing to rent it out for $10 a month and move his family elsewhere on the property.

Walt wanted this job so much he could taste it more than the sulfur, but how could he ask Della to abandon the relative comforts of Trinidad for the absolute bottom of the barrel discomforts of Childress? It was beginning to seem as though the more he went forward, the more he dragged her down.

Back in Trinidad he went for a walk with Della in a secluded leafy area by a waterfall, popular with sweethearts and others who wanted to have a heart-to-heart discussion in a beautiful natural setting. He described Childress and the new house to her in all their awfulness, weighing this misery against the possible benefits that would accrue to them: he would make more money, living in Childress would of course be cheaper, and the job would be worth a lot in prestige for the future. But of course the terrible things were just too horrible to think about, and—

Della cut him off. She was willing to go wherever necessary for him to go to get ahead.

This was the tribute Walter Chrysler paid to her for her decision: "There was never a time when my wife batted an eye to keep me staying on in any place on her account. I've had friends whose wives literally spoiled their careers just by their whines and chronic kicking. Suppose sometime my wife had said, 'No, I won't expose my child to the danger of living in such a place. I think you are foolish and selfish to try to drag me down to such a hole.' Well then, I probably would have stayed in Trinidad, or Salt Lake City, or Ellis. Probably I'd be there yet, but I'd be pretty wistful. Nothing in my life has given me cause for more pride and satisfaction than the way my wife had faith in me from the very first, through all those years when I was a grease stained roundhouse mechanic."

The last thing he did in Trinidad was to introduce John Wicken, his replacement as master mechanic on the Colorado & Southern, around the shops. Wicken was a Swede who had been sent to the St. Louis World's Fair in 1904 to take charge of the Swedish exhibit, after which he set up an electrical plant in Van Buren, Arkansas. According to Wicken's daughter Mae Costigan, Walt made sure he met everyone there, and told him the story of the tools he made as a boy because he had been too poor to buy any commercially manufactured ones. Confident that the Colorado & Southern shops now were in good hands, he said his goodbyes, turned around, and left.

On to the future.

⊞ 12 ⊞

Childress: Springboard
to the Future

Deep in the Heart of Texas

The railroad Walter Chrysler went to work for in Childress was called
the Fort Worth & Denver City, but what that name stood for was practically a paradigm of the upheavals that plagued the railroad business in
the 1890s and early 1900s. It was chartered on May 27, 1873, to run a
line between Fort Worth and Texline, on the border of New Mexico. There
it connected with the Denver, Texas & Fort Worth, which in turn connected
to the Denver, Texas & Gulf, which ran from Denver to Trinidad (these other
lines all had "Texas" in their names because by state law anything connecting up to Texas trackage had to have that word in its title).

The three lines together were known as the Panhandle System, a hybrid
cobbled together from two incompatible types of line by a pair of men who
did not get along. Governor John Edwards built the Colorado portion, and
General Grenville Dodge built the Texas part. Their relations became so
acrimonious that Evans tried to break up the alliance in July 1891. In August 1893 Evans filed suit to become a receiver for the the Gulf line, saying
the Union Pacific had not lived up to its part of the agreement between the
two parties (in 1890 the Union Pacific Denver & Gulf Railway Company
had been formed to mop up twelve smaller companies, including part of
the Panhandle System).

Two months later, the Union Pacific itself went into a receivership that
was a complete mess, with each line in the system getting its own receiver,
which meant that reorganizing the line was a nightmare. On December 19,
1898, the Colorado & Southern Railway Company was incorporated for the
purpose of acquiring by purchase at a foreclosure sale the property owned
by the Union Pacific Denver & Gulf Railway Company and several other
smaller properties. Along with the Union Pacific Denver & Gulf came a
controlling interest in the capital stock of the Fort Worth & Denver City

Railway Company, giving the Colorado & Southern, through an arrangement with the Denver & Rio Grande Western on trackage between Pueblo and Walsenburg, Colorado, a through line all the way from Orin Junction, Wyoming, to Fort Worth, Texas. So in a way, Walter Chrysler in 1904 was not leaving the Colorado & Southern at all, but just transferring to another branch created by the consolidation of and shift in ownership of the U.S. rail system in the 1890s.

Here, for the first time, there seems to be some discrepancy between Chrysler's version of his biography and independently verifiable facts. According to his account, the shops at Clarendon burned down in the autumn of 1904, but the annual report of the Fort Worth & Denver City for 1901 states that they burned down in July 1901. The line had been contemplating the move from Clarendon to Childress for some time and had already decided to upgrade the "woefully inadequate" facilities at Childress; "the decision in this matter was hastened by the destruction by fire of the division shop at Clarendon," the report said.

The *Denver Times* of April 1, 1902, reported that the new shops at Childress were nearing completion. They would be "among the best modern railroad shops in the country. In the general plan the Childress shops are similar to the Denver shops of the Colorado and Southern, though smaller, as they will serve the purpose of a system having only about half the mileage of the Colorado road." The article went on with this description of the new complex: "With the exception of the storeroom and roundhouse, the shops are all comprised in one large structure, L-shaped, with the ground plan devised so that in repair and construction work the material will all be reached for the different stages of work by a scientific method of evolution by which neither time nor energy is lost in long transfers. The buildings will be of fireproof construction, the walls of pressed brick with white stone trimmings, and the roof carried by structural iron. The arrangement of tools is on the plan of the most approved railroad machine shops of the country and the equipment is in every respect modern." The article closed with this: "H. W. Cowan, chief engineer of the Colorado and Southern, acted as consulting engineer, and G. B. Martin of Mr. Cowan's office in this city did the architectural work. General Superintendent Scott of the Fort Worth line was consulted in all matters pertaining to general plans and detail for the arrangement of the plant." By October 11, 1902, *The Denver Times* reported that the shops were up and running.

It seems, then, that George Cotter and Walter Chrysler really had nothing to do with the construction of the Childress shops. Furthermore, according to a long obituary of Chrysler written by Fred L. Haskett in the *Dallas Morning News* on August 19, 1940, it appears that Walter Chrysler was brought to Childress by General Superintendent W. R. Scott, whom he had known from Kansas (Scott later rose to become president of the Southern

Pacific). Of course, it may well be that it was a joint decision by Cotter and Scott, and that Scott as general superintendent would have been the one to make the formal request for Chrysler's services. But there is yet another peculiarity. Walter Chrysler's 1905 Christmas card, sent out just two months before he left Childress, identifies him as the general foreman of the mechanical department of the Fort Worth & Denver City, not the master mechanic.

But maybe there is a clue to what seems to be a fair bit of disinformation on Chrysler's part. Years later, in the 1930s, when General Hugh Johnson was involved in labor negotiations with Chrysler, he noted that Chrysler had a flair for telling very tall tales of his youth for effect, or maybe only a laugh. Perhaps one's life story sounds better gussied up with a few accomplishments that weren't exactly yours but were nearby to yours, shall we say. In Chrysler's version it seems that everything in his life went onward and upward in an unbroken line. In truth, there were many accomplishments for him at Childress; they just weren't quite as vaulting as he made them out to be.

In that same obituary the men who knew him at the Childress shops said he was brought down from Trinidad because some new locomotives were failing to deliver their rated horsepower, or tonnage power. These engines were of a new design and were not able to pull the trains they were intended for, despite the time and money expended on them. Chrysler was expected to make them over. He immediately went on the road with the engine men and studied the locomotives while they were in actual service.

Not only did Chrysler find the faults and correct them, but he made the engines go with greater power and speed than their manufacturers had rated them for. The same men said that Chrysler brought peak efficiency to the shops. "It was Chrysler who placed the first jigs and ideas in use in the big shops, and many are in use to this day." This was reminiscent of his work at Trinidad, where his new type of hydraulic lift for locomotives worked much better than anything previously used.

The article continued: "It is also said by some of Chrysler's friends in Childress that the idea of using rubber in automobile construction came to him from the fact that he used rubber to remove vibration and shocks in locomotives.

"There was a certain class of locomotives on the Denver Road that rode hard, and the engineers claimed that the roughness of the engines injured or made their backs sore. Chrysler investigated these engines and developed a block of rubber that was placed under the driver springs. The rubber absorbed the vibration and shocks."

As always, Chrysler was very popular. "Chrysler was one of the boys. He was known by his men as Walter. He was respected by the railroad men because he was a practical, self made man. He was a machinist by trade and a good one. No mechanic in the shops would even pretend to know more than his big boss. Chrysler was just as eager to gain knowledge as they were.

"None of the railroad men who made the Childress Y.M.C.A. their headquarters will ever forget the small locomotive made by Chrysler when he was a boy serving his apprenticeship as a machinist. The locomotive was made to perfect scale, equipped with air brakes and fired by coal. The little engine was mounted on the mantel of the fireplace in the reception room of the Y building." Apparently Chrysler told Hackett in a letter written not long before his death that he still had the engine in his mansion on Long Island. The pride he took in building it as a boy stayed with him for the rest of his life.

Everyone remembered another bit of ingenuity on his part, this one especially crafted for a Childress situation. One morning he woke up in that miserable little house to discover a raging torrent outside. He found all communication with the outside world cut off because the telephone wires were down. So, in a very clever piece of thinking, he fashioned a cannon out of a piece of metal tubing and used it to shoot a wire across the water, reestablishing a connection in short order.

Among his friends in Childress were Robert G. Fitzgerald, chief train dispatcher; P. A. Caldwell, a passenger train engineer for thirty years; Ernest S. Butcher, general foreman of the paint shop; Jim Hunt, a mechanic with a marvelous mind and fingers that could shape anything of metal; Judge A. J. Fires; J. J. Piggott, who made cowboy saddles; and John R. Scott.

One day, after working very hard through the fall and winter of 1905, Chrysler received a telegram from John E. Chisholm, master mechanic on the Chicago Great Western Railroad at Oelwein, Iowa. The two men had been friends in the West, and now that Chisholm was being promoted to general master mechanic, he was offering his old job to Chrysler, which would mean a raise of $40, to $200 a month. There were other advantages as well. Chisholm bragged about the wonderful facilities in the Oelwein shops. There were transfer tables on which an engine could be treated like a toy, and—miracle of miracles—decent washroom and toilet facilities for the men. At Childress, the men drank out of a common bucket, and they washed in the same sort of trough Walt had used at the Ellis shops.

He couldn't get away, so he wired George Cotter at Fort Worth to come meet him at Childress, and Cotter, being the prince of a friend that he was, did just that. When Walt explained the situation, Cotter encouraged him to take the new job. He could pay Walt the $200, but that was all; at the Chicago Great Western, he would just be starting at that level. Besides, he would enjoy their shops, and bustling Oelwein (population six thousand) would be a nice change for Della. But who would replace Walt at Childress? Walt had just the man: George Little. He had made him roundhouse foreman at Trinidad, and he had been following in Walt's footsteps, job after job. So it was settled.

Walt went to cable his arrival within the week to Chisholm. He was overheard by Robert Fitzpatrick, the chief dispatcher, who asked Walt if he could take over the house Walt was renting. He allowed that he could, if he would buy the furniture, too. Fitzpatrick and his family had been staying in a wretched boardinghouse since they had arrived three months previously, so they were eager to move, and Walt was eager to make a complete new start. The furniture hadn't been much when he bought it for $170 in Salt Lake City four years earlier, and after the depradations of banging around on long journeys in freight cars, in addition to the usual wear and tear, it had come to the end of its usefulness for the Chrysler family. For $100, Fitzpatrick bought everything but the silverware, table linens, bedsheets, and a few personal items. Even the pots and pans were thrown into the bargain.

Five days later the Fitzpatrick family was ensconced in the house, and Walt, Della, and the baby were on a train traveling northward to Iowa. Aside from the baby carriage and a small suitcase, everything they owned was packed into one big box. "All, that is, except the $500 we had saved while living there in Childress."

Before he left however, there was a tribute paid to him by the men he left behind. Fred L. Haskett describes it thus: "That Chrysler was loved and respected by the railroad men and citizens of Childress is evidenced by the reception that was accorded him when he left for the east. In Childress there was a two story frame building on the upper floor of which was the Knights of Pythias lodgeroom, where labor organizations met. On the ground floor was the opera house. The men gathered that evening in the opera house, with barbecued meat, pickles, boiled ham and kegs of beer on hand. The event of the evening was the presentation to Chrysler of a fine railroad watch, the best that money could buy in the little railroad shop town. It is said that the watch cost $65, and Chrysler was very proud of the gift." This was the first of many such tributes to be paid to him as he rose from height to greater height on the railroad, and later in the automobile business.

13

Oelwein, Iowa: Superintendent of Motive Power, and the First Car

Come Away With Me Lucille......
In My Merry Oldsmobile
Gus Edwards and Vincent Bryan

On January 10, 1906, a telegram from J. E. Chisholm, approved by J. A. Goodall, general superintendent of the Chicago Great Western, went out "to all concerned" over the wires, stating that W. P. Chrysler was appointed master mechanic at the Oelwein shops of the railroad. On a balmy day in February, the little family rolled out of Texas on the rails. Walt told Della that Oelwein would be a much better place for her than Childress. It was a good railroad town, bigger and more sophisticated than what they were leaving behind. Besides, it would have plenty of doctors handy, which was particularly important now that Della would be giving birth to their second child in a couple of months.

"We arrived there in the morning, stepping off the train into an Arctic region encased in snow and ice to a depth of 18 inches. In the clothes we had been wearing down in Texas, we began to shiver. I got the baby carriage from the baggageman, and when the baby was tucked in and wrapped with blankets, we set out for the hotel. I pushed the baby carriage, and once I slipped and fell. After we had eaten breakfast and were established in a hotel room, I started for the job; on the way I saw what would be a new responsibility of mine—great snowplows bucking and churning their way through the white mounds that were making all trains late; but nevertheless, they were running.

"Chisholm took me right to the shops, and I was thrilled to the marrow. I forgot all about the cold. They were the biggest shops I had ever seen. Sixteen or 18 locomotives, or entire trains could be hauled inside of them. In the winter darkness they were brilliantly illuminated with the sputtering bluish lights of arc lamps. There were great cranes aloft that could lift a

1908 Locombile Type I seven-passenger touring car. This is an exact model of the car Chrysler bought at the 1908 Chicago Automobile Show. (*Courtesy Bridgeport, CT, Public Library*)

locomotive in their chains. Everything was marvelous, and when I saw the transfer tables, I felt like applauding. Best of all, everything in those shops was to be in my charge. I did not worry for a second. It was a bigger job, but thanks to an abundance of self confidence, I knew I could run it."

He rented a modest story-and-a-half white frame house at 7 5th Avenue South, according to the Oelwein City Directory for 1906–7. It had a pleasant porch that in summer would be shaded with morning glory vines. Since it sat on a half acre of ground, he and Della began planning a garden—almost a farm garden in miniature—in the rear of the house. There was also an empty barn in the rear, where a certain kind of automotive history was to be made. They bought some new furniture, of course, but on time payments, since they wanted to keep their $500 savings in the bank, just in case a rainy day arrived. Walt had more personal responsibilities now, since a new daughter, Bernice, was born to Della and him on April 4, 1906, just a few days after Walt turned thirty-one.

Walt knew how to get along with the men. He could be strong and hard, but he was also fair. Since he was a first-rate mechanic, everyone respected what he said in that regard; he could put the center valves on the ranges so they were set right without asking for help, and very few mechanics could claim that skill. He was a popular man all along the line of that railroad. Thirty years later a seventy-two-year-old retired locomotive engineer from the Grievance Committee at Oelwein came to see Chrysler at his office; he just wanted him to look down in the street to see that he was driving a Plymouth.

The Chicago Great Western had made an excellent choice in hiring

Chrysler, and his advancement was rapid. In May 1907, one year and three months after his arrival in Oelwein, John Chisholm was made superintendent of motive power and Walter Chrysler assumed his job as general master mechanic. But not for long. On December 21, 1907, the following telegram went out along the wires: "Mr. W. P. Chrysler is appointed Superintendent of Motive Power, with headquarters at Oelwein, Iowa, vice Mr. J. E. Chisholm, resigned. Effective this date." It was signed O. Cornelisen, General Superintendent. He was now the mechanical head of the entire Chicago Great Western system. "Over the whole railroad, from Chicago to Oelwein, from Oelwein to Minneapolis, I was in charge of engineers, firemen, carmen, shopmen, roundhouse men and others. That took me up as high as a man could go mechanically in railroad service." It meant that he was in charge of anything that moved along the railroad, and anyone who moved it, and making sure that it moved on time. At thirty-two years of age, he was the youngest man ever to hold such a position in the history of U.S. railroads. His pay was now $350 per month. "I was learning plenty and still seething with ambition."

O. D. Foster, in an article entitled "Watch the Terminals; Not the Way Stations—Chrysler," appearing in *Forbes* magazine on February 1, 1925, spoke of the dilemma in which Walter Chrysler now found himself. "One sweltering forenoon in August, 1906, a man stood in the doorway of the shops of the Chicago Great Western Railroad. As he watched, the noon whistle blew and the men began to file out. In their anxiety to reach the open air they jostled against each other and crowded the forward line impatiently.

"As they trickled out through the doorways Chrysler followed them. He watched them moving on in groups, some of them aimlessly, others taking a more direct route. Many of them were men whose hair was streaked with grey—good mechanics, all of them. He thought of the rows of little brick houses where they lived, two families in a house. Nice, respectable homes, neat as a pin, most of them. But was that all life had to offer?

"As he crossed the yard he took a swift account of his abilities. He knew he had qualities which he had never used. One of them was a certain interest in finance. It irked him to see inefficient management, short sighted policies, waste and ineffective effort. He had vision, but he was often handicapped in using it, for his work lay largely along the mechanical side; he gloried in responsibility, but he was at the top of his particular heap. Regardless of ability, he felt he had reached a place where promotion was impossible, for one of the inflexible laws of railroading is that a mechanical man never reaches the executive's chair.

"Suddenly he came to a stop right in the middle of the yard. In that instant he sensed the difficulty. He was on the wrong side of the desk. Instead of repairing cars and running trains, he wanted to build and sell.

It was not enough to do other people's bidding; he wanted to use his own judgement and foresight. It was the turning point in Walter P. Chrysler's career. From that moment he determined to blaze his own trail." Foster got this account from Chrysler himself, whom he interviewed for this article.

Walter Chrysler would achieve his goal in stages. He had learned mechanics and how to manage men, machinery, plants, and roadways in a vast transportation system. Later, when he entered the automobile business, he was to discover that he had also learned something of inestimable importance in this new field: precision. No one before him would ever calculate the economy of time and movement, material and finance necessary to the building of an automobile as well as he, and this all due to twenty years of training on the railroads. "Chrysler has been called a jack of all trades," said Christy Borth. "What made him different was that he was also master of them." A profound understanding of research, innovation, finance, and publicity were still ahead of him, but they would come based on each advancing step he took in life. One thing that was always with him was a complete lack of pride before his own ignorance; he was always inquisitive about what he did not know. These qualities, combined with hard work, sound judgment, and a positive personality ever willing to take a chance on tomorrow, eventually turned him into the quintessence of American business in the 1920s. By the time he looked down on the world from the top of the Chrysler Building, he was the paradigm of his age.

But if he lived several lifetimes crammed into one, as has often been said, his progress took time, and was nothing if not methodical.

Here in Oelwein he did two personal pieces of business, one quite conventional, and the other quite insane for such a conventional man. The seemingly insane venture proved to be utterly sound, for it formed the basis of his entire future and his calling to greatness.

The conventional business concerned a U.S. patent called "A Packing for Piston Rods," application for which was filed on March 1, 1907, by August C. Schaefer of Oelwein, Iowa. On June 27 of that year, while the patent was still pending, Schaefer transferred one-half of his interest to Walter Chrysler for the sum of $40. Schaefer gave Chrysler a power of attorney to sell his interest on that same day, and the two men also agreed that if a chance for the sale of the whole or any part of their interest should materialize, they would retain at least a 51 percent interest. The patent, number 871,063, was granted on November 12, 1907, and reissued June 2, 1908. On June 1, 1908, the two men, for an unspecified value received, granted to the Ward-Packer Supply Company of Chicago the exclusive right to manufacture, sell, and use their invention, and to license these same activities to others. On June 6, 1908, A. A. Packer wrote to Chrysler that he had almost arranged for a trial of the new device on the Northern Pacific line. Things must have gone well, for on January 16, 1911, Chrysler bought out

Schaefer's interest in the patent for $1,000. At the time he was manufac-
turing huge locomotives at the ALCO works in Pittsburgh, which would
have required packing for a lot of piston rods, of his own choosing, of
course. He was learning. In the immortal words of Mae West: "One and
one are two, two and two are four, and five'll getcha ten, if ya know how
to work it." So far this was all very sound and sensible.

The next piece of business was anything but. However, it involved Walter
Chrysler's first encounter with the romance of the automobile, on which
he would speed to destiny and fame.

Chrysler often went to Chicago on business, and in 1908 he went to see
the auto show in that city. "That is where it happened. I saw this Locomobile
touring car; it was painted ivory white and the cushions and trim were red.
The top was khaki, supported on wood bows. Straps ran from that top to
anchorages on either side of the hood. On the running board there was a
handsome tool box that my fingers itched to open. Beside it was a tank of
gas to feed the front head lamps; just behind the hood on either side of the
cowling was an oil lamp, shaped quite like those on horse drawn carriages.
I spent four days hanging around the show, held by that automobile as by
a siren's song."

The price was $5,000. He found by repeated inquiries that there was no
bargaining room. All he had from years of saving was $700. "I must confess
that I never asked myself if I should, if I could afford to go in hock to buy
that car. All I asked myself was: where could I raise the money?"

He turned to Ralph Van Vechten, who came from a very prominent family of Iowa bankers in Cedar Rapids, by way of the general merchandising
and lumber business in Mattawan, Michigan. His father, C. D. Van Vechten,
came to Cedar Rapids in 1877 to be cashier of his brother Giles F. Van
Vechten's private bank. When the Cedar Rapids National Bank succeeded
the private bank, C. D. Van Vechten became a stockholder and later, a member of the board of directors of the new institution. Ralph Van Vechten
(whose brother was Carl Van Vechten, the noted photograper and novelist)
was born in Michigan in 1862, and after attending high school in Cedar
Rapids and editing an amateur paper called *The Rounce*, he became a reporter for the *Cedar Rapids Republican*. In 1880 he went into the banking
business, first as a messenger boy, then a clerk in his uncle's bank, and in
1887 as a cashier at the Cedar Rapids National Bank. He resigned this
position in 1905 to become second vice president of the Commercial National Bank of Chicago. Four years later he became first vice president, and
when that institution became the Continental and Commercial National
Bank the following year, he was made senior vice president and a director.
Simultaneously, he became president of the Cedar Rapids National Bank.
By this time he had transferred his principal activities and residence to
Chicago, though he still maintained a residence in Cedar Rapids. Later he

became one of the founders of U.S. Gypsum, and figured very prominently in the early financial history of the automobile business as one of the saviors of General Motors during its first great crisis in 1910.

Van Vechten played a vital and ongoing role in Walter Chrysler's involvement with the automobile business from the beginning. And the beginning was now.

At six-and-a-half feet tall and 275 pounds, Ralph Van Vechten was a giant of a man in those days. His full, U-formed face, bushy caret-shaped eyebrows, and well-groomed shock of red hair gave him a manly demeanor that was both hearty and friendly. Walt Chrysler thought him a great companion. Their favorite rendezvous was the basement bar of the Hotel Brevoort, down a flight of marble steps from Madison Street in Chicago, a popular hangout for retired railroad officials. Toward the end of the 1908 auto show, Walt lay in wait there for his friend Van until he came in. Bombarding him with information about the Locomobile, Walt enthused over how and why this car had mesmerized him. Van had heard it all before. "You told me that this morning Walt, and yesterday afternoon." Walt had indeed been worrying the life out of him about the $4,300 loan he needed to buy the car, but despite his respect and friendly feelings in the matter, Van needed some assurances. "What about collateral?", he kept asking Walt, both men knowing that there wasn't any to offer except a chattel mortgage on the car, which was not satisfactory—at least not on anything as frivolous as a car.

Walt argued vigorously for the car loan in his particular case. "Van, you know a lot about the transportation business. You do business with the railroads here in Chicago every day. Well, the automobile is the transportation business too. The railroads have made this a richer country, haven't they? Well then, just ask yourself what this country will be like when every individual has his private railroad and is able to travel anywhere." Van Vechten agreed that he would grant the loan if Walt could come up with a suitable cosigner, someone of financial substance. Walt was ready for him; he had already lined up his friend Bill Causey, superintendent on the Chicago-Oelwein division of the CGW, to sign for the loan with him. That was fine with Van Vechten, who knew well that Causey was a man of means. The following day the deal was done.

Years later Chrysler wrote, "Clearly that car had a fascination for me that must have seemed to others the equivalent of madness. But I really meant it when I argued my case with Causey and Van Vechten. I did not simply want a car to ride in. I wanted the machine so I could learn all about it. Why not? I was a machinist and these self-propelled vehicles were by all odds the most astonishing machines that had ever been offered to men." A dozen years later, when both Chrysler and Van Vechten had become powerful forces in the automobile industry and Van Vechten headed a syndicate of bankers begging Chrysler to save the failing Willys Motor Car Company, he was mighty glad he had finally agreed to that loan. It was not for nothing that by his death in 1927 Ralph Van Vechten had become one of the wealthiest, most influential, and certainly the best loved of all Chicago bankers.

Back home on 5th Avenue South, Walt rolled up his sleeves and set about cleaning out the little barn behind the house of all the dirt and junk left there by the previous tenants. While he was at his task, Della came to ask what he was up to. He told her he was setting up a workshop for the new automobile he had bought, admitting he had spent their entire savings and committed himself to a debt larger than his entire annual income. "She did not scold me, but it did seem to me that when she closed the kitchen door, it made a little more noise than usual; maybe she slammed it."

The Locomobile arrived in a freight car, shackled to the floor. He hired a teamster to haul it to the house and place it in the barn. He didn't know how to operate it, and he was determined that no one but he would be the first to drive it. "I cannot remember that I have ever been more jubilant than when Della, with Bernice in her arms and Thelma jumping up and down with excitement, saw me steer that horse drawn car into the yard. If it had been a jewel of fantastic size, I could not have been more careful of it."

Though he saw that Della was wild with enthusiasm, he turned down her request for an immediate ride. Or any other ride. During the three months it sat in the barn without moving, the only contact Della had with the car was to sit in it forlornly sometimes when Walt cranked it up.

During that time Walt worked on it every night, every Saturday afternoon, and all day every Sunday. He pored over auto catalogs and drawings, and made schematics of his own. Car parts were spread out on newspapers all over the barn floor as he studied every function of the car over and over. Finally he was confident he understood all about the Locomobile, because he could disassemble and reassemble it and tune it to run like a fine watch.

At last the great day to unveil it and drive it arrived. One hot Saturday afternoon after lunch Walt took off his jacket, rolled up his sleeves, and pushed the gleaming Locomobile into the yard. Since the neighbors had listened to the car's engine bang and clatter for months, they sensed that this was an auspicious occasion, and they all gathered round to watch while Walt cranked up the car and sat behind the wheel, one hand on it and the other on the sliding transmission lever. She growled, snarled, and winced, due to the chain drive, every time he went near the transmission lever, but the engine purred and she didn't smoke (much), so he clamped his teeth on the big cigar in his mouth and threw in the clutch. She bucked forward, stopped, then lurched forward again to roll axle-deep into a ditch in his neighbor's yard, the neighbors yelling their lungs out all the while. Crestfallen, he got a team of horses to pull him out of the mud, and after settling with the teamster and promising pecuniary satisfaction to his irate neighbor, he cranked up, jumped behind the wheel, and started off again.

This time he just threw that terrifying, clanky transmission into high and rolled away. He didn't know what to do, so he simply white-knuckled the wheel and steered the enormous behemoth down the road. Rather than risk God knows what by shifting the rattling chains of the transmission at the corner, he took the turn in high gear, swearing that it felt like the car curved around with two wheels off the ground. Leveling off from this hair-raising moment, he soon found himself past the edge of town, in the country.

"A few hundred yards ahead, I saw a cow emerging from behind an osage hedge that bordered a lane. She was headed for the road. I bulbed the horn until it had made its goose like cry four or five times, but the cow, a poor rack of bones draped with yellow hide, kept right on her course and never changed her pace; nor did I change the pace of the automobile. I could not; all that I could do was to grip the wheel and steer, biting on my cigar until my teeth met inside of it. Well, I missed the cow, though I was close enough to touch her."

Sweat pouring down, he dodged ruts and holes and hung on for dear life as he made three more turns until at last he raced up 5th Avenue South pushing 20 miles an hour out of his 80-horsepower car. Finally, he came to rest outside the barn, and his neighbors helped him push the car inside. As he shut the door, he trembled from nervous exhaustion; there was not a dry stitch of clothing on his body. Though it was only six o'clock in the evening, he dragged himself into the house, took a hot bath, and went to bed for a long, deep sleep.

After that he learned about driving quickly, and was soon seen beside Della in their linen dusters touring all over Oelwein and on the country roads beyond it. Even so, he kept taking the car apart and reassembling it again (more than forty times in all) to learn more about it, until he thought he could practically put the thing together in the dark.

Though Walter Chrysler said that this encounter with the Locomobile was his first connection with understanding the workings of an automobile, apparently it was not. Everett L. Hennessey, in a 1961 master's thesis for Kansas State College, revealed that Walter Chrysler had actually built a car of his own in his student days at Ellis. It would have been in the early 1890s, when a number of isolated boys and men, all learning about individual vehicle locomotion from articles in *Scientific American* and similar journals, were building cars in the backyards and barns of America.

Based on an interview with Chrysler's cousin Lee Wagner, Hennessey writes: "Sometime along in this era Walter made a cart like car with a wooden frame and steel wheels. It was steered by the front axle pivoting in the center line like a wagon and barely was large enough for Walter and his cousin, Lee Wagner, to ride upon. This cart was powered by a two cylinder air cooled gasoline engine with power transmitted by a gear drive attached to one rear wheel. It was reported that Walter made the engine himself. His cousin Lee remarked that this was not a particularly successful product since they pushed it about as much as they rode on it." It seems, then, that automobiles and automobiling were on Walter Chrysler's mind for a long time before he took up with this legendary Locomobile. And as usual, his interest in this type of machinery came, from the beginning, through contact with his hands.

Despite the monumental future importance of the Locomobile affair, in 1908 the major consideration in Walter Chrysler's life was his railroad position. No matter what went wrong on the Chicago Great Western, it was the responsibility of the superintendent of motive power. So Chrysler kept on the move among all the line's shops, from Oelwein to Dubuque, Minneapolis, St. Paul, Omaha, and Kansas City. He was in complete control of equipment worth huge sums of money, and in charge of spending millions on new rolling stock, coal, and a vast array of other supplies. All the men in the mechanical department were his responsibility, too. A wallet full of passes on all the major U.S. railroads was the visible symbol of his mobile authority, and he kept it, bulging, constantly in his pocket.

He was proud of all of the men he picked to work for him, and his ability to match the right man to any task. One sentimental day he was able to give a master mechanic's job to old Gus Neubert, who had trained him at Ellis and gave him his first shot at self-discipline. He had heard Neubert was down on his luck and out of work in Arkansas City, and wired him immediately. When they stood face-to-face at Oelwein, they embraced like the old friends they were, and Chrysler set him to work. "I really needed Gus Neubert, and others like him. We had respect for each other because we shared the secrets of a mighty craft."

At Oelwein, too, Chrysler came into contact for the first time with men who had learned what they knew about machinery in college. Among these men was Sam Stickney, son of A. B. Stickney, a lawyer and construction engineer who was the founder and president of the Chicago Great Western; Sam Stickney was the general manager and vice president. Walt admired and envied the degree Sam had gotten from the Massachusetts Institute of Technology, and though it wasn't easy keeping up with men like Sam, "there was no word or term of mechanical engineering used by those college men which lacked meaning when they spoke to me. I had inside of me the essence of their knowledge." This was because Walt had continually pounded away at his engineering courses from the International Correspondence Schools for six or seven years and had mastered them all through hard work and diligence. But there was something Walt had that the college men lacked. Frequently they couldn't turn their learning into commands that could be understood by the rough sort of men who worked in the shops. "I could get out on the floor of any shop, walk into any roundhouse and do any man's job, with calipers or hammer or with a turret lathe," so the men respected him and understood him when he told them what to do. "I had not been handicapped by the overalled route that I had followed." Indeed, his background made him unique along the Chicago Great Western. But he understood how competent he was, and since he knew that he had gone as far as he could go as a mechanical man on the railroads, vaulting ambition was making him itch for something more. Circumstances would soon provide a reason for him to seek his opportunities elsewhere.

❖   ❖   ❖

Later in 1908 the headquarters of the Chicago Great Western were transferred from St. Paul to Chicago, and many important people on the line were replaced. The Stickneys were out; A. B. Stickney had been replaced by Samuel Morse Felton. Walt recalled, "After my first conversation with him, I said to myself, "From now on, life around here is going to be something less than sweet."

Sam Felton was a railroad man of the old school, which was still doing a thriving business in those days. Beginning in 1868, when he was fifteen, Felton had the typical mechanical man's rise through the profession, though he went much further than most. By the early 1890s he was president of the East Tennessee, Virginia and Georgia Railway, and eventually ran more than a score of railroads. "However, somewhere on his upward route he had picked up what seemed to me to be a gouty disposition." Well, if he was going to be hard to please, Walt determined to work nineteen hours a day to satisfy him. He worked harder than ever—even spending four nights a week out of town—to make sure he had the whole spread-out system in his mind and under control. But it all turned out to be of no avail.

One night near midnight a bone-weary Chrysler got a call from the Oelwein dispatcher telling him that Sam Felton wanted to see him in Chicago first thing in the morning. Incredulous, he pulled himself together, took the next train, and arrived in Chicago in time to walk into Mr. Felton's office at 8:30 A.M. Felton ignored his greeting and went on reading a huge stack of correspondence, letting him stand there in silence. At last Chrysler spied a morning paper on the corner of Felton's enormous desk, picked it up, and strode over to a chair by the window, where he sat down, put his feet up on the wide windowsill, and spread out the paper on his lap. He was boiling with rage, of course, and not really reading anything in the paper he clutched in a viselike grip, until Felton shortly barked a question as to what he was doing there. After being reminded that he was answering Felton's summons, the old man glared a minute before he finally remembered. After rummaging through his papers, Felton found what he wanted—a report that a hot box had made one train three minutes late. Felton wanted to know why; Chrysler protested that he couldn't say because he had been out inspecting the division for over a week. He offered that he would have a report on this as soon as he got some time in his office, but Felton yelled, "You ought to know now. I shouldn't have to ask for a report." Chrysler repeated that he didn't know a blankety-blank thing about it because he had been on the line for a week. Felton then began ranting and raving, which, considering Chrysler's temper, was the wrong thing to do. His dander fully up, Chrysler reached deep into his inside pocket; at that, Felton put his hands on the sides of his swivel chair and shut up. Chrysler pulled out his wallet, fat with the railroad passes that were a symbol of his job and authority. "With a wide circle of my arm, I flung it down on his desk so hard that it bounced; and then I said—well, I was explicit. Sam Felton never got a chance to close his mouth before I had stomped out of his office and slammed the door behind me. That is how I became an ex railroad man."

So it wasn't that Walter Chrysler's famous temper had deserted him, it was that by now he knew exactly when and where to exercise it unrestrained. When he knew the situation was right, he let go.

He went off to the bar of the Hotel Brevoort, where he licked his wounds in the middle of the morning on that cold December day in 1909. After a while, who should come in but his old friend Bill Causey, and Walt was glad to tell him all about what happened, start to finish. Later in the morning, as they drank, Causey revealed that he had been sent over by Sam Felton, who knew they were old friends: "Look Walt, Felton's old enough to be your father. He doesn't want you to quit. You just happened to walk into him when he had a grouch." Walt replied, "Well, he fixed the time of my call. I'm never going to give him the pleasure of firing me."

As the day wore on, other friends came into the bar, and Walt began to really enjoy himself, all his pressures finally relieved. Bill Causey stuck right by his side, through drinks, through meals, pulling at his arm or plucking at his lapel from time to time, trying to get him not to quit. Even as Walt walked through the station to get the 9:30 P.M. train back to Oelwein, Causey dogged his heels, still pleading with him. Just inside the barrier, the gate man stopped him to see his pass. He had forgotten that he had left them on Felton's desk, and, cussing up a storm while Causey laughed like a hyena, he dug into his pocket for the fare. Causey sat up with him all through the night, across Illinois and Iowa, trying to persuade him to stay, using sensible arguments and soft words of praise. But it was no good. Walt Chrysler would not go crawling back to Sam Felton under any circumstances.

Back home, he found Della bundling little Thelma off to school, and he blurted out his news. She didn't cry, or blame or criticize him. If she was frightened, she didn't show it. She had great human understanding of her man, great insight into his character, and handled this situation perfectly. She just let him talk and listened quietly, and by the time he had his coffee, he had composed himself.

Back at the office, he let his chief clerk know he had quit and packed up his personal belongings. He hung around the house for a few days and tinkered with his car. When he had made up his mind, he telegraphed Waldo H. Marshall, the president of the American Locomotive Company (ALCO), looking for a job.

The two men were on the best of terms. Chrysler had bought a lot of locomotives from Marshall during his tenure at the Chicago Great Western, and was so much admired by the latter that it was natural for him to look in that direction when he needed a job. Marshall telegraphed back that he didn't believe Chrysler had quit, but after a further exchange of wires and letters, he was convinced. He invited Walt to Pittsburgh to talk with James McNaughton, who was Walt's kind of man, having risen by his bootstraps to become general superintendent of both the Brooks and Schenectady Works of ALCO. "He assured me, with great kindness, that I was coming to a place where I could make my talents count."

He was to be made superintendent of the Allegheny Works. It sounded like an impressive job, but when he translated it into railroad terms, he realized that he had slipped several rungs down the ladder; he was merely a foreman, and for the first time since Salt Lake City, he was back in overalls. But at $275 a month, he would be getting better pay than most foremen.

"The works manager of the Allegheny plant at that time was an elderly fellow who had the crusty look of a cold locomotive's fire box. If he had a sense of humor, I never detected it." The manager had good reason for his sour disposition, though, for he was in the grip of a new work-scheduling system designed to equalize job costs at all the ALCO plants. It must have been quite irritating to the old-timers like him to put up with all the changes around the shops. Chrysler sensed a bit of trouble here, but nevertheless he was being offered a good job with real possibilities, so he signed on to go to work at ALCO.

For $40 a month he rented a substantial-looking red brick house adorned by windows with polished wood frames and fronted by a cut stone porch at what is now 84 North Harrison Street, then Seville Place, in the Bellevue section of Pittsburgh. Then he returned to Oelwein to collect his family and arrange for the move to Pittsburgh. It had been lonely for him there in the wintry industrial smoke, and he hugged his wife and children close when he was reunited with them.

Before he left Oelwein, though, he was given an extraordinary send-off at the opera house on the night of Thursday, December 16, 1909. According to B. C. Forbes, in an article entitled "Chrysler Tells How He Did It," which appeared in the January 1, 1929, issue of *Forbes*, this occasion was a tribute to "Chrysler's magnetic personality and his faculty for inspiring friendship and good will. J. C. Jepson, of Oelwein, who figured prominently on the occasion, recalls: 'The esteem in which W. P. was held, not alone by his employees but also by the citizens of the entire community, was evidenced by the farewell reception tendered him a few days prior to his departure for his new home in Pittsburgh. The opera house was packed, and although it was a bitter cold night, and the festivities lasted until the wee sma' hours in the morning, everyone present realized that he was losing something in Mr. Chrysler's going and was, therefore, reluctant in saying 'Farewell.'

"The evening's program closed by presenting the departing one and his family with a beautiful chest of silverware, and I had the pleasure of making the presentation speech. There were cries, 'Chrysler!' 'Chrysler!' I see him now, mounting the stage, with cheeks flushed and great big tears dropping on his coat, lips quivering in vain endeavor to say something. A deathlike stillness pervaded the auditorium when he finally managed to say, 'I thank you boys. God speed you all. Goodbye.' He left the stage amid ringing cheers and soon everyone joined in singing, *For He's A Jolly Good Fellow*, *Auld Lang Syne* and similar songs.

"It was a night long to be remembered, but little did any of us dream that the name of 'Chrysler' would ere many years be known, not only on this continent but also in foreign countries.

"The big, white, red-upholstered Locomobile went with Chrysler when he left Oelwein." On his way to destiny.

⌘ 14 ⌘

The First Manufacturing Job: ALCO

Locomotion

Walt and Della were determined to have a nice Christmas for the family despite all the upheaval they were going through at the end of 1909. The family had increased during the year, for on May 27, 1909, Walter Chrysler, Jr., their first son, was born. Of all the Chrysler children, he was the one to achieve a permanent measure of fame on his own, though not in industry. Despite his father's urgings that he make a career in business, he was to become famous in the arts, first as a publisher of exquisite books, then as a patron of the performing arts, and finally and most enduringly as an art collector and donor. His taste was both eclectic and catholic, but his eye was unusually good and his financial sense of art was exceptional; he amassed a legacy of enduring importance, most of which can now be seen at the Chrysler Museum in Norfolk, Virginia. On Christmas Day of 1909, however, his sense of art was all involved with pretty baubles in bright colors, pleasing rattles, and tinkly chimes.

The family had arrived in Pittsburgh that week, and just barely managed to unpack and settle in by Christmas Eve. By some miracle, even the telephone was connected. Cash was scarce for the Chryslers, what with moving expenses, train fares for the family, and that monthly bank payment on the Locomobile. But Christmas was Christmas, and that morning saw waves of delight among the squealing children as they opened their presents. Then, just at the peak of merriment, Scrooge came to call.

The phone rang, and it was the old sourball works manager. No Christmas greeting; his 'Bah! Humbug!' was: "Chrysler? Say, your friend, the efficency expert in New York, no longer is vice president. (The expert had been a former Superintendent of Motive Power on the CGW, known to Chrysler.) He got fired yesterday. Maybe you better go down to New York and see where you stand." And Merry Christmas to you, too.

Walter and Della seated in his second car, a 1911 Stevens-Duryea, parked outside their home on Seville Place in the Bellevue section of Pittsburgh. (*Courtesy Frank B. Rhodes*)

Walt wasn't frightened by this news, for he knew, as the other man didn't, that he had been hired by the president of the company. No, what made him feel as if he had been doused with cold water was that he was supposed to go to work for the man on the other end of the wire the next morning, and this man didn't want him.

The man repeated the advice about going to New York. "Say, I've got a better idea," said Walt. "If you want to know where I stand, maybe you better get on the train and go down to New York and find out for yourself." With that he banged down the receiver, picked up a little three-valve trumpet from the Christmas toy melange, and cheered himself up by attempting to play his old standby, the tuba part from the William Tell Overture. "Downhearted? Not me! I had all the confidence in the world. The next morning I put on my overalls and plunged into my work. Three months later I did not have a better friend than the works manager."

A lot of changes happened to the family in Pittsburgh. Della finally got a serving girl to help her out with cleaning and laundry and minding the children. After having three children in eight years, this was the first household help she had ever had, and it was a great relief from what had become a heavy household burden. Walt got a new car, too, selling the Locomobile to purchase a large, dark, and impressive six-cylinder Stevens-Duryea touring car, considered as fine as any manufactured in America at that time. He was often seen with his family and the neighbors across the street, Mr. and Mrs. Van J. Abels, negotiating the hills of Pittsburgh or on long runs to towns like Wexford, Dorseyville, and Zellenopia. Mr. Abels took pictures, and there they all are, the ladies in the backseat wearing frilly bonnets tied under the chin and Walt behind the wheel in a stylish jockey cap, clamping down on a big Pittsburgh stogie. He also joined the Duquesne Club, his first, which was the best in town. All this was possible because, about a year and a half after he left railroading to go into manufacturing, he was made works manager of the American Locomotive Company; it was a high-paying job with enormous prestige.

"What was important was the change in me. The fun I had experienced in making things as a boy was magnified a hundred fold when I began making things as a man. There is in manufacturing a creative joy that only poets are supposed to know. Some day I'd like to show a poet how it feels to design and build a railroad locomotive."

He had been called assistant works manager practically from the beginning, but "sang easy" and lay low on his authority while he roamed about acres of buildings in his overalls trying to get a sense of how activity was organized in the many buildings that made up the Allegheny (or Pittsburgh) Works of ALCO. There was an iron foundry next to the Ohio River, an enormous truck shop, a brass foundry, a forge shop, and—best of all to Chrysler—the erecting shop.

After he'd learned the lay of the land, mastered the intricacies of locomotive manufacture, and set his own system in motion, "the Allegheny plant began doing something it had not done during three preceeding years; it began to make money."

In his memoirs, Nicholas Kelley, counsel both to Walter Chrysler and the Chrysler Corporation, speaks of Chrysler's efforts to turn things around at ALCO: "The American Locomotive Company had hired him to run their Pittsburgh plant, which he had rearranged. He said that the way the old locomotive shops worked was that they would work on one thing which was taken away and worked on somewhere else, and then it would be taken over to another corner [to be worked on], and then brought back. He thought it was the greatest waste in the world. Moving materials was very expensive. He straightened it all out so that the process began at one end and the finished locomotive came out at the other. That was one thing that Chrysler had very clearly in his mind. He had it begin at one end and come out at the other. The thing is what is called progressive. The line is the most striking feature of that." Later we will see that the progressive moving assembly in the automobile business came from many sources, including the ideas of Walter Chrysler. What he brought to the process came from devising quicker, more efficient methods of manufacturing locomotives here at ALCO.

All locomotives are custom jobs individually designed to the specifications of the purchaser. Therefore it was amazing that Chrysler brought the Allegheny Works to the point of erecting a new engine every single day. Each engine was sold before it was built, and Chrysler used to take orders for millions of dollars' worth, mostly at the Duquesne Club from men like himself who had started out as machine shop apprentices in overalls. One day, for instance, he got a huge order from Loren H. Turner, superintendent of motive power on the Pittsburgh & Lake Erie. Turner needed twenty-five locomotives capable of pulling twelve Pullman cars at sixty miles an hour on a 1 percent grade; his order amounted to $1.25 million, an enormous sum of money then.

By now things had changed for Walter Chrysler, big time. He was earning $8,000 a year, a huge amount in 1911, making big deals with important men. He was building all kinds of engines for such lines as the New York Central, the Pennsylvania Railroad, and many others. (He had trouble over the New York Central jobs; ALCO's boilermakers at Schenectady created a job action over the fact that New York Central engines were to be built at the Allegheny works. In a letter to Chrysler dated October 29, 1911, the union machinists and blacksmiths agreed that they were willing to build engines for any line provided that any boilermaker employed in the Allegheny works "shall receive the union scale of wages as heretofore.")

He got one other big order from Turner, in late 1911, "given to me while we sat and devoured a rare steak as big as my forearm." This was for twenty-five switching engines, but in order to seal the deal Walt had to promise he would personally put the engines through his shop. The reason was that Turner had heard a rumor that Walt was leaving ALCO. Walt acknowledged that this was so; but he had a new baby on the way, and wouldn't go until it had arrived sometime in January, so he could guarantee his supervision of Turner's job until completion, "even if I have to work on Christmas."

He was going to Flint, Michigan, to enter the automobile business. This marked the second enormous change in his business life in two years, and he knew this decision would part him from the locomotives and railroad companions he loved forever. "I was afflicted by regrets. Aside from these feelings I had to stop and think that I was taking my wife and children away from the comfort and dignity of the best situation I had ever achieved into a young and somewhat raw industry.

"But the new chance was exciting; it excited me as pioneering chances have always excited my ancestors, causing them to cross the ocean to an unformed America, to move northward into Canada, and then to go westward to the Kansas plains. I felt that same kind of thrill when setting out for Flint."

This new life for Walter Chrysler came about through the good offices of James Jackson Storrow, one of the great American bankers of the twentieth century and eminence grise of the automobile business in the 1910s. Storrow sat on the board of directors of the American Locomotive Company; due to a banking takeover during a crisis in 1910, he was both a board member of the General Motors Corporation (GM) and, for a few months, its president.

Henry Greenleaf Pearson, in his 1932 book, *James Jackson Storrow, Son of New England*, described the events that led Storrow to seek out Walter Chrysler. In a letter of February 2, 1911, Storrow spoke of a need at General Motors "for anywhere from 2 to 6 sound, level headed mechanical engineers. The output of the company last year was $58 million dollars, and this was almost entirely accomplished without the advice and assistance of technically trained mechanical engineers. We also need a few managers and superintendents of facts." He further mentioned that he went to Harvard engineers on the q.t. to find out if they knew anybody for these positions; he promised to give "tender consideration" to any candidates they might propose. The help was especially needed at Buick, where output and quality both needed improvement. For example, the number of shafts shipped out each year exceeded the number of cars manufactured, due to defects in these items; nor was this the only defect that had to be made good after the cars left the factory.

Storrow was very thorough in informing himself about the car industry through long conferences with company officials and visits to company factories. Once he had a Buick disassembled and each and every part spread out on a sheet on the floor. Then he had everything catalogued, so that for the first time ever it would be possible to see and obtain a complete record of exactly what elements went into the making of the company's product. As obvious as the need for such a record may be today, this was an enormous step forward in the chaotic conditions of automobile construction at that time. And Buick was one of the largest and most successful producers.

Storrow's search for a man of alertness and originality who also had manufacturing experience in metals led him to Walter Chrysler. Sitting on the board at ALCO, he saw the changes in the balance sheets, and upon investigation, he learned how much of this was due to Chrysler's efforts at the Allegheny Works. He knew then that he had found his man, and arranged to meet with him.

Chrysler received a telegram from Storrow inviting him to come to his office in New York City. Since he had no idea who Storrow was, he made inquiries of a banker friend at the Duquesne Club, only to be told that in addition to being the head of the famous banking firm of Lee, Higginson and Company, he was also a member of the ALCO board. He was advised that anything Storrow had to say to him would be a matter of some importance.

For the very first time, Walter Chrysler went to New York City, to meet

Storrow at the offices of Lee, Higginson at 43 Wall Street. Bedazzled by his first sight of the tall buildings of the city, he had some difficulty finding this address. Storrow, a man of warm heart hidden behind a grave countenance, greeted Chrysler with words of praise about his performance at ALCO, then got right to the point, inquiring if he had ever given any thought to automobile manufacturing. When Chrysler replied that he had been thinking about it off and on for nearly five years, Storrow told him he could go to work at Buick, the most important of the GM companies. As former president of GM and chairman of the finance committee, he explained that he wanted to see Chrysler become the works manager at Buick. Chrysler would have to meet with the president of Buick, an excellent man with a great reputation as a carriage manufacturer, who knew he needed an experienced machinery man to run the works. That suited Chrysler just fine.

The next week, back in Pittsburgh, he got a telegram from Charles W. Nash of Flint, Michigan, the president of Buick, inviting him for lunch. The legend, probably apocryphal, was that on the way to meet Nash at the Fort Pitt Hotel, he saw a man by the side of the road with a broken-down car, stopped to fix it, and arrived with his shirt greasy, his tie undone, and his hair matted with sweat; Nash, put out by his lateness and taken aback by his appearance, took a while to warm up before a pleasant atmosphere was established. Though Chrysler performed many ad hoc roadside repairs later on, Nash didn't remember such an event in connection with their first meeting, and neither did Chrysler, who said they met at the ALCO works and then went off to lunch. In any case, the two men, though polite, seemed somewhat incompatible at first brush, and things didn't go too well until the meal had finished. "Want a cigar?", Nash asked. "Yes, I smoke panatelas," Walt replied. Nash broke out in a broad grin. "You smoke panatelas? That's funny. I smoke them myself." Chrysler said, "In the time we smoked those slender brown rods down to butts we got better acquainted, and Nash asked me to visit his plant, the Buick Motor Company, at Flint."

Hearing about this situation, James McNaughton boggled Walt's and Della's minds by offering him a 50 percent raise, to $12,000 a year. The raise alone was almost as much as his entire salary when he left the CGW. Nevertheless, he kept his appointment with Nash at Buick.

After five minutes in the office at Buick, Nash gave Chrysler a pass and told him to spend a day looking all through the plant, and then come back to talk things over.

"What I saw astonished me. Of course I was a machinist, and I was looking at workmen trained to handle wood. They did not, I was prepared to bet, know one single thing about metallurgy. The bodies were being made of wood. In a big carpenter shop, long wide poplar boards were being bent and shaped in steam kilns. With wood they were admirably skillful, for most of them had been carriage builders, but wherever they were handling metal it seemed to me there was opportunity for big improvement. I saw a hundred such opportunities, so that I became excitedly eager, saying to myself: 'What a job I could do here, if I were boss.' "

When Walt came back to Nash's office, the Buick president wanted to know the verdict. Chrysler said that he had seen he could be very useful here, and was eager to get involved. "I saw enough to be able to make up my mind." When Nash asked him for an example, Chrysler explained, "Men were painting the chassis of each car as they would paint the panels of a carriage. I drive a car, and I know that by the time you get a new car home, all the under part of the chassis is splashed with mud; thereafter no one ever sees it." After a silence, Nash said: "What salary do you want, Mr. Chrysler?"

Chrysler told Nash about the raise to $12,000 at ALCO, and watched the lights go off and the air go out of the tires of this negotiation. Not possible, Nash said; the auto business didn't pay that kind of money. Besides, Walt knew, Nash didn't really want him; he had been wished upon him by Storrow, and this was a way of getting out of it. But Chrysler wanted this chance, and he persisted. "Mr. Nash, what will you pay?"

Nash pursed his lips, scratched his head, and thought. "Underneath his hair, Mr. Nash was doing sums with pieces of my life."

"Mr. Chrysler, we can't afford to pay over $6,000."

"I accept it, Mr. Nash."

"Just like that; and he had to hire me. But he did not like it, not one little bit."

On November 30, 1911 W. P. Chrysler received a telegram from C. W. Nash stating simply, "Letter just received. We accept your proposition." So it was official.

In six months Nash and Chrysler were the best of friends, and remained so for life.

Jack Forker Chrysler was born in Pittsburgh on January 7, 1912. Though he was itching to get away to Flint, Walter Chrysler remained at ALCO through January 25 to finish the Turner job, according to his word.

Before he left there was another grand send-off with a dinner and florid speeches. The reverend John Dows Hills of the Epiphany Episcopal Church, which the Chryslers attended regularly, had fond memories of them. Close friend H. C. Gibson of ALCO said, "He has all the attributes of a great man. He has energy, modesty and a total absence of that superciliousness we sometimes call 'high hat.' " Finally a huge silver loving cup, flanked by enormous curved ivory handles on each side and mounted on a polished mahogany base, was presented to Chrysler. It was inscribed: "Token Of Esteem To W. P. Chrysler By Employees, American Locomotive Co., Pittsburgh Works." This cup sits today in a display case at the Chrysler Boyhood Home in Ellis, Kansas.

Years later S. C. Corfield, once a stenographer at ALCO, said, "We were mighty sorry to have him leave. But he was through with railroads and locomotives, and we felt that he would put a new kick into automobiles."

In 1925 Chrysler said of the automobile, "As I visualized its future, it far outran railway development, which in a sense had reached its zenith because the automobile provided flexible, economical, individual transportation which could be utilized for either business or pleasure. It knew no limits except a right of way; it was bounded by no greater restrictions than individual effort and will. To me it was the transportation of the future, and as such, I wanted to be a part of it. That was where I saw opportunity." And so, with confidence and courage, he put the first thirty-six years of his life behind him to face the thrill of a new world he knew he could conquer, for all those years had prepared him for what he was now to undertake.

His neighbor, Mr. Van Abel, recalled that he packed up and left for Flint one cold February day. "The old Stevens-Duryea left Bellvue, never to return, and all the folks around here were sorry. The Chryslers were dandy people."

PART TWO

The Automobile
and the Assembly Line

15

The Early History
of the Automobile

Chariots shall rage in the streets, they shall jostle one another in the broad ways; they shall seem like torches,
they shall run like the lightnings.
Nahum

I wanted to build a vehicle
to replace the family horse.
Henry Ford

It never kicks or bites, never tires on long runs
and never sweats in hot weather.
It does not require care in the stable
and only eats while on the road.
Ransom Eli Olds

They claim this motor car is a mystery. It has an
electric plant, a water plant and a whole lot of other
gadgets. But after all it is nothing but organiZAtion.
OrganiZAtion. OrganiZAtion. Bricks and mortar, men
and machinery and organiZAtion. And I am going to
be one of the big motor car manufacturers
of this country.
William Crapo Durant

To succeed is to realize what is possible.
Charles E. Sorensen

We must go ahead without the facts.
We will learn as we go along.
Henry Ford

Walter P. Chrysler was not an automotive pioneer. By the time he entered the automobile business in 1912, the horseless carriage had been thought of and constructed by a host of inventors, and had been superseded by the true modern type of automobile. The business of building automobiles, fifteen years old in the United States by then, had already entered its consolidation phase. But if ever a man was suited to the tasks of such a period, he surely was. He came to understand the automobile and the industry that produces it to the nth degree, from its most niggling little detail to its grandest implication. In this way he became the most knowledgeable of all auto men. Thus equipped, he accomplished what everyone of his day thought impossible: in a late age for the industry, he expanded the number of enduring automotive manufacturing giants from two to three. But you cannot really understand Walter Chrysler without knowing the early history of the automobile, because otherwise you will not know where he fit into it and what he did to continue it.

The great pioneers of the automobile were Charles E. and J. Frank Duryea, Elwood Haynes, the Apperson brothers, Ransom Eli Olds, Henry Ford, Hiram Percy Maxim, Charles B. King, Alexander Winton, and William Crapo Durant, along with a handful of others. First among them all were Gottfried Daimler and Karl Benz. But even these men were not the true pioneers, for although their efforts led directly to the modern automobile and the vast industry that builds it, mankind had been dreaming of and even making self-propelled vehicles for hundreds of years before these men existed.

Arthur Pound, in *The Turning Wheel*, his superb history of the first 25 years of General Motors, points out the incredible accomplishments of human civilization due to the wheel, but notes that no better movement for it than the horse was devised or discovered until relatively recently. "Other animals might outdraw the horse, but no other animal could combine pulling power with as prompt acceleration. The unique conformation of the horse's leg from hoof to hip joint gives him a leverage out of all proportion to his weight. In the practical arts the advance of knowledge had been tremendous, but from the dawn of history down to modern times mankind had available in quantity for land transport no better motive power than the horse."

In 130 B.C.E., Hero of Alexandria, in his *Pneumatica*, described his self-propelled steam vehicle, which he called the Aeolipile, according to Pound. The world, which had other things on its mind, forgot all about such things for almost 1,400 years until a monk named Roger Bacon prophesied chariots without animals in 1250 C.E.; it speaks volumes about the intervening time to note that Bacon could only speculate about what Hero had actually begun to do. With the Renaissance things changed. In 1601 Giovanni Baptista Della Porta continued with Hero's experiments, and in 1629 Giovanni

Branca came up with a steam turbine that was considerably advanced over Hero's design. Wonderously, in 1665 the Jesuit Father Ferdinand Verbiest, at the court of the Emperor of China, had local workmen construct a steam vehicle, about the size of a baby carriage, on the aeolipile principle.

Thirty-two years earlier, in 1633, Edward Worcester, the Marquis of Somerset, had invented the first really useful engine, a double-action one with displacement chambers; it was not, however, a commercial success. Thomas Savery received a patent in 1698 for a water-raising engine, the first to find a commercial application. It was succeeded in 1705 by Thomas Newcomen and his assistant John Cawley's Atmospheric Steam Engine, the first to make the piston engine a practical success by separating the piston from the boiler. This was in turn succeeded by James Watt's steam engine of 1763, which used a separate condenser for the first time, and several others of Watt's design. (16 years later Watt invented the principle of the crank, converting up-and-down motion to rotary motion, which would be of great importance to the development of the gasoline automobile.) In 1740, Bishop Berkeley, with great foresight, said, "Mark me, ere long we shall see a pan of coals brought to use in place of a feed of oats."

By the latter half of the eighteenth century, the stationary steam engine had long since proved its usefulness in coal mines and other places. The problem inventors faced was to make it "portable, gear it to wheels, and get it on the road," as Arthur Pound succinctly puts it in *The Turning Wheel*. For all intents and purposes, history's first solution, and application, came from Captain Nicolas-Joseph Cugnot of France, who in 1769 constructed a huge three-wheeled artillery gun tractor. The single front wheel pivoted and operated under a tremendous load from both the boiler and the engine. It worked, but had the single greatest failing of all such vehicles over the next hundred years: it was underpowered for its intended purpose. After it over-turned on its second trial, the royal government, which had expended great sums upon it, turned on Cugnot, and he went into exile. Napoleon recalled him twenty years later but did not follow up on this notion of artillery transport. Had Cugnot been allowed to continue until he succeeded, the history of Europe might well have been different.

In America Oliver Evans worked on plans for a steam-driven carriage from 1772 to 1784, when he finally completed the design for his engine; he received the first U.S. patent for a self-propelled carriage on October 17, 1789. Evans actually anticipated the famous Englishman Richard Trevithick in creating the noncondensing, high-pressure engine. (Trevithick saw and applied the drawings of Evans' 1787 engine in 1794–95; he had also known that William Murdock, James Watt's foreman, had succeded in demonstrat-ing a model steam carriage in Cornwall in 1784, and he developed Mur-dock's ideas.) In 1804 Evans astonished the citizens of Philadelphia by suc-cessfully operating the *Orukter Amphibolis*, a 21-ton amphibian vehicle, which was a combination steam wagon and flatboat. Previously in London, Trevithick coupled a 60-pound-pressure long-stroke steam engine directly to the wheels of a carriage, and drove his invention at 5 miles an hour through the streets on Christmas Eve of 1801 (he is credited with developing the layout of piston, connecting rod, and crank). Four years later he invented the first steam locomotive, and cut a colorful figure until he died in poverty in 1833.

Many other steam carriage inventors and operators followed, but in America they were hampered at first by bad roads, and in England by the antipathy of railroad and stagecoach operators to this new technology, along with reports of fearful accidents (the first, in 1834, killed several people and struck terror in the hearts of many). Eventually England passed the Act of 1865, wich required a vehicle on the highway to be preceded by a man on foot waving a red flag. This effectively killed nonrailway steam transport in England through the rest of the nineteenth century. Development then shifted to France and America, where both government and public opinion created a favorable atmosphere for the development of mechanized off-rail transportation.

In the 1870s, Amadee Bollée, the inventor of independently sprung front wheels, profitably operated a number of steam omnibuses in Paris. In New York Richard Dudgeon invented a steam carriage in 1860 that still operated in 1903 after thirty-six years in storage. Bruce Mohs, in an article in *Antique Automobile*, tells of Dr. J. N. Carhart of Racine, Wisconsin, who built a steam buggy in 1871, and in 1878 won a $10,000 prize sponsored by the state of Wisconsin to promote the construction of "a self propeller . . . which shall be a cheap and practical substitute for the horse and other animals on the highways and farms." The prize was to be awarded after a 200-mile race from Green Bay to Madison, but because the state found Carhart's vehicle neither cheap nor practical, it awarded him only $5,000 in 1879 after considerable debate.

Accounts of non-steam types of vehicles have come down to us over the centuries too. Heliodorus, a writer of romances who probably lived in the 3rd century C.E., mentions a triumphal chariot in Athens that was moved by slaves who worked machinery. Drawings from the Middle Ages show men moving ornate, heavy carriages by means of worm and other type gears. A 16th-century Jesuit missionary in China, Matteo Ricci, wrote that he had traveled there inside a great wheel, whose forward motion was provided by two fellow passengers operating levers. Around 1600 sailing chariots, previously known in China, came into use in Holland. A two-masted one carrying twenty-eight people and capable of speeds of up to 21 miles per hour was designed by Simon Stevin and used on a regular basis.

Most important of all in the development of the automobile was the creation of the internal-combustion engine. It was invented in 1680 by a

Dutchman named Christiaan Huygens, who also invented the pendulum clock and discovered the rings of Saturn through his work in developing new lenses far more powerful than any previously known. The explosive force he used in his engine was not gasoline, a petroleum derivative that would not be known until the nineteenth century. Huygens used gunpowder.

By the time the nineteenth century was well under way, many experiments involving the internal combustion of some sort of gaseous materials were being conducted. Richard P. Scharchburg in his pellucid, elegant even, biography of J. Frank Duryea entitled *Carriages without Horses* charts the work then taking place in America. *The Road Is Yours*, by Reginald M. Cleveland and S. T. Williamson, *The Automobile in America* by Stephen W. Sears, *The American Automobile—A Brief History*, by John B. Rae, *The Birth of a Giant* by Richard Crabb, and Arthur Pound's *The Turning Wheel*—all these fine books together give a full picture of the early development of the gasoline engine car, and they can be highly recommended to an interested reader on this subject.

Scharchburg tells us that the first internal combustion engine in the United States (it also was the first to use liquid fuel) was patented in 1826 by Samuel Morey, who apparently ran it in a vehicle on Market Street in Philadelphia in 1829; he accidentally fell out of the machine, which ran away on its own and stopped by crashing into a brick wall, creating America's first auto accident. Others in America and Europe also worked on perfecting the internal-combustion engine, most notably Etienne Lenoir of Belgium, who patented a two-cycle engine in Paris in 1862, and Nikolaus Otto and Eugen Langen of the German Confederation, who patented a four-cycle engine in 1867. (In fact, Alphonse Beau de Rochas had patented his own type of four-cycle engine, which lacked the Otto engine's compression phase, in 1862; he never developed his device, but successfully sued Otto and Langen in French courts.) This last was the first whose movements formed the basis of the internal-combustion engine to this day—intake, compression, explosion, and exhaust. It took eighteen years for this design to be refined to the point at which Gottlieb Daimler's version of it could be considered for production in quantity.

In America such men as James F. Hill, George Brayton, Sephaniah Reese, Henry Nadig, William T. Harris, John W. Lambert, and Charles H. Black all produced vehicles powered by internal combustion between 1885 and 1892, according to Scharchburg's exhaustive research. (Hill may also have built an oscillating steam engine vehicle as early as 1868, when he was thirteen years old!)

Of all these men, the most significant was George Brayton, whose two internal-combustion engines of the 1870s used gasoline. The first operated a streetcar on rails in Providence in 1873, the second an off-rail omnibus in Pittsburgh in 1878. Brayton's engine, patented in 1872, formed the basis of the notorious automobile patent applied for in 1879 by George B. Selden, a Rochester patent attorney, and granted to him in 1895. According to Stephen W. Sears, the Brayton Ready Motor was seen by Selden at a Philadelphia Centennial exhibit in 1876, encouraging him to make "an imaginative mental leap. He envisioned it as the power plant for a road vehicle that would use liquid hydrocarbon fuel, be steerable, and have a means of engaging the driving wheels." The Selden patent was the result of this imaginative leap, and eventually it gave the automobile industry a fifteen-year headache during the early part of its consolidation phase.

Over in Germany, as soon as Otto and Langen's "Otto Cycle" engine went into production at the Gasmotorfabrik Deutz factory near Cologne, all sorts of innovations for it ensued. Former Otto engineer Gottlieb Daimler, working with his assistant Wilhelm Maybach, produced an Otto Cycle engine in 1885 that weighed only 110 pounds and was rated at 15 horsepower. Rotating at 800 to 1,000 rpm, it was a vast improvement over previous oil and gas engines that could do no better than 150 to 200 rpm; they installed it in a motor bicycle. Before the year was out, Daimler's chief rival, Karl Benz, had assembled a three-wheeled motor carriage containing his version of the Otto cycle engine, featuring water cooling and electric ignition (battery, coil, spark, and plug); it also had a device allowing variable speeds and an automatic control of the gas supply through a clutch lever operating a stopcock. Daimler's engine featured high compression, like modern ones, but Benz's car had far more modern features, and so the endless squabble over the primacy of their respective inventions is essentially moot.

It should be noted that an article published in *Scientific American* in 1888 describing the vehicle Benz had run successfully in 1886 was read by some forty thousand American mechanics. In some ways it was the most significant document in the early history of the motor car. As Cleveland and Williamson point out, "The Benz article spark plugged the most imaginative ones." There were about three hundred people in America working on some kind of self-propelled vehicle before the turn of the twentieth century, trying to place a mechanical device in a buggy to replace the horse in front of it. Many, like Walter Chrysler, began by reading this and later *Scientific American* articles.

One who did not begin this way was Ransom Eli Olds, who was born to Mr. and Mrs. Pliny F. Olds (his father was a blacksmith) in Geneva, Ohio in 1864. Pliny Olds sold the family farm in Ohio, and eventually father and son were engaged in the manufacture of gasoline engines in Lansing, Michigan. By the early 1880s Ransom Olds became convinced that horses could be replaced by mechanical power. In 1887, at the age of twenty-three, he built and operated a three-wheeled steam vehicle on the streets of Lansing, Michigan, and another with a vertical boiler two years later. This latter vehicle was sold to the Times Company of Bombay, India, in 1893, and so is credited with being the first American automotive export sale; however, it was never delivered, because the boat it was shipped on sank.

The Olds works built its first gas engine in 1885, and soon its products were in demand throughout Michigan, then coast to coast, for marine, factory, and farm use. Pliny Olds made his son one-half owner of his River Street machine shop when the boy was only twenty-one, so he learned how to operate a successful business at an early age. Ransom Olds operated his first steamer almost simultaneously with the vehicles of Daimler and Benz, though, of course, theirs were gas powered. The Germans and Olds were unaware of each other's work, but all of them were proving that small engines, for use on the road, were both feasible and practicable. More attention has been paid to the work of the Germans in this regard, most likely because Olds didn't realize that newspapers or scientific journals would be interested in what he was doing.

Both Daimler and Benz were profitably manufacturing quantities of four-wheeled motor cars by the early 1890s, and Daimler had begun to license out his engine by that time. The Steinway Piano Company of Long Island, New York, was a licensee, but was never able to market a car successfully, despite much publicity. However, great success accrued to the French engineering firm of Panhard et Levassor, who licensed Daimler's engine and proceeded to create what is generally agreed to be the world's first true automobile—with the engine in the front of the vehicle, the passengers arranged in rows behind the motor, rather than over it and the axis of the crankshaft was parallel to the side members of the frame—as opposed to a horseless carriage. (Levassor obtained his license by marrying Mme. Sazarin, the widow of Daimler's patent attorney and owner of the French patent rights to the Daimler engine.)

As early as 1891, Emile Constant Levassor designed the prototype of this machine. Its development came about through the influence of the modern bicycle. In 1885, J. K. Stanley of Coventry, England, invented the safety bicycle, a low-wheeled machine with gearing and chain drive, replacing the velocipede, whose main wheel was moved by pedals and therefore needed to be huge to keep the vehicle upright. As Pound points out, "The influence of cycle design on the inventive French mind freed French inventors from the obsession of carriage design which dominated early English and American efforts—the stagecoach in England, and the buggy in America."

As an *Encyclopaedia Brittanica* article of the early 1930s notes, "The drive was taken through a clutch to a set of reduction gears and thence to a differential gear on a countershaft on which the road wheels were driven by chains. With all recent modification of details, the combination of clutch, gear-box and transmission remains unaltered, so that to France, in the person of M. Levassor, must be given the honor of having led in the development of the motorcar." It would be a long time before the superiority of the "Systeme Panhard" would become indubitable in America, and many factors would combine in its triumph here. In this and in other ways though, as Rae says, "The automobile is European by birth, American by adoption."

In addition to the layout of the modern car, the French also contributed its name. By the mid-1890s everyone knew that this new machine needed to be called something other than a horseless carriage, but what? In the fall of 1895, Herman Kohlsaat, publisher of the *Chicago Times-Herald*, ran a contest in his newspaper offering a $500 prize to the person who could devise the best name for this new type of transporation machine. The winner was "motocycle," a word which was swiftly laughed into oblivion as inappropriate for a four-wheeled vehicle, though in slightly altered form it became useful for the two-wheeled "motorcycle." The French created what would become the universally adopted word, "automobile." By the summer of 1896, *Scientific American* was using the term in its pages, but there was still some confusion about this word, owing to the fact that the French Academy did not officially sanction its use until 1899. Besides, in the beginning Americans did not know whether to accent the first, third, or fourth syllable when pronouncing it. This confusion may be the source of why to this day automobiles are still officially called "motor vehicles" on their registrations. Olds didn't call his cars "Oldsmobiles" until after the turn of the century for this reason.

Early on the French also contributed the terms "chassis," "limousine," "garage," and "chauffeur" to the language, the latter originally indicating a class of servant who was above eating with the kitchen help but below the rank of a governess, who sometimes took her meals with the family.

As can be readily seen from the above list of progenitors, the automobile did not have any one inventor. Many people were to claim to be "the father of the automobile" or "the inventor of the automobile," but in reality each was one of many who contributed to the development of it. Who did what, on what kind of a machine, and when; what he knew of the work of others; and whether his contraption actually worked—these are all aspects of a complex historical phenomenon. We may put milestones by certain names along the path of the automobile's development, and even a few monuments, but there is no temple named for a car god in whose name all was accomplished. There were inventors and organizers and makers, but the automobile was a *movement* if anything in history ever was. The techology for it was lying around the world in bits and pieces for some time, but men turned to concentrate their energies on it only when society called out for them to do so; then, and only then, was it actually created. By the time it came into existence, it was an irresistible idea. The steamboat and the train were the first inventions that meant people could be transported by mechanical means. The bicycle gave them individual semimechanized transport. Motorized transport was the next logical step, and if the men who created the first horseless carriages hadn't done so when they did, somebody else would have, and soon.

Perhaps the main reason Europeans were so far ahead in this enterprise (American auto production didn't overtake French production until 1906) was the matter of roads. European roads were laid out hundreds, sometimes thousands, of years ago, and were well established and well maintained, the envy of the world. In modern times, one of Napoleon's greatest achievements was the splendid system of military roads he established in France. American roads outside the cities, by contrast, were horrendous, rock-strewn, potholed dirt paths. They became mud rivers every spring and were clogged with snow in winter; in summer they were overlaid with choking, blinding dust.

With the coming of the safety bicycle, tens of thousands of people, now including women and children, took to the roads in America (there were ten million bicycles in this country by 1900), and they all had close personal experience of the inadequacy of its roads. A League of American Wheelmen was formed, which successfully agitated on state and local levels for better roads. By 1893 Congress had appropriated $10,000 for a Bureau of Road Inquiry in the Department of Agriculture, whose purpose was to study and inform the public on improved methods of highway construction. Eventually the federal highway program grew out of this beginning, which came at exactly the moment when automobiles began to appear on the streets of American cities.

◈   ◈   ◈

It was not to become apparent for some time that the internal combustion engine was to be the primary (eventually the only) source of motive power for the automobile. The three contenders for primacy in the 1880s and 1890s were the steam engine, the electric battery, and the internal combustion engine. Not until the turn of the century did the inherent superiority of the qualities of the internal-combustion engine sweep all before it.

The great possibilities of steam engines in motor cars had been understood for quite a while, but it was not until Léon Serpollet invented the flash boiler in 1889, that they became truly practical. Previously, steam vehicles were of the steam roller type, which had a boiler in which a large volume of water was heated in bulk to maintain constant or slowly changing steam pressure. It was a bulky and inflexible system. Serpollet's boiler was a capillary metallic tube into which water was injected and immediately converted to steam. It used only a few centimeters of water and held no steam in reserve, hence was much more lightweight and practical than anything which had gone before it. Not all steamers used it, the Stanley being the most notable exception, but those that did had a great advantage in lightness and speed in raising a head of steam.

All steam cars offered great advantages over other types. They were very fast, offered quick acceleration from a standstill, and were terrific hill climbers. No cranking was required to start them, and since they didn't require transmissions, the automobilist didn't have to know how to shift. Since there were comparatively few moving parts, they were very easy and quick to fix. As opposed to problems in a gas vehicle, which might take days to repair, trouble in a steamer could be diagnosed in five minutes and fixed in an hour. This resulted in great popularity. In 1902 over half the registered autos in New York City were steamers.

The White, which introduced the flash boiler to American cars in a design by Rollin H. White, was considered the best steamer by many experts and was also the best seller, numbering as many as 1,500 cars in a single year's production through 1911, when White turned to gas vehicle production. But of more than 120 brands the Stanley was by far the best known and most talked about.

Stanley Steamers were manufactured by identical twins Francis E. and Freelan O. Stanley, who were born in Kingfield, Maine; later they moved to Newton, Massachusetts, where they established several successful businesses. Inventive geniuses who became very prosperous, they made the first violins commercially manufactured in the U.S., patented a useful home gas illuminating device and, most importantly, invented a superior photgraphic dry plate, later sold to Eastman Kodak for a huge sum in 1904. The twins' literary minded parents named the twins for characters in Sir Walter Scott's novel *Marmion;* the trade mark of their dry plate was a shield trumpeting Marmion's death cry "On, Stanley, On!"

The Stanley twins looked and dressed alike, even trimming their beards the same way. According to Cleveland and Williamson, the only way to tell them apart was to tell a joke. The one who slapped his thigh and said, "Godrey mighty!" was F. E.; the one who slapped his thigh and said, "Gee cracky!" was F. O.

After seeing a steam car at the Brockton County Fair in 1896, the brothers decided to build one of their own, which they did in 1897, following a period of experimentation begun some years earlier. They achieved what many engineers said couldn't be done—they constructed a car with a 190-pound boiler and a 35-pound engine. F. O. and his wife climbed Mt. Washington in a Stanley Steamer; another car set a hill climbing record, and a third set a world's speed record, traveling a mile in two minutes and eleven seconds. Orders flooded in and the brothers' new venture prospered. Then a group of financiers offered them ten times the money they had put into the company, and they sold out for $250,000. The new group formed the

Locomobile Company, and assigned it the Stanley patents they had purchased. Instant disagreements caused the new company to split into the Locomobile Company and the Mobile Company, which moved to Tarrytown, New York. When Locomobile decided to move to Bridgeport, Connecticut, the Stanleys bought back their old Newton plant and were back in business in the spring of 1901. They developed a new machine, not infringing on any existing patents, which eliminated chain drive and moved the engine so it was not in direct contact with the rear axle. For $15,000, the Stanleys promptly licensed their patents to the White Sewing Machine Company of Cleveland, Ohio, which began manufacture of the above-mentioned White steamers in a corner of its sewing machine factory.

Speed was an obsession of the Stanleys, and on January 27, 1906, at Ormond Beach, Florida, their factory mechanic Fred Marriott drove an astonishingly modern-looking semi-torpedo shaped Stanley at 127.66 miles per hour; he also clocked a mile in 28.2 seconds, becoming the first man in history to travel faster than two miles a minute. (The car was actually, literally, an upside down rowboat the Stanleys had adapted as an auto body.) These official records lasted until 1910. Two years later Marriott drove at over 150 miles per hour before the same car (known as the Stanley Woggle-Bug) was destroyed after hitting ripples in the sand of Ormond Beach as the wheels were leaving the ground in flight. Marriott survived, though badly injured.

Unfortunately Francis Stanley was not so lucky, dying in an automobile accident in 1918. This took the heart out of his brother, who no longer cared about the firm and let sons-in-law run it into the ground until it closed in 1924.

But in any case it was really over for the steam car by then. It had many inherent drawbacks, which loomed more and more important in the mind of the public as time went on. The boilers could freeze in winter, and even the improved ones took two minutes to get up steam, which became an enormous disadvantage after the electric self-starter was invented in 1912. Though not much water was needed in the flash boilers, it had to be constantly replenished. This was fine in the Northeast, where soft water was readily available, but in the West water was filled with lime that would quickly clog car boilers, just as it did in locomotives. This meant that boiler water would have to be brought in from distant points for steamers, just as the railroads did for their engines, and this would be both expensive and restricting for a self-powered vehicle whose main attraction was that it could operate away from the confines of tracks. Besides, because these cars operated on pressures of 600 pounds per square inch, they needed constant skilled maintenance and so were basically unsuitable for mass consumption. Perhaps most important of all, though, was that people were afraid the boilers would explode, though there is little evidence any ever did. The public had the same fear of internal combustion engines in the beginning, though this was overcome. Somehow the aura of danger never would depart from steamers.

Ultimately however, the problems with steamers could have been dealt with, if manufacturers wanted to make the effort to overcome them. But as John B. Rae says, "The insuperable handicap for the steam-driven automobile was and is that an internal combustion engine has greater thermal efficiency than a steam engine, so that the same amount of technical effort would inevitably produce better results with the gasoline car than the steamer. There is no evidence that the steam automobile was the victim of a conspiracy on the part of the manufacturer of gasoline automobiles, as has sometimes been alleged by its partisans. What happened to it was simply a manifestation of the survival of the fittest."

The other great challenger to the supremacy of the gasoline engine car was the electric vehicle. It was quiet and clean, and had no vibrations, odors, or fumes. It was easy to drive, having no requirements for cranking or shifting, and was easy to maintain. In the early days of motoring it was considered the ideal car for a woman to operate, particularly when her journeys were mostly confined to short trips in town.

The world's first electric vehicle was produced by Robert Anderson in Aberdeen, Scotland, in 1839, astonishing when you realize that the self-exciting dynamo wasn't invented until 1871. Pound tells us that "his carriage was driven by a primitive electric motor consisting of bars of iron on a drum. These were drawn around by electro magnets, probably on the principle of some old toys which had a star wheel to produce the necessary make and break; [perhaps] it was dependent upon intermittent primary cells." Anderson never thought of his vehicle as more than a toy, and considering that the storage battery would not come into being for decades, he had good reason to think this way.

William Morrison of Des Moines, Iowa, designed the first electric vehicle in 1891, and ran it on the streets of Chicago in the fall of 1892. Morris and Slalom of Philadelphia were the first to go into production with their well-designed Electrobat of 1895, and shortly thereafter Colonel Albert A. Pope began production of his Columbia Electric in Hartford, Connecticut. Colonel Pope was the first person to produce cars in large numbers in America. He made more than half the 4,192 cars manufactured in America in 1899, and was an important precursor of mass production in this country. By 1900 his Columbias began to appear as taxicabs, ambulances, and delivery wagons on the streets of New York. Because they were so quiet and trouble-free, they lent themselves to a variety of elegant coach works in limousine, coupe, victoria, and brougham styles; most provided prominent places for the seating of liveried servants. Diamond Jim Brady ordered his with curved glass.

Since these vehicles were pitched to the very rich and socially conscious, every effort was made to get the beau monde to be seen in one. The very presence of one of the "400" in a swanky electric gave it instant cachet and respectability. Cleveland and Williamson recount one unfortunate but hilarious example of the rich trying to accommodate themselves to the motor age. It seems that Mrs. Hamilton Fish had purchased an open electric, and was duly given instruction on how to operate it. Lever forward, go ahead; lever backward, go back; lever upright, stand still. As she began to drive, a man crossed the street in front of her. She pushed the lever forward, and knocked him down. In a panic, she pulled the lever too far back, and ran over him again. By now in a complete tizzy, she pushed forward again and ran over him again. The terrifed victim got up at last, shook himself and shouted, " 'Fore God, ma'am, before you get through you sure is goin' to run over me!", and hopped down the street and around the corner as fast as he could. Mrs. Fish pulled the lever up to a stopping position, alighted from the brand-new car and left it standing where it was in the middle of the street, never to see it again.

Colonel Pope thought electric vehicles were the future of the automobile business. "You can't get people to sit over an explosion," he told his employee Hiram Percy Maxim about the gasoline car. But he was wrong. The success of electrics was only temporary, and due to the insufficiencies of early gas-powered vehicles. In the end, electrics couldn't go much faster than 12 miles an hour, had an extremely limited range, and carried very heavy batteries, which had to be recharged quite frequently. They were about as practical as enormous golf carts. As early as 1899 no less an authority than Thomas Edison said that the need to constantly recharge the batteries was too great a handicap for electric vehicles to overcome, and their day was over quickly.

The reason the gasoline-fueled internal-combustion engine triumphed as the source of motive power in the automobile is that it is small, cheap, and efficient, and most of all, it does not require an external source of power to keep it going. In the beginning, these engines had many drawbacks. They were noisy and dirty, emitted noxious fumes, vibrated excessively, required dangerous cranking to get started, and could not be operated without knowing how to shift a transmission. But they were reasonably fast, shortly became easy to repair and drive, and could go long distances without attention. Scarcely ten years after the automobile began to appear in America, the domination of the internal combustion engine was complete.

For all practical purposes, the beginnings of the automobile in the United States, and the founding of the automobile business there, should be attributed to brothers J. Frank and Charles E. Duryea. Descended from French Huguenots, they were born in Illinois and left there to become bicycle mechanics in Washington, D.C., in the late 1880s. The fact that they were visionary pioneers of transportation could be seen as early as 1882, when upon his graduation from Gidding's Seminary Charles gave an extraordinary oration entitled "Rapid Transit," in which he said that "the time will come when the humming of flying machines will be music over all lands; when Europe will be distant but a half day's journey; and when all people will be brothers in their social and business relations."

In 1888, after their first ride on a self-propelled vehicle (an electric trolley), the brothers began considering the possibilities of lightweight electric, steam, and other vehicles that could replace the horse-drawn wagon. By 1890 the brothers removed to Chicopee, Massachusetts, near Springfield, where they began to work on bicycle designs with the Ames Manufacturing Company. Inspired by *Scientific American* articles written in 1891 on the engines of Karl Benz and Atkinson, Charles began to design a gas-powered engine for brother Frank, a better and more experienced machinist, to build. A nurse named Erwin F. Markham invested $1,000 in March 1892 to get the project started, and the brothers rented quarters at the John W. Russell & Sons machine shop at 47 Taylor Street in Springfield. They spent $70 for a heavy phaeton body for the car, and work began.

All sorts of problems ensued, as they invariably do with anything so new, whatever the field may be. Charles's design was faulty. When it was asembled, the engine's ignition tube lacked a burner, it had no starter, there was no carburetor or muffler, and no piping for either. Nevertheless, as Professor Scharchburg relates, its completion over a period of ten months despite tremendous difficulties and disappointments was "one of the enduring monuments to the mechanical genius and unbounded determination of Frank Duryea and the small band of dedicated associates. They proceeded without benefit of precedents, materials were weak and faulty by modern standards, and neither hand nor machine tools had been specialized to their present utility. Nearly every piece and part had to be laboriously hand tooled and fitted." Scharchburg also makes clear that Frank was on his own by late September, 1892, after which date Charles Duryea gave no more instructions and assumed no more responsibility for construction or financing of the car.

Eventually Frank found he had to build a new engine with many features not found in Charles's original design. He worked on it during the summer of 1893, and by the end of that season all the bugs in the vehicle had been sufficiently dealt with to enable it to go on a trial run. On September 20, 1893, it was upended and taken down from the machine shop in a freight elevator, then hauled by a team of horses to the barn of Will Bemis (Markham's son-in-law) on the outskirts of Springfield, a rural location where its operation wouldn't frighten the horses. The following day, Thursday, September 21, 1893, J. Frank Duryea took a streetcar to the Bemis home, started up his motor carriage without difficulty, and drove it on Springfield's

Spruce Street for a distance of some 200 to 300 feet, and all the way into history. The next day the *Springfield Evening Union* printed an article under the headline "The First Tests Made," with the subhead "Duryea's Gasoline Carriage Makes a Favorable Showing." This was generally considered to be the first successful gasoline vehicle ride in American history. Of course it wasn't, any more than Columbus's landing on Hispaniola on October 12, 1492, marked the completion of the first voyage to the New World. But just as Columbus's landing was a marker for a monumental achievement in the history of Western civilization, so this event became a marker for the American beginnings of what James Womack called "the machine that changed the world."

This first vehicle had been designed and built without the accommodation of such important features as rubber tires and ball bearings, and left much to be desired in terms of any kind of sales appeal. Since Markham's resources, now depleted to the tune of $2,800, were stretched as far as he could stand, more money was found through the good offices of Henry W. Clapp, a local stock promoter, and a new, far more modern vehicle was designed and built in 1894–1895. With other backing from a group recommended by the Springfield Chamber of Commerce, an agreement was signed on August 29, 1895, creating the Duryea Motor Wagon Company, the first American corporation founded for the express purpose of manufacturing automobiles. Though real production wouldn't begin for some time, it was another pioneering milestone for the Duryea brothers.

What really put them on the map was winning a race. In May, 1895, Herman H. Kohlsaat, the publisher of the *Chicago Times-Herald*, inspired by newspaper accounts of an auto race from Paris to Bordeaux (which was the world's second such race, the first having been Paris-Rouen in June, 1894), decided that his paper should sponsor a race of its own. Kohlsaat originally scheduled the race for the Fourth of July, but all sorts of organizational problems beset him, and the race actually took place on Thanksgiving Day, November 28, 1895. $5,000 was offered for prizes and $5,000 for expenses. The course was a 54-mile round-trip from Chicago to Evanston, Illinois, and the day of the event was cold and snowy, after several days of similar weather. Since everyone knew a bicycle race couldn't be run under such conditions, a successful conclusion to this race would prove that the motor carriage was the most effective mode of personal transportation yet devised.

Eleven vehicles were to compete, but three dropped out voluntarily due to the bad road conditions, and two more never made it to the starting point, including the much-heralded and very well prepared Haynes-Apperson. Two electrics, a Sturges from Chicago and an Electrobat from Philadelphia, were entered, though it was really only for publicity, since their owners couldn't arrange for recharging stations along the route;

without that service, the electrics couldn't have gone the distance. There were four gasoline models entered: three imported Benz vehicles and the Duryea, driven by Frank himself, accompanied by an umpire, Arthur W. White. The race began at 8:55 A.M. Despite cold, wet, and darkness, and even under the handicaps of two accidents and driving several miles out of the way in confusion, Duryea and his motor wagon won the day, crossing the finish line at 7:18 P.M. They averaged just over 7 miles an hour, using 3.5 gallons of gasoline and 19 gallons of water. The only other car to finish, one of the Benzes, didn't cross the line until 8:53 P.M.

The Duryea Motor Wagon Company was awarded $2,000 for its victory, along with something far more important: universal acclaim, and yet another place in history. As Professor Scharchburg states, "A thrill swept the United States when morning newspapers announced that an American car, designed, built, and driven by an American, had triumphed over foreign competition under most trying road and weather conditions. In the light of automotive development since that event, the Chicago race deserves to rate along with the voyage of the Clermont and the operation of the first railroad train in the United States. . . . Arthur Pound's concluding paragraph of his seminal account of the "Great Race" was a most fitting conclusion in 1945, and so it remains today: "By means and methods which would now be considered clumsy and awkward, but right valiantly withal, a gate had been pushed ajar through which the world rolled into a new age." "

In 1896 Frank Duryea produced his third Motor Wagon, and from its plans a total of thirteen were built that year. This marked the first time that more than one car was made from the same plans in the United States, and this manufacturing event is considered the birth of the automobile industry in America. George H. Morill, Jr. of Norwood, Massachusetts, bought one of these machines and so became the first known purchaser of an American gasoline-fueled car.

Two years before that, Frank Duryea had been so involved in the constant changes necessary to make his first model practical that he told Erwin Markham it would be necessary to make a new model each year, incorporating his latest discoveries, if the motor car industry was going to amount to anything at all. Thus he had discovered a reason for the necessity of the annual model change even before the first company organized to build motor vehicles in this country had come into existence, and indeed he proceeded to produce a new and improved model for 1897, when he was not occupied with promoting his cars at races in the United States and England.

Unfortunately, the skills of the Duryea workers and the quality of the company's parts were not of the best, and virtually all of the early production had to be rebuilt. In addition, the officers of the company seemed much more interested in selling patents and licensing agreements than they were in building cars, in opposition to Frank's wishes. By 1898 the company was dissolved into a new one called the National Motor Carriage Company. Frank Duryea sold out his interests in the reorganization, and the new company soon faded into oblivion. Frank did design one car for them, a three-cylinder surrey that proved to be a rough-running bomb, though it is remembered as the first car to use metal on its body, in the form of sheet metal side panels.

Subsequently, in 1902, Frank Duryea entered into an agreement with the J. Stevens Arms and Toll Company in Chicopee Falls, Massachusetts, to manufacture the Stevens-Duryea car, one of the finest luxury machines of the early part of this century. The first model, the Stanhope, was essentially the same as the 1897 Duryea Wagon, which was so advanced for its day that it remained modern even four years later. Always innovative, Stevens-Duryea cars were the first to have a single housing for the engine, transmission, and clutch, and in 1912 the company introduced modern instrument panels and hoods faired into the windshield. As we have seen, Walter Chrysler, certainly the most discriminating of buyers, made his second automotive purchase (after the Locomobile) a Stevens-Duryea.

Frank Duryea did very well with this venture and stayed with the firm until he sold out and retired in 1915. Charles Duryea did not fare so well, through a series of unsuccessful ventures that featured outmoded and awkward automobile designs, and he and his brother entered into a protracted, acrimonious dispute (which went on for decades) as to which of them was primarily responsible for the first Duryea car. After Professor Scharchburg's *Cariages Without Horses* book, it seems clear that J. Frank Duryea was the one who did most of the work.

The summer after the Duryea vehicle first ran in Springfield, another car was demonstrated on the Pumpkinvine Pike in Kokomo, Indiana, at a speed of 6 miles an hour; the date was July 4, 1894. This car, a one-cylinder, 820-pound vehicle, was designed and driven by Elwood G. Haynes of that city, and had been built by Edgar and Elmer Apperson (brothers, again) and Jonathan Dixon Maxwell; the latter was one of the most significant of the early pioneers and the ancestor of the Chrysler Corporation.

Haynes was one of the very few of the pioneers who was formally trained as an engineer, with degrees from Worcester Polytechnic Institute and Johns Hopkins University. He was a truly brilliant engineer, and before becoming interested in the automobile, he invented the vapor thermostat and, in 1888, developed the process for making carbon steel. Haynes read German and had undoubtedly been familiar with the work of Daimler and Benz. By 1891 he had come to the realization that he could make more calls per day for the Indiana Natural Gas and Oil Company, for which he worked as a superintendent, with a self-propelled vehicle than with a horse and buggy, and so he set about designing one. He took his plans to the Apperson brothers, who constructed a vehicle from them at their machine shop in Kokomo.

The Appersons had never seen a horseless carriage, but they could read plans and were able to machine the parts they couldn't obtain. Haynes paid them 44 cents an hour to build his car in their slack time only, which stretched out the construction period significantly. After a year at work, they were joined by Maxwell. In any case, they worked independently of the Duryeas, and constructed a fine machine completely on their own.

Haynes and the Appersons built a car named the Haynes-Apperson in Kokomo for ten years and then split up, with separate, and very fine, Haynes and Apperson makes being marketed in that city until about 1925. A tremendous dust-up among the parties caused the split, with the Appersons claiming, but never able to prove, that they were responsible for the design of the first Haynes car. Meanwhile Haynes claimed that he, and not the Duryeas, was entitled to be known as the "inventor" of the American car on the somewhat dubious grounds that he began work on his car before the Duryeas began work on theirs. He got into a huge dispute with another pioneer, Alexander Winton, over this, and until the end of his career he advertised himself as builder of the "first car." He does, however, have a sure claim as the first American motorist to get a traffic ticket. A bicycle-riding policeman gave him one as he ordered him off the streets of Chicago in 1895.

The Massachusetts Institute of Technology turned out another highly trained engineering pioneer. He was Hiram Percy Maxim, son of the inventor of the Maxim machine gun, and later himself the inventor of the Maxim silencer. He knew about the internal-combustion engine but was completely unaware of the work of Daimler and Benz in 1892, when he decided to use such an engine in a self-propelled vehicle. He took 8 ounces of gasoline, a 6-pound cartridge case, and some matches to a corner of the American Projectile Company plant in Lynn, Massachusetts, where he was supervisor; he exploded one drop of the fuel in the case, and thus performed the essential function of internal combustion. A second try with two drops of gasoline got a much tamer explosion, and he discovered that the more gasoline there was, the less violent the explosion, because the gasoline could not mix so completely with air. From this beginning he quickly went on to create a one-cylinder engine with a carburetor made from a kerosene can with a copper tube fixed to its bottom; this device dripped fuel into the cylinder through a valve. In essence he had made a sort of gasoline automobile engine. He tried to attach it to a used $30 tandem tricycle, but it was too heavy for the trike and ran out of control when Maxim tried to drive it; during his ride he was thrown over the handlebars. Postponing any more trials, he saved up his money to buy a four-wheeled body, meanwhile continuing engine work until he had created a sophisticated three-cylinder engine.

An 1894 visit to the Hartford, Connecticut, factory of Colonel Albert A.

Pope, then a very successful manufacturer of bicycles, carriages, and electric vehicles, got him into production. Pope had Maxim's engine evaluated and hired him on as chief engineer. By August 1895 he had a vehicle up and running, and after working on the inadequate cooling system of this car, he had a gasoline-engine horseless carriage ready for sale by Pope's company. Alexander Winton was later to claim the first sale of a gasoline automobile in 1898, but Pope had certainly sold some of Maxim's cars by then, not to mention that the Duryeas had sold some of theirs also. Due to Pope's prejudice in favor of the electric car, Maxim spent more time than he would have liked building those, but he had great fun in the auto business until he realized the days of the little horseless carriages he loved were coming to an end, due to the ascendency of the true motor car. So, in 1900, he quit the vehicle business and went back to munitions, where he did very well with his famous aforementioned Maxim silencer.

Colonel Pope was one of the seminal figures in automobile history. He was the biggest, most successful manufacturer of bicycles in America, and that was one of the major currents from which the automobile came. John B. Rae points out that the automobile inherited steel-tube framing (combining strength and lightness), chain drive, ball and roller bearings, and differential gearing from the bicycle. To this list we can add the pneumatic tire, invented for the bicycle by John B. Dunlop in Ireland in 1888 (or, more precisely, reinvented, as Charles Goodyear stumbled on the formula for vulcanization of rubber by accidentally dropping India rubber and sulfur on a hot stove in 1839, and patented his process in 1844; the next year the Scotsman Robert William Thompson patented the pneumatic tire, but it was forgotten because it wasn't practical for any vehicles of the period). Three years later, in 1892, Thomas B. Jeffery (progenitor of American Motors) invented the cylinder rim for his Rambler bicycles, making the changing of tires a much easier affair than it had been.

We have seen that the clamor of bicyclists created a demand for better roads and, as Rae says, "The combination of the pneumatic tire and the hard surface road was indispensible to the success of the motor vehicle. Without both, highway travel could never have competed with rail transport in comfort or speed."

Many European figures who were to be prominent in the automobile industry began as bicycle manufacturers, such as Morris in England, Opel in Germany, and Peugeot in France. In America, men like Pope, Winton, Willys, the Duryea brothers, the Dodge Brothers, and Pierce and Lozier, famous bicycle manufacturers all, were to become just as famous when they turned to automobiles. As in France, the bicycle made the talents of skilled machinists available to the nascent automobile business. George N. Pierce of Buffalo, New York, was an excellent example. He began by building birdcages out of metal wire, then bicycle spokes, then bicycles, then motorcycles, all with great success. In 1901 he produced the Pierce-Motorette, the direct ancestor of the famous Pierce-Arrow luxury car, which survived until 1938 and was considered by many to be the finest automobile ever manufactured in the United States.

The bicycle also brought a problem with it. Without question, it was a craze, both in the United States and Europe, that reached its apex in the early 1890s. When it ended, many companies were caught up in the widespread financial wreckage caused by the collapse of the bicycle industry. In the beginning, the automobile was a wacky novelty, then a rich man's plaything. It got increasing attention, but it was out of the reach of the common man, since it was far from having the low price, service support, and other accommodations necessary to give it general utility and acceptance. Most people thought it was a fad whose day would pass; almost no one could conceive of it becoming indispensible to the everyday conduct of American life, superseding the horse, the streetcar, and the railway. As a result of all these things, its development required visionaries and daring venture capitalists willing to invest funds. Unfortunately, some of these people were the same kind of shady syndicalists speculators who had come sniffing around the railroads in their early days, and millions of dollars went down the tubes in creaky auto ventures that were little more than conduits for financial fraud. More solid banker types stayed far away from the auto industry for a very long time, until it became too big to ignore. All of this, combined with the necessarily experimental nature of the first automobiles, inspired little confidence in the average citizen, and retarded the acceptance and growth of the industry for a considerable period of time.

By 1896 significant developments were beginning to occur. On March 6 of that year Charles Brady King drove the first vehicle ever to appear on the streets of Detroit. It had a four-cylinder, four-cycle water-cooled engine that King himself had designed and built. Newspaper accounts of it on the following day described it as "a most unique machine," a status it would not maintain for long. On June 4 Henry Ford broke down the wall of his little machine shop on Bagley Avenue in Detroit to push his "quadricycle" out onto the street for its first test run. It was the first of well over a hundred million vehicles produced under the badge of his name. In Cleveland, Alexander Winton produced a two-cylinder experimental horseless carriage, and in the same month Ransom Eli Olds drove a one-cylinder, 6-horsepower car on the streets of Lansing, Michigan. But even as the automobile was in its infant stages, the public was clamoring for it to display its possibilities. The previous month at Narragansett, Rhode Island, a race between two electrics and five Duryeas was so dull that spectators shouted, "Get a horse!" which was the origin of the famous phrase.

August 21, 1897, brought the organization of the Olds Motor Vehicle Company, and that year saw the first experiments of the Studebaker brothers with motor vehicles. They had been distinguished carriage makers since 1852, and although the firm stopped making cars in 1966, their 114-year record as vehicle manufacturers still stands today. Also in 1897 the first car insurance policy was issued to Gilbert Loomis of Westfield, Massachusetts. In 1898 William E. Metzger, one of the greatest automobile merchandisers ever, established the first independent automobile dealership in Detroit. John Wilkinson built his first four-cylinder, air-cooled engine, from which the famous Franklin air-cooled cars (1902–34) developed. The latter were so good that Harry Bennett, who rose to great prominence as Henry Ford's right-hand man in the 1930s and 1940s, drove them in preference even to Ford's prestigious Lincolns.

Also in 1898, Alexander Winton built and sold a quantity of one-cylinder autos, and introduced a commercial delivery wagon. Winton was a Scottish ship engineer born in 1860 who emigrated to the United States twenty years later. By 1890 he became a bicycle manufacturer in Cleveland and involved himself in designing and building automobiles by the middle of the decade. His cars were credited with many automotive firsts. The initial 1896 vehicle had a sort of electrical starter and an engine with a 5-inch bore, which made it very powerful, allowing the vehicle to hold six passengers on two seats that faced each other. He called it an omnibus, and in 1897 formed the Winton Motor Car Company to build six of these vehicles to begin service in Cleveland. However, there were so many lawsuits from the owners of horse-drawn vehicles that he gave up his plans. His early car designs used a steering wheel instead of a tiller, and Winton was the first American to think of moving the engine from under the seat to place it front of the passengers, in the French style. He sold pneumatic tires at $400 a set, and provided touring-car tonneau bodies with an entrance from the rear. In 1905 he offered an eight-cylinder engine, which was an unheard-of source of automotive power at the time. Never an item for the masses, Winton's automobiles were marketed to the very rich. He would typically build a few cars for display and take special orders. In 1899 Percy Owen opened the first automobile sales room in New York to sell Winton cars.

Winton would enter every speed and reliability test he could to keep his name before the public. In the summer of 1897 he gained a lot of publicity by making the first Cleveland-to-New York motor trip in ten days, from July 29 to August 7. He found the condition of the roads between cities to be "outrageous," and complained loudly about the situation. But then he was never one to control his temper or sequester his wrath. Reginald M. Cleveland and S. T. Williamson report that "his Cleveland shopmaster could tell whether his temper was good or bad by what he did with his hat. If he tossed it up in the air, everything was fine. If he threw it on the floor and jumped on it—look out!"

On one such hat-stomping day a young Winton purchaser came to him to discuss ideas on how he could improve the car. Tossing his hat on the floor in a fury, Winton screamed, "All right, if you don't like the car, and you know so much, why don't you make a car of your own?" His listener was James Ward Packard, who promptly went out and did exactly that, establishing one of the great American automobile companies of the twentieth century. (In actuality Packard and his brother William Doud Packard had planned and commissioned drawings for an automobile in 1893, but the depression that began that year prevented them from realizing their plans for automobile manufacture then.)

Best of all was the disgusted Winton purchaser who hitched a team of horses to his unsatisfactory Winton and pulled it through the streets of Cleveland with a sign proclaiming, "This is the only way to drive a Winton." Shortly after came Alexander Winton himself, dragging an open farm wagon with a jackass in the passenger seat and a sign proclaiming that this was the only living creature unable to drive a Winton!

In 1899 and 1900 several automobile publications began to appear, such as *The Motor* and *Automobile Topics*. *The Saturday Evening Post* carried the first national automobile advertising in 1900, and Olds moved from Lansing to Detroit and organized his second company, the Olds Motor Works. On November 6, 1899, James Ward Packard, the founder of Packard Electric, completed and ran his first car in Warren, Ohio. Also in 1899, the first automobile accident occurred in Columbus, Ohio, between the only two vehicles in Columbus, Ohio, at the time. The first National Automobile Show was held from November 3rd to 10th, 1900, at Madison Square Garden in New York City under the sponsorship of the Automobile Club of America. Some 48,000 people saw 300 vehicles selling at prices from $280 to $4,000, and the displays of forty vehicle and eleven parts manufacturers. Test drives were set up on obstacle courses in the Garden to entice buyers, as was a 200-foot ramp, 53 feet high, to demonstrate the hill climbing and braking abilities of Mobile steamers. That year also saw the first Mack bus, and President McKinley became the first American President to ride in a motor car.

But of all the developments of this era, none was as significant as the one that occurred on January 10, 1901, near Beaumont, Texas. On that date the famous Spindletop petroleum well came in. Previously, kerosene was the principal byproduct of petroleum, and indeed the petroleum trust was organized by John D. Rockefeller, Sr., to control the supply of kerosene oil. Until the advent of the car in the 1890s, gasoline was considered a noxious, volatile, and dangerous byproduct of petroleum mainly useful as a cleaning solvent and a fuel for portable space heaters and cooking stoves. When Spindletop came in and the vast east Texas oil fields were discovered, gasoline suddenly dropped below 5 cents a gallon, and huge new discoveries over the next ten years at Glenn Pool in Oklahoma, Kern River in California, and the Caddo Fields in Louisiana meant that supplies of it were seemingly unlimited. Now fueling up the gasoline-powered buggy became cheap and easy, and because of this, and the ascendency of the electric light bulb, gasoline became the chief byproduct of petroleum by 1908.

But the widespread use of gasoline as an automobile fuel couldn't have happened without the right kind of vehicle, produced in sufficient numbers, to spur it. This catalyst was to be the Curved-Dash Oldsmobile of 1901, the product of the most influential man involved in establishing the automobile industry, Ransom Eli Olds.

Perhaps the situation of the automobile in America in 1900 is best explained by E. D. Kennedy in his book *The Automobile Industry—The Coming of Age of Capitalism's Favorite Child*, a very fine explanation of the place of the automobile in the life of America until World War II. In 1900, he says, there were 76,000,000 Americans in 18,000,000 families. About 4,000 of these people owned automobiles, or one family in 5,000. It meant that only one one hundredth of one percent of the potential automobile market had been tapped. Yes, the automobile was an expensive product at an average price of $1,000 in those days, when $100 in cash money represented a considerable sum. But the automobile manufacturer had to reach only a tiny portion of this vast market to be a resounding success, because if every factory then extant were to run day and night only 5,000 vehicles could have been made. In fact, as Crabb points out, of 200 or so firms which manufactured cars between 1894 and 1902, only five had produced more than one hundred cars: Olds, of Lansing; Winton, of Cleveland; Jeffery, of Kenosha; Pope (Columbia), of Hartford; and Haynes-Apperson, of Kokomo. So the car manufacturer of 1900 only had to reach three families out of 10,000 to sell everything he could make. In other words, the market was minuscule but the potential was Blue Sky, limitless. A good product, an efficient manufacturing method, and a reasonable price would all be needed if automobile makers were to reach any significant portion of the great masses. Ransom Olds was the first man to provide all three elements.

On May 8, 1899, he organized his second company, the Olds Motor Works, and in so doing moved his operations from Lansing to Detroit, Michigan. He had been building cars since 1897, but by 1899 he realized that the car was not a toy but "the big venture," and required more capital than he could find in Lansing. S. L. Smith, a Michigan copper and lumber baron, was his backer in the new venture, thus becoming the first significant and successful investor in the automobile business. He put up $199,600, representing 99.8% of the total paid in capitalization of the company; Olds and others from Lansing put up the rest. Smith knew the Olds family well, and had provided the funds for the Olds Gasoline Engine Works started by Pliny Olds in 1892; he put money in the Olds Motor Works to set up his sons Frederick and Angus in business. With Smith's money Ransom Olds built Detroit's first car factory on Jefferson Avenue, completing it in the fall of 1900. It was a four-and-a-half acre site, developed as a small manufacturing complex containing assembly and machine shops in one building, a foundry in a second, a blacksmith's shop in a third, and offices and a display room in a fourth. Here he manufactured the first vehicles to be called Oldsmobiles.

They were not a success. Though he produced 400 cars, more than any other gas buggy manufacturer had done, between mid-1899 and the end of 1900, the firm lost $80,000. The trouble was that the cars cost $1,250, a fair bit of money for what was essentially a buggy with an engine under the seat. The public wasn't yet accustomed to this new type of conveyance, and after all, a good horse and buggy could be had for about $400. Olds needed a new type of product, and in consequence built no fewer than eleven prototypes of new models, some of them electrics, in a quest to find what would be marketable. But on the morning of Saturday, March 9, 1901, a fortuitous disaster occured, one that Fred Smith was later to call "the best move ever made by the management." A fire broke out, destroying the factory and ten of the eleven prototypes stored there. A quick-thinking worker was able to pull out one car only, the one nearest the door. It was a one-cylinder, two-seat, 700-pound gasoline runabout, without top, lights, or fenders, and it was soon to be famous for its most striking feature, a curved dash. Olds spent a sleepless night, and on Sunday morning he realized he had no other choice than to produce it. "I decided to discard all my former plans and build a little one-cylinder runabout," he said, "for I was convinced that if success came it must be through a more simple machine. . . . My whole idea in building it was to have the operation so simple that anyone could run it." He put it on the market at $650, and created the first car ever produced and sold in quantity.

Quantity in 1901 meant 425 cars, with demand snowballing as time went on. By June of the next year orders were piling up at the rate of fifteen to twenty cars a day, but Olds had the capacity to produce only about five. The only thing he could do was to form alliances with other companies to manufacture major components for his cars. He went to Leland and Faulconer in Detroit, the foremost machine shop not only in that city but probably in the entire country, and placed an order for two thousand engines for his cars. This was the first large component order ever placed by a U.S. car manufacturer with an outside supplier. Shortly thereafter he went to the Dodge Brothers and signed a contract for them to supply two thousand transmissions for the Olds runabouts. This outsourcing of component manufacturing established a precedent that continues to this day. This step allowed manufacturers to increase production on short notice. It also meant that new sources of materials and money, trained workers, and experienced management could be added to a company's strengths at the stroke of a pen.

By associating Olds with Leland and Faulconer, the Dodge Brothers, and other component manufacturers in Detroit, and by allowing them to grow tremendously and share in the Olds financial success, Ransom Olds began the chain of interconnections that created the U.S. automobile industry. In a period of fifteen months Detroit went from having no part at all in automobile manufacture to turning out more cars than any city in the world, a situation that would continue for many decades.

Olds quickly doubled his production to 10 cars a day by the spring of 1902, and by the end of the year he was turning out 70 to 80 a week. When production reached 2,000 in the fall, proud workers took up a collection, purchased a $20 gold piece and took it to a jeweler who made it into a watch chain pendant in the shape of a Curved Dash Olds. They happily presented this token of their esteem to a beaming Mr. Olds.

As the company continued to grow, Olds established a kind of progressive production in his factory to speed things up. Rae says, "The flow of materials was carefully controlled to eliminate delays, and the cars were assembled by work gangs whose members each had specific functions to perform." The process began with the chassis, and components were brought to the workstation until the car was complete. Rae speculates that he might have arrived at the full assembly line if Curved Dash production had continued to increase, but by the time the factory reached its maximum output of 6,500 cars per year, in 1905, the little buggy was already hopelessly outdated, Olds had left the company, and Oldsmobile was turning its attention to bigger, heavier, and much more expensive cars that it would produce in far smaller quantities.

But in the first three years of the twentieth century Olds was still involved in the day-to-day affairs of the company, and pioneered many of the marketing techniques still used today. Unlike the Stanleys and the Duryeas, Olds recognized the value of promoting his cars to the public, and was the first man to do so aggressively. He received an order for 1,000 autos from Roy M. Owen and Roy Rainey at the New York Auto Show (they were becoming Olds' New York distributors), and the attendant publicity represented "the first mass marketing of an expensive and complex product. Previously, mass marketing was confined to cheap, small items like kerosene lamps, razors and pins" (Crabb). Even Chauncey DePew, President of the New York Central Railroad, was photographed in an Oldsmobile, which allowed the rich to feel comfortable buying them.

Olds kept his car in the news with races and cross-country expeditions in order to drum up business. In the fall of 1901 Roy Chapin drove a factory equipped car from Detroit to New York for the auto show. He made the journey in seven and a half days, averaging fourteen and a half miles per hour on the 820-mile trip, during which he sometimes drove at train speeds of 35 miles per hour (he knew this because his car was equipped with a Jones speedometer, a 1901 novelty). In 1903, L. L. Whitman and Eugene Hammond made a cross-country trip in an Oldsmobile, and another of the cars set a world's speed record of five miles in six minutes. Also during this period, Olds's cars competed in and won races with Fords and Wintons, but unlike those firms, Olds was able to turn his performances to account, because he had quantities of cars to sell. As early as 1901 he said he could produce four thousand cars, equal to the total car production of all makes in the previous year. It didn't happen quite that fast, but it happened, and at a price of $650, he knew he had a product he could sell to professional men, farmers, merchants, and the rest of the general public. Now he had to turn his attention to making sure they knew it.

Olds was the first to publish sales manuals and magazines for his dealers, and the first to bring his dealers to Detroit for a national convention. He was the first to regularly advertise cars nationally. And he also hired the first full-time sales manager in the industry, Roy Chapin.

It all had results. In 1903 Oldsmobile produced the promised 4,000 cars, more than one-third of the U.S. total. Olds agents went abroad for the first time, selling cars for delivery the next year in England, France, Germany, and Russia, which was an American first. From then until World War II American cars sold in tremendous numbers in Europe, because they were much more durable and easy to service than European ones. In 1904 Olds produced 5,508, or 25 percent, of the country's production of 22,134, and this percentage held in 1905, when Olds made 6,500 (125 per week) of the 24,250 cars produced. In three years' time the Olds Motor Works capital stock increased tenfold in value, and the company paid out 105 percent in dividends. When Olds sold his interests in the firm on January 1, 1904, he received $500,000 for his shares.

He left in a dispute with the Smiths over the future direction of the firm. Olds wanted to continue to build small, light cars, but they wanted to go into the heavier, multicylinder luxury car market then beginning to develop. The Smiths won out, but didn't do very well with the enormous and expensive cars they subsequently produced. However, the touring car with its much larger, more powerful engine was what would eventually allow the automobile to outstrip all other forms of horse-drawn and mechanical transportation, and Olds eventually realized this. When he built a new car, the REO, at a new firm in October 1904, it was a two-cylinder, five-passenger job at double the price of the Curved-Dash Olds. Times had changed, and like all good businessmen, he changed with them.

But the importance of the curved-dash Olds cannot be overstressed. It was the first car, and the only horseless carriage, to become an American institution. Gus Edwards and Vincent Bryan's 1905 song "In My Merry

Oldsmobile" achieved an enormous instant popularity which it maintains today as a symbol of that entire motoring era. "Furthermore, Oldsmobile orders for material, spread through the machine shops, body works and supply houses, set hundreds of wideawake Detroiters to thinking how they could supply those wants, improve on their merchandise, and gather part of the golden stream of profits which Oldsmobile had started in their direction. Detroit rode to wealth and large population down a path in the direction which Oldsmobile had indicated. As John K. Barnes wrote in the *Motor World* of April, 1921, 'It was Old's success in Detroit that fixed the center of the automobile industry in that city.'" This last is from Pound.

Added to all of this, and perhaps of equal importance, was that the Olds Motor Works was a vast training ground for the future leadership of the automobile industry. In addition to its vital importance in drawing Henry and Wilfred Leland, later creators of Cadillac and Lincoln, and the Dodge Brothers into automobile production, Oldsmobile turned out or had close associations with over 150 of the topmost executives at the dawn of the industry. Howard Coffin, the first professional engineer to join a U.S. car firm, and Roy Chapin, who became Secretary of Commerce under Herbert Hoover, later founded Hudson; Jonathan D. Maxwell, inventor of the thermo-siphon cooling system, and Benjamin Briscoe founded Maxwell-Briscoe, an antecedent of Chrysler; Robert C. Hupp founded Hupmobile; Carl Fisher built the Indianapolis Speedway and developed the Prest-O-Lite Company; Barney F. Everitt and William E. Metzger were two of the three founders of Everitt-Metzger-Flanders, the direct antecedent of the Studebaker gasoline car. All these were among the most prominent of those given a start or a big boost through their association with Oldsmobile.

There were two men, however, who towered over all others in importance in the establishment of the American motor car industry, perhaps the most influential business the world produced in the twentieth century. The first was William Crapo Durant, a restless visionary who saw better than anyone the necessity for expansion through consolidation in the industry; without it, he knew that this business of building automobiles could never become firmly established and instill confidence in the financial community and the consuming public alike. He founded General Motors. The second was Henry Ford, who wanted to create a means of far-ranging mechanized individual transportation that anyone could build, anyone could operate and fix, and anyone could afford to own, thus breaking the age-old physical and social isolation in which most human lives were lived. He founded the Ford Motor Company and built the Model T. While Ford is still greatly celebrated and Durant is little known today that is an unjust disparity of fame. But it does not really matter, for the fact remains that without these two vastly different men of vastly different accomplishment, the automobile industry, and the automobile itself, would not now exist as we know them.

❖   ❖   ❖

The General Motors Corporation was founded on a tragedy whose name was David Dunbar Buick. His story, and that of the entire history of the Buick car, is admirably detailed in Terry B. Dunham and Lawrence R. Gustin's *The Buick—A Complete History*. Buick was born in Arbroath, Scotland, on September 19, 1854, to a joiner and his wife who emigrated to America two years later. When he was fifteen he went to work making plumbing fixtures at the Alexander Manufacturing Company in Detroit, rising to become a foreman there. (During this period he also worked as an apprentice machinist at James Flower & Brothers in Detroit, the same firm where Henry Ford would apprentice in 1879.) He and an old school friend named William Sherwood acquired Alexander when it went under in 1882 and turned the company around into a success.

By 1889 Buick had invented thirteen items for valves, lawn sprinklers, water closets, and bathtubs. The most famous was a process for bonding enamel to cast iron, making today's porcelain kitchen sinks and bathroom fixtures possible. (Actually a German firm had invented this process years before, but they held this knowledge as a closely guarded secret. Buick figured it out on his own, and prospered greatly from his discovery.) Buick and Sherwood Manufacturing Company stationery proudly displayed a picture of the factory and, revealed behind a fancy drawn drape and some wispy ferns, its primary product: a toilet.

Like many others, Buick was hooked on the internal-combustion gasoline engine as soon as he encountered it, around 1895. Because of his new fascination, in 1899 he and Sherwood sold out their company to the Standard Sanitary Manufacturing Company of Pittsburgh for $100,000. At the age of forty-five, he decided that he wanted to involve himself in the possibilities of the gasoline engine, and founded the Buick Auto-Vim and Power Company to manufacture these engines for farm and marine use. An engineering genius named Walter L. Marr soon began working with Buick. He was as crazy about gasoline engines as Buick, and they soon turned their attention to experimenting with an automobile. (It seems certain that Marr had built at least one car before his association with Buick, receiving help from none other than his neighbor Henry Ford, and in the process invented the spark advance.)

The two men were both fiery and hot-tempered, and Marr quit or was fired from the Buick organization two or three times over the next five years. During this time another brilliant machinist, Eugene C. Richard, went to work for Buick, and the three men came up with the idea for the valve-in-head, or overhead valve, engine. "It was an important development. With its valves directly over the pistons (unlike the L-head engine in general use at the time), the Buick powerplant had a more compact combustion chamber, and a faster fuel burn rate. It was, in essence, a more efficient machine. And because it was so efficient, it developed more horsepower than other engines its size. Eventually the entire industry would make use of its principle, although not before the Buick engine developed a reputation for power and performance which helped the company survive in those desperate early years" (Dunham and Gustin).

Unfortunately, Buick had no financial sense whatsoever, and was constantly strapped for money. Buick sold Marr the original car and "all my right, title and interest in it" on August 16, 1901, for $225, and he reorganized the company several times; Buick Auto-Vim and Power became the Buick Manufacturing Company in 1902, and the Buick Motor Company on May 19, 1903. Marr joked that every time he came back after being fired, it was to a different company. The 1903 reorganization was an attempt by Benjamin Briscoe to get repaid $3,500 he had loaned Buick; if he didn't get his money by September 1903, Briscoe would get control of the company, which might help other plans of his.

Briscoe and his brother Frank were important sheet metal producers whose major product was the all-metal garbage can. After a surprise investment of $100,000 from none other than J. P. Morgan (Ben Briscoe ran to a New York bank to cash the check before Morgan could change his mind), they invested in equipment to produce more complex goods than they had done before. When Ransom Olds gave them an order for 4,400 radiators for his new Curved-Dash Olds, they were off and running in the auto business. Naturally enough, they began manufacturing sheet metal for a number of car firms, and in a couple of years they were employing twelve hundred workers and making a lot of money. When Benjamin Briscoe asked Jonathan Maxwell to evaluate Buick's car, Maxwell just asked him to go into business manufacturing one of his own design. Seeing what a disorganized man Buick was, and knowing Maxwell's superb credentials, Briscoe readily signed an agreement with Maxwell on July 3, 1903, to manufacture the Maxwell-Briscoe car. As far as Buick was concerned, Briscoe simply wanted to be through with him. If he got his money back, fine; if not, he would get some production facilities for his new venture. In the event, he was able to unload the whole thing on the Flint Wagon Works, which at that time had decided to go into the car business. Briscoe got his money, and Buick got to continue working on his beloved brainchild.

The principal in the Flint Wagon Works was James A. Whiting, one of the largest wagon makers of his time and one of Flint's premier businessmen. He was also farsighted enough to realize the potential of the automobile to completely overtake his business, and decided to become involved in car manufacturing at what was still an early date, while his wagon business still had some years left in which to prosper.

A big deal was made locally of the relocation of Buick to Flint. *The Flint*

Journal of September II, 1903, headlined "New Industry For Flint: Buick Motor Company Of Detroit Is To Be Moved To This City." (On the same page it was reported that at a Flint meeting of the Michigan Master Horse Shoers Association there was a call for the creation of a state horse shoeing college, an idea whose time had come and gone.) A new building for the manufacture of stationary and marine engines, and automobile engines, carburetors, transmissions, and plugs was grandly touted, but there was no statement about car manufacture. When asked, Whiting smiled and deferred to the future on that one. It was pretty clear though that he would be soon going in that direction.

The cash required for the purchase, $10,000, was borrowed from a bank, and before Whiting's Buick venture was over, further bank borrowing almost sank the whole city. The Buick Motor Company of Detroit was reorganized into the Buick Motor Company of Flint on January 25, 1904, and in the process its capital was reduced to $75,000 from $100,000. The new building was completed and enthusiasm ran high. In April the ever wandering Marr returned to Buick, and on July 9th Marr and Buick's son Tom set off on a round trip to Detroit on a stripped-down Buick chassis; the return trip, lengthened to 100 miles, was completed in three and a half hours, and the men were jubilant over the abilities of the little car. Unfortunately, however, Marr and Buick spent the whole of 1904 tinkering and testing, and not a single car was built. By the fall of that year the Flint Wagon Works had borrowed $75,000 from three banks in the city, which was a very considerable sum for that place at that time and actually threatened the financial stability of the city of Flint. The town went to Billy Durant, who gave it salvation and a heaven beyond all imagining.

William Crapo Durant was born in Boston on December 8, 1861 to a ne'er-do-well father and a mother who was the daughter of Henry Howland Crapo, a man who by dint of unremitting mental labor and Yankee frugality had risen to become one of the wealthiest and most respected citizens of the state of Michigan. He became a lumber baron through giddily overextending himself to buy a huge tract of woods in 1854, dealing with the specter of bankruptcy for the next half dozen years until at last he found himself on firm financial footing. After founding a small railroad between Flint and nearby Holly, Michigan, he rose through a merger to become president of the famous Flint and Pere Marquette line. In politics, he served as mayor of Flint beginning in 1860, and then was twice elected Governor of Michigan, in 1864 and 1866. He died in 1869, and three years later his daughter Rebecca, now divorced from William Clark Durant, moved to Flint with her children Rebecca, called Rosa, and William, called Willie.

The boy, whose life is arrestingly chroicled in *The Dream Maker*, by Bernard A. Weisberger, grew up in a way very typical of the place and time of his youth. Though Billy came from an illustrious family, little was made of social and class distinctions, and he was treated in the same manner as other young people of the town. Thus, when it was time to go to work in his grandfather's lumber mill, he was given the job of piling up lumber at 75 cents a day.

To earn extra cash, he began selling patent medicines for a local drugstore and found his true calling in salesmanship. In fact, as you might say of Walter Chrysler that he was a mechanic and Henry Ford that he was an engineer, you could say that at base Billy Durant was a salesman, and that it informed everything he did.

In short order he went on the road for a Flint cigar maker named George T. Warren, and immediately returned from Port Huron, the nearest town of any size, with an order for twenty-two thousand cigars. He had simply bypassed the wholesalers by going directly to the merchants and offering factory-direct prices. Soon he was out of the lumber mill and earning $100 per month.

He was constantly in motion during this time, trying his hand at any number of jobs to learn and get experience. He sold real estate, kept books for the water company, and worked for the gas company, too. Sensing the money to be made selling fire insurance in the lamplit wooden buildings of Flint, he acquired a partner and gathered several agencies into one of the largest insurance firms in the state.

Though he was a salesman, he was the opposite of a "drummer," the backslapping, buttonholing, girlie-chasing slicker then beginning to push goods of various kinds and qualities in communities large and small throughout the land. No, Billy Durant was something else entirely. He was a believer. He had to have 100 percent faith in everything he sold, so that you could see in his eyes that he knew what he was selling was of the highest quality, and you could believe in his merchandise the same way he did.

Weisberger tells us: "He was, all who knew him agreed, soft spoken and often the last to speak. He dressed neatly but not conspicuously, his smile was gentle and winning, his eyes serious. His power rested on an ability to project his own unswerving faith in the product. 'Assume that the man you are talking to knows as much or more than you do,' was his advice to other salesmen. 'Do not talk too much. Give the customer time to think. In other words, let the customer sell himself. Look for a self-seller.' His art was to turn the eyes of the prospect inward, to give him a vision of himself as somehow improved, transmuted, assisted in worthy undertakings by the product, so that the salesman became a mere window through which the customer perceived vistas to which he had been previously blind. The end result was not merely an order signed, but a friend made."

The problem was to find goods worthy of his approach to selling, and in a way this would occupy him for the rest of his life, bringing untold opportunity when he succeeded, and downfall when he no longer could. But this is just a practical view of Mr. Durant's activities. In a larger sense, his visionary flights, his pure invention could take him to places mankind did not know existed, much less that it needed to enter; but he had to have faith that these dream destinations could be achieved and conquered. Otherwise he failed, as completely as anyone in our times ever has.

"Time and chance happen to them all," says Ecclesiates of the affairs of men. Fate came to Billy Durant in a roadcart one fine September day in 1886. A friend offered him a ride in the little contraption when he was rushing to an appointment. He expected to be bounced around on his short drive in this flimsy sulky-type vehicle, but was amazed to find that he was not. Examining the vehicle, he discovered it was the unusual springing arrangement that cushioned his ride. Impressed, he found out where it was built and bought the company, in part with money raised at a local bank on his signature, in part with money raised by a young hardware clerk named J. Dallas Dort. On September 28, 1886, they formed a partnership to manufacture vehicles under the name of the Flint Road Cart Company. Durant promptly hired himself to an agricultural fair in Wisconsin, where he demonstrated his superior product at a competition and came home with an order for six hundred of them. The trouble was, his factory had a capacity of two carts a day.

Durant solved the problem by ordering 1,200 of his carts from the biggest manufacturer in town, W. A. Paterson, at $12 apiece; shortly afterward the order was increased to 3,200. Within a year Durant's bulging order book disposed of about 4,000 of his carts at $22 each. After Paterson tried to cut his throat on two different occasions by offering to sell Durant's carts to his customers directly, Durant came to the conclusion that he had to do the manufacturing himself, including all the components, down to the whip sockets.

To that end, he began hiring key employees, such as Fred Aldrich, who became secretary of the company, A. B. C. Hardy, a production supervisor who became indispensible to the firm and a legend in the industry, and Charles W. Nash. The last of these survived a Victorian childhood at the bottom of the economic scale. When he was six, his parents separated and he was bound out to a farmer who promised to feed and lodge him, and permit him to attend school three months a year in return for his labor. At 21 he was to get his release with a new suit and $100. It is hard to believe nowadays, but until the 1920s poor children were thought of more for their economic worth than anything else, and Nash's situation was not unusual. Beaten, starved, and overworked, he ran away at the age of twelve, worked very hard at anything he could find, and saved every penny he could. In 1890 he got a job at the Flint Road Cart Company, and so distinguished himself in his work that he soon rose to the highest supervisory ranks of the firm. Eventually, of course, he followed Durant to the peak of power at General Motors, and founded the Nash Motor Car Company, one of the largest, most successful, and long-lived of any of the independent manufacturers. Of all the motor car giants, none came from such an unfortunate beginning, or rose so far, as Charles W. Nash.

In 1895 Durant's burgeoning firm changed its name to the Durant-Dort Carriage Company, by this time manufacturing vehicles for everything from the grandest to the most utilitarian of purposes. Soon Durant began acquiring component subsidiaries such as the Flint Gear and Top Company, the Imperial Wheel Company, and the Flint Axle Works. He created the Flint Varnish Works, and made alliances with William F. Stewart (bodies), the J. B. Armstrong Company (springs), and the Flint Specialty Company (whip sockets). Durant-Dort added a major division in seven of the ten years between 1892 and 1902. This was all in the service of what today would be called vertical integration. By owning or controlling the means of making component parts, the company would never be caught short of any of the items necessary for the manufacture of its products. The control of production could now rest completely in its own hands. This experience of Durant's certainly set the stage for his attitude toward vertical expansion and acquisition years later, when he ran the General Motors Company. In some ways he would be running Durant-Dort all over again.

The company continued to do well, even in the terrible depression year of 1893. Its sales rose and rose, eventually reaching an absolute peak in 1906 of 56,000 vehicles. In addition to outselling its Flint competitors (Flint was now known as 'Vehicle City', the wagon capital of the U.S.), Durant-Dort outsold Studebaker Brothers of South Bend, the Velie Works at Moline, the Fisher Family Carriage Works at Norwalk, Ohio, and many others. Its products were sold from coast to coast and as far away as Australia, sometimes under the brand names of such firms as Montgomery Ward and John Deere. Durant and Dort had both become millionaires in the process, but Durant, by 1901 or so, ever itching to seek out new opportunities, became restless and left the company's affairs mostly in the hands of the capable people he had assembled as a management team. One of them would tell him where that great new opportunity he so longed for was to be found— right in his own backyard, as it turned out.

It was Fred Aldrich who suggested that Billy Durant consider involving himself in the tangled affairs of the Buick Motor Car Company in the fall of 1904. Nobody knows exactly why Aldrich went to Durant, or why the latter accepted the challenge. But surely Durant, as the world's largest wagon manufacturer, must have been well aware of the mushrooming auto business. All the other major firms had already experimented with horseless carriages or were about to. The Studebaker Brothers, the most profitable of the carriage makers, began their auto experiments in 1898 and were already manufacturing electrics as an adjunct to their wagon lines. A show-down between the horse-drawn vehicle and the car was surely coming, and Durant needed to be prepared to streak ahead of the pack with the most forward-looking kind of transportation imaginable.

But as always, he knew he had to proceed with complete confidence. So on September 4, 1904, he began to put a demonstration Buick through a grueling set of trials on the backwoods roads of Michigan. For almost two months no pothole was avoided, no mud lake went untraversed. Previously he had said autos were noisy, foul-smelling, and obnoxious, but as with the little road cart eight years before, he knew he had found a "self-seller" in the Buick, and decided to sell others on it as well. He took over the Buick Motor Car Company on November 1, 1904.

On that day he raised the capitalization from $75,000 to $300,000, and 18 days later raised it again, to $500,000. In January 1905, in typical Durant fashion, he returned to Flint from the New York Auto Show with orders for 1,108 cars. In all of 1904, Buick had only managed to produce 37 automobiles, and some 350 of these show orders would go unfilled in 1905, despite the fact that plant foreman William Beacraft was sleeping in the shop to turn them into cars. Through a dizzying set of financial maneuvers, Durant increased Buick's capitalization again on September 11, 1905, to $1,500,000. This time it wasn't so easy. When company attorney John J. Carton found the capitalization was $60,000 short at the last minute, he included an item of that value called "ownership of invention of combustion engine construction not patented for business reasons." It was a good thing Carton was one of Michigan's top Republican leaders, or he would never have gotten that one past the good Republican Secretary of State in Lansing. By the time capitalization was boosted again, to $2,600,000 on June 12, 1907, the company was booming and there was no need for any of this kind of "creative financing."

Early on, Durant solved the financing problems that had plagued Buick company since its inception. He also had a terrific product, beginning with the 1904 Model B and continuing over the next few years with an improved series of new models in various price ranges starting at $1,250. And the public was buying in ever-increasing numbers, until in 1908 Buick sold 8,487 units, moving twice the number of cars as the next two makes, Ford and Cadillac, combined and becoming the best-selling car in America.

The secret of his success was systematization of his business in all departments from finance to manufacturing, sales, and service. He would identify objectives and problems, and worked out ways to achieve the former and overcome the latter. If he needed cash, he sold stock; if he needed new product, he stayed close to the ideas of his superb team of engineers; if he needed good dealers, he went out and found them, and created a whole department to support his dealers with first-rate service and parts. Harry

Shiland, Buick's blunt, demanding service director, admonished Durant, "You aren't selling cars to mechanics. Cars have to be foolproof for the average doctor or lawyer or businessman to want them," and Durant took this advice to heart. Almost all sales then were first-time sales, and if your neighbor didn't like the car he had bought, you wouldn't buy one when you were in the market. "When better cars are built, Buick will build them" was a slogan Durant dreamed up at that time. It rang true then, and re-verberated through the rest of the century, because he gave the public good cause to believe in it.

By the summer of 1905 an old problem Durant had experienced in the carriage business surfaced in the automobile manufacturing process. A se-vere bottleneck in the delivery of axles from the Weston-Mott company of Utica, New York, had developed, and Durant, after complicated negotiations with Charles S. Mott, eliminated the problem in the future by convincing Mott to open a new company in Michigan solely devoted to furnishing Buick with axles. This event was emblematic of Durant's entire modus operandi in establishing and running General Motors: starting up, controlling, or acquiring other companies that would keep critical parts supplied to him.

By bringing Weston-Mott to Flint and relocating the W. F. Stewart body-making operation there too, Buicks were now completely built in Flint, just like the Durant-Dort carriages. In the process, Buick acquired two superb new executives: William Little, a body man who became general manager, and Harry Bassett, who would eventually become president of the Buick division of General Motors after the departure of Walter Chrysler.

No matter how fast Durant expanded and everybody under him worked, the factory could barely keep up with demand. Now that there were better products and greater public acceptance, the market for automobiles seemed to be exploding everywhere, beyond the capacity of manufacturers to supply it. Alfred P. Sloan, who sold his Hyatt Roller Bearings to Weston-Mott, said the watchword of the auto business then was "tempo." "Speed! Do what you have been doing, but do it faster. Double your capacity. Quadruple it. Double it again. At times it seemed like madness. Yet people clamored for the cars. There were never enough automobiles to meet the demand. The pressure on production men was desperate."

Buick production rose to 14,606 in 1909, or 11 percent of the national total, and 30,525 in 1910, which was over 15 percent of the 187,000 cars built that year. Flint exploded, too, in the first decade of the century, going from a population of thirteen thousand in 1900 to over thirty-eight thou-sand in 1910, including a workforce of fifteen thousand. Everyone was roll-ing in money, and housing was so short that people slept in boardinghouse beds in shifts timed to match the work shifts at the plants.

The only one who didn't prosper was David Dunbar Buick. Theodore F. McManus summed him up this way: "Fame beckoned to David Buick. He sipped from the cup of greatness, and then spilled what it held." He had some shares of the company in the various reorganizations, but his presence in the plant became first erratic and then superflous after 1904. By 1906 he was broke again, and after a payoff from Durant, he left the company he had founded with optimism and hard work just seven years before. An old-time Buick employee named Fred Hoelzle told Dunham and Gustin in 1980 that Buick "never seemed to fit himself in with others. Nobody seemed to take to him. I think he was most interested in finances. He was quiet and we didn't see him very often. Finally, he just kind of faded away. Nobody seemed to notice."

Buick drifted into further financial misadventures in California oil and Florida land later on. With his son Tom, he tried manufacturing their patented carburetors, but this didn't work out. There was the presidency of a short-lived car firm named Lorraine Motors in 1921, and involvement with the Dunbar car in 1923, which never existed as anything but a prototype. One night in 1920 Herbert R. Lewis encountered Buick at the Ben Franklin Hotel in Philadelphia. In a room off the lobby Buick showed him "one of the most beautiful cars I had ever seen." Buick had designed it, and was going to show it to backers the next day. When asked its name, Buick replied, "Just call it Dave Buick's best." It was probably the Lorraine.

Tom Buick prospered supplying all the brass to Buick until the company didn't pay its bills in the financial crisis of 1910 and caused him to lose everything he had. After this, his son recalled that the family was thrown out of thirteen apartments for nonpayment of rent. He died a Fuller Brush salesman in 1942.

In 1928 Bruce Catton, later a famed Civil War historian, tracked David Buick down and interviewed him for a Detroit newspaper. He was by now completely broke, not even able to afford a telephone, and made his living as an obscure instructor at the Detroit School of Trades. Later, as he became more enfeebled, he was given a job at the information desk. But he was bright and cheerful, and not one word of complaint or regret about the past came from his mouth. "I'm not worrying," he told Catton. "The failure is the man who stays down when he falls—the man who sits and worries about what happened yesterday, instead of jumping up and figuring what he's going to do today and tomorrow. That's what success is—looking ahead to tomorrow."

He died the next year of colon cancer, on March 3, 1929, at the age of 74. To date, over 35,000,000 motor cars have been built in his name, which will never be lost to history.

The wheel of fortune turns and turns, and as one spins down, another rises. While David Buick was slipping from the automotive scene, Billy Durant was about to embark on a venture that would eclipse anything anyone else had ever done not just in the transportation business, but in any business. He was going to found General Motors, whose practices would become the model for most modern corporations. But even if he had not done this, Richard Crabb's assessment of his achievements up until that point would still mark him as a monumental figure: "Durant accomplished what no man had then done, or would ever do. He had moved from horses to horsepower, and had been a pacesetter in both. He had directed the production of more horse drawn vehicles than any other man who had ever lived. Within four years, he had also scaled the same heights with the self propelled vehicle." In so doing, he had prepared himself well to make his greatest mark on history.

As with the road cart, as with Buick, General Motors wasn't his idea. Benjamin Briscoe dreamed it up, but it was Billy Durant who had the scale of vision and the skills to push it through into reality.

At that time the automobile business was growing but still shaky. Some forty-four producers manufactured about forty-four thousand cars in 1907, but about three-quarters of those were built by one-quarter of the firms. Due to industry practice of the time, the actual construction of the cars was pre-financed by their sale. The buyer, either a dealer or a customer, paid 20% down in cash, and the balance was attached to the bill of lading in the form of a sight draught on the customer's account. The manufacturers, however, bought their components on credit and paid for the parts with the draughts on the finished cars. Benjamin Briscoe called this method of doing business "manufacturing gambling." As long as things grew and prospered this system was fine, but any sales downturn would have a domino effect throughout the industry. This was precisely what happened in the brief but sharp recession that followed the panic of 1907, causing several companies to go out of business. What was the buyer of one of the cars of such a failed firm to do? He had invested as much as $3,000 in a car, and now where was he to go with his complaints, or to get parts or service? In short order, his shiny new investment became balky scrap metal.

Then again, there were companies that were little more than excuses for stock manipulation in the first place. They would spiff up an old factory, cobble together a few snazzy-looking models, and put out an elegant brochure, using this as a front for issuing flimsy securities. Often the companies collapsed before any actual cars got produced.

Even the strong companies were vulnerable. When weak companies failed, both the buyers' and the bankers' confidence was badly shaken, and credit dried up for the survivors, which was a very bad thing for a rapidly growing industry.

Added to this situation were the products themselves. Autos were just barely in their adolescence and quite unreliable, without much standardization and interchangeability of parts. Often a batch of steering knuckles from one manufacturer would be quite different from another batch made by a different, or even the same, manufacturer. It could take days, and the services of skilled mechanics, to fix even simple problems, which severely limited the usefulness of autos. If the automobile was to penetrate deeply into the American market, more systematization and control over production was needed. And if the industry wanted the trust of the public—and sobersided bankers—something important had to be done in the way of building confidence.

Briscoe thought a huge combination of the principal automobile producers would end the abuses and shortcomings that plagued the industry. His model was U.S. Steel, the largest of all combines, whose financial consolidator was no less than J. P. Morgan, the most powerful of all financiers, and, as we have seen, a sometime backer of Briscoe's.

Initially Briscoe thought the auto combine should have about a dozen members, but Durant thought that might stretch it too thin and defeat the purpose. He wanted only a few top firms, stong enough to be pacesetters for all the others. Of course Buick and Maxwell-Briscoe would be part of the group, and in addition Durant wanted Ford and REO, Ransom Olds's new company. Briscoe agreed, though he lost out on his idea of the form the combination should take. He wanted a full operating merger, whereas Durant wanted a holding company with fully independent constituents. "Durant is for states' rights, I am for a union," Briscoe said. Eventually Briscoe's idea would be close to what GM was to become, but for now it was Durant's vision that prevailed.

Financial talks with Morgan's son-in-law Herbert L. Satterlee at his law offices in the spring of 1908 went well until, to everyone's surprise, including Durant's and Briscoe's, Ford and Olds demanded 100 percent cash on the barrelhead for a complete buyout of their respective interests. A stock buyout was one thing, but Satterlee blanched at the propect of putting up $6 million in cash to retire Ford and Olds. The bankers would come up with their own plan, and inform the principals of it when they were ready. Durant turned to Briscoe and said, "Let's go it alone. We two."

But after another unsuccessful pass at Morgan (their lawyer, Francis L. Stetson, thought Durant was deceiving Buick stockholders by asking them to give him their shares without informing them of his negotiations for the new concern), Durant broke it off with Briscoe, who didn't want to defy his powerful New York banker friends. Durant went solo with his own plan. He bypassed the bankers completely and went to Satterlee with all the stock of Buick and an option to buy no less than 75 percent of Oldsmobile, which was foundering under a policy of building huge luxury vehicles only. With these assets he proposed at last to start up his new company. Curtis R. Hatheway, one of the Satterlee lawyers, investigated possible names, and suggested General Motors, which was adopted. On September 16, 1908, the company was incorporated, with an initial capitalization of $2,000 to make it legal. When the Buick shares were tendered two weeks later, capitalization was raised to $12.5 million, and Buick was paid off with $2.5 million of GM preferred stock, $1.25 million in GM common stock, and $1,500 in cash. Six weeks later Olds was paid off with $3 million in GM stock, the assumption of $1 million in Olds debt to Samuel L. Smith, and $17,279 in cash.

It was done. The auto combine was born. The underlying concept wasn't original; industrial combinations of every sort had been transforming America for years, and at least one man, financier and traction mogul Anthony N. Brady, had thought of an automobile consolidation even before Briscoe. But it was Durant, with a combination of dogged determination and unfailing ingenuity, who saw it through. Without his realizing it, and in part as a reaction to his own policies, General Motors would become an entity that would reconstruct the entire concept of the corporation, which remains the basic, dominant unit of business organization throughout the world. But in a very real sense General Motors, at base, was Billy Durant's baby; over the next dozen years, his understanding of what that meant would turn out to be both his triumph and his tragedy. He now had freedom and capital he never dreamed of before, and with them he expanded himself into oblivion. Twice. But what a world he left behind.

He bought out the Oakland car from Edward Murphy, the head of the Pontiac Buggy Company. He set his sights on Cadillac, the ultraprestigious luxury car whose reputation was based on the exacting standards of its founder, Henry M. Leland. After three passes at it, during which the price rose from $3.5 million to $4.5 million, Durant acquired it through a clever combination of cash and promissory notes taken from the coffers of Buick. He made another pass at Ford, and came within a hair's breadth of buying it. By the fall of 1909 Ford, who was by now producing the Model T, told Durant he would sell out for $8 million, "and I'll throw in my lumbago." All that was required was $6 million in cash, since Ford's partner James Couzens was willing to raise his Ford stake to 25 percent and take his payout in GM stock. But in what would seem to be a supreme example of gutless stupidity on the part of the banking community, Durant was not able to raise the money from any of its members. Ford might be very profitable (though no one in 1909 had any inkling of just how profitable), but the bankers were afraid of Durant. He seemed like a loose cannon whose corporate acquisitiveness might eat up every dime General Motors could make (which was considerable: $9.1 million in profit on $29 million in sales the first year). When a similar chance came up for Durant to acquire Maxwell-Briscoe from Benjamin Briscoe for only $2 million, the bankers refused again, and another extraordinarily valuable asset was lost to GM.

But perhaps there was more than a little reason for this. It must be said of the bankers, as Arthur Pound has done, that they could not be overly blamed for not understanding the future value inherent in these companies.

After all, even their sellers didn't realize what they were worth. Cadillac was sold for $4.5 million, a little more than two times its 1908 earnings; if Durant had paid $20 million for it, he would still have had an asset paying at the rate of 10 percent a year. At $8 million, Ford was willing to sell out his company for little more than three times its 1908 profits. Durant alone seemed to have had both the vision to understand what these companies were worth and the intestinal fortitude to persevere in creating a financial instrument that would combine them.

Unfortunately for his project with the bankers, in addition to winners such as Oakland and Cadillac, he also bought some real dogs. There was the Elmore, which had a two-cycle engine that was a pile of junk and the Welch, which one Durant associate described as "the super passenger car of its day, as big as a freight car," something which nobody needed. He bought Marquette Motor Car of Saginaw, Reliance Motor Truck of Owosso, and the Randolph, which hailed from Illinois, none of which had a market. The Cartercar, another car from Pontiac, Michigan, had a friction drive. "How was anyone to know that Cartercar wasn't going to be the thing?" Durant explained later. "I was for getting every car in sight, playing safe all along the line." But by 1909 everybody knew what 'the thing' would be: a four-cylinder auto with a front-mounted four-cycle engine, delivering its power to the rear wheels through a driveshaft, and equipped with an H-slot, sliding-gear transmission, was becoming 'well-nigh universal' " (Weisberger). It was amazing that the head of the biggest auto company in the world couldn't see this, but it was an example of the problematic way in which he did business. It was all scattershot and intuitive, rather than systematic and considered. When he was right, he was very, very right, but when he was wrong, it was a disaster. So it wasn't too hard to see why the big conservative Eastern bankers of the day were not willing to back up such an imprecise and overextended man even on his good ideas. (They did manage to get themselves caught, however; in 1910, the hapless Benjamin Briscoe managed to raise $30 million to start a second giant combine known as the United States Motor Company. It was an aggregation of some 130 companies, almost all of which turned out to be manufacturers of useless, outdated automotive junk. When it collapsed in 1912, only its one solid asset, the Maxwell, survived. That one asset was enough to pay off the backers eventually, the principal one of whom was Anthony N. Brady.)

Crystalline examples of both good and bad judgment on Durant's part occurred in the early days of GM. Durant was at the head of the pack running toward vertical integration of manufacture in the car business, as he had done in the carriage business. In 1909 he sold GM his interest in Champion Spark Plug, which he had acquired from the debonair French inventor Albert Champion for the Buick. Later, as A. C. Spark Plug, it was a major profit center for the company. He acquired Weston-Mott, which made axles, for GM, and a host of other companies that manufactured engine castings, body panels, brakes, transmissions, springs, electrical and ignition parts, and many other automobile components, all in the first year and a half of the company's existence. But he also bought out the Heany Lamp Company for $7 million, mostly, as usual, in stock. Its claim to value was based on a patent application for a type of incandescent lighting that Durant was convinced would solve the problem of night lighting for cars, then illuminated by highly ineffective gas or acetylene lamps. The head of the company, John Albert Heany, claimed that he had invented the modern tungsten filament for the electric light. The trouble was that the patents Heany had applied for were in part falsified as to their priority, and eventually invalidated by the Commissioner of Patents. So GM was forced to write off as worthless an investment larger than what it had paid for Buick and Oldsmobile combined. By 1929 the stock paid out to Heany was worth $325 million, and had earned another $50 million in dividends.

By the end of two years Durant had bought over $54 million worth of properties for under $33 million, four-fifths of which had not been cash. But in the process he had brought the corporation's cash reserves to a dangerously low state and raised its obligations to a dangerously high one, making the company extremely vulnerable to cash flow interruptions. The company was overburdened by a mix of good and bad investments, and there was no systematic oversight to sort things out and provide relief. A red flag could be seen in the company's results for 1909; in that year business increased by over $10 million, but it brought in a profit of only 12.75 percent, as opposed to 1908's overall profit of 31 percent. Trouble began early in 1910 when sales began to falter. This situation reflected a market adjustment, with many old firms aimed at the high end of the market yielding to newer ones selling their products to people of more modest means. Buick was producing at an extraordinary rate, but for a while the customers weren't there, and more importantly, the firm had frittered away its cash reserves in Durant's buying bonanza. Buick had some $8 million in bills, and there simply was no cash around to pay them. Anything that came in couldn't even be put through Buick's regular accounts without being seized for overdraughts. The big banks wanted no part of helping a man they saw as reckless, so Durant was forced to borrow millions in small amounts from little country banks he had once dealt with in the carriage business. One night while returning from a loan-seeking trip to St. Louis and Kansas City with A. B. C. Hardy and Arnold Goss, he saw an illuminated sign flashing the word "BANK" down the street from the small town train station where they were stopped. He shook Goss awake, pointed to the sign, and said, "Wake up, Goss; there's one we missed!"

Production at Buick was shut down to adjust inventories, putting 4,250 men out of work. Trouble spread even to rock-solid Cadillac. An emergency meeting of the First National Bank of Detroit and the Old National Bank of Detroit had to be called at one point to approve a $500,000 loan to Cadillac just hours before it had to meet its payroll.

In the end nothing availed; even when the Continental and Commercial Savings and Trust Company of Chicago looked as if it might help in a substantial way, a lack of proper bookeeping made it impossible to tell how much money was actually required to save the situation, and in the confusion, the Chicagoans retired. By September, company directors were starting to sell off parts of the firm to keep it afloat, and desperate measures would be needed to save the enterprise.

Some good things had happened by then to make a rescue possible. For one thing, economy moves started to have an effect. By cutting off expansion and selling off some of its companies, GM's flow of red ink was stanched somewhat and revenues began to flow back into company coffers. Expenses were cut and production made more efficient, so that despite the fact that the workforce was reduced from its high of 14,000, sales began to rise without a problem in filling orders. Things were showing signs of improvement at GM, even without Ford's orderly routine in ordering parts, or Packard's tight management controls. Then, too, all the financial conferences were giving the bankers a better sense of the profits and stability that could be derived from designing and producing a car largely in-house. Henry Leland was attending these meetings and giving scores of bankers a good education in the difference between the dozens of assembled cars then in their heyday in 1910 and such specifically engineered makes as Cadillac, Buick, REO, and Ford. They were starting to understand why these brands represented superior business practices.

The showdown finally arrived at the offices of the Chase Manhattan Bank in New York during a long session on September 10, 1910; the net had closed in, and GM was one day away from bankruptcy and dissolution. All the bankers had assembled to hear the company out. Durant opened with a request for $15 million, stating that GM was a good risk with 1909 earnings of over $10 million, surely to be bettered in the following year. He was quickly cut off with a dismissive statement that despite the fact that it was number two in sales, GM had low profits (!) on high sales and mounting debt. After the major GM divisions gave reports, the bankers stated that they would give no more loans. At 4 P.M., J. C. van Cleef of the National Park Bank noted that Cadillac, without debt and with great profits, had been little heard from. Wilfred Leland then gave a forty-minute account of its success, and an hour of questioning by the bankers gave them a new sense of the money that could be earned by a stable, well-run car company over a number of years. They began to think that a well-run version of the entire General Motors enterprise might indeed be worth saving. They adjourned until 10:00 A.M. the following morning, but asked to talk further with Leland at the Belmont Hotel at 8:00 P.M. At that meeting he began to reorient their thinking as to how GM could be saved rather than dissolved. He made them see portents of success in its operations, pointing out that a $15 million loan was not a bad risk to a company earning at the rate of $10 million a year. By midnight all the talk was of how to save GM, and by 2:30 A.M. the bankers agreed to make the loan when the conference resumed the next morning.

Wilfred Leland was not authorized to say anything to anybody of the agreement, and Durant got the shock of his life when he found out about it at the meeting the next day. None other than Ralph Van Vechten, who had loaned Walter Chrysler the $4,300 he needed to buy his Locomobile two years before, spoke in favor of the loan. He was the Vice President of the Continental and Commercial Savings and Trust Company of Chicago who had been willing to loan millions to Durant just that past July, until GM's accounting proved to be a hopelessly entangled mess. Now he spoke with confidence of General Motors' future as a means of bringing stability to the automobile industry, something he felt should be strongly encouraged (it seemed that Durant had primed that pump particularly well). When the amounts each banker was willing to contribute were totalled up, the sum came to $17.5 million. Van Cleef turned to Leland and said, "I want to congratulate you, and I want to say that you have saved the General Motors Company."

The above account comes from Crabb, and is based on Wilfred Leland's own version of events. When he gave it, he no longer had any love for Durant, and may have been more than a little self serving, as Weisberger thinks. It is clear though that a lot of hard, fast talking was done on the night of September 10–11, 1910 to salvage GM, and there was credit to be given on all sides. GM gave a good enough account of itself that the bankers, representing the major financial interests in the United States, recognized that the automobile industry would make a great contribution to the American economy, and that a relatively few well-managed firms would provide the industry with stability through constantly improved products and service. Crabb concludes: "The actions of the bankers that September night in 1910 were a major factor in pointing the face of the car industry to the future. A shuttered General Motors, with its potential for better cars, would have turned back the clock. GM and Ford became the chief architects of better cars and service. That led the industry out of its wilderness into an economic contribution so broad that a new level of life evolved."

The banks were not, however, eleemosynary institutions. The price of the banks' participation was very steep. GM issued $15 million in five-year notes at six percent, discounted to $12.75 million. They were secured by a mortgage on all of the company's properties and assets, which bank auditors valued at $37.7 million, far less than GM's own auditors had claimed at the end of 1909. Furthermore, they demanded a bonus of $2 million in GM common stock and $4.169 million in GM preferred.

"Outrageous!" screamed Billy Durant, who had good reason to be upset, for they also demanded that he give up control of the company. He would only be allowed to be one of a five-member, five-year, voting trust that would control the company, the other four being James N. Wallace of Central Trust of New York, Albert Strauss for J. and W. Seligman, James J. Storrow for Lee, Higginson, and Anthony N. Brady. A wave of bankers would join the board, and a number of loyal Durant supporters, many seasoned auto men like Wilfred Leland, would have to retire.

Most galling of all was the fact that within weeks of the takeover some 14,000 Buick orders poured into the factory, proving to Durant that he was right in saying that a few dollops of cash at the right moment could have gotten the company through without a reorganization. On top of that, the new management was sanctimoniously calling itself the savior of a wrecked corporation, which justified in its own eyes the charging of outrageous fees for its services. Durant was humiliated and vilified in the press at every turn. Of his departure from GM, *Motor World* said, "The feeling is . . . that an element of real peril to the entire industry has been circumvented and chastened."

And so William Crapo Durant was effectively cut off from the idea he had created and the corporation that idea had engendered. But he was not cut off from the wellsprings of his own genius, which lay in the ability not only to envision the future, but to reify it for great masses of humanity. "To him," said a contemporary, "the immediate future was remote; the remote future near and vivid."

What he dreamed up now was nothing less than the most spectacular comeback in American corporate history. In the next five years he would found Chevrolet, turn it into a howling success, and use it as a lever to regain control of a much larger, vastly better organized, and more sophisticated General Motors. He was still the same Billy Durant, though, and out of the clash between his personal style and the implacable needs of the evolving corporate supergiant came the problems and solutions that would lead both to his own downfall and to the basic model of the modern corporation.

❖   ❖   ❖

One day Theodore McManus, a Detroit newspaperman and P.R. man, wrote down a little verse during a long wait in Durant's office. He shoved it over to him when he finally got inside. It read:

I'm glad I'm not a vacuum
I'm glad I'm not a myth
I'm glad I'm not the sort of stuff
They fill pin cushions with

But most of all I'm glad, O Lord,
You did not make me Henry Ford.

Weisberger reports that Durant gasped, "oh, you villain!", and doubled over with laughter. And that was exactly the point. No one ever would have confused gregarious, fun-loving, charming, gracious Billy Durant with old Henry Ford. Henry Ford was a sour pickle. With little sense of humor and none of aesthetics, Ford was greedy, censorious, and abstemious, never touching alcohol, meat, or tobacco, abjuring the company of gamblers, drunks, and loose women. He was a politically regressive nineteenth-century populist and an anti-Semite. Though longing for the sweet simplicity of old-fashioned 19th-century America, he did more than any other human being to create the basic conditions of life for twentieth-century man, both physically and socially. He invented prosperity. As R. L. Bruckberger said, his revolution, Fordism, turned out to be far more important to the twentieth century than Lenin's. Ford's revolution was not ideological, but it was carefully thought out and planned over a protracted period of time, and he implemented it with a fanatical, single-minded determination rarely fulfilled to such great effect in all of history.

Henry Ford, the son of Irish immigrants, was born in a little clearing in the Michigan woods called Dearborn on July 30, 1863, the same month the Battle of Gettysburg in the Civil War was fought. He was a farm boy raised on the uplifting sentiments of the McGuffey readers in school, like most American children of his time. He was devastated by his mother's death when he was only twelve years old; later, when he was asked the secret to his success as one of the richest men in the world, he answered, "I have tried to live my life as my mother would have wished."

Just four months after her death, young Henry encountered a steam engine moving toward him out in the fields; on investigation, he discovered it was operated by a chain connected to the rear wheels. It was the first such contraption he had ever seen, and by his own account, it marked him for life with a fascination for self-propelled vehicles.

Young Henry displayed quite a remarkable mechanical aptitude, and when he was sixteen he became an apprentice at the James Flower & Brothers machine shop in Detroit, the selfsame place where David Buick had apprenticed ten years before, and where the Dodge Brothers would subsequently work for a time. Later he worked at the Detroit Dry Dock Company, earning extra money repairing watches at night. Interestingly, while repairing watches he figured out that he could make good, serviceable timepieces for 30 cents apiece, if he were to produce 2,000 a day. But when he realized that would mean he would have to sell 500,000 watches a year to make real money, he gave up his scheme.

Having completed his apprenticeship by the time he was nineteen, in

1882, he went back to work on his father's farm, where he remained until he was thirty. While there, he repaired a neighboring farmer's Westinghouse portable steam engine, and then he went to work for the farmer, traveling from farm to farm with the machine, doing various heavy tasks with it. After one season he became the official demonstrator and repairman for the Westinghouse Company in the southern Michigan territory.

Ford's life in those days seemed to be a bucolic idyll, but it wasn't. Increasing mechanization meant greater agricultural production on the farm, and improved railway and steamship transportation meant worldwide competition for farmers, both of which lowered farm income. The farmers were confused, not understanding why increased machine-based productivity wasn't raising their income. Then there was the great currency saga. The farmers were behind the National Greenback Party, which took its name from the currency issued without gold backing during the Civil War. Paper currency was inflationary, which was good for the farmers. It meant they paid back the dollars they had borrowed on mortgages and other loans with cheaper dollars later on, and this was a big help, especially in times of falling income. Bankers, of course, brought back old-fashioned gold-backed dollars as fast as they could, to the farmers' dismay. "Railroad tycoons, eastern bankers, city slickers in general, middlemen, moneylenders, Jews—this was the demonology of rural Michigan at the end of the nineteenth century," says Robert Lacey in his superb biography of the Fords, *Ford: The Men and the Machine.* "Though the Greenbackers did not last, the grassroots movements that took their place shared the same assumptions." The whole business culminated in the Populist Party of the 1890s and the presidential candidacy of Williams Jennings Bryan; at the Democratic Party convention which nominated him to the presidency in 1896, he gave an impassioned speech in favor of bimetallism which contained the celebrated phrase, "You shall not crucify mankind upon a cross of gold." But despite all the Populist hubbub, Bryan lost, and gold continued to back the currency.

The populist beliefs of a late-nineteenth-century Michigan farmer were to stay with Henry Ford for the rest of his life. Some were quaint, like his support of temperance; some became damaging to the commonweal, like his distrust of bankers; and some were vile, like his hatred of Jews. But they were all of a piece with his background, and though he became the richest man in the world, they never changed.

He married Clara Bryant, one of the great influences of his life, in 1888. Three years later, he was amazed by an Otto internal combustion engine gave him an idea that changed everything for him. He thought this engine could be mounted in a wheeled vehicle and adapted to propel itself. However, he needed to know more about the electricity required to fire up an internal-combustion engine, so he found a job at the Edison Illuminating Company in Detroit, packed up his family, and left Dearborn.

While at Edison, in late 1895 or early 1896, Ford began cobbling together a gasoline engine out of metal scrap. He met Charles Brady King there, and when King took that historic first ride in his gasoline car in Detroit on March 6, 1896, Ford followed beside him on a bicycle. Three months later, on June 4, 1896, Ford broke down the brick wall of his little workshop on Bagley Avenue and pushed his Quadricycle out into the street, where he ran it. Unlike Brady's 1,300-pound horseless carriage, Ford's vehicle was a lithe 500-pound job capable of speeding at 20 miles an hour. Shortly thereafter, when Charles G. Annesley offered him $200 for it, he sold it to get money to build another one. Thereby, Henry Ford sold America's first used car.

Early on Henry Ford got encouragement in his work from a very distinguished source, which he lived on emotionally for some time. Alexander Dow, Ford's boss at Edison sent him to the annual convention of the Association of Edison Illuminating Companies in 1896, which took place at the Oriental Hotel in Manhattan Beach. He was seated next to Edison at dinner, and while speaking into the great man's good ear, he sketched for him his idea of a gasoline engine suitable for use in a horseless carriage. When he was finished, Edison pounded his fist on the table and said, "Young man, you have the right thing. Keep at it!" Edison's emphatic encouragement was something he never forgot, and in later years the two men became the closest of friends.

It is important to remember of Henry Ford, as Lacey points out, that unlike Thomas Edison, Alexander Graham Bell, and the Wright Brothers, Henry Ford's fame does not rest on invention. Many people think he invented the automobile, but he did not. His achievements are based on the work of others. But he knew what to do with the work of others better than anyone.

He was also a later starter, and not an early success. His initial venture, the Detroit Automobile Company, formed on August 5, 1899, was the first automobile company to be set up in Detroit. The backers who furnished the capital were a prestigious lot, including William Maybury, the mayor of the city. Fifteen months later, after producing a dozen vehicles, the firm was dissolved. He blamed the backers, whom he characterized as a rapacious group interested in money rather than making better cars for the public. Fred Strauss, a longtime associate, explained it differently. "Henry wasn't ready," he said. "He didn't have an automobile design."

He was learning, though, and now set about building a reputation through successfully racing vehicles of his own design. On October 10, 1901, he won a tremendous victory over a challenge from Alexander Winton to all comers at Grosse Pointe. (The car featured a spark coil wrapped in a porcelain insulating case fashioned by a dentist—the forerunner of the spark plug.)

Six weeks later, on November 30, 1901, the Henry Ford Company was incorporated, with capital coming from five of the men who had lost their entire investment in Ford's previous venture. Four months later, Ford was shown the door by his backers. It seems that he secretly began to work on a new racing car, neglecting the work he was supposed to be doing on a new car engine for his firm. Henry Leland was brought in, initially as an adviser; then, as things got worse, he was given a mandate to run things on the shop floor. He began giving orders to Ford, which led to a showdown. Ford was let go with $900 cash and the plans to his new racer. The backers kept the designs for the firm's new car and replaced the engine with a superb new one of Leland's design. Management agreed not to use Ford's name, so the car was rechristened a Cadillac, in honor of Detroit's founder, and a new firm, the Cadillac Automobile Company, was formed. Under Leland's guidance, it was to produce one of the great luxury car marques in the world, and the rock that saved General Motors in 1910. But for all intents and purposes, except for the Leland engines, the first Cadillacs were Fords.

Ford was now close to forty and a two-time failure at car manufacturing, mainly because he was never sufficiently organized to develop a marketable product. On his own once again, Ford now hooked up with a bicycle racing champion named Tom Cooper, who gave him backing for two new racers named "The Arrow" and "999," after famous express trains of the time. He also began work with one of the great auto engineers of all time, the Byronically named C. Harold (for Childe Harold) Wills, as fine a mechanical draughtsman as there ever was. (Ford never learned how to draught precise mechanical drawings, and some said he couldn't read them either.)

The 999 was a monster of a car, its engine a four-cylinder brute displacing 1155.3 cubic inches. Cooper didn't want to drive it, so he brought in another famous bike racer, Barney Oldfield, who had never driven a car before. He was game though, as he was a bit down on his luck; "I might as well be dead as dead broke," he said.

On the day of the race, October 25, 1902, Oldfield tromped on the accelerator and never let up until he won, driving the Ford to victory over Winton once again. Six weeks later he drove the 999 a mile in one minute and one point one seconds. Lacey says, "In later years he liked to say that he and Henry Ford had 'made' each other, Ford by building the car and Oldfield by driving it. 'But,' Oldfield used to add, 'I did much the best job of it.'"

By the time of the race, Ford had broken with Cooper, accusing him of "sneaky tricks" and thinking only of himself, which was by now a pattern with Ford when things went wrong. But the real reason was that he had found a new backer, Alex Y. Malcolmson, a multimillionaire coal dealer Ford had bought supplies from as part of his duties at Edison. The two men signed an agreement to go into business to manufacture a car on August

16, 1902, months before the October race; it would seem that the sneaky tricks were all Ford's. Lacey notes: "As a child of rural populism, Henry Ford always expressed contempt for the ethics of "big business," but when it came to the pursuit of his own interests, he demonstrated an opportunism to rival that of any robber baron."

Malcolmson set a tough, dyspeptic coalyard clerk named James Couzens to work supervising the enterprise, and he was a hard taskmaster. Ford and Wills together developed a wonderful two-cylinder engine for the new prototype Ford, one in which for the first time the cylinders were set vertically instead of horizontally. This reduced vibration greatly and was a big improvement over other designs. The new car was to be known, appropriately enough, as the Model A, and would be the company's first product. On June 13, 1903, the company was incorporated, and a month later the first Ford runabouts were loaded onto a freight train for shipment.

The original investors in the Ford Motor Company were a motley, rather unimpressive crew who put money in it because they were heavily involved with Malcolmson in one way or another. In addition to Malcolmson himself, there were John S. Gray, Malcolmson's banker-uncle to whom he was heavily indebted; Couzens and his sister Rosetta, who put in half her life savings of $200 when her brother couldn't come up with the last $100 of his $2,500 committment; the Dodge Brothers, who had contracted to build all the mechanical car components for Ford; Vernon C. Fry, Malcolmson's cousin; Albert Strelow, a painting and woodworking contractor who had built Malcolmson's coalyards; John W. Anderson and Horace H. Rackham, two lawyers who collected Malcolmson's debts and did the legal work for his business expansions; Charles J. Woodall, a Malcolmson bookeeper; and Charles H. Bennett. This last was an airgun manufacturer who invested after he tested the Model A prototype and was very impressed by it. He was the only outside investor in the group. The total cash paid in was $28,500.

Within a month, however, the company was next door to bankrupt. For the first month there were nothing but expenses, and by July 10 the bank balance was down to $223.65. Then on July 15 the company made its first sale, to a Dr. E. P. Phennig, a Chicago dentist, who ordered a Model A at $750 and a $100 tonneau to go with it, for a total of $850. From there on out, the company was deluged with orders, and sold 1,700 cars in the next fifteen months. Within a year the investors had been paid $100,000 in dividends.

Everybody worked like demons to keep up with the company's success, putting in days as long as sixteen hours. Ford and the other engineers were constantly trying to put improvements into the car. When they found the original carburetors were no good, they designed a much better, cheaper one right away with a young Pennsylvania designer named George Holley. But steely-minded James Couzens, the sales manager, refused to interrupt deliveries of the new cars for the sake of improvements. When Henry tried to delay the very first shipment of cars, Couzens admonished him not to interfere. "Stop shipping," he said, "and we go bankrupt." He then escorted the cars to the railroad station and personally nailed the doors of the freight cars shut.

Couzens began establishing a dealer network of 450 very strong members, who aggressively sold Ford cars. In so doing he created the idea of the car dealership system. It was probably his greatest contribution to the company, for thereby he got wide and reliable distribution for the company's production in an era when most cars were sold as a sideline by blacksmiths, bicycle dealers, and the like.

By the time he reached his fortieth birthday, July 30, 1903, just fifteen days after the Ford Motor Company sold its first car, Henry Ford was at last a success after more than a decade of apprentice car manufacture. Within a year he had made a profit of $25,000 on his Ford shares. One day in 1904, Eugene Lewis, a salesman for Timken Bearings, commented to Ford that Packard had just paid out a dividend. Ford reached into his pocket and pulled out a much-folded-over check for $10,500 in his name, dated forty-five days before. "Other people get dividends too," he said.

The new and more expensive models B, C, and F followed the original Model A in 1904, and in 1905 the grande luxe Model K was marketed to the luxury trade. But Ford and Malcomson were developing big differences about the future direction of the company. Like the Smiths at Oldsmobile, Malcomson wanted to build large, expensive cars, but Ford, like Olds, did not agree with him. A May 1905 interview with Ford in the *Detroit Journal* headed "Ten Thousand Autos at $400 Apiece" said it all. Ford could have gone into the prestigious luxury trade, but his background and instincts did not incline him that way. Besides, an open conflict with Malcomson provided him a way to get rid of him.

The Ford, like all others of its time, was an assembled vehicle. Everything but the body, wheels, and tires was made by Dodge Brothers, and those external parts also came from outside sources. The car company was essentially a designer, assembler, and marketer of vehicles, not a manufacturer of its components. This meant that before it made its own profits, Ford had to pay out profits to the manufacturing companies for their services. Ford and Couzens wanted to eliminate this situation by forming a manufacturing arm, which they realized would meet with growing success as its operations and volume grew. This meant a low-priced product was the way to go. By setting up an outside entity, the Ford Manufacturing Company, without Malcomson, they were able to force him and his supporters Bennett, Fry and Woodall out of the Ford Motor Company. (Strelow sold out at the same time to put his money in a Canadian gold mining company, of all things.) Since the company's articles of association specified that shareholders had to sell their shares within the company, by the middle of 1906 Henry Ford wound up with 585 of the 1,000 shares outstanding, and he never had to answer to any business associate for the rest of his life.

At last, in his early forties, Henry Ford had found his own springtime. He was now free to pursue the genius of his vision, which was simply this: "The way to make automobiles is to make one automobile like another automobile, to make them all alike . . . just as one pin is like another pin when it comes from a pin factory," he told John Anderson in 1903.

The day he got rid of Malcolmson and the others in 1906, he told his mechanic Fred Rockelman, "This is a great day. We're going to expand this company, and you will see that it will grow by leaps and bounds. The proper system, as I have it in mind, is to get the car to the multitude."

Of course, there is a big difference between a pin and an automobile. The one is just a piece of metal as simple and functional in design as can be, and though it takes several processes to complete, it is simple to manufacture. The other is intricate and complex, a unified design of myriad smaller designs, each one of which must be not only elegantly functional on its own terms, but able to work perfectly with all the others. To turn out cars one like the other, the minds of men and the functions of their bodies must work together on materials in a grand concert of systematized harmony. To accomplish what he wanted to do, Henry Ford worked to organize the movement of untold numbers of people, materials, and machines toward a particular, dedicated purpose. He succeeded in this, and his method was called at first Fordism, then mass production. It was a movement that was all about movement, and it would change the material and social circumstances of everyone it touched, faster and more fully than any other movement in history. Henry Ford did not create it himself, as its fathers were legion, but he was the master who brought all of its elements together and set it working in the world.

16

The Development
of Mass Production

> I am going to democratize the automobile. When I'm
> through everybody will be able to afford one, and about
> everybody will have one. The horse will have disappeared
> from our highways, and the automobile will be taken for
> granted.
>
> Henry Ford

> Put all your eggs in one basket, and watch
> the basket.
>
> *Puddin' Head Wilson*, Mark Twain

Henry Ford didn't invent the assembly line, which, after all, was only one element of mass production. For that matter, he didn't invent mass production, either. The term *mass production* stands for the culmination of a 120-year-old process that proceeded in fits and starts from French theory through English boatbuilding and Yankee armory shop practice. It was disseminated by mechanics through half a dozen U.S. industries, the last of which was the automobile industry, but its roots went back hundreds of years before that.

The sine qua non of the whole process is interchangeable parts. Unless a manufacturing process has these, mass production can never develop. Johann Guttenberg's invention of moveable type in 1453 was perhaps the earliest important application of the notion of interchangeable parts, though textile printing blocks, stencils for decorating, and dies and stamps for coins were important antecedents of moveable type, as were molds for writing tablets used by the ancient Babylonians.

To have interchangeable parts, you have to have standardization "the principles of which were known to the builders of the pyramids, as well as the textile makers who introduced the factory system to England in the early 16th Century," according to Merrill Denison, author of *The Power To Go*.

In order to proceed on to mass production, standardized interchangeable parts must be used in a process in which they are brought to an object being constructed along a moving line. Around the same time as Guttenberg's invention became known, an early type of moving assembly was used in the construction of warships in Venice. Ship hulls were towed through the Arsenal while various stores and components were fitted onto them. At the finish, the completely fitted galleys were ready for sea duty; as many as ten a day were manufactured in this manner. All these instances were crude but clear precursors of what was to come.

But as John B. Rae points out, the real beginnings of mass production came about with the industrial revolution in the eighteenth century. Perhaps the earliest man to try out predecessor ideas was Christopher Polhem, a Swedish engineer and manufacturer who tried to make iron products with mechanized processes that didn't use skilled workmen. However, because he came before the development of efficient metal working tools, his success was limited. Things go in a more direct line after this.

The great study of the origins and development of mass production is David A. Hounshell's *From the American System to Mass Production, 1800–1932*. As James P. Womack of M.I.T. said to this author, Hounshell put on his miner's hat and went through every seam of every archive to put together a convincing and comprehensive view of the development of this system.

The French, as we have seen, were pioneers in many areas of self-propelled vehicle development, and Hounshell tells us that they were the beginners in mass production too. Fittingly, for we are speaking of the French, they began with Enlightenment theory. "Le système Gribeauval" was propounded by General Jean-Baptiste de Gribeauval, beginning in 1765. He believed that French armaments should be put on a rational basis through the use of standardized weapons with standardized parts. With his "uniformity system" of complete parts interchangeability, he theorized that all arms could be interchanged one for the other, just as soldiers could be interchanged in the same manner. Thus he sent armsmakers and the governments which supported them on a course that would take almost a century to complete.

The fulfillment of Gribeauval's desires came in America, and it was appropriate that America's champion of Enlightenment, Thomas Jefferson, first brought the General's new ideas to his country's attention. While he was minister to France in 1785, he wrote a letter to John Jay telling of the work of Honoré Blanc in the French royal arsenals. Blanc, under Gribeauval's patronage, had produced interchangeable parts for musket locks, and Jefferson enthusiastically described assembling several complete locks himself from the scrambled parts of fifty such locks. Three years later Jefferson spoke with Blanc about moving his operations to the U.S., and wrote a glowing letter about Blanc's work to Secretary of War Henry Knox. But in

1790, after Blanc's funds had been cut off by the Assemblée Nationale in the wake of the Revolution and a move to the U.S. became a real possibility, Knox did not reply to Jefferson's plea to bring him here, and an important early opportunity was lost. But Blanc's ideas were in the air, and by the end of the century the U.S. would start on a quest for interchangeable parts in its arms manufacture.

Of course Americans were quite familiar with French arms practice, as both French military equipment and personnel were important to the American side during the American Revolution. Major Louis de Tousard, who served under Lafayette, fled from the French Revolution to America in 1793, and became a great champion of *le systeme Gribeauval* in the States. In 1798 he wrote a document based on French military-technical experience which became the blueprint for the establishment of the United States Military Academy at West Point; even earlier, at George Washington's urging, he wrote a book on military artillery which was finally published in three volumes as the *American Artillerist's Companion* in 1809. It became the standard textbook for military officers at West Point and elsewhere, and as such its ideas were deeply ingrained in the American military mind. Uniformity was its guiding principle.

Federal armories were established at Springfield, Massachusetts, in 1794, and at Harper's Ferry, New York, in 1798. It was in the latter year that the federal government made a decision of great importance to the future of standardized production. It let out substantial cash advance contracts for the production of small arms with standardized parts, the first to Eli Whitney and the second to Simeon North.

Whitney was advanced $10,000 to deliver 10,000 guns by the middle of 1800, but apparently he set out upon his contract without a clue as to what he was going to do. In fact it was only after the Secretary of the Treasury sent him a pamphlet on foreign arms manufacturing techniques that he even began to espouse the uniformity principle. He also began to talk about special machines to make these uniform parts, "machines for forging, rolling, floating, boring, grinding, polishing, etc."; probably this talk came both from the knowledge that he would have to come up with revolutionary methods to manufacture such machines and a familiarity with nailmaking and other metalworking machines which used these processes.

When his contract reached the end of its term he hadn't produced a single gun, and he devised a scheme to buy time and money through a famous demonstration before congressmen, President Adams and President Elect Jefferson in January, 1801. He assembled ten different locks to the same musket with only a screwdriver, craftily interchanging only the assembled locks, not the lock parts. Taking the bait, Jefferson assumed that the parts were interchangeable as well. Granted new money, Whitney finally began to deliver muskets in the late summer of that year. When he fulfilled his contract at last in 1809, it was with guns of abysmal quality containing no interchangeable parts. As Hounshell puts it, "Whitney was a publicist of mechanized, interchangeable parts, not a creator."

North was another matter. He contracted for five hundred horse pistols, which he delivered in February, 1800. This led to other lucrative government contracts over a period of many years, including a famous 1813 document for 20,000 pistols, specifying that "the component parts of pistols are to correspond so exactly that any limb or part of the pistol may be fitted to any other pistol of the 20,000." This was a first, and shows how far the construction of arms with interchangeable parts had gone by this date.

In building his guns North brought about many innovations. He made interchangeable parts by fitting them to a standard gauge, rather than making them similar to a standard pattern and fitting them by hand to form a unique instrument. He created a system of assembly in which one person worked on great quantities of the same component, thereby saving labor costs and motion. He also created the first kind of special-purpose machinery, a milling machine, which did the work previously accomplished by hand filers. By one of the many quirks of the writing and teaching of history, the public commonly believes that Eli Whitney invented interchangeable parts and was the father of mass production, when in reality much more on this account may be attributed to Simeon North.

In the last analysis however, it was the United States Ordnance Department which was the prime mover in creating interchangeable parts. It provided both the cash and the specifications for manufacturers to work with in creating machines constructed according to an idea that, like many other things in this area, was French by creation and American by adoption.

Innovations followed hard upon North's work. In 1822 Thomas Blanchard patented a sequential battery of 14 machines for turning gunstocks, virtually eliminating hand labor. The heart of the sequence was the Blanchard lathe, an invention that could reproduce in wood the shape of any irregularly shaped object, such as, in this case, a gunstock. His immediate inspiration was a machine he created in 1818 to turn musket barrels, which are flat and oval, rather than cylindrical, at the breech end. Blanchard used the desired irregular form as a cam in his manufacture.

Without any problem Blanchard acknowledged important sources for his battery invention in his patent application. He knew that Diderot's *Encyclopedie* contained descriptions of turning regular forms by lathe, and he knew of the English work of Marc I. Brunel, Samuel Bentham, and Henry Maudslay, who had a factory in Portsmouth which turned out blocks for the Royal Navy without the use of skilled labor. They had forty-five machines of twenty-two different kinds which sawed, drilled, mortised, recessed, turned, and shaped the shells and sheaves of wooden blocks. With ten unskilled employees, they turned out 130,000 blocks a year, in three different sizes.

But Blanchard's contribution is original, because neither the French nor the English used lathes or any other kinds of machines to turn irregular objects.

In the 1820s John Hall's Rifle Works became an inside contractor at the Harper's Ferry Armory. In addition to using sixty-three different gauges in three sets (work, inspection, and master) to create a far greater manufacturing precision than had ever been known before, Hall set forth the principle of fixture design, one of the basic tenets of precision manufacture. Fixtures are devices that secure objects during machining. To eliminate constantly increasing inaccuracy as each object of his manufacture was fixed several times as it was processed, he proposed that each piece should be located in each fixture relative to one point on the piece, which he called the bearing point. All fixtures for a part, he reasoned, should be constructed relative to that bearing point. Hall's ingenious principle was universally adopted, and became one of the basic tenets of mass production.

It was at the Harper's Ferry Armory, that the basic principles of what became known in the 1850s as the American system of manufactures came together for the first time. This involved interchangeable parts made through a combination of jigs, fixtures, and gauges; sequentially arranged special-purpose machinery; and the use of unskilled, rather than skilled, workers in the manufacturing process (skill came to bear in the construction and maintenance of machines, not in their operation). It was called the American system to distinguish it from the European and British system of manufacture, which called for the extensive use of highly skilled hand labor, the result of centuries of craft training and guild organization. (Indeed, it was the British and continental prejudice for their ancient system of production which gave America the lead in the world automobile business after 1906.) But Hounshell is right in saying the American system should more properly be called the "armory system" or "armory practice," because that indeed was where it originated and developed. It is interesting to note that the desire for uniform products originated in the military mind, and that the uniform system of manufacture which resulted from it has very much of a military simplicity, economy, and discipline as its hallmarks.

Soon the American system began to spread, first to other armories and then beyond to other industries. The Springfield Armory took up Hall's improvements quickly, just as previously improvements had circulated swiftly between the two armories as well as among patent arms manufacturers.

In 1855 Samuel Colt opened what he called the largest, most modern private armory in the world in Hartford, Connecticut. Colt had patented the revolving pistol in 1835 and formed two different firms to produce them since then. At his new armory he hired Elisha K. Root, a famous mechanic and inventor who had manufactured axes at the Collins Company with great success. Root applied seventeen years of axe-making experience to die making and the drop forging of revolver parts. His techniques were heavily involved with special-purpose machinery, and soon after the new armory's opening some 400 machines performed over 350 machining operations in the construction of each Colt revolver; later 1,500 machines, each made in the Colt shops, turned out the guns.

Colt's major contribution to mass production wasn't his production techniques, however. It was the fact that many brilliant mechanics worked out problems of parts manufacture as sub- or inside contractors at Colt, then left to exploit their newfound knowledge in other businesses in the outside world. Pratt & Whitney and the Weed Sewing Machine Company were just two of the myriad firms that came into existence through the application of principles learned at the Colt Armory. Though the inside contract system, in which a contractor hired and paid his own staff and was responsible for their work, was a long-standing fixture of New England manufacturing, its particular application at Colt, along with highly developed drop forging, machine milling, special-purpose machinery, turret lathes, and rational fixtures and gauges, can be said to represent the ultimate expression of the American system; indeed, Englishmen often referred to it as "Colonel Colt's system of manufacturing."

Of course the armory system wasn't developing in a vaccuum. Root's axes helped it along, and many other items such as nails, barrels, pins, locks, clocks, knives, and swords were produced by mechanical processes outside the armory system. The manufacturers of these items, especially the clockmakers, differed from armorers in that they had to develop extensive private markets, rather than selling all of their products to the government. Also unlike the armorers, they needed to develop economies of scale to keep prices down and increase sales and production to make a profit.

A good example was Connecticut clockmaker Eli Terry. He used the Yankee peddler system to distribute large quantities of his goods, and in the process created installment selling as a marketing device. At $25, Terry's clocks were rather expensive for families in the early nineteenth century, but still, many people who couldn't afford to lay out this sum in advance nevertheless wanted a clock for their parlors. So the peddlers, who extended credit for one or even two years, went around both adjusting clocks and collecting payments at the same time. Little is known of Terry's production practices, but it is sure that he mechanized them both to increase output and lower the cost of his goods to the public. In many ways the sewing machine industry, the reaper business, and later the bicycle industry and others owed more to the clockmakers for their development than to the armsmakers. All needed to create a profitable market for their goods, and such necessity dictated much about successful business practices to them.

The development of the sewing machine embodies some of the most important trends in the progress of nineteenth-century American manufacturing. Perhaps its greatest contribution was The Great Sewing Machine

Combination, the first major patent pooling agreement in American history. Elias Howe contributed his basic 1846 patent for a grooved needle with an eye point, used in conjunction with a lock stitch forming shuttle. Allen B. Wilson's 1854 patent on a four motion cloth feeding mechanism went into the pool, as did many patents from I. M. Singer & Company, including one on the needle bar cam (1851). The man who constructed the pool, Orlando Potter, added patents from his Grover and Baker Sewing Machine Company. Pool members could use the various companies' patents freely, and other companies could license them for $15 per machine. This arrangement ended confusion about manufacturing techniques by allowing companies to choose their own technologies without fear of lawsuits or reprisals.

Sewing machines were not inexpensive (Wheeler & Wilson sold them complete for $125 in 1853, the equivalent of thousands in today's money), and once the patent problems were settled in the mid-1850s, they were in great demand, so the sewing machine industry was an exploding, profitable business. From producing just a few hundred units per annum in the early 1850s, Wheeler & Wilson grew to a production of 174,000 by 1872. Though its machines were hand made early on, rapidly increasing demand soon caused the company to hire armory trained workers who introduced armory practice to the production of Wheeler & Wilson's products.

A much smaller company, Willcox & Gibbs, was formed to exploit its patented 1858 machine which used a single thread to make a chain stitch rather than a shuttle or rotary hook with bobbin to make a lock stitch. These machiness could be made and sold for much less than previous ones. The company contracted with Brown & Sharpe of Providence, Rhode Island, to produce its machines. Though it was a small firm that had previously only done custom work on mostly precision instruments, Brown & Sharpe immediately decided to produce the Willcox & Gibbs's machines by means of armory practice. Starting from scratch, it wasn't easy or quick for Brown & Sharpe to get production up and running, but its implicit faith in this method of manufacture eventually worked out very well. The Willcox & Gibbs sewing machine had an excellent reputation for quality and sold briskly, though in quantities that were only a fraction of the major companies' production.

Perhaps Brown & Sharpe's greatest contribution was its 1872 acquisition of the services of Henry M. Leland, known as the Master of Precision and inventor of both the Cadillac and Lincoln automobiles. (Leland named the latter car after Abraham Lincoln, the first president he voted for.) A veteran of both the Springfield and Colt armories and several famous machine shops, Leland's contribution was his interest in, and refinement of, manufacturing processes. At Brown & Sharpe, he developed much better grinding machines, eliminated a contract system in favor of a much more efficient piecework system, and instituted a strict procedural approach to manufacture. By recording all operations on paper, Leland's foremen were able to follow the work more closely and move materials more quickly and smoothly in their proper sequence. After he established his own shop, Leland & Faulconer, in the 1890s, his superb reputation for high standards of precision in manufacturing eventually led him to become one of the most important figures in the strengthening and consolidation of the automobile industry.

What the largest of the sewing machine companies, Singer Manufacturing Company, proved was that the armory system was not the only way to build and sell vast quantities of consumer goods, for Singer produced millions of its machines by the old-fashioned European methods, only slowly combined with armory practice, to become far and away the largest and most successful manufacturer of sewing machines. By 1880, it was making over 500,000 a year at a huge profit; its machines were sold at five to ten times their cost. Singer bought parts from jobbers and fitted them together at the bench, believing that this was the best way to assure the highest quality, in direct opposition to the beliefs of Willcox & Gibbs. It refined its processes of manufacturing only when the pressures of massively excessive demand forced it to, and in the meantime it made its fortunes through the use of advertising and marketing—eventually a major contribution to extending the system of mass production.

Singer's production, though huge, was not mass production but quantity production, and there is a big difference. As Cleveland and Williamson pointed out in 1950, 27 million cows can give 60 million tons of milk a year, and that is quantity production, but only about 20 auto plants produce 16 million cars a year, and that is through the benefit of mass production, which substitutes power for labor. Quantity production has its limits, which Singer slowly discovered. It is labor intensive and expensive, and most important, inaccurate on a large scale. The company had to maintain a huge repair department to deal with all the problems that showed up in its machines. Despite the fact that all of its major executives were "up from the bench," expanding production forced the company to introduce machine tools gradually into the construction of its goods.

Beginning with the purchase of ten milling machines from the Manhattan Firearms Company in 1863, Singer slowly began to bring machine tools into its factories, until by 1880 it was filled with all types of such instruments. By 1873 the company was so sold on the advantages of interchangeable parts that it specified them in a contract with an outside supplier, the Providence Tool Company, for production of its popular Domestic sewing machine. It was not until 1881 though that complete interchangeability was achieved in Singer's own plants.

In between these two dates the company used a combination of armory and European practices to get the results it wanted; this was due to the failure of Providence Tool to produce machines of sufficient quality to satisfy Singer officials. Symbolically, sometime during this period Singer changed the name of the department where the sewing machines were put together from the fitting department to the assembly department, though it appears some fitting was still done until the mid-1880s. In fact it wasn't until 1883 that company management finally decreed that every part should be finished to gauge in its own department and ready for assembly, and that nothing should be made where the final machine was to be assembled. Even then there was still some measuring going on in various departments because the company used absolute gauges rather than the limit gauges of a rational gauge system until 1886.

During the 1880s Singer's production spiraled ever upward, to a peak of a million sewing machines a year. During its dizzying climb, the company wound up pushing the American system of manufacture to its utmost limits, due to the technological imperative necessitated by relentlessly increasing demand. The next leap forward, into better, simpler technologies and continuous flow, was beyond this business, possibly because it could never completely escape its origins at the bench. Another industry would take up the standard as the direct precursor to true mass production. Before we go into it, there are two interesting sidelines.

One is the woodworking industry. There was quantity, but never mass production in the wooden clock business, in part because it was superceded by the brass clock industry by 1837, before vast numbers of clocks were produced. Mass production techniques never really caught on in the manufacture of furniture or housing either, despite a large and rising demand for both items. Some thought it was because of the very nature of wood. It was reasoned that there were no improvements to be made in the woodworking industry after the implementation of machines to replace hand work, since woodworking was not a heat-using industry, like metalworking. But the real reason was that the products of both the furniture and housing businesses were considered by their consumers to be durable goods whose form was a deeply personal expression of their owners' tastes, social position, and aspirations. No one wanted a sofa that was exactly like a million others, which was quite different from what they wanted in a sewing machine, whose main qualification was that it would work. Someone might not object to standardized outside panel sizes in a house, but that was only a small element of its total cost. Everyone had his own ideas of what a house should look like and how it should function inside, and that is where the real costs came in. Mass production is impossible without a simplified, standardized product, and therein lay these two industries' real dilemma. Furthermore, housing assembly must be done on site, so even when gangs of dedicated workers built standardized housing elements into large numbers of homes at Levittown in the late 1940s, the bench type of assembly used of necessity was far from a mass production technique.

The other important woodworking industry was the wagon business. While also a quantity production industry it was technologically advanced, and before it was finished it drew near to the processes of mass production, even if it never really achieved them.

The Studebaker wagon works, begun in 1852, was located in South Bend, Indiana, nearby to the factory that Singer had established to manufacture its sewing machine cabinets. Henry and Clement, blacksmiths, were brothers who founded the company; later, several other brothers became involved. Studebaker Brothers benefitted from an abundant supply of nearby timber and the availability of special purpose wagonmaking machinery, particularly wheelmaking machinery. This machinery was developed to satisfy the needs of ever more numerous small-town wheelwrights, who were no longer in a position to make entire vehicles by themselves. Thus the Studebakers did not have to devote their energies to creating their own machinery, and could concentrate on production.

At the incorporation of the Studebaker Brothers Manufacturing Company in 1868 the company was turning out 4,000 vehicles a year; six years later, production had risen to 11,050. An 1874 fire allowed them to build a completely new plant, and through a strict, controlled adherence to an American system of manufacture, they were able to bring the cost of their wagons down from $140 to $70 apiece, while at the same time improving quality.

Studebaker Brothers was always at the leading edge of technology, constantly aware of the latest developments in other industries, and seeking to adapt them to its own. For instance, it began using resistance welding and sheet steel construction of important metal parts as it became aware of the usefulness of these techniques in wagon manufacture. The success and growing effectiveness of its methods can be seen in the fact that while 190 people were required to manufacture those 4,000 vehicles in 1868, only 1,900 built 75,000 of them in 1895. Altogether Studebaker Brothers built one million horse-drawn vehicles over forty-three years, before it decided to concentrate completely on automobile manufacture in 1911. Though its products were constructed primarily of wood, such a record would not have been possible without many of the practices, and much of the philosophy, of armory practice.

The woodworking industry did get involved with mass production, however. After all, those millions of sewing machines needed and got cabinets made of wood, and Singer and others were able to mechanize their construction extensively, eventually using heat methods of laminating and forming wood; in the 1920s and 1930s the radio industry would do the same. The point is that these items were simple, low-end furniture items without much individuation, the opposite of what was the case with furniture and housing. So as far as mass production was concerned, the market determined what was possible in the woodworking industry. Without a developed market, there is no need for mass production in any field.

The second sideline involves the legendary McCormick Reaper, the great anomaly in the history of mass production. It has an entirely unearned reputation as a landmark in the development of this system. In the first place, the interactions of a reaper's parts are not upon one another but upon soil and crops, so interchangeability of parts with precise fit was not a priority in its construction. Also, special-purpose machinery for these machines was not available, so Cyrus McCormick had to rely on general-purpose machinery manipulated by skilled machinists in its building processes. This, coupled with constant changes and new models, some for genuine improvements and some just because the farmers wanted them, made the reaper far from an ideal candidate for armory production practices.

Until about 1880 the company was run like a big blacksmith shop by Cyrus McCormick's brother Leander, whose only previous experience had been as a country blacksmith. Cyrus McCormick was a great believer in publicity, and as with the Singer sewing machine, great demand for his reaper was built up in this way. But as Hounshell points out, the McCormick reaper, bench built as it was, was not a model in any manufacturing sense; it was "an ephemeral machine, a marketing rather than a manufacturing concept."

Only after a rift between the brothers did the company move into modern practice. Leander was fired in April, 1880, and production was put in the hands of Lewis Wilkinson, an experienced worker at various armories, sewing machine, and other companies back east. Though superintendent of the McCormick works in Chicago for only a year, he taught Cyrus McCormick, Jr., the rudiments of armory practice during that time, and sold him on the validity of such methods. When Cyrus Jr., took over as supervisor in 1881, the new system was firmly in place, and production increased by almost 50 percent; the next year it increased by that amount again, to over 46,000 units.

Because of the wonder people felt at the reaper, they were led to assume early on that it was produced by modern armory methods. But in reality it took over forty years and a basic management change for that to become true. As is true in many other aspects of history, the legend remains fixed in many minds, long after it has been effectively debunked.

(There was one important contribution the McCormick reaper made to the history of mass production, however: labor unrest. By 1885 the skilled workmen long employed at the factory were chafing under the increasing control of their work processes that the new system entailed. The molders, joined by machinists and other metalworkers, went on strike at that time, resulting in the famous Haymarket Riot. As David Hounshell points out, "The hardware, processes, and customs of the armory system provided powerful instruments of control over labor. When they were installed suddenly, such as at McCormick, strife was bound to result.")

❖   ❖   ❖

The last stop on the path to full-fledged mass production was the bicycle industry. Invented, once again, by the French, the bicycle was originally a velocipede, with a huge high wheel in front and a small trailing wheel behind. It was dangerous to ride, and only used by brave and agile men. Since it was expensive too, it had a limited market. Still, between 1876, when Colonel Albert A. Pope brought the velocipede from England and began making it here, and 1887, when the safety bicycle was introduced, he and a few other manufacturers turned out about 250,000 of these machines. From 1887 on the bicycle market exploded, since the new safety bicycle, coupled with the pneumatic tire, meant that everyone, including women and children, could ride bicycles easily and safely. Increased production efficiency and volume brought prices down so that large numbers of people could afford them.

From the beginning, the Pope Manufacturing Company was an armory-type manufacturing organization. Colonel Pope contracted with the Weed Sewing Machine Company of Hartford, Connecticut, to build his machines; this company, ten years earlier, had contracted with the Sharps Rifle Manufacturing Company to manufacture its sewing machines in the self same factory. When Sharps moved from Hartford to Bridgeport in 1875, Weed took over Sharps' plant, machines, and many of its employees to manufacture its own sewing machines. So the armory tradition of manufacture can be traced through in a single line in the same plant from arms to sewing machines to bicycles (and eventually to automobiles when Pope began to manufacture them too). The technologies of these various industries commingled as production problems were worked out on the same machines in the same place. However, the only important innovation introduced by the bicycle at this time was the ball bearing, the use of which was to spread through all types of manufacturing.

Pope's great and lasting contribution at this time was in the area of marketing. He sponsored books, periodicals, and clubs all dedicated to proselytizing the good news about the bicycle. He also sponsored monthly bicycle poster contests, which perfected this very popular nineteenth-century form of advertising (Maxfield Parrish would later win one of Pope's poster contests in 1895, and see his work and that of many others exhibited in special showings around the country). The result of this activity was that Pope's annual sales of 1,200 in 1880 increased to 1,200 a month by the middle of 1881.

Most importantly, he started a bicycle trade show in Springfield, Massachusetts, in 1883. An instant hit, such gatherings brought together exhibitors, sales agents, journalists, and the paying public, and were excellent means of disseminating information about the bicycle. In 1896 the Chicago bicycle show drew 225 exhibitors and 100,000 visitors, while the one in New York attracted 120,000 people to 400 exhibits.

With the safety bicycle came two major new manufacturing techniques. The first was resistance welding, developed by Elihu Thompson between 1886 and 1888. This automated one of the most difficult tasks of blacksmithing. Weed used this technology as soon as it became available, to weld bicycle rims for Pope's famed Columbia models.

The other innovation came from an entirely different tradition in bicycle manufacture. Sheet-steel stamping of parts came from the Western Wheel Works of Chicago. This company, like all the other bicycle manufacturers in the West, did not come from the armory tradition. It had been the manufacturer of toy wooden wagons; others came from the ranks of toy and novelty specialists; had been wagon, carriage, or agricultural implement makers; or were entirely new enterprises. All worked mostly in wood. When metal wheel rims almost totally replaced wooden ones in the early 1890s, these companies began to make them, and soon turned to manufacturing entire bicycles. Since none of them had been used to working in metal, they had to learn the techniques of working with it from scratch. Instead of using forgings, they decided to make their bicycles from pressed steel.

Beginning with pressed frame joints imported from Germany, Western Wheel soon developed its own techniques for working with pressed steel and found American toolmakers who could build equipment to its specifications. By 1896 almost every part of its fast-selling Crescent model was made of this material. Sheet steel, combined with resistance welding, meant that there was practically no machining to be done, and it made workers far more productive, since many never had to leave their seats at the machines to make adjustments. A constant stream of material was brought to these workers by runners; possibly, as Hounshell suggests, Western Wheel might have developed a conveyor system for this factory function if the bicycle business had not collapsed suddenly and completely in 1897. In any case, Western Wheel's production methods brought prices way down.

At its height, the bicycle business produced 1.2 million vehicles a year. For a while Western Wheel, with its new techniques, outproduced everyone, even Pope. But Pope, with ever-improving systems and quality control, was able to keep almost even with Western Wheel in its output. Both claimed their systems led to superior-quality products, though by objective standards Pope's product was clearly better. The ultimate question in all of this was whether Western's quality, though not as good as Pope's, was nevertheless good enough for all practical purposes.

Some years back the 3M Company was capable of producing a hair set-ting lotion that would allow a woman's hairstyle to last for three weeks or more. But beauticians didn't want it because it cut into their weekly busi-ness, and their customers didn't want it because it promoted unsanitary conditions and took away the pleasure and novelty of getting a new weekly hairdo. The weaker, cheaper products of competitors amply fulfilled the needs of the marketplace, and the 3M product disappeared in short order. In a similar vein the "good enough" quality of Western Wheel's product, coupled with the lower prices it allowed, might have forced Pope either into a decline or to follow Western Wheel's lead. The industry collapse rendered the issue moot, but it would come up again in the automobile business.

Because of the bicycle, people learned to want individual transportation; because it was so widely disseminated, they learned to want something not only fast but cheap. From its origins as a rich man's toy, it became an ordinary expectation of the common man. This couldn't have happened without the technology to make it possible to turn out large numbers of good-quality machines at low prices. The same would occur with the au-tomobile, but not without the tremendous leaps of faith, organization, and vision that Henry Ford would eventually bring to its production. Fordism took the strains of all the predecessor industries of the automobile and combined them with new techniques to create the system-market that is now known as mass production.

Henry Ford wanted to turn the automobile from a plaything of the rich into a general utility for everyman. However, in order to do so, the first thing he needed was the right car. He got it with the Model T.

Charles Sorensen, Ford's production manager, said that the inspiration for the T came from Ford's experiments with vanadium, a steel alloy, and heat-treated steels. He realized that with them he could make much stronger, lighter, and faster cars than any built before. As he envisioned employing these new materials in a completely new car, his enthusiasm grew. Joseph Galamb, the engineer in charge of the Model T project, said Ford sketched out his idea for the new design on a blackboard and came in at seven or eight o'clock each night to check on the progress being made with it. By the end of 1907 the designers were working until ten or eleven all the time. "Mr. Ford followed out the design very closely and was there practically all the time," said Galamb. "There was a rocking chair in the room in which he used to sit for hours and hours at a time, discussing and following out the development of the design." The rocking chair had been his mother's.

The final product was filled with innovations. All the cylinders in the engine were cast in a single block with a separate, bolted-down cylinder head on top, creating the basic configuration of the modern internal-combustion engine. The transmission was a refinement of an old system using continuously circulating fabric bands. In its final form it was the renowned planetary transmission, a primitive sort of automatic device operated by pedals, one each for forward, reverse, and braking. Once mastered, it was capable of a considerable range of movements. In place of the dry batteries then in use, the Model T had a device called a magneto, a heavy flywheel with sixteen copper coils and magnets studded over its surface. It produced sparks for the cylinders, a first for a low-priced car. Ford himself came up with the idea for a baked-on varnish that made the magneto trouble-free. The Model T's body and springs were designed to keep the car high off the ground, making it ideal for the muddy roads of the rural areas Ford's farmer customers lived in. Finally, there were two sets of brakes, one that operated through the transmission and another, completely independent emergency set for the rear wheels.

The vanadium steel that had so captured Ford's interest was used extensively in constructing the Model T. Until Henry Ford encouraged a small company in Canton, Ohio, to experiment with vanadium, no one in the United States knew how to alloy it with steel. It made possible extraordinarily strong, flexible, and lightweight machine parts, and could be found in the crankshafts, springs, axles, and gears of the Model T. Also, through the influence of Sorensen, for the first time lightweight pressed steel casings protected the engine, transmission, and other mechanical parts of the car against mud, dust, weather, and the myriad shocks of abysmal contemporary driving conditions. The ones for the rear steel axle housings manufactured by Keim Mills of Buffalo were modeled on the bell-shaped telephone receiver. These features of the Model T, combined with its transverse springs and very "loose" wheels, gave it an extraordinary flexibility perfectly suited to the rural roads and farms where most Americans lived until the 1920s. Most T's were sold to and used by farmers, and Ford designed his car primarily with these customers in mind.

The Model T was introduced on October 1, 1908, little more than two weeks after General Motors' incorporation on September 16 of that year. It turned out to be so good that not only farmers but practically everyone else bought one as a first automobile. The advertising claim that "no car under $2,000 offers more" was absolutely correct; for a price that began at $950 in 1908 and sank to as low as $260 fifteen years later, customers bought what was not only the strongest, most durable car on the market but also the most advanced. It was the only truly revolutionary car ever built in America, in that it turned the car from a luxury into a utility, and, in the space of ten years, replaced the horse and wagon as the primary means of personal transportation in this country. Concepts of mobility, time, and distance were altered, and American society was forever transformed from a rural entity into an urban one.

"You know, Henry," a farm wife from Rome, Georgia, wrote to him in 1918, "your car lifted us out of the mud. It brought joy into our lives. We love every rattle in its bones." But the rich and famous also viewed it with the same affection. Author E. B. White christened his "Hotspur" and drove it across the country in 1922, on completely unpaved roads along the stretch from Minnesota to Spokane. John Steinbeck had one, as did another eventual Nobel Prize laureate, Sinclair Lewis, whose wife claimed his Model T gave him more pleasure than that august honor ever did. "Gertrude Stein loved her Model T, demonstrating her liberation by driving it through the the snow and mud of Flanders, where she served as a volunteer nurse during the First World War. . . . According to Ernest Hemingway, Stein's famous phrase about a lost generation, *une generation perdue*, originally came from a French garage owner's diatribe against a young mechanic who had failed to look after Miss Stein's Ford properly" (Lacey).

Many people treated the Model T like a member of the family, just as they had the horse which it replaced. It was given names, mostly female, the most famous of which was the immortal sobriquet, "Tin Lizzie." Humor about the model T abounded, all of it encouraged by Henry Ford, who knew it was good, amiable, free publicity. Songs like "Your Tin Lizzie Mamma's Gonna Reel You In" and "The Packard And The Ford" (they got together and had a little Buick) were amusing novelties. Stephen W. Sears's *The Automobile In America* lists thirty-one titles under the heading "Labels for Lizzie"; Some of the better ones are: "I Do Not Choose To Run"; "Abandon Hope All Ye Who Enter"; "Capacity 5 Gals"; "The Mayflower—Many A Puritan Has Come Across In It"; "Quiet Please, Violent Ward"; "The Tin You Love To Touch"; "You May Pass Me, Big Boy, But I'm Paid For"; "If We Had Milk And Sugar, It Would Be A Milk Shake"; "Barnum Was Right"; and "Don't Laugh Girls, Think How You Would Look Without Paint." Perhaps the ultimate tribute to the Model T was paid in this immortal parody of Rudyard Kipling's *Gunga Din* published in the *American Field Service Bulletin*:

"Yes, Tin, Tin, Tin,
You exasperating puzzle, Hunka Tin,
I've abused you and I've flayed you,
But by Henry Ford who made you,
You are better than a Packard, Hunka Tin."

As with any such legend, myths abound about the Model T. One of the most important was exposed as such by David Hounshell. This was the notion that it did not change from its introduction in 1908 until its demise in 1927. In fact, practically every part of it was modified in some way to improve production techniques, to keep up with improvements in auto design, or to adjust to the incorporation of these changes, and at an ever-decreasing price. But change was not what the company was selling, so it was done on the q.t. over the years. Henry Ford has often been criticized for being unwilling to change the Model T. However, although it eventually came to seem staid and old fashioned, it was not a static product. Ford simply made a marketing decision not to inform the public of this fact.

To achieve his goal of bringing the Model T to the masses, Henry Ford had to have something besides a wonderful product. He needed a system to bring it to the people, and that, in its fullest flowering, turned out to be mass production.

"Henry Ford had no ideas on mass production. He wanted to build a lot of autos. He was determined, but like every one else at that time, he didn't know how. In later years he was glorified as the originator of the mass production idea. Far from it; he just grew into it, like the rest of us. The essential tools and the final assembly line with its many integrated feeders resulted from an organization which was continually experimenting and improvising to get better production." So said "Cast Iron Charlie" Charles Sorensen in his 1956 book *My Forty Years With Ford*. As Ford's production man, he was the most important man in the entire organization, next to Ford himself. What he says here is spot-on accurate.

Mass production was the end result of the refinements of armory and other production practices which took place over a period of 115 years, coupled with unique twentieth-century innovations. The final stages of the process were the work of about a dozen men who combined their extraordinary skills in a concerted effort to bring mass production to its ultimate fruition. Henry Ford was only one of them, and in a funny way, his greatest contribution, like Billy Durant's, was as an idea man. He was the symbol for Fordism, not in the strict sense its creator. The others, out in the trenches, did the actual job. As David L. Lewis notes in *The Public Image of Henry Ford*, the Reverend Doctor Samuel S. Marquis, a close, observant friend of Ford's and head of the company's Sociological Department until 1921, stated: "The wise Ford official, when handed "bouquets" for an achievement, hastily tossed them over to Henry, and when there was no one around, explained to him what it was all about. And Henry kept the flowers."

Even the world-famous article explaining Fordism which appeared in the 1926 edition of the *Encyclopedia Brittanica* was written by someone else. William Cameron, the editor of Ford's notorious *Dearborn Independent* newspaper ("The best weekly ever turned out by a tractor plant," according to *Detroit Saturday Night*) was the one who wrote that piece. Cameron was later to say that not only had Ford not written the article, but he doubted he had ever even read it.

The Henry Ford we know, or think we know, was in part a figure created by his own mythomania. In addition to accepting bouquets for things he didn't do, he went back over his life and reimagined it for public consumption, cleverly disseminating the new, improved version everywhere and in all media so well that generations of the public came to believe in it as history written in cement. Still, he was not unique among great men in doing this, and in the last analysis he made contributions that were both real and indelible.

As early as 1902, when others thought him a crackpot, he wanted to build a universal vehicle to replace the family horse. He stuck with his idea even when all others who had it, like Olds, Hupp (Ford later said "I recall looking at Bobby Hupp's roadster at the first show where it was exhibited and wondered whether we could ever build as good a small car for as little money"), Buick, and E.M.F. one by one moved out of the production of small, light vehicles to concentrate on building larger, more expensive ones. Ford participated in and oversaw the design of what became his universal car. He wanted, oversaw, permitted, and paid for the system that brought it to the masses. And he and he alone was responsible for the extraordinary advances in social thinking which completed the mass production process by making it possible to deliver his product into the hands of the very people who made it, which included anyone, absolutely anyone, regardless of race, color, creed, sex, physical handicap, educational or national background, who wanted a job and could do the work. The automobile was the first large machine ever that could be bought by the workers who made it. Ford's idea, and its instrumentation to completion, was a revolution in human history, the most profound since 1789.

Anterior to his own organization, there were two other factors that were vital to the development of his work, both involving quality and standardization of materials.

He couldn't have done it without Henry Martyn Leland, who was called the Master of Precision because of his complete dedication to and unbending insistence on the utter interchangeability of parts in building automobiles. From Civil War work at the Springfield Armory through many years of sewing machine manufacture at Brown & Sharpe and his own firm of Leland & Faulconer, Leland's obsession was to create ever higher standards of manufacture through better parts and better systems.

Among his innovations was the introduction of the Swedish Johansson Standard Gauging System to America in 1896. This very expensive system, which was a great improvement over anything that preceded it, worked with exact and unchanging permanence. It consisted of jewel-like steel blocks, kept in a velvet case, that were accurate to millionths of an inch. Characteristically, this gave his firm's products a precision vastly superior to anything else on the market.

Crabb speaks of an incident in which he threw an entire day's production of his firm's castings on the floor; those which remained unbroken, he considered good enough. When the workers complained to his partner Faulconer, Leland's reply "was the manifesto of the yet unborn automobile industry: 'There always was and there always will be a conflict between "good" and "good enough," and in opening up a new business or a new department one can count upon meeting this resistance to high standards of workmanship. It is easy to get (worker) cooperation for mediocre work, but one must sweat blood for a chance to produce a superior product.'" In short order there were no broken castings on the foundry floor.

The Dodge Brothers witnessed this event, and Henry Ford heard about it, as did every machinist in Detroit. Soon firms were willing to pay three times the going rate for L & F castings, which wouldn't break even if they were *indavertently* dropped on a shop floor.

Leland proceeded from manufacturing bicycle and auto parts of the highest quality to manufacturing Cadillacs. By 1908, these vehicles were advertised as "the Standard of the World," due to winning the English Dewar's Trophy given for standardization of parts. On February 29th of that year three Cadillacs were driven around the Brooklands racetrack, completely diassembled, and their parts were mixed together along with sixty-five brand new parts. Three cars were then reassembled from the pile, driven 500 miles and shown to perform up to new car standards. No other car in the world could then have matched that performance, and Cadillac's already fine reputation was greatly enhanced.

Sometime before this, Alfred P. Sloan, who later as President and Chairman of General Motors introduced both flexible mass production and the basic structure of the modern corporation, had an encounter with Leland which profoundly affected his life. He describes it in his book, *My Years with General Motors*. Sloan got to know the automobile business and automobile men by selling them his Hyatt Roller Bearings to use in their cars. One day during a call on Leland, he measured Sloan's bearing with calipers and said, "Mr. Sloan, Cadillacs are made to run, not just to sell. You must grind your bearings. Even though you make thousands, the first and last must be precisely alike." Sloan reflects: "A genuine conception of what mass production meant really grew in me with that conversation."

Industry standards of interchangeability might also have taken much longer to develop without Albert B. Selden. He was a clever patent lawyer from Rochester, New York, who, having seen the Brayton engine at the 1876 Centennial exhibition in Philadelphia, made a mental leap to imagine it as the motive power behind a self-propelled vehicle. He made a patent application for such a vehicle on May 5, 1879, and as was then permitted, he developed his patent over the next sixteen years, incorporating any new improvements he heard about. Selden knew delay was important, as a patent lasted only for seventeen years and this one could not be brought to account unless the automobile were sufficiently advanced to have a commercial application. The patent was finally granted on November 11, 1895.

Four years later Anthony F. Brady, the Wall Street financier, entered the picture. He was involved with Colonel Pope in the Electric Vehicle Company, which sought to put electric cabs on the streets of New York. The venture was not going well, and in desperation the company acquired Selden's patent, hoping to make money licensing gas autos. It wasn't easy in the beginning.

Early in 1903, the Association of Licensed Automobile Manufacturers was formed after suits for patent violation against Winton and others were won by Electric Vehicle, which charged a 5 percent royalty on each car manufactured under its license. Winton and nine others, including Olds, joined up and paid their royalties. Eventually, more than one hundred manufacturers were included. A.L.A.M. did perform a very useful function, in that it set standards for automobile manufacture. Previously, it seemed that every mechanic with a pile of parts and a barn was manufacturing cars willy nilly, with no real idea of how to do it well. A manufacturer had to prove to A.L.A.M. that it knew what it was doing before it was allowed to join the organization.

Eventually James Joy at Packard and Leland at Cadillac succeeded in having the royalties on the patent reduced to 1.25 percent; later they fell to .8 percent. More significantly, Joy and Leland got Electric Vehicle to divert 2/5 of its royalties to A.L.A.M. With this new financial backing, A.L.A.M. broadened from a mere protective group into something larger which performed a variety of functions. Among them was the setting up of a mechanical department, which paralled and later merged with the American Society of Automotive Engineers, subsequently known simply as the S.A.E.

Early in its existence A.L.A.M. made a foolish move which would eventually prove fatal to it. Fred Smith of Oldsmobile, A.L.A.M.'s acting president, turned down Ford's inquiry about membership. He claimed that the Ford was just an assembled car, not up to A.L.A.M. standards. Incensed, Ford and Couzens invited a lawsuit, which was enjoined and continued flagrantly and famously until 1911. The lawsuit, which loomed large over Ford's future, was probably the main reason why Ford twice considered selling his company to Billy Durant's new General Motors combine. At a low ebb on September 15, 1909, a New York Circuit Court ruled against Ford, but on January 9, 1911 he was finally vindicated. On that date the Court of Appeals ruled that Selden's patent, though valid, was based on the two-cycle Brayton engine, not the four-cycle Otto engine which was the basis of all manufactured gasoline autos that had been subject to the patent's licensing claims. The struggle and the victory made Ford a folk hero and famous public figure for the first time—in the public eye he was the man who fought the "Motor Trust," and won.

The A.L.A.M. collapsed around the time of Ford's victory, but a new organization to continue some of its positive contributions was organized in 1913. This was the Automobile Chamber of Commmerce, later the National Automobile Chamber of Commerce, which changed its name to the Automobile Manufacturers' Association in 1934. Ford never joined any of these organizations, even after the N.A.C.C. gave a huge banquet in his honor in 1928.

The main benefit of this organization was the cross licensing of patents, which was controlled by the patents department of the N.A.C.C. Though not a member, Ford offered free access to his patents to anyone, and assumed the same privilege from N.A.C.C. members. It was an amicable arrangement.

The S.A.E., of which Ford was a member, was even more significant in clearing up car production standards and bringing a necessary universality to the industry; certainly it encouraged and expanded Leland's quest for standard manufacturing practices, without which mass production of automobiles could never have developed.

The early days of car production are well characterized by James P. Womack in his book *The Machine that Changed the World*. Skilled workers employed by independent contractors or machine shop owners made special parts and components for cars. There was no standard gauging system, and in addition machine tools of the time couldn't cut hardened steel, not to mention that steel pieces warped as they were baked. All these factors produced highly irregular parts. At the carmaker's assembly plant they were then filed by still other skilled machinists until they fit. Sequential fitting produced dimensional creep, and each of these craft-built vehicles differed significantly in dimension from others built to the same blueprints. Consistency and reliability were elusive, causing much trepidation among car buyers, especially when the auto began to spread beyond wealthy customers who had trained chauffeurs to deal with any problems that might arise.

The S.A.E.'s main function, of inestimable importance, was to standardize parts, names, and other basic automobile items throughout the industry. Henceforward spark plugs, carburetor flanges, screw threads, bolts, nuts, and myriad other items would all be built to the same standards everywhere, from Pierce Arrow at Buffalo to Buick at Flint. Specific S.A.E. identification systems were worked out for a host of metals, bearings, frame sections, carburetor parts, locks, washers, and thousands of other auto parts. On one item alone, seamless steel tubing, the number of sizes was reduced from 1,000 to 50. Some manufacturers feared that standardization would reduce their claims of superior workmanship, but eventually they all saw that it would in reality create a higher universal standard of quality that would both reduce costs and instill confidence in the consumer. It would also free auto makers to be creative in areas where it really counted, instead of concerning themselves with thousands of petty details. Through monumental work and attention to detail by the S.A.E., the chaos in which a completely unstandardized industry was floundering around diminished and finally disappeared. Mass production was also brought a good deal closer to reality.

The S.A.E. was begun by a New York consulting engineer named E. T. Birdsall, who took steps to organize a professional association of automobile engineers in 1903. In January, 1905, 30 engineers adopted a constitution, and the American Society of Automobile Engineers was formed. Andrew L. Riker of Locomobile was the President, Birdsall was the Secretary Treasurer, and Henry Ford was the First Vice President.

Henry Ford immersed himself completely in the activities of the S.A.E., and it was mainly here that his abiding respect for interchangeability developed. At the organization's second annual meeting in 1907 Ford read a paper called "Simplicity," which outlined his plans for a perfect car. It was just twelve months before the appearance of the Model T.

So the standardizing efforts of the N.A.C.C. and the S.A.E. were a welcome benefit to manufacturers and customers alike, and gave Ford a foundation from which to build his revolutionary new production concept.

Ford knew what his aim was, but it was only bit by bit that he came to understand how to achieve it, through the work of the bright men and real geniuses who set it up.

Walter Flanders was the one who initiated the process. He only worked for the company for two years, from 1906 to 1908, but in that time he set Ford on the road to mass production by introducing it to the refinements of armory practice. A huge (275 pounds), lusty, red-headed man, the very opposite of Henry Ford, Flanders came to the company after delivering an order for 1,000 crankshafts on time, a rarity in those days. He was not so much interested in cars per se as in their production. Ford hired him to take charge of this area. He invented multiple drill, vertical boring mill, and valve grinding machines, but his great contribution was in arranging production more efficiently. Most of his time was spent moving machinery around and changing plant procedures to make processes run better, more logically, and more economically. He also got suppliers to fill up nearby vacant buildings with parts so that they were readily available, and production would not be subject to costly parts delays. Ford, seeing what sort of man he was, gave him a good incentive to do his best. He paid him $1,000 a month, with a $20,000 bonus for building 10,000 cars a year. Flanders made it, and in the process brought considerably more order to the way the Ford factory was run.

There is some controversy as to whether Flanders introduced interchangeable parts to Ford, even though he was a typical New England mechanic who had introduced various armory practices to the company. But his longtime associate Max Wollering claimed that Henry Ford was well aware of the benefits of interchangeability before Flanders showed up, though it is clear that Flanders hammered home its value to Ford and his associates. He also gave Ford ideas on how to sell the cars. "Charles Sorensen aptly summarized Flanders' contributions to the Ford company, saying that he 'created greater awareness that the motor car business is a fusion of three arts—the art of buying materials, the art of production, and the art of selling.' Clearly, as Sorensen recognized, Flanders—particularly in his rearrangement of machine tools—'headed us toward mass production'" (Hounshell).

Childe Harold Wills, who had worked with Ford since at least 1902, was the great draughtsman and engineer who reduced Ford's ideas to paper and helped to refine them. Throughout his long automobile career he was known as one of the industry's most meticulous craftsmen. He was a major figure in the design of Ford automobiles and the layout of Ford factories from 1902 through the construction of the Highland Park facility some years later.

Though Wills was supposed to be in charge of manufacturing operations after Flanders left, it was actually Peter E. Martin, a French Canadian associated with Ford since his early days, who oversaw production as factory superintendent.

The aforementioned Charles E. Sorensen, a pattern maker who had joined Ford in 1905, was Martin's assistant. Flanders's production organization and development functions were taken over by him. This was fortuitous, for Sorensen turned out to be a true mastermind who played a key role in the development of the moving assembly line. Allan Nevins, one of Ford's biographers, said that "Charles E. Sorensen was a man who could have been head of a great country or played a decisive role in any of a hundred other callings and acquitted himself with distinction."

Oscar Bornholdt was in charge of tool design and construction until the first assembly line began to run, at which time his assistant, a technically trained German immigrant named Carl Emde, took over.

August Degener, a draughtsman whom Ford had hired before the company was formed, rose to be superintendent of inspection by 1910.

Joseph Galamb, a Hungarian whose engineering training had mostly been done in Europe, was hired in 1905 to work on designs and plans. The engine of the Model T was largely his creation, with the close collaboration of Wills and Ford himself.

Fred Diehl joined the company in 1907, originally as a timekeeper. He soon rose to be placed in charge of purchasing materials, originally as an assistant to James Couzens. Couzens himself, of course, was the number two executive man in the company, ultimately responsible for its day-to-day operations.

Albert Kahn, the German-born and -educated son of a rabbi, was the architect who created Ford's Highland Park factory, where the assembly line was born; indeed he designed most of the major assembly plants in the industry. The reason was his interest in and understanding of a fabulous new building material—reinforced concrete. Through this building method, usually brittle concrete beams were given enormous added strength by pouring this material around a basketwork of steel rodding. This was a much cheaper, more flexible construction method than building just with bricks or solid steel skeletons. "Using reinforced concrete an architect could, for the first time, create really wide, open factory areas which had the added advantage of being virtually fireproof, since concrete, unlike steel, is a poor conductor of heat" (Lacey). It also meant that the walls could be made of great expanses of windowpanes for the very first time, giving much greater light and ventilation to the workplace. With the construction of the first of these Kahn-designed buildings for Packard in Detroit in 1905, the factory was changed from a dark, dusty dungeon-like place into a bright, open, airy, modern space. Ford and Kahn saw eye to eye, and when the Highland Park factory, with its 50,000 square feet of window panes lighting the building from the sides and above, opened in 1909, it was hailed as Detroit's own Crystal Palace.

William S. Knudsen, a Danish immigrant who later went on to become President of General Motors, joined Ford in 1911 through its acquisition of the Keim Mills stamping plant in Buffalo. When the plant was closed down by Ford after a strike halted production, the critical presses were shipped to Highland Park, and Knudsen went with them. He was to finish off the production end of mass production by figuring out the proper layout of the Ford plants. Cleveland and Williamson explained what he did this way: "First determine what machinery should be used. Next decide where every machine tool would be placed. Be sure the flow of materials coincides with the sequence of operations. Be certain, as Knudsen said, 'that all noses are pointed in the same direction.' Then erect the building around the layout." Indeed, Albert Kahn's Detroit success was due to his grasp of the rightness of doing things this way, rather than simply refitting old buildings around this new production idea. When Ford built branch plants, Knudsen was put in charge of arranging them in the correct way.

Those new plants came about due to Norval Hawkins, the man who succeeded advertising genius E. LeRoy Pelletier (originator of the slogan 'Watch the Fords Go By') as Ford's "publicity engineer." According to Crabb, it was Hawkins who discovered that costs could be greatly reduced when freight cars were shipped with the maximum weight of components to be assembled into complete cars at plants near the point of sale. The first branch plant, designed by Albert Kahn, was built in Kansas City; it was supplied by spurs from two railroads. Soon branch plants were being built around the country, thus expanding mass production in an exponential manner.

The actual laying out of the first assembly line was the work of Clarence

Avery, who joined Ford in 1912 as Sorensen's assistant; he was a young man who had caught Henry Ford's eye when he was Edsel Ford's manual training teacher in high school. Bright and well educated, he was instructed by Sorensen to learn conceptually every manufacturing idea at Highland Park. Avery did extensive motion and time studies on the well-laid-out stationary chassis assembly process at Ford, and from that beginning he and Sorensen began to lay out the plans for the first chassis assembly lines. It was mostly Avery "who made the moving, fully mechanized assembly line, and complete synchronization of its manufacturing procedures, possible. . . . the idea of the moving assembly line had taken root at Ford, but Avery translated the idea into reality in less than 18 months" (Crabb).

William Klann was the foreman of Ford's motor assemblies at the time the assembly line was put in, and it was he who responsible for the conveyor systems that were used, having been a close observer of how these devices were used in other businesses.

The story of the development of the assembly line at Ford cannot be fully appreciated without understanding the contribution of the Dodge Brothers, Horace and John. They were the true builders of Ford cars, contributing everything but the bodies, wheels, and tires until 1913; as such, they were by far the largest manufacturers of automobiles in the world. Thus, until the assembly line, the Ford car was really an assembled car, and Ford quality was Dodge quality, built to Ford specifications. The Dodge Brothers' high standards gave Ford an important base from which to finally organize its own fully integrated production.

From the moment Highland Park was built it was clear that the arrangement between Ford and the Dodges would not last; they were important stockholders in the company, and with ever-increasing production, Ford had realized that he was paying the Dodges twice, for their work and as stockholders. Self production had become an economic imperative for Ford. On the Dodge's side, they were dismayed by Ford's refusal to incorporate any of the improvements they were coming up with. Eventually, it became imperative for them to produce their own car. Thus in August of 1913, just four months after the first assembly line was put into operation at Ford, John Dodge resigned from the board of Ford and gave the required notice of termination of the agreement between the two firms, agreeing to help the company replace Dodge parts with its own within a year.

On July 17, 1914, Dodge Brothers was chartered in Michigan, and announced the production of its new car, to be produced in Hamtramck, within 100 days. The first car was produced there on November 14, 1914. John Dodge explained his decision to go into production by saying, "Just think of all those Ford owners who will someday want an automobile." Because of the Brothers' tremendous reputation as builders of Ford components thousands of people lined up to become dealers of Dodge Brothers cars, and huge orders piled up for the cars themselves. Stressing the new car's main attraction, the company introduced the word "dependability" to the English language in its advertising. The Dodge Brothers were well launched on their own new venture, but it is safe to say that the legacy of quality they left behind at Ford was in no small way responsible for the success of the new assembly-line technique.

It must also be noted that James Couzens of course kept the whole Ford enterprise together, as he had since the days when Malcolmson had brought him into the company. He gave it a structure in which all the other structures could operate. His importance cannot be overestimated.

Above it all, below it, behind it, in front of it, informing every aspect of the Ford Motor Company's existence and direction, was Henry Ford, the prime mover of the organization. Without Ford, Fordism, or mass production, would never have been called into existence at that particular time and place.

The idea of the assembly line existed at Ford by 1908. Sorensen claimed that on Sundays in July of that year he, Henry Ford, Wills, Martin, and an assembly foreman named Charles Lewis laid out a crude sort of chassis assembly line at the factory. Sorensen's men pulled a chassis on skids past places where various chassis components were located, going through the motions of assembly. It was a slow, tedious process. Wills and Martin didn't think much of it, but Ford, though saying little, told Sorensen to continue with his experiments. They would take a long time, because Ford's team was just beginning to think about the areas that would prove crucial to the success of this radical new process. Still, this event does show that the men of Ford were concerning themselves with assembly problems even at that early date.

Until the installation of assembly lines in 1913, Fords were made like other cars. There were departments where various components were worked on. The pieces were located at work stations, and gangs moved from station to station performing their functions. Gradually, through the efforts of Walter Flanders and others, more and more rational planning and sequential ordering of production was introduced, which made operations not only cheaper but faster as well, allowing for ever-increasing output.

Because of his financial success and the fact that he was the sole arbiter of company policy, Ford was able to give his production engineers considerable freedom in trying new machines and systems and scrapping old or unsuccessful ones. Then too, because neither armory nor Western Wheel practices were firmly entrenched at Ford, his men were free to borrow from each tradition and bring their own creative processes to bear in overcoming the difficulties of older methods and in creating new technologies that led to constantly improved production techniques. "When they were finished, they had created—in Allan Nevins's words—a lever to move the world" (Hounshell).

When Ford decided that his Piquette Avenue plant had become too small and that he needed to build a newer, much larger one at Highland Park, he was still producing several different models. In 1909 he simplified planning for the new factory by deciding to concentrate all his production on the Model T. This meant there would be no duplication of single-purpose machinery for several models, a great saving in energy, space, and money.

The new building was 865 feet long by 75 feet wide. Next to it was built a single story 840 × 140 foot building with a sawtooth glass roof, which served as Ford's main machine shop. An 860 × 57 foot glass-enclosed craneway connected the two. All floors of both buildings were totally opened to the craneway, so materials could move easily between them. Thus the craneway served as the major distribution point for all the components that went into the Model T.

Fred Colvin, in a series of articles that appeared in *American Machinist* in the spring of 1913, spoke in detail of how he found the Ford shops just before the assembly line was introduced. This well-known and highly respected technical journalist was very impressed with the success Ford engineers had achieved by concentrating on the "principles of power, accuracy, economy, system, continuity, and speed." At this juncture components were so standardized and production so well organized that Model T engines weren't even started until the cars were ready to leave the factory. It was a measure of Sorensen's and others' confidence in Ford's manufacturing quality that the cars weren't even road-tested. Ford's success was about "system, system, system!" according to a reporter from the *Detroit Journal*.

Good as the system was, it would make a quantum leap in productivity when a new idea was recognized at Ford. This was the basic principle of mass production, the notion of moving the work to the worker, rather than the other way around. This was where the moving assembly line came in.

Like everything else in mass production, it came from somewhere else. Oliver Evans's late-eighteenth-century automatic flour mill used conveying devices to process wheat into flour, and many other businesses, from farming to canning and shipping, eventually came to use them as well. In February, 1913, Sorensen began using a conveyor-type mold carrier in the Ford foundry, but it wasn't a novel idea. As long ago as 1890 the Westinghouse Air Brake Company used a similar system, also, like Ford's, to carry machine-made molds past pourers. Conveyors that moved sand were part of both systems, eliminating all hand shoveling and wheelbarrows. Because of its conveyor system, Ford's foundry capacity was considered a marvel.

William Klann, the head of the engine department who was perhaps most responsible for the adoption of the conveying system at Ford, had direct experience of two industries in which it played a major part. Before he joined Ford in 1905, he had worked for Heutteman & Cramer Machine Company of Detroit as a machinist repairing grain elevators and other mechanical conveyors in breweries. Apparently such devices had been used in breweries since shortly after the introduction of Evans's mechanized flour mill. Klann said that breweries and foundries used the same hoppers and conveyors in their respective malting and moldmaking operations, and claimed that a fellow Heutteman & Cramer employee first interested Henry Ford in mechanical conveying by showing him an H & C catalog of the devices used for such purposes in these industries.

Another influence was the Chicago slaughterhouses. William Klann toured the one at Swift & Company and was very impressed with its system of overhead conveyors and gravity slides. Of course, the slaughterhouse system was one of disassembly, but Ford himself said it was a model for flow production in the auto industry. After his tour of Swift's, Klann told P. E. Martin, "If they can kill pigs and cows that way, we can build cars that way and build motors that way."

According to Klann, H & C, the breweries and the stockyards all contributed directly to Ford's development of its conveyor system, though apparently there was one more influence. Edwin Norton, who later began both the American Can Company in 1901 and the Continental Can Company in 1904, had developed automatic can making machinery, which had both special purpose machinery and a conveyor system bringing the work to the worker, by the mid-1880s. In 1913 Oscar C. Bornholdt compared Ford's sequential layout of its machine tools to that of food-canning machinery. It would not have been much of a leap of imagination for him to compare the flows of materials in the factories of the two industries as well.

The first assembly line at Ford, to manufacture magnetos, started operations on April 1, 1913. Each man did one operation on the line, then pushed the work down to the next one, and so on, until the magneto was finished. By the end of the day, assembly time had dropped by about 50 percent. Raising the height of the line relieved the workers of back pain, and putting the operation on a moving chain regulated the pace of their work, speeding up the slow and retarding the speedy to an even, continuous flow. Eventually the twenty-nine workers on the line were reduced to five, and assembly time dropped to 5 minutes from the original bench time of 20 minutes.

This first line worked out so well that assembly lines were swiftly emplaced wherever possible in the plant. Overnight, this was the new way to do things, and in short order tons of expensive, and suddenly obsolete, equipment was tossed out in the mad rush to change over to the new method of assembly. Klann began the process of developing a final engine assembly line from several subassemblies almost immediately, achieving his goal by November 1913. There had been a lot of tinkering with the engine assembly line, but by the time it was finished, engine assembly time was cut from 594 man-minutes to 226.

The crown jewel of the process was the chassis assembly line, finally achieved some five years after that early rough experiment in July 1908. One morning in August 1913 a 250-foot rope was attached to a windlass in a long open space in the Highland Park factory. Clarence Avery's study of 250 men at stationary assembly stations and 80 parts carriers who worked with these men had shown that the best possible assembly time for a chassis was twelve and a half hours. Based on Avery's figures for optimal installation times of different chassis components, engineers placed the components at intervals along the path on which the chassis was pulled; six assemblers followed the work along from station to station. When it was completed, this very first attempt at final chassis assembly had taken five hours and fifty minutes, or less than half the previous best possible time.

Avery continued his time and motion studies. (It is important to note that they were different from Taylorism, the work of Frederick W. Taylor, which suggested ways for workers to move the work faster; Avery figured out ways to make *the work* move faster to the men.) Still unmechanized improvements on a 300-foot assembly line using 177 men dropped assembly time to two hours and thirty-eight minutes before Christmas of 1913. One hundred and ninety-one men pushing the cars along the line by hand after Christmas actually increased assembly time, so by early January, 1914, the chassis were finally moved by an endless chain. After a great deal more experimentation, three different assembly lines were turning out 1,212 chassis assemblies in an eight-hour day, which worked out to 93 man-minutes for each. This was a phenomenal success, and naturally led to all sorts of attempts to save labor in every area of the Ford shops. Like the politicians of the French Revolution, once the new era was proclaimed, the men of Ford threw out the precedents and traditions of the past wholesale.

It is important to note however, that contrary to popular opinion fostered by stories of Henry Ford's not giving a hang about records, all the processes of the company and improvements thereto were based on exhaustive and extensive recordkeeping. Costs were laid out on graphs and charted to the penny, so that Henry Ford had an excellent basis for the production and financial decisions he made. David Hounshell shows that the workings of few companies in history were so well documented, and that the development and refinement of the mass production system could never have been achieved if this had not been the case. As with everything else, this was the direct result of the wishes and policies of Henry Ford.

Exciting as all this was, it did not come without problems. The most important was labor. In a nutshell, the workers hated the new system and quit in enormous numbers. Assembly-line work was regimented, rigorous, and very hard. It was also dehumanizing, making the workers feel like part of the machinery themselves. By the close of 1913, Ford had to hire 963 workers for every 100 workers it wanted to add to its staff, which was very disruptive to the whole organization. There was even talk of unionization and the possibility of strikes. Greater pay parity among jobs and even a higher minimum wage of $2.34 per day beginning in October of 1913 didn't solve the problem. Discontent grew. Perhaps the final shock came on December 31, 1913, when Ford offered a 10 percent bonus to every worker who had been with the company more than three years. Only 640 out of a total of 15,000 qualified. Clearly, something had to be done.

The solution proved to be the last stage in the development of mass production. Ford never did anything in conducting his business that was not for the sake of the profit motive, and this was no exception. But it also shows the benevolent face of modern capitalism, and its long-term positive effects. If Henry Ford himself did not have a developed sense of social justice, he never could have come up with as good an idea as he finally put forth.

Ford knew there were gross inequities between the workers' compensation and that of himself, his executives, and his production experts. General compensation needed to become demonstrably fairer for him to have a truly stable workplace. James Couzens thought it was a good idea, too, because of the enormous advantages of the favorable publicity he could foresee for such a move.

On or around New Year's Day of 1914, Ford and his top executives met to discuss raising the daily wage at the company to somewhere between $3 and $5. At a stroke, Henry Ford cut off all discussion and came to a decision—he would pay a wage of $5 for an eight-, rather than a nine-, hour day; $2.34 would be a base wage and $2.66 would be a bonus paid to deserving workers of at least six months' service and twenty-two years of age who could prove they were using their money for the purposes of leading "a clean, sober, and industrious life."

When the announcement of the $5 day came in January 1914, all details were swept aside. Ford was treated like a great hero of the common man. Huge headlines proclaimed the news all over the country. It was an astonishing event: a cutting of hours from nine to eight per day, a doubling of the daily wage, and the addition of a third shift to handle the crush of unfilled orders the factory was trying to cope with—and all of this in the middle of a major economic recession, too. People could hardly believe it. "A magnificent act of generosity," said the New York Evening Post. "God Bless Henry Ford" was the headline in the Algonac Courier for a story describing the car maker as "one of God's noblemen."

By dawn of the next day 10,000 unemployed men, some dressed in rags, were massed around the Highland Park employment office in the bitter cold seeking between four to five thousand jobs on the new shift. By the time signs were posted in several languages that hiring was over on the 14th, 15,000 men were appearing each day; when they turned unruly after reading the signs, fire hoses were turned on them in the nine-degree temperature, instantly turning their clothes into frozen cement.

Other businesses were horrified at Ford's action, predicting social ferment from an action Ford would find he couldn't afford. In reality, though, Ford could well afford what he had done, for he knew that his new production techniques were bringing him incredible savings. In fact, he could probably have afforded to pay his workers $20 a day, and by the end of the year he was able to pay his shareholders over $11 million in dividends, even after the extra costs of the $5 day were taken into account. It must be said, however, that on January 5, 1914, Ford had only a vague idea of the profits he was going to make on his new system, and even with enormous back orders he was taking a big chance.

Ford was an avid reader of Emerson and believer in his ideas. Biographer Robert Lacey tells us that Ford's favorite Emersonian essay was "On Compensation." In it Emerson wrote, "In labor as in life, there can be no cheating." An employer gets what he pays for, and it is his duty to educate his workers and uplift their vision and the quality of their lives. Since the universe exists in a perfect balance of give-and-take, the employer who does not pay the proper price for labor gets something else instead. In Ford's case the "something else" was enormous labor turnover, which threatened all the gains his new system promised to bring. His solution was to conclude with Emerson, "Always pay; for first or last you must pay your entire debt. . . . He is great who confers the most benefits. He is base—and that is the one base thing in the universe—to receive favors and render none . . . Beware of too much good staying in your hand. It will fast corrupt, and worm worms." So, ultimately, profit motive or no, it is fair to say that Henry Ford created the $5 day at least in part out of an Emersonian sense of social justice.

As an adjunct to the $5 day, he created the Sociological Department, headed by his good friend the Rev. Dr. Samuel S. Marquis. This was a progressive move at the time, though it may seem like an unconscionable example of Big Brother-type meddling in employees' lives to people of today. It was this department that went into workers' homes and determined their fitness for the $2.66 bonus part of the $5 wage. But it must be remembered that Detroit was a wide-open boom town then, like the railroad and mining towns of old, filled with saloons and whores, slick operators and corruption. Many of these newly "rich" workers had no stabilizing influences in their lives, and many could not even speak English. The Sociological Department served a very useful function by encouraging clean, safe, and sanitary living conditions, and trying to make sure that workers' families were properly provided for by the breadwinner. It also took steps to overcome the language barrier at Ford, caused by the fact that over 70 percent of the workers were foreign-born. From May 1914 on, non-English-speaking workers had to take

English courses taught by unpaid fellow workers after hours in order to be subject to the profit-sharing plan. Though alien as a concept to people today, the Sociological Department unquestionably performed a welcome and useful social function until the need for it was obviated by the very success Fordism brought to its workers by the beginning of the 1920s.

But more than money came to the Ford workers through this new system. The badges they wore identified them as the American workers with the highest prestige—everyone wanted to join in the prosperity they enjoyed. It meant they could afford better homes, food, and clothing than their peers at other firms—and something else, of much larger significance. Henry Ford had been lowering the price of his cars as he saved money with more economical ways of producing them, thereby broadly extending the number of consumers able to become his customers. By 1914 he had cut the price of the Model T virtually in half from what it had been at its 1908 introduction. Coupled with the doubling of the workers' wages, this meant that Ford's workers could actually afford to buy the cars they produced. This was the first time in history that workers could purchase any large machine they made. In a few short years the car had gone from a rich man's toy to a middle-class man's expectation to a working-class man's reality.

In 1907 Henry Ford had said: "I will build a car for the great multitude. It will be large enough for the family, but small enough for the individual to run and care for. It will be constructed of the best materials, by the best men to be hired, after the simplest designs that modern engineering can devise. But it will be so low in price that no man making a good salary will be unable to own one—and enjoy with his family the blessing of hours of pleasure in God's great open spaces." Now he had done it.

Because Ford was not secretive about his discovery, opening up his plant and methods to all who wanted to copy them, his system spread like wildfire, first through the automobile business and then into other businesses as well. Wherever it spread, the previously undreamed-of prosperity for the common man that went with it spread also. Between 1910 and 1920, the number of horses and the number of automobiles displaced each other, and the age-old era of animal-driven transportation was virtually at an end. New prosperity meant that farm people who came to the cities to work in industrial plants were never to return to their farming roots. The population of the great cities exploded, and after nearly 150 years America turned from an agrarian civilization into an urban one practically overnight. Indeed, what Henry Ford invented was not really mass production, but mass prosperity, a state of being never before within mankind's reach.

Amazingly for his time, place, and background, he really did extend his offer of employment and prosperity to any capable person who wanted it, not excluding women, blacks, the handicapped, ex-criminals, and Jews.

He talked as condesendingly as other employers of his time about women workers, but he gave them more employment at better wages than others in Detroit. Though the $5-a-day offer was not originally made to them, that changed in short order.

Ford hired his first black worker in 1914. Typically of Henry Ford, he was William Perry, a man he had known and worked with before he left the farm in Dearborn. Perry was given lots of publicity as reporters swarmed over the Ford plant at that time, but he was neither a curiosity nor a token. "By the early 1920s there were more than 5,000 blacks working for Ford, and by 1926 there were double that number—a tenth of the entire work force. The Ford Motor Company employed more blacks than all the other car companies combined" (Lacey). When Detroit mayor John W. Smith formed an interracial committee in 1926 to reduce racial tensions through better employment policies towards blacks, Ford was the only employer who did something about the problem. He made a personal effort to increase and upgrade jobs for blacks in his plants, even making some of them foremen. When whites objected and fights broke out, Ford responded to the committee's request for some degree of segregation by placing the entire foundry operation of his company, up to plant superintendent, in the hands of blacks. "Henry Ford liked to boast that the foundry was the most efficient unit in the entire Rouge complex" (Lacey).

Even more extraordinary was Henry Ford's attitude towards the handicapped. He declared that the only reason not to hire a worker was contagious disease, and even there he made an effort, setting aside a separate building for tuberculosis sufferers. Ford's personnel chief, John R. Lee, analyzed 7,882 jobs at Ford to align them with specific physical disabilities. By 1919, 9,563 of a total of 44,569 Ford employees had some kind of handicap. All were paid at full rates, with full profit sharing. The same was true of the 400 to 600 ex-cons who worked at Ford through a private arrangement with the courts. Never one to want anyone to think he pursued these amazingly enlightened policies for eleemosynary reasons, Ford used to boast that these workers gave him a much better day's work out of gratitude to him.

Still, the Reverend Marquis quoted Henry Ford as saying: "Blindfold me and lead me down the street and lay my hands by chance on the most shiftless and worthless fellow in the crowd and I'll bring him in here, give him a job with a wage that offers him some hope for the future, some prospect of living a decent, comfortable and self respecting life, and I'll guarantee that I'll make a man out of him." In other words, Henry Ford had made himself a justified man, in Emersonian terms.

Then there was the matter of Henry Ford and the Jews. Personally and professionally he got along quite well with them. Albert Kahn was his architect, and the two men were never on anything but the best of terms.

Rabbi Leo Franklin was an old friend and neighbor from the Edison days to whom he gave a new Model T every year. His butcher and antiques dealer were both Jews too. Ford never employed fewer than 3,000 Jews in his business, and in fact seems to have gotten on with every Jew he ever knew in his whole life, according to Lacey.

Henry Ford hated the Jews in the abstract. It was a hangover from the agrarian, populist, bi-metallism of his youth. "It was quite simple, said Henry. The world was controlled by gold, and the gold was controlled by the Jews. . . . The Jew is a mere huckster, a trader who doesn't want to produce, but to make something out of what somebody else produces" (Lacey). At the time, it was quite common to use the Jews as scapegoats for all the world's economic ills, and Henry Ford was not alone in his beliefs. A scabrous series of anti-semitic attacks appeared on and off in Ford's notorious *Dearborn Independent* from 1921 to 1927. Typically, they were written by the editor, his brilliant, sybaritic amanuensis, William Cameron, and were based on the ideas of Ford's rabidly anti-semitic Prussian private secretary, Ernest Liebold. In the "Henry's Page" editorials of this newspaper, Jews were blamed for everything from the international Zionist conspiracy proclaimed by the soon to be discredited *Protocols of the Learned Elders of Zion* to the jazz music and rolled stockings of 1920s Flaming Youth.

Under Liebold's influence, these articles were collected and reprinted as a series of books called *The International Jew*. Along with Ford-financed reprints of the *Protocols*, they were widely distributed and had great influence, particularly in Nazi Germany, where no less a personage than Adolph Hitler read and admired them. Hitler hung Ford's picture on the wall, and based several sections of *Mein Kampf* on his writings; indeed, Ford is the only American mentioned in Hitler's book. It can probably be said, as Lacey does, that no American contributed as much to the evils of Nazism as Henry Ford. On his seventy-fifth birthday in 1938, Ford received the German Eagle from Hitler, the highest civilian award that could be bestowed on a foreigner by the Third Reich. Though in response to widespread criticism of this award Ford professed it had come from the German people who were generally not in sympathy with their leaders' anti-Jewish policies, his private response the next year to the coming European war showed nothing had changed. "The whole thing has just been made up by the Jewish bankers," he said.

Before he died however, the vicious reality behind his impersonal paranoid fantasy about the Jews was made known to him. Lacey quotes the testimony of Josephine Gammon, who worked at Ford during World War II and got to know Henry Ford well. She claims that when the films showing the opening of the concentration camps were brought to Ford and he finally saw the unutterable horror that anti-semitism had caused, he collapsed with a stroke, the last and most serious one before his death.

Yes, the man who had done these things was ignorant, unschooled, re-calcitrant, reactionary. This made it even more astonishing that he did so much to create what we think of as modernity in the physical circum-stances of men's lives. Shouldn't such a man have been some sort of latter-day saint, like Mohandas K. Gandhi, we wonder? But he was not. For all that he was so far away from being such a man however, his world-shaking achievements were nonetheless indubitable.

The future uses of history are unfathomable to the people of any given time. The Guelphs and the Ghibbelines were of enormous importance to the history of the thirteenth century as it was lived, but who among the readers of this book has any but the vaguest notion of who they were or what they did? Similarly, who knows what the reputation of John F. Ken-nedy or the assassination of Archduke Francis Ferdinand will mean to the peoples of the twenty-sixth century? But some people will stand as icons for our age, as Leonardo, Shakespeare, and Robespierre stand for theirs.

Einstein, Hitler, Gandhi, Stalin, Chaplin, Picasso, Freud; these will prob-ably be among the very few names that will always be thought of when the twentieth century is recalled. Another will surely be that of Henry Ford.

As far as the automobile business is concerned, our subject, Walter Chrysler, was the great anomaly. He was the genius of a late age, the only other man to achieve on the scale of Ford and Durant, and at a time when this should have been no longer possible. He didn't build guns, sewing ma-chines, wagons, bicycles, gas engines, or any of the other items that were anterior to automobile assembly. In fact, until 1909 he didn't build any-thing. Walter Chrysler was a railroad mechanic, and what he knew about machinery came from that fact. Popular engineering magazines, correspon-dence courses, and nearly twenty years' experience in roundhouses were responsible for what he had learned and would prove vital to his achieve-ment. It is interesting to note, for instance, that in a roundhouse the work, a locomotive, comes to the worker, is acted upon, and then moves away, just as in the basic process of mass production. Jobs of ever-increasing authority fully taught him all aspects of railroad precision, as he learned to be completely responsible for every screw, every nickel, every person, and every minute along a railroad line. What he knew about cars came from buying the best one he could find, taking it apart, and analyzing it in min-utest detail until he understood how it was made and how it operated. "Discovery favors the prepared mind," said Louis Pasteur, and when the call came, Walter Chrysler immediately realized he could apply all the self-taught learning and railroad knowledge he had acquired over the previous thirty-six years to the automobile business, to enormous effect. As he grew in capacity and skill, he went far beyond his background to create an ex-traordinary new company of lasting power and worth, one that would affect the lives of millions and become one of the chief symbols of its age.

PART THREE

Greatness

⊡ 17 ⊡

Chrysler at Buick

What is paint, my little man?
Gooey stuff, that's in a can.
It isn't good to drink or eat,
But for grief, it's hard to beat.

Is it tough, and is it lasting?
Will it adhere to a casting?
Will it stand the heat we give it?
Would another type outlive it?

Can it dry without a "tack"?
How much pigment does it lack?
Should it brush, or spray, or flow?
Is its solids content low?

Can it stand before the arc,
And for hours show no mark?
When you bend a panel back,
Will the film on it crack?

Can it withstand acid and lye?
Does it contain a bleeding dye?
Paints must pass our every test,
For Chrysler must have the best.
Fred B. Shaw, Chemist, Dodge Main Plant;
Chrysler Motors Magazine, October, 1936

Walter P. Chrysler went to meet the challenges that lay ahead for him at Buick in 1912 with his customary pioneer enthusiasm. His railroad history had prepared him well for what lay ahead in this new business, but, like all pioneers, he encountered many surprises, none of which stumped him. He flexed and expanded his knowledge with every problem solved, every new success. Within a very few years at Buick, he was much more of a man of business than he was when he began; in fact, he was fast becoming a giant.

Walter Chrysler, third from right on bench, surrounded by other Buick ex-ecutives at the Buick plant in Flint, Michigan, 1912. (*Courtesy Menno Duerksen*)

He had taught himself about the inner workings of the automobile when he tore apart that Locomobile over and over again back in Oelwein in 1908. He learned how to construct complicated vehicles when he erected those huge locomotives back at ALCO. His time at Buick was to be all about learning how to build fine automobiles in minutest detail and enormous numbers and at a vast profit. In a few short years he would turn himself from a tyro into the most valuable executive General Motors had ever known.

The problem he faced at Buick was Billy Durant's overarching cry: "OrganiZAtion!"; how to get the greatest financial return out of humanity, time, materials, plant, systems, and everything else that made up the Buick Motor Car Company.

A good summation of the sort of analytical force he needed to bring to bear on his new position is contained in a speech given by Henry M. Leland at the Westminster Presbyterian Church on October 30, 1910. It is quoted in his biography, *Master of Precision, Henry M. Leland*: "If you take a ton of iron from the ground, remote from a railroad, it is worth very little. Take this ore any place where it is accessible to a railroad or a boat and it is still worth very little. If you take it to a smelter and put it into pig iron, it is worth from $15 to $20 per ton. Put that same ton of ore into steel bars,

Walter P. Chrysler, about 1919. (*Courtesy DaimlerChrysler Corporate Historical Collection*)

and it is worth $50 a ton. But if you then put it through fine automatic screw machines and develop little screws, so small that it is necessary to use a microscope to see them, for use in holding jewels in watches, the same ton is worth $30,000." Chrysler had to consider everything at Buick to be like that raw iron mined from the ground; it was up to him to figure out the best way to make all elements of the company as valuable as possible.

He found out immediately how daunting his task would be. On his very first day as works manager he went into the plant and asked a clerk for the piecework schedule, since the men were being paid on piecework. Met with a blank stare and a lot of casting about, he discovered that there wasn't any. His eager assistant over at the stamping plant did little better. He had one, all right, but it was just a little folded-over scrap of paper with scribblings that told Chrysler nothing of importance. He was aghast.

At ALCO it would have been impossible to do competitive bidding without knowing all costs, down to the drilling of holes, on the construction of a locomotive, which usually ran around $40,000. The building of locomotives was scheduled to completion on a certain day at a certain price, and that could not possibly be done without knowing time, motion, labor, and materials to the last degree; if not, ALCO would lose money. They used slide

A family portrait - Left to right - Bernice, Thelma, Mr. and Mrs. Chrysler, Walter Jr. and Jack.

Walter Jr.   Bernice   Thelma   Jack

Chrysler family portrait taken in Flint, Michigan, about 1920. (*Courtesy Frank B. Rhodes*)

rules for their estimates, and everything was laid out on a scientific basis before construction began. By comparison, ALCO was building only one or maybe two machines at a time; at Buick they were making over two score a day, without any hard knowledge of what was involved. From that day forward, Buick had a real piecework schedule, which was used as the basis for what became a precise cost analysis of the construction of each car.

In Walter Chrysler's effects there is a slender black leather looseleaf book, about eight inches long by three inches wide, containing parchment sheets folded over once lengthwise. On these sheets are typed the precise costs of each component of each model made by Buick from July 1912 through April 1913. Not each model is listed for each month, though some models' costs are broken down over several months; thus, the motor of a Model 31 cost $133.47 in September, $119.36 in October, $122.24 in November, and so on; the price of a stripped car is added up, and finally that of an equipped

GM executives, 1919. Right of center, Walter Chrysler stands directly behind William C. Durant; only known photograph of the two men together. (*Courtesy Frank B. Rhodes*)

car (with mohair top, windshield, etc.) is computed on the bottom of the page. There are tables showing the monthly and daily average cost basis numbers on each model finished and shipped from July 1, 1912, through either February 18 or April 30, 1913. Small enough to fit into his inside coat pocket, the book is an example of the precise documentation Chrysler used to measure constantly the performance of his company.

He made good use of his figures. The first time new models were laid out after his arrival, he presented a scientifically devised cost estimate for their construction, rather than simply taking the previous year's figures and adding to them the cost of changes and new features. The figures—even his high estimates—were so low that the board said it was impossible to build Buick cars for what he proposed. Since Chrysler knew how cautious he had been in preparing his figures, he offered to take as a salary the difference between the total of his high estimates and the total actual cost of the cars. Inexplicably, the board refused his offer and, covering all bases, turned around and added $30 to his cost figures, just to be on the safe side. When the cars were actually built, the board was astonished to discover that the cars did indeed cost less than Chrysler had predicted, and that he would have earned a fortune if they had accepted his offer.

The reason this was so was that his sums were based on cost-saving changes he instituted all over Buick from that very first day. When he began working for Buick, there were no testing grounds at the plant, so drivers came in and out of the plant all day to take cars out for test runs on country

Paris, France, autumn 1919. GM trip to explore the possibility of buying Citroën. André Citroën, far left; Chrysler third from left; Albert Champion center; Alfred P. Sloan, third from right. (*Courtesy Frank B. Rhodes*)

roads outside of Flint. But he noticed that neither the drivers nor the cars were assigned control numbers, and after a week's close scrutiny he found out that every day between one and four more cars were taken out than were returned. As soon as he told his findings to Nash, a registration system was started immediately. Chrysler later remarked, "I saved the Buick Motor Car Company my first year's salary the first week I was in Flint."

He wasn't afraid to make improvements by finding out he was wrong, either. Beverly Rae Kimes says that soon after he arrived at Buick he asked for money to build a larger sheet metal plant, but some investigation showed him that the reason he needed the additional space was only to alleviate congestion. After he made a study of the situation, he instituted a new system of staggered hours at this factory. He brought some trackers in an hour earlier in the morning, had others work through the lunch hour, and made still others stay an hour after production stopped at night to clear the plant of finished product and lay out new materials for the next work force. In this manner no time was wasted on layout congestion and bottlenecks during the day, and he was able to tell the company that no new sheet metal plant was necessary after all.

Perhaps the most important changes he made were modifications in standard practice in the chassis room, a large brick building about 600 feet long by 70 feet wide. He studied operations there with Chet Smith, his new production manager, and did not like what he found.

Big wooden posts, lots of them, held up the roof, not a one more than 20 feet away from another. Of course, they were in everyone's way all the time. The room was laid out with workstations in long rows at which the chassis were assembled by gangs of men who moved from one to the other. Four men would bring pieces of a frame and rivet it together, then others would come with axles, and still others with springs. When these men moved on, painters went to work, first sanding and then painting the frames with a putty-rich primary coat that took twelve hours to dry. The next day there was more sandpapering and another coat of liquid primer, with another twelve-hour drying period. After yet another light sandpapering, the frames got a finishing coat of varnish to make them shiny, which meant yet another twelve-hour drying time. This was precisely the kind of inefficiency Chrysler knew he had to eliminate if he were to increase Buick's production capacity.

Among the things that were wrong here was that the frames were being painted as if they were wood instead of metal. He told Smith to cut out the sandpapering and the final coat of varnish, which cut two days off production time. There was some griping from men who thought it was a lessening of quality to work this way, which was understandable, since many of them had been carriage makers. But Chrysler pointed out that a chassis was caked with mud the very first day a car was used, so that shiny underpinnings were of no value to customers. The changes stuck.

The effects of such modifications were felt throughout the organization, because if chassis construction were finished in half the previous time, that meant that other operations would have to be speeded up also. Six months later chassis production got speeded up again as two coats of paint were dried in just half a day by stepping up the room temperature to 85 degrees and closing the windows. Through this and other ways of adapting carriage craft methods to true automobile construction, Chrysler increased chassis production from forty-five to seventy-five a day in the same workspace at a much lower cost.

The next thing that went were all those posts supporting the roof, which instead was braced with stronger trusses. This was needed in order to implement a major innovation in the way Buicks were assembled. All but four or five of the worktables in the chassis room were eliminated, and benches were set up near them. Beyond them, clear to the end of the room, was a pair of tracks made of two-by-fours. Chassis completed at the stations were lifted by chain hoist onto the tracks, then pushed by hand from station to station, where men put on fenders, gas tanks, and at last the bodies. It was hardly mass production, but it was certainly a big step in that direction, using the basic mass production principle of bringing the work to the worker rather than the other way around.

This wasn't the first time such an idea had been tried; Wayne Lewchuk in *American Technology and the British Vehicle Industry* points out that Max Wollering, machine shop superintendent at Ford in 1906–1907, claimed that Ford and Sorensen had tried pushing partially completed chassis from station to station around 1909, but for some unknown reason discontinued the experiment. When his boss at Ford, Walter Flanders, left the company to become a founding partner in EMF (the predecessor to Studebaker), Wollering went with him. Flanders of course was the New England mechanic who had organized production at Ford in a rationally progressive way, and he worked along similar lines at EMF (whose unfortunately varying quality led some customers to refer to its products as "Every Mechanical Fault" and "Every Morning Fix-It").

There was a 30-station production line at EMF from the beginning, but it was not a continually moving one. A clerk recorded when each task was completed, and when all of them were done, the entire line moved forward one station. About one hundred chassis per day were completed that way. According to Wollering, the cars were first pushed along, but later, "we took two elevator drums, put a couple of motors on them with cables, and had proper hooks attached to the cable that would grasp the front axle of the car to tow it along."

Alanson P. Brush, manufacturer of the sprightly little $500 Brush Runabout ("Wooden wheels, wooden axle, wooden run," said one wag) that disappeared in the U.S. Motors combine disaster of 1911, also had a chain link track along the floor of his plant. However, he manufactured about ten cars a day this way, so one can hardly see the benefit of using it.

Everybody pretty much knew what everyone else was doing in those days. Manufacturers met for lunch at the famous Pontchartrain Hotel in Detroit each day and routinely put new ideas and inventions on the table for comment. Employees moved from firm to firm also, and naturally spread ideas around when they did.

At Buick, a key figure in disseminating information from Ford was a man named Frederick G. Hoelzle, christened "Mr. Snoop" by James Couzens. According to reminiscences found in the GMI Alumni Foundation's Collection of Industrial History and Dunham and Gustin's *The Buick, A Complete History*, Hoelzle frequently had dinner with Henry Ford and came back to Flint with interesting bits of information as to what he was up to, after having returned the favor by giving Ford the latest news from Buick. It is not at all inconceivable that Ford and Buick interchanged ideas on centralized assembly through this conduit.

Chrysler claimed that Ford operated his final assembly line on a chain conveyor after Chrysler had begun his own nonmotorized system at Buick, which probably was so, since Ford did not begin his line until January 1914. But as we have seen, the development of the final assembly line was actually a complex process in which it is almost impossible to assign temporal priority. Several, including Chrysler, have legitimate claims to part of the credit. Automotive mass production in all its complexity, however, was first achieved by Ford.

Once Chrysler had his assembly line, he went backward through the plant tying everything into it. He said his biggest cue for a needed change was the sight of a worker idled by the lack of a continuous flow of parts. In each case he found out what the holdup was and eliminated it. "Every new thing was an invention," he said. "As soon as one problem was revealed and straightened out, twenty other problems had arisen. The motors began to get their shapes riding on a conveyor line; then the axles, crankshafts, camshafts; until now it would be difficult to find an operation which requires men to exert their muscles like they used to. The workmen have machines to do their bidding."

As we have seen, this was the exact opposite of the way Henry Ford approached centralized assembly. There the magneto line came first, and as soon as his men saw how well it worked, they rushed to put the construction of as many parts as possible on similar lines. Months later came the first chassis line, and months after that came the first final assembly line. In other words, Ford built up the process, whereas Chrysler worked backward from the end result, just as he apparently did erecting locomotives at ALCO. "Most men pay too much attention to way stations and not enough to terminals," he said, betraying his railroad background.

The effects of these new assembly-line techniques are worthy of some analysis. In the last full year before the new methods at Ford, 1912, the company produced some 95,000 cars, which more than doubled to about 225,000 the next year as more and more assemblies went on the line. The following year, the first of the final assembly line, only about 10 percent more were built. So production in reality plateaued for almost two years until the new system was straightened out. Only in 1915, with some 372,000 new cars assembled, and 1916, with 586,000, did production actually begin to climb to stratospheric heights. There was a lull before the company felt the full effects of mass production and the previously unimaginable prosperity it would bring. In such circumstances one sees in higher relief the courage it took for Henry Ford to cut his prices (he even gave his customers a $50 rebate at the end of the year, believing that they should share in the profits of his new system) and institute the $5-a-day wage at the beginning of 1914, no matter how much a wage stimulus was needed in his organization.

Things are even more interesting at Buick. While it is certainly true that Chrysler increased production at Buick, in the first few years he did not raise it to previously unheard-of amounts. In 1909 and 1910, respectively, the company built 14,606 and 30,525 cars, using old-fashioned stationary construction methods. A brief, sharp recession in 1910, coupled with management disarray after Durant's departure and the inexplicable discontinuance of Buick's most popular model, the 10, caused production to fall to only 13,389 in 1911. (Actually the Model 10's disappearance was due to the fact that the board preferred not to compete with Henry Ford in producing "cheap" cars—which turned out to be a shortsighted mistake, though typical of the times.) This meant that daily production had actually been somewhat more than 100 cars a day before falling to the 45 that Chrysler encountered at the time he joined the company. Though he undoubtedly saved Buick a fortune and thus helped it to make huge profits through his new methods, the company's output didn't surpass the 1910 figure until 1914, when 32,889 cars were made. During this time he had also set things up so that Buick could make far more cars than it ever had before, since production rose by a third, to 43,946, in 1915 and exploded to 124,834 in 1916. Buick might have been able to continue on with quantity rather than mass production methods to keep up with demand for a while, but Chrysler, with a mandate from Nash and Storrow, worked as hard as he could to establish the newer, more rational production methods both to increase profits and to prepare for the rapidly expanding markets of the future.

For nearly three years Chrysler was at the plant night and day, not once taking time off for a night out with Della. Changes were everywhere. Buick began painting and stockpiling parts ahead of time to cut down on assembly time, an industry first, as was the use of atomizers to spray paint, making the coats much more even and less subject to puddling and "tears." The *Buick Bulletin*, a monthly factory publication from those years, gives a detailed picture of all sorts of new construction methods the company started to introduce during that time. One issue publicized the cost savings and increased quality of metal stamped in improved drop forges. Another explained the quality-control benefits of testing all steel shipments after they arrived at the plant, despite the fact that they had been ordered to rigid specifications from steelmakers—by doing its own testing, Buick's heat-treating department could if necessary modify any steel that fell short of its own standards. Still another *Bulletin* trumpeted the value of drying wood in uniformly heated kilns, ensuring that worms could not attack unevenly dried wood hidden in the frames of cars after they had left the factory. Fred W. A. Vesper, an advertising man who joined Buick in 1910, had coined the world-famous slogan "When Better Automobiles Are Built, Buick Will Build Them" around 1911, and the *Buick Bulletin* gave ample evidence that Chrysler's new techniques bore out the truth of this statement.

As with Ford, one of the keys to Chrysler's success with the introduction of mass production techniques was simplification of the product line. Buick offered three model levels in only two styles, roadster and touring, from 1912 through 1916; two truck models were made from 1913 through 1916, and a coupe and sedan were offered in 1917; in 1918 the most expensive roadster and touring models were dropped. Though Ford just offered the Model T in those years, it was produced in five body styles; because Buick only manufactured two styles in three models, that meant it was producing only one more car offering than Ford. As at Ford, changes were made in the cars, but they were relatively small, and in the area of "refinements." Grease cups were added at important places, brakes and pedals were redesigned, the gearshaft moved inside the car and was enclosed, the splash lubrication system was improved, lines were softened and rounded, and the battery box and other items were moved inside the car from the running boards. But these were hardly revolutionary alterations. Dunham and Gustin point out that feature writers of the day had a tough time coming up with things to talk about in their annual articles about new Buick cars; one man was reduced to writing about torque tube attachments two years in a row. Indeed, Chrysler had almost two full years before he had to deal with really important changes in Buick cars, and this gave him a good deal of leeway to concentrate on the all-important area of improving production techniques.

The big changes came in the 1914 model year. One was a new six-cylinder engine, Buick's first. It was a 48-horsepower, 331-cubic-inch valve-in-head affair that sold for $1,985. Work on it began in 1912, so it had been developed with considerable care, and was a high-quality unit. Only 2,045 of these cars were produced, but after the introduction of a smaller companion six in 1916, the company turned out 100,000 six-cylinder cars that year. By 1919, all Buicks were sixes.

The other big change at Buick in 1914 was the adoption of the Delco battery-run electric light and starter system. These were the items that made Walter Chrysler aware at the end of 1911 that a huge new female car market could now be tapped, and decided his immediate entry into the automobile business. But even so he took all the time he felt was necessary to make sure these items were perfected before they were introduced on the Buick. Advertisements and brochures made it plain that Buick would not add these items to its cars until it had found the best way of doing so. The story of how it was done gives a good idea of the pains that were taken to assure that Buick's reputation for the best quality was upheld. Often even a good measure of foolishness had to be endured before this goal could be achieved to the satisfaction of all parties involved.

Cranking the motor to start a car was one of the most onerous and dangerous tasks associated with operating an automobile. It required great strength to do it, and if the car backfired during the operation, an arm could be broken, or worse. Indeed, it was such an accident that caused the development of the electric starter. On Christmas Day of 1910, Byron T. Carter, developer of the friction-drive Cartercar (one of Durant's early GM purchases), stopped to help a stalled motorist in Detroit's snowy Belle Isle Park. The man's Cadillac backfired when Carter cranked it, breaking his arm and jaw; a few days later, he developed pneumonia and died. Carter was a true gentleman, one of the nicest, most respected men in Detroit. When Henry Leland heard of this incident he became extremely depressed, especially since it involved one of the cars he himself manufactured. "Cadillacs will kill no more people," he declared, and instructed his firm to develop a safe and foolproof method of starting motors. As Crabb points out, this marked the beginning of modern automotive research. From that time on research was done by teams of men combining their abilities and working full time to improve the automobile, ending the era when new devices were dreamed up by lone experimenters trying desperately to perfect their inventions on their own.

In 1911 many companies, including Winton and Packard, used self-starting devices operating on acetylene, springs, or compressed air, but none was reliable and all required constant checking and maintenance. There were many types on display at the auto show that year, including an underdeveloped one patented by Thomas Edison. Cadillac engineers looked them all over but decided to work on a generator they had developed for Leland's estate. The system they worked out would operate from a small electric motor powered by a storage battery, which in turn would be charged by a small generator operating all the time the car was on. An engineer named Frank Johnson cut teeth in the flywheel so that the starter's power could be applied to the motor at that point.

The problem with the whole business was to build an electric motor small enough and powerful enough to start the car dependably all the time, even in cold weather. Earl C. Howard, the assistant sales manager at Cadillac, recommended that Leland speak with a young engineer at National Cash Register who had developed a similar motor to eliminate the hand crank on the company's cash registers. This was Charles H. Kettering, who turned out to be one of the greatest engineers in motor car history. He worked with Cadillac engineers to create the required motor, and on February 27, 1911, it was started for the first time, turning over an engine in a fraction of the time required by hand cranking.

A few hours later elated Cadillac engineers decided that since their cars were going to have a storage battery and generator, why not operate the ignition and headlights electrically also? Most cars used Prest-O-Lite acetylene gas for their headlights then; they had to be refilled, and could blow out in wind and rain. Ford's electric lights operated on the magneto and were terribly underpowered, working neither when the motor wasn't on or when the car went slower than 25 miles per hour. Now a Cadillac's lights could be turned on instantly whether the motor was running or not, and worked even in wind, rain, or snow.

The company had a devil of a time getting the devices installed in its 1912 line, as neither small-enough batteries nor tough-enough generators existed then. Kettering assumed responsibility for manufacturing the non-motorized parts of the self-starters and electric lights. He got associates from NCR to work nights and weekends for his Dayton Electric Laboratory Company (Delco), using their own credit to get the men, materials, and cash to get the job done. Furthermore, Kettering talked the Electric Storage Battery Company into making ten thousand of the required batteries, which made them very nervous, since they had never had such a huge order before.

They weren't the only nervous ones. Storrow and the rest of the bankers on the GM board had to be convinced. Remembering the disaster of the Heany Lamp Company and knowing how precarious the company's finances were at this moment, the board had to be sure this new system wouldn't bankrupt the entire parent firm. Only after outside engineers from Westinghouse, General Electric, and the Haltske Company unanimously approved of the device did the board give the go-ahead to use it on Cadillac cars.

The crowning touch to the whole process was when Leland decided to eliminate the hand crank on Cadillacs, thereby throwing his engineers into shock. Then he told them he had taken it off and hidden it two months previously, without anyone missing it. "Why not take it off?" he said. "Haven't you any faith in your starter?"

By August 1912 Cadillac announced that cars equipped with the new system would be off the line in six months' time, and though the first ones had problems, within two years all midpriced and luxury cars had installed it or were forced out of business. After extensive testing, Cadillac was awarded an unprecedented second Dewar's Trophy for its "improved" starter-lighting-ignition system in 1913. (Apparently, they expected the award in 1912 when the originally troublesome system appeared, for in October of that year Cadillac began advertising itself as "The Standard Of The World.")

The reminiscences of Louis Ruthenberg, a key employee of Delco Labs in the early days, provide a clear picture of what the company had to go through to get Buick to adapt Kettering's device to its cars; the account is found in his article, *Ten Years With "Boss" Kettering*, published in *Ward's Auto World* in 1969.

Sometime in 1913 Charles Nash, the president of Buick, decided that his cars had to have electric starters, despite the protests of the company's chief engineer, Walter Marr, who had been vociferous in his opposition to it. Leland told Nash that Kettering's system was the way to go, and Delco worked furiously to put together a version of it to demonstrate to Buick.

Before this was done, the company sent Ruthenberg to discuss the situation with Walter Chrysler, who spoke of a need for a self-starter in Buick's popular four-cylinder models but also warned Ruthenberg that many thought a magneto would power it better than a battery. When Ruthenberg protested the superiority of his product, Chrysler concluded with, "All right, young fellow, you are going to have a fight on your hands. I'll be in your corner as long as you are right. If you are wrong, I can't stay in your corner."

The fight turned out to be a battle royal. When the badly machined sample part arrived from Delco, Guy Tressler, foreman of the experimental shop where the Delco parts were to be hooked up for demonstration, bluffed Buick's engine department into thinking it had sent over a badly machined crankcase and got them to do the work necessary to align Delco's parts correctly to the Buick one. After an all-night effort by Tressler and Ruthenberg to get the irregular Delco piece mounted in a Buick, it was ready for testing, and Chrysler told them to put it on the company's cinder test track.

The car's carburetion was adjusted for top speed, and when Chrysler sent over Marr and his assistant DeWaters, all they did was complain that the car didn't accelerate well and "pull" from low speeds, which Ruthenberg pointed out they all knew couldn't be done with the carburetor adjusted for top speed. Marr then drove it into a mudhole and condemned the ignition when it wouldn't pull the car out. The next day, after the demonstration to Chrysler and Nash, the latter told Marr this device worked just as well as a magneto equipped one, and that he was just prejudiced against it. Recognizing that they had "a little family affair to settle among themselves," Ruthenberg was sent home to Dayton.

Marr, who knew a battery ignition was going to be shoved down his throat by management whether he liked it or not, kept up his assault on the Delco system, next cabling Dayton that "laboratory tests prove your ignition less than half as effective as magneto." In a slap at the youthful Ruthenberg, he added, "Please send competent engineer at once." Ruthenberg, this time accompanied by Delco's best field engineer, Bill Mooney, arrived in Flint to discover that Marr's tests were a jerry-rigged affair to show that a magneto raised more heat than a battery ignition. This was meaningless, because the battery raised a spark only when it was needed, at the moment of ignition, whereas a magneto had an unnecessary trailing spark, which burned the plugs unnecessarily.

But, like dutiful courtiers in ancient China, Mooney and Ruthenberg did silly things to raise the temperature the battery put out, so that Marr could now be delighted and tell them they were at last getting somewhere and should arrange a road test for the "improved" system. They did, and Marr now approved completely. He had won his battle, and so he approved the system. Neither he nor Nash nor anyone else ever knew, however, that Delco shipped the original units after the first few "improved" batches went out, and no one was the wiser.

Ruthenberg was mightily impressed by his contacts with Chrysler during the Delco days. Whenever he visited Flint, Chrysler would pull out his file of Delco complaints and ask for corrective measures. "Again and again I was impressed by the directness and effectiveness of his methods," Ruthenberg said.

On one occasion he had to deal with a complaint that owners had about failure of the Delco system upon depression of the clutch pedal a few days after taking delivery of their new Buicks. After he told Chrysler he was pretty sure the short-circuiting was coming from the clutch pedal and that he needed to go to the plant to find the problem, Chrysler had a characteristic reply: "Don't stop there. Find out how to fix it. When you've done that, call me on the phone. The assembly line is half a mile away, but I'll be there in ten minutes after you call."

At the line, Ruthenberg found that the wiring was being abraded by the clutch pedal, and solved the problem by encasing the wiring in a piece of flexible loom. He also made sure the stockroom clerk had enough of this material on hand to make an immediate change.

"After he reported affirmatively, I called Chrysler. He came to the assembly line almost immediately and inspected the change. He then asked the foreman if he thought the remedy would be effective and whether more loom was available. He then jotted down in his notebook the serial number of the car on which the change had been made and said to the foreman, 'This car and all of higher serial numbers will have the change. We shall notify dealers to change all cars of lower serials. I'll see that engineering specifications are changed. So long.'"

"In other automotive plants, the change Mr. Chrysler had made within an hour might have been made within a week, after lengthy conferences, much discussion, changes in engineering specifications and records, transmission of change notification to factory, sales and field service."

Years later, Chrysler was to say, "I always tell a young man to make decisions promptly." By doing this, on a constant basis, those decisions would get better and better until they were right nearly all the time. "All I am," he said, "is just a man who wants things done and done quickly. Give me a quick decision, even if a mistake happens. That's all right. The same mistake won't happen a second time." It was one of his main principles of doing business, and this incident shows how effective such a policy could be.

Whatever Walter Chrysler did at Buick was not done in a vacuum, and he was always proud to acknowledge the accomplishments of an excellent group of men working with him.

Among these were Walter Marr, the engineer who built the first Buick and remained its chief engineer until a health crisis caused him to retire to Tennessee; when it passed, he remained with the company on a consulting basis until 1923. He was succeeded by Enos A. DeWaters, who gradually eased into the job during Marr's increasing absences. "One day Chrysler asked DeWaters why he still signed letters under the title assistant chief engineer. He replied that no one told him he was chief. Chrysler responded, 'Well, I'm telling you now.' in those informal days, that is how things were often done" (Dunham and Gustin). He served as chief engineer until 1929, and consulted for another two years.

Harry H. Bassett arrived at Buick when Weston-Mott was absorbed into Buick in 1916. Bassett became assistant general manager under Chrysler at Buick from 1916 to 1919, eventually succeeding him as president and guiding the company's fortunes superbly from 1920 to his sudden and untimely death in 1926.

Richard "Trainload" Collins was sales manager of Buick until 1916, after which he became president of Cadillac before moving on to run Peerless in 1921. As the name implies, he was famous for selling Buicks by the trainload, and was in large measure responsible for the tripling of Buick sales between 1914 and 1916. Of Chrysler and him, Ruthenberg quotes the following exchange: "The former told me, 'Dick Collins is a great sales executive—probably the best. But we can build a hell of a lot more cars than he can sell.' On the same day Collins said, 'Walter Chrysler is undoubtedly the greatest production man in the industry, but, with the distributor and dealer organization I've built, we are going to outsell production.' Quiet, shrewd Nash was quite happy to encourage the rivalry, and Buick prospered greatly."

Edward T. Strong came to Buick from the harvester business. After two years as manager of sales in the Buffalo and Chicago branches, Strong succeeded Collins as Buick's sales manager from 1916 to 1926, after which he took Bassett's place as president of Buick for six years.

Cady Durham was the beloved and respected superintendent of Buick's engine plant who became general master mechanic, works manager, and finally assistant general manager of the company in 1920. He was a colorful, spontaneous man who boasted that he could call each of his men by their names, and do all their jobs, too—which wasn't surprising, since he had designed most of the machines on which they worked.

As mentioned before, Chet Smith was the production manager who was instrumental in effecting all the plant changes Chrysler introduced when he first arrived at Buick, and was of invaluable assistance to him.

Most famous, and most important to Chrysler in the future, was K. T. Keller. Chrysler first noticed him when he worked for the GM central office staff, and found in him a kindred spirit with a love of all things mechanical. He kept an eye on Keller's career even when he went on to work for other companies, and hired him away from the Cole Motor Car Company to become master mechanic at Buick before he had turned thirty. In 1926 he hired him for the Chrysler Corporation, where he was groomed to succeed Chrysler himself in 1935.

Some of these men were inherited by Chrysler; some he picked out and moved along himself. W. A. P. John, in an article called *Chrysler Punches In*, originally published in *Motor* magazine in May 1923, asked him how he picked men. "I don't know. You just do it," he replied. "On the basis, I suppose, of what you can deduce from their character, training, experience and personality and your hunch as to how they will fit into the job and work with the others around them. Sometimes you're right and sometimes you're wrong. . . . It's lots of fun handling an organization and more fun watching the men grow and preparing for the organization's future."

The story of Ruthenberg and the Delco ignition also points to how Chrysler dealt with men outside the organization. He identified the company's needs and then demanded improved machine tools from all the salesmen who called on him. "A machine tool salesman would no more than show his head inside my office than we'd be after him: 'We have to have a machine that can—' Then he'd take his pencil out and write down what we needed; back in his home factory he would feed the problem to the engineers: 'How can we do thus and so?' They would work it out, sometimes swiftly, sometimes not for months or even years." Chrysler and his staff would do all they could to help get what they needed, but in the end that salesman and his company had to be on their toes to get and keep the Buick business. The same applied to suppliers of such raw materials as cotton, steel, and other metals. "We kept on reaching out for better ways, for better things, until evolutionary changes were occurring . . . everywhere raw materials came from. We were insistent—imperiously sometimes," Chrysler said. After all, "we were making the first machine of considerable size in the history of the world for which every human being was a potential customer."

These officials and the thousands of men who worked under them inhabited a vast Buick plant in Flint. A company publication of 1913 outlined its scope. A total floor area of 2,453,124 square feet was divided among many buildings. Two assembly factories measured 758 by 74 feet, one was 782 by 74 feet, a fourth 800 by 74 feet; all were three stories high, and contained a total of 16 acres, just in those four buildings alone. The transmission and general machine building measured 349 by 268 feet, and the shipping department building, the largest in the world, was 308 by 211 feet. The drop-forge building occupied 59,630 square feet, and the brass foundry another 27,590 square feet. A sheet metal and radiator building was 690 by 140 feet, an enameling department covered 21,750 square feet, a body plant 121,800 square feet, and a motor castings foundry 65,000 square feet. The pride of the whole organization was the engine plant. At 782 feet long by 360 feet wide, it covered 6 acres; it was the largest motor-manufacturing plant under one roof, and the largest machine shop in the world. Eleven other buildings contained power plants, garages, sales rooms, offices, and other departments whose function was vital to the company.

The Buick was completely manufactured in house from scratch, and was in no way an assembled car. The company had its own spring works, gray iron foundry, brass foundry, forging plant, sheet metal plant, radiator plant, spark plug plant, aluminum foundry, body plant, wheel plant, axle plant, and motor plant, all making parts from chemically tested raw materials. These parts were then sent to machine, motor, gear cutting, axle, forging, and milling plants, after which enameling, upholstery, and top shops did their jobs. Finally all the pieces went to assembly plants, one for each model. Everything was made at Buick, down to cap screws, nuts, and bolts.

Unlike Ford, the company didn't have to learn this method of construction, for it had always been this way. It was the way of the future, for it meant that costs and quality could be company controlled, both for the benefit of the company and the consumer. Buick literature touted the advantages of the manufactured car over the assembled one, noting that a Buick owner never had to worry about a car disabled by the unavailability of a part that had been sold to a manufacturer by a supplier who was out of business or had discontinued the item in question. Buick was always there for the owner to rely on, no matter what the problem with its products.

On November 7, 1913, in what was probably the most extravagant single gesture of his life, Walter Chrysler had a photograph made of all the men and women of Buick, standing outside one of the company's factories. The December 1913 edition of The Buick Bulletin shows this extraordinary human document of Buick under the heading: "THE MEN WHO WORK UNDER ONE COLOSSAL SYSTEM BUILDING THE CAR THAT SELLS BY THE TRAINLOAD; PAY ROLL AVERAGES $406,645 A MONTH; TOTAL OPERATING EXPENSES ABOUT $110,000 A DAY." The accompanying article states that five thousand handbills were distributed the previous day to the workmen in the plants, telling them to show up on a triangular piece of ground just east of the factory #6 at 11:20 A.M. the following day. "The men filed into the field with the precision of a fire drill. The seats, regular circus chairs, two box car loads of them, had been brought into town especially for the occasion. There weren't enough places for all, but those who couldn't stand up without somebody behind them sat on the ground, and the ground was awfully wet too, as some of us know by experience." There they stand, five thousand men lined up in rows before the huge plant, on which is hung a banner hundreds of feet long proclaiming in enormous black letters: "BUICK MOTOR CO. LARGEST AUTOMOBILE MANUFACTURERS IN THE WORLD ANNUAL CAPACITY 40,000 CARS." (Remember that at this point Ford, whose capacity was larger, was still in large measure *assembling* Dodge Brothers parts.) Right down in front, ramrod straight and leaning on his knee like a star quarterback, is Walter Chrysler, Works Manager—not alone, mind you, but in a line with other top executives of the company. Leadership, cooperation, solidarity: these were his trademarks, and this photograph says it all.

Considered the largest photograph of industrial personnel taken up to that time, it intends to leave a gargantuan impression of manufacturing power, which the article reinforces by quoting the value of the materials used by the factory, and the value of the plant to Flint. The 2,973,300 square feet of leather Buick used cost it $768,332 a year, and 13,000 tons of steel cost $532,785; the company paid out $1,355,240 for aluminum, $5,175,000 for tires, and so on. Millions of dollars in wages meant a great deal to the local economy, it said, and the company itself was the occasion of great civic pride: "The Buick system of operation is on such a scientific basis that the shops turn out 165 and 170 cars a day with a little more than 5,000 men while some other manufacturing concerns employ nearly twice as many men for a similar output."

The plant had been quite famous for some time. According to an article in *Auto Topics* of October 19, 1912, appearing under the headline "Bull Moose Gazes into Buick Factory," presidential candidate Theodore Roosevelt and his party stopped off for two hours on a trip between Detroit and Saginaw to inspect the Buick factory and take in its wonders, and incidentally to do a bit of speechifying to the workers.

A rather touching page from the *Buick Bulletin* of April 1913 shows a time-honored way in which the men of Buick were able to express their company pride. On the top of the page is a photo of the Buick band, looking for all the world just like the Union Pacific band Chrysler had played in twenty-five years previously; it was described as being composed of "high class musicians, some of whom have played with Sousa and Creatore and other bandmasters of world wide reputation." On the bottom of the page is a photo of the Buick soccer team, with a list of its triumphs leading to a first-place win over Packard. The honorary president of the team, Walter Chrysler, sits in the midst of the team, just above its victory cup.

In addition to music and sports, there was another kind of activity the men participated in. Through the efforts of William E. Beacraft, a major in the Salvation Army who was superintendent of the engine works, there were religious meetings at the Buick plant every noontime, beginning around the time Chrysler started with the company. By the end of the 1910s there were hymns and homilies by Flint clergymen in most of the city's plants during the lunch break, a practice that continued up to the Depression. Odd though this may seem to modern readers, this sort of thing was hardly unique to Buick. A decade before, Henry Leland would have his men get down on their knees for prayer breaks during the day (as opposed to other shops, such as Flanders's, where men got beer breaks instead). Leland's practice gave rise to a famous remark. One day a Cadillac worker, upon seeing the firm's three principals, Henry Leland, his son Wilfred, and Ernest Sweet, two of whom were bearded, remarked, "Well boys, our troubles are all over now. Here comes the Father, the Son and the Holy Ghost."

It is important to note that Chrysler's new position hadn't turned him into any starched-collar stick-in-the-mud, some lofty figure presiding over the men below him. Fred Hoelzle recalled that one day during an inventory period when production was suspended, he and some of the other Buick boys decided to play hooky and go to see their beloved Southern Michigan baseball team play. As they sat in the bleachers, who should walk in and take seats a few rows ahead of them but Walter Chrysler and Charles Nash, skipping school just as they were. But they were the bosses and could do what they wanted. Needless to say, the boys were mighty uncomfortable. When the snack vendor came along, Chrysler and Nash bought some popcorn, whereupon Chrysler turned around and asked, "Fred, what would you fellows like?" They had peanuts, which somehow or other didn't taste too good. The next day, Chrysler never mentioned a word about the whole business. Having done the same thing all those years ago to see the circus parade in Wellington, Kansas, he knew exactly what his men were going through and did his best to put them at ease. As the Jesuit novelist and poet John Louis Bonn once said, "A gentleman is a man who knows the precise moment to put his feet *on* the table."

There were "official" good time breaks at Buick too. An interdepartmental memorandum invited all the major Buick executives to a banquet at a place called Bridgeport on April 10, 1919. The invitation said that the banquet was given "Prior to putting in our crops for the coming season, and to commemorate the breaking up of a hard winter." Walter Chrysler was to be the toastmaster, and the diners were to be transported by a special car leaving from the front of the office building at 6:00 P.M. that evening.

Chrysler did more for the men than buy them the occasional bag of peanuts, however. He made sure Buick factory buildings were well lighted and ventilated, with plenty of fresh water always available, and provided pleasant lunchrooms for the workers to eat in. An efficient maintenance corps was always at work keeping the buildings clean and well painted. There were trained nurses on duty to deal with any medical problems, and an ambulance for emergencies. A 1916 Christmas note from Chrysler's friend the Reverend J. Bradford Pengelly commends him for starting a department of personal services at the plant also. Eventually his concern for decent living circumstances for his men and their families would lead him to do important work on their behalf in this vital area of their lives.

Under Chrysler, production at Buick expanded, expenses declined significantly, and profits went way, way up. The only thing that didn't go up was Chrysler's salary, and the reason was the parsimonious Charley Nash. Chrysler characterized him as a fellow who was never "reckless with any-body's money. . . . I'd tell him he was tighter than a barrel without a bung. 'Charley,' I'd say imploringly, in the manner of a little boy, 'please show me the first nickel you ever earned. Mr. Storrow says you've got it hidden some-where.' " After working at Buick for three years without a raise from his original $6,000, Chrysler finally got mad about it. Flint was a boom town, and Chrysler felt conspicuous by his lack of increasing prosperity, especially compared to other executives of similar station to his. One day he walked into Nash's office, put his knuckles on the table, and asked for $25,000 a year, otherwise he'd quit. All Nash could do was screech, "Walter!" before calming down and mumbling that he'd have to speak to Storrow. Two days later, in a conference with both men, Chrysler was told he'd gotten his raise. He replied, "Yes? Well, thank you; and by the way: next year I want $50,000."

Elated, he went home to tell Della, who was thrilled. They lived in a modest frame house and were not in the least extravagant, as were many of their acquaintances. He attributed this mostly to his wife's steady influ-ence. On this occasion he told her to go ahead and get an evening gown they had been discussing; ever the sport, he said, "Aw, get two." But she turned him down, content with just the one she needed.

This was the spring of 1915, a time when big changes began to happen at GM. They involved none other than Billy Durant, who was about to stage what is still today the biggest comeback in American business history. After the bankers deposed him as head of General Motors in 1910, he remained in an influential spot as chairman of the finance committee until Novem-ber of 1911, when Storrow succeeded him. Slowly, painstakingly, but surely, he regrouped and reorganized his affairs around a new company, Chevrolet, using it as a lever to regain control of GM by the autumn of 1915.

He did it by doing what he had done before. Durant returned to Flint, where he had started out with Buick just seven years earlier, and formulated his plans to start a new company using the talents of Louis Chevrolet, a famous Swiss-born race car driver who had recently driven Buick's little "Bug" racers to big victories around the country. When Durant made up his mind to go back into business, he simply called on Chevrolet, told him, "We need a car," and set him up in a rented Detroit loft to design that car.

Durant actually set up two companies in Flint in the summer of 1911, one the Chevrolet Motor Car Company, one the Little Motor Car Company, which manufactured a low-priced car bearing the name of company su-pervisor William Little; he also bought a substantial interest in the Mason Motor Company, which under Arthur Mason manufactured engines for the other two companies. As in the case of the founding of GM, next to no cash was paid in, perhaps $36,500 in all, with Durant relying on the credit he commanded among his friends in Flint to enable the first year's production of three thousand cars to be financed from sales receipts alone. It was like the early Durant days at Buick all over again.

Luck was with him in other ways, too. Just at this moment all the carriage companies in Flint, seeing the writing on the wall, were closing down, and Durant bought out the assets of the Flint Wagon Works for $200,000 on his personal note. Little was sent off to Detroit to help with the Chevrolet, and A. B. C. Hardy, the great production man who had built Flint's first cars before running afoul of the Selden patent, took Little's designs for four-cylinder light runabouts to be priced at $650 to $690 and manufactured them. He made three thousand of them in 1912, plus extra motors, several thousand buggies, and assorted parts. In 1913 Durant-Dort sold Durant more factory space for $200,000 in Chevrolet stock.

All Durant was doing here was trying to fill the gap in the Buick line that he perceived had opened up with the cancellation of the Buick Model 10, its best-seller. In fact, the Little had many of the same features of the Model 10, at a much lower price. And in other ways, too, Durant returned to business on the back of the Buick retrenchment that came after he left GM: He hired many laid-off Buick workers, and purchased the now-abandoned factory on the west side of Flint where Buicks were originally made.

Down in Detroit the first Chevrolets began coming off the line in the form of the Classic Six, a surprisingly large, ponderous five-passenger touring car that was priced at $2,150. Though the three thousand units that were sold the first year were a tribute to Louis Chevrolet's racing fame and Durant's marketing ability, the car was basically a flop. It was a solid car, but heavy in appearance and handling, and almost a thousand dollars higher in price than Durant wanted it to be. Still, its advent in the middle of 1912 was much delayed, and Durant needed to put it into production, so he did. But he quickly started to figure out a way to save the situation.

His first notion was to produce the Little Six in Flint at $1,285, a much more attractive price. The trouble, however, was that the car was a piece of junk. Durant's own tests told him it wouldn't last more than 25,000 miles. But, unlike the Chevrolet Classic Six, it sold.

Durant knew this situation wouldn't hold, and tried to remedy it as quickly as he could. He had already commissioned a new prototype but scrapped it when he realized it would be too expensive to produce. He also tried to convince Louis Chevrolet to design a smaller, lighter six for the Little, but to Chevrolet, a big, expansive man with grand ideas, that was unthinkable. By the middle of 1913 he quit his namesake company, an event that was probably preordained by the lack of compatibility between his personal style and Durant's. The blowup came when Durant, who loathed

Chevrolet's constant cigarette smoking, told him to give them up in favor of cigars, which he thought were more seemly for an important company official. In a typically volcanic outburst, Chevrolet yelled at Durant, "I sold you my car and I sold you my name, but I'm not going to sell myself to you. I'm going to smoke my cigarettes as much as I want. And I'm getting out." He sold his shares at a modest profit, "And so Louis Chevrolet departed, not too gently, into the peculiar night that enveloped David Buick. Both men would have their names mentioned literally thousands of times a day throughout the United States and parts of the world, but those who spoke the names would rarely have any idea that they once belonged to men" (Weisberger).

At last in 1914 the solution to lasting success was found. Durant took the best from both the Chevrolet and the Little and combined them into two new models, the Royal Mail, a coupe, and the Baby Grand, a touring car, both wearing the Chevrolet badge. They were priced attractively, and an ebullient Durant announced that he planned to sell twenty-five thousand of them in 1914, after which Hardy gently pointed out he could only build five thousand, which in the end was the amount sold. No matter; the new cars were a hit, and the following year the introduction of the 490 series (that was the price) caused sales to explode: By 1916 almost 63,000 cars were produced.

Durant was busy on the stock front, too. He had closed down operations in Detroit and moved all production to Flint, but he personally began to spend more and more time in New York, where he increasingly concerned himself with high finance. A banker friend, Louis Graveret Kaufman, got Hornblower and Weeks to support a new Chevrolet stock issue, and later helped Durant consolidate three companies into the main Chevrolet one, changing it from a Michigan company to a Delaware company capitalized at $20 million. Kaufman also claimed that he was the one who first interested Pierre S. du Pont in buying GM stock, an event of signal importance; du Pont himself, however, said it was John J. Raskob, his financial adviser, who did it. At any rate, du Pont, beginning with a purchase of 2,000 shares, began acquiring GM stock in 1915, until by 1919 he and his family's interests owned 28.7 percent of all outstanding shares. From 1917 on, he controlled more and more of the company, until eventually he ran it.

Durant, knowing the conservatism of GM's bank management and the profits the company was building up, thought the company's stock was undervalued and began buying it up, believing this would be a way to regain control of his "baby." It was all done on the quiet, so the price of the stock would not boom. Chrysler, in *Taking the Lamp Apart*, tells of a major transaction during this period that speaks to Durant's shrewdness. Durant recalled that one night he met with Albert Strauss, one of the banker board members of GM who had deposed him, at his offices at J. &

W. Seligman for the purpose of purchasing all that company's GM stock, "a wagon load," at $30 a share. When the transaction was complete, Strauss inquired as to what the stock was worth. " 'Well', said Billy, with a merry gleam in his eye, 'I have certificates engraved the same as yours, signed by the same officers. I consider mine worth $1,000 a share.' Mr. Strauss blinked. What he had just sold to Durant at $30 a share was to sell on the New York Stock Exchange at $975 a share."

In the spring of 1915 he made his intentions plain and began soliciting GM stock more openly. He took any shares he could find, and convinced loyal business associates and cronies who held large blocks of it to give him their shares to control. Storrow didn't believe that Durant or anyone else could gain control of the company, but he saw that Durant was a dynamic figure who would be an important force in the company's operations, and so he retired from the board and his position as finance chairman in June of 1915, replaced in the latter position by Durant's man Louis Kaufman.

Durant decided to use the GM board meeting of September 16, 1915, to put his position clearly before it. This was a very important meeting, coming on the seventh anniversary of the founding of the company. An announcement was supposed to be made to the effect that the company's bank debt would be retired on October 11, three months earlier than planned, due to the profits that had been built up. It was also expected that GM would declare its first common stock dividend at that time.

On September 13, Durant showed Wilfred Leland an enormous stack of GM certificates, which he claimed represented control of the company, and firmly predicted that they would allow him to take it over once again. All through the night before the meeting on the fifteenth, he and three associates stayed up counting each certificate and passing it through all four hands to make sure it was recorded accurately. On the sixteenth Durant, Nash, Storrow, and "certain other parties" had a meeting downtown, after which the board meeting took place. It was at first a standoff, with neither side having the votes to assert control. Storrow broke the ice by proposing an expansion of the board to seventeen members, with each side electing seven and du Pont proposing three neutral directors. At the regular board meeting bouquets were tossed around as the debt was paid off, a $50 dividend was declared on each $100 share (the largest dividend ever declared up to that time on a listed NYSE stock), and the board proposal was approved (it was actually approved on November 16, at which time du Pont was elected chairman of the board and Charles Nash was reaffirmed as president). But this was far from the end of the matter. Before the end of the meeting, Durant offered to bring in Chevrolet as part of the company, but the board turned him down, saying it wasn't clear he actually controlled it. Within the year they would find out how wrong they were.

Chevrolet was dutifully recapitalized at $40 million one week after the meeting, and when demand for the stock proved overwhelming, it was re-capitalized again ninety days later at $80 million. By the beginning of January 1916 Durant made clear what the new $60 million in stock was for. He offered to exchange five shares of Chevrolet common stock for every one share of GM common, and one share of Chevrolet common for every one share of GM preferred. Since he ran a syndicate that made sure the Chevrolet stock was supported at $140, and GM stock was selling at no higher than $558, there was money to be made, and stockholders rushed in like crazy to turn in their GM stock. After all, they couldn't lose even if GM stock rose, for its dividends would now accrue to Chevrolet, which would pay out to its own shareholders.

Durant cinched his situation one Sunday when he went down to see Pierre du Pont and his family in Delaware. He sold them on his position, and left with permission from them to buy up enough GM and Chevrolet stock to gain control of GM; that turned out to be $27 million worth.

The bankers fought back, claiming that their good management had caused the company to roll up huge profits, pay off its debts, and declare big dividends, but it was all to no avail. Durant's cash offer won out. By May he announced that he controlled some 450,000 of the 825,589 GM shares outstanding. He made sure that any profits he made from his syndicate were liberally dispensed to his loyal supporters, even allowing non-players such as du Pont and Raskob in on the five-for-one action on a late basis.

His triumph was complete. Chevrolet had in effect swallowed General Motors, and if he had been so inclined, Durant could have even changed the name of the whole company to Chevrolet; he did not, though, realizing the value of the General Motors franchise. He did allow himself to be named president of GM despite his abhorrence of titles. Most important of all, on the following October 13 General Motors dropped its identity as a holding corporation and became General Motors Corporation, a manufacturing company chartered in corporation-friendly Delaware. The former operating companies that had made up the company, such as Buick, Cadillac, Oakland, and so on, now became divisons of General Motors, and all the company managers now became division managers, vice presidents of the corporation, and members of the corporate board of directors.

There were two big, immediate problems for Durant to clear up relative to the future of GM. They were called Nash and Chrysler, and he dealt with them immediately.

Nash was a protégé of Durant's, whom he had moved along from Durant-Dort's early days all the way to the presidency of Buick at General Motors. Nash himself rose to the presidency of GM under the bankers after Durant's departure. During the proxy fight in 1916 Durant assumed Nash would be on his side, and made big plans for his continuance at GM; Nash even said he had been offered a huge sum of money to stay on. However, when it became apparent that Nash was on the bankers' side, Durant was livid, for he was a man to whom friendship and loyalty were everything. After he regained control of GM, he wasted no time getting rid of the man he now saw as an ingrate and a turncoat. At their last meeting Durant reportedly said, "Well, Charley, you're through."

For Nash, it had been a question of Durant's executive style. He told Chrysler, "I'll never work for him again. . . . It upsets me too much to have anybody else monkeying with an organization I'm supposed to run. I owe Durant a lot; I admire him, too; but I won't work for him. I can't. You won't be able to either, Walt. You'll suppose yourself to be the boss, and then he'll come along—well, you'll find out. He's got princely charm, he is the soul of generosity, but—"

In the spring of 1916 Durant knew that Nash was making plans to leave. Storrow thought that he, Nash, and Chrysler should go into their own producing venture, and they approached Packard as a group with a buyout offer for the whole concern. It all seemed to be going smoothly, with Packard Chairman James Joy interested, but enough members of the board felt otherwise for the deal to be squelched.

The men next turned their attention to the Thomas B. Jeffery Company of Kenosha, Wisconsin, builders of the pioneer Rambler car, which had metamorphosed into the Jeffery in 1914. The company became available after Charles Jeffery, the forty-year-old son of the company's founder, decided to retire after surviving the harrowing ordeal of the 18-minute sinking of the *Lusitania* off the coast of Ireland in May 1915, during World War I. Storrow told Chrysler that Jeffery would be available at the bargain price of less than $5 million, which Lee, Higginson would advance on the strength of Nash's reputation. He urged Chrysler to join, pointing out that he would be one of the principals in the company and would have the satisfaction of working for himself. It certainly was a tempting proposition, but it would mean that Chrysler and his family would have to move to a new town once again, which they were loath to do, since they all felt settled and comfortable in Flint. He turned Storrow down, though the two men remained on the best of terms for the rest of Storrow's life. The same was true of his relationship with Nash, who, together with Storrow, took over Jeffery on July 29, 1916; he had resigned as president of GM on June 1, 1916.

Durant of course was well aware of what was going on, and after Nash resigned, he offered Chrysler a promotion to president of Buick. Chrysler demurred, saying that he was considering another proposition, which he would take if it worked out. Upon Durant's further inquiry, he said it would take about thirty days to know for sure. Durant asked him to call when he had decided what he was going to do.

When Chrysler realized he wished to remain in Flint and finally made the call, he arranged a 7 A.M. meeting with Durant at the Buick factory, since that was when his day began. Durant was waiting for him. They sat at opposite sides of a table, and Durant got right to the point. "I'll pay you $500,000 a year to stay on here as president of Buick," he said. Just like that. Flabbergasted by an offer that was far beyond what he had expected, Chrysler took a few moments to collect himself. Then Nash's warning flashed through his mind, and as he started to speak, Durant broke in: "Now Walter . . . , you just put aside, for the time being, all your plans of getting into business for yourself. I don't blame you for the ambition, but I ask you to give me just three years of yourself." He then appealed to Chrysler's loyalty to his own men, who had stood by him in all the upheaval with Nash. "They have stood by me, as you say," Chrysler acknowledged, "but I'm standing by them when I say that I can accept only if I'm to have full authority. I can run this property by myself. I don't want interference. I don't want any other boss but you. If you feel that anything is going wrong, if you don't like some action of mine, you come to me; don't go to anybody else and don't try to split up my authority. Just have one channel between Flint and Detroit from me to you. Full authority is what I want." By this time Durant knew he had made his sale; his face beamed, and he touched his fingers lightly to the tabletop. "It's a deal," he said.

Chrysler later recalled: "I cannot hope to find words to express the charm of the man. He has the most winning personality of anyone I've ever known. He could coax a bird right down out of a tree, I think. I remember the first time my wife and I entered his home. The walls were hung with magnificent tapestries. At that time I had never experienced luxury to compare with Billy Durant's house. In five minutes he had me feeling as if I owned the place."

At the end of his deal with Durant, he would feel as if he owned a large part of General Motors too. The deal was sweetened before it was signed, with Durant doing one of his famous stock manipulations, which turned out to be very much in Chrysler's favor. He arranged for Chrysler to draw $10,000 at the end of each month, with the right to draw the balance at the end of each year either in cash or in GM stock, priced as it was the day the agreement was signed. In other words, he had a direct stake in his own hard work, with nothing to lose if the profits of the corporation as a whole didn't hold up. In the event, he made a fortune by the time he left the company.

Walter Chrysler became president of Buick on June 7, 1916. On June 27 he was elected a member of the board of directors of General Motors, and on December 14 he became a vice president of the corporation.

Chrysler and Durant were two fiercely energetic, forceful men with diametrically opposed management styles. Chrysler wanted everything bolted to the floor, and Durant wanted to be able to move anything and everything around at a moment's notice. Conflict was inevitable, and it came.

The first major blowup was over a dispute with Richard "Trainload" Collins, Chrysler's old rival who had headed Buick's sales department and was now a member of GM's corporate board (the following year he would become president of Cadillac). A crony of Durant's, he appeared one day in Chrysler's office to inform him that he had bought Buick's Detroit branch house from Durant (it was the most profitable of the sixteen the company owned, earning about $200,000 annually for GM). Chrysler became apoplectic. He put on his coat, jammed his derby on his head, and told Collins on his way out the door, "You might as well go downstairs and get in your otherwise-than-Buick automobile and drive on back to tell Durant that you have not bought the Detroit branch. I'm going to be there about as quick as you are, because I'm going right now." In Detroit he laced into Durant, reminding him that their agreement specified that he and he alone would run Buick's affairs, including this one. Durant countered that Collins had been trying to wheedle this out of him for months, but Chrysler was adamant: If Collins got the branch, he was through. If Durant wanted to change corporate policy, fine, but at Buick he was to be the undisputed boss. Durant backed down, and that was that.

About a year later came another dispute. This time Durant wanted to hire Chrysler's drop forge superintendent for General Motors at $12,000 a year, $4,000 more than he was being paid at Buick. Again Chrysler threatened to quit if Durant interfered with the running of his plant, and Durant offered to cancel the arrangement. Chrysler declined, because he didn't want to stand in the way of the man's advancement, but he made it plain that he was very unhappy.

More and more of these incidents began piling up, until in exasperation Chrysler went to Durant and pleaded for some order in their relations. "Billy, for the love of—please now, say what your policies are for General Motors. I'll work on them; whatever they are, I'll work to make them effective. Leave the operations alone; the building, the buying, the selling and the men—leave them alone, but say what your policies are." Durant laughed and said, "Walt, I believe in changing the policies just as often as my office door opens and closes." Chrysler shook his head and replied, "You and I can never get along."

He knew Durant couldn't help it; when he saw someone or something he wanted, he just threw money in the right direction, consequences be damned. He had done the same thing to keep Chrysler at Buick. Whenever the two men would fight, he'd try to smooth things over by raising Chrysler's salary. But Chrysler kept saying he didn't need more money, he just wanted Durant to keep his hands off Buick. Nash's warnings never left his mind.

Buick was by far the most successful element of General Motors. Other divisions made money, but up to half the profits of the whole corporation were coming from the Buick division. This worried Durant, who wanted all divisions to be equally successful. He would try to deflect any situation that would give Buick too much power. Still, money was being made at Buick, lots of it, and no one could argue too strongly with that.

◆   ◆   ◆

Chrysler's progress at Buick continued apace. It had been announced that all Buicks for 1916 would be sixes, with a new 224-cubic-inch 45-horsepower small model to sell for only $985; sales that year nearly tripled to an all-time record of 124,834 units. Even restrictions on materials such as steel as the country geared up for wartime production in 1917 didn't depress Buick sales much, with the company turning out 115,267 cars that year (with the four-cylinder model now back in the product line).

During this time he set the company on the path to producing all-steel panelled bodies. The poplar bodies the company had been using were both heavy and not very durable. They had to be sawed, steamed, bent, shaped, and glued, processes that were both time-consuming and expensive for something that shouldn't have been made of wood in the first place—metal was much stronger and could be expected to last much longer. The problem was how to turn out metal bodies. One day, in a Toledo plant, Chrysler watched steel oil barrels being made, and suddenly an idea hit him. He ran out and found the man who had made the expanding dies for the barrels, and hired him on the spot, taking him to Flint to work on dies for a steel-panelled Buick body. It took months and a lot of money, but Buick finally got those steel-panelled bodies.

In 1917 Chrysler harnessed Buick to the war effort, without even getting formal approval from Durant, who characteristically was too preoccupied to talk with him about it during a quick trip Chrysler made to New York. Chrysler hopped on a train for Washington and met with Colonel Edward Deeds, a former Delco man now in charge of aircraft production for the War Department. He collected an order for 3,000 twelve-cylinder Liberty motors from Deeds within three hours, and took rolls of blueprints back with him to Flint. He plunged forward into the work needed to get the job set up, at one point not even returning home for two weeks. He worked very closely on this project with K. T. Keller, his master mechanic in charge of tooling, and gave him a great deal of credit for the speed with which it was done.

There were problems, though, mainly derived from the fact that the Liberty motors were a joint venture in a way, with certain parts the exclusive province of designated manufacturers. Ford made all the cylinders, and could hold up Buick production if they didn't come through fast enough. Chrysler found out that Ford was having problems producing the overhead camshaft cylinder heads that Buick was making easily, so he struck a deal with Harold Wills at Ford to exchange cylinders for cylinder heads (he had brought some of the cylinder heads with him to the meeting with Wills). After Henry Ford and the government gave their respective approvals, the deal was struck, and Buick was testing its first Liberty motors within two months.

Shortly thereafter Buick got an order for eight-cylinder aircraft engines and began producing them, too, along with a variety of other war materiel. By the time the war was finished, Buick had produced 1,338 Liberty motors (mostly twelve-cylinder ones), 1.2 million 3-inch mortar shells, 1.2 million mortar bases, 1.05 million shell casings, 397,000 cartridge containers, 13,500 trucks, and 11,000 sets of axles, plus tanks, trench helmets, hospital equipment, and other metal objects.

The most famous single item Buick produced in World War I was an ambulance that resembled a small house attached to a Buick chassis. It saw service ministering to the Allied wounded from 1914 to 1917, was taken by the Germans, and was recaptured by the Americans in 1918. The French government awarded the battered but unbowed little vehicle the Croix de Guerre for its wartime service, and later on it was returned to the United States and put on display in the Red Cross museum in Washington.

Largely because of the work of Buick, British munitions minister Winston Churchill sent GM a gracious note of thanks for its wartime help. Durant read it at a Flint dinner given in his honor, and returned a note of good wishes and sincere thanks to Churchill on behalf of his company and the citizens of Flint.

The war turned out to be a good thing for Buick's future in unforeseen ways. With production strained to capacity and thousands of orders unfilled during this time, it was clear that the factory needed to expand. As reported in *Horseless Age*, an explosion in the brass and aluminum foundry at Buick in January 1917 caused this building, the only wooden one in the complex, to burn to the ground, at a loss of $40,000. It was swiftly replaced with the largest gray iron foundry in the world. This incident impressed on Chrysler the need for fully modern facilities, and later that year adaptation of the plant to wartime production made him realize that new buildings that could both accommodate the manufacture of a tremendous amount of war materiel and later serve as an expanded plant for pent-up postwar car demand were needed immediately. Therefore, he began supervising an enormous building program at Buick that featured bigger, improved buildings equipped with the latest type of machinery. The ones needed for the war effort were built with great speed, and plans for the others were so completely laid out that they were put up and finished shortly after the armistice at the end of 1918. By 1920 the company had a factory more than a mile long and four city blocks wide, completely devoted to the progressive assembly of six models of Buick cars; each of three final-assembly plants had lines for each model. By supervising the erection and/or modification of the whole business, Chrysler put Buick in an excellent position to take advantage of the booming car markets of the 1920s with well-built products efficiently produced.

♦ ♦ ♦

During this whole time, from his arrival in Flint, Walter Chrysler's personal life was a thing created by Della and visited by him whenever he could find time to do so. For three years the family lived in the same unpretentious white frame house Walt had found when he arrived in Flint, until prosperity allowed him to build his own home for the first time in his life. He constructed a handsome stucco-and-timber A-frame residence, combining elements of both a Cotswolds cottage and a Swiss chalet, at 514 East Kearsley Street in Flint. Attractive and unusual, it had eye-catching appeal on the outside and large, comfortable rooms within. From indications in a local newspaper, *Flint Saturday Night*, it appears that Thelma and Bernice, now teenagers, were both very popular and enjoyed a full and happy social life. The boys, much younger, passed these years uneventfully, as far as anyone knows. There are particularly sunny, smiling photos of Walter Junior surviving from those years. In one he stands with wrinkled knickers, rumpled white shirt, and bow tie askew, the smile in his pudgy face revealing several missing teeth, his arms oustretched in the pleasure of a bright and beautiful day.

Of Della we know little except her long-suffering patience, which her husband lavishly praised. He plunged into his work from the beginning at Buick, and even after 1916, when the big money finally began to come in, he didn't have much time to give to his family. During the production of war materiel in 1917 and 1918 he barely even got home at all. Della was probably spending less time with Walter than ever before, and it could not have made her very happy.

Not much is known about her attachment to religion, but a curious document from this period is extant. It is a baptismal certificate in her name, dated Easter Even, 1915. Apparently the service was performed by the Rev. Mr. Pengelly, Walter Chrysler's friend and admirer, who was pastor of St. Paul's Episcopal Church in Flint; Charles Stewart Mott and Harriet Monroe were her sponsors. About a month later, on May 30, she was confirmed by Bishop Charles D. Williams in the same church. Among Christian churches a baptism in one denomination is considered valid in all the others, so one wonders why Della did this. She might have been some sort of freethinker until this time, but that would have been highly unusual in the small Kansas town in which she grew up, where so much social life centered around the church. Additionally, she was married to Walt in the Methodist church at Ellis, and members of the Forker family were known to be churchgoers in Pittsburgh. Perhaps her original baptismal and confirmation documents had been lost and she had decided to formalize her situation. No one knows today. However, it appears that religion played an important part in her life from this time forward, no matter what it had meant to her in the past. Eventually she was to collect Christian religious art and artifacts of many types, and she had a small chapel in her Long Island home.

At the same time that Walter Chrysler's success at Buick was confirmed by his appointment to prestigious posts within the corporation, his father, Henry, died. The U.S. government had pensioned him off for his Civil War service at the rate of $24 a month in 1905, and illness forced him to go on the retired list at the Union Pacific in 1908, at the rate of $50 a month. By then Henry and Anna had moved to Salina, Kansas, where he was to spend the rest of his days. The couple came to Flint quite frequently to see Walt and Della, as did Irene and Ed with their respective families. There are a number of photos of the family in shirtsleeves and summer dresses at family outings, even some taken shortly before Henry's death on May 23, 1916. Though Anna remained at Salina after her husband died, she also traveled a fair bit to see Irene and Ed in California, in addition to her trips to Flint.

❧   ❧   ❧

Business life bustled along for Chrysler. He paid very close attention to detail in all things, and surviving documents attest to this fact.

A June 26, 1917, memorandum from the Buick archives finds him concerned about recent problems in the quality of Buick workmanship after consultation with branch managers and distributors; furthermore, the same people were complaining about undue noise in the Model 49 motor and worrying that there would be serious trouble if the new Model 45 motor was just as noisy. Chrysler directed Bassett, Marr, and DeWaters to drop everything in the engineering department and get to work on the engine problems that very afternoon.

On February 17 of the same year he wrote to a Mr. Rankin of a reception on March 2 to be given for former president William Howard Taft by the Flint Board of Commerce, with a "glad hand" supper to be given at the Masonic Hall before Taft's speech. As chairman of the reception committee, Chrysler informed Rankin of the price (75 cents), the dress (everyday), and the promise of "a rousing good time"; since time was short, he asked Rankin to please sign and send in his acceptance at once as a personal favor.

The Hagley Library in Wilmington, Delaware, contains a goodly amount of correspondence between Chrysler and John J. Raskob from this time. Chrysler shipped Buick Coupelets to Wilmington for Pierre S. du Pont the same day the order arrived; he gave a long and thoughtful recommendation for F. O. Benzer, a vice president and one of the founders of Hudson, whom he had known for years; he interviewed a Frank G. Talman, Jr. on the request of Mrs. Durant; he straightened out a short shipment of Buicks to the Wilmington agency (taken over by Raskob and others for $180,000); most touchingly, he wrote a tender note of condolence on November 18, 1918, to Raskob upon the loss of his daughter, probably from the Spanish influenza. This happened at the very end of World War I, and Raskob's reply is worthy of note: "I appreciate very much indeed your kind thought of me as expressed in your letter of the 18th. It is indeed hard to lose one's child, but when we look about and see the suffering of others it really makes us ashamed to complain too much."

Soon after, there was an exchange between the two men on a happier occasion. At New Year's Raskob sent Chrysler a copy of the General Statutes of Kansas regarding automobiles, which apparently contained some howlers about Jayhawkers. Chrysler replied, "Under normal conditions I certainly would have had a good laugh, but inasmuch as I laughed so much New Year's Eve in New York [at Raskob's house] I was entirely laughed out. I appreciate your sending this very much, however, because it has a tendency to smooth out my erratic mind and temperament."

By the beginning of 1919 a fair amount of smoothing needed to be done. Walter Chrysler was now vice president in charge of operations at General Motors and a member of the corporation's Executive Committee, and he was clearly the most important profit maker the corporation possessed; that year Buick alone contributed $48 million in profits, more than half what the whole corporation made. Also, having slowly convinced the Fisher Brothers body works of the advantages of building all-steel paneled bodies, Chrysler persuaded the General Motors board to buy out 60 percent of Fisher Brothers stock in September 1919 for $26.8 million. Fisher was a progressive concern, and the first to realize the enormous potential of closed car bodies, but its products were expensive, since they were made the old-fashioned way, by hammering steel panels on wooden molds. (Chrysler had a paper in his files estimating that GM would require 95 million board feet of lumber for its products in 1920.) After the inspiration of that barrel maker in Cleveland, Chrysler developed his own new process for making drawn-steel bodies on expandable dies, lowering the cost of production and maintenance of car bodies; in lowering their weight, he lowered the cost of freight while at the same time increasing the cars' performance.

After convincing the GM board of the savings to be realized from his new methods, he then convinced them that buying out Fisher would be a lot cheaper for GM than building new body plants of its own. Then he had to spend a lot of time convincing the reluctant Fishers of the superiority of his new process. At last they decided to use it, though their steadfast belief in the superiority of wood meant that it would not be completely eliminated from GM bodies until 1937. GM began buying up Fisher stock in 1918; in September 1919 GM entered into its contract for control of the company. Shrewdly, the agreement called for cost plus 17.6 percent on the bodies GM bought from Fisher, with the right to purchase bodies elsewhere if this figure was not met. The deal would turn out to be one of the best investments the company ever made, and by the time the Fishers sold out the balance of their company to GM in 1926, they had become vastly wealthy men. Chrysler was in the main responsible for the whole thing.

Nevertheless, despite such successes, Durant, who liked him and had an enormous respect for his judgment, couldn't manage to keep his promise to let Chrysler alone to run Buick. This fact, combined with other Durant actions Chrysler couldn't abide, led to his rising gorge.

Somehow he managed to deal with Durant's waste of his time, infuriating as it was, in hastily summoned trips to New York or Detroit. Alfred Sloan recalled in *Adventures of a White Collar Man* that frequently Chrysler would drive 65 miles from Flint to Detroit without breakfast for an early-morning meeting with Durant that wouldn't actually start until 4 P.M. and then continued very late, with no provision made for food; when he and Sloan would ask if they should go for lunch, the reply would always be, "No, no! Mr. Durant regrets the delay. He'll return to you gentlemen in just a minute," though he would then make them wait hours longer.

Once Chrysler went to New York in response to a call from Durant and for a couple of days tried to find out what he wanted. "But he was so busy with big deals that he could not take the time to talk with me. It seemed to me that he was trying to talk with half the continent; eight or ten telephones were lined up on his desk. He was inhuman in his capacity for work. . . . Men, big men, came and went at his command. . . . Once, in a lull, I gained his attention for a fraction of a second. 'Hadn't I better return to Flint and work? I can come back here later.' 'No, no. Stay right here.' Into a telephone he gave an order. 'Buy 10,000 shares. . . . ' I waited four days before I got mad and went back to Flint. And to this day I do not know why Billy had required my presence in New York."

Walter Chrysler persevered through all this demeaning, annoying nonsense, but when it came to direct interference in his job, that was another matter. Things came to a head over the issue of frames for Buick cars, certainly his complete responsibility.

Chrysler had been negotiating for over a month with the A. O. Smith Company of Milwaukee for Buick frames for the following year, 1920. Smith was anxious to make a deal with Buick because it was operating at only

40 percent of capacity, and Chrysler was bargaining for a very attractive price. One day he attended a big Flint Chamber of Commerce booster luncheon at which he, as president of Buick, was expected to speak. The president of the chamber, Durant's former carriage-business partner Dallas Dort, preceded him. Waving a telegram over his head, Dort shouted, "Boys! I've got great news for you. Here's a wire from William C. Durant. He says he has just authorized the spending of $6,000,000 to build a General Motors frame plant in Flint."

The men of course cheered wildly, but Chrysler was eating his guts up in fury. When called on for his remarks, he remained seated and said, "I haven't anything to say—only this: Not so long as I stay here will General Motors have a frame plant in Flint. Right now you lack the facilities to house the men and women who have been attracted here by work. What sort of a mess will we be in if a bigger crowd is attracted into Flint?" He got up and left, to a deafening silence.

He was absolutely right. Frank Rodolph, in his fine *Industrial History of Flint*, gives a picture of how things were. "Flint was a veritable Eldorado, a swashbuckling boom town, in that period. It was literally swamped by prosperity. The fastest expansion of any industrial city in America was marred by growing pains. Flint was gay and colorful, but not without pathos. . . . The motor and parts factories could not get men fast enough. . . . Unemployment was not in the Flint vocabulary. . . . For many newcomers the Flint prosperity was only in their pocketbooks. Money could not buy adequate housing. . . . Housing, schools, streets, water and sanitation systems—nearly everything was overtaxed. . . . Hotels and rooming houses could not accommodate the inrush of workers, not even by renting to day workers by night and night workers by day. Hundreds of families lived in shacks and tents hurriedly set up in any open space near the plants. . . . Even on its main thoroughfare Flint had a disgraceful 'mile of mud' on North Saginaw Street and another 'half mile of mud' on the south end. . . . The *Flint Journal* reported September 3, 1915, 'There is not a rentable house to be had anywhere in this whole city of more than 10,000 homes.' Yet Flint invested over $2,000,000 in buildings in 1915 and twice that much in 1916. Bank clearings gained 210 percent in 1916. The city went heavily into debt for new schools, pavements, sewers, water mains; hundreds of thousands of dollars annually in bond issues." Yet with all of this, as Buick and Chevrolet expanded, it was never enough. Walter Chrysler was keenly aware that any more of Durant's unconsidered foolish boosterism for the town would lead to disaster, for General Motors as well as for Flint.

The day after the Flint luncheon, at a General Motors board meeting in Detroit, Chrysler let the ever-smiling Billy Durant have it with both barrels. How did he know the frame plant would cost $6 million, and where was the layout? It turned out that some overworked Durant crony had done the estimate in jig time, and as to the layout, there was none. Chrysler hammered home that it would take two years to build such a plant and another three years to learn how to run it. "It will cost more in five years than we would pay for frames in ten years," he shouted. "I can go out right now and buy frames for General Motors, for all of you, every car division, at a price that will save a million and a half a year." A du Pont man on the board, Jonathan Amory Haskell, defused the explosive argument between Durant and Chrysler by suggesting that a committee composed of Raskob, Chrysler, and himself should investigate the matter. Durant agreed, "but at the time I realized that Billy Durant would be no more able to forgive such an affront than an Indian. The way he saw it, I suppose, was that I had put myself athwart important plans of his."

Chrysler then sent for A. O. Smith, to whom he gave an enormous order, subject to the right price. Smith would make the frames for all General Motors cars for a period of five years, at a downward sliding scale of prices as quantities increased. The GM board approved the contract, which saved them $1.75 million over the next year alone. After five years, it renewed the contract for another five years. "Billy was nice to me after that, as nice as only Billy knew how to be, but I felt, indeed, I knew, he could not forgive me for my heated opposition."

Chrysler and Durant continued to argue over various issues throughout the summer and into the fall of 1919, and late in September the point of no return in their business relationship was reached over the Janesville Machine Company.

Since resuming control of General Motors, Durant had reverted to his old expansionist ways, though now with more oversight than the first time around. In 1916 he created United Motors, a GM subsidiary consisting of the Perlman Rim Corporation of Jackson, Michigan, the Remy Electric Company of Anderson, Indiana, the New Departure Ball Bearing Company of Bristol, Connecticut, the Delco Corporation of Dayton, Ohio, and the Hyatt Roller Bearing Company of Newark, New Jersey, all of which made important components for GM cars. With the $13.5 million he paid for Hyatt he obtained the services of Alfred P. Sloan, and with the $8 million he paid for Delco he got Charles F. Kettering; in the former instance GM got the man who was to be perhaps the most important business executive of the twentieth century, and in the latter one of the automobile industry's greatest inventors. It was a terrific piece of business to create this new GM division, with Sloan at its head. Equally good was the Guardian Frigerator, an electric icebox Durant purchased from an inventor named Alfred Mellowes, who had been financed by an executive of a GM supplier, the Murray Body Company. Durant put personal money into it, reorganized it completely, named its product Frigidaire, and sold it to GM for $56,366 in 1919. In so doing he created a whole new industry, of vast profit to GM, whose product name was one of the very few, like Victrola or Thermos, that came to stand for all such objects manufactured. But typically of Durant, he couldn't control his acquisitiveness, and not all his purchases were good ones. One of the stinkers was the Janesville Machine Company.

Durant wanted to get into the farm tractor business and to that end had been buying into the Janesville Machine Company of Janesville, Wisconsin. He sent Walter Chrysler to Janesville to report on what GM was getting for its money. At a GM board meeting in the summer of 1919 Chrysler's state-ment on the matter was none too tactful. He told the assemblage that they had paid too much for a business that would take three to five years to return its investment. "Leave that kind of business to the corporations that are geared for it," he said. The board didn't listen, and eventually the com-pany lost a great deal of money on Janesville Machine.

At the meeting, though, the argument between Chrysler and Durant continued and escalated, centering around the fact that there was a great deal Chrysler didn't like about the extensive GM spending plan Durant was overseeing for the company then. Chrysler got louder and louder. Finally he shouted, "What am I roaring about? I'm roaring as a stockholder, if you really want to know. Everything I have in the world is tied up in this com-pany. I don't want to lose it." After Durant made a smart remark, Chrysler said, "All right, Mr. Durant, I resign," picked up his portfolio, and walked out of the meeting to repair to the Book-Cadillac Hotel across the street. Board members were dispatched to urge his return, but he was obstinate. Finally Haskell came, acknowledged that both men had just flown off the handle, as everyone does from time to time, and told him that Durant wanted him to forget it all and return the next day to finish the meeting; Chrysler, cooler now, agreed.

He went back, but much as he considered these men friends as well as business associates, he could not cancel out the fact that his business judg-ment told him the company was expanding too fast and too far. During 1919 GM had become a billion-dollar corporation by increasing its capital stock from $370 million to $1.02 billion (although only a third of the stock had been issued). But that was not what Chrysler objected to. His difficulty was with the physical expansion of the company. It invested in tractors, refrigerators, airplanes, and a variety of other items that had little to do with its basic business; the Dayton Wright Airplane Company alone cost $1.2 million. In addition, with investments in companies such as Fisher Body and the Pontiac Body Company, GM was taking control of various sources of its supply; it was buying makers of gears (T. W. Warner at $5 million), bearings, batteries, fuses (International Arms and Fuse Company at $1.175 million), and other items. It was building new factories and, of necessity, new housing for its workers. And then there was the new GM office building it was constructing in downtown Detroit at a cost of $20 million. "They kept buying this and budgeting that until it seemed to me we might come to a dismal ending. Buick was making about half the money, but the corporation was spending much faster than we could earn. So I quit, this time for keeps, saying, 'Now, Billy, I'm done.' "

The problem was Billy Durant, but not him alone, as it was in 1910. The country was in the grip of postwar prosperity and euphoria in 1919. Prices were high, and everyone was sure that markets would continue to expand, particularly in the automobile business. It took a cool and perspicacious head to realize that there might be trouble in the offing for actions based on such assumptions. Durant's investments for GM, both good and bad (and Chrysler readily admitted that some were very, very good), were watched over closely by the du Pont interests, which now owned a significant piece of the company, and it is fair to say that Durant did not make any large moves without the knowledge and complicity of du Pont.

In 1916 Pierre du Pont had insisted on a finance committee for GM, which met twice a year to set up capital expenditure budgets for the next six months, and met monthly to approve any expenditures over $300,000 and any appropriations over $150,000. There was no problem with this arrangement until the following year. GM's stock price began falling, and Durant, as its largest stockholder and ever the speculator, began to buy up its stock on margin, until he wound up in serious financial difficulties in a continually falling market. In November 1917 he approached the GM finance committee for a million-dollar loan, which was turned down; the GM board instead voted him a $500,000 annual salary retroactive to the beginning of 1916, which settled his difficulties, but marked a turning point in control of the company.

Shortly thereafter Raskob, in a burst of creative financial thinking called "The Raskob Memorandum," proposed that du Pont, ever more flush with profits from selling munitions to the Allies, buy out a large interest in GM (until then only various du Pont family members owned a few thousand shares of the company). After all, he reasoned, du Pont was now a huge company that could never return to being a small one; GM was an excellent, growing concern, and a superb prospect for du Pont products, which could replace the customers du Pont would lose at the conclusion of the war; eventually, du Pont could even take over GM. (Years later this memorandum would form the basis of a huge U.S. Government antitrust suit against du Pont and GM.) Du Pont's board agreed, and bought up 24 percent of GM common, 90 percent of it on the open market, which caused the stock to rise and stabilize; they also bought up a large number of Chevrolet shares. Du Pont insisted on the merger of GM, United Motors, and Chevrolet, which was also accomplished with no objection from Durant, who had skated too close to ruin in this affair. Everything was done in a typically low-key du Pont way, with lavish support of Durant's management and derogation of its own importance in running GM's business. But control had definitely shifted.

Chrysler had noted it while the crisis of November 1917 was going on, though he wasn't privy to the details of that event. On the day he went to see Durant about GM's wartime mission, he walked into the eye of the storm. "His door was standing open, which was extraordinary in itself; Billy was standing there, staring at the wall as if in a daze. He seemed completely unaware of me and just stood staring blankly, as rigid as if he had been turned to ice. I entered and closed the door behind me quietly, hardly knowing what to do. Here was a friend, and plainly he was in some kind of trouble." He noted the presence of Durant's son-in-law, Doc Campbell, Pierre du Pont, John Raskob, and a few others. "I seemed to be in a room full of Napoleons at various stages of Napoleonic careers. I decided to vanish from the scene. There was nothing I could do. . . . From that day forward it seemed to me that the du Ponts were more active in their excercise of power." Eventually the board of du Pont voted to keep the company from buying up any more GM stock, so great was its investment and influence in the latter concern.

When Chrysler heard Durant say that some of the methods of expansion GM was pursuing were not his idea nor to his liking, he knew that this could well be true. But he also knew what he was up against when he bucked the board's ideas. Durant was bad enough to deal with, but Durant plus du Pont was an implacable force. This time he had really had it.

After he quit the second time Alfred Sloan came to see him to try to convince him to reconsider, but it didn't work. "No, I'm washed up," Chrysler told him. "I just can't stand the way the thing is being run. All I'm anxious about now is to sell my stock."

Then came Amory Haskell, with a new brand of soft soap. It seemed that GM was thinking of acquiring the Citroën plant in France, and was buying up francs to that end. Would Chrysler go along to give them a report on the physical properties from a mechanical standpoint? He allowed that he would, to help the company, as long as it was understood that he was getting out. "We'll talk about that later," said Haskell. "What is this going to be, this boat ride? A peace ship trip?" Chrysler inquired. "Whatever you want it to be. Just come along," came the reply.

He went, but as much as anything else the trip was a chance for Della to get something out of her husband's hard-won success for the first time. They were in their mid-forties and had waited all their lives for a chance to see Europe, so she wanted to go along. Walt thought it was a great idea, and insisted on it to Haskell. But her coming meant that the wives of Alfred Sloan, Charles Kettering, and Charles Stewart Mott were also coming along, and Haskell had the unenviable job of arranging for passports in those still unsettled postwar days; he got the job done. The only "stag" member of the party was French-born and-speaking Albert Champion, a definite asset during these particular negotiations. (He had his limitations, though. The Rev. Mr. Pengelly told of a night in Madrid during this trip when an exhausted Champion, Chrysler, and Mott tried to get dinner ordered from an uncomprehending Spanish waiter. "Albert had exhausted all of his elegant French trying to make the waiter understand his order. Finally Walter conceived a bright idea. He drew a picture of a cow and then pointed to the flank of the cow and held up three fingers, ordering, as he thought, three fine porterhouse steaks. The waiter beamed all over for he had gotten the idea. In about ten minutes he came back all wreathed in smiles and produced three tickets for a bull fight.") Nattily handsome and charming, Champion was a well-known ladies' man who reputedly met his end at the hands of an irate husband some seven years later (though this was not the official account given out; sudden illness was what was alleged).

Despite the ostensible point of the trip, every conversation Chrysler was involved in centered around his staying on at GM. But he was determined to leave. The trip was delightful, though, and one thing that came out of it was a close personal friendship between the Chryslers and the Sloans that continued to the last.

As for Citroën, Chrysler approached it with his customary thoroughness, combing through every part of the plant before writing up a report of close to twenty pages. The report boiled down to this: don't touch it. The plant was old and would cost as much to modernize as it would to build a brand-new one fitted out to American ideas of mass production. Besides, there wasn't sufficient business in France to warrant the cost of taking over Citroën. On the basis of this report, GM backed away from the deal, and made $140,000 buying back its dollars. The Chryslers, however, became quite friendly with André Citroën, and remained so for many years.

The year was now winding down, and arrangements needed to be made for Chrysler's exit. Prior to the official announcement of his severance from the company on November 1, Chrysler wrote private letters informing his business associates of the situation. In a typical letter to Winthrop Ingersoll, of the Ingersoll Milling Machine Company, he attributed his success at GM to good friends such as Ingersoll and hoped their friendship would continue into the future.

Of course Durant and du Pont did not want to see all of Chrysler's GM stock dumped on the market. He had accumulated quite a bit of it at minimal prices due to his lucrative arrangement with Durant, and also through stock splits, which at various times were on a three-for-one, five-for-one, and ten-for-one basis. A public sale of Chrysler's GM stock might well have had a destabilizing effect on its price, which was the last thing the company needed. According to Durant's unpublished memoirs, he handled the situation personally. He went to Chrysler and offered to buy all of his GM stock for his own account. Chrysler remembered that he was offered $46 a share, which in fact amounted to only a small fraction of an original 1916 share. The sum Durant offered was $10 million for the lot. Since he didn't have that much cash on hand, he offered a one-year payout, commencing with a one-quarter payout, or $2.5 million, on the spot, the rest to be paid in quarters every three months over the next nine months. Chrysler accepted the offer, pleasantries were exchanged, and papers were signed canceling Chrysler's contract with GM. Durant then wrote out the first check and gave it to Chrysler, and the deal was sealed.

Nobody knew it then, but within a year all of Chrysler's fears would be realized and Durant himself would be forced out of GM for a second and final time, under circumstances considerably less pleasant that those surrounding Chrysler's departure.

Suddenly, beginning around the spring of 1920, the postwar boom collapsed, and GM was caught with heavy expenses related to the huge expansion plan that it could not finance. Banks were not lending, so Durant decided to offer $64 million in new stock for underwriting. An English-Canadian banking group agreed to pick up $36 million of the offering at $20 a share, then selling at $38.50 on the open market. The other $28 million was unsubscribed, a situation complicated by the fact that several major GM shareholders were threatening to dump their holdings out of unhappiness over the inappropriately timed expansion of the company.

Durant decided personally to support the stock with his own funds, without telling any of the other board members. But it continued to sink, and the only way Wall Street firms would support the $28 million left in the stock issue was if the company would sell them an aditional 200,000 shares at $10 each. Durant was forced to agree, but when word leaked out that GM stock was available for $10, the bottom fell out. Durant began this affair with $105 million, but when then stock slid even below the $10 level, he found he was actually $20 million in debt, owed to three brokers and twenty-one banks. If he were to go under, the banks and brokers might go with him, and the future of GM itself might be compromised.

Du Pont and Raskob saved the day. They decided that the future of the company could not be so closely tied to one individual's financial problems, and forced Durant out. In exchange for his handing over control to them, the du Ponts arranged for the house of Morgan to assume his personal debts to banks and brokers. They also gave him $500,000 to clean up his problems, and allowed him to keep about $3 million in stock. Later, however, he was to say that "there were many things I had forgotten and so when I really cleaned up and protected everybody else, I had nothing left." He resigned from the presidency of GM on November 30, 1920. Famously, when he did, he put on his hat with a flourish and said, "Well, it's moving day." Then he turned around and left.

A few days later, after he had called his people together and asked them to support the new management, he received a friend in a small office he had rented near the grand new GM building. The man said that the du Ponts had asked him to carry on at GM, and Durant advised him to do so. "Then, going to the window, Mr. Durant raised the shade full length, and said with his head high, 'It's a new day' " (Pound).

Indeed it was. He was over sixty and broke, but though he was down, he was not out. His knowledge of Wall Street and his reputation in the automobile business made it possible for him to attract new money, and with it his life had a third act, as he became one of the highest-flying of all high flyers in the fantastical Roaring Twenties, before he, like the world, came apart in the Great Depression.

Pound brings up the old saying that a man has three chances at riches in the course of a business career, and that they correspond to the three complete swings in the business cycle which typically occur in a quarter of a century. A man usually goes broke in the first depression he encounters, squeaks by in the second, and having learned his lessons, emerges from the third in the full strength of his powers. Billy Durant squeaked by in his first crisis, went broke but learned a lot and recovered from his second, and went broke for good in his third. The trouble was his incurable optimism. He fancied himself a financier, but he was really a salesman, out there on a smile and a shoeshine, like Willy Loman. He could never quite convince himself of the periodicity of the business cycle, hence he was never really prepared for the inevitable downturns it brought. Even P. T. Barnum realized he had to deal with the consequences of fires and other calamities, and steeled himself to do so, with great success. Not Durant, however, though any disinterested observer would have to admit that for fifty years he gave the world a circus attraction to rival any fascinator Barnum brought along to captivate the public's attention. Fortunes were made, fortunes were lost, and made again and lost again, while he changed the world as much as any businessman of his time. Not a bad epitaph to a life, that.

❧   ❧   ❧

Walter Chrysler's prescience had paid off for him. He was out of GM stock entirely when it slid to as low as $9 a share, then rebought what he had sold to Durant when it climbed back to a price between $12 and $13 a share. By that time Pierre S. du Pont had taken over as president of the corporation, and the stock continued to rise.

During his last hectic year at GM, Chrysler became heavily involved in a Flint civic project on behalf of the corporation, showing that his concern for the workers of the town was not of the sort that did not go beyond hand wringing and conversation. It involved the town's biggest problem, housing.

There wasn't enough of it, and what there was became overpriced when the wartime prosperity dried up at the conclusion of World War I (Rodolph said that at the height of the wartime affluence men had silk shirts made to order at $18 apiece, and some even wore them to work). According to a November 8, 1919, article in *Flint Saturday Night* regretting his departure from GM, the first helpful thing Chrysler did was to come up with an idea to force an arbitrary decrease in rents in the spring of 1919, when local industries confronted with the task of changing from a wartime to a peace-time economy had left many workers without jobs to support themselves and their families. But this was only a stopgap measure for a temporary situation.

By Frank Rodolph's account, GM itself, heavily influenced by the du Pont interests, began to become concerned about the welfare of its workers, and instructed its Executive Committee of Durant, Haskell, and Chrysler to in-vestigate industrial conditions in the communities in which the company had plants. They did so, and the result of their study was a large-scale corporation-sponsored housing program in such cities as Detroit, Pontiac, and Lansing, in Michigan, and Bristol, in Connecticut, though none of these was nearly as large as the one it launched in Flint. The company sponsored other social programs to improve the lot of its workers, too, but housing was the main thrust of its efforts.

The Modern Housing Corporation was formed at a capitalization of $3.5 million, and on February 1, 1919, it acquired 1,000 acres of what had been the Stockdale and Durant farms, plus adjoining acreage, in the northwest part of Flint. Within a year it constructed 950 homes on this land, which became known as the Chevrolet Park and Civic Park developments. These were among the very first housing projects in the United States, and had an enormous influence throughout the nation. Chrysler was very much involved in this project from the beginning, both as a representative of the corporation and as a director of the Flint Chamber of Commerce, which he served tirelessly throughout the city's great period of expansion in the 1910s. He was a major figure in the city's Civic Building Association also, and much praised for his role in it. Leonard Freeman, president of the Chamber of Commerce at that time, later said of Chrysler, "He was the most constructive man I ever knew."

❦   ❦   ❦

Walter Chrysler lived and worked at Flint for eight years, and had become one of its most respected and beloved citizens. On January 22, 1920, almost eight years to the day after his arrival in the city, more than 250 men attended a dinner in his honor at the Flint Country Club, sponsored jointly by the Kiwanis Club, the Rotary Club, and the Exchange Club. The official signed testimonial printed in the program spoke of the deep regret felt by all at his departure from Flint, and eulogized him thus: "We rejoice in the privilege of having known you and worked with you during these nine years. We admire you as a business leader; we respect you as a willing servant of the public interests; we honor you as a man and love you as a friend. You have exhibited great efficiency in the administration of an industry which has shown remarkable expansion during your management; you have never turned a deaf ear to any appeal on behalf of human good, either private or public; in you the people of this City, whether in your employ or that of others, have always found a loyal friend. . . . None can ever dim the lustre of your name or lessen the warmth of genuine affection in the hearts of the citizens of Flint."

After a generous dinner of oysters, roast turkey and trimmings, bisque tortoni, cakes, and coffee, the speeches began amid the smoke of cigars and cigarettes. Fred Aldrich introduced the toastmaster, J. Dallas Dort, who introduced the speakers, each of whom had an identifying relationship to Mr. Chrysler listed in the program, along with an appropriate verse: there was W. W. Mountain, "The Associate"; Charles Stewart Mott, "The General Motors Corporation"; C. M. Greenway, "The Community"; The Reverend Pengelly, a last-minute substitute for an ailing John North Willys, who was by now Chrysler's next business associate; and John J. Carton, "The Friend," whose verse read:

"As o'er the glacier's frozen sheet
Breathes soft the Alpine rose
So through life's desert, springing sweet,
The flower of friendship grows."

Last of all was Mr. Walter P. Chrysler, "The Guest."

Pengelly outdid himself on this occasion, and though his remarks were couched in terms both more florid and more emotional than those of our own day, there is a clear and heartfelt sentiment behind his words that still comes through today.

Pengelly drew on the imagery of rivers, streams, currents, and eddies to speak of the composition of American life, in which he found the influences of Adams, Washington, Jefferson, Lincoln, and Roosevelt, along with the Declaration of Independence and the Constitution. "All these are part of the great main current of American life," he said. This he contrasted with the dangers of Bourbonism ("paralysis of the body from over eating and paresis of the mind from under-thinking") and bolshevism ("under feeding of the body and under training of the mind"), both of which threatened our fair land if not curbed. But he saw Chrysler as a bulwark against such troubles. "In this time of great unrest he has kept things flowing prosperously and harmoniously forward. . . . He is a real American and one who understands Americanism and keeps things in the main current of American life."

Pengelly next stated flatly that "we are living in the highest pressured age and area of the world," and that "we can reasonably say that in his particular field of manufacturing [Chrysler] is the highest pressured man of all." Nevertheless, he was "full of brains and vitality . . . a dominating figure. If you don't think so take a look at his eye, isn't it clear? Listen to his voice, isn't it masculine? Watch his action, isn't it forceful? Here is to Walter P. Chrysler, the High Pressured Man of this High Pressured Age and Era. And through it all he remains a human being, unaffected and friendly."

Then Pengelly remembered the tears in Chrysler's eyes when he came to him and spoke of his sadness at leaving the men of GM and the work he had done there. He pointed out that the men themselves held "The Big Chief" in great affection "because they could always get to him with their troubles and be assured of a fair and sympathetic hearing." He also noted that though Chrysler asked his men to share responsibility, "he is quite willing to share the glory. That is the spirit of a big man, a man around whom others can gather, and in whose life they can find a common meeting place. Mr. Chrysler thinks in terms of fellowship, he feels in terms of friend-ship and acts in terms of grateful service."

After quoting Henry Van Dyke and Rudyard Kipling, he included their words in his final remarks: "Chief: You are a 'Good Workman'; you have 'real ideas to draw from'; you have not worked for money or fame alone, but for man, and 'for the joy of working.' I hope that 'The God of Things as They Are' will still more abundantly prosper you, your family and your work. Walter, old boy, here is God-speed to you and all of your enterprises."

On his program, next to the scribbled names of men such as Champion, Durant, and Nash, Chrysler wrote, "Will not have a talk of this kind again."

The evening concluded with songs with special lyrics for the occasion crafted to popular tunes of the day, like "The Stein Song," "Dear Old Pal of Mine," "Ja Da" ("Chrysler, Chrysler, Walter, Walter, Walt, Walt, Walt"), " 'Til We Meet Again" ("Though we have to bid you sad adieu/ Wishing every good may come to you"), and finally, "*Blowing Bubbles*":

Walter Chrysler always bubbles—
Bubbles with good nature rare;
We've admired his way
Steadfast day by day,
So as he leaves, we want to say
Flint will greatly miss you,
You're liked everywhere,
May whatever seem like troubles
Prove but bubbles in the air.

On this note Walter Chrysler once again departed a city and a workplace on which he had left an indelible impression as a worker, as a civic leader, and just as a man.

Looking back on that evening of so many years ago, you can almost see the sad happiness of the occasion on Walter Chrysler's face: the crinkle of a smile beneath his eye, the cloudy marble within.

⌸ 18 ⌸

Chrysler at Willys

Restlessness is discontent—
and discontent is the first necessity of progress
Thomas A. Edison

Menno Duerksen, the lively popular auto historian who wrote in *Cars and Parts* magazine for many years, made this astute comment about Walter Chrysler in his four-part series on the man in his "Free Wheeling" columns: "Virtually every shop he had taken over in the railroad industry had been in trouble. In fact, that was usually why they called for Chrysler. Taking run down shops and whipping them into shape was what the Chrysler reputation was all about." This is also what it had been about when he went to Buick. Chrysler's success in turning ALCO into a moneymaking proposition was what led James J. Storrow to offer him the job as works manager at the faltering Buick plant in 1911. His stunning performance there gave him a reputation as the greatest turnaround man in the auto industry, and what he did with this reputation would form the basis of a matchless industrial achievement: the creation of one of the three pillars of the American automobile industry from tens of millions of dollars' worth of bad debts, worthless stock, and useless cars.

When the Chryslers got back from Europe in the fall of 1919, Walt was faced with a dilemma. He was forty-four years old and his work at Buick had turned him into a man rich beyond his imagination or expectation. For the first time since he left high school in Ellis in 1892 he did not have a job to go to, nor did he have a need for one to support himself and his family.

At first he took an office in downtown Detroit. All the years of super-human devotion to his work had caused him to neglect his personal business affairs, now complicated by the millions he was acquiring through his GM buyout. Since he clearly understood his own ambition to go into car manufacturing for himself, he cleverly decided to protect his family from the vagaries of such an enterprise by placing in trust for each of them large sums of money that he could never touch, no matter what his business circumstances. He was very careful and precise in all of this, and had the advice of brokers and bankers from Flint.

Years of habit had accustomed him, like an old drayhorse, to be wide awake at 6 A.M., so he would dress and jump into his car to drive the 65 miles from Flint to Detroit, where he would work and putter around the office until he drove back home. He did this four or five days a week, and the rest of the time he just hung around the house. Of course, knowing that he was at liberty, the men of the town involved him in all sorts of civic projects, from the development of a golf course to the building of a new hotel. When the hotel was discussed at a Chamber of Commerce meeting, Chrysler became uneasy and said, "I don't believe in putting this thing off. Flint needs a new hotel and needs it badly. The Buick Motor Company will keep it filled with men who come here on business. Let's get the money for it today." The money was subscribed and the new hotel a certainty before the men left the room.

Civic boosters weren't the only ones who came to see him at home, however. All kinds of men visited him, from friends of his youth and railroad days to old employees of the various concerns he had headed. Nobody was standing guard outside his door, so in they came. One problem was that all of them seemed to puff on cigars and cigarettes constantly, leaving a permanent blue haze of stale tobacco smoke throughout the house, to Della's great annoyance. Finally she had had it, and told him she wished he would go to work. "Because of her tone, I was relieved when she said 'work.' She added: 'This isn't a home anymore. It's just a place crowded with men. A sort of railroad station.' I grinned widely. She had said it first. It wouldn't seem like quitting on a promise if I changed my mind. 'Do you know what?' I said to her. 'I will go back to work.'"

It was a bit of a subterfuge to get her to desire fervently what he had already decided he wanted to do. Walter Chrysler was a man of many things, but leisure had never been one of them. He had been approached by a group of bankers to take over the ailing Willys-Overland Company. Figuring importantly in the group was none other than Ralph Van Vechten, who had loaned him the $4,300 to buy his Locomobile eleven years before, and played a major part in the salvation of General Motors during the crisis of 1910. The announcement of Chrysler's association with Willys came on January 6, 1920, completely surprising the auto industry. An article in a Detroit paper, noting that Chrysler had turned Buick into the third-largest auto company in the world, earning the second-highest profits, said that Chrysler and Willys would together "make a bid for what will be practically world supremacy in motor car manufacture." Chrysler was to become both executive vice president and general manager, and turn the company into the world's largest manufacturer of four- and six-cylinder engines.

All of this dynamic enthusiasm was in the service of gilding a particularly bedraggled lily, for Willys-Overland was very far down on its luck, and Chrysler had in fact been brought in at the behest of a group of New York bankers very concerned about the money they had tied up in what was then a badly stumbling enterprise.

Since 1907 the car company had been run by John North Willys, one of the great automobile executives, who was solidly in the Billy Durant super-salesman mold. Willys began in business before 1900 with a sporting-goods store specializing in bicycles in Elmira, New York. By the time he was twenty-seven he had a half-million-dollar-a-year business, mainly as a bicycle wholesaler. Though the bicycles continued to sell well and seemed to have a bright future, the moment Willys saw his first horseless carriage, he thought such machines "semed to possess larger possibilities, for, undoubtedly, more people would want to have themselves propelled about the country than to do the propelling themselves on a bicycle. So I got two auto agencies." This was in 1906.

Demand for automobiles was on a rising curve, and Willys had no problem selling them. The problem was in getting them. These were the early days, when production of even 5,000 cars in a single year was practically an unheard-of feat for any company. Willys organized a distribution company and contracted to sell the entire output of two Indianapolis firms: American, whose product became famous as the low-to-the-ground American Underslung, and Overland, whose total production in 1906 was forty-seven cars.

Pleased with the Overland, Willys contracted for and presold five hundred more of its cars in 1907, depositing a hefty down payment of $10,000 on his order. Unfortunately, this happened just at the moment that the brief but very sharp Panic of 1907 occurred. The Overland cars were not delivered and even factory correspondence ceased. Facing complete ruin, Willys took a train to Indianapolis on a Sunday to find that Overland employees had been paid in uncovered checks on Saturday night, which would mean the company would have to file for bankruptcy the next day. The total amount needed was $350.

The problem was that nobody, not even millionaires, had any money at this moment. Willys took the situation in hand by commandeering all the restaurant and barroom receipts at the hotel where he was staying, and covered the checks first thing Monday morning. He now assumed complete financial responsibility for the company, and became a car manufacturer on the spot.

Fortunately the Panic subsided quickly, and he borrowed wherever he could and persuaded the banks to advance him money on the sight draughts that went out with the bills of lading covering the cars. He showed them orders for far more than the $80,000 the company owed, and pointed out that if they pressed their old claims, they would get nothing, whereas if they didn't, they would both get their money back and develop a new market.

They went along, and Willys dug in. Having lost the factory, he set up operations in a circus tent, where he manufactured 465 cars in 1908. In 1909, after he acquired regular facilities, Willys turned out an astonishing 4,907 cars, at a million-dollar profit. During this year he bought out both the Marion Motor Car Company of Marion, Ohio, and the huge, vacant Pope-Toledo plant in Toledo, where he tripled production to 15,598 in 1910. In 1912 he sold 28,572 cars, and in 1916 140,111, for the number-two position in the industry, behind Ford. Profits in 1915 amounted to $10 million.

His success was truly astonishing, but just like Billy Durant, he eventually overdid it and wound up in big trouble.

He bought out the Garford and Edwards Motor Car Companies, and began production of a variety of popular Willys-Knight sleeve-valve-engine cars. By the middle of the decade he was offering a dizzying variety of models, some thirty in all on eleven different chassis in 1915 alone. In October 1917 he promised to bring out a strong competitor to the Model T in the form of an Overland four complete with a self-starter and electric lights for under $500.

But by the time this model appeared two years later, wartime inflation had upped its price to $845, very far above the price of the Model T, which by then had been provided with a self-starter and completely outclassed the Overland as a low-priced car. This wouldn't have happened if the company had not been mismanaged in a variety of ways. Willys himself had moved to New York to oversee his much-expanded holding company, which now included Moline Plow and, through a merger, Curtiss Aviation, of which he became president. He installed a former hardware executive named Clarence A. Earl in Toledo to manage production. Earl had no previous automobile experience, and was incompetent to do the job. He presided over a disastrous eight-month strike at Toledo, the first major one in the auto industry, and bumbled along through the maze of problems connected with wartime production. It was his lack of ability as a production man that caused the overpriced Overland to be completely uncompetitive in the marketplace.

John Willys had two major things going against him. The first was that he knew very little about cars themselves, which meant he had a very limited understanding of his actual products. There was a famous story recounted by Carl Breer that illustrates this situation. One day Walter Chrysler brought Willys into the factory to see the wooden dummy of a new model, with its crude wood axles set on blocks. "As they arrived from the freight elevator, Walter hurriedly led John N. directly to the wooden model and said proudly, 'Here it is!' John took one quick look after scanning us standing by, and in enthusiastic acclaim with quick emphasis said loudly, 'Have you had it on the road yet?'," not realizing that it was non operational. Chrysler and the others were both amused and somewhat taken aback that Willys could not recognize a self-apparent wooden facsimile.

Willys also fell into the trap of a certain kind of megalomania. First off, Willys, one of the largest producers of wartime materiel, mistakenly decided to devote the entire production of his company to the war effort just ten days before the armistice was announced. Then, in addition to announcing the $500 car he couldn't produce and buying into industries he didn't understand, his Willys Corporation bought out the Duesenberg plant in Elizabeth, New Jersey, in 1918, where he planned to manufacture a new six-cylinder model based on his four-cylinder Willys-Overland. He had Tobe Couture, whom he inherited from Duesenberg, demonstrate two prototypes of the new car to bankers, who put up $15 million for a new plant to manufacture the cars on the Duesenberg site. This building, five stories high, 3,500 feet long, and 460 feet wide, was completed in April 1919. Unfortunately, the new car was not nearly ready for production, and in addition Willys did not foresee the big postwar slowdown that began developing in 1920. The result of all of this was that Willys's operations became one of the first victims of the inventory depression that lasted into 1921.

Buoyed up by the brisk sales and inflated prices that accompanied the end of the war, when materials were hard to find and cars were easy to sell, Willys made commitments for hundreds of thousands of items, including bodies, tires, and all sorts of parts, in addition to new machine tools that would turn these things into automobiles. That, combined with his $15 million commitment on the Elizabeth plant, was heading the company toward financial disaster. He owed 127 bankers a total of some $46 million, and they wanted their money.

A bankers' committee, headed by Chase National, was formed, and Ralph Van Vechten approached Chrysler about taking over the situation. John Willys, who had known Chrysler from Flint, was also enthusiastic about the idea, though by then he had little to say in the matter. He admired Chrysler and had often tried to get him to come to work for him until Durant made Chrysler president of Buick at that enormous salary.

Chrysler was very apprehensive about taking the job, because if he failed, he could ruin the spectacular reputation he had so painstakingly built up at Buick. Van Vechten and Willys argued strongly to get him to accept. Finally he agreed, but only after demanding a never-before-heard-of salary of $1 million a year, net, for each of two years. The bankers were taken aback, but they knew all was lost otherwise, and so they agreed. One other thing Chrysler demanded was to be fully in charge, the boss of everything, even though Willys was to retain his title as president. He would not allow his efforts to be circumscribed by another Durant-type executive. Chrysler was to be the doctor that would save the company, and Willys was to get out of the way and let him apply his medicine any way he saw fit.

Since Chrysler's time in Flint was now truly finished, he sold his East

Kearsley Street house to Albert Champion and his wife for $40,000 in April 1920. Willys was headquartered in New York, so Chrysler moved there, at first to the Biltmore and later to the Carlton House. Strong ties to Flint remained, however, and his daughters in particular returned to the town many times over the years to see old and dear friends.

Whatever he may have thought privately about the latest turn of events in his company's fortunes, Willys's public enthusiasm for Chrysler ran very high in the beginning. The telegram he sent to Chrysler's farewell Flint dinner in 1920 was effusive. "I rejoice in the fact that I am able to have associated with me in a business way and also a personal way such a wonderful man as Chrysler has proven himself to be," he said. "He is a great executive and has wonderful constructive ability, and above all he typifies to me what the philosopher has so ably termed a man who is clean both inside and outside, who neither looks up to the rich nor down to the poor, who can lose without squealing or win without bragging, who is too brave to lie and too generous to cheat, and who takes his share of the world and lets other people have theirs. The organization in my interest is delighted that we are to have his counsel and his advice. Long may he live and prosper."

Willys's first swallow of Chrysler's medicine may have caused his state of joy to abate somewhat, though he never showed it. At the very beginning of his regime Chrysler strode into Willys's office ("You never saw another like it—magnificent"), lit a cigar from his ornate gilded humidor, and promptly cut Willys's salary in half, to $75,000 a year. When the look of puzzlement fell from Willys's face, "He gave his head a little toss and then he laughed. 'I guess we've put our problems in the right man's hands,' he said."

Beverly Rae Kimes notes that this little exercise may have been a bit silly in light of Chrysler's enormous compensation. "It was clearly a power play to show who was boss," she said.

Willys gave a detailed and penetrating analysis of Chrysler's qualities and value in his article "The More People You Can Direct—the More You Are Worth," in the *American Magazine* issue of August, 1920. Referring to Chrysler in everything but name, he said that this earner of the country's largest salary was just a workingman with no college background. "But," he noted, "on the way up he seems to have learned something about everything.

"During his first month in his present job he made two manufacturing suggestions which should have occurred to almost anybody—but did not. They were merely in the way of cutting out extras which nobody wanted on automobiles, but which had been supplied as by habit. The first suggestion saved the company $250,000 a year and the second $45,000. He considerably more than earned his salary during the first month!

"This man watches the affairs of nearly a dozen corporations, and he is not an officer in all of them. He has demonstrated that he knows all about manufacturing; that he knows all about selling; that he knows all about finance. I cannot imagine where or how he got all of the information that is stored in his head. But he has it; and he not only uses it with unerring common sense and judgment, but he never makes a show of his knowledge or capacity. In fact he would not shine at all in comparison with some smart sales manager or advertising agent. He uses his ability not to make speeches but to get things done."

Willys noted Chrysler's method of getting an important decision made by gathering all the parties to it together in a room, then getting them mad both at each other and at him, in order to find out what was truly on their minds. When everybody had everything off their chests, he smoothed over the situation nicely "because each man discovers that, although he may have been wrong in part of his stand, he was right in another. . . . What he always does take away with him is exactly the idea that the big man wanted to put over. That is, this man has the marvelous faculty of getting a group together, of completely changing their minds on a subject, and then sending all of them out with the new idea, but without their knowing that their minds have been changed by any outside force.

"Why is this man so valuable? Any employer can handle any number of specialists in single lines. . . . With somewhat more difficulty you can get men who are specialists in perhaps two subjects. With a still greater difficulty you can hire men who are not specialists, but who have the ability to manage other men. With a great deal more difficulty, you can find an occasional specialist who can also handle men successfully. But the rarest man on earth is the man whom I have just described, who seems to be a specialist in nearly every subject and can also manage any kind of men. Such a man is worth practically any amount of money, for there is no limit to the amount of business he can direct. . . . Thereby you extend the power of your own hand."

Chrysler himself, in an address given to three hundred men of the factory management class at Toledo University on June 22, 1920, put it this way: "We are all made out of the same clay; human nature is pretty much the same everywhere in life. . . . I have always felt, and believe it is true now, that no one man ever accomplished any one thing worth while alone. Through confidence, maintaining good faith and holding loyalty while surrounding himself with specialized men of various types, the successful man attains the real ideal, and that is the rounding out of a whole organization, through co-ordination and co-operation, as one great big man."

After cutting Willys's salary, Chrysler rolled up his sleeves and went to work. Unnecessary, redundant, and uneconomical factory equipment was disposed of. He moved the Knight Motor plant from Elyria, Ohio, to Pontiac,

Michigan, where better motors could be manufactured for $85 less each. A huge and in large part useless office force was cut to the bone, and the sale of excess office equipment that this move occasioned raised $150,000 for the company's coffers. (Shortly thereafter, Henry Ford took a similar action in his own offices, in a move that was considered wildly eccentric but was actually financially shrewd.) Willys boasted of employing 100,000 men, but the practical Chrysler slashed away at the employment rolls until they made sense. Clarence A. Earl was quickly replaced by Charles B. Wilson, president of the Wilson Foundry and Machine Company of Pontiac, Michigan, one of the Willys subsidiaries that Chrysler held in the highest regard for its efficient principles of operation. "A lot of things had been going on inside that vast and sprawling company that had wholly escaped the attention of its management," Chrysler said of the Willys organization in general.

As always, he began collecting men to fill assignments vital to the completion of his aims. One was Colonel A. C. Downey, a tough-minded man with whom Chrysler had once wrangled for three days during the war over a government contract for shells. He had been so impressed by Downey that he told him to come by for a job if the time ever came when he needed one. One day in Toledo he did just that. When Chrysler asked him about salary, Downey left it up to him, and on the spot Chrysler hired the man who would one day become the general purchasing agent for the Chrysler Corporation. "I knew three things about him," Chrysler said. "He was honest; he was loyal; he had ability. That is all I ask from any man. I don't care how raw the ability is; that can be developed through experience. But unless a man is loyal and honest, I don't want him associated with me."

At that moment Chrysler was plagued by a subsidiary about which he was, to say the least, suspicious (when he spoke about this company in later years, he would never name it). Three days after he hired Downey, he gave him the job of cleaning it up, an assignment as tough as anything the former colonel ever had to do in the army. He gave Downey the company's name, told him what city it was in and what it made, and said to him: "It's rotten. That's all I can tell you. I want you to go there, stay a month or six weeks, and then come back and tell me what's wrong." The Colonel, who knew as little about this business as Chrysler did, was sure his curiosity would win the day for him, as indeed it did. Within a little while they fired the company's president and Downey had it running as smooth as silk. Chrysler didn't even bother to read his report. "He found out plenty; I know that," he said.

Chrysler could have told similar stories about a great many of his men. He now had the management of them firmly in his grasp. "From the day that I had left Flint to go to New York, I had been aware that for my purposes men were what I wanted," he said.

His greatest contribution to Willys, and his strongest effort there, lay in reducing the commitments Willys had made to parts suppliers. "All that was bad in the Willys-Overland Corporation was due, really, to lack of competition, to the wartime boom and its easy money. Prosperity had made some of its officials too tolerant of things that, in any better managed corporation, would have been regarded as shocking," Chrysler said. He made some officials restore monies that he believed they had squandered on inappropriate expenditures. But mostly he vastly improved Willys's finances by canceling contracts with suppliers for unnecessary parts figured at unrealistically inflated wartime prices. Because of his experience at Buick, Chrysler knew all these people and could talk turkey with them in a way that no mere banker could. He could tell them they would be foolish to put a good customer under, and point out that for every bad old contract they canceled, lucrative new ones would come through in the future. Furthermore, in dealing with Chrysler, they knew they couldn't claim hardship unless it was true. "I traveled everywhere that parts were made," he said. "I talked over long distance telephone wires until my voice became hoarse. I argued. I cajoled." Within a few months he had managed to cut the company's debt from $46 million to $18 million, which was a truly amazing feat.

John North Willys was soon to be performing rather amazing feats of his own in revitalizing the company. The crape hangers were out in full force. "They got Billy," they said around Detroit, referring to Durant, "now they'll get John." But Willys just pushed up his sleeves and went to work doing what he did best—selling. He spent months crisscrossing America, reselling both himself and his cars to his dealers. He was forthright about his troubles: "Wall Street didn't get me, I got myself," he told them, shoring up their morale by promising that he was back on his game with the old accustomed vigor. The eyeball-to-eyeball honesty paid off, and the dealers stood behind him. Walter Chrysler said, "This trip of Mr. Willys out among the dealers has been wonderful. The whole situation has been turned directly about."

In September of 1920 Willys went further and announced big price reductions in Willys-Overland cars, in the range of $100 to $200 per car, reducing the price of the popular roadster and touring cars from $1,035 to $895. According to Menno Duerksen, he also worked very hard behind the scenes with Chrysler to reduce deadwood in the ranks of management.

All manufacturers then were trying desperately to reduce costs to be able to reduce prices into a range more in tune with the realities of the postwar economy. Over the next few years this would prove vital to economic survival. By late May of 1921 Willys had reduced his prices even further, with Willys-Knight cars cut by $300 and Willys-Overland cars by yet another $200, so that the Willys-Overland touring cars now sold for only $695, a reduction of 32 percent from wartime prices.

But Willys and Chrysler had fundamental differences over the product line. Chrysler didn't think very much of Willys cars, and disagreed with John Willys' idea that the way to interest the public was by adding on a few new gadgets and painting the cars in bright new colors.

Having realized that he was not able to bring out a car to compete with the Model T, Willys eventually revised the Overland into a slightly larger, more attractive car with appealing model designations such as Blue Bird and Red Bird, and at good prices in the $700 range, he did very well with them. In fact, by June of 1922 he was making a monthly profit of $1 million, and by 1925 he cleared almost $20 million on sales of 215,000 cars, which were just somewhat modernized from the 1921 models that only sold 48,000 copies. Willys's formula was successful.

But Chrysler's interest was in the revolutionary new six-cylinder car that Willys had announced for production in the Elizabeth factory, and it was with this car that he would find the lever to propel himself into a new position as an independent car manufacturer.

Part of his job at Willys was to get this car designed and built, though work on it had begun before he arrived at the firm. The two men had agreed on adding the car to the Willys line, and furthermore that it would bear Chrysler's name. An article in *Automotive Industries* on December 9, 1920 stated that production of the Chrysler car would begin at Elizabeth in the spring of 1920, after an advantageous delay that would make it easier to find both materials and customers for the car. As it turned out, it was because of this new vehicle that Chrysler first became associated with the three men who would become the linchpins of his destiny in the automobile business: the engineers Fred Zeder, Owen Skelton, and Carl Breer.

Chrysler said of them: "Those three automotive engineers were wizards. They seemed to be part of a single extraordinary engineering intelligence. . . . You would never find, hunt high or low, three friends more harmoniously attuned, unless it might be those men of fiction, the Three Musketeers." Indeed, this was to be the sobriquet by which they were known throughout the automobile business for the rest of their lives.

Fred Morrell Zeder, the front man for the team, was born in Bay City, Michigan, on March 19, 1886, and graduated from the University of Michigan in 1909 with a bachelor of science degree in mechanical engineering. He became erecting engineer for the Allis-Chalmers Company in 1910, after serving an apprenticeship with the company that began right after his graduation. Late that year, after putting up a power plant in Detroit, he joined the EMF Company as head of their engineering laboratories, while at the same time leading a consulting firm whose specialty was power plant engineering. When the Studebaker Corporation took over EMF in 1912, Zeder signed on as consulting engineer and rose to the position of chief engineer the following year. The man he replaced, James G. Heaslet, though associated with cars since 1897, was one of the old-fashioned type of auto en-

Walter Chrysler and "The Three Musketeers," 1925. Seated, left to right, Walter Chrysler and Fred Zeder. Standing, left to right, Owen Skelton and Carl Breer. (*Courtesy DaimlerChrysler Corporate Historical Collection*)

gineers—really little more than a good mechanic whose work method was to proceed by trial and error. Zeder represented the future of auto engineering. He was a trained university graduate, a technologist whose experiments were done in a laboratory under controlled conditions before they were ever tested on actual cars.

After initial difficulties organizing and directing a department that contained some very temperamental engineers, he got production on track, and sales rose steadily through 1916. However, this success masked some important product problems that came home to roost at that time, steering the company into heavy financial seas. Zeder acknowledged that many of the company's problems were due to the shortcomings of his engineering department, and he convinced Studebaker's management that the hiring of some top-quality, proven engineers would pull them out of their difficulties. This gave him the opportunity to hire the other two members of what would become the Zeder Skelton Breer triumvirate.

First he sought out Owen Skelton, a very quiet, unassuming man of great skill who had worked for many years at Packard. Skelton hailed from Edgerton, Ohio, where he was born on February 9, 1886, and later graduated from Ohio State University. His first job was in Toledo working for

Pope-Toledo, which manufactured one of the most advanced cars of its day. He gained a reputation there for his ability in working with axles and transmissions before leaving to join Packard in Detroit, where he worked for the next seven years. From 1914 to 1916 he and a partner produced an assembled car called the Benham, which was notable for its early use of streamlined bodies. He left the company to take up Fred Zeder's offer to join Studebaker.

Fred Zeder had known Carl Breer from Allis-Chalmers where both men had apprenticed at the same time. Breer was the oldest of the Three Musketeers, having come into this world at Los Angeles on November 8, 1883; the son of German immigrants, he was the last of nine children. After graduating from Commercial High School, he went to work in his father's carriage and blacksmith shop, where he learned the craftsmanship and machining that went into the building of vehicles. Armed with this knowledge, he built his own steam car in 1901, and demonstrated it to get his first job with the Tourist Automobile Company, then a major west coast auto manufacturer. He then went to work for Toledo Steam Cars, Spalding, Northern and White, before helping to design a very advanced two-cylinder car called the Duro, which featured opposed cylinders, a transmission set forward of the engine, and a solid driveshaft to the rear axle. His real desire was not to work but to continue his education, and to that end he entered the Throop Polytechnic Institute, where he was given one year to graduate and meet the entrance requirements for Stanford, his real goal. After successfully completing his courses at Throop, he entered Stanford, from which he graduated in 1909 with a degree in mechanical engineering.

During his apprenticeship at Allis-Chalmers immediately following graduation he met Fred Zeder, and when after four years of separate careers Zeder approached him with a job offer at Studebaker, the two men, together with Skelton, began a lifelong engineering partnership without parallel in the automotive industry. The personal relationship between Zeder and Breer was just as intimate as the professional one, for Carl Breer married a sister of Fred Zeder's, and their families became as close as any two families could be. Interestingly, their sons, Fred Breer and Fred Zeder, Jr., are just as close as their fathers had been, living today just a few doors away from each other in Palm Springs, California.

Of the three men it could be said that Zeder, the front man and salesman of the group, was a superb engineer whose conservatism emphasized solid quality above all else; Skelton, the quietest and most elusive, was the superb design analyst and technician; Breer, as professor Scharchburg says in his succinct article "Zeder-Skelton-Breer Engineering," "was a careful and thorough thinker. Not an inventor, his forte was the application of existing technology to solve perplexing problems. His expertise was engines; but he was interested in every aspect of a car's design from front wheel drive to aerodynamics."

Now that he had his group together, Zeder's job was to create a new line of cars to replace the outmoded and clumsy Studebaker models. The new team approach to design turned out to be a winner, for through their interaction the three men managed to avoid most of the expensive mistakes that led to financial disaster for many another firm. (Indeed, Walter Chrysler's post-Buick career at Willys and later at Maxwell was due to just such mistakes.) Scharchburg gives a great deal of credit on this project to Skelton's superb personalized leadership in organizing and directing the design activity of other members of the team. "His spirit of cooperation in the design of engineering innovations was immense," Scharchburg says.

The three Studebaker models introduced in April 1918 were completely new, and for the first time marked a total break with the old EMF cars. Underslung springs with bronze bushings and new frames narrowing at the front made possible much lower bodies with smooth, rounded lines. Underneath, the transaxle was eliminated, and an aluminum cone clutch replaced a pressed-steel one. Hotchkiss drive, a clutch brake, and detachable cylinder heads on the Bix Six model were all introduced. Though production was held down by wartime shortages and other complications of the business of war, the cars were a big hit, and in 1919 Studebaker, now completely confident of the triumph of the automobile, stopped making horse-drawn vehicles entirely.

Zeder, Skelton, and Breer were not happy at Studebaker, however, feeling that their excellent efforts on behalf of the corporation were underappreciated. For instance, as the trio was developing its new Studebaker line in 1917, a worried management had Alanson P. Brush design an alternative line "just in case." Though the new cars set a worldwide standard for toughness and durability that allowed Studebaker president Albert R. Erskine to say in 1924, "These are the cars that made Studebaker famous," the three engineers felt their confidence undermined. Luckily for them, a fateful opportunity to make a fortuitous change of employment was about to come their way.

According to Tobe Couture's reminiscences, the new Willys Six was running into big problems as it was redesigned for actual production. Engineers who had been brought in for the redesign work completed six experimental cars and began testing them. As miles were built up on the testers, all sorts of problems began to show up. First the frames began to fail in various places, and then faults occurred in the bodies. Later, with the accumulation of still more miles, defects began to show up in the engines. All this was happening while tooling was being set up in the Elizabeth factory for what was clearly a very flimsy car. Something had to be done.

By this time Chrysler was on the scene at Willys, and one of the first things he did was arrange for Couture to give him a demonstration ride in the new car at Schooley Mountain in Pennsylvania, a very difficult grade that few cars could climb in high gear. Impressed by the car's performance, he left the other admiring Willys officials at the top of the hill and went down again with just Couture in the car. At the bottom they pulled off to the side and Chrysler asked, "Tobe, what do you *really* think of this car anyway?" "I replied, 'Do you want to hear the truth, or do you want me to say the car is wonderful?' He said: 'It had better be the truth.' So I told him: 'The sooner you scrap the whole program and start with a new design, the sooner we will have a good car.' " Chrysler blew a gasket. " 'Tobe, do you realize we are all tooled up for production?' he cried out. I said: 'Yes, sir, but you asked for the truth.' "

The two men somberly drove back up the hill, where they gave the bad news to the Willys officials, among whom were Donald S. Devor, general manager, Mr. Segardi, chief engineer, and Bill Cleary, the purchasing manager. After a discussion, everybody went home.

Next day Chrysler called a meeting of the whole organization, and each man in turn was asked his opinion of the new car. They all pronounced it terrific, even Segardi, the chief engineer, who was too afraid to tell the truth. When it was Couture's turn, he laid it out flat: "The sooner we scrap the car the better off we will be," he declared. Of course he was questioned very closely by everybody, but he held his ground, telling the meeting he had all the reports of all the test failures on the car. The result was that, based on his report, the company spent the next six months experimenting and changing things to try to save the design. Needless to say, Couture was not the most popular man in the organization after this.

In the early summer, Chrysler set out to obtain the services of the Three Musketeers for Willys. Carl Breer's reminiscences, published in part by the S.A.E. as *The Birth of the Chrysler Corporation and its Engineering Legacy*, state that the original contact between Chrysler and the engineers was made through a Detroit tailor named A. G. Brown, who told Breer to get in touch with Chrysler. Willys general manager Donald S. Devor, who had been an apprentice at Allis-Chalmers with Zeder and Breer, suggested to Walter Chrysler that Zeder, Skelton, and Breer could solve the engineering problems he was having with the new Willys Six at Elizabeth. After several productive meetings among the men, the three engineers, along with their fifteen-man staff, left Studebaker to join Willys on July 14, 1920.

They began immediately with a full investigation of all the design and experimental work that had been done on the new six over the past year and a half. Chrysler had informed them of Couture's negative opinion, so they gave him a detailed grilling. But he remained steadfast in his judgment that the whole thing should be tossed on the scrap heap. The engineers tried out a lot of solutions to the problems they found, but finally they had to agree with Couture that the design was unworkable and should be abandoned.

Armed with this report, Chrysler asked Couture to join him in a meeting with the bankers at his New York office on Vanderbilt Avenue. The two men gave out the bad news, and it was a stunner. By this time tooling for the car was practically complete, so this was a considerable blow to the financial men, who were already dealing with the ill effects of the depression that had set in, causing massive layoffs and production shutdowns in Toledo. But Chrysler thought this car was a "boggle" that, if produced, would complete the ruin of the Willys Corporation, and he knew it was his duty to say so.

Chrysler proposed to save the situation by setting the Musketeers on a crash program to produce a totally new car. Willys's philosophy of cobbling together a new car from existing parts had been a big flop, so now it was time to try Chrysler's idea: "I was convinced that the country was waiting for a better automobile than had yet been offered to it."

Chrysler, knowing all along that there was a good chance the old design was unsalvageable, had given the engineers permission to work on a new design at the same time that they were trying to save the old one. For the sake of morale, it was clear that work on the new job had to be conducted in secret, so this operation was moved to the Beechwood Hotel in Summit, New Jersey, which was where Owen Skelton and some of the other engineering men were then living. Drafting tables and other equipment were set up on one of the upper floors of the hotel and kept tightly under wraps. The men working on the project were in effect living double lives at the Elizabeth factory and at the Summit hotel, just twelve miles away. It all worked out perfectly, and no one but the top Willys executives was ever the wiser.

The Willys Four had been advertising a terrific ride due to its having a 120-inch spring base on a 100-inch wheelbase, but Breer and the rest of his crew were unimpressed by this claim, knowing it to be nothing more than advertising puffery. In fact, this chassis and spring setup lent itself to a lot of problems and had to be completely redesigned. They wound up with a chassis with longer, heavier side frames, on a car that featured an L-head, six-cylinder in-line engine, with a shorter stroke than bore and a seven-bearing crankshaft; an updraft carburetor at the center of the engine, with a hot-spot intake manifold providing more uniform distribution spreading to the three cylinders on each side; a unit power plant; a Hotchkiss rear end; and semielliptic front and rear springs.

Skelton said that when the engine alone was completed there was a good deal of hesitation about how to approach Chrysler with it. The seven-bearing engine, featuring high compression and interchangable bearings, had been developed in secret, without advice or suggestions from Chrysler.

In the event, when he was told, he came to Summit immediately with Willys' general manager, Jay Hall, and was so enthusiastic that he went to work selling the engine to Hall and the bankers from the first moment he saw it.

All the new features on the car necessitated a completely new body and hood design. Chrysler partitioned off a corner of the Elizabeth plant for this work, and the engineers set up a styling division there, headed by Oliver Clark, in which all the men participated. Chrysler ran over frequently from New York to check on their progress and make suggestions, and was delighted both by their own momentum and by their ability to understand and utilize his ideas. Clay models were made as soon as the full-scale drawings were done, and then an Elizabeth woodworking shop built a full-size model complete with leather upholstery, a canvas fold-back top, and "jiffy" side curtains. It was mounted on wooden axles equipped with disc wheels supplied by the Budd Manufacturing Company. (This was the completed model that John Willys later saw and mistook for a working prototype.)

After the go-ahead was given, the prototype was built quickly. The engine itself was finished in record time, just ninety days after the production department was handed the blueprints. All department heads cooperated to the fullest to turn out the work.

By the spring of 1921 the first car was ready, and two top test drivers, one of whom was Tobe Couture, drove it 800 miles a day through all types of terrain, from the Jersey coast to the hills of the Orange Mountains, over surfaces ranging from dirt and gravel to the cobblestone pavements of Frelinghuysen Avenue in Newark. Couture used to demonstrate how smooth and quiet the vehicle was either by driving it on the cobblestones or rolling its 56-inch tread along the 56-inch wide streetcar tracks of Newark. After 30,000 miles the car was torn down and found to be in perfect condition.

By now Chrysler was very high on this car, and sent all sorts of people over to Elizabeth for demonstrations, most of which began on the third floor of the factory, which was two-thirds of a mile long (it was said to be the largest building under one roof in the world) and permitted speeds of up to 60 miles per hour. Couture was in charge of impressing the visitors, and always did a bang-up job. This was how Carl Breer described Couture's dog and pony show: "First he would take the newcomer for a demonstration on the long and empty [third] floor of our factory building, filled with round concrete columns about 20 feet apart. At the far end five or six hundred feet away was an elevator shaft surrounded by these columns around which Tobe would make a sudden turn to the right, swing around the elevator shaft and back up the same straight stretch, circle about in similar manner to return, and in this way would demonstrate the car's ability to the newcomer at fairly high speed.

"After making four or five runs like this, all at once he would let out at a much higher speed, rushing for the turn around the elevator. About this time the newcomer would sense the danger, and in sudden excitement shout out loud, 'Tobe! You can't make it!' Tobe, knowing all the time he's not going to take the turn, goes straight ahead and slams on the brakes! After realizing what happened, the passenger would come to in real excited ecstasy and really sensed the car's ability. Tobe then would demonstrate in the heavy street traffic and over the highways and the steepest grades of the Orange Mountains. Invariably he won the acclaim of the newcomer."

Chief among the people sent over for a demo ride were some of the country's most important car dealers, including the largest Buick dealer on the West Coast and the biggest Cadillac dealer in Cincinnati. The first time Chrysler himself was taken on the special Couture demonstration on the third floor and was treated to one of those 35-mile-per-hour turns around the elevators, he yelled, "Don't ever do that again!" But when the dealers came for their rides, Chrysler pulled Couture aside and told him, "Give 'em the works!"

Perhaps the greatest measure of the car's quality came when Chrysler arranged a sporting contest between his car and the Wills Sainte Claire. This ultrarefined luxury vehicle was just then going into production under the aegis of C. Harold Wills, Henry Ford's master engineer, who was touting his new V-8 car as "ten years ahead of its time." The event covered speed and acceleration, and also hill-climbing tests on a famous long New Jersey hill that Wills had selected. Some twenty men and a half dozen cars were involved, and even Wills had to admit that Chrysler's new job outperformed his in hill climbing and everything else. It was a great day for Chrysler and the team who designed and built it. Everyone was so encouraged that a huge electric sign spelling out the name CHRYSLER, which was the name of the new car, was erected on top of the Elizabeth plant. Walter Chrysler's papers contain a booklet with a complete breakdown of all costs for building one hundred of these new Chrysler touring cars, which totaled $69,674.74; the handwritten date on the booklet was April 9, 1921. It seemed only a matter of time before production would begin.

From here on out everything should have gone right, but it all went wrong. By March of 1921 business conditions were beginning to improve, and Willys was starting to hire back men who had been laid off by the severely curtailed production of the previous six months. But financially there were still problems. Creditors were pressing for payment, and bankers were urging the merger of the separate Willys and Willys-Overland companies, for reasons of economy and streamlined operation.

A New York Times article of March 20, 1921, noted that Willys-Overland debt had been reduced to $20 million, but that the company still faced problems because of the cutback in production and profits in the recent slowdown. The banks were still lending it money, however, because they felt that the recent increase in automobile business meant it could pay off its debts and reduce inventories. The Willys Corporation had no merchandise credits, a bank debt of $11 million due to the new factory, and capital assets of $26 million, so all in all the bankers thought the merger advisable. But those creditors remained insistent.

By late April John Willys was announcing a 30 percent increase in employment and a 50 percent increase in production for May, and pointing with pride to a record factory driveaway of five hundred cars. "It looks good to see them rolling away," he said. "The old times are coming back."

By midsummer, though production was near normal, the company noted that it still owed $20 million, which was not comforting, and it was in this atmosphere that the new "Chrysler" job had to be financed.

    ❧   ❧   ❧

According to Tobe Couture's memoirs, Chrysler had been trying to get backing to arrange to take over the Elizabeth plant and build the new car himself. "A few days before the Fourth of July, Mr. Chrysler called Messrs. Zeder, Skelton and Breer to his office on Vanderbilt Avenue and said: 'Boys, it's all set. I am taking my family on a boat trip to Europe and when I come back we will start manoeuvers to build this car at Elizabeth.' Mr. Chrysler's group had made an offer for the Elizabeth property, which Mr. Chrysler had reason to believe would be accepted." Papers in Chrysler's own hand dated June 30, 1921, show that he was stitching together a plan in which he would invest $3 million of his own money (on which he would get a stock bonus) in the issuance of $14 million worth of 7 percent debentures joined with the issuance of 250,000 shares of class A and B stock, all of which was necessary to complete the Elizabeth plant.

But there was a villain in the piece who foiled these plans. He was J. R. Harbeck, chairman of the Willys Corporation and vice president of American Can. There was no display of friendship between Harbeck and Chrysler, and indeed there was a degree of rivalry in this undertaking. Couture said that Harbeck hated Chrysler and tried to foil him at every turn. "I believe Mr. Harbeck recognized the worth of the new car and its importance to the future of the Willys Corporation, and no doubt in his own mind, he had hoped to out manoeuver Mr. Chrysler," he wrote. What he didn't realize is that Chrysler and Harbeck were equally involved in the complicated affairs of the Maxwell Corporation at that time, and that a good deal of the rivalry and bad blood between the two men had been generated in that situation.

There was a lull in the production process, which alarmed no one particularly. After all, steps had to be taken to disassemble the tooling for the abandoned Overland Six and prepare the new car for production at the plant. No one thought there would be a money problem. Breer stated that when the team joined Willys they believed there was enough capital to cover all contingencies, despite any immediate problems that might have to be dealt with.

But nothing happened. Eventually word got around that Harbeck had blocked the sale to Chrysler's interests, so that plan was off. Apparently he said he thought Chrysler was trying to pull off a fast deal. To an extent he might have been right, for those same June 30, 1921, papers of Chrysler's show that he intended to resell the $3 million of debentures he was going to purchase from Willys-Overland while keeping a profit of between $2.5 and $3 million on the 100,000 shares of stock that went with them. After that deal went sour, the Willys bankers no longer wanted to finance the Elizabeth operation and the new car as they tried to straighten out the organization's finances. When conditions improved in 1921, the stockholders and the officers of the corporation wanted to go forward with the new project for the future, but they met intractable opposition from these bankers, and the two sides were pulling in opposite directions. Chrysler recalled one acrimonious meeting of the banking committee at which only one man, Edward R. Tinker of Chase, was willing to authorize payments for further engineering work on the new car. Tinker lost then, but was to play an important role in Chrysler's subsequent automobile career.

Things had come to a standstill. Willys was seen no more around the Elizabeth automobile plant, and Chrysler was losing interest.

Late in 1921 there was a board meeting to consider renewing Chrysler's contract at Willys. There had been much commotion about his million-dollar salary from the moment it was announced in big newspaper articles around the country. At a Society of Automotive Engineers meeting at the time, George Crane had said nobody was worth a million dollars a year. But in practical terms, his reduction of the company's debt by over $25 million meant that he was worth every nickel of what he was paid. Still, there was a lot of resentment. At the board meeting one of the bankers said that a million dollars a year was quite a lot to pay anybody, and a big discussion ensued. Nicholas Kelley, Chrysler's lawyer, recounted what happened next. "Chrysler looked at these fellows and said, 'You think that's too much, do you?' They said, 'Well, that's a great deal of money to pay anybody.' Chrysler said, 'If that's the way you feel about it, you can stick that job up your ass.' "

Then one day right at this time, suddenly and without warning, word came through publicly that Willys-Overland in Toledo was in financial difficulties, causing all monies to be drained from the Elizabeth operation and sent there. John Willys, in what turned out to be a clever stock manipulation to regain control of his company, threw the Willys Corporation into receivership on November 30, 1921.

That was really the end for Chrysler. He told Tobe Couture, "I have more money than I know what to do with. I want to get out of this thing," and left for Europe.

However, though tough times were ahead, it was far from the end for Chrysler, Zeder, Skelton, and Breer, and for Chrysler's long-held dream of getting into manufacturing for himself. At the same time as his rescue of Willys was taking place, he was involved with an equally difficult rescue operation at the Maxwell-Chalmers Corporation, which would give him the basis for his new company and his new car. Never were his leadership and ability to instill loyalty in a group of dynamic men of more value than during this next period, for out of it at last came the Chrysler Corporation.

◨ 19 ◧

Putting Together
the First Chrysler Car

Side by Side by Side

At his retirement dinner in November 1956, Tobe Couture got up to speak of the formation of the Chrysler Corporation. In his speech, he said that most people in the room that night didn't realize it, but the Chrysler Corporation almost never came into existence at all. A good deal of the reason that it did was the cohesion of Zeder, Skelton, and Breer, and their loyalty to Walter Chrysler's vision.

The sudden turn of events at Willys in the autumn of 1921 was a real blow to the engineers. They had left the security of good jobs at Studebaker and induced fifteen valuable men and their families to go with them. Fred Zeder had bought a home in South Orange, New Jersey, and Carl Breer had done the same in nearby Summit. Bills had to be paid, and everybody needed to earn a living. Besides, the three engineers had worked very hard to build an efficient and proven team, and they were loath to let it go now. There was only one solution they could see.

All three of them went to Chrysler and told him they wanted to set up a consulting firm. He said fine, that was what the three of them should do. But they countered that they felt they needed to hold their entire group together, as their men were first-rate and the engineers felt a responsibility to them. Chrysler understood their predicament and arranged to help them get started.

All the men the engineers had convinced to leave Studebaker and go to work for them had been given relocation allowances for moving to New Jersey, so they had a bit of money to fall back on. Besides, the three engineers were dedicated to the idea of this new Chrysler Six and didn't want to give up working on it. They hoped that Chrysler would be able to find backing in another way.

Their firm was incorporated as the Zeder Skelton Breer Engineering Company. It was billed this way to avoid the unfortunate associations of being known as the "BS" Z or Z "BS" company. We will refer to them as ZSB from now on.

To set up their operations they found a fourth-floor loft at 26 Mechanic Street in Newark. It had previously been a furrier's shop and was very quiet, fronting an old cemetery.

There was no time or money to waste, so everybody pitched in immediately to do what they could. Zeder was out selling the new firm's services, and everyone else was turning out the work. Tobe Couture got a good commission from the Daniels Motor Car Company, which advertised its $5,000 superluxury autos as "The Distinguished Car to the Discriminating." Its new Model 90 had some supersized problems, and ZSB was glad to help out. But pickings were slim, and the engineers had a difficult time meeting their heavy payroll, especially since they decided to continue everyone at their previous wage scale.

ZSB had good reason to hope that Chrysler would be able to get his own production company organized, however, because just eight months after taking on the job at Willys, Chrysler was approached by another group of bankers to take over the equally sick Maxwell company, and was guiding their affairs with great success. ZSB viewed this situation as another possible source of income, and another possible launching platform for Chrysler's new car.

The Maxwell was one of the great successes of the early car industry. Believing that David Buick would never straighten out his car production problems, Benjamin Briscoe had happily sold out his Buick interests in 1904 to go into business manufacturing the new Maxwell car, named for Jonathan Dixon Maxwell, the engineering genius who had done pioneering work at Haynes, Apperson, and Olds, and who, with Charles B. King, cofounded the Northern Manufacturing Company, makers of the famed Silent Northern. He also invented thermo-siphon cooling. With uncharacteristic backing from J. P. Morgan to the tune of $350,000, the Tarrytown, New York, Maxwell-Briscoe Company was a big success from the beginning, with sales climbing each year to mark it as one of the top firms in the field.

The Maxwell was a very fine car, but a lot of its success was due to its indefatigable sales manager, Cadwallader Washington Kelsey, whose ability to dream up publicity stunts was matchless. Teeterboard rides and police chases involving Maxwells were filmed and shown in nickelodeons; five Maxwells made an excellent showing in a light-car race preceding the Glidden Car Tour of 1908; an unheard-of 1909 cross-country trip by two women driving a Maxwell brought undreamed-of press coverage. In 1910 sales climbed to 20,500, good for third place in the industry, behind Ford and Buick.

Then trouble ensued. As we have seen earlier, Briscoe, frustrated by his inability to continue with Durant in the formation of General Motors, decided to imitate him by forming his own gigantic motor combine, U.S. Motors, in 1911. He combined the Maxwell with a long list of other makes including Stoddard-Dayton, Columbia, and Brush in a new company that was practically an unmitigated financial disaster. Aside from Maxwell, almost none of the components of U.S. Motors was viable, and indeed some were dead on arrival. The whole thing collapsed into bankruptcy in 1912, with Maxwell as the only important survivor. Though most of Maxwell's factories were gone, somehow Jonathan Maxwell was able to take over the company and become its president, moving operations to Detroit.

In a direct precursor to what was to happen with Walter Chrysler in 1920, a group of bankers approached Walter E. Flanders, late of EMF and Studebaker, to take over the Maxwell operation, and on January 25, 1914, the Maxwell Motor Company was formed with Flanders at its head. Flanders worked out a deal whereby the bankers paid him $1 million and gave him $2.75 million in Maxwell stock. He tore right into the situation, coming up with a steady stream of new models and new engines over the next few years. Production rose from 17,000 in 1913 (sixth place in the industry) to 44,000 in 1915, which was good for fourth place, just barely behind the new Dodge. Production reached a peak of 75,000 cars and 25,000 trucks in 1917, with huge profits. In fact, the company earned some $18 million between 1913 and 1918, and that period saw the stock price rise from $1.75 to $99 a share.

Things continued to go well through the First World War, but by 1920 big problems had shown up. Flanders was a terrific production man, but he was not very well attuned to engineering, and after several years of success, Maxwell products were becoming outmoded and quality was declining. Then too, in 1917 he leased a large plant in Detroit from the Chalmers Motor Car Company for five years on a profit-sharing basis that turned out to be a bookeeping nightmare.

Chalmers's story began in 1907 when Howard Coffin and Roy Chapin convinced the natty and successful former vice president of the National Cash Register Company, Hugh Chalmers, to come out of retirement and buy out the Thomas-Detroit Company of Buffalo, New York, manufacturers of the famed Thomas-Flyer, which was to win the New York-to-Paris auto race in July 1908. Chalmers, destined to become yet another of the great salesmen of the auto industry, had done so well at NCR that he had retired from it a millionaire at the age of twenty-seven. (Historian Christy Borth points out that Chalmers was only one in a line of extraordinary men NCR contributed to the auto industry, including Charles Kettering of GM, Packard's president Alvin Macauley, Chrysler's sales manager Joseph Fields, and Edward S. Jordan of Jordan Playboy fame.)

The three men formed the Chalmers-Detroit Motor Car Company in July 1908 and began manufacturing cars in the $1,500-to-$2,800 range as 1909 models. When Coffin and Chapin decided to produce an under-$1,000 car, they parted company with Chalmers and went on to found Hudson, named for J. L. Hudson, the Detroit department store magnate who put up most of the money for the venture. On his own, Chalmers was successful selling his prestigious and highly regarded Chalmers cars, with sales reaching a peak of 20,000 units in 1915. But sales declined rapidly after that because Chalmers and his general managers concentrated all their efforts on sales and promotion and little on the actual product, which had fallen behind the times. By 1917 the company was stuck with excess capacity, and Chalmers made the deal with Maxwell, which needed expanded production facilities. But the bookkeeping problems meant that the deal was fraught with suspicion and animosity on both sides for as long as it continued, and Maxwell began to experience financial problems as a direct result of losses from its association with Chalmers.

As a consequence of material shortages, Maxwell production dove to only 34,000 in 1918, though it made good money producing war materiel, as did many other firms. This was the same year that Flanders left, originally to retire and later to join his old EMF partners Barney Everitt and William Metzger in manufacturing the new Rickenbacker car, named after the renowned World War I flying ace Eddie Rickenbacker. (Flanders died in a car crash in 1923, a blow from which the Rickenbacker never recovered.) Maxwell was now run by W. Ledyard Mitchell, a good executive who nevertheless was unable to stanch the flow of profits from Maxwell's arrangement with Chalmers. (Later Mitchell would figure prominently in the Chrysler Corporation.)

Sales rose to 50,000 in the 1919 postwar boom, and Maxwell's bankers, believing like everyone else that the boom would continue, loaned it large amounts of money, eventually amounting to $26 million. Unfortunately, the boom collapsed into a depression. Maxwell was stuck with 26,000 unsold cars, some 16,000 of which were on railroad sidings with demurrage owed by dealers who couldn't or wouldn't take them. "All of the borrowed money had been converted into shapes that were totally unlike money," Chrysler said. "On top of that, Maxwell, like Willys-Overland, had contracted for many millions of dollars' worth of parts to be manufactured into cars of a design that was no good." What made matters worse was that the parts were priced at postwar boom levels, so even if they were assembled into cars, those cars would have to be sold at unrealistically inflated levels.

James Cox Brady approached Walter Chrysler on behalf of the bankers who had backed Maxwell. He and his brother Nicholas previously played a major part in making the arrangements for Chrysler to go to work at Willys, and the three men had become close personal friends. "We enjoyed great

times in one another's society, Nick and Jim and I," said Chrysler. "Often
we rode between New York and Detroit in their private car, a party of a
dozen or more, including other bankers, such as Harry Bronner, Ed Tinker
and Waddill Catchings." Tinker, of the Chase National Bank, and Chrysler's
old friend Ralph Van Vechten, of the Continental and Commercial National
Bank of Chicago, were involved in both the Willys and Maxwell situations,
so there were several familiar faces for him to deal with in these new circumstances. Though Jules Bache wanted a Chalmers man to head the new
situation, he was overruled by the Bradys. Even so, Chrysler was at first
reluctant, considering all the problems between Maxwell and Chalmers. After one bitter meeting, he told Tinker, "I would not touch it with a ten foot
pole." But eventually the Bradys prevailed, and he agreed to do the job.
After getting permission from John North Willys (who was hardly in a position to deny it to the same bankers who were rescuing him), Walter Chrysler joined Maxwell in August 1920.

At first he was in an advisory capacity as chairman of a reorganization
committee, formed in the late summer of 1920. His salary was $100,000 a
year. Later, when things were going well and the board was anxious for
him to devote his full energies to the corporation, they agreed to a tough
contract that granted him generous stock options that were the real in-
ducement in the situation; those options, in fact, were on a considerable
part of the Bradys's holdings. Nicholas Kelley said they allowed him to buy
around $1 million worth of stock for a pittance. Furthermore, Kelley said
he got a very lucrative profit-sharing agreement that eventually, added to
his salary, was paying him $800,000 a year. (When this arrangement was
later questioned for tax reasons, all they had to do was point out that he
previously had been paid $1 million a year at Willys-Overland, where he
was on straight salary with no control of the company at all; the agreement
held up.)

When the board proposed the sweetened agreement, Ed Tinker pointed
out to Chrysler that the bankers were hiring him to run Maxwell because
he had proved he was more than just a production man, as he was known
at Buick; the Willys situation now showed him to be both a merchandiser
and a finance man, too. Under the Maxwell deal, if he could turn things
around at Maxwell and raise the stock price, he would have the opportunity
to obtain a major stake in the company. This might be the springboard from
which he could at last plunge into manufacturing his own car. Chrysler
recognized the wisdom of Tinker's advice, for what he needed now was the
leverage to catapult himself into his long-dreamed-of future as a car manufacturer. The cash in this arrangement, much less than in the Willys deal,
was just lagniappe.

He had his work cut out for him. All those cars lying around were in
terrible shape. They were poorly assembled in the first place, and had been

left without proper maintenance in warehouses and on railroad sidings. On top of that, there were big problems with the cars themselves. A redesign in 1919 moved the gas tank from the cowl to the rear of the car, but it was insufficiently braced and constantly broke its mounts. Then there were the infamous rear axles, which were not strong enough for the weight they carried. One good jolt from a pothole, and they snapped. Chrysler immediately shut down all production and the plant turned away any new supplies, then coming into the factory at the rate of $1 million worth a month. Then he concentrated on fixing up and selling the distressed merchandise on hand. Since the cars were in the field, he sent out mechanics and materials to fix them where they stood. They braced up the shaky gas tanks and put strong new struts on the axles, replaced bad transmissions, and got rid of anything else on the cars that was no good.

In order to accomplish this, the first thing Chrysler did was to go to the bankers and ask for another $15 million. Shocked, they asked what he could possibly mean, since the reason they had hired him was to get back the $26 million they were out already. He told them in essence that they had piles of unusable junk in the form of unsold and unassembled cars, and that the only way to turn them into cash was to fix up the bad cars and assemble the parts into new, better ones. He suggested one-, two-, and three-year notes to be paid in cash at 6 percent.

But there was more. In order to sell these cars, he proposed to cut the price of the touring car to $995, which would show a $5 profit on each one; the roadsters, at $935, would be even cheaper. The bankers were up in arms, saying they should get a profit of $100 per car. But he told them he was liquidating an inventory, and the cars wouldn't sell at higher prices. In the end they had to go along with him, and the tonnage moved, as Chrysler told them it would.

The day after he took the Maxwell job Chrysler sought out A. E. Barker, a marketing and distribution man he knew only from his successful reputation at Dodge. "Here's this Maxwell job—the hardest one you or any other sales manager ever had to tackle," Chrysler told him. "You can't even start with nothing—you've got to overcome a lot of trouble before you can even begin to build. Can you whip it?" "Hell yes!" came the reply, and Chrysler hired him on the spot.

He wasn't the only one hired. Lots were fired, too; one released executive shot himself while "cleaning a friend's revolver." Chrysler had done a similar housecleaning at Willys, and he was becoming known as a rather ruthless hatchet man. But desperate times called for desperate measures, and clearly both of these inefficient organizations needed to be shaken up and mightily improved, or they would go out of business. He was applying the techniques of management and deployment of men he had learned so well over a decade and a half of running railroad shops and Buick. For a man charged with heading a vast, faltering organization, the ultimate in humane treatment of employees is to keep such an organization operating and eventually return it to robust health, for the benefit of the greatest number of its workers. Though his methods were undoubtedly tough on many individuals, that is what Chrysler did, both at Willys and at Maxwell.

Realizing that the company had over fifteen years of goodwill among the car-buying public, Chrysler decided to support Barker's efforts by creating the "Good Maxwell" advertising campaign, so called to distinguish the re-done cars from the bombs it had been selling. Years later Chrysler said he gagged every time he saw those "Good Maxwell" ads, but there was little he could do about the fact that he had to shore up the company's reputation. Somehow or other the public believed the publicity, and a combination of a truly better product, the right price, and the right ads saved the day.

Looking to usher in a brighter future as quickly as he could, he also ordered the design and production of a new Model 25 for the 1922 model year. It featured a higher hood line, barrel headlamps, crown fenders, and, most important, a new three-bearing engine designed by former Willys-Overland engineer Henry T. Woolson; it ran much more smoothly than the one it replaced. Throughout 1921 Chrysler proceeded cautiously, fixing up and selling off the old inventory and trying to put the company back on an even financial keel while producing few actual new cars; total output that year was only 16,000 Maxwells. But after the new Model 25 came out, sales improved markedly, with production up to over 55,000 by the end of 1922, a sharp improvement over the 34,000 sold in 1920. Maxwell went into the black once more, earning close to $900,000 in 1922, even after deducting a $1.1 million loss on the Chalmers operation. Chalmers sales were to keep on sinking, and the resultant losses were a continual drag on the newfound profits of the Maxwell over the next several years.

The company had been trying to deal with the Chalmers problem for several years. A new company, the Maxwell Motors Corporation, had been formed on May 7, 1921, subsuming both Maxwell and Chalmers into a new, combined operation that was supposed to pay down debt and operate at a considerable savings. This was actually the result of a friendly receivership worked out over several months in which corporation president W. Ledyard Mitchell, as receiver, sold the assets of Maxwell-Chalmers to the company re-organization committee, led by Chrysler and Harry Bronner, for $10,915,000. The new corporation began functioning on June 1, 1921, and by August 21 its president, William Robert Wilson (yet another banker brought into the situation) was able to say that contingent liabilities had been reduced by $12 million over the previous year and that inventories were down by 60 percent, running only slightly higher than daily production. Everything in Maxwell's balance sheet was conservatively valued, with inventory reflecting the fall in car prices during that period and allowances made for continuing problems in that area. (All car companies, beginning with Ford, Maxwell, Studebaker, and Packard in the autumn of 1920, had been lowering their prices, and by May 1921 a price-cutting stampede began that was to see the Model T touring car go down to $355, the Chevrolet sedan drop from $1,375 to $875, and the Willys touring car go from $895 to $695. Nobody knew how far this trend would go.) Maxwell was clearly on the right track, but only a final drastic move with regard to Chalmers would end the problems it brought to the parent company.

In the summer of 1922 Chalmers had been hit with both a mortgage foreclosure and a general creditors' suit, and a Noteholders' Protection Committee of the Chalmers Motor Company was formed to deal with the problem. In September it sent out an offer to exchange ten series A and ten series B Maxwell shares plus $60 in cash for each $1,000 Chalmers note or $860 cash debt of the company. Debt holders had until October 5 to make the exchange or risk getting only a distributive share of Chalmers assets from an impending judicial sale. This took place on December 7, when Boyd G. Curtis, a local Detroit attorney representing the Maxwell interests, paid $1,987,000 for the assets of Chalmers. The only bidder, he assigned the property to Maxwell immediately after Federal Judge Arthur J. Tuttle confirmed the sale. This meant that after 1922 Chalmers would stop hemorrhaging the profits of the now smartly turned-around Maxwell Motor Corporation. The company continued to sell the Chalmers for a while, but in ever-decreasing numbers. In 1924 Chrysler dropped it entirely. The last cars were produced in 1923, with some 2,022 of them sold as 1924 models.

Chrysler pulled Maxwell-Chalmers through its problems, but it was not an easy row to hoe. In 1923 he reminisced with W. A. P. John on just how tough it had been when he first signed on. "If ever there was a mess," he said, "that was it. Bankruptcy was 48 hours around the corner and if the break came, only 20 cents on the dollar would have been paid.

"They showed me that the company owed the banks over $12 million; that accounts payable were $6 million; that other items of indebtedness brought the total up to over $20 million. That was bad enough, but it wasn't the half of it. There were only 50 active dealer accounts on the books. The old Maxwell car was discredited everywhere, with $10 million in notes receivable against them needing liquidation. I doubt if you could have given one away under the conditions that then existed.

"I went over the list of creditors. Three-quarters of them were old friends of mine! Right then and there I knew I was in for a job if we could evolve a reorganization that gave us a ghost of a show to succeed.

"We worked out a plan to take care of the creditors by issuing new stock and notes. The bankers provided working capital and . . . here we are."

In 1929 he confided to B. C. Forbes that shortly after he started at Maxwell he realized that he could truly build his future on it; Ed Tinker's advice was prescient. " 'Here's the place for me to start,' Chrysler told [Forbes]. True, the conditions I found were far from encouraging. But I could see possibilities. I went at it full steam, surrounding myself with a very able organization.' "

In addition to W. Ledyard Mitchell, Chrysler picked up another man at Maxwell who was later to figure significantly in the future of the Chrysler Corporation: B. E. (Bernice Edwin) Hutchinson, familiarly known as "Hutch." After leaving MIT at the dean's invitation, Hutchinson got a job as a reporter for the *Boston Globe.* Next he shoveled cinders and then served as superintendent of the open-hearth department of his father's Grand Crossing Tack Company. Following this, he became an accountant, first with Ernst & Ernst and then for the American Writing Paper Company, where he first reorganized accounting and subsequently became treasurer. When he joined Maxwell as treasurer, he looked at its books and immediately wrote down inventory by $11 million. Though it made the books look anemic, this move earned the respect of the bankers, who now knew more than ever that the company meant business. Hutchinson was shrewdly aware that as treasurer he had to be a salesman to convince the banks that the company was willing to take a realistic look at its present so that its great team of executives could build it a glorious future. He did this so well that in six months he became vice president of the company.

Having put Maxwell on the right course early in the game, Chrysler naturally concentrated on extending his gains. After the sudden Willys bankruptcy in late 1921 it seemed to ZSB that he had lost all interest in the possibility of manufacturing the new Chrysler job they had all worked so hard on under his direction. Early in 1922 Chrysler took another trip to Europe, and ZSB heard little from him. The two Willys receivers from New Jersey, James Kerney of Trenton and Clifford J. Voorhees of New Brunswick, were favorably disposed to ZSB, and rented them the same engineering space and facilities they had formerly been using at the Elizabeth plant for only $100 a month. There they and their associates toiled away in sometimes very precarious circumstances during the first few months of their new firm's existence. Owen Skelton, then still a bachelor, was living in the Robert Treat Hotel and often went broke handing out ten-dollar bills to help the married men keep their families fed. But through it all they kept on working on perfecting that Chrysler job, hoping that somehow, someday, it would see production.

After Chrysler returned from Europe, the boys decided to rekindle his interest in the project. One night Zeder, Skelton, and Breer invited him over to the Robert Treat Hotel for dinner; following a very pleasant time, he was anxious to have his chauffeur drive him back to New York. But after some very persuasive language from Zeder, Chrysler—who, according to Couture, had "a good brannigan on"—went out to the Elizabeth plant, the men driving mostly in silence. The whole ZSB organization was waiting for him and showed him things about the improved new engine he had never seen before. It was perched up on a block, and he was fascinated by it, poring over every detail as the hours went by. He examined part after part of the engine, listened to it hum, and studied its design, growing more and more enthusiastic. He scrutinized every aspect of a wooden model of the proposed car that had been set up nearby, too. One o'clock came and went, and then two o'clock; by three, he had seen enough to get all the juices flowing once again. According to advertising man Ted MacManus, "He pushed Zeder outside into the immense assembly room, reached for a hand, found it and in a ringing voice shouted: 'Fred, I'm with you.' In the thin light which filtered from the partly opened door of the experimental laboratories these two men, with their right hands clasped and left arms thrown about each other's shoulders, wept unashamed." Skelton later said, "That night he showed his old determination. He wanted to see that car built with his name on it."

Chrysler now began taking steps to do just that. He knew that the Willys receivers had decided to sell off the Elizabeth plant, which he told Nicholas Brady he thought was the best-laid-out automobile plant in the East. With it were to go the plans for the Chrysler job. He set about getting backing to purchase the whole works at the sale, scheduled for June 9, 1922, on the site of the plant. The Maxwell interests were behind him, tempting him. Ed Tinker of Chase, who knew the inside affairs of both Maxwell and Willys, told him, "You could buy that new Elizabeth plant for Maxwell for much less than it cost," and with such support Chrysler thought he had a good chance of making a winning bid. Needless to say, ZSB, having got wind of what was going on, was keenly interested in the outcome.

The sale of the Willys buildings at Elizabeth was announced on April 28, in compliance with an order signed by Justice Bodine of the U.S. District Court in Newark. By this order the Willys receivers—Messrs. Kerney and Voorhees, and Clement O. Miniger of the Auto-Lite Company of Toledo, a man fiercely loyal to John North Willys—were directed to dispose of this property at auction. These receivers were appointed when a bill was filed sometime previously by the Ohio Savings Bank and Trust Company of Toledo, requesting liquidation of the company's affairs. The bank alleged that the corporation owed more than $10 million and that the value of the plant and other properties was considerably greater than that. The receivers were to report back to the court on the results of the sale on June 19.

The Sunday New York Times on June 4 carried the advertisement of the sale, which was to be conducted by Charles E. Gerth of Gerth's Realty Experts on the following Friday at 11 A.M. The property was to be sold in four separate lots. The first consisted of the land, buildings, appurtenances, and fixtures; this lot included the main plant, but machinery, material, supplies, and other chattels were not included. The second lot consisted of a baseball park, including all appurtenances and fixtures, but not machinery and other items stored there. The same restrictions applied to the third lot, a garage. The last lot was made up of property to be listed by the receivers at the time of sale, and included a vast assortment of machine tools. The court directed that $200,000 had to be deposited beforehand by anyone bidding on parcel one. Ten percent of the highest bid on parcel two had to be deposited, with 20 percent on parcel three and 15 percent on parcel four. All bids would be submitted to Judge Bodine on June 19. This was the plan, but the actual events of June 9 blew everything sky high.

The auction was expected to be a perfunctory affair, but it turned out to be charged with high drama. Hundreds of people assembled outside the entrance of the vast three-story red brick factory waiting for the auction to begin. (It was said to be the largest building of its kind in the world, over 3,500 feet long and having 32 acres of floor space; 80 carloads of materials could be unloaded at its incoming sidings, and 125 boxcars could load up on the outgoing side. In addition, it was self-contained, with its own refrigeration and power plants, and its cafeteria could serve 1,200 at a time.)

Nicholas Kelley was sent out to run the bidding on behalf of Walter Chrysler and the Maxwell interests, though old Senator James Smith, Jr. of New Jersey was to do the actual bidding. Among those present were representatives of two other large concerns prepared to do serious bidding. One was J. Clarence Davies, who claimed only to represent himself but who was rumored to represent Studebaker or General Motors interests. The other was Joseph P. Day, a New York real estate expert representing none other than Billy Durant, who was also present, though not as a direct bidder. (Clement O. Miniger, one of the receivers, resigned his position in order to bid, possibly representing the Willys interests; in the event, he failed to do so.)

Durant had quietly visited the site several times during the spring and had been shown three cars in which the new Chrysler six motor was mounted; like many another before him, he had ridden in one of the cars through the vast reaches of the plant. As a result, he offered the receivers $3 million for the whole property, knowing that under the rules of a receiver's sale the blueprints and specifications of the new car remained the property of Willys-Overland and would be sold with the other assets of the plant. He was turned down, but on auction day he claimed he would not bid a nickel more than his previous offer for the property. Durant was serenely confident that he wouldn't have to, either, for he arrived thinking there would be no other bidders. But when all three representatives went into the huge main room of the plant and put down the requisite $200,000 on the long tables that had been set up for the auction, he knew it was not going to be quite as easy as he had thought.

Gerth began by accepting bids for the individual parcels amid the usual noise and hullabaloo surrounding an auction, but in the process, Kelley noticed that the car plans were not being offered. He told Smith to protest, but when the reticent old man refused, he did it himself, claiming that holding back in this manner was illegal. The receivers said they were indeed holding them back and that it was legal. But when all was totted up, the aggregate was only $3,030,000, much less than was hoped for, and so it was decided to accept bids on all the properties considered as a whole. That's when things really livened up.

Under the new plan, the bidding started at $4 million, rising steadily and quickly in increments of from $5,000 to $100,000. According to *Automotive Industries*, "excitement became intense among the 500 or 600 spectators. Each new bid was received with cheers. Nicholas Kelley said pandemonium broke loose, because many of those who attended the auction held mechanics' liens on the property, and they realized that the higher the bid, the more they would receive on their claims."

Davies bowed out of the bidding at $4,465,000, and then Smith suddenly raised his offer to $5,500,000. By then everyone was choking with excitement. But it was all over in a flash. Joseph Day raised him $25,000; Smith bowed, smiled, and retired. In yet another triumph, the day, and the plant, now belonged to Billy Durant. Knowing that he had bested his old rival Walter Chrysler probably added to his victory, even if it wound up costing him almost double the amount he had originally expected. (In actuality, Kelley said, "I took a walk past the old boy, and he was wild. He said, 'Young man, you have cost me $2 million, which didn't do you any good, but which I have to pay.'")

As for Chrysler, "When I got that news, I was wild," he said. Smith had stopped bidding because of a lack of authority to keep on going against Durant, who everyone thought would be cleaned out by the $5.5 million bid. But Chrysler said, "I told Tinker I would have been willing, if the bankers had agreed, to bid up to $7.5 million."

Now Walter Chrysler had lost his new car for a second time, and this time the loss seemed irrevocable. It had been his dream to go into auto production ever since he began tearing apart that Locomobile back in Oelwein and decided to leave railroad management for manufacturing. He had become adept enough at running automobile businesses to become the highest-salaried man in history, and worth every penny. But, "God bless the child who's got his own," as Billie Holiday said, and every time he tried to get his own, he failed. First it was the obstinate pride of John North Willys and the malice of J. R. Harbeck that had thwarted him; now it was shrewd, lucky Billy Durant, risen like a phoenix from the ashes of his second collapse at General Motors, who went the extra inch to snatch Chrysler's creation from under his nose at the eleventh hour. This new car had been created at Chrysler's behest as a standard for him to carry as a captain of industry.

Suddenly he was back where he had always been in the automobile industry: prominent and well paid, but still an employee in someone else's enterprise. It bids fair to say that this was the worst setback of his entire life.

Maxwell gave out a statement that it had intended to buy the plant to produce a new Chrysler Six, in recognition of their confidence in his ability to produce a new line in addition to the Maxwell and the Chalmers. But plans for the new car went with the factory to Durant, and since Maxwell now had no factory in which to produce such a vehicle, they did not foresee making an offer to Durant for the rights to it.

The night before Chrysler left for Europe, the Maxwell directors gave a dinner for him at the Metropolitan Club in New York, in recognition of his achievement in putting Maxwell back on its feet in so short a time. Clearly this was timed to be a celebratory announcement of the inauguration of the new Chrysler Six, and it was now rather an awkward occasion. Ed Tinker presided, and announced that Chrysler would be the only speaker, reducing the possiblities of any protracted funerary unease.

In his speech Chrysler outlined his accomplishments at Maxwell while he was still vice president of Willys. He was proud of selling 40,000 of the redone cars at profits of $5 to $15 each, and now was excited to have a new model being turned out at the rate of 6,500 a month, showing a profit of $100 per car; he expected 1923 production to be at least 100,000 cars. Pointedly he noted that he had often been asked if he planned to stay with the company, and replied that since the Maxwell directors had stood by him, he intended to stand by them.

Four days after the auction Walt and Della, accompanied by Thelma and Bernice, sailed on the Aquitania for a two-month vacation during which they were to visit France, Switzerland, Italy, Austria, Czechoslovakia, Germany, Belgium, and Holland before stops in Paris and London prior to sailing for home on September 9. A highlight of the trip, which Walt had promised to Thelma upon her graduation from the National Park Seminary, was a visit to Oberammergau to attend a performance of the Passion Play there. The trip couldn't have come at a better time, for after all he had been through, Walt needed a rest.

As for Durant, he announced that his new superplant would immediately begin producing 550 of his new cars a day, 400 Stars and 150 Durant Fours. Though the value of the entire Elizabeth package was estimated at $15 million before the sale, the knockdown value announced on June 9 was actually $12,843,133. Since he intended to sell off the garage, valued at $50,000, and the ballpark, valued at $72,000, in addition to twenty-four lots of machinery inventoried at $2,340,000, the actual plant, at $5.525 million, cost him not much more than the $3 million he had originally intended to pay—a superb bit of financial maneuvering.

The problem, as always with Durant's new company, turned out to be product, which inadvertently turned out to be advantageous to ZSB.

❖   ❖   ❖

Almost immediately upon Durant's leaving GM he announced that he would form a new car company. Durant Motors was incorporated in New York on January 12, 1921, after Durant announced a Chevrolet-like scheme allowing certain badly burned GM investors to exchange their shares for ones in his new company on a seven-for-five basis, giving them a chance at the success of his new venture, plus a $12-per-share tax write off on the old one. He then set about selling one class of $10 shares to the public, even allowing them to be purchased on time in lots of no more than twenty, so that the "little fellow" would not be excluded from the new prosperity Durant was creating. By the close of 1922, his clerks were handling up to a million dollars a day in checks, and he had 146,000 stockholders, a figure that eventually rose to 350,000, second only to AT&T.

The initial car he produced was the Durant, and he had prototypes of it on the road forty-seven days after he first announced it. It was an assembled car, as all of Durant's creations would be, designed by Alfred T. Sturt. The four-cylinder Durant, with a Continental engine mounted on a 109-inch wheelbase, sold for $890, joined a year later by a six at double the price. But what really got enthusiasm up was the announcement of his new low-priced car, the Star, meant to compete directly with the Model T at $348, despite having features far in advance of its competitor. Thirty thousand people showed up to view its unveiling in Washington, D.C., on March 10, 1922, and similar crowds attended its debut in New York, Boston, Detroit, Houston, and Philadelphia. The Model T seemed like something out of the Stone Age next to the Star, which offered such modern conveniences as demountable rims, a self-starter, and a sliding-gear transmission. No one could believe it could be built and sold for $348, and as it turned out, they were right. The touring car wound up selling for $442 with the self-starter and demountable rims, which looked even more expensive after Henry Ford cut the Model T's price to a bargain-basement $298. But that didn't keep the stock from flying out of the company's coffers. One million Star shares were sold immediately at $15 each, and another million followed close upon.

True to his word, Durant quickly got his indispensable production man, Hoelzle, and his son to tool up the Elizabeth plant for progressive manufacture of the Star. Durant announced an order of 250,000 motors from Continental, and soon the cars were rolling off the line to the dealers in volume. Though the numbers are controversial at best, some say eventually 1.5 million Stars were produced; actual figures were probably only a fraction of that, but still, the numbers were substantial. In any case, the boom didn't last because the car was badly produced and eventually field problems over-whelmed its reputation among dealers and consumers alike.

Occasional ZSB visits to see the Star being built in the Elizabeth plant showed why. For instance, on one trip along the line they saw such things as spring shackle bolts being driven into place with sledgehammers, which meant they were never going to last. Then there was no such thing as follow-up on design and assembly problems. An example was the car's thermo-siphon radiator. It was held in place by a large-diameter hose con-nection through which the hot water flowed. The result was that engine and car vibration caused fatigue in the thin brass radiator top tank walls, which cracked and broke loose. This was not a difficult problem to correct, but nothing was done about it, and the factory continued turning out cars with this fault. Either there was no centralized engineering supervision to seek out problems, or if there was one, nobody wanted to spend the time and the money to correct them. Either way, it was trouble just waiting to happen, and eventually it did. After a meteoric rise, the Star's customers disappeared, and it was out of business by 1928.

Walter Chrysler's loss of his Chrysler Six turned out to contain some good financial luck for ZSB. The engineers were doing the best they could with consulting work, but times were lean. Zeder and Breer had mortgaged their houses to keep the firm going, and the only reason Skelton didn't was that he didn't have one. Then one day out of the blue Tobe Couture got a call from Billy Durant, who wanted to see him at his office in New York. When he arrived and was immediately shown in to Durant ahead of the typical mob in the reception room he found out what it was all about. Durant had decided to use the Chrysler Six plans to build a new car, to be called the Flint. It seemed that Durant had built several prototypes from the Chrysler Six plans and found that their performance was not up to the old Chrysler prototypes he had ridden in months before. In particular, the Flints could not make the grade on Fort George Hill in New York City, which he knew the old Chryslers could do, because he had ridden up the same hill in one of them the previous spring. Did Tobe think he could tune up an old Chrysler car to ride the way it had when he had been in it? Tobe replied that he really didn't know, Durant would have to talk to Zeder about this, and the firm was so busy that he didn't know if it could take on any extra work. (Actually, ZSB hadn't had any substantial work in over six months.) Durant had never met Zeder, so Couture introduced them on the phone, and they talked for an hour. Somehow Zeder allowed as how, busy as the firm was, he could fit in designing work on the engine of this new job for $150,000, and Couture was put to work. This proved to be the salvation of ZSB.

Couture and Durant went out to Long Island to pick up one of the old Chrysler cars from a rather unwelcoming group of Flint engineers. Couture went to work the following day and immediately found out what was wrong. The car had old-fashioned two-wheel brakes, and the linkage from the brake pedal to the brake drum was incorrect, so if you drove over a bump with a full load, the brakes would apply. All that was needed was a readjustment in the geometry of the brakes. This he did, and the car got over Fort George Hill at 30 miles per hour without any problem. He never told the Durant engineers what he had done ("Oh, I adjusted the carburetor," was what he said), but the job was good enough for Durant to order ZSB to design the engine of the new Flint for production by Continental Motors.

According to Carl Breer, the engine size of the Flint was determined in a meeting between Durant and Ross Judson and his team of engineers from Continental. Then, in a fixed-sum contract made directly with Billy Durant, ZSB delivered complete designs for an L-head straight-six engine with seven main bearings and an updraft carburetor. Unfortunately, however, Durant stretched out the car, styled it to resemble a junior Locomobile, and sold it at prices from $1,195 to $2,085, which never allowed it to develop sufficient volume for a permanent place in the car market. It was discontinued in 1927. Later on, Durant said it was the best car and engine he ever produced, and its quality led him to commission several hundred units of a ZSB-designed engine for the ultraprestigious Locomobile line he had acquired in an effort to cover all price levels in the car market, just like GM.

One of the great benefits of ZSB's new association with Durant on the Flint engine design was that ZSB now had access to the dynamometer laboratory at the Elizabeth plant. Tests on a dynamometer were very expensive propositions, and were of vital importance in monitoring the firm's progress on improvements to the new high-compression engine they were continuing to design in Newark for the never-say-die Chrysler car. It wasn't exactly ethical, but at least they were able to do this all-important testing for free.

There was a sidebar that could have derailed the new Chrysler, at least as a Chrysler. Early in their association with Durant, he suggested to ZSB that they might take a look at reestablishing the failed Mercer car in the old brewery building where it had been manufactured, but upon examination of the facilities, this proved impractical. More seriously, as 1922 dragged on and the Durant funds were dwindling, ZSB decided to try to promote their new car on its own, under the brand name of Zeder. They had talks with Dillon, Reed, a fast-track brokerage firm with a reputation for raising funds for new businesses, but nothing came of this. Then their friend Rayal Hodgkins, manager of the Cleveland Tractor Company, suggested Cleveland as a good site for manufacturing the Zeder. It was the home of several important car companies over the years, including the Peerless, Winton, and White, so it seemed reasonable to set up shop there. Zeder and Hodgkins went through the city trying to promote the car and make plans for its manufacture, but all to no avail.

Something had to be done as 1922 was drawing to a close, because ZSB's cash was running out and Fred Zeder was not able to promote the firm's main brainchild on his own. Once again he decided to go back to Chrysler.

Skelton contacted Chrysler in New York on Armistice Day, finding him not in the best mood. When asked if he would see the three engineers right away, he replied curtly, "All right, but make it damn fast." However, by the time they arrived at his office his mood had changed completely, into one of docile affability. He said, "It is not only Armistice Day, but it is Saturday afternoon; I have cancelled everything, and the afternoon is ours." They went off to the plant where he was shown the updated plans for the car. Once again impressed with what he saw, he approved the specifications for the new job and signed a contract with ZSB for further development of it. "Now we are going to build the car," he said. "It is your job to get it ready for production. I don't know where it will be built, but I know some factories we can have," apparently thinking of the underused Chalmers plant under his direction.

Newark was just an easy stop away from New York on the Hudson and Manhattan Tube Train, and Chrysler began making a lot of visits to the ZSB shop, poring over all sorts of details of the new automobile as it was being prepared for manufacture. Skelton said, "He always had many ideas, and we worked with him and planned how this new car would be built." Chrysler remembered, "Any time I vanished from New York to go to that drab little factory building in Mechanic Street on a Friday, as had become my habit, I would be lost to my family for the several days of the weekend. I'd call my wife, apologize and start to explain when she would interrupt to mock me: 'Yes, I know, you're in New Jersey and you're going to stay through Saturday.' Then quickly her voice would change; 'Of course I understand. Go ahead and stay.' " This car creation had gone on for so long now that she could not possibly have misunderstood. As Chrysler later said of his and ZSB's relationship to the whole enterprise, "The Chrysler car? Nobody had heard about a Chrysler car. But we had dreamed about it until, as if we had been its lovers, it was work to think of anything else."

Sometimes they would stick one of Zeder's new high-compression engines under the hood of an old jalopy and try it out on the local roads. If they happened to stop at a light next to a big, fancy limo, they delighted to see the shocked expression on the snobby chauffeur's face when they left his car in the dust as they pulled away. There they were, grown men as excited as hot-rodding teenagers, but they just couldn't help it.

Finally it was time to show Chrysler a dynamometer test on the new engine. The date was April 11, 1923. Carl Breer was not there, for on the very day that Chrysler chose, he and his wife were scheduled to leave for California on a train trip to show off their new baby to relatives and friends, and it was decided that Zeder and Skelton could manage alone. First there was a lunch at their favorite spot, the Robert Treat Hotel; then Tobe Couture drove them out to the Elizabeth plant. Atop the factory the huge old "Chrysler The Six Cylinder Motor Car" sign was illuminated; it had been put up soon after Chrysler joined Willys and never taken down by Durant. The sight of it aroused quite a bit of emotion in Chrysler's breast as he was driven up to the plant.

Inside, Frank Schwartzenberger, the engine dynamometer man ZSB had acquired, like Tobe Couture, from Duesenberg, put on quite a show. The engine, rather small at 201 cubic inches, turned at 3,600 rpm. In those days, when high-compression engines were unheard of, this was amazing, and Chrysler was mightily impressed. Tobe Couture did his usual buildup routine, taking Chrysler for a demonstration drive through city streets, then over hills and past Thomas Edison's lodge in the Orange Mountains, all the time extolling the thrill of this latest job. On their return, Zeder and Skelton reminisced with Chrysler on all they had been through. Gazing up at the huge illuminated Chrysler sign, they finally put it to him: Why not build a real car with the engine they had just demonstrated to establish, at last, the Chrysler automobile? Breer later said: "Evidently they built up his enthusiasm from what he saw to the extent that he put his arms around the both of them and with enthusiasm said, 'We'll do it; let's go.' In true Chrysler fashion that was the initial sounding gong of the Chrysler Corporation."

Chrysler had one stipulation, though. ZSB would have to complete five prototypes by September 1. That meant that the finished design and procurement of all necessary materials to build these cars would have to be accomplished in four and a half months. It was rather a daunting job, but the engineers knew they were up to it and agreed.

Chrysler seemed to have a momentary hesitation when Skelton called him the following Monday in New York, but later that day the principals met at Chrysler's apartment to lay out the groundwork for proceeding full speed ahead on the project.

Over at Mechanic Street, ZSB got to work quickly. The complete car design was worked out in detail, and the engine reached the final stages of its development. At his retirement dinner, Tobe Couture said he had been sent out to engine shops to procure parts for the new job. It was the way things were done in those days. When he finished his rounds, the whole thing cost $400, and as he handed in the bills Fred Zeder joked that it was too expensive. As other parts were obtained, first chassis and then complete cars were built and tested locally.

Apparently hard testing of the engines had been going on for some time at various points throughout the United States. Roy Moore, a local Maxwell mechanic in Federal, Arkansas, remembered being called upon to service experimental engines in two unmarked cars in 1922. Two drivers arrived to test the cars for over 200,000 miles each during a one-year period, and similar tests were being conducted on two cars in the Midwest and two in the West. Moore was told these tests were being done on behalf of a group of engineers who had developed this new engine, but neither the group nor the car was identified, even to the test drivers. Moore, however, recognized the unmarked car body as a Chalmers one, and thus was one of the few who knew what this testing was all about. After each type of weather and terrain test he recorded the results and serviced the cars. They were a smashing success, fully living up to everyone's expectations.

Things were buzzing on Mechanic Street throughout the spring of 1923, and eventually it became clear that it was time for ZSB to pull up stakes in Newark and move on to Detroit, where the new car was to be manufactured at the Chalmers plant on Jefferson Avenue. As part of the move, ZSB was absorbed by Maxwell and became a formal part of that company when the engineers set up shop at Chalmers on June 6, 1923.

The engineers were now to oversee all engineering at the Maxwell-Chalmers concern. The very first thing they did was to convince Charlie Morgana, in complete charge of Maxwell production, to make all parts exactly as they were laid out in the schematics, rather than making undocumented changes based on the exigencies of actual production along the line. From now on, all changes had to be approved in a meeting between production and engineering, duly dated and noted on the mechanical drawings and disseminated in departmental notices. Morgana later called the resulting central control and elimination of confusion the greatest thing that ever happened to him and his men.

Upon looking into the engineering department at Maxwell, ZSB saw that it was a jumble, with three different groups working competitively on three different projects. As for the company's product, this was their assessment: "The Maxwell plant at the time was building a four-cylinder car, as was the Chalmers plant. Both were on the borderline of the horseless carriage era." They rated the Maxwell product a sturdy, worthwhile one, quite popular then. But they saw Chalmers embroiled in huge field problems due to an underdeveloped, expensively priced overhead-value six they had just put on the market. It was decided that Chalmers production would taper off to make way for the new Chrysler.

They were not there to make waves in the existing company, which is why they set up at Jefferson Avenue, eleven miles away from Maxwell Engineering. All went smoothly. Offices and design studios under Skelton were established on the upper floors of the plant, while laboratories, under Schwartzenberger, were installed on the ground floor. The two departments worked simultaneously and harmoniously until the sample cars were ready for road testing. By then the company was tooling up for production of the new car under the supervision of Billy Kirkpatrick and his assistants, Lou Breedy, Scotty Smith (who figured importantly in developing the new engine at Elizabeth), Vern Drum, and Frank Keller.

Changes in the car's design began to come about through Walter

Chrysler in New York. He approved the addition of a western development called Lockheed four-wheel hydraulic brakes to Chalmers cars and, since he wasn't any too familiar with it, suggested that ZSB "better look into what it is all about."

Malcolm Loughead (the name was altered to Lockheed for business purposes), the brother of the man who founded Lockheed Aviation, thought he had provided a perfect braking system to Chalmers. Carl Breer met him while he was supervising the installation of this new system on the Chalmers production line. The ultraexpensive Duesenberg had pioneered a version of Loughead's four-wheel hydraulic brakes a few years before, but this was the first time such a system was to be commercially applied to a large production vehicle. Upon examination, Breer determined, much to Malcolm Loughead's chagrin, that the system was not at all correctly developed for automobile use. He set about rethinking it, and by the time he was finished there was almost nothing left of the original system outside of the idea of using hydraulic fluid to apply stopping force in place of the metal rods and other parts used in mechanical systems. Maxwell's patent coverage was so extensive by the conclusion of revisions that the brakes could truly have been featured as a Chrysler development. After discussion between the Lockheed company and Maxwell, it was decided to give Lockheed all the patent rights in exchange for a royalty-free licence. This was great for Lockheed, as it allowed that firm the opportunity to sell licenses to other auto firms as well, in addition to establishing its own brand of hydraulic fluid in service stations throughout the country. This would prevent mechanics, despite all sorts of company warnings, from substituting lubricating oil for the hydraulic fluid and damaging the brake systems (much of the new system was made of natural rubber, which is not at all compatible with lubricating oil).

Chrysler also put ZSB onto new items such as the oil filter and air cleaner, both of which were added to the car. ZSB also dreamed up the idea of the ornamental radiator cap for the Chrysler. They had designed a beautiful cap with Mercury wings to symbolize speed, and did not want to ruin its look with a Motormeter in its center; this was a thermometer placed over the regular plain radiator cap to show the driver how hot his engine was running. To accomplish this, they devised a remote temperature gauge for the dashboard, and almost instantly put the Motormeter Company out of business.

Perhaps most important of all was the final form of the engine itself. They wanted a high-compression, low-volume engine that could be driven full throttle at 3,000 rpm for fifty hours, and that is what their testing proved they had achieved. They got it from a nondetonating (knocking) L-head six-cylinder engine combined with a seven-bearing crankshaft (for greater strength and stability). Its 201 cubic inches turned out an authentic

68 horsepower (Packard was turning out 54 horsepower from 265 cubic inches) at a 4.7:1 compression ratio, which was obtained by using a modified version of the free-breathing Ricardo cylinder head developed in England. This engine used fuel with an octane rating of 50 to 55, and it was capable of driving the car at 75 miles per hour. Such figures were extraordinary in 1923 for a car of any size, at any price, much less the medium range the car was destined for.

This Chrysler was to be small, with a 112.75-inch wheelbase, as a direct result of Walter Chrysler's desires (it was actually 113 inches but never referred to as such out of superstition—Maxwell had gone bankrupt on a Friday the thirteenth, and nobody wanted to invite bad luck). It seems that sometimes when he was stuck in traffic he would think of the small, chic cars he had driven in Europe and wonder why such cars were not manufactured in the United States. Then, there was the fateful day when he looked down from his office window in New York and saw a gigantic traffic jam caused by a chauffeur trying to maneuver a huge limousine around a corner he had misjudged. Why couldn't a quality car be small and nimble instead of gargantuan and unmanageable? he mused. Out of those thoughts came his dictates for the size of his own automobile.

The prototype car bodies were cobbled together out of Chalmers parts. Restoration of one of them, now on display at the Chrysler Historical Museum in Auburn Hills, revealed that a good many of the parts were clearly stamped "Chalmers," so good use was made of whatever was to be found at hand in the Chalmers plant. Nobody actually styled the car in the modern sense. Oliver H. Clark, a junior member of the ZSB team, was the "body engineer" responsible for coordinating it. Clark confirmed to *Ward's Quarterly* that it was indeed Chrysler himself, true to his vision of a compact vehicle, who set the body guidelines for his new car. "The boss, who invariably viewed himself as a marketing expert, chose the wheelbase 'scientifically at random,' hoping the available engine, not to mention the ultimate passengers, would fit. The Chrysler targets were a 110-inch wheelbase, 2,400 pounds dry weight and a top speed of 60 mph. The production version came amazingly close."

Clark's "styling department" consisted of a drafting board, a large blackboard, and himself. He said the shape of the first Chrysler, and many thereafter, "just kind of happened." In fact, some of the first Chryslers, which came in nine models, bore more than a little resemblance to the Chalmers. The only real styling went into the radiator shape and ornamentation, including that winged radiator cap, shaped to resemble a Viking's hat to emphasize the supposed daring, exploratory nature of the car. The later gold radiator emblem was a copy of the corporate seal, a cartouche formed to look like ribbons and sealing wax that would suggest quality, with the name *Chrysler* emblazoned on it diagonally; the lightning bolts above and below the name are actually Z's meant to memorialize Fred Zeder's contribution to the founding of the make.

Clark had no administrative problems to hamper him, and came up with a finished design approved by the board of Maxwell-Chalmers on June 4, 1923. By July 31 the first operable prototype had been completed and demonstrated to Chrysler on a midnight drive up Kercheval Avenue in Detroit. Elated, he insisted then and there that Clark come up with a roadster version of the car to display at its premiere the following January at the New York Auto Show. Chrysler pointed out that the excellent but slow-selling Wills Sainte Claire automobile had been sustained solely by demand for its roadsters, and he didn't want to take any chances by not having one in his line. Not only did Clark come up with a roadster, but he made it a stunner by huddling with the Ditzler Paint Company to come up with a range of "King Tut" colors. They provided the basis for dazzling three-tone paint jobs, an industry first. (The most popular was pyramid gray over desert sand, set off by Egyptian red striping and black fenders.) As a result, Chrysler roadsters were best-selling eye catchers from the beginning, and remained in high demand throughout the rest of the Roaring Twenties.

Work at Jefferson Avenue continued apace, and the rest of the required five cars were completed by the September 1 deadline. They all had mechanical two-wheel brakes, but upon ZSB's assurance that the four-wheel hydraulic brake system was perfected, Chrysler agreed to add it to his car. Thus in what the engineers believed was record time the new car was fully developed, and the drawings were released to the production department.

There was much joy in the corridors of the company, but in the inner offices there was trepidation, too, as once again Walter Chrysler had to deal with the possibility of losing his new car. It was the talk of the town, and this time Studebaker was casting greedy eyes upon it. Only a combined effort of skillful manipulation and fierce determination on Chrysler's and Fred Zeder's parts saved the day for the men who had worked so hard to make the Chrysler car a reality. But before they did, the success of their own labors very nearly ate them up.

In the fall of 1923 Nicholas Brady abruptly told Chrysler that his family wanted to take their money out of the automobile business. Chrysler couldn't quarrel with the reason, either. James Brady was very ill, and it was possible he would not live. Considering the situation, Brady said he didn't want to be tied to Maxwell. Good friend that he was, Chrysler did not hesitate in his reply. "I was perfectly willing to toss in my options and step aside, provided an arrangement could be worked out that was acceptable to the stockholders." It was easy to see why the bankers doted on Chrysler; when it really counted, he was every bit as much a mensch as he was a businessman.

He knew what it would mean for him. "It was clear that if Studebaker bought out the Bradys, Frederick F. Fish, Chairman of Studebaker, would want to head up the combined enterprises with their President, Albert R. Erskine. There would hardly be room for Erskine and Chrysler in one pasture lot."

Painful as it must have been, he did his duty toward the stockholders with the same enthusiasm he brought to all his tasks. The stock price had been rising smartly since he had taken control of Maxwell, and he had every reason to believe that if he gave the Studebaker boys a big buildup on his new Chrysler prototype, he could bump it up quite a bit more in a buyout situation.

Chrysler met with the Studebaker officials and brought them out to Detroit for a demonstration of the new car. It was all hush-hush, though, because he didn't want to stir up anyone while negotiations were going on.

Tobe Couture was the man on the spot, and it was a pretty tight one. This is how he later described it: "One afternoon Mr. Chrysler came down to the experimental room and asked how the cars were running. I said, 'Fine.' He asked if we had two cars we could demonstrate that night and I told him yes. He said, 'All right, I'll be here at eight o'clock, but don't say a word about this to anybody.' At eight sharp he arrived with five men. After about two hours driving all over the east side of Detroit, we came back to the plant and they left about eleven P.M. It turned out that the five men were Studebaker people, and they came back full of enthusiasm, ready to buy the car from him. Mr. Chrysler again asked me not to tell anyone about the ride.

"Well, I didn't have to tell anyone, as the guard at the gate told Mr. Zeder when he came in the next morning. He said, 'We had a lot of company last night—Mr. Chrysler and five men—and Tobe took them for a ride in the new car.' Well, about 9 A.M. my office phone rang and it was Mr. Zeder's office saying he wanted to see me right away. I had no idea he knew about what went on the previous night, but I soon found out as he asked me how things were going, and I said, 'Fine.' Then he said, 'You worked pretty late last night, and I hear you had company.' Just then Mr. Chrysler walked into his office, and was I ever relieved! I said, 'Mr. Chrysler, am I glad to see you!' I turned to Mr. Zeder and said, 'Ask him.' So Mr. Chrysler explained it to Mr. Zeder. Then he said, 'Fred, the Studebaker people want to buy us out and you can name your own price.' (Mr. Chrysler thought so much of Mr. Zeder and his organization that he felt this was a wonderful opportunity for them.)

"Walter P. and Mr. Zeder then proceeded to have a big fight. No matter how much Mr. Chrysler said it was a big opportunity for all of them, Mr. Zeder yelled back, 'Don't you believe it, all they want is the car, not Walter Chrysler or Zeder, Skelton and Breer.' Mr. Zeder absolutely refused to have any part of it."

One day shortly thereafter Tobe Couture prepared a new Chrysler phaeton and he, Zeder, and Skelton drove it from Detroit down to Washington, then back up to New York. From there Couture drove it out to Mr. Chrysler's estate at Great Neck, Long Island, in order to present it to him on Thanksgiving Day.

The reason for the trip was the final showdown with Studebaker. According to articles in the *New York Times* and various other accounts, this took place on November 27, 1923, and played out over the next several days. Maxwell stock had jumped up to $58.50 per share over rumors for the past week or so that the two companies would merge. On that day closemouthed directors of both companies met at offices of their respective financial advisers on Wall Street, Studebaker at H. P. Delafield at 20 Exchange Place and Maxwell at the Brady Estate at 80 Broadway. Rumors flew along the street all day, as people rushed in and out of meetings at the two firms, denying that anything at all was going on; when leaving the Brady offices, Jules Bache, a Maxwell director, said none of the officers of the company had ever said negotiations were under way to merge with Studebaker, and he knew nothing of such a proposal. "If someone has been buying the stock in the open market and has gained control he can tell the directors what to do, but until he shows up we know nothing." But he knew well that banking connections close to the situation had been whispering for days that the deal was on, and that this was the first time anyone had denied that a deal was in the making.

Maxwell stock began to break sharply when two Studebaker directors suddenly left their meeting and returned forty-five minutes later, trailing the rumor that the deal was off. Previously the stock had held steady as people thought there was an even chance the deal would still go through. Now the Studebaker directors referred all inquiry to Maxwell, where Bache stonewalled. At one point the stock slid $10 before closing the day down $8.375, to close at $49.75.

What was going on that day was this. While Skelton and Couture stayed by a telephone in Newark, Zeder went to the big meeting at the Brady offices in New York. Apparently he was required to sign the takeover papers. At the meeting he told Chrysler and the Maxwell directors in person and the Studebaker people by phone that if the deal was made without his signature, he would call Carl Breer in Detroit and have him destroy all the blueprints for the new Chrysler automobile on the spot. It was not, under any circumstances, going to become a Studebaker. After this, there was really little else to be said. Studebaker had offered $26 million; Chrysler then wrote another, much higher figure on a slip of paper and passed it along. These terms were much too stiff for Studebaker, and everyone knew it. Zeder's declaration had determined the outcome of this situation. Everything else was pro forma; the negotiations were at an end. Thirty-three years later Tobe Couture said that was how close it came to there not being a Chrysler Corporation at all.

The following day it was announced that the merger talks had failed and that William Robert Wilson had resigned as president of Maxwell. According to the *Times*, only one Studebaker director had carried on the negotiations on behalf of his company; when the deal was proposed to the entire board of directors, they objected strongly, and this was the reason the merger was definitely off. The result of this situation was that by the close of the year Maxwell would bring out a new car from the Chalmers division to be known as the Chrysler Six, expected to sell for around $1,500. On December 6 in the same paper James Cox Brady asserted that it was Albert Erskine of Studebaker who originally proposed the merger, which he said was turned down by the Studebaker board. He also denied a printed report that negotiations were begun on the part of the Brady-Maxwell interests, further denying that the Bradys had a controlling interest in Maxwell—all of which was disingenuous, to say the least. He ended by reassuring the public that neither he nor the interests he represented sold Maxwell stock or profited by the recent run-up in its shares during the period when rumors abounded.

With Studebaker now out of the way for good, the efforts of the Bradys and the others turned back to Walter Chrysler. They told him he now had his greatest chance, and he agreed. He and Hutchinson had been working both sides of Wall Street to create financial enthusiasm for a new, non-Studebaker Maxwell enterprise, and it was in fact at this time that a Chrysler Corporation was first spoken of. It was still premature, though. For the moment there was the matter of some $3,889,000 worth of bonds maturing the following June that the board wanted to trade at par; Chrysler balked at this, and they came to terms at $85. This was the last item that needed clearing up. Finally Walter P. Chrysler was in full command of the situation at Maxwell and completely assured that he would at last bring out a new car with his own name on it. Nothing could stop him now . . . could it?

When Tobe Couture brought the new Chrysler phaeton to Walter P. on Thanksgiving Day, the two of them, proud and happy, went for a long ride on the highways near Great Neck. Toward the end of it Chrysler had Couture pull off onto the side of the road and asked him what he really thought of the car. Couture looked at him gravely and asked in a serious voice, "Do you want me to tell you the truth?" Remembering the exact same scene on Schooley Mountain with the disastrous Willys-Overland prototype three years before, terror suddenly stabbed Chrysler in the breast, and he mournfully said to Couture, "Aw, tell me you don't mean it." When Couture looked back at him with a mischievous gleam in his eye, Chrysler screamed, "Don't you say a damn word!" and the two of them fell on each other, laughing and yelling like schoolboys.

⊞ 20 ⊞

The Significance
of the First Chrysler Car

What's New?

> "I gave the public
> not only quality,
> but beauty, speed,
> comfort in riding,
> style, power,
> quick acceleration,
> easy steering,
> all at a low price."
> Walter P. Chrysler

Upon assuming his position at Willys-Overland, Walter Chrysler left behind Michigan, as a place of residence, for good. The offices of his new concern were on Vanderbilt Avenue in New York City, and though he traveled a lot to Toledo and Detroit, the major part of his work was in New York, and therefore so was his home. First he took up residence in a hotel; later he acquired an apartment on Park Avenue. No one has ever figured out where he stayed when he was in Detroit, though it appears he stopped at the Detoit Athletic Club and the Book-Cadillac Hotel. Furthermore, the historian Eugene Weiss has made a good case for the possible existence of an apartment for Chrysler in one of the main buildings of the Chrysler complex at Highland Park.

In February 1923 he made his first big splash in real estate, purchasing a huge, elegant estate at King's Point, Great Neck, on Long Island Sound.

Walter Chrysler introduces the first Chrysler car, 1924. This is one of the most famous photographs in industrial history. (*Courtesy DaimlerChrysler Corporate Historical Collection*)

He purchased the building from department store magnate Henri Bendel, who had built it in 1917 from reinforced concrete and stucco in a Beaux Arts version of French Renaissance style. The mansion, designed by Henry Otis Chapman, was considered one of the most elegant on what was called the Gold Coast. It consisted of twenty-three rooms, including seven master bedrooms and six servants' rooms; the house had ten bathrooms. Its entrance hall was two stories high, with an overhanging balcony and a beamed, beautifully hand-painted ceiling. All the major rooms had fireplaces and were decorated individually, one with French paneling, one with brocade-covered walls, one in the Italian Renaissance style, and on and on.

The music room and chapel featured a mammoth keyboard organ whose music could be heard throughout the house by means of a special remote control system. The basement contained a built-in swimming pool, gymnasium, massage room, and billiards room.

Outside, the 12 acres of grounds displayed gorgeous, perfectly maintained lawns and gardens, an 82' by 30' swimming pool, a nine-room superintendent's quarters, an eight-car garage, a kennel, a chicken house, and a greenhouse. The estate, complete with a 150-foot concrete-and-timber pier and a boathouse, fronted on 450 feet of Long Island Sound. Walt loved swimming in the pool, and shortly purchased the first of several yachts, the *Frolic*, with which he indulged his newfound love of boating.

He was forty-seven years old, and in twenty-five years had gone from

Walter Chrysler affixes a license plate to one of the first Chrysler cars. (*Courtesy DaimlerChrysler Corporate Historical Collection*)

wiping down locomotives for 5.5 cents an hour and living in furnished rooms to possessing the multimillions that bought him one of the grandest mansions in one of the toniest spots in the country. Though the big money had been coming his way since 1916, he hadn't had the actual cash in hand to radically alter his life until just three years earlier. Now, having set up iron-bound trusts to take care of his family, he was using his fortune to achieve his dream of becoming an automobile manufacturer. He celebrated this by acquiring some of the major accoutrements of an industrial mogul. If anyone had ever earned them, it was he.

This was the age of *The Great Gatsby,* and the Gold Coast of Long Island was *the* location of that age. Diaphanous summer evenings on sweeping lawns, mad parties in impossibly big waterfront mansions, and over it all the smell and feel of fresh money, crackling and new, pervaded the whole atmosphere. Walter Chrysler planted himself in the middle of it all, but though he was in it, he was not of it. The Chryslers entertained well but not lavishly; Walt loved to relax in a robust and hearty manner, but he never let that aspect of his life run away with him. Work and increasingly, empire building were never far from his mind.

There was one way in which Walter Chrysler was very much of his age, however: His new product was sui generis. It was a long time coming, but the new Chrysler automobile was made out of whole cloth by men who had no preconceptions of what a car should be, and because they were not burdened with a preexisting corporate culture dictating design and manufacturing traditions, they were free to burst onto the world with a brand-new kind of car. This was the essence of the 1920s, an age that created a society filled with glorious new things that had never been there before. Radios, refrigerators, unconstructed clothes, art deco designs—shortly the Chrysler car was to join them as one of the sensations that defined the excitement of these heady times. Walter Chrysler himself rode this wave to its crest. Unknown outside the automobile business in 1923, he would become a household name for creating a vast, forward-looking enterprise within five years, and one of the totemic symbols of its time, the Chrysler Building, within seven.

❖   ❖   ❖

Tooling for the new Chrysler was completed and set up at the Chalmers plant in the fall of 1923, and cars began rolling off the line by December 20. The week before Christmas the complete line of Chrysler Six cars was shown at the Jefferson Avenue plant to important bankers, material and parts suppliers, automobile dealers, and other leading lights, who all acclaimed it.

Tobe Couture, as always, was whipping up enthusiasm for the new car with his wild and wooly demonstrations. He recalled showing it to a Jewish dealer who foolishly didn't believe the car would do 70 miles per hour. When he got it up to 70 in the rain, with the man beside him, Couture tooks his hands off the wheel and tromped on the brake pedal, the better to illustrate the accuracy of the steering and the brakes. The poor guy was trembling like a leaf but signed on to sell the car. Another skeptic was Jules Bache. Where Chrysler was concerned, there was always a certain dubiety on his part. He was doubtful about this car, too, but after he was given a ride in it, he became quite a convert. Couture recalled seeing him sitting by the hour and talking with Chrysler, whittling away at some pieces of soft pattern pine he had picked up. Eventually he became the second-biggest stockholder in the company, after Walter Chrysler himself.

Now the advertising juggernaut was set on its course. Chrysler had obviously felt very confident of himself during those fateful days of the Studebaker negotiations in late November. He had already commissioned auto advertising genius Theodore F. MacManus to write the first Chrysler ad, and on the very day the Studebaker negotiations were called off, he gave him permission to run it.

The first ad was a two-page stunner that ran in the December 8, 1923, edition of *The Saturday Evening Post*. As described by Chris Sinsabaugh, the first page contained a salutation from "Walter P. Chrysler, car manufacturer"—no corporate name. The name Chrysler was asterisked, with a note at the bottom that said, "Pronounced as though spelled Cry-sler," acceding to the fact of his anonymity to the general public. Following was another page in which there was a centered box reading, "Walter P. Chrysler, motor car manufacturer. See preceding page." "The Maxwell Corporation paid $7,000 for those nine words—$14,000 for the two pages," said Sinsabaugh. "The *Post* boasts today that these two lines on the second page were 'the loudest whisper ever printed.' Followed in another issue another two page blast in which Walter Chrysler took off his mask for the first time and blazoned forth his plans."

The second ad, which appeared in the *Saturday Evening Post* on December 29, 1923, became famous in advertising annals because it was conducted in the form of an interview, and was in fact often reprinted under the rubric "An Interview with Walter P. Chrysler." It was another example of the sagacity of MacManus. Having brought forth the name Chrysler to the public, he next acquainted them with the man himself in the form of an intelligent but chatty conversation. Starting with "Mr. Chrysler, why did you build the Chrysler Car?" a series of simple questions gave him the opportunity to expand on the features and virtues of his machine, and let the public in on his philosophy of motor car manufacturing.

To the first question he answered, "Because I have been convinced for years that the public has a definite ideal of a real quality light car—one not extravagantly large and heavy for two people, but adequately roomy for five; economical to own and to operate. And, above all, real quality from headlights to tail-light.

"My conception of an ideal quality light car is that of scores of thousands, whose requirements are practical, not visionary. For them, I saw a car with the power of a super-dreadnaught, but with the endurance and speed of a fleet scout cruiser."

He listed all the car's features, told of its four-year gestation, and gave full credit to his engineers, Zeder, Skelton, and Breer. "They began with a clean slate, and designed from the ground up. There were none of the usual handicaps—no existing machinery, tools, jigs and dies to be considered; no pre-determined plant capacity or manufacturing lay out to fit to; no executive fads or whims to be satisfied. We have made no compromises. . . . While owners will appreciate the fine features of our design, every engineer in the industry will *know* that they mean the highest quality job that can be built."

Chrysler then proceeded to romance his vehicle in a manner calculated to set the pulse of every status-conscious car buyer racing: "You will sense in the Chrysler that difference which we are in the habit of describing as 'foreign' or 'French' or 'European'—or custombuilt. Your good taste will tell you at once that here is perfect balance of proportion and blending of line. You will also feel that here is an exceptionally racy car, largely because it is built so close to the ground." He followed this up with a description of a small car so well styled as to give an optical illusion of length, and listed the many striking features of its body and interior. Then he gave a hard sell on the exceptional quality of the car's engine and mechanics, hammering home such innovations as air and oil filters and hydraulic four-wheel brakes.

After waxing rhapsodic on its ease of maintenance and head-snapping, vibrationless performance, he left the reader with a terrific teaser, of which he would make a great deal in the coming weeks. When asked, "But isn't such a car—one of such wonderful abilities and built of the best materials on the market—beyond the reach of the very people to whom it is the ideal?" he replied, "I'll leave that to you; for the one thing in the whole car of which I am most proud is the price." Then he didn't tell what that price was going to be. The bottom of the ad states, "If, without knowledge on the subject, the average motor car owner were asked to estimate the price of the Chrysler Six, he would be bound to rank it among the costliest of cars. The price when revealed will prove a profound sensation." In other words, McManus prefigured the advice of Rose Havoc, Gypsy Rose Lee's mother, on the fine art of ecdysiasm (that's stripping to you): "Find out what they want, and then don't give it to them." This ad got everybody in the country talking.

With a fine car, great staff, wonderful manufacturing facilities, and terrific hoopla all in place, one would think it would have been nothing but clear sailing ahead for the Chrysler galleon. But before he reached open seas, there turned out to be another huge obstacle in Walter Chrysler's path: money. It seems that in November 1923 two banking groups, Blair & Company, joined by Chase Securities, had pledged to take $6 million in bonds at $92 per hundred to get the new Chrysler project started; this would net the company $5.52 million which Chrysler thought adequate to his purposes. Then, at the last moment, the bankers got cold feet, told him he was overextended, and withdrew. The car could not be produced without this money, and suddenly everything was up in the air once again. Chrysler's solution, as before, was to dare and dare again to overcome his problems, admitting no impediment to the momentum he had built up.

The account to be given now diverges from Chrysler's own account of this event. His version is a romanticized telling of what actually occurred, elevated from mythmaking to the status of truth through decades of repetition. Only in the 1980s did researchers uncover the reality of the situation.

Chrysler claimed that on top of the bad news from the bankers, he received notice from the American Automobile Association that the new

Chrysler cars could not be exhibited at the upcoming New York Auto Show because they had not been both produced and sold, and thus would violate the rules of eligibility established for that event. Of course, he had counted on making a public sensation at the auto show with his spectacular new cars, and he hoped to thereby induce the bankers into changing their minds about the loan. His credit had been stretched to the snapping point in re-tooling for the new cars, and new capital was essential to buy the materials to make them. "It seemed to us that we were pretty close to ruin before we had made a start," he said.

As gloom and doom pervaded the executive offices of the new company, Chrysler claimed he suddenly got an inspiration and shouted for his sales manager, Joe Fields. Since the show would take place at the Grand Central Palace, very near the Commodore Hotel, where all the industry people were staying, why not simply hire the lobby of the hotel and set up the Chrysler exhibit there? Everybody in the auto business would be swarming through the lobby night and day, and Chrysler felt this would be a surefire way to create the sensation he needed. He yelled, " 'Joe, you've hired plenty of hotel rooms. Go and hire the lobby of the Commodore. We'll have a show, all right!' Joe Fields did not stop to ask any questions; he simply vanished. When he came back he fluttered a sheet of hotel stationery with some writing on it. 'Boss,' he said, 'we own the lobby.' "

Historian Christy Borth in 1965 was the first to make note of the inac-curacy of this account. Eighteen years later, researcher Anthony Yanick concurred. Both men reached their conclusions through an examination of contemporary accounts of the auto show, which took place between Jan-uary 5 and 12, 1924. In the first place, it wasn't held at the Grand Central Palace, but at the 258th Field Artillery Armory, nine miles away in the Bronx, because the Palace was no longer large enough to house the exhi-bitions of 73 motor vehicle manufacturers, plus those of manufacturers of components and parts. Due to overcrowded conditions even at the armory, "the Commodore Hotel, headquarters for many automobile and accessory manufacturers. . . . was the scene of several private and 'overflow' exhibits. Automotive exhibits included the Stutz, Rollin, Chrysler and Federal truck," according to an account in the January 12, 1924 edition of *Automotive Industries*. Furthermore, on January 6, 1924, the *New York Times* reported, referring to the Chrysler, "The most important new car of the year is on exhibition at the Commodore Hotel and in space 35 [actually it was space 34] at the Automobile Show." An ad in the same edition of the *Times* pro-claimed, under the Chrysler seal, "The most important new car of the year is on exhibit at the Commodore Hotel and in space 35 at the Automobile Show [then underneath in fancy script] The Chrysler Six." The official cat-alog for the 1924 New York Auto Show lists Chrysler cars in area 34 at the armory along with Chalmers cars, and Borth even shows a picture of the

Chryslers on display at the show. So though it was true that Chrysler cars were exhibited in the Commodore's lobby, so were several other brands. And they were *not* banned from the official show in the Bronx.

The actual story of what went on, though not quite as dramatic, is in its own way equally interesting. We have it due to a letter deposited in the Chrysler Historical Archives by Michael Kollins, a distinguished automotive scholar and former engineer with the Chrysler Corporation. Though the armory was only thirty minutes from Times Square by subway, almost nobody showed up there on opening night due to wrecks on the subway lines that halted all underground traffic out of midtown Manhattan. In addition, there was a blizzard and a sudden drop in temperature to subzero levels. "Chrysler had six models displayed in space "34", along with the Maxwell exhibit, which also had two Chalmers models," says Kollins. "It is true that Joseph E. Fields, Sales Manager for Chrysler, had arranged with the Commodore Hotel management for the use of the lobby as exhibit space. I believe Chrysler also had six models displayed in the lobby of the Commodore Hotel.

"So while Samuel Miles, the show manager, was wringing his hands and fretting in the Bronx, Walter P. Chrysler was happily packing people in to the Commodore Hotel, where he was proudly displaying his Chrysler car. The Chrysler exhibit, along with the cooperation of Mayor Jimmy Walker [actually, he didn't become mayor for another two years] and the New York Police Department, made the introduction a sensation."

So the story up to this point wasn't exactly untrue; it was just rouged up a bit for public-relations purposes. No one has ever questioned the veracity of the tale from here on out, however.

Walter Chrysler proclaimed the exhibition a complete triumph. "Although we were not in the show, we stole it! From morning until late at night a crowd was densely packed around us. Even before the end of that first eventful day we knew that our models were attracting more attention than was being excited by anything on display in Grand Central Palace [sic]. All my old friends of the trade came to speak to me in the lobby, to shake my hand and slap me on the back."

Crabb tells us that Mr. and Mrs Herbert Lewis arrived that first day, astonished to find both Chrysler and his cars on display in the Commodore lobby. "He ignored Lewis, but walked over to Mrs. Lewis, the image of an excited man having a wonderful time. 'Now I know your old man is a General Motors man, but we've got something over here that I want to show you,' he said, as he took her arm and escorted her to the new Chrysler. As she was leaving, Chrysler, still speaking in a voice that everyone in that part of the lobby could hear, said, 'This is a great new car and I'm going to sell you a new Chrysler.' " In 1929 he told B. C. Forbes, "In designing the Chrysler we took very special pains to make the steering easy. Women caught on to this. Easy steering, which did not require any great strength, coupled with quick acceleration, gave many women courage to drive in cities. They found they could easily handle a car even in the most congested traffic. My own opinion is that this bringing of women into the picture did more than any other one thing to broaden the market for cars in the last five years."

There was no doubt that the car was a sensation, with its high-compression "engine of tomorrow" and other innovations, but many of the auto men were shrewdly appraising the value of the car's components to figure out its great mystery—its retail price, which Chrysler still held secret.

"Then there came what I was looking for," said Chrysler. "A nice plump banker," in the form of none other than Jules Bache. They chatted amiably about the car and the attention it was getting. "I was trying manfully to keep from showing any eagerness. Yet Jules Bache had the means to give us what we so desperately needed: money. As I talked with him the car exhibits were only a part of the show I was putting on there in the lobby of the Commodore. The rest of it was what I was doing by pretending to be carefree. Watching me you would have thought I did not know how to worry."

Bache cleared his throat and got down to business. He offered to buy $5 million of new Maxwell bonds—at $70. "My heart seemed to drop down on my stomach. Then I got mad." This meant that Maxwell would realize only $3.5 million for issuing $5 million in bonds. After a few minutes Bache left, having heard from Chrysler in no uncertain terms what he thought of the offer (which probably meant he called on his old roundhouse vocabulary to give full expression to his feelings).

Other bankers came to talk a bit. Finally Ed Tinker of Chase Securities, who had let him down two months before but who also Dutch uncled Chrysler about Maxwell, stepped out of the crowd, ready to talk serious business. They got inside one of the cars, closed the doors, and started dickering, "with a ring of faces staring at us as if we had been fish in a bowl."

"I wanted 96, I told Tinker.

'You'd have taken 92, and glad to get it, Walt, a few months ago.

'Ed, these people are wild about this car. It's got qualities they can't get in a $5,000 automobile.

'You'll sell this car all right, Walt. 94, I guess, if we get a bonus.

'96 Ed, and no bonus.

'Mister, if you don't let me out of this automobile right this instant I'll scream.' Ed was mocking me with a voice that he had transformed into the shrill falsetto of a desperate woman.

'96.

'94, and I'm going downtown right now.' And he went."

Suddenly Chrysler became fearful. Tinker could change his mind, after all, or some of the other Chase people might not go along with the deal. The anxiety became overwhelming, and Chrysler decided he had to seize the moment to settle this thing. He found Hutchinson, and the two of them bundled up and went through the icy streets down to Wall Street to seek out Tinker. While Chrysler shivered in the street, Hutchinson went into Chase to talk to Tinker. The banker was not there. At last he caught up with him on the second floor as he reclined under a mound of soapsuds in a barber chair in a tiny, one-man private barbershop. Hutchinson accepted the offer at $94, but said Chrysler insisted the deal be closed that day, by three o'clock. Tinker agreed.

When Hutchinson conveyed the news, Chrysler went to a public phone and called his law firm, Larkin, Rathbone and Perry, where he spoke to Nicholas Kelley, who was to represent him and the Chrysler Corporation for many years thereafter. He said the papers on the notes had to be signed by 5 P.M. Kelley agreed to begin right away but pointed out that it took time to draw up a mortgage. "Get started," came Chrysler's succinct order.

Kelley and Hutchinson went over to the offices of Chase's law firm, Rushmore, Bisbee and Stern, and started in on the papers. At midnight Eldon Bisbee, dressed in white tie and waistcoat, returned from a dinner and pitched in. At 6 A.M. everyone was still hard at it, and all, including Chrysler, saw the sunrise. Shortly thereafter the papers were signed, and Walt knew that "the Chrysler Corporation, but still called Maxwell, was out of the woods. We had our money, we had our car and we had a live organization."

What Joe Fields still didn't have was a price for the car. He told Chrysler he could tire his arm out writing orders for the new car if only he had a price—and if the price was right. Chrysler gave it to him; he said it would be $1,595, the same as the Buick. (Actually, though there are several different versions of Chrysler's 1924 prices, it appears that none of the nine models was priced at $1,595, but rather in a range from $1,335 for the touring car to $2,195 for the Crown Imperial Five-Passenger Sedan, with an above-the-line Five-Passenger Town Car going for $3,725. The closest thing to the oft-mentioned $1,595 figure was the Four-Passenger Roadster at $1,525. Nor did Buick have a $1,595 car for 1924; the closest thing was a Seven-Passenger Touring Car at $1,565; its Five-Passenger Touring Car went for $1,295. The point is, however, that the Chrysler was indeed similarly priced to the Buick throughout its line.)

Years later Chrysler reminisced to a reporter for *Auto Topics* about this event: "I'll never forget how I went down to the New York Automobile Show with the price of the car in my pocket—and its specifications there too. I wouldn't tell anybody the price. And I wouldn't even tell them the wheelbase that first day. They all guessed the price higher than it actually was. And we were swamped with orders. It was a better automobile than anyone had ever offered before for the money and people want value. Give them something better at a competitive price and they'll buy your product."

Fields was indeed swamped with orders for the new Chryslers, and the cars were an immediate hit; in fact, they sold as fast as the old Chalmers factory could produce them. Within a few months they were rolling off the line at the rate of 110 a day, and by the end of the year 32,000 of them had been produced, a record at the time for a brand-new make.

Combined with strong sales of the Maxwell Four, the company had a sharp uptick in total sales, from 67,000 to 79,000. This meant that a profit of $4,115,000 was earned by the parent corporation for the full year. All of this happened in a bad year for the automobile business, with the sales of most companies, aside from Ford, who always did well in a downturn, staging a retreat. Walter Chrysler was doing very well for himself and all who depended upon him for their success.

❖   ❖   ❖

Clearly Walter Chrysler had managed to do an excellent job of assembling a first-rate team to design, build, and sell his new Chrysler car, but what of the machine itself? What was its true place in automotive history? Was it really new and better than anything that preceded it, as Chrysler said, or did it just represent the public's fond acceptance of a lot of well-churned-out hype?

Historian Mark Howell's article *The Chrysler Six—America's First Modern Automobile* is the best analysis yet to see print of the significance of Mr. Chrysler's new car. In it he makes the daring claim that "this little machine stands second only to the Model T Ford in its revolutionary impact on the industry. Beyond a doubt, this car stands alone as the dividing line between what may be termed 'old' and 'modern' cars."

He reasons that the Chrysler car was the first whose value was due to the importance of technical research and knowledge, rather than simply fine materials and high-quality workmanship. At the time of the Chrysler's debut, "it appeared our cars of all classes were designed on the premise that America's economy was rural, its roads the worst in the world, and its people of an austere and puritan outlook. Thus the poor should be satisfied with cheap, poor cars, the middle class with ordinary, drab cars, while only the rich should experience the joy of luxurious performance"—even if that performance came from huge, inefficient engines of 1910-vintage design, which imposed costly and needless penalties in size and weight. Chrysler recognized that this premise was no longer valid, as America had been industrialized by World War I and its population was now in large measure sophisticated, affluent, and urban. Says Howell, "How about a compact, medium priced car with a combination of the more salient features of all classes? Wasn't the prime objective of technical progress creation of a machine attractive to all?"

Chrysler realized he had to give the public one truly extraordinary feature in his new car to make it stand out from all the rest, and since he knew that performance was more important to car buyers than anything else, he decided that would be what he would emphasize. "Not merely as measured in power, speed and acceleration, but in the manner in which it was delivered. . . . .to endow the car with a sharply elevated *quality* of performance."

To achieve this, Chrysler and ZSB set themselves the following goals for their new engine: high power output relative to capacity, silence and smoothness, and simplicity of design (to minimize production costs). With the inclusion of one costly feature, a statically and dynamically balanced 7 main bearing crankshaft, they achieved their goal. "Through its own research and that of other pioneers, the Chrysler team had incorporated for the first time in an American engine the latest knowledge concerning combustion chamber design, fuel distribution, valve timing and cooling, cam contour (for silence), intake and exhaust manifold design, etc. These were the areas most neglected by other designers, and, as suspected by the Chrysler team, they were the keys for the solution of the problems imposed by any attempt to combine high power output with silence and smoothness. Once the functions of these various areas had been brought into proper balance and relationship, victory was assured."

In the end, the Chrysler's power per cubic inch equaled that of the mighty $6,500 Duesenberg, and could have exceeded it if the engineers had been willing to accept a slight loss in smoothness. But Chrysler didn't need to do that. All he required was that the engine should meet the power output standards of its class while its compact, lightweight engine permitted the entire car to be scaled down in size, weight, and cost. He then added subtle crossover luxury features to the car, such as the first instrument panel under one piece of glass to appear in a car priced under $3,000 and a horn that made a modern beeping noise instead of the old-fashioned *oogah* sound of the past. Such things gave distinction and class to the car, and allowed Chrysler to charge a price for it that garnered a profit double the normal amount. It was not greed but the need to establish his company financially that led him to do this. Notes Howell, "Chrysler knew that as soon as his car reached the market, his engine would be subjected to the most intimate scrutiny. And there was nothing that could be protected by patents. Superiority was based solely on sophisticated refinement of conventional design. Within a few short years, these refinements would be common to all progressive and alert competitors. Survival, then, depended on gaining wide acceptance and financial security in the shortest possible time."

Even though the Chrysler was indeed outstanding, as Howell says, "A work of merchandising and engineering genius," and as Fortune added in 1935 "the car could give for $1,500 the thrills of a $5,000 car," it still had to be financed, and initially, as we have seen, that was quite a problem.

Since it was so far ahead of its time, the bankers at first refused to lend Chrysler the $5 million he needed to go into production. The reason was that despite their great respect for his business acumen, they had no conventional way of judging the value of so revolutionary a vehicle. "The answer lies in the simple fact that his new car failed every single important test devised by recognized authorities to determine the success potential of a new machine. . . . The public was more interested in horsepower per dollar than in horsepower per cubic inch. By the same token, the most popular measure of overall value was the ratio of size and weight to the dollar," Howell writes.

The bankers looked at the competition in this class, such as the Buick, which was the benchmark, and thought the Chrysler clearly offered much less car for the money, dollar for dollar. "The most casual observation revealed Buick superiority in both strength and finish," says Howell. "Actually, the Chrysler's size and weight were minimal even in the next lower price class. Based on appearance alone, the Chrysler belonged in this class, and as an unknown its chances then would not have appeared outstanding."

This, then, was why the bankers were not eager to come across with the financing—they couldn't see that Chrysler had invented a new standard for automotive value. Hence the need for Chrysler's dog-and-pony show in the lobby of the Commodore. He knew that beyond the quantifiable features of his car, there was an invisible ingredient built into it that would sell it. He was confident that once he got the public whipped up into a publicity frenzy, the bankers would come through and make it possible to put his cars into the buyers' hands. Once they drove it, he knew his magic ingredient would explode in the minds and bodies of the motoring public throughout the country.

What was that ingredient? "Beyond question, the Chrysler did have something both irresistible and unavailable in other cars. Obviously that something had to be related to performance. But it was not superior power and speed. Buick could equal Chrysler's 70 mph, and Hudson could exceed it. Chrysler was the master in acceleration, but by no great margin.

"The difficulty in explaining the Chrysler charisma lies in the fact that its impact was felt more on the senses than on reason." Anyone with wide experience driving pre-1928 cars would know what that impact was. Simply this: for the first time a motorist had the feel of driving a modern car. Howell enthuses about his first drive in a Chrysler in 1927: "within a block I knew it was the most exciting car I had ever driven!"

"On starting the engine, I was struck by the uncanny absence of those sounds so common to others. No clicks from the valve gear; no whine from the camshaft drive. Just a comforting tautness, as though each part was perfectly shaped to fulfill its function. The engine seemed to run with a freedom that suggested total absence of friction."

"The controls were exceptionally light and precise in action. Touch the brake pedal, and the perfectly equalized hydraulic system responded immediately. Touch the throttle, and response was so instant as to suggest eagerness. Even gear shifting had been transformed from heavy drudgery to an act of swiftness and ease."

"Delightful! But these sensations rapidly faded once under way, for here was a quality of performance startling in its contrast with the conventional. It was as though one had driven for the first time free of dragging brakes and retarded spark."

"There was also a brand new kind of smoothness, so utterly lacking in effort it reached the senses as a dynamic flow—backed by a torrent of power in reserve. With an engine that clearly bubbled with life and revelled in motion, only the most stolid failed to sense the presence of sunny, spritely and uninhibited personality. Could there be a more charming traveling companion?"

"The modestly priced little Chrysler equaled our most costly machines in silence and smoothness, but added to this a sparkling new ingredient—mechanical effortlessness. And it united for the first time luxurious performance with lightness and and ease of control. This was the combination that proved irresistible to nearly everyone and it is the hallmark of modern performance. None of our pre-Chrysler cars had it and none since have appreciably improved on it." The new Chrysler's influence was so pervasive that by 1928 virtually every car had copied it, and so it is only by going back to its debut in 1924 that we can realize how revolutionary a vehicle it was.

The contributions of Fred Zeder, Owen Skelton, Carl Breer, and their team of engineers in creating this first Chrysler car are enormous, for it was they who engineered it. But it is equally clear that *what* they engineered was determined by the ideas of Walter Chrysler, who dreamed it up. The kind of vehicle it would be, the reasons for it, its final physicalization—all were the products of his mind and judgment.

"I gave the public not only quality but beauty, speed, comfort in riding, style, power, quick acceleration, easy steering, all at a low price," Chrysler told *Forbes*. "These qualities used to be given only in cars selling for $5,000 or $6,000. But I realized that the country's buying power at that price was limited. So, years before the first Chrysler made its appearance, I reasoned that if I could build a small car, embodying all these advantages, and at a price within the reach of millions, I would be doing a constructive thing for the public and would, I felt sure, reap a substantial reward."

Like Henry Ford with the Model T fifteen years earlier, Walter Chrysler wasn't a good enough engineer to have designed his car himself, but he oversaw its direction every step of the way and scrutinized each detail of its composition. Like Ford also, he understood that the state of the world was such that it needed his kind of car at the precise moment he produced it. In other words, he knew exactly *why* this car had to be made, and everything else flowed from that knowledge. True genius in any business enterprise consists in recognizing the obvious, then bringing it to the world's attention.

How did Walter Chrysler recognize the obvious? Study, observation, insight, and conclusion. When he was on the brink of the two months of furious activity that led to the debut of his new car, Chrysler wrote an article in *The Annalist* titled "What Is Ahead for the Automobile Industry?" In about a thousand words he gave the history of the automobile business and its social and economic impact on the U.S. This was all done with accurate and well-chosen figures, leading to sound conclusions about the future of the car industry. It shows he knew exactly what he was doing, and that as he analyzed and predicted for his own business, everything was well and carefully reasoned out.

He told us: 25,000 cars were manufactured in 1905, 2,659,604 in 1922; 1 million cars were registered in 1913, 13 million in 1923; 112 companies manufactured cars, but Ford did 55 percent of the business, and he and five others did 85 percent; 94 percent of all cars sold for $1,500 or less. It seemed that the cities were jammed with cars, but 75 percent of them were in cities and towns of 50,000 or fewer, 30 percent in towns of 1,000 or fewer; only 9 percent were in cities of 500,000 or more. So in other words the car was everywhere, with the great majority owned by the middle and lower classes; it was a pervasive aspect of American life.

He noted that the auto industry was larger than steel, and smaller only than slaughtering, meat packing, and petroleum. But where would steel, petroleum, rail shipping, road construction, and a host of allied industries be without cars? And then there was the matter of tax revenues—the auto industry was responsible for $335 million in federal, state, and miscellaneous taxes in 1922.

"The motor car is a revolutionary influence," he said. "For example, it is responsible largely for the disintegration of urban residential life and the development of suburban life. Think of what a creator of economic wealth the automobile has been in making possible suburban development. Think of the extent to which salesmen have been able to increase trade through the use of automobiles."

After pointing out that any business connected to so many others is of vital importance to the nation's economic health, he predicted with perfect accuracy: "There is no question but that in the years to come new cars will be seen, but there will be fewer makers of cars and large companies making those cars. The larger companies will continue to find ways of eliminating waste and of reducing costs by standardization, and the result will be cheaper cars and more of them. Where the banker thinks of saturation, the automobile manufacturer thinks of replacements."

By 1923, he realized that those replacements would be something better, dollar for dollar, than what the car buyer ever was offered before. Chrysler was a great production man, not a great inventor, and his background led him to produce the world's first scientific car. Small and simple, with the elegance of true efficiency, it produced power and strength in an environment of luxurious good taste, without any trace of shoddiness, inaccuracy, or waste. This sort of vehicle, once only a hope in consumers' hearts, would now become a demand, and he was determined to satisfy that demand as quickly and as expansively as he could. "Personally," he said, "I never understood why progress should crawl when it can be made to leap."

21

Maxwell Becomes the Chrysler Corporation

Riding High

He seemed to have
his finger firmly
on the pulse
of the times.

Theodore MacManus succinctly analyzed the misgivings with which industry people contemplated Chrysler's new automobile. "It is not hard to understand how and why every now and then a man like Ford or Chrysler springs out of the obscurity with almost a full fledged genius for mechanical things. But it is rather difficult to comprehend how a man like Chrysler, with little in his boyhood circumstances to warrant it, likewise manifests a sort of an intuitive mastery of both management and finance. Having been a mender of broken business at the outset of his automotive career it was cynically reasonable to assume that when he was given the opportunity to build a business of his own all might not go so blithely and well. In fact, it was quite generally said when he assayed to produce the Chrysler that it was a pity that such a splendid executive should undertake so late in the day to produce a new car. This was said quite sincerely and seriously and even solemnly by brother manufacturers, motor car merchants and bankers alike."

Menno Duerksen added, "In fact it was none other than Old Number One himself, Henry Ford, who warned Chrysler that if he tried it, 'You'll go broke.' " But despite all the naysayers and crape hangers, "he was able to do something which nobody, but nobody, else would be able to do—butt his

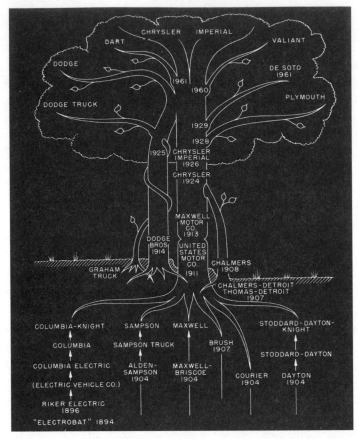

Chart showing Chrysler Corporation antecedents, with corporate family tree traced through 1961. (*DaimlerChrysler Corporate Historical Collection*)

way into an already established motor car industry and make a roaring success of it at a time when, so folks said, all the top spots had long ago been nailed down."

He did it by daring to believe in his own knowledge, intuition, and judgment, and then backing his ideas to the full extent of his resources. "To attain this ideal, I maintained, out of my own pocket, a plant—a sort of experimental factory—in Jersey, for three years, employing as many as 35 engineers, before one Chrysler car was exhibited publicly. I actually spent $3,000,000 of my own money in designing, creating and perfecting the Chrysler in this Jersey plant," Chrysler told *Forbes*.

He also did it by being a great leader of men. In 1947, in a speech given to the Newcomen Society, Fred Zeder spoke of how much the creation of the Chrysler had taken out of everyone connected with it. He recalled a press luncheon Chrysler had arranged at the Ritz in New York shortly before the car's debut. Representatives of New York newspapers and national periodicals, people like Ochs of the *New York Times* and McClure of *McClure's* magazine, had been invited to "get together and become a little better acquainted," as Chrysler put it. He began by explaining the background and aims of the Chrysler organization, not neglecting to tell of how he met ZSB and they began to design his dream car. "When he told that group at the Ritz about the sacrifices of our little group of engineers in our work of developing this new car, even to the point of our resources dropping below our bread and butter needs, he was so overcome with emotion that he sat down and buried his face in his hands and wept. Yes, wept. It was a tense moment; no one moved or spoke. Some were embarrassed, others, like myself, were deeply moved by the humility of this man. I had to say something, and I finally arose and stammered my disclaimer of such credit. Somehow I got through a few words and sat down. Afterwards, these publishers told me that they had never met a more human man."

Zeder's words made the audience see how Chrysler got his men through the trying times connected with the birth of his automobile. "Mr. Chrysler supplied leadership. He built with men, not with companies or machines; and in so doing he showed a wisdom and a foresight which illuminated the darkness ahead. Mr. Chrysler was not a synthetic leader; his love for the men he worked with was genuine. He was not given to backslapping or fulsome praise for insignificant accomplishment; but nevertheless his most typical pose is remembered by his associates as one in which he stood with his arm over the shoulders of a friend, listening to his story, and encouraging and guiding him. His leadership was honest and sincere.

"As a good manager, he had the ability to surround himself with men who knew their professions and trades supremely well; and yet every man who worked for him felt that Mr. Chrysler knew his subject as well as he did himself. But Mr. Chrysler never assumed the prerogative of doing the man's work for him. If one had the responsibility and the ability to act, he did so with confidence, realizing that his leader would depend on his judgement and would sustain it.

"He was in no sense a figurehead; he became 'all things' to these men. To the salesman he became the Master Salesman; to the production man he became the Genius of Production; to the engineer he combined both the practical wisdom necessary for the accomplishment of a specific objective and the vision necessary for the protection of the future."

In short, in a business that created motive power, he was a motivator beyond compare.

❖   ❖   ❖

The public took to the new Chrysler car from the beginning. "As a matter of fact, we made money from the start," Chrysler said. "To be exact, in three months, we were in the black." By this time, production had reached 100 cars a day. By the beginning of June, it was up to 150 a day, and by September, the Chrysler was outselling the Maxwell line. As has been noted before, the first year's production, at 32,000 units, was a record at the time for a new car.

In a letter dated February 11, 1924, accompanying the 1923 annual report of the Maxwell Motor Corporation, Chrysler took note of some $999,305.90 spent as the remainder of development costs for the new Chrysler car, which expenses were to be deferred and amortized out of earnings in future years. Despite a loss of $878,459.94 on the Chalmers line, which included "the absorption of substantial expenses incurred incidental to rearranging and improving the Chrysler plant for the production of the new line of Chrysler cars," the company made an overall profit of $2,667,851.57. In a similar letter of April 9, 1925, detailing the 1924 results, Chrysler is able to point to a profit of $4,115,540.20, after deducting $2,474,493.17 for amortization, $489,345.65 for federal income taxes, and $463,730 as the entire discount on the corporation's newly issued $5 million debentures. Cash on hand rose to $5,680,610.07, an increase of $4,596,361.92. The company had no bank debt, having cleared it up in 1922.

These results, which came from a sales increase from 67,000 units to 79,000 units, were truly striking, particularly when set against the business climate of 1924. After coming off a banner year in 1923, with industry sales so good that auto producers began pouring millions of dollars of profits into expanded plant capacity, sales turned down more than 10 percent the following year. Profits were markedly lower also. Ford, who always did well when others did not, and Dodge joined Maxwell as the only manufacturers whose profits rose significantly. Hudson and Nash's profits remained even, and everyone else's fell precipitously. The investors were happy, and the bankers breathed a big sigh of relief, as their faith in Chrysler had proven to be a matter of sound judgment.

Chrysler himself, very proud of his new machine, shortly resorted to an old method of proving automobile prowess—racing. On July 16, 1924, Ralph De Palma began what was to be a long association with Chrysler by taking a Chrysler touring car to Los Angeles for the nine-and-a-half-mile Mt. Wilson Hill Climb, with its 4,636 foot rise and 144 hard corners. He completed the course in 25 minutes and 48 seconds, obtaining speeds of 44 miles per hour in second gear! "Not only did he win the event, but his time was two minutes faster than any previous stock car's and better than a minute less than the racing car record," said Cullen Thomas.

Menno Duerksen pointed out that Chrysler proved something with this victory. "It will be remembered that one of the features of that brilliant new Chrysler engine was a compression ratio of 4.7 to one, at a time when few engine makers had ventured beyond the four to one ratio. Even an amateur engineer knows how important high compression is to high altitudes. So it was an astounding measure of Chrysler's success in gambling on high compression engines when the new car not only won the hill climb but shattered all previous records by more than two minutes."

Later that year, in the same car, Ralph De Palma set a number of stock car records by driving 1,000 miles in 1,007 minutes at the Fresno, California, board racing track. The car averaged almost 60 miles per hour, but when you discounted time for stopping and refueling, its actual moving average was 68.3 miles per hour.

◈   ◈   ◈

Not all Walter Chrysler's happiness at this time came to him from business alone. On December 3, 1923, his daughter Thelma became the wife of Byron Cecil Foy. Foy was born at Dallas, Texas on June 20, 1893, to Walter F. and Frances (née Smith) Foy, whom he later characterized as "strict, home loving family people." After graduating from the University of Texas in 1916, he attended Cornell and, during World War I, served as an Ensign in the Naval Aviation Service. After the War he became a Ford salesman at the Dallas Factory Branch, and by going after fleet sales from large corporations and the city government, he outsold salesmen from dealers in much larger cities, winning first prize in a nationwide sales conference. This success led the factory sales manager to take him under his wing and promote him, first as a travelling representative to such eastern cities as Baltimore and Boston during the years 1916 to 1918, and later to other more responsible positions at Ford.

By 1921, he had become President of the REO Motor Car Company of Los Angeles, a position he held until 1925. After this, he became Vice President of two major Chrysler dealerships, in Detroit (J. H. Thompson Company, 1925–1927) and New York (Simons, Stewart and Foy, 1927–1929), before joining the Chrysler Corporation, where he was to rise to very high positions. Apparently, this was due to real executive ability, notwithstanding the fact that he had married the boss's daughter. (As was said of the great Irving Thalberg at MGM, who had married boss Louis B. Mayer's daughter, actress Norma Shearer, "the son-in-law also rises.")

Thelma was very well educated in the finer points of music, poetry, and art, and spoke French and German fluently. Later on, she was to amass an outstanding collection of eighteenth-century French furniture and one of the best modern art collections in the world, concentrating her interests in this area on French Impressionism. Perhaps she was best known, however, as one of the great clotheshorses of the twentieth century, constantly appearing on worldwide best-dressed lists and eventually owning what may have been the finest private collection of New Look dresses from couturier Christian Dior. (Characteristically, immediately after her engagement was announced at a dinner at the Chrysler home in Great Neck on September 23rd, Thelma and Della set sail on the *Berengaria* for a six-week trip to Paris to assemble a trousseau for the prospective bride.)

The wedding took place at Elm Point, the Chrysler family home on Long Island, which was gorgeously decorated with red roses and white chrysanthemums for the occasion. The Reverend Kirkland Awske of All Saints Church, Great Neck, officiated. Ranking officials representing almost every automobile enterprise in the country attended the reception, as well as a party of thirty-one guests from Los Angeles, where Foy had his position with REO, and his parents resided. Following the honeymoon, the bride and bridegroom left on a honeymoon itinerary which included White Sulphur Springs, Pinehurst, and Palm Beach. After Christmas with the Chryslers in New York, they went to the Hotel Ambassador in Los Angeles, where they made their home.

But most of Chrysler's attention at this time was on business. Things were going well. By late 1924 he was telling *Automotive Industries* that he predicted business for 1925 would be "very satisfactory," which in the event turned out to be quite an understatement. Though it wasn't the highest production year of the 1920s, nor the most profitable, it was in many ways the healthiest for the industry, because everyone made money, and the profits were liberally distributed. Independent companies (then everyone but Ford and General Motors) all saw their earnings soar, and they wound up with 40 percent of the total $331,391,000 profit listed by the industry. Ford got about 25 percent, with the balance going to General Motors. After this, GM produced an ever-greater share of the cars, and earned an ever-greater share of the profits. "The distinguishing characteristic of the 1925 season was that in 1925 there was still room for nearly everybody not merely to get along, but to register new records in sales and profits. An increase in the output of one manufacturer was not accompanied by a decrease in the output of his competitors. The purchasing power of the country was well able to absorb 4,000,000 passenger cars a year. And—in 1925—an output of 4,000,000 passenger cars was sufficient for an almost universal prosperity" (Kennedy).

Having come on so strong with his new car, Chrysler rode into 1925 with his basic product, the Model 70 (model numbers were supposed to indicate top speed) little changed; windshields were now one-piece, and rubber engine mounts were used to reduce vibration for the first time (formerly engines were bolted to the frame, greatly adding to the shaking transmitted to the passengers).

On January 5, 1925, Ralph De Palma triumphed again for Chrysler in the 1,000-mile endurance run, which took place this time at Culver City, California. He took a stock five-passenger phaeton with wire wheels, removed the fenders and running boards, and completed the 1,000 miles in

786 minutes, thus averaging 78.6 miles per hour. Quite an astonishing feat for a car that was supposed to have a top speed of 70 miles per hour!

Later in the year famed race car driver Sir Malcolm Campbell piloted a Chrysler to a 100-mile-an-hour lap record at the the Brooklands race track in England. Another Chrysler entered the French Grand Prix at LeMans the same year, placing seventh in the race.

The big news of 1925, however, was the transformation of the Maxwell name and products into a new entity called, at last, the Chrysler Corporation. By the end of the year, not only would the Maxwell identity disappear, but, through cosmetic changes and some mechanical banging around, the Maxwell cars themselves would be transformed into Chryslers. The dawn of the new day at Walter Chrysler's rescued and transformed company would finally be completed, and its bright morning begun.

The Maxwell cars had been doing very well in this period. The "Good Maxwell," the fixed-up old bomb of a model that had made Walter Chrysler choke, was replaced in 1922 by the New Series Maxwell, a modernized, restyled model that featured a higher hood line, barrel headlamps, crowned fenders, and an engine revamped (it hadn't been changed since 1914) by former Willys-Overland engineer Henry T. Woolson. With prices cut to as low as $885, the 1922 Maxwell sold 44,811 units, rising to some 67,000 the following year, good for ninth place in the industry in both years. In 1924 Maxwell fielded ten models and sported yet another revision of the old engine that increased horsepower from 30 to 34. Despite the general slowdown and the introduction of the new Chrysler car, which cannibalized Maxwell sales, the company moved 48,124 Maxwell units, a more-than-respectable showing.

But momentum was not in the Maxwell's favor. The company's new Chrysler car was the car of tomorrow that you could buy today, and all the glamour the company could offer attached itself to that name. As its reputation spread, everybody wanted to buy a Chrysler, despite the fact that its prices began where the Maxwell's ended; by the end of 1925, production of the Chrysler outstripped the Maxwell by nearly four to one. It was clear that the usefulness of the Maxwell trademark had outlived its time, and that the parent company would place all its bets on the Chrysler from there on out.

First came the transformation of the company into the Chrysler Corporation in the spring of 1925. Of course, Walter Chrysler, having made a big splash with the new Chrysler car, wanted to change the Maxwell company into the Chrysler Corporation, to reflect the new reality of the whole situation. But the real reason it happened was due to legal problems connected to the reorganization of Maxwell in 1921.

Under that plan, previous stockholders obtained stock in the new company according to the amount and type (common or preferred) of stock they held in the old company. In addition, depositors of ten preferred shares of the old stock had the right to purchase four and a half shares of the new Class A preferred stock and twelve shares of the new Class B common stock for $450. By this means, the syndicate that had put up the $15 million additional cash to turn Maxwell into a going concern again hoped to spread their investment around, if not indeed make a profit on it.

By 1925 the company, now profitable, found itself facing a legal conundrum relative to these two classes of Maxwell shares. When B. E. Hutchinson wrote down the inventory of the company by $11 million in 1921, it left the capital of the company impaired, which meant it couldn't declare any dividends. But in 1925 there was a ruling in a New Jersey court that said in effect if a company that had noncumulative stock-earned money, the dividend must be paid to the preferred-stock holders. Maxwell Class A was noncumulative but participating preferred stock, while its Class B common stipulated that if the dividend wasn't earned, it didn't accumulate. The preferred got the first monies, at 5 percent, and the common got second monies, also at 5 percent, with the remainder divided equally.

But with this new ruling the company directors found themselves in an untenable situation. As Nicholas Kelley explains it, "The question was whether, when they hadn't made [declared] dividends for certain back years, and then made enough money to pay them off, these rulings seemed to say they had to pay the back dividends even though the [preferred] stock wasn't *cumulative* preferred stock. That was a question to which a lawyer couldn't give an answer that he could be sure of.

"The new Maxwell company was a Delaware company. If it did pay those dividends out to the common stockholders, and not to the preferred, it did not know whether the preferred would come after it or not. On the other hand, if the preferred were paid it, and were not entitled to it because that wasn't to be made cumulative, the company might have the common stock holders coming at it for wasting assets. To get out of that dilemma, and for a lot of other reasons, they got a new Delaware corporation called the Chrysler Corporation. It bore Chrysler's name. He was going to be Vice President of it."

The reorganization, however, turned out to be quite a roller-coaster ride. According to an article in the *New York Times* on April 10, 1925, the Maxwell Class B common shares were to be exchangeable for the new Chrysler common shares (no par value) on a one-for-one basis. The Class A shares were to be callable at $115 each, or were exchangeable for Chrysler preferred shares on a one-for-one basis, and were entitled to a one-share bonus of Chrysler common stock for every ten Maxwell shares tendered; holders of Class A shares could also retire their Class B shares on a share-for-share basis from the new bonus shares. A sinking fund of not less than 10 percent of the amount of dividends paid on common shares was to be created to pay for retirement of the preferred shares. (Class A shares were entitled to a $4.23-per-share dividend; Class B shares were entitled to a $2.06-per-share dividend, after the A dividend had been paid.) The new Chrysler preferred shares were to be without par value, and were to pay a cumulative dividend of $8 per share per annum, as of January 1, 1925. "The new year has begun most auspiciously," the company announced, "and there is every indication that the progress already accomplished will be continued into the current year."

The Maxwell board approved the merger plan on April 16. Walter Chrysler urged stockholder acceptance of the plan, and called for immediate deposit of the old Maxwell stock at the Central Union Trust Company on Wall Street. He said a large part of the stock had already been deposited, and that the certificates of deposit of the new stock would be listed on the New York Stock Exchange the following week. May 6 was to be the deadline for depositing the old stock at Central Union Trust.

On May 26, George W. Davidson, president of Central Union Trust and chairman of the Maxwell Motors Stockholders' Committee, announced that "since more than 90% of both the Class A and Class B Maxwell shares had been subjected to the plan and agreement dated April 25, 1925, the Committee has declared the plan and agreement to be operational."

On May 28, all hell broke loose. "Confusion reigned around the Maxwell Motors post on the Stock Exchange during the forenoon trading yesterday, and for a time many Wall Street firms were unable to advise their customers as to their market position in regard to the shares," reported the *New York Times* the following day. "The confusion first developed at the opening, when it was reported that the specialist in the stock found orders on his books for the purchase of more than 15,000 shares of Maxwell Motors B, stock undeposited, and no orders on his books to sell. When this situation became generally known, the report was circulated that the stock had been cornered."

The problem was that the merger plan, in calling for the deposit of outstanding Maxwell shares, had left very few of them available for trading. All anyone buying the stock could get from the seller was a certificate of deposit of the stock rather than the stock itself, and this was not a good delivery. This was particularly acute for short sellers, who sold stock they didn't own, and were now forced to buy it back at any price, to avoid falling victim to the old Wall Street maxim on short sellers, "He who sells what isn't his'n, must buy it back or go to prison." With so little actual Maxwell stock available (a stock exchange investigation showed only 25,940 of a total of 213,665 Class A shares and 40,258 of 633,187 Class B shares on the market), there existed a situation known as a "short squeeze."

The problem was due to the actions of the exchange itself. As Nicholas Kelley explained it, during the period set aside for the deposit of the Maxwell stock, "Stock came in and we asked them to strike the old Maxwell stock off the list at the Stock exchange. They wouldn't do it. There was less and less Maxwell stock all the time, and more and more holders of C.D.'s. Finally there was very little Maxwell stock left." So it wasn't a real corner but a technical one, caused by the conversion plan and the exchange's failure to deal with it in a judicious manner.

Kelley solved the problem by getting Davison at Central Union Trust to lend the actual stock to the brokers who were caught in the squeeze. "You can't have an affair like this. It's a scandal," he told him. "You don't want it. It will be safe to lend it, because the stock will come back to you. They should have struck off the stock as soon as we asked them to, at the Stock Exchange. They declined then, but they'll now strike it, and make the deliveries of the certificates. Lend them the stock.

"So he did. Making the stock available was just like putting a pin in a balloon. Borrowing stock took the pressure off."

But one important Maxwell stockholder put a different kind of pressure on, and began to apply it with his thumbs to the company's throat. This was John Thomas Smith, general counsel and vice president of General Motors and a member of its Board of Directors. There was bad blood between him and Walter Chrysler, who told Nicholas Kelley that he didn't trust Smith at all. It seemed that Chrysler had had to deal with Smith on his severance arrangement from GM, and felt he had been cheated in certain aspects of the agreement. Smith had great regard for Chrysler, though, and had made a substantial investment in the Class A preferred stock of the reorganized Maxwell company a few years earlier. During the changeover from Maxwell to Chrysler, Smith suddenly showed up with a large number of the Maxwell Class A preferred shares and demanded a better deal than what was being offered. "John Thomas Smith took the position that we couldn't force him out of his preferred stock," said Kelley. "For what it was worth, he threatened to enjoin our proceedings." In the end, Chrysler brought in his good friend John Raskob from GM to settle the matter. He arranged a meeting in his office among himself, Smith, and Raskob, and they came to an agreement. Unwilling to allow Smith to hold him up, Chrysler made concessions in securities that were said to be worth $1 million to Smith. Now the thing was truly done, and no more obstacles remained.

On Saturday, June 6, 1925, the Chrysler Corporation was born. It was chartered at Dover, Delaware, as a holding company for a Chrysler Corporation that had recently been formed in Michigan with minimal capital to conform with certain legal matters necessary to the Maxwell-Chrysler merger plan. The incorporators were Nicholas Kelley and Sewell T. Tyng, both of New York City, and Albert B. Maginnes of White Plains, New York. They paid a state tax of $5,475 with the filing. The next day the Maxwell directors called for a special stockholders' meeting on June 24 for the purpose of approving plans to turn over the assets and goodwill of Maxwell to the Chrysler Corporation.

According to the *Times* report of June 25, "Walter P. Chrysler stated that the new company was beginning its career under the most auspicious circumstances. The new 4 cylinder car to be shown to the public tomorrow has been most enthusiastically received by the dealer and distributor organization. The company has orders on its books to assure capacity production for three months on its 4 and 6 cylinder lines. 'Never in the history of the company has it been in so strong a position with respect to forward orders, organization, facilities and cash,' he declared."

The one peculiar thing in all this was the syndicate of bankers that had saved Maxwell by taking a chance on Walter Chrysler's reorganization of it in 1921. Some of them had taken stock in the company in place of debt that had been wiped out in the reorganization, and when the stock rebounded from a low of around $3 to $16 and they could get out with their losses fully recovered, they sold, against Chrysler's urging. "Listen, I protested, you have seen this thing come up from nothing. Aren't you foolish to sell now, just when you might hope for profit?

"That's not the way we do business. We loaned money, and the loan went sour. We were in the hole, and now we're out."

Chrysler bought up whatever they sold, and later saw the stock split four for one. By the late 1920s those shares were worth over $130 apiece, so one of those $16 shares became worth in excess of $500. As Kelley said in 1953, after they had split again and were worth $720 each, "If one asks if the old stock was worth anything, the answer is, that is what it was worth, *if you had kept it.*"

The Bradys, Nicholas F. and James Cox, and Jules Bache were among those who did keep it, and on September 30 the *Times* reported that they had earned some $20 million in profits since the new Chrysler Corporation was formed, for its stock by then had climbed as high as $194.875. (By the time the four-for-one stock split was announced on November 18, it had risen to a peak of $253.)

Some wound up completely out of the money. One imprudent investor, who dawdled along and did not exchange his original Maxwell shares either for new Maxwell shares or Chrysler shares by the ultimate cutoff date of the 1925 creation of the Chrysler Corporation, subsequently shook off his torpor and filed suit to have his shares exchanged. He pursued his suit for decades, to no avail. In 1952, after explaining things to the man's grandson-in-law for the umpteenth time, Kelley said, "He was finally shut up, after 30 years. These things do drag out sometimes."

Concurrent with the announcement of the new corporation was the announcement of a new Chrysler four-cylinder car, the very first to bear the Chrysler name. But in many ways it wasn't new at all. The Model 58 was essentially a Maxwell with deeper-skirted fenders, lower running boards, and a Chrysler radiator shell, cap, and belt moldings. With the old Maxwell's antiquated thermo-siphon cooling and mechanical brakes, there were many who questioned Chrysler's wisdom in putting his name on this car. But the bankers were convinced that the Maxwell name was a liability and wanted to be rid of it, so all the company's cars would now be Chryslers.

In reality, though, the car was much improved over its previous incarnation. Hydraulic brakes were offered as an option from the beginning, and were made standard on the rear wheels by the end of the year. The engine was changed considerably, thanks to the ministrations of ZSB. Having modified the original Maxwell two-bearing engine into a three-bearing engine with much more efficient cooling for the "Good Maxwell," the designers set about developing a brand-new four of more modern design. "Using all split half main bearings with a crankshaft flange to hold the flywheel, and a pressed steel underpan for the oil and complete enclosure, this was a much more sturdy L-head design with a full pressure oil system and greatly added range of power and endurance," said Carl Breer. "In defense, one could hardly tell the difference in normal driving between the six and the four."

Ads for the Model 58 appeared proclaiming, "58 miles per hour! 25 miles to the gallon! 5 to 25 miles in 8 seconds!" And with prices $400 to $600 lower than those of comparable Chrysler Six models, the customers grabbed up all the 58's the factory could produce. After all, glamour sells, and now the public could get all the glamour of the Chrysler look and name for as little as $895. The company was right on track, and by the end of the year Chrysler had established himself as one of the major players in the auto industry, with his company earning $17,126,000, more than four times what it had earned in 1924.

With success came problems, of course. The biggest was a huge wrangle with fire commissioners throughout the country due to the company's decision to sell fire and theft insurance on its cars at the time of purchase; it was interested in protecting vehicles sold on time, as were 75 percent of vehicles then. The company claimed it was saving consumers money by selling at group rates. The policies were sold through the Palmetto Fire Insurance Company of Fort Sumter, South Carolina. The problem was that Palmetto wasn't licensed to sell insurance outside South Carolina, and Chrysler salesmen weren't licensed to sell insurance anywhere. The issue raged in the press and the courts for fifteen months, centering mainly on who had the right to sell insurance in various states, and what rights states had to regulate the sale of insurance within their borders. Chrysler gave up on its plan in June 1926 because it couldn't find companies willing to be reinsurers of the Palmetto plan. B. E. Hutchinson announced that Chrysler would consider renewing its insurance service in October after the Supreme Court issued a decision on the issue of the master insurance contract involved and its status relative to local agency restrictions of the various states. In October the Court duly issued its decision: The states won, and Palmetto lost. The states had a right, said the Court, to ban nonresident agents from writing insurance within their boundaries, and had the further right to forbid insuring property within their borders unless the insurance was written in accordance with laws passed by those states.

But the Palmetto affair was the only dark cloud on the Chrysler horizon in 1925. Everything else was sunny indeed. As was his wont, he spent the early fall in Europe, this time accompanied by Lawrence P. Fisher, one of the Fisher Body brothers, who was now president of Cadillac. On his return from a trip to Germany, France, and England on the *Berengaria* on October 24, Chrysler said his company now had forty agencies in France, thirty-two in England, and three in Germany, plus others in Belgium, Switzerland, Spain, and Italy. He expected Chrysler to sell 10,000 cars in Europe in 1925, and another 25,000 in 1926.

As good as 1925 was, 1926 looked to be even better. The world had altered remarkably since the War, and the pace of change was ever accelerating. As for Walter Chrysler, he seemed to have his finger firmly on the pulse of the times, and was now entering the period he would come to epitomize.

⌨ 22 ⌨

Art and Color
Take Over the Car Business

In clothing, housedecorating and furnishing, and in general personal, appearance by 1927 the American of modest income had spruced up. He was no longer satisfied
with utility alone. And when it came to automobiles, he
wanted "a blonde who could cook," as Charles Wilson,
President of General Motors, said.

The Road Is Yours
Reginald M. Cleveland and S. T. Williamson

"On July 4, 1920, more by accident, I think, than by intention, a chemical reaction was noted in one of the du Pont laboratories which led
to the development of a nitrocellulose lacquer eventually called Duco," said
Alfred P. Sloan in his 1964 autobiography, *My Years with General Motors*.
When Duco finally appeared on the 1924 "True Blue" Oakland late in 1923,
it revolutionized the way cars looked. Duco was a lacquer base that could
carry more color pigment in suspension and produce more brilliant colors
than the paints, varnishes, and enamels that had been used on car bodies
in the past. "Duco, by reducing the cost of color finishes and increasing
enormously the range of color that could be applied economically to cars,
made possible the modern era of color and styling. Furthermore, its quick
drying removed the most important remaining bottleneck in mass production, and made possible an enormously accelerated rate of production of
car bodies."

No more did practically all cars have to be black, because that was the
fastest-drying color. No more would it take two to four weeks for the paint
on car bodies to dry. Combined with the slightly later construction of
continuous-strip mills for manufacture of rolling sheet steel and the introduction of a continuous-process technique for manufacturing plate glass,
the new paint process meant that cars could be made ever faster and
cheaper. But mostly what Duco did for the public was to make cars bloom

Walter Chrysler in his study at his home in Great Neck, 1925. (*Courtesy Frank B. Rhodes*)

into a riot of shiny colors. Dozens of shades of blues, greens, browns, and grays, flaming reds and yellows, even exotic maroons and oranges, all began appearing on cars in dazzling high-gloss finishes. Many were festooned with contrasting stripes, belt lines, cowls, and fenders. Suddenly, a car seemed less like a utility and more like a sculpture, a living room, and a fashion statement all rolled into one. The amazing thing was that this new aspect of the car wasn't just available to the rich. Everybody could have color, and by 1925 even Henry Ford was offering it on the Model T.

But there were other novelties in this era, too. Since 1922 cars had been rolling along on balloon tires, low-pressure tires that gave a much softer, cushier ride. Then in 1924, at the same time that balloon tires became the industry standard, Essex lowered the price of its closed coach to within $5 of its open model, and the rush to buy this much more comfortable, desirable model became a stampede as other manufacturers followed suit. In 1925, for the first time, more closed than open cars were produced, and by 1929, 90 percent of all cars manufactured were closed models. In 1924 also, tetraethyl lead, an antiknock gasoline additive developed

Walter Chrysler and Dr. William F. Mann, Superintendent of the National
Zoo in Washington, D.C., surrounded by the Bachelor Lions of Washington,
D.C., March 1926. The occasion was the departure of a Walter Chrysler-
financed Smithsonian expedition to Africa to collect rare species of plants
and animals. (*Courtesy Frank B. Rhodes*)

painstakingly since 1916 at Delco Labs by inventor genius Charles F. Kettering and his assistant, Thomas Midgley, Jr., became widely available, just
in time to be soaked up by the Chryslers and the other high-compression
cars soon to follow them on the market. (MacManus said that Kettering
performed perhaps a hundred thousand experiments to develop no-knock
gas; he was determined to prove that the knock came from the gas, not
from the electric ignition and the self-starter, as engineers generally thought
at the time.)

In fact, according to Carl Breer, Chrysler was the first to acknowledge
the virtues of Ethyl gas, as it was known. After Walter Chrysler was approached by Kettering about this new product, he had ZSB look into it. "Ket
had been trying to interest the various General Motors car divisions but, as
in the past, they were indifferent to his 'anti-knock' ingredient claims, so
he turned to Chrysler," said Breer. The engineers came back with glowing
reports, and because of Ethyl they set about developing an extraordinarily
effective high-compression cylinder head that gave the new gas a great
boost. In appreciation of Walter Chrysler's initial interest, the Ethyl Gasoline

Walter Chrysler greets Bob Penny, close friend and marble-playing partner of his youth, on Chrysler's return to Ellis in 1926. (*Courtesy Walter P. Chrysler Boyhood Home*)

Corporation was to maintain offices in the Chrysler Building in New York City for many years after it opened.

Now that auto companies had something glamorous to sell in their show-rooms, advertisers appeared with the ability to sell these romantic new dream machines to a waiting public. In 1923 Edward S. Jordan created the most famous auto ad of all time to move his pert, colorful Playboy Road-sters. While traveling on a train across the flat and monotonous Wyoming plains, a tall, tan, and athletic horsewoman suddenly appeared, racing her horse toward Jordan's window. For a brief moment the horse cantered be-side Jordan as the woman smiled up at him; then she turned and was gone. Jordan asked a fellow traveler where they were: "Oh, somewhere west of Laramie," came the desultory reply. Within minutes he composed an im-mortal ad, which appeared within days in the *Saturday Evening Post*. Be-neath an illustration of a cloche-hatted girl racing a sporty Jordan Roadster against a cowboy straining to push his fleet-looking steed to catch up with her, there appeared these words:

> Somewhere west of Laramie there's a broncho-busting, steer-roping girl who knows what I'm talking about. She can tell what a sassy pony, that's a cross between greased lightning and the place where it hits, can do with eleven hundred pounds of steel and action when he's going high, wide and handsome.
>
> The truth is the Playboy was built for her.

Built for the lass whose face is brown with the sun when the day is done
of revel and romp and race . . .

Step into the Playboy when the hour grows dull with things gone dead
and stale.

Then start for the land of real living with the spirit of the lass who rides,
lean and rangy, into the red horizon of a Wyoming twilight.

The Playboy, which retailed for $1,895, wasn't expected to sell in great
numbers, but on its own terms it moved like hotcakes, and more important,
its advertising galvanized the automobile industry. The ads didn't mention
a single feature of the car. Instead they sold freedom, speed, and romance.
Everybody caught on, and by the late twenties museum-quality ads, masterpieces of the illustrator's and copyist's arts, were selling cars in unprecedented numbers to a willingly entranced public.

Manufacturers helped by continuing to lower the prices of new cars,
from Packard, which lopped a quarter of the price off some of its most
popular models, to Ford, who in the mid-twenties sold the basic Model T
roadster for an all-time rock-bottom price of $260. They also offered ex-
tremely generous credit terms to dealers and consumers alike. The big companies got into large-scale financing, with GM developing the General Motors Acceptance Corporation and Ford financing cars through its Universal
Credit Corporation. As John B. Rae tells us, "Other manufacturers relied on
independent finance companies like Commercial Credit Corporation and
Commercial Investors Trust, and on banks attracted by opportunities involved in underwriting installment buying of cars. By 1925, 75 percent of
all sales were on time, both new and used alike, and this technique was
rapidly becoming the accepted method of selling all types of durable consumer goods." The finance companies evidently did a very good job of as-
sessing credit risk and giving the public feasible, if not really the much-
heralded "easy," payments, because in 1925 only 1.75 percent of the cars
sold had to be repossessed.

Dealers helped new-car sales along by taking cars in trade and maintaining a used-car market larger than their new-car market. By the late
twenties very few new cars were sold without a trade-in, and every one of
those cars had to be resold, in large measure to people who couldn't afford
new ones. The effort to sell used cars wasn't a very profitable one, but as
the 1920s wore on and first-time buyers became as scarce as hen's teeth,
it was an essential one, and the dealers shouldered it manfully.

Ubiquity was the automobile's most salient feature. The 10.5 million passenger cars on the nation's roads at the end of 1921 ballooned to over 17.5
million by the end of 1925. New roads appeared everywhere, encouraged
and in part financed by the government. In 1916 the $75 million Federal
Road Aid Act was passed to give an incentive to the states to develop high-

Aboard Alfred P. Sloan's yacht, the "Rene," about 1932. Standing, center, Sloan, and to his right, Chrysler. Della is seated at left. (*Courtesy Frank B. Rhodes*)

way departments and to map out their roads in a systematic fashion; aside from the monies spent on the Panama Canal, this was the largest sum ever spent for public works up to that time. The Federal Highway Act of 1921 gave impetus to highway development by requiring each state highway department to designate up to 7 percent of its nonurban road mileage as primary. These were the intrastate trunk-line systems that had been mapped out under the 1916 law, and under this new act, these roads were welded into a system of numbered interstate federal highways. The federal government gave out funds for the development of the roads on a fifty-fifty matching basis, with about 200,000 miles of trunk roads initially receiving support. State and local authorities soon realized that relatively painless gas taxes were a good way to pay for further road construction. Merrill Denison puts it this way: "The automobile literally built its own roads. The automobile provided horsepower to do the work and taxes to pay the cost. The realization that the automobile could be taxed was the key."

By the end of the decade there would be over 3 million miles of surfaced roads in the United States, with the first transcontinental road, the Lincoln Highway, completed in 1927, after a fourteen-year effort spearheaded by Henry B. Joy of Packard. As the decade progressed, gravel and cobblestone roads were replaced by smooth, hard surfaces of asphalt and concrete, and highways were constantly improved in design to permit traffic to move with greater speed and safety. The study of highway construction problems was a new science called highway engineering, and was subsidized by the federal government.

In short, everything possible was done to put America on wheels, and America responded with a full cry of enthusiasm. Even the man who couldn't afford a new Model T at $260 could manage to scrape up $25 or even $10 for an old jalopy he could haul out of somebody's barn or backyard and put on the road.

Emblematic of the whole era was the disappearance of the Model T, which finally occurred at the end of May 1927, after more than 15 million had been built. More than 2 million were made in 1924, but sales stagnated in 1925, and they fell off by some 20 percent in 1926. In 1927 sales fell off a cliff. The old Model T was simply outmoded by the mid-twenties despite some halfhearted attempts to modernize its appearance and make it available in colors. But as one New York dealer stuck with a load of these barely saleable cars said, "You can paint up a barn, but it will still be a barn and not a parlor."

Henry Ford resisted the inevitable for some time, even railing against the new types of advertising and salesmanship he was convinced were leading consumers to buy jazzed-up cars they didn't need. No longer did the customer buy cars he said, "he is being backed into a corner and sold." (Ford hadn't advertised his cars since 1914.) But like it or not, that was exactly what was happening, and the great man was forced to acknowledge that times had changed.

"It could almost be written down as a formula," said Henry Ford in *My Life and Work* in 1923, "that when a man begins to think that he has at last found his method, he had better begin a most searching examination of himself to see whether some part of his brain has gone to sleep." Painful as it was, he eventually decided to follow his own advice. Without any advance warning (though there had been rumors), he shut off production of the Model T, and seven months later he came out with a new car, the Model A, that was as spiffy and handsome and modern as the Model T had been antediluvian. Contrary to what F. Scott Fitzgerald thought, there *was* a second act to this American life, and before Henry Ford was through, there would be yet a third.

❖   ❖   ❖

Chrysler had fortunately started out with a car several years ahead of its time, so he was not faced with the problem of modernizing his basic Model 70 Six in 1926. He concentrated on diversification. If the public wanted Chryslers, he would give them an ever-expanding number of types to choose from, in price ranges he had not sold in before. In August of that year he discontinued the Model 58 in favor of a smaller, lighter Model 50. This model was the first Chrysler product to feature an all-steel body, with a wheelbase 4 inches shorter than before. The lower unsprung weight meant the car could perform just as well as its predecessor with regard to pickup and top speed, and reductions in size and weight meant that Chrysler could slash the price by anywhere from $140 to $265, depending on the model. The two-door coupe and roadster and the four-door touring models could all be had for $750.

The big news, however, was the creation of the Imperial as a separate series, rather than just a style name for fancier-bodied sedans. Once again a teaser announcement came in a full-page ad in the *Saturday Evening Post*, this time on December 16, 1925. In big bold letters it read simply: "As Fine As Money Can Build—Utmost Luxury For 2 To 7 Passengers—92 Horsepower—80 Miles Per Hour," then underneath in smaller letters, "Watch *The Saturday Evening Post*." The two-page spread formally announcing the new Chrysler Imperial appeared in the *Post* on January 26, 1926. Four body styles, out of a total of eight, were illustrated on one page, with the car's features described in the expected silken prose on the other.

Under the hood was a scaled-up, more powerful version of the original Chrysler Six, with new skirted, slot-type aluminum alloy pistons that had nickel-alloy Invar struts, which permitted very close tolerances without scoring or seizing. Although such competing companies as Packard, Auburn, and Stutz were offering straight-eight models, and Cadillac, Lincoln, and Peerless featured V-8's, most also offered sixes, and the ultraprestigious Pierce-Arrow made sixes exclusively, so the Imperial's lack of an eight was not a big sales problem.

The Imperial bodies, much longer and heavier than the Model 70 bodies, were a thing of beauty, resting on wheelbases of 120, 127, or 133 inches. As Warren Erb described it, "The Model E-80 Imperial featured a unique radiator treatment. Although rounded like all Chryslers, and adorned with the same Chrysler gold seal emblem and 'Viking hat' ornament, the Imperials had concave channels sculpted into each side of their nickel-plated radiator surround. This sculpting continued back into the top of each hood side in graceful 'V's,' disappearing just behind the cowl. This hood and radiator styling were unique in America, but entirely too similar to the English Vauxhall (designed by Lawrence Pomeroy); Vauxhall tried unsuccessfully to file a formal complaint over this matter, but they didn't have the money to pursue it. Chrysler also sculpted, in similar manner, the surrounds and tops of the Imperial's bullet headlights, in pleasing harmony with radiator and hood. It was, indeed, a distinctive look among contemporaries."

In its first year, the new Imperial sold 9,119 units, impressive indeed for a new car in the luxury field. Overall, Chrysler sold some 162,000 cars in

1926, up more than 50 percent from 1925 levels, and good for a profit of more than $19 million. Business couldn't have been better.

❖   ❖   ❖

By this time Walter Chrysler was beginning to think more expansively; in the full flush of success and for the first time he did something for the common weal that was not connected with the car business in any way. On March 1, 1926, newspapers throughout the country wrote with great admiration of an African expedition to be conducted by the Smithsonian Institute and financed by Walter P. Chrysler. "WALTER CHRYSLER TO FINANCE GREATEST AFRICAN ANIMAL HUNT," proclaimed an article in *The Boston Transcript*. "Smithsonian Institute and Auto Magnate Co-operate to Get New Stock for National Zoo." Dr. William F. Mann, superintendent of the National Zoo, was to lead the expedition, originally inspired by a lack of both rhinoceroses and giraffes at the zoo. From that point on, the plans expanded to have a very broad scientific scope beyond just the collection of live wild animals.

"Our keepers at the National Zoo are asked by children continually, 'Where are the giraffes?' " said Dr. Mann. "We grew tired of disappointing them with the information that the National Zoo hasn't any giraffes to show them, but we could not help ourselves. Then Mr. Chrysler heard of our difficulty, and offered to the Smithsonian Institute [sic] to finance an expedition to collect giraffes and whatever else we need. So we have primarily the desire of the children to see a giraffe for arousing Mr. Chrysler's interest and for making possible an expedition of first rate importance to science."

The State Department had gotten permission for trapping from the government of Tanganyika, and a party of experienced field naturalists under Dr. Mann was to depart from Dar-es-Salaam for a six-month field expedition in the interior of that country, chosen because of its large numbers of both protected and unprotected species. The *Times* said they hoped to get samples of a hundred species. They noted that though the Smithsonian had sent out hundreds of field expeditions to get specimens for mounting in its eighty years (this number included those that came from a big-game trip to Africa under Theodore Roosevelt in 1909), "the trapping of wild beasts in the Smithsonian-Chrysler expedition for zoological exhibition is almost without precedent."

The list of creatures they wanted to capture reads like one of the most exotic pages from a boy's true adventure story. In addition to the rhinoceroses and giraffes, they sought the topi, hartebeest, bushbuck, kudi, aardvark, armor-plated pangolin, the diminutive potto, monitor lizard (which ravages the nests of crocodiles to eat their eggs), and hyrax (known as the cony in the Bible; smaller than the rabbit, it is yet the closest known relative of the elephant). The scientists were to capture all sorts of antelopes, gazelles, zebras, monkeys, lions, leopards, and other cats, hunting dogs, wolves, hyenas, and wild hogs. Not to leave out reptiles, they would seek out pythons, spitting cobras, puff adders, black mambas, boomslangs, and giant leopard tortoises, which grow to nearly 100 pounds. They expected to find many previously unknown species too, particularly among the smaller animals and insects.

The grace note was to be the birds, among which they hoped to encounter various types of parrots and lovebirds, the giant ground hornbill, the fish eagle, the secretary bird (or snake killer), the colorful plantain eater, and a selection of vultures and smaller brilliant-colored finches, including the paradise whydah, whose body is scarcely larger than a canary's but whose tail is eight to ten inches long.

A photographer, Charles Charleton, accompanied the expedition so that a motion picture record of the trip would be preserved. The only thing left out was Rudyard Kipling, who could have made a portrait in words as grand as anything the eye could see.

There is extant a series of photographs taken on the deck of the *Leviathan* on the freezing cold March day when the expedition departed for Africa. Typically, one shows a jovial Walter Chrysler shaking hands with a very somber, stiff-looking Dr. Mann, both men wrapped up in huge overcoats and topped with enormous hats. They are surrounded by men in bedraggled lion, monkey, and tiger suits, the lion holding a sign reading, "The Bachelor Lions of Washington, D.C.," and the monkey holding one proclaiming, "Happy Voyage! Don't Let Our Brothers Make Monkeys out of You!" It is all a wonderfully silly way of conveying the happiness Walter Chrysler's help brought to a large number of children and a great institution.

In a way it was appropriate that this expedition should have been done to bring happiness to children, for six months later a child would bring great happiness to him. On September 18, 1926, his first grandchild was born, to Thelma and Byron Foy. This was a little girl named Joan. Her appearance in this world was providential, a kind of rebirth and new hope, for just the previous month, on August 3, 1926, Walter's beloved mother, Mary, had died at the home of his sister, Irene Harvey, in Glendale, California. She had lived in Salina until 1923, when she decided to relocate to Glendale, where she could spend her time in the beautiful Spanish-style home of Irene and her husband, Charles, surrounded by the warmth and palm trees of southern California. There, too, she could enjoy her charming granddaughter Edna Harvey, born in 1915 and later to become accomplished and acclaimed as the ballerina Edna Breymann (surnamed in honor of her grandmother) before her untimely death from cancer in the late 1930s. Glendale had the added virtue of proximity to her other son, Edward, who lived in nearby Riverside with his wife and children. Mrs. Chrysler had an unspecified long illness before her demise, but died with the comfort of her family around her.

Walter, who was not able to be with her in California when she died, met the funeral party in Salina, where Mrs. Chrysler was buried in the family mausoleum. As he often said, it was his mother, with her hairbrushes and lectures and buffalo steaks, who molded his character and turned him into the strong-minded, strong-willed individual he became. Her passing was a very emotional moment for this very emotional man. He provided a contingent of Chrysler cars for the funeral, and upon its conclusion, gave them all away to the relatives and friends of his youth who attended the event.

❖   ❖   ❖

When Walter Chrysler left Kansas to seek his fortune in the late 1890s, it wasn't because he disliked the place or had any ill will toward the people who lived there. In fact, he harbored deep and abiding nostalgic sentiment for all the people and events of his youth. He simply wanted to make something of himself, at first to be worthy of Della's hand in marriage, and later because he saw he had the chance and ability to be a real force in the business of transportation. To do any of it, though, he knew he had to get out of Ellis and seek his opportunities in the great world outside. Except when he returned for one day in 1901 to get married, it was a long time before he was to see little Ellis again.

On April 5, 1919, Walt and Della visited Ellis (on the way back from California) in the summer of 1918. His old negro gaming partner Bob Penny was there to greet him, which warmed him greatly. They discussed the state of craps in Ellis, which Penny said had never been the same since Walt left. Later that day, Penny was seen in the general store where Walt had worked as a boy, waving a large banknote. When asked where it came from, he replied, "Walt." Six years later, when Walt returned to Ellis again, this time as a newly famous auto magnate, Bob Penny was the first one to step out of the crowd to greet him as he got off the train. He was holding a bag of marbles in his hand. Walt took off his jacket, rolled up his sleeves and pants legs, and got down in the dust for a game right there on the spot. He won, just as he did in the old days when he was the undisputed marble champion along the Union Pacific line in Kansas.

That day in 1924 was a memorable one both for Walt and for the town that had nurtured him in his youth. The *Ellis Review* reflected on his short visit, which took place during a return trip from California, where he had seen his mother: "A deep study of human interest centered around Chrysler during his brief sojourn here, for he picked up threads of friendship and association apparently just as he had left them. To him they were still friends—all of them—regardless of race, creed, color or station in life. He had a handshake and slap on the back for everyone, even if he was obliged to run out into the middle of the street to greet an old acquaintance. A greater part of his time, while not in private homes, was spent here, there, and everywhere, reviewing a panorama of boyhood reveries with as much side-splitting merriment as in days gone by.

"Gazing into the faces of a score of guests seated around a banquet table in the early afternoon Chrysler became tense and serious; for among those present were his early bosses who many a time had raked him over the coals, and when he arose to address them he was deeply touched. But Chrysler spoke, not to a sober board of directors, but to a little group of fellow men in whose breasts reigned the true spirit of brotherly love and esteem, not because of his achievement in the industrial world, but because he was Chrysler, whom they knew when he was a boy and when they were boys together.

" 'Walt,' as he was familiarly addressed, spoke almost three hours, briefly covering an elapse of 26 years since his departure. Prominent in his talk were the ups and downs of life in a mighty struggle to accomplish visionary aspirations that ultimately resulted in a marvelously successful career. Pointing a finger at a number of railroad men, now retired, Chrysler said, 'It was you men who forced upon me years ago the basic principles of a winning fight that I have long since treasured as a thing priceless.

" 'Sometimes I am led to believe that there is no limitation to what a man, especially a young man, can accomplish, and until the so-called impossible is forced upon him in a sink or swim manner, he doesn't know what he can do.' "

One of the things Chrysler did with his success was to give somthing back to the people of Ellis. Anne Hedge of the Chrysler Boyhood Home has said that Walter Chrysler hired quite a few men from Ellis in his various auto businesses. "Whenever they had a problem, they'd go to his office and talk to him personally. The office was always grand of course, and they'd want to take off their shoes so as not to dirty his carpet, but he'd always say, 'Hell, no!' and wave them right in, just like back home in the old days.

"As for Bob Penny, Mr. Chrysler sent him $100 each Christmas for the rest of his life. Back in those days, that was a heck of a lot of money. He always gave generously to local charitable causes too, whenever he was asked."

❖   ❖   ❖

In this period, the mid-twenties, his interest in his family's genealogy continued and quickened. It began when an inquiry from John North Willys on the subject in late 1922 awakened his curiosity. A letter from a Chrysler associate on December 1, 1922 advises Willys "that we have taken this matter up with his relatives and give you all the information which we have been able to gather from family bibles and other sources." After listing what was discovered, the letter concludes: "Mr. Chrysler now feels that he should carry this still further and is employing a genealogist to make a complete search." He hired a Miss M. E. Buhler of 140th Street in New York City to do the search for him in 1923, and enlisted family members to aid him in the project.

Miss Buhler did a very good job, corresponding with Chrysler's secretary, D. R. McClain, on his behalf. There still exists a brilliant two-page analysis from March 1924 done by Miss Buhler on just one claim to a connection with Chrysler. She also created a Grafton Chart Index of the family background, which has proven to be of great value (this is a fan-shaped chart providing spaces for the names of all one's ancestors for ten generations back).

Chrysler's great-grandson, Frank B. Rhodes, has an extensive correspondence file of Chrysler's on this matter, beginning with a letter written by him on December 28, 1922, requesting that "Aunt Laura" Montgomery of Detroit send him information on his father's family and suggesting she might find it in family Bibles. When Chrysler hired Miss Buhler in the early spring of 1923, he sent her to see his aunt on her way up to begin her researches in Canada. On January 9, 1923, he requested background family information from a maternal relative; the reply came on April 18, 1933, when John Campbell of Kansas City wrote that he had found the Breymann family Bible and made a photostat of it. These are just a couple of instances, but they show how painstaking this sort of research can be.

The stream of letters continued throughout the 1920s and '30s, as leads came in and more and more people became aware of Chrysler's search. He studiously followed up each one with detailed and thoughtful replies, whether or not they proved to be fruitful. One letter from a Mrs. George Chrysler Featherly of West Orange, New Jersey, in 1929, stated that when she had applied to Chrysler for a secretarial job way back in 1917, he had written her requesting information about a New England minister from the eighteenth century named Chrysler, so we see that his interest in genealogy was of long standing; Willys's inquiry was simply the catalyst that began the formal search. Some of the inquiries were done for merely the price of a postage stamp, while others were very costly. In November 1933 Chrysler paid out $1,550 to the American Historical Society to research various branches of the family, for instance. But however it was done, Chrysler looked into his family's connections and past with vigor and enthusiasm.

Later, in the early 1930s, Walter Junior began his own investigations, which built on the work his father had initiated. It wasn't only curiosity on his part, however, for he had social aspirations that required the establishment of an "acceptable" family background. By the end of 1934 a letter from M. M. Lewis of the American Historical Society proclaimed that complete research on all the related Chrysler families had been done. In the end, though, it took the substantial subvention provided by Thelma and Bernice in the 1950s to produce the exhaustive volume of Chrysler genealogical research that is one of the proudest achievements of the Chrysler family.

❧   ❧   ❧

Back in the realm of business, by the end of 1926 Walter Chrysler was talking like the compleat capitalist of his day. "The chief reason why I anticipate a continuance of good times is the diffusion of wealth in this country," he said in *Auto Topics*. "The War gave a tremendous push in the direction of democratizing wealth, and this trend has continued. Every employee of intelligence today is an embryonic capitalist, and, with labor well employed and wages rising, the spread of wealth should continue with improvements in motor cars by the progressive manufacturers in the past two years." Now producing up to 750 cars a day, he looked to expand his own volume to over 200,000 cars the following year.

He didn't achieve that figure, but he came awfully close, manufacturing 192,000 Chryslers in 1927, a number that would not be surpassed until 1965. The only addition to the line was a new Series 60, which was a six-cylinder car on a 109-inch wheelbase, priced a bit higher than midway between the Series 50 Four and the Series 70 Six.

Outside Chrysler, significant innovations were being made at GM. In 1926 it introduced the Pontiac, a companion car to the venerable Oakland. It was in many respects an unremarkable car, but it offered something that made it sell like hotcakes: a six-cylinder engine for the price of a four. At $825, almost 77,000 of them were moved in the marque's first year, far more than doubling Chrysler's record for initial-year production two years earlier. The times were such, however, that even this record would be broken the following year by the new Graham-Paige.

More important than the appearance of the new Pontiac was the inauguration of another new GM make in 1927, the LaSalle, intended as a less expensive companion to the Cadillac line. By this time GM had decided to cater to the car buyer from the cradle to the grave by offering a "car for every purse and purpose," as a *New York Times* ad on January 9, 1927, proclaimed, "from the Chevrolet Touring car at $510 to the Cadillac with special coach work at $9,000." To that end, it decided to fill in the price gap between the most expensive Buick and the least expensive Cadillac. What made the LaSalle a milestone in the development of the motor car was that it was the first automobile to be consciously styled from bumper to bumper. At Chrysler, Oliver Clark was the chief body engineer, not head stylist, because at that time no such position existed. Chrysler bodies were formed according to the needs of the engineers, which was then the universal practice in the automobile business. All this was changed by a dashing, even flamboyant, young man from California named Harley Earl.

Earl was born in Los Angeles on November 22, 1893. Tall, tanned, handsome, and athletic, he was the son of coach builder J. W. Earl, who went from the carriage business to the custom car body trade in the 1910s in order to capitalize on the new market for beautiful, exotic, and expensive auto coach work demanded by Hollywood stars and other wealthy southern Californians.

After attending Stanford and the University of California at Los Angeles, Earl joined the family firm, where his natural interest in color and style helped him rise quickly to become chief designer. By 1919 his designs were gaining him considerable notice in the press, and when Don Lee, the West Coast Cadillac distributor, bought out J. W. Earl's firm later that year, young Harley stayed on in his position, eventually rising to become general manager of the new company. Among the hundreds of custom designs annually turned out by the firm were those built for the likes of Cecil B. DeMille, Tom Mix, Roscoe (Fatty) Arbuckle, Blanche Sweet, and Mary Pickford. One customized Pierce-Arrow was a gift from multimillionaire oilman E. L. Doheny, Jr. to his wife. Doheny liked it so much he allowed a picture of himself sitting beside Earl in the front seat of the car to be published in the *Los Angeles Times*. Along with the car, Doheny gave his wife a chauffeur, which was a big mistake, for a short while later the wife and the chauffeur ran off together in the car, causing quite a scandal.

In 1925 Don Lee placed an order with Cadillac for a hundred chassis, to form the basis for his custom designs. Lawrence P. Fisher, the flamboyant, high-living one among the seven Fisher brothers, had just been appointed president of Cadillac. He had no intention of selling Lee or anyone else a hundred Cadillac chassis, but he decided to go to Los Angeles to see for himself what had made Lee become so successful. There he met the attractive, impeccably dressed Earl, and the two men hit it off right away. "They shared a basic love of fun, and while Earl wasn't in Fisher's league as a playboy, he could keep up with L.P. on a barstool, on the fairway, as a clotheshorse, and on the topics of cars, sports, money, and people. Larry Fisher and Harley Earl had a lot in common," said historian Michael Lamm.

It was propitious that their meeting should take place just then, for big changes were taking place at GM under Alfred P. Sloan, who was president from 1923 to 1927 and would dominate the company's affairs for forty years. Author Stephen Bayley, author of *Harley Earl And The Dream Machine*, described Sloan as "a dark suited Michigan WASP who combined the organizational authority of the British Civil Service with the analytical powers of a Karl Marx." It was he who created the fully thought-out hierarchical business structure of General Motors that would become the universal organizational model of the modern corporation. Henry Ford had realized the potential of the mass market, but under Sloan GM was to realize the potential of the "mass class" market, with vehicles designed to appeal to everyone from farmers to executives.

At this very time in 1925, the company's sales committee had just voted to institute the annual model change, which would famously introduce the concept of "planned obsolescence" to the motor car—an idea that has sold more automobiles than any other in the history of the industry. In their eagerness to implement this system, they unwittingly created the whole notion of "styled" cars. Larry Fisher, who had been in on formative discussions of this annual model concept with his brother Fred and with Alfred Sloan, brought Earl along to Detroit, at first as designer of his division's new LaSalle. His success with that project led to his being placed in charge of all styling for the whole of GM, where he instituted the practice of restyling each of the company's lines every year.

Harley Earl was hired in January 1926 and produced his designs for the new LaSalle in three months. He was actually hired by Cadillac as a consultant and given only one assistant, a wood modeler named Ralph Pew. The first thing he did was to introduce the custom-shop technique of using a sculptor's model, meaning that car models were produced by molding clay over wooden armatures. This made it possible to produce more unified, sculpted, less stiff designs than resulted from hammering them out of metal, as was the usual practice. "I produced one design for four different bodies," he told the *Detroit Free Press* some years later. "A roadster with a rumble seat, a convertible coupe, an open touring car with the fold-down windshield and little canvas top, and a sedan. I made clay models which I had done in California. They had never seen this done in Detroit."

The LaSalle was copied completely from the car then most admired by Earl, the Hispano-Suiza. He imitated it right down to the car's emblem. It was of course consciously designed to look European. "No effort was made to create a profile that suggested a long, smooth flowing line. Instead, Earl deliberately broke up and separated the lines of the car. At the same time, however, his design blended all the elements of the car into a single dominant theme: that of a short, compact automobile with plenty of power," said Robert P. Ackerson. Its side view was sharp and angular, set off by twelve large vertical engine louvers. The front featured two large headlights, connected by a short tie rod centered by a "LaS" monogram and supported by vertical tubular posts. "The mixture of vertical and horizontal lines, reinforced by the high, narrow radiator with its vertical shutters created an impression of speed and grace never before seen on a mass-produced American car," Ackerson continued. But what was most important was that every single element of the car, from roof to running boards and from headlights to taillights, was consciously styled to be in harmony with every other element.

"The original LaSalle was a watershed in U.S. automotive design. Being the first production car to really have been thoroughly styled, it symbolized the growing maturity of the American automotive market. No longer were Americans content with basic transportation. The automobile had become an expression of one's good taste and lifestyle, and the owner of a LaSalle was recognized as a person of discriminating judgement in the choice of his automobile," was how Ackerson summed it up.

When the model for the LaSalle was finished, Larry and Fred Fisher were called in to look it over, followed by the Executive Committee of GM. They were so enthused that Sloan told him on the spot that his design had been accepted. "Mr. Sloan said, 'Larry, I think we should send Earl to the Paris Auto Show,' and Mr. Fisher replied, 'Mr. Sloan, I already have his ticket',", Earl recalled.

Earl and Sloan went to Paris together, where they forged a deep and lasting friendship. When the LaSalle debuted on March 5, 1927, it caused a sensation, and was hailed as one of the most beautiful designs ever. In its first model year, the LaSalle went on to win several design awards and sell 12,000 cars.

"I was so impressed with Mr. Earl's work," Sloan wrote in his autobiography, "that I decided to obtain the advantages of his talents for other General Motors car divisions. On June 23, 1927, I took up with the Executive Committee a plan to establish a special department to study the question of art and color combinations in General Motors products. Fifty persons would make up the department, ten of them designers, and the rest shop workers and clerical and administrative assistants. I invited Mr. Earl to head this new staff department, which we called the Art and Colour Section. Mr. Earl's duties were to direct general production body design and to conduct research and development programs in special car designs." On January 1, 1928, the Art and Colour Section officially became a part of General Motors' central office. (The name was a good choice—by that time all manufacturers were conscious of sprucing up their styling with more graceful designs and color, color, and more color; one manufacturer alone was said to offer 150 different shades to his customers.)

Earl was the ideal design chief for GM, for he managed his division according to standard GM practice. Everything was done through a rigid hierarchy of communication. He was at the top, dictating the parameters of an automotive style that would then be filled in by his subordinates, whom he watched over like a hawk. "He would give the ambiance of a theme, but would not define the theme as far as hardware or proportion," noted Stephen Bayley. Earl couldn't draw himself, but his design process always began with flat, two-dimensional drawings, very sensitive to line variation and subtlety. "Like a Beaux-Arts class, everything was up against the wall," said a designer of his named Garfinkle. He would come in, look at the drawings, and make his inimitable cryptic comments, such as: "I want that line to have a duflunky, to come across, have a little hook in it, and then do a rashoom or a zong." He would then sit in his director's chair while his minions raced about trying to interpret and carry out his wishes. Only when he was fully satisfied was a design modeled in clay.

So, in essence, in this new collective manner of designing cars, he set himself up as the master and dealt with everyone else as apprentices, moving them around at his command. In the shop, which he ran like a great artist's atelier, the going saying was: "Our Father, Who art in styling, Harley be thy name."

Harley Earl's lack of original visual ability, added to the fact that he couldn't draw or effectively communicate his ideas, should have made him a disaster as the leader of a design department. But, as Bayley put it, "He might not see it, but when he saw it, he knew it. He had a tremendous feel for line." That was also coupled to a critical, synthetic, and administrative genius that made him the perfect leader of Art and Colour. "When I refer to myself," he said, "I am merely using a shortcut to talk about my team," which for him was a creative group responding to the collective will of the corporation and buying public, not an individual person's will. Ultimately, he viewed his job as knowing what that collective will wanted, and making sure his designers served it.

The Chrysler Corporation's approach to styling was quite different and much simpler, but it was quite successful in its own way. Oliver Clark's design department initially consisted of a drafting board, a blackboard, and himself. His design for the first Chrysler was approved by the Maxwell Board of Directors on June 3, 1923, and was on the road in prototype form by July 31. Throughout the 1920s and through the Depression his design team consisted of a total of eight men; meanwhile Harley Earl's ballooned to nearly 150. Engineering dictated the look of the cars at Chrysler in large measure, but Clark and his small staff managed to turn out some enormously attractive and popular cars nevertheless.

Like everything else at Chrysler, the styling department was small, creative, and alert. Its modus operandi was the polar opposite of the way things were done at GM. Art and Colour was effective but byzantine. And in the end, would anyone say that the 1932 Plymouth, for instance, was any less attractive than its counterpart at Chevrolet? Was the Imperial of the same year a lesser design than the Cadillac? No one thought so then, and no one thinks so now. Chrysler managed to achieve the same result as Art and Colour, but in a much simpler fashion, even though Earl's method eventually became the industry standard.

◆   ◆   ◆

Chrysler did do something in 1927 that no other car manufacturer attempted: It went into the marine engine business. This came about directly due to Walter Chrysler's interest in boating. When he bought the house in Great Neck, he decided to buy a yacht to go with it. After all, the house was right on Long Island Sound, a yachtsman's paradise, and it had wonderful boating facilities. His neighbors, including Alfred Sloan and Alfred S. Sinclair, all had expensive, beautiful yachts of their own; Sloan's had a crew of forty-two. It was considered de rigueur for the successful mogul or society figure of the times to own such a floating palace.

His yachts were all commissioned, and all were called *Frolic*. According to the August, 1926, edition of *The Sportsman*, the *Frolic I* was 62' long, its beam was 12', and it was powered by two six-cylinder, 180 h.p. engines, capable of moving it at 24 miles per hour. The *Frolic II* was 70' long, with a 12'6" beam, with two 350 h.p. engines that let it cruise along at a top speed of 26 m.p.h. The *Frolic III*, which was designed by John H. Wells, Inc., and built by the Mathis Yacht Building Corporation, was bigger still, at 75'. Mr. Chrysler used all of them for his daily commute across the Sound between King's Point and the New York Yacht Club on East 26th Street during the warmer months of the year. One publication featured a picture of him in a summer suit and straw boater, seated in a rattan chair on the polished deck of the *Frolic III*, reading his morning paper on the way to work.

He thought this mode of transportation might catch on in a more general sense. On January 9, 1927, he told the *New York Times*, "The time will come when New York City will consider the use of water taxis to transport passengers from lower New York to different sections of Riverside Drive. These taxis will be motorboats capable of carrying from 6 to 10 passengers." He thought rates would be comparable to those of regular land taxis.

Auto Topics announced on May 7, 1927, that Chrysler was going to produce marine engines. "Long interested in speed boats, Walter Chrysler has crystallized that interest by entering on production of a marine engine. For some months he has devoted considerable time and money to this project, developing a separate plant, and now has ready what he has elected to call the Chrysler Imperial Marine Engine. It has already been adopted by Chris Craft. All Chrysler service facilities near a large body of water will be included in a plan of personnel training to service the marine engines."

An article in *Auto Topics* in 1933 on Amplex, the Chrysler division into which Chrysler Marine was folded in 1933, gives the early background of Chrysler Marine: "Chrysler brought into this new field the mass production and standardization methods which had proved so successful in the motor car field. It possessed tremendous plant facilities, precision machinery, and methods of manufacture which enabled it to produce an engine of higher quality and at lower costs.

"Exclusive manufacturers of marine engines, whose methods of manufacturing were limited by their comparatively small production, could not afford to invest in the necessary expensive tools and equipment to produce marine engines at a price and of a quality to meet the requirements of an advancing industry."

Automobile engines were not looked on very favorably at first for boating puposes. They suffered because of small bearings, a small crankshaft, splash-feed oiling systems, and undersize piston pins. In general, they were not considered rugged enough for marine service. But engines created specifically for marine purposes were made by small firms that did not have the capital to invest in the equipment they would need to make a sufficient number of high-quality engines to meet growing demand.

"Up to that time such installations had been largely made by amateurs who considered that it was only necessary to add a reverse gear, a water-jacketed manifold, a water pump and a few other parts to obtain successful marine engine performance."

To the surprise of many Chrysler did not turn out anything like this. "Chrysler speedily proved to the industry that Chrysler marine engines were not adaptations of those in automobiles. Rather, they were designed specifically for boats, and were economical and sturdy."

Jeffrey L. Rodengen explained the impact of the revolutionary new Chrysler Imperial marine engine in his book, *The Legend Of Chris Craft*. "Evidence suggests that Chrysler developed the new Chrysler Imperial marine engine specifically for the Chris Smith & Sons Boat Co. products, knowing that if the Smiths would standardize on their engine, he would hardly need any other clients within the marine field. As one periodical of the time commented, 'the engine is the product of the combined genius of Walter P. Chrysler and the Chris Smith & Sons Boat Company.'"

"With a slim weight of only 835 pounds, and packing over a hundred horsepower, the new Imperial was perfectly suited for the 22-foot Cadet, and promised 32 to 35 miles per hour, as opposed to 25 miles per hour for the 70 horsepower, 800 pound Kermath. For a penalty of only 35 pounds and $100, Cadet buyers could now get a substantial improvement in performance.

"Beyond performance, however, the successful application of the Imperial in the Cadet made available to owners the nationwide service of Chrysler, and an army of Chrysler factory trained mechanics. 'Designers are congratulating the Chris Smith & Sons Company on having been the first to adopt the new engine and avail themselves of the wider market afforded by the Chrysler prestige and widespread organization,'" said a contemporary publication. As Maryland researcher Weldon Ferguson has pointed out, these Chris Craft Cadets were sold side by side with cars in Chrysler show-rooms throughout the country.

Within two months of its debut Chrysler claimed over $500,000 in sales of boats powered by the new engine. By May 1927 three Cadets a day were being turned out and orders were backlogged, causing Chris Smith to take steps to further automate his company's production process beyond what he had done already. By the end of the 1927 racing season, Chris Craft boats were the undisputed stock runabout champions, winning regattas from Boston to Newport to Greenwich to Miami, even adding victories in such faraway spots as England and Barcelona. Now other leading runabout builders, such as Gar Wood, Hacker, and Sea Lyon, were featuring Chrysler engines in their powered boats. The following year the Royal engine, with 20 more horsepower, was added to the line, and production of Chrysler marine motors tripled, increasing still further in 1929.

Chrysler did not cause boats to be mass-produced, for by their very nature, boats, like airplanes and locomotives, cannot be so made. But he did bring very important benefits of mass production to boat manufacturers, by providing them with powerful, precision-made, reliable motors developed by mass production techniques. That was his contribution to their trade.

❖   ❖   ❖

There were other, much more personal contributions he made in 1927. One involved Great Neck, Long Island, where his mansion was located. The town had a very famous institution called the Alert Engine, Hook and Ladder and Hose Company, organized in 1901 with fifteen charter members and five trustees. The fire company needed to raise money, so on Wednesday evenings in the summer its members, attired in their uniforms and accom-panied by the Great Neck band, visited several of the millionaires in the area. After the rendition of several popular numbers by the band, The Com-pany's First Foreman (forerunner of today's Fire Chief) Egbert E. LeCluse, would introduce the members, explaining what they had done and what they proposed to do, providing they could raise enough money toward con-struction of a building.

"The men who helped foot the bill for the Alert Fire Company, each of whom was several times a millionaire, were pictured in newspaper cartoons as socialite "fire laddies," who ran with the apparatus and horses of the Alert Fire Company. Usually pictured at the head of the smoke breathing horses were J. Pierpont Morgan, king of American financiers, and William R. Grace, merchant prince of the seas. Following these leaders were other "moneybag" firemen, including such notables as Cord Meyer, William G. Brokaw, Joseph P. Grace, Roswell Eldridge, J. B. Webb, H. P. Booth, J. A. Jones and George P. Dodge."

The Alert Company firehouse, a wooden structure with towers on either side of its fascia, was opened on July 25, 1904, and remodeled in 1928.

Walter Chrysler became one of the first honorary members of the Alerts in 1927, under Chief Herbert R. Ninesling, when he donated a Chrysler Imperial fire engine to the Company. A platform consisting of the chassis, engine, running gear, running boards, and body from the cowl forward was delivered to the Bell & Post Motors Corporation of Farmingdale, New York. There a fire engine body was cemented to the frame, and all was painted a glorious shade of fire engine red, striped with gold. This engine remained in service for decades thereafter, and Walter Chrysler could sometimes be seen at the firehouse working on the truck's engine himself; he remained an interested and generous contributor to the company for the rest of his life.

At the end of 1927, he made still another contribution, this one much more unusual. Chrysler, by then an Episcopalian, heard that the Catholic Church of the Sacred Heart in Boulder, Colorado, was in need of a set of chimes for its bell tower. He contacted its pastor, Father Agatho Strittmatter, O.S.B., and donated the chimes to the church. They cost $15,000, then a considerable sum of money. At Christmas, Father Agatho joyously told his congregation of the gift of "a musical instrument to the church by one of America's wealthiest and foremost industrialists." Months later, they learned the identity of their benefactor when a plaque was placed in the church. It read: "The tower chimes dedicated to the honor and glory of God. A gift of Walter P. Chrysler, A.D. 1928. May religious liberty always triumph." To this day congregants of the church stop by the Chrysler Boyhood Home to express their gratitude for his gift. Father Agatho himself was so touched that he researched and wrote a long article on Mr. Chrysler which appeared in the *Detroit Times* on April 15, 1928; later, he printed up and distributed thousands of copies of this piece throughout the country.

❖   ❖   ❖

As usual, though, his business was the main focus of Chrysler's life at this time, and engineering was the main focus of his business. Engineering at Chrysler had gone extremely well from the beginning under the direction of Zeder, Skelton, and Breer. The first Chryslers were famous for their excellent, advanced engineering, and were often bought by mechanically minded people. Ford, of course, was pretty much a one-man band and didn't have great need of anything beyond basic engineering until he decided to discontinue the Model T in favor of an all-new Model A in 1927. This meant that, contrary to what most people thought, he had absolutely nothing on the drawing boards when he decided to create the Model A. It could be said that this lacuna allowed for the rise of the Chrysler Corporation and the consolidation of General Motors into the permanent industry leader. But it took GM quite some time to organize its engineering as well as Chrysler had.

GM engineering had its origins in Charles Kettering's Dayton Engineering Laboratories, which merged with GM in 1920. But though marvelous things like Duco and tetraethyl lead were developed there, it wasn't until O. E. Hunt of Chevrolet was made corporate vice president for engineering in 1929 that coordination of the advanced engineering work of the whole corporation was begun. According to Alfred Sloan, GM "did not have a department or section of the corporation under the title 'Engineering Staff' until 1931." They got one then, of course, but as we see, it was only after a long and lumbering process. Things were different at Chrysler, since engineering was a major component of the organization from the beginning. In fact, if such things could be reduced to one word, the watchword at GM would have been organization; at Chrysler, that watchword would have been engineering.

Auto Topics for December 10, 1927, carried the news that Chrysler was erecting a new research facility at Highland Park to house its engineering department: It would be four stories high, 600 feet long, and 60 feet wide. "Complete facilities will be provided for mechanical, physical, electric and metallurgical labs, an experimental machine shop, design and drafting rooms, experimental body building and painting departments, and experimental car garages." The building was set to include such up-to-the-minute items as an ice plant, with a capacity of 75 tons a day; dynamometer test rooms, with exhaust systems underground; and an air-washing system to provide fresh air in all working spaces. Other features would be chassis roll testing machinery and hydraulic lifts for car observation. Completion was scheduled for March 15, 1928.

On January 17, 1929, a crowd of seven hundred members of the Society of Automotive Engineers were given dinner at the Book-Cadillac Hotel in Detroit, and then conveyed by motor coaches to the Chrysler Engineering Building at Highland Park. They were greeted by members of the Chrysler Engineers Club and shown the building's exhibition hall, where twenty-five Chrysler cars were displayed amidst a bower of hothouse plants. Then they sat in the lecture hall for a speech by Fred Zeder explaining the transformation and new eminence of the automotive engineer, which was the justification for the grand edifice in which they were all now gathered:

"Engineering of the product has in the past been dominated by the management; by the production man, whose viewpoint is and should be his tools, dies, jigs and fixtures, his direct labor, his overhead and his capital investment; by the purchasing man, whose viewpoint is and should be the cost of the material entering into that product; and by other members of the organization's personnel. Naturally, cut and dried, high and mighty and guesswork methods were employed. With the help of a good advertising agency that studied human psychology and had the peculiar knack of converting a mechanical defect into a sales asset, the companies got by.

"But those methods are not fair. The engineer must assert himself. Successful companies today are entrusting this phase of their business to the engineers, and the engineer is coming into his own."

He then praised the Standards Committee of the SAE, which now served as a clearinghouse for all manufacturers' findings, eliminating chaos and the corruption and graft it spawned, while making new technological advances quickly available to all.

"The blueprint is nothing more than the engineer's method of shorthand writing," he continued. "To write the specifications of a connecting rod, for example, would require at least a dozen sheets of closely typewritten matter." Because of the S.A.E., "Engineers now talk the same language, and there is no mystery about automotive engineering. The design of a motor car is nothing more than a composite problem of thermodynamics, metallurgy and mechanics."

Harry T. Woolson, who had come along with Walter Chrysler from Willys to Maxwell and was now chief engineer of the Chrysler Corporation, then took over and told the story of the glorious new engineering palace in which they now sat, which had been opened for service on July 2, 1928. He extolled its very existence as evidence of the high position to which engineering had been elevated by Chrysler management, praising the engineering leadership that had thus been demonstrated.

After noting that the department now included 850 individuals, Woolson gave the layout of the 120,000 square foot reinforced concrete building. In the Iron Age account, Woolson stated that under that one roof were all of the chassis and body designing, drafting, building, and assembling departments and electrical, chemical, metallurgical, physical testing, and research laboratories of the corporation. Complete experimental cars were built there after each of their component parts had been subjected to rigorous tests in various sections of the building.

Physical, mechanical, metallurgical, and chemical laboratories equipped with modern testing apparatus were located on the first floor, along with chassis and engine dynamometers and the cold room, where tests could be made at −20 degrees Fahrenheit in a 40-mile-an-hour gale produced by blowers. There too full power breakdown tests were made by a battery of water brakes in the power plant section. The washed air in the dynamometer rooms was changed every 1 ½ minutes.

The second floor contained the service garage, and also the display room, auditorium, and offices. The experimental chassis assembly department was on the third level, where testing was done on transmissions, propeller shafts, rear axles, and brakes. An experimental body construction department and paint shop were on the fourth floor. A fifth floor was added only three months after the building went into service, and here design, development, and specialized research work were conducted.

After films on the various departments were shown the crowd was broken up into small groups, each of which was given a guided tour through the building. The guests were suitably impressed, even astonished, by some of the building's features, such as the cold room. When they returned home, everyone started wondering how they could get their own firms to create such wonderful facilities.

The best and latest equipment and the brightest engineers were all assembled in that building to work under the creative guidance of ZSB. Extraordinary things were to come out of it, but even so, it was just one part of the amazing manufacturing enterprise that Walter Chrysler was about to create. In January of 1928, he was one of the major independent car manufacturers. By December 31st, he would become one of the Big Three.

23

Chrysler Makes It
the Big Three

> While the water is stirring I will step into the pool
> *Sojourner Truth*

On April 1, 1926, the most important of Walter Chrysler's employees joined his firm. This was K. T. Keller, the man whom Walter Chrysler thought to be most like himself, and the man he picked and groomed to succeed him. As early as 1911 Chrysler called him a production man after his own heart. "When Keller was told to go ahead," said Chrysler, "the job was as good as done."

He was a long time coming. Kaufman Thuma Keller was born in Mount Joy, Pennsylvania, a small hamlet 12 miles west of Lancaster, on November 27, 1885. A sturdy, bright lad, he spent his youth involved with small village and farm life, doing typical after-school chores and making spending money by working in small factories and raising pigeons and squabs. He graduated from high school at sixteen and took courses in commercial law, shorthand, bookkeeping, and typewriting at a business school in Lancaster. At eighteen he decided to broaden his horizons by going to England, where he spent three years as secretary to a temperance lecturer. There he led an introspective existence, reading and contemplating works of philosophy and literature. Among his papers in the National Automobile Historical Collection at the Detroit Public Library there is a marked-up copy of *The Poems, Plays and Essays of Oliver T. Goldsmith*, on which he has written, "I carried this book all through my three years in the British Isles, 1903–1906."

From one of Goldsmith's speeches he underlined these words: "As we were born to work, so others are born to watch over us while we are working. In the name of common sense then, my good friends, let the great keep watch over us, and let us mind our own business, and perhaps we may at last get money ourselves, and set beggars at work in our turn."

Upon his return to the United States, he took a $75-a-month office job at the Westinghouse Machine Company, but within a year he jumped at a

Twenty-fifth anniversary photograph of the first Plymouth ever made. Manufactured on June 14, 1928, it was sold to Mrs. Ethel Miller of Turlock, CA, who also bought the one-millionth Plymouth in 1934 and the two-millionth two years later. (*Courtesy DaimlerChrysler Corporate Historical Collection*)

chance to become an apprentice mechanic, even though it meant a big pay cut, to 20 cents an hour. His apprenticeship completed, he went off to Detroit early in 1910, where he became chief inspector of the Detroit Metals Products Company, whose main product was motor axles. Thence he jumped to the Metzger Motor Car Company, and after letting himself get carried away there with his own success, he endured three months of unemployment and near-starvation. At the end of this period there was a greasy job at Hudson for 40 cents an hour, and soon he was back on track, with a $200-a-month inspector's job at the Maxwell plant at Tarrytown, New York.

Within a short time he took $50 a month less to get a position at GM in Detroit, where he could see possibilities for advancement. He was hired to go there by the mentor of his youth, Henry L. Barton, former works manager at Westinghouse, who had now become an important executive at GM. There Keller circulated among the machine shops of the company's various car lines in an effort to determine which were the best production methods to be installed in each. It was at this time that he first came to Walter Chrysler's attention.

"I had liked Keller's looks the first time I had seen him," Chrysler said. "He was only twenty-seven then, but already he was an old hand in the

Popular film star Jack Oakie with his 1929 DeSoto. (*Courtesy DaimlerChrysler Corporate Historical Collection*)

automobile business. He had that same love for machines that had dominated my life, and a further bond between us was that he had served a special apprenticeship in the Westinghouse machine shop, erecting, designing and engineering. . . . Thereafter, deliberately, as a part of his own scheme of education, he had worked at many jobs." In a lot of ways, Keller's story sounded like a replay of Chrysler's own.

Within a short time again he became superintendent of GM's Northway Motors division. He got a lot of good experience there, and developed lasting friendships with great men of the auto industry, including the Lelands, Charley Nash, Dallas Dort, and Harry Bassett, in addition to Walter Chrysler. But his salary was stagnant, and during the mid-1910s turmoil at GM, he decided to leave, this time for a job at the Cole Auto Company in Indianapolis. When Chrysler heard about his departure, he came down to Detroit. "He called me at my home and he said, 'Won't you come down and have dinner with me?' " Keller later recalled. "I went down. He said, 'It is none of my business, but why are you going to leave General Motors?' 'Well,' I said, 'opportunity.' He said, 'Why don't you come up and work for me? I will give you opportunity.' I said, 'I am committed to where I am going.' He said, 'If you ever want a job, just come up and work for me.' Now, to me, that was the sign of a big man, and that first hand of friendship from him had a great deal to do with my entire life."

Keller quickly got bored at Cole. "I missed the excitement of being in the

Jack Chrysler, Sr. and Walter P. Chrysler, Jr. at the wheel of a 1928 Chrysler Imperial Roadster, photographed in front of Cleopatra's Needle in Central Park, NY. (*Courtesy Frank B. Rhodes*)

center of things. Remembering Mr. Chrysler's remarks, I shipped my furniture to Flint, put my wife and son in a car, and in two days arrived there myself. Mr. Chrysler did not know I was coming.

"I called at his office. He was glad to see me and asked me what I was doing. I told him I was working for him. He said, 'Fine, how long have you been here and what are you doing?' I told him I had been there three minutes, and right then I had progressed no farther in Buick than saying 'hello' to him. He laughed, and I went to work."

This was just prior to World War I, and Keller, not yet thirty years of age, was now master mechanic of Buick. Within a month Chrysler had the order for those three thousand Liberty Motors, and Keller was put in charge of retooling Buick to produce them. During the war Durant had also put him in charge of all GM chassis operations. By 1919 Chrysler, now elevated to a GM vice president, brought Keller, now Buick general master mechanic, back to Detroit from Flint to work with him. When Chrysler and Durant both left GM in 1920, Keller was afraid he'd be stranded, but instead he found himself vice president and general manager of the fast-growing Chevrolet division, a position he held until 1924. On April 1 of that year (always a talisman day in his life) he took the place of R. S. McLaughlin as general manager of GM's Canadian operations; during his years there he felt he learned a great deal about the importance of both sales and service.

Through it all, however, Keller said, "I always had my eye on that man Chrysler. I knew him thoroughly. I was captivated by his untiring energy and his resourcefulness and courage. He was absolutely fair to his people, square with his customers, and faithful to his stockholders. I once heard him say, 'If it isn't good for our stockholders, our customers and our employees, it is no good for me.'" Keller had wanted to come along with Chrysler when he joined Willys, but Chrysler told him, "Stay here, and whenever I see a job that will pay you enough, I'll send for you."

"By 1925, Mr. Chrysler asked me how I'd like to work for him. I told him I had two questions I wanted to ask, and upon the answers to those I'd base my decision.

"Number 1: Was he going to make it his life's work, as I was reaching the age when I wanted to settle down.

"Number 2: Would he bring out a car to compete with Ford and Chevrolet.

"I'll long remember how he looked at me and said, 'I'm not ready to answer those questions now.'"

The first question looked to Chrysler's past. After all, when he quit Buick, he told the world he was going to retire. His job with Willys lasted just two years before he moved on. And after he restored Maxwell to health, it took all the persuasive powers of ZSB and the bankers to convince him to stay with the company and launch the new Chrysler car. Was it possible that he might want to cash in his chips and leave to enjoy the good life? Keller didn't want to be stranded by Chrysler again.

The second question looked to the future. By 1926 it had become apparent that although he was still at the top, Ford was starting to hit the skids, and a great opportunity was shortly to open up in the burgeoning low-priced field. Competitors such as Willys and Chevrolet were offering improved products at ever lower prices, but it was clear that there was a lot more room in this part of the market. Though he was doing very well in the middle- and upper-price brackets, a production genius like Chrysler would clearly be able to make an enormous splash with a low-priced car. If he did, that would make the difference for Keller between one more ride on the merry-go-round at an independent firm and grabbing the brass ring at a potential giant.

The following year Chrysler sent him a telegram saying that he wanted to meet with him at the Chicago Automobile Show. "When Keller came I was standing beside our show exhibit, and if you had seen us you might have supposed it was just a casual conversation; but it was a warm reunion, for we two are kindred spirits."

Chrysler's greeting to Keller was this: "Now I can make you a real offer; I want you to come with me."

"Are you going to devote your life to the Chrysler Corporation?" Keller asked.

"You bet I am!," was Chrysler's emphatic reply.

"Will you build a car to compete with Ford and Chevrolet?"

"Yes!"

That was that, and on his signature date in 1926, April 1, K. T. Keller joined the Chrysler Corporation.

In 1939 B. C. Forbes claimed that Chrysler already knew then that one day he wanted to make Keller president at Chrysler, with the founder remaining as chairman of the board. "But, as Mr. Chrysler said to me several years ago, 'In a large organization, you cannot always do immediately what you would like to do. You have to take many things into consideration. You must 'time' your important moves.'" So Keller's first title was vice president in charge of manufacturing.

Timing was everything indeed, in this and all other areas of Chrysler's business.

Almost as soon as Walter Chrysler's name was on his own car and company, he began to realize that the main chance lay in expansion beyond the parameters he had set for himself. The Chrysler, successful as it was, nevertheless was a midpriced product, and as such, it had a limited number of customers. In 1925 half the new cars sold were the low-priced Ford, Chevrolet, and Willys models, while more than fifty other companies divided the remaining market.

As the car became universal in the 1920s, the number of first-time buyers who paid cash was dropping, and the sale of new cars was increasingly propped up by trade-ins and and financing. Competition became ever fiercer as technical innovations and the economic benefits of mass production made better cars available to the public at cheaper prices. Smaller companies, unable to mechanize successfully and match the lower prices, dropped by the wayside throughout this period.

Though it was profitable from the start, big money started to roll into the Chrysler Corporation when it reengineered and rebadged the Maxwells into Chrysler Fours and made the Chrysler name and identity available to the public for half its initial price. Chrysler's plants produced 162,000 cars in 1926 and 192,000 cars in 1927, and it became apparent that their production capacity was being pushed to its limits.

Chrysler was a production man, and as such, he knew that volume and economies of scale were what made huge profits, particularly in an era of rising costs like the 1920s. So he was finding himself hamstrung both by the lack of potential new customers in his price category and by the lack of plant capacity to expand into the much larger low-priced market, where Ford- and GM-style money could be made.

Henry Ford didn't announce the demise of his superannuated Model T until the spring of 1927, but Detroit was rife with rumors of that possibility for some time beforehand. It had had a great run, but everyone knew the public would have its fill of Ford's product sometime soon. When that finally happened, someone both clever and prepared could become a major player in the American automobile business. In an important way, then, motive and opportunity were combining to give Chrysler the incentive to plunge into the biggest leagues of automobile production.

Rumors about Chrysler started appearing in the press. A report in the *New York Times* of April 12, 1926 had sources close to Chrysler denying for a second time that he wished to merge his interests with those of Durant, whose car combine was now beginning to falter, particularly after he was injured in a terrible train wreck in Florida the previous January. Then the *Wall Street Indicator* of September 21, 1927, announced in a headline that "Chrysler May Head General Motors in Great Battle with Ford." Mars Covington's long, long article on Chrysler went on to suggest that Chrysler had a lot of support among several very important board members of the company to become president of GM. Covington singled out the Fisher Brothers, and claimed their fortunes had been made by Chrysler's insistence on better, cheaper body production methods when he was at Buick, which ultimately caused the Fishers' company to be bought out by GM. But Chrysler didn't want to join GM, either. What he really was up to was something else entirely.

On August 14, 1926, Walter Chrysler told *Auto Topics* that he saw a large and undeveloped market in the small-car field for a greatly improved product. "There is no question in my mind but that people who prefer a low priced, quality automobile are desirous of having built into that car certain features that heretofore have not been made available to that field. The industry has not given sufficient attention to the man who drives a small, low priced car. It simply has gone on the assumption that the same measure of comforts that must be incorporated into every car of higher price, if it is to be successful, could not be built into the smaller cars.

"I disagree most emphatically with that position. The person who prefers to drive a small car is entitled to every consideration that can be given him. It is possible to build the qualities of comfort, roominess, easy riding and long life into a small car. The possibilities with such a car are so tremendous that it can actually be built in great quantities at remarkably low cost, if the manufacturer has the capacity and organization to do it.

"There is a ready made market of 100,000 cars the first year for the company which produces that type of car. We are going to do it. Unless we are far astray in our judgement of what the American public wants in the so called small car field, it will appreciate such a car to the extent that it will make it an outstanding success."

He certainly had the organization to do it. ZSB were probably the best engineers in the automobile business. B. E. Hutchinson was a first-rate finance man. Joseph E. Fields was an excellent sales manager. In K. T. Keller he had just acquired a top-flight production man. Oliver Clark and his team were wonderfully skilled, adaptable "body engineers." Having first used Widman and Fisher bodies, Chrysler now had acquired its own body plant, the American Body Company, located just across the street from the old Maxwell plant. In all these areas Chrysler was well prepared to meet the challenge of entering the low-price field.

What he lacked was capacity. Henry Ford hadn't built the Rouge plant for nothing. It was said that after the Model T was created, production was Henry Ford's problem every day of his life for the next fifteen years. He had to ask himself continually, how do you build more Model T's, and where do you build them? GM, which produced about two-thirds as many cars as Ford but six times as many as Chrysler in 1926, had built, expanded, and acquired all sorts of production facilities since its inception. But Chrysler did not have a completely integrated plant. He had no foundry, forge shop, or other facilities for making many of the major structural elements of an automobile. He couldn't build a truly low-priced car without these facilities, because all his profits would go to the parts manufacturers from whom he purchased his car's components. In any case, he abhorred assembled cars, because there was no central control over their manufacturing processes, and above all Chrysler wanted to be in complete control of the quality of his products. So Walter Chrysler knew that if he was to compete with the giants of the industry, he had better find a way to come up with the plants in which to manufacture all the parts of the vast numbers of wonderful cars he knew he could create.

He was faced with two choices: build or buy. Yet building an integrated plant would be prohibitively expensive, costing perhaps as much as $75 million. That would have entailed assuming a great burden of debt, which Chrysler knew was unwise, even for a company earning between $15 million and $20 million a year.

There was only one solution: buy something that already existed, and pay for it with equity. As it happened, the perfect something existed in the shape of the Dodge Brothers company.

The Dodge Brothers, Horace and John, born poor in Niles, Michigan, in 1864 and 1868, respectively, were sons of a blacksmith and utterly devoted to their mother. Burly, red headed and hot tempered, these inseparable brothers were perfectionists on the job and brawling boozers off it. No one ever worked harder than they did, and the extraordinary success they eventually achieved was due to unrelenting effort.

Their original training as machinists came through jobs at the Murphy Engine Company in Detroit, beginning in 1886, where they obtained great practical knowledge of all kinds of machine and manufacturing operations. Four years later they found work at the Canadian Typothetae Company in Windsor, Ontario, where they made their mark as developers of a bicycle they patented that rolled on an adjustable ball-bearing hub. Their machine caught the eye of a Detroit manufacturer named Fred S. Evans, who backed and organized the Evans and Dodge Bicycle Company in 1899 and produced the Dodges' bicycles in the leased Canadian Typothetae works. By 1901 the firm was sold to the Canadian Cycle & Motor Company and, with $7,500 in cash and $10,000 worth of machinery, the Dodge Brothers went to Detroit and opened the Dodge Brothers Machine Shop in the Boydell Building on Beaubien Street. To get established, they took any job that came their way, making miscellaneous parts for steam engines, bicycles, firearms, and a variety of other items. Often they labored far into the night seven days a week, designing, engineering, and planning out future work. From the beginning, John was the front man and Horace the production man.

In March 1901 Ransom E. Olds gave them one of the first large orders for automobile parts ever placed, two thousand transmissions to be installed in his popular new Curved Dash Olds runabouts. Through 1903, Olds relied entirely on Dodge Brothers to supply his transmissions.

As their reputation for the highest manufacturing standards grew, Henry Ford and Alex Malcolmson approached them with an offer to build the motors for Ford cars. After difficult negotiations, it was finally agreed that Dodge Brothers would build all the mechanical parts for Ford. The Brothers' respect for Ford's engine was a big factor, but the main reason they took the job, which required them to give up their work for Olds, was that Malcolmson, who lacked cash, offered them a far more lucrative arrangement than anything they could get elsewhere. His bad credit induced him to offer to pay cash on delivery for the first hundred Ford chassis Dodge Brothers produced, instead of paying in forty or sixty days, as was the usual custom. Thereafter, he had fifteen days to pay for shipments, and if he failed, all unsold machinery would become the property of the Dodges. So on February 28, 1903, the parties signed an agreement for Dodge Brothers to supply 650 Ford Model A engines, transmissions, and axles at $250 each. A month later the Brothers each took fifty shares of Ford stock in lieu of payment for $7,000 worth of materials, with a promise to pay in $3,000 cash. Their shares were equal to a 10 percent interest in the Ford Motor Company.

This arrangement proved to be unique, and one of the best ever made in the automobile industry, for as Ford's business expanded, the Dodges made a profit both on the work they turned out for him and on their stake in his company. From 1903 until 1914 Dodge Brothers made every part of the Ford cars except for the frames, wheels, tires, and bodies. Together with architect Albert Kahn, they designed and built a huge new plant in Hamtramck in 1910 that became Dodge Main, and by 1914 they shipped from it some 1,200 motors, transmissions, and axles for Ford cars each day. With the opening of this new plant they became the world's largest suppliers of automobile parts, piling up millions of dollars in profits as Ford's output expanded in leaps and bounds. It should be noted, however, that everything they got, they earned. The Dodges risked their capital and their business on Ford at the beginning, when he had no capital at all. Furthermore, until 1914 it was primarily the Dodges that built Ford quality into Ford cars.

Though personally they were great friends, there was always a certain mutual distrust between Henry Ford and the Dodge Brothers. As stated previously, Ford hated the fact that he had to pay the Dodges a profit twice, first as suppliers and then as investors. On their side, the Dodges always feared that Ford would either find another parts supplier or decide to manufacture his own, and in either event, there was nothing they could do about it, since Ford owned 58.5 percent of the stock in his company and thus was in complete control of it.

Ford built a huge new factory on Woodward Avenue in Highland Park in 1910, and it was to be close to this facility that the Dodges built their new Dodge Main facility nearby. As Crabb points out, the relationship between Ford and the Dodges was essentially doomed from the moment the new Ford Factory opened its doors, because now Ford had the staff, money, and space to take over the work that Dodge Brothers had been doing for him. In fact, in 1912 Ford and the Brothers came to an agreement in principle, to become effective in 1914, for Dodge Brothers to lease its factory to Ford and integrate their space and their employees into the Ford organization.

This contract gave John Dodge time to think hard about Dodge Brothers' entire situation. After all, he reasoned, in reality it was they and not Ford who were actually producing the increasingly popular Model T. Furthermore, Ford had brusquely turned down any of their suggestions to improve the Model T, even ones that would save money. Dodge knew he could build a much better car than the Model T, and began to think more and more that now that the Brothers were in their mid-forties, the most experienced car builders in the world, and very rich, it was time to seize the day and strike out on their own. Perhaps even more tellingly, he also remarked around the same time, "I am tired of being carried around in Henry Ford's vest pocket."

After the Brothers argued between themselves over this matter in their customary manner, the die was cast. On August 18, 1913, John Dodge wrote to James Couzens of Ford, resigning as vice president and director of that company, and gave the required one year's notice of termination of the agreement between Dodge Brothers and Ford. There was no bitterness involved, and indeed Dodge Brothers churned out 500,000 Ford motors by the end of the year.

On July 17, 1914, Dodge Brothers was chartered in Michigan, and the firm announced that a new car would be produced within a hundred days. The company was capitalized at $5 million, all of which was paid in by John and Horace Dodge themselves. It was a far cry from the Ford Motor Company's start eleven years before, when Alex Malcolmson had to scramble to raise just $28,500 for that company to go into business.

The country went wild with anticipation of the new Dodge Brothers car. Some 22,000 people applied for dealerships alone in the next four months. Theodore F. MacManus, the same advertising wizard who was later to orchestrate Walter Chrysler's entry into the public consciousness, organized one of the most effective advertising campaigns of all time to introduce the car to the public. It was simplicity itself. He rented billboards from one end of the country to the other, and on them he put nothing but the legend, 'Dodge Brothers,' in white lettering on a blue background. Richard Crabb describes it this way: "That was all—just two words. After enough public curiosity had been aroused, and it was plenty, two more words—'Motor Car'—were added. A bit later the word 'Dependable' appeared (the word 'dependability' was added to the language by Dodge Brothers; customers wrote in again and again, coining this word to describe their cars—dealers beagan using the word, and eventually it was placed on billboards across the nation). Finally in the summer of 1914, newspapers and magazines carried this announcement:

'Dodge Brothers of Detroit, who have manufactured the vital parts for more than 500,000 motor cars, will this fall market a car bearing their own name.' "

And what a car it was. At $785, it was 50 percent more expensive than a Model T, and worth every nickel. The Dodge Brothers Touring Car boasted a 35-horsepower engine, compared to 20 for the Model T; it had a sliding-gear transmission, rather than the Ford's clunky planetary one, which required a lot of servicing; its pioneering all-steel welded body, designed by Edward Budd, was sturdy and less subject to vibration than the typical wood-based body; it sported a speedometer and windshield, a Cadillac-style electric system (which included a self-starter and electric lights powered by a wet battery and generator), and demountable rims (which made it possible for a motorist to carry a fully inflated spare).

Furthermore, since the Dodges thought the Model T was flimsy and in constant need of repair, they built "dependability" into their cars, which would be apparent no matter what conditions they were driven in. To that end, John personally bounced tires off a four-story roof until he settled on U.S. Chain Treads; Horace created the forerunner of the modern proving grounds by building a sloped track on which to test engine strength on the upgrade and brakes on the downgrade; and John crashed new models into brick walls at 20 miles per hour to determine their safety, saying, "I might as well, because someone else is going to do it when these cars get out on the road" (these were the industry's first crash tests).

These efforts show that the Dodges knew that all the talk about dependability wouldn't have meant a thing in the long run if it wasn't really true, so through experience, good design, and unrelenting effort, they made sure that it was. Frederick Haynes, who had known the Brothers since their bicycle manufacturing days and was to rise to become president of Dodge Brothers nine years after joining the firm in 1912, put it most succinctly: "The car was designed on honesty, it was built on honesty and it was marketed on honesty."

For reasons that remain obscure, the Dodge Brothers chose as the focus of their car's radiator badge the six-pointed star known as "Solomon's Seal" since it was adopted from Hinduism by the Jews. According to C. T. Schaefer, "Solomon's Seal was first used by the Hindoos as a charm against evil; later it was found in drinking vessels and other cups of the Arabs. It was revived again in the middle ages and appears at that time on the insignia of certain German and Austrian free municipalities." The seal (also known by the Jews as the "Magen David," or "Star of David") was superimposed on a map of the world, and inside it were the interlocking initials, "DB."

"Its symbolism relates to the two triangles interwoven; the one pointing upward is supposed to be white and to be typical of the soul, and the one pointing downward is supposed to be black and typical of the body. Interwoven as they are, they stood in medieval times for the mysterious union of the body and the soul. The ideal can be typical of any of the various dualisms, such as the union of mind and matter, of truth and beauty, etc. The meaning of the Dodge insignia thus centers largely on the six-pointed star, as the meaning of the world behind it is self evident. The use of the circular band separated by a white field (this surrounded the star) provides room for the name and product of the company (Dodge Brothers Motor Vehicles)."

The Dodges never publicly explained why they used this symbol, and they left behind no documents to clear up the matter. Dodge biographer Jean Maddern Pitrone found no explanation for it. Dodge scholar Joel R. Miller heard of two possibilities. One was that the Dodges used the Magen David to honor a Jewish venture capitalist who supported them; but the identity of this purported benefactor has never surfaced. The other was that it bespoke the Brothers' interest in mysticism. "Who knows?" Miller said.

The first Dodge Brothers Touring Car rolled off the line toward the expectantly waiting John and Horace on November 14, 1914. They got in the backseat, a driver put his foot on the self-starter button of the car, and, as Crabb puts it, " 'Old Betsy' chugged to life; at idle, the car had a sound of its own, a chug. 'A Ford rattles, a Packard purrs, and a Dodge chugs' " became the saying. The car was delivered to a customer in Nashville, and by the end of 1915, 45,000 others just like it found buyers.

The Brothers themselves were lucky to survive the introduction. They arranged an enormous party for the occasion at the Book-Cadillac Hotel, but it turned into a huge drunken brawl. John Dodge provided an impromptu finale to the party by mounting the long white-cloth-covered banquet tables and marching up and down each one with gusto as he gradually darkened the great hall by smashing out the electric bulbs in the chandeliers with his cane. Excessive though this was, it was not atypical of the wild parties the Brothers gave in their prime. They could be pugnacious brawlers, too; this author met a man whose grandfather recalled seeing the Brothers even engaged in a fistfight on the floor of the Dodge Main plant in 1919.

Within two years after their introduction, the Dodge Brothers touring cars became the stuff of legend. The U.S. Army bought three of them to use in Mexico in the fight against Pancho Villa. For the first time, motor vehicles were used as replacements for beasts of burden, driven over open terrain, not roads, like horses, camels, or elephants. General John J. "Black Jack" Pershing's officers were so impressed by them that he ordered six more. One morning in May 1916, near Chihuahua, Mexico, Pershing carried out the first motorized charge under combat conditions in the history of the U.S. Army. He put fifteen heavily armed men in three Dodge Brothers touring cars and had them charge in tight formation over open country at their maximum speed of 40 miles per hour toward the rebel headquarters, located in a ranch house. The rebels were so surprised that they jumped out of windows and ran. Colonel Julio Cardenas was killed, but there were no U.S. casualties. The young lieutenant in command of Pershing's forces, George S. Patton, said, "We couldn't have done it with horses. The motorcar is the modern warhorse." Pershing ordered another 250 of the cars in July 1916, which were used by his entire staff. Two years later America's great air hero Eddie Rickenbacker was among the soldiers who drove them in Europe during World War I.

Despite chafing at Ford's policy of everlasting changelessness on the Model T, in the end the Dodge Brothers followed in his footsteps with a similar policy. "Constant improvements but no yearly models" was what they advertised. As the Dodge Brothers factory ground out hundreds of thousands of cars over the next ten years, there was indeed little change in the cars themselves, other than a slight modernization of appearance and the introduction of the industry's first all-steel closed body in late 1922. But why argue with such success? Nineteen years after its debut, "Old Betsy" #1 was found to have run over 350,000 miles before being retired for display purposes, and several others from the first year's production had chalked up amazing mileage figures like 100,000, 236,000, and 250,000, sometimes without even needing to have the valves ground or the oil pan lowered. The public had been aware of the car's toughness and durability from the beginning, and that, rather than style or innovation, was what sold it.

In addition to providing America with its step up from the Model T, during World War I the Dodge Brothers also gave the U.S. government a dramatic display of the superiority of mass production over hand craftsmanship, while at the same time demonstrating an important new way of making long-distance commercial shipments.

The long war caused a great need for replacement of cannon in France, and though both Britain and France could mold almost any amount of cannon barrels and running gear, they could not turn out the firing mechanisms, since all of these were handmade. In desperation Marshall Joseph Joffre of France led a delegation to Washington to confer with Secretary of State Newton D. Baker about a solution to this major problem. After no other industrialists were found who were capable of helping, in October 1917 Baker finally called on John Dodge, who, after looking at the blueprints, immediately recognized the recoil firing mechanisms as suited for a mass production job. Joffre and Baker indignantly disagreed, insisting that this was not a mass production situation. "The hell it isn't," Dodge said. "Look here, Mr. Dodge," Baker said, "I am not accustomed to being spoken to in that kind of language." Dodge retorted, "The war would be a hell of a lot better off if you were. Do you want this job or don't you?" Baker gave his approval on October 27, 1917, and John and Horace Dodge went to work.

Within a week after John returned to Detroit, utility lines were staked out on an 18-acre tract they had set aside for the factory, carloads of building materials had been delivered to the site, men were operating steam shovels, cranes, cement mixers, and switch engines, and the Detroit Terminal Railway was building a railroad spur onto the property. Within a month 11 acres of concrete floor had been poured and the factory was taking shape. Throughout a desperately cold winter eighteen hundred men worked feverishly to complete the $10 million building, while Dodge designers and engineers labored furiously to design and build 129 separate machines to produce the parts for the firing mechanisms. On March 1, 1918, Horace Dodge gave the signal for the huge factory to begin working, just four months after the original commission was given. Mesta Machine and Carnegie Steel supplied the forgings for the recoil mechanisms, and production time dropped from the thirty-five hours common in France to just five hours, largely due to a lapping machine designed by Horace. The firing mechanisms worked perfectly, and were rushed to the fastest available ships crossing the Atlantic. To do this, the Dodges loaded them onto military trucks also to be sent to the front, bypassing bogged-down railroads and saving time and money on shipment and handling. In so doing they (and Roy Chapin, who loaded thirty thousand military trucks with supplies and sent them on the road in similar fashion) demonstrated for the first time the viability and flexibility of long-distance shipment by truck. For his efforts, John Dodge and his eight thousand workmen were awarded the Legion d'Honneur by the French government after the war.

During the War the Dodges also won a protracted court battle with Henry Ford, who did not want to give out profits from his business to these men who were now his competitors. After much maneuvering, Ford bought out the Dodge's interest in his company in April 1919 for $25 million, having already paid them some $9.5 million in dividends over the years. Not a bad return on an original investment of just $10,000!

The Brothers were at the peak of their game when tragedy struck. While in New York in January 1920 for the auto show, Horace caught pneumonia and almost died. While nursing him, John also caught pneumonia and died on January 14 at age fifty-five. The grief-stricken Horace died, officially of cirrhosis, on December 10 of the same year, age fifty-two. Each left an estate valued at approximately $37 million, but unfortunately neither left a son capable of carrying on the business, even though both of their boys were trained to do so by Fred Lamborn, who was chief mechanic at the firm when the Brothers died. "They were both capable, but being rich men's sons, it just didn't work out," Lamborn said. Each was gone from the company by 1922. Horace Junior was a playboy who married six times and devoted his life to polo. John Duval, known as "John Devil" around the factory, was a true hellion and wastrel who had been pensioned off by his father at $150 a month when he eloped with a classmate. Anna and Matilda, the widows of Horace and John, respectively, decided to continue their ownership of the firm, and placed their trust in its leadership in Frederick Haynes, an auto pioneer and right-hand man to the Brothers who was a knowledgeable and diligent executive. He was once quoted as saying, "I don't say that a man's whole life should consist of business and nothing but business but I do say and I do know that the man who puts his job first is the man who gives the orders in the end." Haynes was elected president and general manager of Dodge Brothers on January 11, 1921.

He was a good manager, but he was hampered in two ways. The widows themselves often interfered, and because of the nature of the trusts established for their benefit, nothing of importance could be done at the firm without recourse to the courts. Still, the firm prospered, with sales rising from a low of 81,000 units in the depression year of 1921 to over 200,000 by 1924, on which the company earned just under $20 million. Furthermore, Haynes had also formed a very lucrative alliance with the famous Graham Brothers, Joseph B., Robert C., and Ray A., in 1921 to distribute their Graham Brothers Trucks, manufactured on Dodge Brothers chassis, exclusively through Dodge Brothers dealerships. Despite all this prosperity, the widows decided to sell out, as they saw that it was inevitable that the fortunes of the company would sooner or later fall to the direction of a succession of managements with much less connection to the family than Frederick Haynes. In addition, Matilda had projects of her own with which she thought she could have success, and she needed cash for these purposes. For these reasons, the firm was put on the market in 1925.

First Matilda contacted Henry Ford, who was greatly saddened by the Brothers' deaths, for despite their business animus, an abiding personal friendship seems to have remained among the men. (Indeed, the Brothers waited to file suit against Ford in 1916 until the day after Edsel's wedding.) Ford declined to bid, however. A rumor spread around Detroit that a new combine would be formed to rival GM, consisting of Dodge, Hudson, Packard, and Briggs, but this idea never came to fruition. In the end there were two bidders. The first was GM, which made its offer through J. P. Morgan and Company. It offered either $124.65 million in cash, or $50 million in cash plus $90 million in non-interest-bearing notes to be paid off in nine yearly installments of $10 million each. The other offer was from Clarence Dillon of Dillon, Read & Company, who offered $146 million, all cash; it was he who had dreamed up the Dodge-Hudson-Packard-Briggs idea, but in the end he decided to try to purchase Dodge Brothers on his own. Though the offers were not that far apart, the widows preferred the all-cash offer, and Dillon, Read got Dodge. The money was paid on May 1, 1925, in a single check, said to be the largest industrial check ever written at the time. Photos of the check were widely published, and for the rest of his life Clarence Dillon was known as the man who wrote a check for $146 million.

Within two weeks of completing the transaction, Dillon, Read sold the public $75 million of Dodge Brothers bonds and $85 million of preferred stock; they gave a bonus of one share of Class A common stock with each share of preferred. The entire issues of stocks and bonds were eagerly snapped up by the public, earning Dillon, Read an immediate profit of $14 million. In addition, they retained complete control of the company, as only a special type of common shares, Class B, held entirely by Dillon, Read, had voting rights. This meant that once again President Haynes did not have control over the company, since Dillon, Read seated Edward G. Wilmer, a Wisconsin public-utility executive who had been chairman of Goodyear since 1921, as chairman of the Dodge Brothers board. Haynes retained his presidency, however, and earned profits of $28.7 million on the sale of over 300,000 vehicles in 1925. The company did almost as well on slightly higher sales in 1926. Actually though, those 1926 profits came mainly from operations in the early part of the year. In April of that year Haynes and Wilmer switched positions, with Haynes acting mostly in an advisory position and Wilmer now responsible for major decisions and daily operations. For reasons never explained but probably related to this state of affairs, the Graham Brothers, who had sold a 51 percent interest in their company to Dodge Brothers in November 1925, becoming major investors and top executives of the firm, decided to quit Dodge Brothers, sell out the remaining 49 percent of their truck operation to that company, and dispose of all their Dodge stock in April 1926.

Wilmer was not an auto man and simply didn't know what he was doing. Sales declined by 117,000 units in 1927, and profits were cut in half. By 1928 Dodge Brothers had skidded to thirteenth place in the industry and was unable to meet its payroll in May of that very prosperous year. It was really no wonder. The Dodge had built its reputation, sales, and prosperity on giving the public a much better car than the Model T for only $100 more. But by 1928 the cheapest Dodge cost $875, while the spiffy new Model A could be bought for $495. Wilmer was refusing to lower his price at a time when everybody else was doing so, and in addition he was abandoning the old reliable four in favor of a series of new sixes. As Oldsmobile had done twenty-five years previously, Dodge Brothers was abandoning its well-established market niche, with dire consequences.

By April of 1928 the handwriting was on the wall, and Clarence Dillon was desperate to get out of the car business. He went to GM, but, having lost out three years previously, they were not about to go after Dodge Brothers a second time, especially now that its luster was considerably dimmed by bad management and outdated plants and equipment. So at last he went to call on the logical buyer, Walter Chrysler.

"I had done plenty of figuring, and I knew that to exercise our full manufacturing power and talents we would have to acquire plants that would cost, if we had to build them, about $75,000,000. Where and how was I going to round up that kind of money?" said Walter Chrysler. "Every time I gave the matter thought I found my head was full of visions of the splendid plants of the Dodge Brothers." Certainly there would be no volume-produced, low-priced car to compete with Ford and Chevrolet without them.

Chrysler's visions of these plants were not only in his head. "Chrysler had known John and Horace Dodge well and favorably," said Crabb. "He had visited Hamtramck many times to see the new shops and equipment added there from year to year. He knew that as a manufacturing center for motorcars Hamtramck stood next to Ford's River Rouge factory."

Furthermore, Eugene Weiss, a former Chrysler employee and historian of automotive buildings in Detroit, points out that from Chrysler's office at the top of the Maxwell Building he could see the seven-story Dodge Main Building every day. One could say that Walter Chrysler's vision of Dodge Brothers plants fairly taunted him on a daily basis.

Clarence Dillon and Walter Chrysler had become acquainted after Dillon, Read had acquired Dodge, and since Chrysler was constantly trying to achieve economies to make his own car more competitive with the Dodge, he was well aware of the problems Dillon was facing. "I knew Clarence Dillon was worried," he said. "I believe he realized that the momentum given to the business by John and Horace Dodge was lessening. We had some talks about the Dodge business."

In 1923, Walter Chrysler had predicted, "The day will come when Chrysler will usurp the position of the Dodge Brothers." In fact, this might have happened as early as the spring of 1925, for Clarence Dillon spoke to Chrysler about selling Dodge Brothers to him shortly after he had bought it himself. But then such a discussion was premature, for Walter Chrysler's day as a great captain of industry had not yet come. Now that day was about to arrive.

◆   ◆   ◆

One morning in April 1928 Clarence Dillon walked into Walter Chrysler's office in New York and asked him if he would like to do a little trading.

"Hell, Clarence, I don't want your plant. What would I do with it?" came the hearty reply.

Of course Dillon knew perfectly well that Chrysler wanted Dodge Brothers, and his casual dismissal didn't fool Dillon one bit. Good salesman that he was, Dillon stayed on for a couple of hours extolling the virtues of the plant and his sales force, reputed to be the industry's best. Naturally Chrysler let him go on, but he never let himself be pinned down. When he finally got up to go, Dillon said he would go back to talk things over with his Wall Street associates. "All right, Clarence. Come in again anytime," was Chrysler's friendly goodbye.

A few days later Dillon was back to talk some more, but this time Chrysler was gruff and short. "It's too much money. We aren't interested. Of course, if it was a bargain—but it's not. So what's the use of talking?"

"Now Walt, don't shut your eyes to this. How else are you going to make the Chrysler Corporation into a first rank competitor of Henry Ford, of General Motors?" Dillon said. He knew he had Chrysler with this argument, for the whole automobile world knew Chrysler's aim was to become an automotive giant.

"Clarence, we're doing pretty well. Can you show me another company with a record to compare to the Chrysler Corporation? We've been getting better, year by year."

"That's true, Walter. But you've got your head pretty close to a ceiling right now, unless—"

"It's too much money, Clarence. You keep right on worrying about Dodge. Maybe it will come on the market a whole lot cheaper next year, or the year after. When a big outfit like this starts slipping, it can go down fast."

"Dodge isn't slipping, Walter."

"I hear different."

"They've got a fine name. They have a fine product, year after year."

"Sure, Clarence. I know. You paid $30,000,000 just for the good will. But that was when the company was making lots of money. How're you doing now?"

"We're doing splendidly. Only I think your crowd could do much better with it," was Dillon's final remark that day.

Over the next month and a half, Dillon kept on feeding him information, but Chrysler remained diffident. And in addition he put up a splendid smokescreen. It was called the DeSoto.

"We started on the DeSoto idea in 1926 right after I joined the corporation," K. T. Keller recalled. "Walter called me into New York and told me Dodge was in trouble. 'I think we can pick it off,' he said. We were watching the old Dodge Brothers firm go to pieces and it had a good distributing setup. But first we needed another car to compete with Dodge and to line up dealers as a hedge. We decided to bring out the DeSoto." To do this Chrysler hired the Dodge Brothers sales manager, a man widely liked by their dealers. "We sent him out to unsell Dodge dealers on Dodge," Keller continued, noting that by the time the Dodge merger was nearing completion, about 60 percent of Dodge dealers had lined up to sell DeSotos. Keller laughed, "We had to go out and sell them on Dodge again" after the merger.

It was a brilliant strategy, for the Chrysler people were devaluing the car they were trying to buy, which was really important to them only for its plant, while at the same time they were adding a new line that turned out to be a wild success solely due to Walter Chrysler's reputation as a car builder. In the event, Chrysler's organization was so good that they were able both to rebuild Dodge and establish DeSoto as a medium-priced car. Thus in one fell swoop Chrysler added two valuable lines to his company, positioning them to be his competitors to General Motors' Pontiac and Oldsmobile divisions.

Though DeSoto was never intended to be anything but a ploy, that ploy worked because it was presented to the public and the industry as a thoroughly serious proposition, laid out and pursued with full vigor and optimism. In addition to Chrysler's reputation for building exciting high-quality cars, the sell-anything-you-can-build atmosphere of the late 1920s certainly contributed to its initial success. But no one, not even Chrysler on his wildest day would have predicted he would pull out of thin air a car whose first-year sales established a record that would last for almost three decades.

The core DeSoto group was formed in March 1928, and in May the DeSoto Division of the Chrysler Corporation was officially organized. The name DeSoto was officially said to have been chosen from among twenty possibilities to honor the sixteenth-century Spanish explorer Hernando DeSoto, Governor of Cuba and discoverer of the Mississippi River. It was thought that the name would symbolize "travel, pioneering and adventure," according to press releases of the time. However, Joe Frazer, the Chrysler sales whiz who was there when it happened, said, "WP thought Plymouth was such a good old American name that he just grabbed a history book and picked out another one that had a nice ring to it." A Spanish flair was very much in vogue in advertising throughout the United States at that time. Monikers such as Sedan de Lujo, Sedan Coche, and Faeton were attached to various models, along with such Spanglish denotations as Cupe Business and Roadster Español. Officially a 1929 model, the DeSoto was a pleasant-looking car featuring the new Chrysler narrow "ribbon" radiator shell, which distinguished its cars at that time. The car was powered by a 174.9-cubic-inch, 55-horsepower in-line six, and it featured Lovejoy shock absorbers, Lockheed hydraulic brakes, and Delco-Remy ignition, all for prices ranging from $845 for open models to $955 for the Deluxe four-door sedan.

When the car was announced in May 1928, five hundred dealers took franchise options without even seeing the car, and after going to Detroit for a preview, 95 percent of them signed franchise agreements on the spot. By the following January, there were 1,500 dealers selling the cars. By the end of 1928 some 34,518 cars had been shipped to them, a number that rose to 81,065 by the end of its first twelve months of production, enough to wipe out the first-year sales records of Chrysler in 1924, Pontiac in 1926, and Graham-Paige in 1928.

In actuality this car was one of two, the other being the Plymouth, that came out of the Chrysler Four parts bin; the Plymouth was really a made-over Maxwell. The cars shared the same bodies, fenders, hoods, and even chassis dimensions. In fact, the basic difference between the two cars was that DeSoto was a six and the Plymouth was a four, though there was only a 4-cubic-inch difference in their engine displacements. Nascent in the simultaneous development of these two cars was a corporation policy of standardization and interchangeability of parts among lines, a policy that gave the Chrysler Corporation a terrific cost advantage over its competitors during the 1930s. It has long since become standard policy throughout the industry.

With Dodge collapsing and the DeSoto introduction looming large, Dillon was becoming desperate, which was exactly what Walter Chrysler wanted. "One day, Dillon strode into my office and began to moan," Chrysler recalled. It was no surprise. After all, if Dodge Brothers had stopped paying its preferred dividends, not to mention the $3 million a year in interest payments it owed on its bonds, the people who had bought Dodge securities from Dillon three years before might take a very jaundiced view of any future underwritings Dillon, Read might offer. God knows what they would have thought if they knew Dodge Brothers was not even able to meet its latest payroll.

"Walter, bankers got no business trying to run a great big industrial enterprise. What do I know about making automobiles and selling them? That's your game. Why don't you take this Dodge business?" Dillon pleaded.

Chrysler looked at him for about a minute before he spoke.

"Clarence, I haven't time to talk endlessly. You are wasting your time and you are wasting mine. Do you really want to trade? Then put your proposition down on a piece of paper. Mind, your lowest price! And don't forget: I'm not making the proposition; you are bringing it to me. So you had better make it tempting. Set your price and then I'll tell you, yes or no."

Dillon said he would arrive at a price and then come back.

Chrysler could see he was doing figures in his head as he walked out the door, and before he hit the street, Chrysler was on the phone to Hutchinson in Detroit, who began turning everything he could learn about Dodge Brothers into sums on paper. Engineers were sent by both sides into each other's plants for a survey. Then they and the respective companies' accountants met in a Detroit hotel suite to exchange statistics and facts, covering every detail of the operation of each company. Hutchinson gave the Dodge facts to Chrysler, and Dillon's men gave the Chrysler facts to him. Ten days after the previous meeting Dillon came back with sheets of paper on which he had figured everything out from his perspective. Of course, Chrysler had done the same. It was time for the big deal, make or break.

Dillon was drawing up a chair right beside Chrysler's desk.

"Not here, Clarence," Chrysler said.

"What?" asked Dillon, nonplussed.

"Not here. I'm bringing two people into this conference and you can bring in a couple for yourself. You may get a sore throat from talking before we've finished." It was Chrysler's intention to bring in Hutchinson and Albert Rathbone, his personal lawyer as well as the corporation's.

"Where do you want to talk?" asked Dillon.

"We'll go over to the Ritz and get a suite of rooms and, Clarence, we'll stay in that suite until we come to a conclusion, stay until one of us says yes or no."

That is exactly what happened. "We stayed there in that Ritz suite, arguing, eating, smoking and drinking until five days had gone. When we finished, all of us had bloodshot eyes from weariness; but we also knew a feeling of triumph," Chrysler said.

From the beginning, Chrysler insisted that Dillon deliver 90 percent of all classes of Dodge Brothers stock. "We were quite certain that we did not want to merge ourselves with a disgruntled minority." He knew this was a distinct possibility, because one of the classes of Dodge Brothers stock was a preferred class that paid a $7 annual dividend against Chrysler's $3, and also had a market value of $115 against Chrysler's $68.

"Ninety percent of all classes of stock, Clarence, or else—"

'All right, Walter. Give me time enough."

"Two months. If we give you longer the time for creating new car models will be on us and passed before the new management can get a chance to function." Dillon agreed that all the stock would be delivered by July 31, 1928.

As for the shape of the deal, Kennedy summed it up most succinctly. "For the company which had cost Dillon $146 million—and into which the investing public had put $160 million—only three years before, Chrysler did not give one penny in cash." He agreed to take over $57,276,000 in debenture bonds and $2,750,000 of notes connected with Dodge Brothers' acquisition of the Graham Brothers Truck Company. By assuming this debt, he acquired a first-rate trucking concern, which to this day is one of the mainstays of the Chrysler Corporation. (Since Walter Chrysler had never previously shown any interest in trucks whatsoever, it is fair to say he might never have gotten into the trucking business without acquiring Dodge.) "Otherwise, the merger was made through an exchange of stock. Chrysler offered one share of Chrysler common for one share of Dodge preferred, one share of Chrysler common for five shares of Dodge nonvoting common, and one share of Chrysler common for ten shares of the Dodge voting stock held by Dillon, Read." The new stock was valued at some $170 million. In all, 1,253,557 new Chrysler shares were to be issued to the Dodge Brothers shareholders, which at the $3 dividend rate, always capable of being amended, would cost $3 million a year. The Dodge bond interest, which could be and was reduced substantially by retiring some of the debt, cost only $3,360,000 a year. So, for next to nothing, Chrysler was to acquire not only the Dodge car but also the enormous manufacturing enterprise that went with it.

To an outside observer, it looked as if Dillon was making a bad deal. But Dillon knew it was the only way he could save his own neck as well as those of his stockholders. It was a matter of this deal or complete disaster.

At this time Nicholas Kelley was returning from a European trip having to do with tax matters in England, Belgium, and Germany. While his ship was delayed in quarantine, Rathbone wired him to go up to Chrysler's office immediately upon landing. When he set foot on shore, a brother of William F. Kenney, a very wealthy friend of John Raskob and Alfred E. Smith, met Kelley and told him to take a taxi right away, which he did. There he found Chrysler, Rathbone, and the directors of the company. "Rathbone gave me some kind of a sheet of paper, longer than an ordinary sheet, which didn't have much typewriting on it. That was the deal by which Chrysler was to take over the Dodge Brothers company." Kelley revealed in his memoirs that, his own advantage in the stock deal notwithstanding, Chrysler could not have purchased the stock of Dodge Brothers for antitrust reasons. So, there was "some kind of a trade whereby the Dodge stockholders would deposit their stock. We never turned the stock in to the Dodge company, but gave the new Chrysler stock to the Dodge holders, according to what the different classes were entitled to."

"Later on," said Kelley, "I asked Chrysler and Rathbone whether that piece of paper had been a contract or not. Rathbone said he never could make up his mind. He worked very hard on some of the documents, and was very close to the whole thing. But I was great friends with B. Edwin Hutchinson, who was treasurer and vice president of Chrysler, and a very active fellow. Rathbone said I was to put it through."

Kelley worked out the strategy of the deal that night and the next day, which was Memorial Day. Though it was very complex, the basic agreement had been sketchily written out on that one piece of paper, and Kelley realized that to a certain extent, as things went along, "you had to make it up." He came to the conclusion that the essence of the deal was that the Chrysler side had to demonstrate continually that it was both willing to perform what it said it could perform and capable of doing so. Kelley had to make sure that he was on top of things at every moment, especially since "it turned out that Dillon's strategy was to say he couldn't perform it and to try to get concessions from us. There were all kinds of things to be done, and you had to work on everything so that it would be ready in time," Kelley said. "You couldn't get in something that might delay or defeat the deal from our side.

"Every step of this thing required making up your mind one way or the other. In order to be able to perform, you had to be careful that in every one of those decisions you didn't get yourself into something that might jeopardize your capacity to perform. For instance, you couldn't get into a squabble with the Stock Exchange over some demand they made on you for listing the new stock and get yourself into a position where they wouldn't list it, or delay listing it." Hutchinson and Chrysler were on his back to make sure there was nothing he was doing that would cause such a delay; they wanted to be sure they were ready to deliver the stock if the deal did go through.

For purposes of economy and simplicity, they also wanted him to call in

Chrysler's cumulative preferred Chrysler stock. This meant that in addition to everything else connected with the merger, Kelley had to track down 220,937 Chrysler $8 preferred shares and get them redeemed at $115 each by August 6. Then, too, Kelley had to amend the Chrysler Corporation's charter and increase the number of the company's authorized shares.

"There was a lot to do. There was an agreement between Dodge Brothers, Incorporated, and the Chrysler Corporation. This was where we undertook to borrow all their assets and business and pay for it in stock. Then there were deposit agreements we had to draw for the deposit of the new classes of stock. We had to read the investment law in all kinds of stuff."

Everything boiled down to two big agreements. Kelley drew one up with Joseph P. Cotton, later Under Secretary of State, who represented Dillon, Read, and Rathbone drew up the other with George Franklin, Cotton's associate. (Arthur A. Ballentine of Root, Clark, Buckner, Howland and Ballantine represented Dodge Brothers in the deal.)

"The agreement said that Dodge Brothers had to deposit 90% of all classes of stock. I put into those agreements—I always drew things that way—that the amount of stock deposited should be determined by the certificate of the depositaries, so that it would be conclusive," just as Chrysler had instructed.

It's a good thing he did, for just as Chrysler had anticipated, trouble showed up, and the 90 percent deposit requirement gave the Dillon side an excellent incentive to resolve it, for Chrysler made it clear he wouldn't budge from this provision under any circumstances.

"Some strikers came along, to enjoin this thing. They got hold of some stockholders. I think they hoped to do a sort of John Thomas thing on us [he was the GM man who had used undeposited stock to hold up Chrysler for a million dollars in the Maxwell reorganization]—they didn't know about that, of course—to make us pay more, or threaten us with getting under the appraisal staff, claiming that they didn't have to take the stock we were offering and would get it appraised for cash."

The problem appeared in the form of an injunction sought by Colonel Calvin Hooker Goddard, an officer in the United States Reserves, who was represented by House, Holthusen & McCloskey. Goddard, who owned a hundred shares of Dodge Brothers $7 preferred, claimed that the Chrysler-Dodge merger was in fact a dissolution, and that therefore the preferred shareholders were entitled to redeem their shares at $105 each, which is what the initial sale of the shares had provided. Goddard contended that under the proposed exchange, Dodge Brothers' shareholders would be contributing over 50 percent of the assets of the merged corporation while receiving only 29 percent of its stock. He said that in the process they would be giving up preferred stock "for a minority common stock interest of a speculative nature." Since that stock was valued at only $68, the preferred shareholders would be losing a third of the value of their shares, and over half their $7 dividend, since Chrysler stock paid just $3.

Cotton got right on this problem. He contended that the proceedings were indeed a merger, rather than a dissolution, and that under the laws of the state of Maryland, where Dodge Brothers was chartered, the plaintiff was entitled to fair value for his stock without regard to the merger. In other words, the value of the stock before the merger was announced, which ranged between $69 and $71.75. Cotton suggested that the effect of the plaintiff's action was to have a hundred shares of preferred stock run the whole Dodge Brothers corporation. Maryland Supreme Court Justice Mullan agreed with Cotton, specifying that as long as the Chrysler Corporation set up a bond to pay for any dissenter's stock redeemed for cash, the merger plan could go forward.

Cotton performed his function with a good deal of style. Kelley recalled that during one tense meeting with the strikers, Cotton got up, "picked up a little black suitcase, and said, 'Goodbye. I'm going to Ireland. I've promised a friend I'm going to see the races there. He's got a horse.' And he just walked out," leaving everybody nonplussed, and the situation defused.

Eventually, most of the preferred-share holders did accept the tender offer, but as the July 31 deadline approached, Dillon was having difficulty coming up with the last of the preferred shares he needed to fulfill the agreement, and several times he came around to ask for an extension from Walter Chrysler, who always refused. He simply would not allow this deal to become a Pandora's box of problems because of these preferred shares.

On July 26 the deadline for the big Dodge Brothers stockholders' meeting to approve the merger in Baltimore was only forty-eight hours off, and Dillon still did not have enough of the preferred shares in hand. So he and his son, C. Douglas Dillon, later U.S. Ambassador to France and Secretary of the Treasury, went up to see Walter Chrysler, hats in hand. Knowing he had his back against a wall, Clarence Dillon gave it his all.

Kelley was in the room with Chrysler, and according to him, after Dillon explained his situation, "he went up to Chrysler, put his arm around him, and asked about this. Chrysler put his head down, and was that way for a long time. Then he got up, put his hand on Dillon's shoulder, and said, 'I'm sorry, Clarence. I can't do nothing for you.'

"Dillon stood to lose a great deal. I suppose he had spent a lot of money trying to get in this stock, going around to see stockholders and all. Also, he had a customer for Dodge in Chrysler. Otherwise he'd have the whole thing on his hands, if this thing was a failure. This was 'Black Thursday' to him because it looked like the collapse of this deal."

Walter Chrysler's account of his conversation with Dillon continued: "I can't do something for you at the expense of the Chrysler stockholders. You know that."

"Great grief, Walter, I've got 85% of the stock. That's more than is ever brought in on a deal of this kind."

"Well agree on that, Mr. Dillon," said Albert Rathbone, "but this is another deal. We said 90 per cent. You agreed."

"But Walter, you want to make this deal."

"Yes, but on the terms agreed upon."

"Here's what I'm up against. One of the large stockholders is in Paris. Her stocks are out in the vault in Detroit. She's got the key. That's why I can't put my hands on those 60,000 shares of preferred."

"Clarence, when the day comes we ring the bell and the deal is off—unless you deliver."

"Walter, I can't do it in two days."

"Clarence, it has not been a matter of two days. It has been 60 days, lacking two. I think you can do it. But if you don't, the deal is off." These were Chrysler's final words on the subject.

He recalled: "As Clarence rushed out of the office, seemingly in despair, even my own lawyers seemed to be looking at me with reproachful eyes." But he was obdurate.

So it was back to the lawyers for the final countdown. Kelley recalled calling up Chrysler out in Montauk point, where he was fishing, and speaking to him for hours and hours. "One night I was sleeping with Hutchinson in the Biltmore Hotel. We had gotten to bed fairly late. The telephone rang about three o'clock in the morning. I guess it was Ferdinand Eberstadt, who was with Cotton and Franklin then. He said that National City Bank (one of 14 depositories nationwide, a number necessitated by the wide geographic distribution of Dodge Brothers' shareholders) had over certified by 37,000 shares the preferred stock, and that there was actually 37,000 shares less than they thought they had. They were that much deeper in a hole. We said that was too bad, but told them, 'Go and get it.' That was all we could do at three o'clock in the morning.

"I don't know what magic they used, but they got in 90% of each class of stock by the specified time. It was all done, and the deal went through."

Actually, it was accomplished through a great deal of nail biting maneuvering on the part of Clarence Dillon between July 28 and the absolute deadline on July 31. At the stockholders' meeting on Saturday the 28th, it was determined that Dillon was still 100,000 shares short of Dodge Brothers' common Series A and 50,000 shares short of the preferred. After E. G. Wilmer endured the taunts and caustic comments of dissident preferred shareholder Hagop Bagigian (300 shares), mostly with silence, it was decided to reconvene the meeting on Monday morning at 10:00 A.M. to determine how many shares had come in by midnight Saturday. On Monday morning it was determined that Dillon was still lacking a small number of preferred shares, so the meeting was postponed several times during the day to allow him to make up the deficit. He did it by going into the market and buying up what he needed, which turned out to be about 12,000 shares which he bought for about $80 each. As soon as he bought the shares, he gave assent for them to the merger. Long after the market closed a telegram was sent to Walter Chrysler in New York from Baltimore announcing that the Dodge Brothers stockholders had approved the merger. (Only 300 preferred shares were voted against it—those of Hagop Bagigian.)

Chrysler summed it all up this way: "There was a happy ending because Clarence, before the time limit expired, produced the 60,000 shares. I never asked him how, or when, he got them. That deal was closed July 31, 1928." At the moment of the signing, the new, enlarged Chrysler Corporation, the third-largest automobile company in the world, came into being.

The following morning Dillon came over to Chrysler's office to smoke a cigarette and assure Chrysler that he needn't worry about anything, since the Dodge organization could run by itself for three months if Chrysler wanted it to.

" 'Hell, Clarence,' I said, 'our boys moved in last night.' They had too, with K. T. Keller in command. Just before 5 o'clock in the afternoon, as the papers were signed, I had picked up the telephone to talk with Keller in Detroit. 'We've bought the Dodge,' I told him. 'Put up your signs.'

"Those canvas signs, prepared several days before, bore this legend: CHRYSLER CORPORATION, DODGE DIVISION. Squads of Keller's men had the signs in big trucks, and when he got my word, Keller gave them the signal to nail them up on the Dodge plants. At the same time Keller, with half a dozen of his men, entered the Dodge headquarters and told the president of Dodge that we were running the plant from that moment. The next minute they were running it and the Chrysler Corporation, by that act, had become a larger organization by five or six fold."

Wilmer courteously went to Chrysler to offer the services of the top Dodge executives to help with the transition, but Chrysler declined, saying he did not require it. Two days later Wilmer resigned as president, along with chairman of the board Haynes and Arthur T. Waterfall, vice president of traffic. A public statement said they all had desired to retire from the company for some time. Under this top level other executives of the company were retained. As could be expected, Walter Chrysler became president of the Dodge Division, K. T. Keller became vice-president in charge of operations, J. E. Fields, also president of DeSoto, was appointed vice president in charge of sales, and B. E. Hutchinson was tapped to be in charge of Dodge's finances. In 1929 K. T. Keller was appointed president of Dodge.

They all had their work cut out for them, as the Dodge line was slipping and no one had figured out where it would fit into a line in which it overlapped with both the Chrysler and the new DeSoto. It took quite some time to straighten things out, but in the end Dodge (its name was changed from

Dodge Brothers in 1930) did better than a good many other lines in the economic crisis to come.

The new company had a production capacity of 750,000 cars. Its market capitalization was somewhere between $450 million and $500 million, or an eighth that of GM and between a third and a quarter of privately held Ford's net worth. It also had combined tangible assets of approximately $235 million, or about a third that of Ford and 23 percent of GM's. There were 4,423,484 shares of stock issued out of 6 million authorized shares. Total debt was some $461 million.

"Downtown, in New York, in 1928, the consensus was: Chrysler's bought a lemon," Walter Chrysler reflected. "That was the opinion of some minds that contained little understanding of industry, and especially of the automobile industry. Buying the Dodge was one of the soundest acts of my life. I say sincerely that nothing we have done for the organization compares with that transaction."

There was indeed a great deal of talk on Wall Street. One wag characterized the transaction as "a minnow swallowing a whale," since the Dodge Brothers' properties were a good deal larger than Chrysler's. But Chrysler's annual dollar volume had caused it to zoom from twenty-seventh place in industry rankings in 1924 to third in 1928, even before the merger, and its profits were among the industry's highest; as we have seen, Dodge's were collapsing, even on volume of 150,000 cars.

It didn't take very much time for everyone to realize that Dillon had made a very good deal for his stockholders—and himself. Only eleven days after the merger, Chrysler stock rose to $94.75 a share, up $9.50 on that day alone, pushed up in tandem with the remaining Dodge Brothers preferred still on the market, mostly by the former dissenters who had now done an about-face on the merger. This meant that, as pure lagniappe, Dillon, Read made a profit of about $180,000 on the shares it was forced to buy on July 31. On August 23, Chrysler issued 30,000 new shares of stock that were snapped up immediately for nearly twice the base asking price of $57.50. By October 11 Chrysler stock was up to $132, and the remaining holders of Dodge Brothers common Class A stock had created a technical corner in it at $167!

From the time of the merger announcement, rumors abounded about Walter Chrysler. The *Detroit News* on May 30, 1928, said that "a report current in the financial district is that the present move is only part of a larger plan whereby, when the present deal is completed, Chrysler will enter the General Motors Corporation through an exchange of one share of General Motors common for two shares of Chrysler, and that Walter P. Chrysler will become president of General Motors." It also suggested he might have bought Dodge to produce his new DeSoto car in its plants. On June 6 the *New York Times* said, "At the time of the first announcement of the merger last week, it was reported in the financial district that the manufacturer and bankers who had arranged the deal were looking about for other properties and that the aim was to make the combination a formidable competitor of the General Motors Corporation." By August 11 the *Times* was reporting rumors that GM executives were buying up Chrysler stock, and that John J. Raskob, having left GM, was preparing to join Chrysler (not true; he left GM to manage Governor Alfred E. Smith's campaign for the Presidency of the United States). On October 17 a third *Times* article reported European rumors that Ford might be combining with Chrysler to fight off competition from GM.

As early as that June 6 *Times* article, Chrysler was giving out denials of all this. "In recommending to our stockholders a proposal to acquire the great Dodge Brothers properties, we have been actuated by a disposition to benefit both businesses, and also to contribute to the economic efficiency and soundness of the industry as a whole. We have no disposition to attain mere size or volume. We have no thought of rivalry with existing great companies or combinations. We do not look beyond Dodge Brothers to the acquisition of other properties." To the *Literary Digest* he said, "If we grow, we will grow according to our financial, marketing, and manufacturing capacities—not beyond them—in a straining after domination. Sound business is not best subserved by endeavoring to outdistance other manufacturing factors."

The next year B. C. Forbes asked Chrysler, "Why did you buy Dodge?"

"When you are riding a bicycle, you either have to go ahead or you fall off," he replied. "We had been going ahead, and the opportunity to acquire Dodge afforded opportunity to make another advance, to take a constructive step. It so happened that both Clarence Dillon, the dominant factor in Dodge, and I felt that the property was more valuable to our company than to anybody else. If we hadn't taken over Dodge, we would have found another channel for expansion. Dodge is going to prove a great asset."

Throughout the 1920s things were changing rapidly in the auto industry. The number of firms producing cars shrank dramatically, and the merger of Chrysler and Dodge in 1928 made it clear to even the dullest observers that huge combines were going to produce most of the cars in the United States in the future. By the end of the year, GM, Ford, and Chrysler were producing in excess of 80 percent of American cars, with the remaining thirty-four manufacturers scrambling for the balance. William L. Ayers observed in the Chicago *Journal of Commerce*, "The consolidation era in the industry is at hand. Men who know say that in three to five years there will be only about eight or ten big automobile companies." The *Literary*

Digest detailed a more extreme prediction, which turned out to be prescient in many ways: "Noting that Ford, General Motors and the Chrysler-Dodge combination now control about 80% of the total output of cars, the Providence *News* thinks it is very likely that within five years the three will make practically all the cars produced in the country, and 'what will happen then is hard to foresee.'

" 'If the "Big Three" are wise they will come to some arrangement by which they will make a scientific division of the market, at the same time contenting themselves with reasonable profits. If they are not wise, they will form some huge supercorporation, and try to sell cars at exorbitant prices that will soon kill off demand. The present prosperity of the automobile industry rests on the fact that it is giving good value for the people's money. If it will continue that practice, it will have nothing to fear from the future.' " It turned out that they were wise in the way the *News* prescribed. But who then knew that despite their good sense they were going to have a great deal to fear in the future?

Others, such as automotive financial analyst Ralph C. Epstein, saw things a bit differently. While thoroughly recognizing the advantages of great size in the automobile industry in terms of finance, research, and flexibility, he nevertheless thought a well-managed smaller firm could find and maintain a niche in the field. After all, the automobile had gone from a utility product to a style product in a few short years, and even a small manufacturer who could give the public what it wanted could succeed, as long as it maintained its managerial and financial integrity. Therefore he thought the thirty-odd manufacturers of 1928 might be whittled down to half that, rather than the five or six some were predicting.

"Efficiency Without Volume," a study of Stutz that appeared in *Iron Age* in May 1927, highlighted the company's viewpoint that successful car manufacturing called for individuality rather than standardization, as long as opportunities for production economies were not overlooked. The article told of Stutz's budget plans, inventory control, mechanical handling of materials, minute mechanical inspections, waste reduction, daily meetings of foremen to inspect rejected materials for possible salvage, and bonuses to foremen who reduced losses. Stutz didn't have the volume or the finances to justify becoming a mass production company, but the article showed it was trying hard to do its best on its own terms.

Five months earlier, Henry Ford told J. Younger in *Manufacturing Industries* that the basic principles of manufacturing are the following: "1) Do the job in the most direct fashion without bothering with red tape. 2) Pay every man well and see he is employed all the time through a 48 hour week and no longer. And 3) Put all machinery in the best possible condition and keep it that way." But Henry Ford was applying these principles to mass production, and that made all the difference. By 1934 Ford was still one of the automotive giants and making millions, even after the depradations of the Great Depression. Stutz was out of business.

Chrysler was not out of business. In fact, by 1934 his firm had risen to be the second largest in the industry, bigger than Ford, which had been number one until Henry Ford shut down Model T production in 1927. Chrysler did this by realizing two things. First, he understood how right Clarence Dillon had been when he told Chrysler he was bumping his head against the ceiling in the midpriced field. Ralph C. Epstein shrewdly noticed what no one else did—that the new Chrysler-Dodge combination in 1928 was producing almost as many vehicles in this price range as General Motors, showing that the newly merged firm had made a strategic coup that strengthened it as a mass production firm. Between them, Chrysler-Dodge and GM now had 50 percent of the middle price category—though, as Dillon had noted, that category was limited in the number of buyers it could attract due to sheer economics.

Second, Chrysler realized that the real action, the place where the big sales increases could take place, was in the low-priced category dominated by Ford and Chevrolet. More value than ever before was being packed into cars in this price range, and buyers were becoming much more demanding. In addition to mechanical value, they also wanted style. Even Henry Ford was forced to realize this, and his snappy new Model A was jam-packed with power, sophisticated mechanical features, and Lincoln-inspired good looks for as little as $460. The mass production market had become the mass-class production market, bringing in the buyers through a mixture of trade-ins, low prices, E - Z credit, and prosperity. To expand in any meaningful way, Chrysler knew he had to get into the market at this level. The way he chose to do it was with a new four-cylinder car called the Plymouth.

The first inkling of this car appeared in the press on August 17, 1927, in an article in the New York Times. "Chrysler Plans Mystify Wall Street" was the headline; the subhead read, "Announcement of New Car Is Thought to Presage Race with New Ford Model." The previous day ads had appeared stating that Chrysler would announce a "an entirely new motor car" the following Saturday. Since the announcement of Ford's new "mystery car" replacement for the Model T had been delayed, there was much Wall Street speculation that the car itself would not actually appear until late 1927 or early 1928. For this reason it was thought that the ambitious Walter Chrysler might be trying to beat Ford to the market with a new low-priced car, though no one actually knew what Chrysler had in mind. It would be some nine months before they did.

A full year before that little flurry of speculation Chrysler made plain what was on his mind with regard to the low-priced field in an interview he gave to Automobile Topics, on August 14, 1926. "A large undeveloped market in the small car field for a larger and greatly improved product is seen by Walter P. Chrysler, president of the Chrysler Corporation," the article said. "This belief persists, he says, in spite of the fact that there are 20 million motor cars owned in the United States.

'There is no question in my mind,' Chrysler states, 'but what the people who prefer a low priced, quality automobile are desirous of having built into that car certain features that heretofore have not been made available to that field. The industry has not given sufficient attention to the man who drives a small, low priced car. It simply has gone on the assumption that the same measure of comforts that must be incorporated into every car of higher price, if it is to be successful, could not be built into the smaller cars.

'I disagree most emphatically with that assumption. The person who prefers to drive a small car is entitled to every consideration that can be given him. It is possible to build the qualities of comfort, roominess, easy riding and long life into a small car. The possibilities with such a car are so tremendous that it can actually be built in great quantities at remarkably low cost, if the manufacturer has the capacity and organization to do it.

'Medical authorities have definitely established the fact that the man who continuously drives a small car suffers from abnormal and excessive fatigue and nervous strain because of the noise, jolting, bouncing and excessive vibration he has always undergone to date in that type car. He has been compelled to put up with these discouraging conditions because, up to the present, no one has gone about the task of designing a small, low cost car that remedied them.

'There is a ready made market of 100,000 cars the first year for the company which produces that type of car. We are going to do it. Unless we are far astray in our judgement of what the American public wants in the so called small car field, it will appreciate such a car to the extent that it will make it an outstanding success.' "

This statement is a blueprint for Walter Chrysler's vision of his entry into the low-priced field. Though by this time he was already making a Chrysler Four which allowed him to remain in the lower regions of the mid-priced field formerly covered by the Maxwell, this was only a stopgap; he would have to go through another two years of careful planning before he could fully realize his ambitions in this area.

The development of this car was kept as a closely held secret until May of 1927, at which time sketchy reports of a new Plymouth car from an unnamed company began to appear in the press. Actual production of the car, designated the Model Q, began at the Highland Park plant on June 11, 1928.

In some ways the Plymouth was yet another version of the old Maxwell, though you would have to look hard to know that. It was quite an attractive package, styled to resemble the new Chrysler Model 65. (Bodies were built by Briggs, with some four-door sedans built by Hayes.) It had the corporation's signature ribbon radiator shell, which made the car look longer and more substantial, and full crown fenders and bowl-shaped headlamps. The body sat on a 109.75-inch wheelbase, and its fenders had a baked enamel finish. The engine was the same 170.3-cubic-inch in-line four that Chrysler had bored out for its Model 52 the previous year, to raise its horsepower to 45; the compression ratio was 4:6 to 1, which shows how far such things had advanced since the debut of the original Chrysler car in 1924.

Plymouth historian Jim Benjaminson notes, "Rubber body mounts helped isolate road noise and vibration from the passenger compartment; rubber was also used in the three point engine support system—the forerunner of what would eventually become Plymouth's famous 'Floating Power' engine mounts. . . . The rubber was vulcanized to the steel, making it virtually a one piece unit." Among the many high-quality features included in the car were full-pressure lubrication, waterproof distributor and coil with semi-automatic advance, aluminum alloy pistons, and internally expanding four-wheel hydraulic brakes. "Among the low priced cars on the market, Plymouth was the only one to feature these brakes," says Benjaminson, and it was many years before Chevrolet, and finally Ford, gave in and matched Plymouth in this area.

Why was it called Plymouth? In the first ad, signed by Walter Chrysler, which appeared in the *Saturday Evening Post* on July 7, 1928, he said: "We have named it the Plymouth because this new product of Chrysler engineering and craftsmanship so accurately typifies the endurance and strength, the rugged honesty, the enterprise, the determination of achievement and the freedom from old limitations of that Pilgrim band who were the first American colonists." The ad headlined, "A New Car . . . a New Car Style, a New Zenith of Low Priced Car-Luxury and Performance," just as Chrysler had been promising.

Chrysler vice president and general sales manager Joe Frazer, later to become a principal in the Kaiser-Frazer combine after World War II, actually named the car. According to Richard Langworth, he thought it was "a good old American name," but other executives balked. Then Frazer asked Chrysler, "Ever hear of Plymouth Binder Twine?" "Hell," replied Chrysler, "every farmer in America's heard of that!" Chrysler was very much trying to focus in on Henry Ford's traditional rural farmer's market, so Plymouth it was. Jim Benjamin's fine history *Plymouth 1946–1959* shows a photo of an old Plymouth Rope sign featuring the legend, "Plymouth Rope, The Rope You Can Trust." Beneath these words is a circle of rope tied into several fancy knots, surrounding an illustration of a sailing ship and the words, "Plymouth Trade Mark 1824." The similarity between this and the Plymouth sailing ship badge and hood ornament which survived in many guises for thirty years after the car's intoduction in 1928 is obvious, lending considerable credence to this account.

Sales kits sent out to dealers for Plymouth's introduction contained Pilgrim costumes and blunderbusses that dealers and their staffs were encouraged to make use of in dealership displays. "Plymouth Parades" were held in many localities. When the cars were shipped, they were covered with canvas with the letters of the Plymouth name scrambled so that bystanders had to figure out just what kind of car lay underneath. Little pictures of Pilgrims and homilies to their virtues appeared in Plymouth ads for quite some time. The cars were available at all five thousand Chrysler outlets, and having learned his lesson about the value of the Chrysler name on the car, it was originally advertised and badged as a "Chrysler Plymouth" until the Plymouth name was deemed to be well enough known and respected on its own.

The car ranged in price from $670 to $725, matching the prices of the previous Chrysler Model 52 Four. But this was only temporary, as Chrysler intended to follow the example of his idol Henry Ford, using the benefits of volume mass production to increase the quality of his new car at ever lower prices. As time passed, this is exactly what he did.

Legend has it that Walter Chrysler himself drove the first Plymouth to come off the assembly line over to Ford's River Rouge plant to show it to Henry and Edsel Ford. Though the Fords admired the car, Henry's response to it was: "Walter, you'll go broke trying to get in the low price market. We and Chevrolet have that market sewed up, and as sure as you try to step in, we'll stop you." With his usual aplomb, Chrysler spent a pleasant time with them, and paid them no heed whatsoever.

The official inauguration of the car took place at Madison Square Garden in New York City on July 7, 1928. World-famous aviatrix Amelia Earhart, who just the previous month had become the first woman to fly across the Atlantic Ocean, drove a Plymouth into the arena, and introduced the car to a clamorous public. Within a week thirty thousand people crowded into the Chicago Coliseum to see it. The totally new Ford Model A had debuted to tumultuous acclaim and unprecedented public interest only eight months before, and a beautifully redesigned Chevrolet had been greeted with wide public acceptance a month after that, but already the public was ready to line up for the latest automotive novelty.

The very first Plymouth, a $670 coupe, was sold to Mrs. Ethel Miller of Turlock, California.

Costing nearly 50 percent more than comparable Ford and Chevrolet models, this new Plymouth was not really a low-priced car. Willys-Overland's remarkable $525 Whippet, the number-three-selling individual make after Ford and Chevrolet in 1928, was the true low-priced competition that year. But eager buyers snapped it up, and after only three months Chrysler was selling every Plymouth it could build. On top of this, it was also selling every DeSoto, announced August 4, it could push out of the factory.

This meant that almost before the dust had settled on the announcements of his new products, Chrysler was finding himself in a production bind of the highest order. The problem was that all these cars, plus the Chrysler Model 65, were being produced at the Highland Park plant, which had a capacity of about 1,000 cars a day. Then in September, Chrysler added its new line of Fargo trucks, which also came from the same facility. It was sheer madness. According to Eugene Weiss, the problem was that the bankers behind Chrysler were getting scared. He had just arranged this enormous takeover of Dodge, but no longer seemed interested in it. It looked as if all his attention was going into the new lines.

In August a two-story mezzanine structure 1,000 feet long was added to Chrysler's Jefferson Avenue plant to make a total assembly line of 1,400 feet, and Chrysler 65 production was moved there from Highland Park, giving extra capacity for the new brands. But even this wasn't enough help. Inaugurating all these new lines was "a big gamble for Walter Chrysler," says Eugene Weiss. "He didn't have the capacity for volume production. Now that they were a smashing success, he needed new production facilities fast. He was looking over a cliff." If he couldn't deliver cars, all the momentum he had built up could be lost quickly, and for good.

What needed to be done was obvious. "Quick decision and quick action have always been characteristic of the automobile industry," said an article in *Machinery* in May, 1929. "The achievements of this industry have been due largely to the imagination and courage of the leaders in this field and to the ability of their engineers to complete a new project in a short space of time. The latest example of this is furnished by the Chrysler Corporation in building and equipping an exceptionally modern plant in Detroit for the new Plymouth car. The story of this achievement is one of the finest examples of what can be accomplished in a brief period of time by sound business judgement and capable engineering talent, backed by ample financial resources."

On August 16 Walter Chrysler made the decision to build a new plant for Plymouth production. *Machinery* described the process he set in motion: "In five days, complete cost estimates were prepared, covering a new building and machine tool and other plant equipment. On August 22 the appropriation for the new plant was made, and immediately an organization was gathered together, factory layouts were made, and building plans were completed." Albert Kahn, the inventor of the reinforced concrete modern factory building, designed the plant, which was to be located at the corner of Mt. Elliot and Lynch Roads. It would stretch for 2,490 feet, cover 22.7 acres of floor space under one roof and on one level, and would be the largest automobile plant in the world. Dodge Main was served by a huge railroad yard to its east, and Mt. Elliot was located on the other side of this yard, so the new plant automatically would have access to railroad shipping, which was an enormous plus. The nucleus of the operation was a 1,950-foot sawtooth-roof Dodge building that had been built just before the Chrysler-Dodge merger.

Ground was broken for the new building on October 10, and despite the depradations of an exceptionally cold winter, the first cars rolled off the uncompleted assembly line on December 28, just seventy-nine days later.

"This building was state of the art in construction methods," notes Eugene Weiss. "It was built so fast because it was a prefabricated building, with an all concrete floor and steel reinforced concrete walls cut to size. You could just pour the concrete and roof in the building from whatever point you wanted, which gave a great deal of flexibility to its construction."

What they decided to do was employ four teams of workers, both to build out from the center and simultaneously to build in from both ends. Huge canvas drapes were hung over the ends of unfinished portions of the factory to protect workers from the bitterly cold weather, but they and a fired-up New York Central locomotive parked next to the factory could do little to alleviate the frigid atmosphere inside the unheated building. Nevertheless, as soon as a portion was completed, the company put people to work inside it, so great was the need for personnel to turn out cars.

By January 15 the entire plant was completed, and two 1,500-foot assembly lines, each with a capacity for 500 cars daily, went to work. The plant itself was cutting-edge, with 14.5 miles of conveyors and practically no trucking inside the building. It was laid out with a view to eliminating all waste effort, and every operation that could be performed automatically was so handled. "The total time from the moment that the frame enters the assembly line until the completed car, with gasoline in the tank and a driver on the seat, leaves the assembly line, is two hours and 40 minutes," *Machinery* said. "Eight different models of the Plymouth car are built, but through variations in the painting and striping of the bodies, the types of wheels used, upholstering, etc., 250 different combinations are available. It takes about one hour from the time that the wheels and bodies are placed on the chassis until the completely assembled, tested, and inspected car is ready for delivery, and it is literally possible for the sales department to ask a customer to sit down and wait for an hour while a special combination to his own specifications is assembled and made ready for him to drive away. Thus the speed and efficiency of building and equipping this plant has been carried right through the building and assembling of the product."

K. T. Keller was in charge of the whole project, as Chrysler had a well-founded confidence in his ability to get the job done. In 1931, with sales slipping because of the Depression, DeSoto production was moved to this facility from Highland Park. A body shop and engine plant were added to the setup in 1932, along with a third assembly line. By this time the plant could produce 2,800 of the DeSotos and the ever more popular Plymouths each day, turning out 90 cars an hour on the three lines in three shifts.

By the time that first Model Q Plymouth ceased production on February 4, 1929, some 66,097 had been produced under extremely makeshift circumstances. This was more than double the production of the Chrysler car in its initial year, and when added to the 81,000 DeSotos produced in the same plant in what was also its first year, Chrysler Corporation had totted up quite a performance. All in all, including Chrysler and Dodge, the corporation turned out 360,000 cars in calendar 1928, which indeed placed it third in the industry, though admittedly a distant third, behind GM and Ford.

Other things were going on in the company then, too, things that would have been important items in an ordinary year, but in 1928 at Chrysler, they just seemed to be minor happenings of passing interest. For one thing, Chrysler now fielded a brand-new Imperial model, the L-80, introduced in November of 1927. It featured the much-heralded "Red Head," a 112-horsepower high-compression engine. Displacement of the six-cylinder power plant was increased from 288.7 to 309.3 cubic inches by increasing the bore from 3.5 to 3.625 inches. The compression ratio, formerly 4:7 to 1, was raised to 6:1 to 1, made possible by the new no-knock Ethyl gasoline. With a top speed of 80 miles per hour, the new Imperial was touted as "America's Most Powerful Motor Car." (A lower-compression "Silver Dome" engine, rated at 100 horsepower, was available for the less adventurous motorist.)

Five standard factory bodies were joined by an array of custom bodies for the first time, from such prestigious firms as LeBaron, Dietrich, and Locke. Starting in 1927, all retained the rounded radiator with Vauxhall-style fluting extending back into the hood. (Vauxhall finally filed suit over this, but the matter was settled out of court, on terms that have never been publicly disclosed.) Prices ranged from $2,795 to $6,795.

Perhaps the most striking of all these 1928 Imperials was the Locke-bodied Touralette, provided to Chrysler under license from the man who actually designed it, John Tjaarda, later to become world famous as the designer of one of the most graceful modern automobiles, the 1936 Lincoln Zephyr. The Touralette was a two-door convertible sedan featuring an integral trunk with leather-covered lid, a continuation of the Imperial hood styling flutes around the entire car body, and, most notably, hand-painted canework on the complete rear portion of the body. At $4,485, it attracted twenty-one customers and was quite an attention getter for the company. One photo preserved by Dwight Cervin shows President and Mrs. Calvin

Coolidge and their son John in the backseat of a shiny Chrysler Imperial Locke Touralette, being driven to an American Legion convention in Wausau, Wisconsin. A typically taciturn Coolidge is tipping his silk top hat to the crowd as he glides by in the brilliant sunshine.

Chrysler cars were increasingly used to demonstrate power. In 1927 a Chrysler Phaeton was used in a cross-country run to illustrate the efficiency of Stover Signal Engineering Company headlights. It went from San Francisco to New York and back to Los Angeles in one minute less than a week, averaging 40.2 miles per hour. The car's performance was so much on target that its drivers, L. B. Miller and J. B. Weiber, used to telegraph ahead for ice cream without worry of arriving to find a melted mess in their plates.

In 1928 Chrysler entered four Model 72 roadsters in the Twenty Four Hours of LeMans, with the two cars that finished the race placing third and fourth in their class; the better of the two averaged 64.56 miles per hour for the race. This showing was truly extraordinary for what were basically 85-horsepower, $1,595 stock cars with much of the comfort features removed, up against some of the world's most exotic sports cars. The race was narrowly won by a $6,500, 110-horsepower, 4.5-liter Bentley, barely trailed by an overhead-cam $5,750 Stutz 125-housepower straight eight. This marked the best showing for American cars at LeMans for thirty-eight years.

An Imperial L-80 took second place in the Belgian Twenty Four Hour Grand Prix at Spa several weeks later. It was backed up by two Chrysler Model 72's that placed third and sixth, respectively, in the same race. Model 72's also placed second and third in the Mille Miglia, second in the Burgundy Four-Hour, and first in class in the Spanish Grand Prix. It was the most successful year ever for Chrysler in European road racing.

That same year, too, five Chryslers were purchased by representatives of the Japanese government for the ceremonies surrounding the coronation of the new Mikado.

Any one of the things Walter Chrysler and his cars did in 1928 would have been at least noteworthy, and many of them were extremely impressive. But all of them together constitute what is perhaps the most compact and significant series of major events in automobile history. Mass production was of monumental importance to the car industry, of course, but it took Henry Ford and his team over half a decade to work it out. True, Billy Durant created General Motors in a few short strokes in 1908, but the job was so badly done in important ways that it almost collapsed beyond repair in two years' time. It took seven years before it became clear that the combination was out of the woods and poised to become a worldwide industry leader. Chrysler's combination worked right from the start, and continued to do so during the greatest economic crisis the country would ever know. It worked because, when the opportunities were at hand, Chrysler was prepared to seize them.

At the beginning of 1928 Walter Chrysler knew as much as any man alive about product design, production, finance, promotion, and, most of all, how to build, deploy, and keep a team of personnel. It had taken thirty-five years from the time he began to recognize his own abilities for life to carve him into some kind of a great man. But at last it had happened, and he made the most of it. At fifty-three he was at the peak of his abilities, the lifetime top of his form.

Emerson said that any institution is but the elongated shadow of one man. Ford was a one-man band. General Motors, which by 1928 had created the modern hierarchical corporation, reflected the combined vision of Alfred P. Sloan and Pierre S. du Pont. Chrysler was an organization of extraordinary minds and abilities that took their direction from the eponymous man at the top, but operated with flexibility, freedom, and devotion. The molding of that organization so that it could function like a fine jeweled mechanism was the great thing Walter Chrysler had learned in his life. Now his accumulated wisdom would bear manifold, ripe fruit in the successes of his company.

This is what he did in 1928: May 30th, Chrysler announces the acquisition of Dodge Brothers; July 2, 1928, the Chrysler Engineering Building is opened; July 7, 1928, the Plymouth car debuts; July 31, 1928, Chrysler completes its acquisition of Dodge Brothers, and becomes the third-largest automobile company in the world; August 4th, 1928, the DeSoto car debuts, going on to establish a first-year production record that will last for almost thirty years; October 10th, production begins on the Lynch Road Plymouth plant, which, together with the acquisition of Dodge, fully assures Chrysler's basis for ever expanding mass production in the 1930s. Following upon each other with astonishing speed, these accomplishments seen together form a magnificent platform of achievement for Walter Chrysler.

Upon it he was about to place one of the twentieth century's greatest monuments. On October 16, 1928, he announced that he would build what would briefly become the tallest building in the world, and perhaps its most beautiful expression of Art Deco architecture: the Chrysler Building.

If ever anyone had an *annus mirabilis*, surely 1928 was it for Walter P. Chrysler, the "Great Mechanic of the Plains." As he told B. C. Forbes, "I like to build things."

24

The Chrysler Building

The Chrysler Tower. . . . stands by itself, something apart
and alone. It is simply the realization, the fulfillment in
metal and masonry, of a one man dream, a dream of
such ambition and such magnitude as to defy the
comprehension and the criticism of ordinary men
or by ordinary standards.
The Architectural Forum, October, 1930

A skyscaper is a machine that makes the land pay.
Cass Gilbert

Look on my works, ye mighty, and despair
Ozymandias
Percy Bysshe Shelley

Everyone knows that the Chrysler Building contains seventy-seven stories that rise to the height of 1,046 feet, 4.75 inches. But it actually contains 84 stories, Sort of. Above the sixty-ninth story none of the distances between floors correspond to the standard 11 feet to be found in midtown New York office buildings. From the sixty-ninth floor on up you are never exactly on floors but between them, with the tower's famous dart-shaped windows sometimes barely illuminating a given floor, sometimes illuminating three at once. The 158 flights of stairs in the building end at the seventy-sixth story, the highest one rented out. To rise beyond the seventy-sixth floor you climb a steel ladder less than a foot in width, emerging on to a platform at seventy-seven (and a half) stories, surrounded on each of four sides by three glassless chevron-shaped window openings, allowing dazzling sunlight, creamy moonlight, and all the elements to rush through at will.

From there, where all traces of human life in the building stop, an even narrower ladder rises to the eighty-fourth floor. David Michaelis describes the eighty-fourth-floor experience of the Chrysler Building: surely one of the most rarefied known to mankind: "Deep sea divers in deep sea depths

The Chrysler Building. (*Courtesy Walter P. Chrysler Building Corporation*)

are said to experience something called rapture of the deep. A diver's euphoria proves so overwhelming that he fails to return to the surface even when his air runs out. From the eighty-fourth floor of the Chrysler Building, the city below appears as dreamy, distant, and unnecessary as the mercury covered surface of the sea must look to an enraptured diver. . . .

"Inside pyramidal walls four narrow openings face the cardinal directions of the compass. The floor is about a yard square. Directly overhead there is a small trapdoor, inside of which is a small ship's ladder and then another—smaller—Alice sized trapdoor, beyond which is another tiny ladder climbing up into the sepulchral darkness of the needle. The needle is, in fact, a very tall, very slender pyramid, and at the tip stands a lightning rod. . . . Inside the needle, the susurration of the wind diminishes and a sense of tranquility and enchantment and rapture takes over. Everything in and about the needle—its shape, the little ladders—points upward.

"Up there at the top, when you're outside, it's another story."

Dome of the Chrysler Building. (*Courtesy Walter P. Chrysler Building Corporation*)

Somewhere in the archives of the Art Deco Society there exists one of the strangest, most breathtaking photographs ever made. It is like a scene from E. L. Doctorow's novel *Ragtime*, in which real historical figures do fictional things. But this shows real people doing something that seems so unreal that it couldn't be true—except that it is.

Late in 1929, after the spire, or "vertex," as it was called, of the Chrysler Building was put into place, Walter P. Chrysler, the builder of the Chrysler Building, and William Van Alen, its architect, stepped out onto a scaffolding platform surrounding its summit. They posed for a photographer on opposite sides of the pyramid-shaped needle, each man with one hand on the very tip. At that moment the creators of this monument were in effect standing on thin air, touching the apex of the tallest object ever designed and manufactured by man. On this dazzlingly bright azure day, high up in the empyrean, these men could see vast distances, perhaps a hundred miles, in all directions. "As the builder and the architect grasped the chrome nickel steel tip of the building, it felt smooth and warm, like the hood of an automobile after a long summer's drive" (Michaelis).

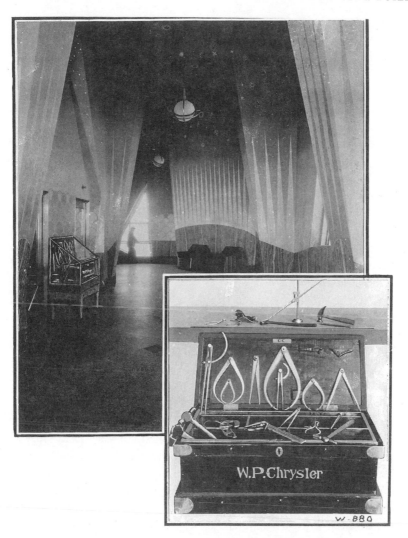

Observation floor of the Chrysler Building, 1930. Inset: Chrysler's hand-made tools from Ellis, on display. (*Courtesy DaimlerChrysler Corporate Historical Collection*)

In the words of the promotional book *The Chrysler Tower*, published in 1930, this is what was underneath that needle: "The Chrysler Building is really five buildings placed one on top of another: the first to the twelfth floor, the thirteenth to the twenty fifth, the twenty sixth to the forty fourth, the forty fifth to the fifty seventh and the fifty eighth to the seventy seventh."

But when you look at it from a distance, the divisions seem different. The best description of it was given by Eugene Clute in *Architectural Forum* in 1930: "The tower rises in impressive, unbroken vertical lines from the four story portico at the center of the Lexington Avenue front to the great semi-circular dormer head 69 storys above the street. The dome grows out of the tower; its surfaces are carried down between the dormers, the sides of which are splayed and metal sheathed, tying it to the tower. The dome above repeats upon its surfaces the semicircles of the dormer heads, elongated so that they grow more slender with each of the seven repetitions until they reach the base of the tall, needle like finial of polished nickel chrome steel, the top of which is 1,050 feet above the ground. The tower is firmly planted in the base formed by the lowest four stories and is buttressed at the north and south by setback masses so composed, proportioned and treated as to surface, that each has the character suited to its functions in the design, by which unity is secured."

He goes on to describe the squareness of the first sixteen stories, noting that they are relieved by a basketweave pattern of gray bricks and white marble. David D. Levine comments that this touch comes from "the 19th Century German theory that the proper form for walls was a woven one. This theory had apparently reached New York by way of Chicago along with the skeleton frame."

The next seven stories, up to the second setback, feature piers of white brick alternating with vertical lines of windows. Aluminum spandrels of three different types, located on the twentieth, twenty-first, and twenty-second floors, "are enlivened by highlights on the burnished portions of the relief ornamentation." The first of the building's large metal ornaments appear on the corners of the second setback on the twenty-fourth floor, in the form of 9-foot-high stylized Art Deco pineapples.

A 1978 Chrysler Building promotional brochure described in detail the use and function of the floors to the thirty-first-story setback: "Just below the 26th floor, a series of inverted V-shaped figures deftly break the optical illusion of distortion. Directly above are corner angles which bend outward tending to throw the vision out at the sides and permit the tower to assume its proper shape.

"At the top of this flare is a frieze of automobiles worked out impressionistically in white and gray brick with mudguards, a shining Nirosta steel hubcap at the center of each wheel and winged radiator caps at the corners." The radiator caps, of course, were duplicates of those found on Chrysler cars of the day. Eugene Clute explains: "The treatment of these four storeys is expressly intended to attract the eye to this point and give the necessary width to the tower where it emerges from the setbacks, overcoming an optical effect which would otherwise cause the tower to appear wider at the top than at this point."

He goes on to note that one of the most interesting features of the building is the height effect of the vertical lines in each of its faces, accentuated by the contrasting horizontal banding carried around the corners of the tower, "leaving rectangles of white brick that give an effect very like that of quoining.

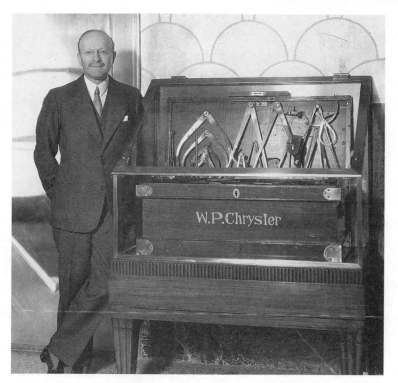

André Citroën with Chrysler's tools at the Chrysler Building, 1931. (*Courtesy Frank B. Rhodes*)

"This horizontal banding creates a remarkable impression of lightness, as one floor above another is emphasized and the verticals are suppressed. The genesis of this happy treatment of the tower was structural and came about quite naturally, for the earlier studies for the design for this building showed a tower on the plan of a Maltese cross. When the plan of the tower was made rectangular, the features arising from the original plan became a decorative surface treatment in white, gray and black brick, that gives depth, lightness and vibrancy by very simple means.

"In the 60th and 61st storeys the plan of the tower is in the form of a maltese cross, bringing about the transition from the square shaft of the tower to the finial." It is here that the eight great metal eagles' heads jut out from the sides of the building, two splayed out from each of the four corners. For the next six stories the ribbed metallic dormers rise up to the base of the dome, which consists of seven arches of the same ribbed metal on each side of the building, each succeeding arch rising higher and narrower than the one beneath it. Each of these arches is pierced by triangular shaped windows, eight on the lowest level, five on the next three, three on

Interior of Walter Chrysler's office in the Chrysler Building. (*Courtesy Frank B. Rhodes*)

the next two and only one on the highest. This highest and smallest arch supports the metal finial, which rises 185 feet from a base eight feet, seven inches square, to a peak of infinite smallness."

❖   ❖   ❖

To this day many people think that the Chrysler Building was a project of the Chrysler Corporation, organized, paid for, and owned by that entity. But it was not. To reflect its true origin it should perhaps have been called the Walter P. Chrysler Building, for it was erected and financed by the man himself.

He did it for his sons, Walter Junior and Jack. He had given all his children and his wife financial security by establishing trusts for them out of his Buick severance agreement. But the notion that his boys might become parasitic rich man's sons was abhorrent to him. "They had to work. I was well aware that a rich man's sons are likely to be cheated of something. How could my boys ever know the wild incentive that burned in me from the time I first watched my father put his hand to the throttle of his engine?

Walter Chrysler makes it emphatic. Chrysler's office, the Chrysler Building. (*Courtesy Frank B. Rhodes*)

I could not give them that, but it was through this thinking that I conceived the idea of putting up a building."

He wanted them to have a business that they could own, work hard at, and take pride in—something that was not connected to the automobile business. "They took no interest in stepping in behind me. That was all right with their dad." Since his boys had lived a good deal of their lives in New York, he thought that would be a the best place to set up a business undertaking on their behalf.

Therefore, he became involved in the building of the skyscraper in 1928. But the idea of constructing such a building on the northeast corner of 42nd Street and Lexington Avenue was not his. He took over the languishing and eventually bankrupt plans of the colorful one-term New York State Senator William H. Reynolds, who announced to the world in 1921 that he would erect a skyscraper on that very spot. He hired William Van Alen to design first a skyscraper and then a hotel for the parcel of land but eventually lost out completely on the project due to his inability to raise money on a completion bond for the project. It was at that point that Chrysler became involved.

In a sense this building, down to its foundations in bedrock, was a Dutch project whose origins could be traced to old New Amsterdam. The land under the building, then as now, was owned by Cooper Union, founded in 1859 and endowed by Peter Cooper, a seventh-generation descendant of Hudson Valley settlers who eventually was known as the "First Citizen of New York."

He was born in 1791, and began his career as an apprentice coachmaker to a firm at Broadway and Chambers Street. In 1828 he built the Canton Ironworks in Baltimore, Maryland, which became the foundation for his great wealth. The next year he designed and built the first locomotive to run on a railroad in America. It was called the *Tom Thumb*, and when it outdistanced a horse-drawn carriage in a race, it electrified Americans everywhere. Now that they saw for themselves what the steam driven iron horse could do, people began to realize that with this machine's potential America could expand into the west and settle it.

Cooper became involved with locomotive construction for the Baltimore & Ohio Railroad, and though he did well with this endeavor, his real fortune was made in the iron business. He had a real feel for this; for instance, he made $300,000 through a 51 percent ownership of the Trenton Iron Company, where iron structural beams were first made in 1854 and the Bessemer process was first tried in America in 1856. Associated with Cyrus Field, he also became the chief promoter and backer of the laying of the first transatlantic telegraph cable. Later, he was president of the North American Telegraph Company, which controlled more than one half of the telegraph lines of the United States.

Though known as a hard money Democrat, he joined the Greenback Party after the Civil War, and in 1876 he was its candidate for the presidency.

Despite his great wealth and business success, he is today best known as the founder of an educational and eleemosynary institution, Cooper Union, established to be "for ever devoted to the advancement of science and art, in their application to the varied and useful purposes of life." Cooper spent two years creating it, and by the time it was chartered in 1859, he had pledged $1.1 million of his $2 million fortune to it. In the over 140 years since it was founded, it has been an enormously successful and high-minded promoter of free education in the arts and sciences. It has also provided extensive free library services, and an important lecture platform in its great hall for many of the major thinkers and speakers of any given time.

Peter Cooper had managed to amass many tax free land holdings in New York, and as he lay dying at the age of 92 in 1883, he gathered his children and grandchildren around him and advised them as to how they might use these holdings to endow Cooper Union in the future. One of these holdings was the 37,555 square feet of goat pasture and squatters' huts surrounding Mrs. White's farmhouse on Lexington Avenue at the northeast corner of 42nd Street.

Mrs. White's little white building lay on a small rocky hill surrounded by grazing pasture attended to by the goats she kept. Squatters' shanties were the other occupants of her plot of ground. Her pasture fence faced Lexington Avenue. The land value of her plot was estimated to be $280 the lot, or two cents a square foot.

A panorama from 1876 showed 42nd Street as it then appeared from Mrs. White's to Madison Avenue. Across Lexington stood the bulbous Hospital for the Ruptured and Crippled, later the site of the Commodore Hotel, now the Grand Hyatt. Along the street were single-story buildings occupied by Schoonmaker, a druggist, Abrams, a purveyor of cigars, Brandeis, a grocer, Tyson, a butcher, and Gibson's bakery. At Madison was another huge Victorian pile which was Doctor Tyng's church, flippantly known as the Church of the Holy Oilcloth. Commodore Vanderbilt pastured his famous trotting horse Maud S. on the empty Madison Avenue block between 43rd and 44th Streets.

It was the building in the middle of this stretch of 42nd Street that made all the difference. Commodore Vanderbilt, yet another Dutch descendant, decided to build Grand Central Depot there, which changed the course of the city's history. Streams of traffic were now converging on this area, which swiftly caused building activity to move northward. Gradually hotels, apartment and office buildings, and new stores crowded around Grand Central, and in the 20th century, subway lines were laid beneath it. By the 1920s it became one of the most concentrated areas of development in the world.

By the time Mr. Chrysler and Van Alen were perched at the top of the Chrysler Building, the land beneath it was valued at $239 a square foot.

Both of these men were Dutchmen too. Chrysler was the direct descendant of Teunis Van Dalsen, the first male child born in New Amsterdam. Van Alen descended from Petrus van Haelen, burgess of New Amsterdam. So the forces that made this land economically and socially viable were Dutch. And the men who formed this building and flung it up into the heavens were Dutch also. Thus one of the ultimate expressions of the life and meaning of New York was built on the historic bedrock of its founders and most important shapers.

❧   ❧   ❧

The first mention of Walter Chrysler's involvement with this building project appeared in the New York Times on October 4, 1928. Senator Reynolds' plans had been known for some time, and a few weeks before this it had been announced that S. W. Strauss & Company, a big real estate mortgage company, would provide him with $7.5 million in financing for the construction of a sixty-seven story office tower. But by now it was being bandied about that Chrysler might be purchasing Reynolds' leasehold on the site from Cooper Union. Affirmations or denials were not forthcoming from any quarter.

In fact, Reynolds, basically a real estate and theatrical promoter who did not enjoy an especially savory reputation, obtained the mortgage from Strauss and then found he had no money left to secure a completion bond on the building, and therefore had to sell his lease. Whatever Walter Chrysler's feelings about creating security for his boys, it was true that he had wanted to obtain a major office building in New York for some time, and this situation was very attractive to him. When some real estate people (Willis H. Putnam, associated with Frank D. Veiller) approached him with the proposition that he take over Reynolds' lease, he responded immediately.

His lawyer, Nicholas Kelley, handled the thing for him, and a good bit of business it was. Kelley went to see Gano Dunn of Cooper Union and initially got nowhere fast. Dunn had barely heard of Chrysler and couldn't place either Kelley or his firm. Only after Kelley let drop that he was a member of the Century Club and the Downtown Association did Dunn decide he was all right to talk to.

Kelley led off by making it clear that Walter Chrysler had plenty of security for completion, and that the negotiations should be based on that assumption. After protracted conversations it came down to the matter of the nature and amount of Chrysler's security.

"Chrysler had barrels of Chrysler stock, which was then about $140," Kelley said. "He had about three million dollars of second and third rate municipal bonds of all little municipalities, school bonds, road bonds and all kinds of stuff like that. I went over and told Mr. Dunn that this was what Chrysler had. I asked him how much he wanted.

"He talked with his Cooper Union people and came back with two proposals. One was for a certain amount, to be kept good, kept at the value it then was. The other was for a much larger amount, but Chrysler would not have to put up any more."

His own people all urged Chrysler to take the smaller amount, but Kelley insisted, "For God's sake don't do that, Don't promise to keep anything good." For Kelley had remembered a horrific real estate downturn in Manhattan commercial real estate during his early days at Cravath in 1911. In previous years conservative investors like the Scottish Widows Fund Life Assurance Society of Edinburgh had ironclad rules of real estate investing that did not permit financing of any building worth more than 40 percent of the land on which it stood. But with the construction of skyscrapers that were worth far more than their underlying land, caution was flung to the winds, and when times turned bad and rentals were not coming in, financial disaster followed. "People who owned buildings subject to mortgages were giving them away to anybody who would undertake to pay the mortgage,"

Kelley recalled. "If they couldn't pay the mortgage, they would lose the building anyway. In this way, if they got someone who would take it over and pay the mortgage, at least the thing wouldn't be in default and be a scandal." He knew what he saw in 1911 could happen again, and was determined not to leave Walter Chrysler vulnerable to such happenstance.

Chrysler listened to him and took the larger amount, in the form of a 6 percent first mortgage leasehold sinking-fund gold bond issue in the amount of $7.5 million. Before the building was completed the stock maket crashed, and all Chrysler's holdings slumped greatly in value. "If he'd had something he had to keep good it could have wiped him out, I suppose. It would have put him under a horrible strain. But this way he was all right. He didn't have to put up anything more. It was part of the agreement that at certain stages, as the building went up, certain parts of the collateral would come down, and he would get it back. He was all right." As for Kelley, by 1930 he looked like some kind of a seer.

On October 13, 1928, *Auto Topics* reported that the W. P. Chrysler Building Corporation had been formed at Albany, New York, with the express purpose of constructing the tallest building in the world. Four days later the *New York Times* gave more details. Frank B. Rogers, Nicholas Kelley, D. R. McClain, and Harry C. Davis were associated with Mr. Chrysler's Building Corporation. The completed building, to be known as the Chrysler Building, and leasehold would be appraised to be worth $14 million. There would be 68 storys, and the edifice would be 16 feet higher than the Woolworth Building, then the world's tallest. Shops were planned for the ground floor, surmounted by offices up to and including the sixty-fifth floor. In two of the upper floors there would be a duplex apartment, and above the sixty-fifth floor a three-story observation dome constructed of bronze and glass, and culminating in a spire. Thirty-three elevators would service all floors. The first five floors were to be faced in stone, with brick and terra cotta above that level.

If it sounds as if the building being proposed at the moment of its inception was quite a bit different from what actually materialized, that is because Reynolds had never really made up his mind during the eight years he had shepherded this project along. After first calling for an eighty-eight-story office building, he changed his mind and thought he would build a forty-story hotel before finally settling on the idea of a sixty-eight story office tower. Along the way he drove his architect, William Van Alen, crazy. Most builders don't exactly know what they want and change the look of a building during the planning stages. But Reynolds didn't even know what kind of a building he wanted. In the end, it was the direct and concentrated personal involvement of Walter Chrysler that was instrumental in giving the building its final form, inside and out.

In Van Alen, Chrysler had an apt associate. He was one of the great iconoclasts of American architecture. The best information on him is contained in a 1929 article by Francis S. Swales in *Pencil Points* magazine. He was born in 1882, and from a very young age had an overwhelming interest in becoming an architect. Fortuitously, he found a job with Clarence True, one of the most flamboyant architects of his day. As architect, speculative builder, and contractor, True made a fortune and an enormous reputation erecting mansions along Riverside Drive in New York. He was also a futurist, not in the design of his work but in his self promotion of it. When he began practicing, the most prestigious members of the architectural profession considered the notion of advertising their services to be unthinkable, both vulgar and déclassé in the extreme. It must be remembered that in those days the advertising business was in its infancy, mostly a staid and informational affair centered around products rather than people, except for theatricals and similar social outsiders. But True advertised his name on billboards all over New York, like Coca-Cola or Nestle, and just like them, he became a household name. He paid no attention to any of his peck-sniffing social detractors, and was fabulously successful.

Van Alen spent three years and three months with True, rising from office boy to draughtsman. During the latter part of this period, he entered the atelier of Masqueray, where he learned the rudiments of academic architecture by making drawings of the Parthenon from plates, studying the orders and their applications, etc. By then Masqueray himself had gone to St. Louis, but Van Alen got the benefit of the master's pithy remarks about the art of architecture. Of the Parthenon: though it was fine architecture whose refinements were worth studying, "it might not make the best design for an office building if a dozen Parthenons were piled one upon another and hung to a steel skeleton." And though Vignola made a good set of rules for setting out Roman and Renaissance orders, arcades and other simple elements of pseudo classic design that were easily learned and assisted in training the eye to observe proportion (whose litmus test was 'does it look good?'), still, "Vignola has been dead a long while, and besides, he did not know everything while he was alive." Sometimes, Masqueray taught, a thing had to be done because it was "the sensible thing to do." Above all he reminded his students that "a good architect would pay more money to a draughtsman who knew how to get good proportions—one who had a good eye."

At the conclusion of his apprenticeship, Van Alen rose rapidly. After a few months at Copeland & Doyle, he got a lot more money at the office of Clinton & Russell. A short time after joining this company he entered the atelier of Donn Barber, and set his sights on winning the Paris Prize. He designed *A Loge* for this purpose in 1906, and finally won the prize in 1908 with his design for *A Grand Opera House.*

Clinton & Russell was an important design firm in the field of commercial building, and shied away from competitions. But they did enter one for a tall office building with a bank below it in New Orleans. Here Van Alen earned his first notoriety. The building's lot was insufficient to accommodate the window bays for the facade in a proportionate manner, so Van Alen proposed a startling solution to the problem. He put a classical pilaster right in the middle of the facade, dividing it in two, which was an affront to the conservative academic precepts of that time. He won the contest for the firm, and a lot of notoriety for himself. "Who was the designer?" everyone wanted to know. In the end, stuffy old Clinton & Russell eliminated the pilaster, but Van Alen's reputation as a comer was made.

He now had acquired enough money to study at the Ecole des Beaux Arts in Paris, as a protégé of M. Laloux, in whose atelier he worked. There he won medals in the concours for both *A Bath House* and *City Hall*. His *A Monument to be Erected on an Island in the Sea to Commemorate a Great Naval Battle*, a design of haunting, almost mythical beauty, displays a comprehension of monumental quality and scale seldom seen in what was still, after all, student design.

In Paris he was still perhaps too influenced by touches of the classical orders on the designs of his facades, but underneath all that his compositions had true merit and displayed a clever turn of mind that was the evident product of a sort of training that was teaching him to think independently of the constraints of his academic background. Eventually he was to kick over all traces of neoclassicism, revolting violently against it. That pilaster for the building in New Orleans proved to be just the opening shot in an all-out war. He came to detest early skyscrapers, which he saw as "encrusted from top to bottom with heavy masonry forms, rows of columns and heavy stone cornices." "No old stuff for me," he proclaimed. "No bestial copying of arches and columns and cornices. Me, I'm new. Avanti!"

Returning to New York, he hooked up with a man who built cooperative apartment buildings. One of those he designed contained a tiny garden in the courtyard. To describe this building, Van Alen invented the description "garden apartments," a concept and a term that swept the United States almost immediately. Thereafter, he entered into a series of partnerships in which he became celebrated for his flashy and sometimes startling designs for stores, shop fronts, shopping arcades, restaurants, and other such popular establishments. In so doing he was able to try out all sorts of design novelties appropriate to businesses that expected to keep up with the times by redoing themselves every few years in order to retain old customers and attract new ones.

For the Standard Arcade in lower Broadway he created windows without reveals that were applied to their openings like posters on a wall. They became an instant American classic. His Lucky Strike cigarette shop in Times Square featured three great elliptical windows, one of which was bent to a quadrant, which created a truly startling effect, whether one liked it or not. In his concept for the Prudence Bank Building the huge main lobby served both the bank and its adjacent shops on an equal basis; the shopkeeper paying $30 to $50 a square foot for his space was in no way subordinated to the building's "anchor" bank.

Van Alen recast the godawful industrial stove and griddle and stock pressed-tin ceiling decor of the various Childs retaurants in New York into something so modern and sleek that even fashionable Fifth-Avenue types were happy to be seen in these establishments. They featured several floors of huge plate glass windows without curtains facing the street, perhaps inadvertantly providing passersby with, shall we say, a living hosiery display. Complaints from ladies who were none too happy being gawked at finally caused Childs to put up curtains. But curtains or no, the storefronts were spectacular. Of the one on Fifth Avenue, Dan Klein said its "corner of plate glass and stone was so neatly rounded that the whole thing looked as though it might have been bent by a single operation around a gigantic roller."

This experience with Childs taught Van Alen the true potential of the word "show" in "show window." It must attract the eye from a distance by form; attract attention closer up by movement in the window; and present only the articles for sale to the observer standing in front of it. Perhaps his masterpiece in this line was the Delman Shoe Shop on Madison Avenue, built into two houses converted into several storys of shops. As Swales describes it, "A large ellipse raised to the second story is the form to catch the eye; the attraction—shoemakers at work in the window—does not cause a crowd of idlers to gather in front to obstruct the view of articles for sale. Instead of an eye paralysing array of numbers of shoes, just four kinds are shown, in four small showcase windows, at and below the eye level. The effect is interesting and dignified both as to the display of goods and the architectural facade as a whole. The outlines of the black and gold marble against the grey stone wall above impress with grace rather than with anything approaching shock. The beautifully detailed bronze window frames and ventilating registers add to the general effect of the design."

Van Alen's work was a matter of great controvery in the architectural community. Perhaps Richard Haviland Smythe, the renowned designer of quaint, original, and beautiful shop fronts in Manhattan, said it best; when Swales asked him how he liked Van Alen's design for the Giddings store on upper Fifth Avenue, Smythe replied, "How I *don't* like it is what you mean." But in answer he replied, "Van Alen's stuff is so darned clever that I don't know whether to admire it or hate it."

Senator Reynolds hired Van Alen when he was forty years old and his fame was escalating as an innovative and flashy architect. At first he set him to the task of designing that eighty-eight-story office tower, supposed to reach a height of 1,040 feet, some 56 feet higher than the Eiffel Tower. No building this tall had ever been constructed before, and it posed many logistical and practical problems; but it also caused considerable comment, which it was intended to do. After Van Alen designed it, Reynolds changed his mind and wanted the hotel; then in 1927 he was back to the office building idea, which was the design on which Reynolds raised the mortgage money. It was at this point that Walter Chrysler came into the picture.

❧   ❧   ❧

When Chrysler took over the project, the first thing he insisted upon was that everything above the sixty-first floor be changed. He increased the number of floors to seventy-seven and wanted a very different look for the tower. "We have his artistic judgement to thank for the fact that he insisted on Van Alen changing and improving his original concept for the tower," said Dan Klein. At that time the whole thing appeared rather squat, with a dome that architect Kenneth M. Murchison described as "looking for all the world like Governor Smith's famous brown derby." Van Alen had a mandate for change from Chrysler, and his solution to the problem of the dome led the building to what it eventually became—a cathedral of modern industrial design.

Every major style of architecture through the ages is a sociological statement of its time. Medieval artisans did not construct vast cathedrals for the ages in the shape and materials of antique Roman villas. Malibu beach houses do not resemble 17th-century New England farmhouses either. Herbert Muschamp has pointed out that the monumental public buildings of the late 19th century in Europe, with their massing of forms, gaudy over-decoration, and allegorical figures perched on every outcropping, expressed both the confidence and fear of the times, raising up aspirations and covering up dissent in the body politic. Anything out of sync with society's symbolic self view was covered up or modified. Was the iron train shed ugly? The genteel façade on the train station gave it the lie. The real genius of that age, which gave it its vibrancy, may have been in the raw expansive power of engineering, but architecture was determined to suppress that notion with the lie of beauty and civility. "The angel on the skyline stood for hollow idealism, the hypocritical tribute of a society that strongly preferred matter over mind," said Muschamp. It was not until the 20th Century that austere geniuses like Auguste Perret in Paris and Adolf Loos in Vienna exposed the real currents of the 19th Century in their architecture. The 20th century would emphasize these things: industrial simplicity, inner workings made plain, manufactured, rather than raw, materials, all combined to give a sense of unencumbered physical and mental speed.

Once the pioneers showed the way there was no turning back, and everything changed. Van Alen was in the thick of this current of modernism during his time in Paris, and long before the late 1920s he had absorbed its meaning into his bones. One also cannot underestimate the influence of the 1925 Paris *Exposition International des Arts Decoratifs et Industriels Modernes*, which introduced the Art Deco style to every item of modern life, from opera houses to earrings. It gave Beaux-Arts trained architects like Van Alen license to turn to a variety of modernist tendencies that had been in the offing for some time, and that he had explored in his up-to-the-minute storefronts. Theatricality and advertising display were already thoroughly ingrained in Van Alen, and art deco modernism allowed him to attach these principles to industrial architecture on the grandest scale when he turned Reynolds' project into the Chrysler Building.

❖   ❖   ❖

It was in 1896 that Louis Sullivan set forth the basic principles for the building of skyscrapers in "The Tall Office Building Artistically Considered." He thought that the ground floors of these buildings should contain banks, shops, and similar service-type businesses, set off by a "main entrance that attracts the eye to its location" and an exterior treated in a "liberal, expansive, sumptuous way." Above the ground floor, the office levels should "look alike because they are all alike." At the top of the building "the series of office tiers should come definitely to an end." He also thought that a tall building must emphasize height. Its "dominant chord . . . must be tall, every inch of it tall. The force and power of altitude must be in it, the glory and pride of exaltation must be in it. It must be every inch a proud and soaring thing."

Such buildings wouldn't have been possible, however, without the invention of the steel frame as a basis for skyscraper architecture. As Douglas Haskell said, "you can hang almost anything on a steel frame. It is a poor suffering helot that carries the burdens of the building and accepts any livery." Without this new technology, Sullivan's ideas would have remained dreams, rather than the forces of architectural and social change that they became.

Sullivan designed what he preached. Frank Lloyd Wright wrote of Sullivan's Wainwright Building, "It was the very first human expression of a tall steel office building as architecture. It was tall and consistently so. . . . The vertical walls were vertical screens, the whole emphatically topped by a broad band of ornament fencing the top story, resting above the screens and thrown into shade by an extension of the roof slab that said, emphatically, *finished*." This was the definitive form of the skyscraper for the first half of the twentieth century, and Van Alen's Chrysler Building did not significantly deviate from it, except insofar as it conformed to the 1916 New York Zoning Law.

The law was put into effect as a reaction to the construction of the Equitable Building in 1915. This building was extruded straight up from its site for thirty-nine stories, and in the process caused considerable environmental and economic damage to property owners in nearby neighborhoods. It blocked the sunlight, casting a great shadow on the surrounding streets, and sucked up tenants from all the other buildings in the area. To prevent this from recurring, the 1916 zoning law required that a building step back at a given angle from the edges of its site to admit light and air to the streets. It did not restrict the height of a tower, but permitted it to be thrust up over no more than 25 percent of the property.

This law had far-reaching and long-lasting consequences. In the first place, it encouraged builders to obtain the largest possible lots, in order to get the maximum economic benefit from their towers; eventually, some building lots took up entire blocks. This gave a sense of sheer size and isolation that led builders and architects to think of their creations as complete cities within themselves, with their own unique style, functions, and services. Rem Koolhaas said that they practically became theme parks, advertising themselves to the public at their entrances and for many miles around by the forms of their towers.

Certainly the 1916 zoning law was responsible for the characteristic "wedding cake" appearance of New York skyscrapers, with their mandated tiered setbacks, for decades to come. It also altered the public's conception of the massing of skyscrapers, at least until the box-shaped glass towers came into vogue in the 1950s.

With these three elements—the steel frame, the tall multiuse form, and the staggered setbacks—skyscraper architects were loosed from the moorings of traditional commercial building design. That steel frame, Haskell pointed out, "will not only support your floors inside, but stand quietly in outer garments with whole courses of Corinthian columns for a belt, cartouches at a couple of tons apiece for spangles, and for a cap a 'spire' a hundred feet high all covered with stainless steel or aluminum." Now anything was possible.

Dan Klein, writing in 1978, put it succinctly: "It was no longer necessary to build in the 'Classical revival style,' or 'Colonial,' 'Georgian,' 'Gothic revival,' 'Greek revival' or 'Italianate' styles. One could be unashamedly modern, experimenting with new ideas and new techniques of amazing ingenuity. There was no need to worry about precedent; there simply was none. There was no conscience about borrowing from France, ancient Egypt, Aztec civilizations, or Hollywood. The spirit of American modernism accommodated them all.

"The cubist painters had shattered all recognizable shapes, and following in their wake modern architects and decorators had no conscience about transforming and streamlining ancient cultures. In America particularly nobody worried about adapting European or Middle Eastern or Far Eastern traditions and combining them with the liberated forms and shapes of the jazz age. The combination became known as American modernism, and the Chrysler Building is a prime example of it, where traditional designs and brilliant new ideas harmonize perfectly to create what was then and still remains something completely fresh and exciting."

The zoning law was Van Alen's bible, but the sermon he preached from it was new and original. As Cervin Robinson describes the Chrysler Building, "Its lowest 16 stories rise straight up from the sidewalk (with the inclusion of an airshaft on one side which gives a U-shaped plan above the fourth). There are setbacks at the 16th, 18th, 23rd, 28th and 31st floors, which conform to the Zoning Law and give the building the appearance of a 'ziggurat' on one side and a U-shaped palazzo on the other. The tower continues straight up from the 31st floor to the 60th, where it becomes a maltese cross which blends the squarish shaft into the finial. The finial design continues above the 71st floor, the highest inhabitable level, to the very tip of the spire 1050 feet above the street." In its combination of styles and ideas, it was novel indeed.

Though the Chrysler Building's form abided by the dictates of the zoning law, each of the setbacks up to the 31st floor served an intelligent function. The first 16 floors were as large as possible to maximize valuable rental space near the ground. The U-shaped cutout above the fourth floor was to admit light and air to the building. Though the first three setbacks simply conformed to the law, the area between the 28th and 31st stories "serve multiple functions in the building," says Robinson. "They add visual interest to the middle of the building, preventing it from being dominated by the heavy detail of the lower stories and the eye-catching design of the finial. They provide a base to the column of the tower, effecting a transition between the blocky lower stories and the lofty shaft. They are pinched out at the corners, with giant Chrysler radiator caps in chrome steel and a frieze of hubcaps and fenders, to attract the eye to the base of the tower and make it appear larger. This was an attempt to overcome an optical illusion, common to tall buildings with horizontal bands, which made the top appear larger than the base of the tower."

The dome of the Chrysler Building is a direct outgrowth of the tower: it adds height upon height. Robinson describes: "Its 'dormers,' each smaller and higher than the previous one, continue the wedding-cake layering of the building itself. This concept is carried forward from the 61st floor, whose eagle gargoyles echo the treatment of the 31st, to the spire, which extends the concept of 'higher and narrower' forward to infinite height and infinitesimal width. This unique treatment emphasizes the building's height, giving it an other worldly atmosphere reminiscent of the fantastic architecure of Coney Island or the Far East." Truly, New York had never seen anything quite like it.

The area the Chrysler Building could occupy was restricted by the zoning law, which also specified its setbacks; but its height had other determinants. Chrysler wanted the world's tallest building and was determined to have it; it was he who dictated that the number of stories should go from 68 to 77, in order that he could raise the world's tallest building. "Thinking of Paris, I told the architects, 'Make this building taller than the Eiffel Tower.' But there were problems. The belief then, according to F. D. McHugh, writing in April, 1930, was that it would be "impracticable to attempt to support an elevator car and its cables for a direct run of more than approximately 1,000 feet, and furthermore that shafts in a number of relays would take up too much revenue producing space." Another problem was "the capacitof the human ear drum to withstand the vibration in an elevator car travelling at a speed which would have to exceed 1,500 feet a minute." Eventually, these difficulties would be surmounted with great displays of ingenuity, in order to get the supreme elevation Mr. Chrysler required.

At first Walter Chrysler seemed somewhat diffident when it came to matters concerning the design of the building, but eventually he became more involved. "The architects had made a plaster model—and in the toy sized lobby, tinted Morocco red to simulate marble, the ceiling was supported on four free standing columns," he remembered.

" 'It looks a little cramped to me,' I said. Until that point I think the architects had felt I was taking rather little interest.

" 'A terrific load is carried by those columns in the plans as drawn,' they replied.

" 'Um, but when people come into a big building they should sense a change, get a mental lift that will put them in a frame of mind to transact their business—how about this?' I reached my fingers through the ground floor of this skyscraper in miniature.

" 'Pull it out,' said one of the architects. 'That's just a piece of cardboard, pegged in there.' I did, and that little action involving a change in the plans cost about a quarter of a million, for even as we made the change the steel for the subsurface of the building was being fabricated.

" 'Could it be done?" I asked.

"One of the architects was sketching on an envelope. He held up his sketch. He said: 'It could be done this way, by making the lobby triangular.'

"From that point on I had all kinds of fun; spent lots of hours down on my hands and knees creeping about the floor of my office—then at 347 Madison Avenue—carpeted with the blueprints and other drawings of the architects; made the final choice for the marbles in the corridors; chose the veneers that make the interior of each elevator cab seem to be the work of some extraordinarily gifted cabinetmaker." And he did a lot more, working with Van Alen to make many contributions of permanent value to the building in systems, materials, and design.

On October 27 Chrysler announced that Fred T. Ley & Company would be the general contractors for the building; there would be some seventy-seven subcontractors, and as many as twenty-four hundred men would work on the job. The razing of existing structures on the site began on October 15, 1928; demolition was conducted by 200 men from the Albert A. Volk Company. By November 11th, blasting for the foundation commenced; the excavation was done by the Godwin Construction Company. They blasted down 69 feet to the famous Manhattan (mica) schist, or bedrock, that makes the construction of New York's great towers possible. This is 450-million-year-old rock, whose surface "has the texture and appearance of a densely woven, brightly beaded evening bag"(Michaelis).

It appears at varying depths in different parts of the city, not five feet below the surface in some parts of midtown, beneath as much as 40 feet of quicksand and 25 feet of gravel cemented by clay downtown. Before construction of any building begins, drills are sent as much as 50 feet below the excavation to be sure that there is no break in the mica schist; no one has ever found a fault in Manhattan's bedrock. Truly, without this remarkable foundation New York would only be a city of six-story buildings, like London, and not at all as we know it.

The total load of the building is 224 million pounds, and to excavate its foundation, the contractor removed 105 million pounds of rock and 36 million pounds of earth, or 63 percent of the building's total weight. When the excavation was completed, the Ready Mix Sales Company poured 4,856 cubic yards of columnar concrete foundations. The first billet was set into the excavated foundation on March 10, 1929, and steel construction began on March 27, 1929; the steel was supplied by the Carnegie Steel Corporation, and fabricated in a Brooklyn steelyard by the American Bridge Company. The first steel uprights were put in place on April 9, 1929; erection by Post & McCord.

Once construction started, it went like a "bat out of hell." Just a few floors were done by June 3, but only six weeks later, thirty-five stories had been added. Tower construction began on September 16, 1929, and the building was topped out on September 28. This was a new record for steel construction; even more amazingly, not a single life had been lost, nor had a single serious injury occurred.

This remarkable achievement was a matter of safety consciousness on the part of the builders and foremen working in close collaboration with the scaffolding firm, the Patent Scaffolding Company, and the Pelham Operating Company and Cheseboro-Whitman Company, who respectively fabricated the hoist machinery and erected it. The unusual weight of many of the steel columns and trusses, some of which were two stories high and weighed 25 tons, coupled with the narrow setbacks on the building, made it necessary to use a creative combination of derricks, cantilevered platforms, and huge hoist towers (one was 800 feet high) to allow the work to proceed swiftly. By having certain derricks lift the steel while others were engaged exclusively in setting it, all could work at maximum speed. Construction went on twenty-four hours a day for the first two months on a double shift; there were lunchrooms on site and staggered work shifts, which eliminated congestion both at the site and in the surrounding streets, streamlining the whole operation.

But equally important to Walter Chrysler was that safety records went with the building records. In an article called "Is Safety on Your Payroll?" he spoke of staring up at workers on the scaffolding with a friend on the street below. " 'My, that's a risky job,' my companion remarked. 'A man just about takes his life in his hands working on a building like this.' "

" 'I suppose it does seem that way,' I replied. 'But it's not so dangerous as you think. If you knew the precautions we have taken to protect those workers, you might change your mind. . . . Not a single life has been lost in constructing the steel framework of that building.' " To give an idea of how much of an achievement this was, it should be noted that the rule of thumb at that time was one death for every floor above fifteen in the construcion of a building; by this measure, the Chrysler Building should have been responsible for sixty-two deaths.

There were many reasons why this job was so safe. There was a hospital on the grounds. When any accident occurred, the cause was immediately found and removed. A bulletin board with constantly updated safety information was maintained. Watchmen were stationed at each entrance to keep out all unauthorized visitors. Fencing and a sidewalk shed of tubular steel protected pedestrians while allowing them unobstructed passage by the site. All passageways, both inside and outside the building, were kept free of debris at all times.

Durable three-stringer ladders extended three feet above the floors they were serving, which reduced any danger of slipping. Stairways throughout were of metal with wooden planking for good footing. Large floor openings were surrounded by adequate railings, and small holes were covered by planking.

Scaffolds came with guard rails, toeboards, and tarpaulin-covered plank roofs. "One admirable feature of their construction was the use of wire netting in the space between the toeboards," said Chrysler. "Catch scaffolds or aprons were placed about three floors below.

"Exterior hoist towers were built of tubular steel, enclosed on three sides with wire netting of half inch mesh, and secured with bars across the opening. The hoists themselves were of durable construction with a cover of netting No. 10 gauge, three quarter inch mesh.

"Eight foot high enclosures for inside hoists were made of wood slats, placed vertically instead of horizontally to prevent the men from using them as ladders. A pivotal bar, two feet from the opening, blocked the entrance to the shaftway. Slats also surrounded the hoisting cable. Across unused elevator shaftway there was placed a pivotal bar instead of the usual gate."

There was also an auto-call horn system throughout the building, through which various subcontractors' personnel could be located, summoned to telephones by means of code numbers. In addition to saving time, this system could avert all sorts of problems by allowing personnel to be contacted instantly at vital moments.

All hoist equipment, engines, and cables were inspected weekly, and all dark corners were lighted.

Walter Chrysler was proud of these safety measures, but he cautioned that "they would be comparatively useless without the cooperation of the workers themselves.

"What makes for protection? Merely the obedience to all the rules of common sense and good practice that have been devised through years of experience. It sounds simple enough, and it is simple enough; but the difficulty is that those who are superintending construction work are very often not constantly on the alert to see that the men under them protect themselves by observing all the 'safety first' laws of building.

"Whether building companies employ the practices which have proved successful in the erection of the Chrysler Building is unimportant. Whether workers obey the same laws that were prescribed for the Chrysler workers is equally unimportant. What is of importance is that owners, builders and workmen combine to make their jobs as safe as is humanly possible."

As soon as the steel was set in place on any given level, the surfacing of the building began. The first three floors were clad in a dark green, almost black, Norwegian granite known as Shastone. Flaked with iridescent mother-of-pearl, this exquisite material framed the shop windows and outlined the entrances of the building in a most imposing fashion. Above this rose some 3,826,000 bricks, half white and half common, except for some 220,000 gray and black bricks used for trim, and 10,000 stored in the basement against the possibility of some future disaster.

Now, in addition to the steelworkers, there were hundreds of stonemasons and brickmasons, soon to be joined by sheet metal workers, plying their trades on the exterior of the building hundreds of feet above the street. They were perched on scaffolds suspended on steel wires that looked like mere threads against the building. A total of 264 safety scaffolding "machines" were used during the erection of both the exterior walls and the elevator shaft walls, for the security of the men. Of course this equipment was installed and operated at a higher point above grade than ever before.

But the greatest achievement in raising the building had to do with the erection of the scaffolding for the cladding of the dome and finial. Forty miles of "Tubelox Scaffolding" Tubular Framing and forty thousand couplers were used from the base of the dome at the sixty-first floor, at 600 feet, to a point 6 feet above the extreme tip of the finial, at 1,046 and ¾ feet. Men working on birdlike perches at gale-swept heights were able to perform their tasks in complete safety. This constituted the greatest height to which structural steel had ever been carried in the history of the world, and this operation was undoubtedly the greatest engineering achievement up to that time in the history of scaffolding.

The covering for the planished metal dome and finial, the first of its type ever placed on a first-class building in America, was made of a new type of chromium nickel steel called Nirosta, formally known as KA2, and commercially known as "Enduro," created in the Krupp steelworks in Germany. Chrysler chose it himself after having it tested exhaustively in the metallurgical laboratories of the Chrysler Corporation. He said of it: "The characteristics of this alloy made it exceptionally well suited to our needs. It has an attractive, dignified color similar to platinum. It shows complete resistance to corrosion present in architectural uses. It possesses the exceptional color of retaining its color and luster; its surface does not tarnish; and, the metal being resistant throughout, there is no danger of surface deterioration, peeling, chipping, or other change. Perhaps the most important result of all is the fact that maintenance expense is eliminated; there is no need of polishing, replacement or refinishing." Van Alen avoided any possibility of corrosion from dissimilar metals by using only nails, screws, bolts, nuts, and rivets of the same material in constructing the cap and spire. Chrysler's faith in the metal was justified, for today, in 2000, after more than seventy years, none of the forty-five hundred sheets of Nirosta in the tower has ever been replaced. The spire was recently cleaned, and gleams as brightly as the day it was set in place.

The irony of the dome of the Chrysler Building, created at the behest of one of the world's masters of the standardization of metal parts and mass production technique, is that it is a triumph of hand craftsmanship of the most careful and considered sort. The metal itself was furnished by three of the Krupp Nirosta Company's fifty one American licensees—Crucible Steel Company of America and Republic Steel Corporation produced the sheets, and Ludlum Steel Company made the bars and accessories. The domelike nature of the construction above the sixty-sixth floor made the steelwork extremely complicated. "Many of the members are made up of very long curved angles that had to be laid out on the mold floor loft of the Federal Shipbuilding and Dry Dock Company, which fabricate these parts. The erection of this complicated structural frame required the most exacting effort on the part of the erectors." The sheet metal contractors, Benjamin Reisner, Inc., found themselves fabricating a good deal of the work in two metal working shops located on the 67th and 75th floors of the building. "The complicated and unusual formations of the dome made it advisable to fabricate the larger portion of the work in these shops, because it could be done only according to field measurements. Speed was maintained by this arrangement."

The needle had a latticed steel framework, onto which sheets of the Nirosta were directly attached. "A base of nailing concrete (nailcrete) was provided for the sheet metal work completely covering that portion of the dome and spire below the needle, and extended down on both sides of the circular-head dormers to the 59th floor level. The sheet metal ribs were fastened to fireproofed wood nailing strips placed on top of the concrete and fastened to the structural steel frame. Standing or lock seams, made without solder, were used throughout, except where they were impossible or undesirable, where soldered seams were used. The radial ribs on the fronts of the metal covered dormers of the dome and similar ribbed construction are formed by sheet metal covered wooden battens." In other words, the dome was built by methods not dissimilar to the methods used to build car bodies when Walter Chrysler entered the car business in 1911, and for many years thereafter.

The winged gargoyles of the thirty-first floor and the sleek, commanding horizontal eagle heads of the sixty-first floor are especially interesting examples of sheet metal construction. "Small scale models were made for studies, and, when approved, full size models were made to which the various pieces of sheet metal were fitted in the stamping shop. These full size models also served as a basis for designing the steel frames which support the gargoyles," explained Van Alen. They had heavy angle iron frames with subsiding bar iron supports for the sheet metal work. (Getting closer to the all-metal body and frame construction that would soon dominate the auto industry.)

These flying wings and eagle heads thrusting out from the body of the building almost make it seem as if it wanted to burst forth from its moorings into flight. Certainly the Chrysler Building is making a statement about the soaring technology of the age, which made its existence possible. If you wanted to know what the times were about, this building would tell you.

David D. Levine writes, "The cap makes the entire building look airworthy. Through its use of gleaming steel and its somewhat aerodynamic shape, it calls to mind airplanes and perhaps prefigures spacecraft. This impression was enhanced by the rocket like appearance of the spire on its top in only an hour and a half on a day in 1929. This concept of rapid motion, precise construction and reference to existing technology is part of the optimistic outlook the designers of the era had toward science and technology. It was felt that new forms of technology . . . could save the world."

The sudden appearance of the hidden, secret vertex was the culmination of the whole Chrysler Building project. One of the most astonishing occurrences in New York history, there has never been anything like it, before or since.

This is how it came about. William Van Alen and H. Craig Severance had once been partners but had fallen out completely, and by the time the Chrysler Building was announced, they were bitter rivals. Van Alen and Chrysler had loudly proclaimed at the start that their building was to be the world's tallest, at 925 feet. Severance, who was the architect for the new Bank of the Manhattan Company building at 40 Wall Street, then announced that his building was to top out at 927 feet. Needless to say, Walter Chrysler was flabbergasted and more than a little annoyed at this turn of events. But he knew he wouldn't take it lying down. So he told Van Alen to do something to remedy this situation in a definitive manner. Van Alen got hold of his steel engineer, Ralph Squire, and went to work.

Van Alen's description of his solution was a somewhat dry understatement, to say the least. "When it was decided that the topmost part of this building should out-top every other existing structure, it was necessary to resort to the unusual because of its after consideration nature. Such problems are the special joy of engineers and constructors. A high spire structure with a needle like termination was designed to surmount the dome. This is 185 feet high and eight feet square at its base. It was made of four corner angles, with light angle strut and diagonal members, all told weighing 27 tons.

"It was manifestly impossible to assemble this structure and hoist it as a unit from the ground, and equally impossible to hoist it in sections and place them as such in their final positions. Besides, it would be more spectacular, for publicity value, to have this cloud-piercing needle appear unexpectedly."

The entire operation was carried out in complete secrecy. Walter Chrysler and Van Alen said nothing publicly about the situation, and seemed to take the loss to Severance philosophically. No one had an inkling of what they were up to.

"The spire was fabricated and delivered to the building in five sections. The lowest of these was hoisted to the top of the dome and let down through an opening (actually the fire tower which ran straight up through the building) to the 65th floor level, where it rested on two 12 × 12 timbers, 20 feet long, placed on the floor framing. The other parts were placed in sequence and connected with the needle portion projecting above the top of the dome.

"The derrick which raised these parts and afterwards raised the spire to its final position was erected on one of the four sections of an outrigger platform built at the top of the dome. These also served as hitches for the derrick's guy lines. Although a twenty-ton capacity derrick was used, it was capable of raising safely the twenty-seven ton spire because the derrick mast was placed close to the opening at the platform level and the boom raised and held close to the mast, practically vertical. Derrick capacity is rated on its safe strength with the boom horizontal.

"When the spire was finally assembled and riveted up securely, the fall lines were lowered and attached to the spire at its approximate center of gravity to prevent its tipping from a vertical position while being raised. The signal was given, and the spire gradually emerged from the top of the dome like a butterfly from its cocoon, and in about 90 minutes it was securely riveted in position, the highest piece of stationary steel in the world. Post & McCord, steel contractors, and H. G. Bolcom, consulting engineer, had finished their work—the spire was in place."

Down below in the street there was a lot of anxiety. People looking up didn't know what was going on, and as the needle emerged from the dome, they were petrified that it might fall over. One of them was Walter Chrysler, who watched from across the street. He had confidence in his men, of course, but still, such a feat had never been attempted before. William Van Alen was anxious, too, and both men were greatly relieved when the operation was completed. An American flag flew from the pinnacle, and there it was before them: the tallest structure ever built by man. Both the city and the world at large were taken completely unaware, and stood amazed along with Walter Chrysler, the mechanic from Ellis, Kansas, who had started his career wiping locomotives for 5.5 cents an hour in a Union Pacific shop thirty-seven years before, and now had built the world's tallest structure. The date was September 28, 1929. And despite the fact that this was one month and one day before the stock market crash that ended the way of life and the view of life the Chrysler Building stood for, his monument would perdure.

But what did people make of it? Instantly the dome and needle became famous as a symbol of New York, and today the Chrysler Building ranks with such structures as the Taj Mahal, the Parthenon, and the Eiffel Tower as among the most recognizable architectural works in the world. But in 1929 many people weren't at all sure they liked it, thinking it garish and excessive. The dome was compared to all sorts of unusual items—a decidedly "unthrilled" Dr. Harvey Davis of the Stevens Institute of Technology harrumphed, "I cannot see the function of a Chinese pagoda on top of a New York office structure, nor can I see any reason for introducing in such a structure the exotic extravagance of Coney Island."

But on the other hand, in commenting on its automotive embellishments, Kenneth Murchison said, "As it is a commercial proposition, embodying the emblazonment of automotive progress, why should the architect have hesitated a moment in being in the Ziegfeld of his profession?" One of the things Ziegfeld did was to glorify the American girl with fantastical costumes topped by amazing headpieces, and indeed one critic saw the Chrysler dome as a "chorus girl's fluffy headdress." In fact just about everyone seemed to think of it as a grand headdress, comparing it to Nijinsky's headpiece from a Diaghilev ballet, or a Balinese dancer's headpiece, or an exotic monarch's crown. Van Alen himself dressed as his building, dome and all, when he attended the Beaux Arts Ball in 1930, and cut quite an astonishing figure. (Architects are supposed to dress as their buildings at this event.)

Back in the realm of architecture, comparisons with cathedrals were obvious, considering the building's spire and gargoyles. Claude Bragdon, who thought all skyscrapers were metaphorical fountains, opined that "the needle pointed fleche of the Chrysler Tower catches the sunlight like a fountain's highest expiring jet. The set backs of the broad and massive lofts and industrials appear now in the semblance of cascades descending in successive stages from the summits to which they have been upthrust." David Levine, noting that the dome's windows recalled the rays of the sun, said it "gleams like a beacon in reflected sunlight, blends with the sky on cloudy days, and hangs like a silver ghost over the city at night." Whether one liked it or not, the power of its attraction was permanent and unavoidable.

People could read about the Chrysler Building and see its progress in newspaper photographs, or they could simply look up at the work, which was visible for miles around. Teaser articles spoke of the richness of its materials and the speed of its construction, and interest on the part of the public was kept up throughout the fall of 1929 and the winter of 1930. But it was many months before they could get inside to look around for themselves.

Meanwhile, Walter Chrysler himself kept busy working on it. He spent a good deal of time concentrating on the elevators, a vital part of a building that rose so high and could accommodate some eleven thousand people at once. For him, safety and convenience were major considerations. " 'If the elevator cabs travel less than straight,' I said to myself, 'they will be more noisy than pistons in cylinders that are out of round.' So I gave orders on how the plumb lines should be taken." Frank Rhodes, his great-grandson, has a photo of him consulting with the engineers and workmen as this was being done.

Then there was the matter of speed. "The city laws only tolerated speeds of 750 feet a minute when we built," he said. "I insisted on preparations for speeds of 1,000 feet a minute." This was done, and as a result, when city codes were changed to permit such speeds a few years later, the building was prepared for it. As early as March 10, 1929, it was given out that the building's elevators would be the longest vertical transportation in the world, and that passengers would be able to ascend its heights in less than a minute. This immediately set people's minds fantasizing about a novel experience to be had someday soon, and added a certain thrilling new cachet to the building.

But Chrysler did more than technical work on the elevators; "I chose the wood veneers that make the interior of each elevator cab seem to be the work of some extraordinarily gifted cabinet maker." These elevator interiors were perhaps the single most beautiful and, next to the dome, most important feature of the entire building.

There were 32 of them in all, in banks of eight or six cabs each, with varying levels of the building served by one or another of the elevator groups. Van Alen, assisted by L. T. M. Ralston, who was in charge of concocting the various mechanical parts of the building, spent a year carefully designing these elevators. They were manufactured by Otis Elevator, with the interior work, and the door surfaces, done by the Tyler Company. Each cab was 5' 6" by 8' in dimension. The doors were made of 'metyl,' which was metal covered in various shades and types of exotic wood veneers. When closed, the elevator doors looked like tall fans set off by metalllic palm fronds rising through a series of silver parabolas, whose edges were set off by gently bending lilies. When the doors were open, each cab seemed like an exquisite Art Deco room.

There were four basic patterns for these cabs, but no two were alike, due to a dazzling array of inlays made from varied selections of rare woods, including Japanese ash, English gray harewood, Oriental walnut, American walnut, dye-ebonized wood, satinwood, Cuban plum-pudding wood, and curly maple. There were arching patterns, triangle patterns, pyramid patterns, Mondrian-like patterns, and even plain ones whose only form came from the wood color and the direction of the grain. Levine points out, "If anything in the building is based on print fabrics, these certainly are. Three of the designs could be characterized as having 'geometric', 'Mexican' and vaguely 'Art Nouveau' motifs, reflecting the various influences on the design of the entire building." Each ceiling was crowned with a different molded metal cartouche, beautifully set in a polished wooden veneer pattern of its own. Truly these are among the most beautiful small enclosed spaces in New York, and it is fair to say that no one who has ever seen or been in them has forgotten them.

In a way the whole working arrangement of the cars was got up to look like curtains opening on a fabulous setting for a scene in a Ziegfeld extravaganza. Indeed, the elevator lobbies feature cove lighting in the form of raised curtains that peak in the old style from the middle and cascade off to both sides. The only thing missing is Gladys Glad emerging from one of the elevators in full regalia, trailing ostrich plumes and satin trains.

Brochures promised quite a trip on these Chrysler Building elevators. "Few thrills are comparable with a trip to the top of the Chrysler Building. One enters the impressive lobby, gazes in admiration at the mural, notes the time as it is indicated by a clock with speedometer-like figures, and then sets out on the longest vertical ride on earth. All about are courteous attendants immaculately uniformed." (Around this time there was a very funny cartoon relating to this. It showed a Chrysler elevator lobby with a sign on the left saying, "Chrysler Limited," and underneath, "Sleeper Jumps." To the right of it was an open elevator revealing two men reclining on upper and lower Pullman berths. Above the doors was a sign saying, "Through Elevators," with a round dial and arrow indicator above that; the stops listed around the dial were "Venus," "Mars," "Saturn," and "Heaven." To the right of the elevator was a comically charicatured black trainman in full livery pointing to the elevator and bawling, "All Aboa'd!" at the top of his lungs.)

"As each passenger enters, he names the floor at which he desires to stop, and the operator pushes a numbered button on the board before him for each floor called. At a signal from the starter, the operator moves a lever and the doors close—the lobby door and the door of the car. There is a stimulating feeling of floating aloft but no sensation of speed because there is nothing with which to compare the movement upward. Above the door are numbers that light one by one: 53, 54, 55 . . . one a second they flash on and off. Now the car passes the fifty-sixth floor which is devoted solely to the offices of Mr. Chrysler and his personal staff. At the fifty seventh the car nestles to a gentle stop." At this level, passengers transferred to two shuttle cars that sailed up to the Observatory on the seventy-first floor, where they could have a matchless view of the surrounding land, sea, and sky for fifty miles in every direction.

Of course, the public needed to be reassured about safety, and particularly that they would not get stuck in their ascent to the empyrean. So the brochure dutifully proclaimed that "the 13,800 volt power system provides for eleven feeders from three powerhouses with spare feeder conduits to provide against in the load requiring additional capacity."

All went well until a sweltering day in July, 1933. The *New York Times* of July 20th devoted two columns to the incident under the bold headline, "Score Marooned High in Chrysler Elevators When Electric Power Fails for 41 Minutes." A transformer blew at 9:34 A.M. and halted all 30 regular elevators until 10:15; the two service elevators were out for 36 minutes. First the lights in the building flickered, and then the elevators halted.

"Everywhere along the seventy-seven story building groups of anxious men and women stood in cars, most of which were suspended between floors. The main lobby, fronting on Lexington Avenue, and those on Forty Second and Forty Third Streets soon were jammed with about five hundred persons waiting for service to be resumed. Only those who had business on the lower part of the 1,046 foot building dared to climb the stairs in the oppressive heat."

Management said twenty people were trapped in the elevators during this time, but an operator estimated the number at close to three hundred. In any case, no one was overcome by the heat in the cars, which only had openings in the ceilings for small ventilating fans; apparently they provided sufficient air circulation to avert real trouble. Nevertheless, this was one bit of publicity the building didn't need.

❖   ❖   ❖

Mr. Chrysler kept on with his interest in the building, making the final choice for the marbles in the corridors and working on the design of the lobby ceiling mural with the artist, Edward Trumbull.

The lobbies were floored in Siena travertine from Germany; on the walls were immense slabs of Moroccan "Rouge Flammé" marble, an extraordinarily beautiful material that is a sort of Pompeiian red in color, with large vertical streaks of variegated beige and buff running through; its scalloped, water marked texture, riven from top to bottom with explosive bolts of lightning, bespoke the very essence of the Jazz Age. The Traitel Marble Company did a terrific job of matching the slabs and framing various openings cut into it, so that it was perfectly proportioned, and seemed to be formed all of a single piece. Each metal fronted vertical fluorescent light bar in the lobby was backed with Belgian Blue Marble and Mexican Amber Onyx, which dulled and suffused the light with a softened glow that illuminated and blended in with the red marble walls to give a rich luster to the entire room.

"The lobby's one puzzlement, the one detail that fits architecturally but doesn't make much sense otherwise," as Paul Goldberger has put it, is two grand staircases opening from corridors on the north and south sides of the lobby. The walls of the staircases are faced in white-veined polished black marble, with the same material used for the stair risers, which are accented with gray and black terrazzo treads. The stair railings are of polished Nirosta in a striking modern design, footed by massive square newel posts of the ubiqitous Moroccan red marble. Above are ceilings made of concentric circles of aluminum leaf, from which splendid Deco glass and aluminum chandeliers, in the form of small cylinders encircling large ones, are suspended. "They are almost worthy of Radio City Music Hall," Goldberger remarks. Curiously, these stairs lead not to great promenades or grand mezzanines, but to unmarked doorways. What was Van Alen's intent? No one knows. "Like all objects of romance, the Chrysler lobby, too, retains a shred of mystery."

The main entrance of the building, on Lexington Avenue, was through a huge multi-storied Shastone portal, which some said was coffin shaped, others said resembled a proscenium arch, and still others compared to a stylized palazzo facade on the Grand Canal in Venice, with four slender long arches resting on the lintel. Above that was yet another Nirosta Chrysler radiator cap, this time splayed and supporting an upraised flagpole on its platform. (Nirosta trim was everywhere on the building, from storefronts

and window sashes to those lobby light reflectors and many other items;
the revolving entrance doors and the complex, geometrically patterned door
frames were of the same material; David Lupton's Sons fabricated these
detailed, finely wrought items for the building.)

As one looked straight ahead upon entering, one saw what was purported to be the world's first digital clock above a semicircular red marble
reception booth. As one looked up, the walls narrowed to focus on the
ceiling, and one saw a painting of the Chrysler Building pointing like a
rocket towards Lexington Avenue, about as bold a statement as the building
could make. This was the first glimpse of the Trumbull mural.

Edward Trumbull, whose boyhood was spent in Detroit, studied with the
celebrated English muralist Brangwyn from 1906 to 1912, before returning
to the U.S., where he received his first commission to do nine panels for the
Heinz administration building in Pittsburgh. Early on, Trumbull and Chrysler concurred in the idea that the mural should depict not a series of graceful allegorical figures representing the spirits of Industry, Architecture, and
Transportation, as one might have expected of such a grand building, but
rather images of the raw manpower that made the Chrysler Building possible. His was not an easy task, for in addition to making an aesthetically
pleasing and sociologically apt work of art, he had to fill a very peculiar
space, shaped like an inverted Y and approximately 110 feet by 97 feet.
Furthermore, this was to be the largest mural in the world, larger even than
the Tintoretto brothers' painting of "Paradise," which adorns the entrance
hall of the Doge's Palace in Venice, which at 72 by 22 feet, was long considered the world's largest painting.

The Chrysler Building, a 1930 advertising brochure for the building, described what was done, and the symbolic thinking behind it. "Trumbull's
idea had to be suitably arresting and majestic to suit the size and grandeur
of the building. His first study was to devise a theme in keeping with the
vastness of the whole plan, a theme that should carry out the boldness of
a scheme that involved thrusting steel and stone farther into the clouds
than ever before.

"He then made his preliminary sketch, a sketch that was not appreciably
altered from the beginning. Dividing his space, Trumbull found that it easily
and naturally fell into triangles, and this was a happy discovery, for the
building inside and out is a combination of firm line and sharp corners.

"At the east end then, Trumbull painted his first triangle and in it a single
figure, the naked torso of a man with sleek head, with rippling back muscles, with sturdy spine whose resilient strength was characteristic of the
lithe power of the building. Here was the base and also the central theme:
brawny man power, symbolic of the vitality and the force typical of our
age. Here too, at the root of the mural was the symbol that Mr. Chrysler
wished to dominate the whole: the power of the individual worker who

labors with his hands, the muscled giant whose brain directs his boundless energy to the attainment of the triumphs of this mechanical era in that never ending struggle to bend the elements to his will.

"In the next triangle, Trumbull placed symbols of the natural forces that are associated with energy: fire and water and lightning. And then the servants of these harnessed elements: electricity, heat and steam; the telephone, the telegraph and the wireless.

"Superimposed on these forces in the third triangle are the workers of today: Riveters, steel riggers, plasterers, carpenters, stone masons, brick masons, laborers—the men who made the dream a reality from the excavation to the tip of the tower. In this triangle there are ten groups consisting of about 50 figures, every one of whom was painted with a worker on the Chrysler Building as a model. These are the men who use power, who have subdued the forces of nature, whose courage and skill lifted this mass of steel and stone to heights never before attained.

"In the fourth and last triangle are the symbols of transportation imposed on a map of the world which runs in the legs of the triangle to the north and south. Here are great ocean liners, railroad trains, airplanes, dirigibles. Lindbergh's plane is shown and the Graf Zepplin. And all these swift instruments of man are winging their way over two hemispheres, graphically picturing the defeat of time and space by energy when it is driven by determination and inventiveness. Nowhere—and here again Chrysler the builder had his way—is there an automobile in the work." Officially, the triangles were to represent Energy, Result, Workmanship, and Transportation, respectively.

At the axis of the lobby is a compass suggesting, along with the map of the world, the boundless scope of the will to achieve.

"Finally, through the center rises the building itself, reaching into the stem of the 'Y.' This is the result of the energy of man, symbolized by the crouching, straining figure of muscular power at the base. This is the structure that has come to reality because natural forces have been made to serve the will of man, the master, because time and space have been dwarfed by the marvels of fleet transportation, because the elements have been subservient to the brain of the builder.

"Into a glorious sky of eternally blue and billowy clouds springs the shining finial, fashioned of gleaming metal and flaunting its triumph like the upraised lance of a knight of old. About the tower drifts a lovely rainbow, a favor flung to the gallant knight, a token of good fortune, a promise of fealty, a pledge of faith. This is the mural by which the artist has sought to express man's mind and body working with the natural forces to make life brighter, happier and easier."

The Trumbull mural epitomized the meaning of this building. It was both a very modern thing and a very ancient one, a talking building that spoke in images of its own history, and the history of its age. Its shapes, its materials, and its systems would tell you everything you wanted to know about why it was there and how it was used. Its ornament told you in hieroglyphs of the society and the times that created it. And like Cheops' Pyramid or the Tomb of Julius II, the Chrysler Building bespoke its progenitor. But though a monument as extraordinary as these, it was not a tribute to the grandeur of greatness in death; rather, it was a celebration of human industry and the possibilities of life, movement, energy, and progress. In a way it could be said that the end of the 1920s marked the culmination of the forces that drove the industrial revolution to a paroxysmal climax; after this came a failure of mechanism and a cessation of implacable social propulsion in industry and basic life, which led to a new understanding and consensus for the future. The Chrysler Building stood and gleamed on the outer edge of the Old World, and though it was instantly antique, it functioned beautifully as a reminder of what untrammeled imagination and spirit could accomplish. Over time it has become one of the world's classic statements of the purpose and will of an age.

❧   ❧   ❧

The building's construction continued with abandon throughout the fall of 1929 and the winter of 1930. Terazzo was laid on main corridor floors, with rubber tiling on secondary ones. Mouchette marble from France was used on upper floor wainscoating. Georgia marble, similar to Parian in its properties, was used in the bathrooms, "Creole" in the men's room, pink "Etowah" in the ladies'. Steel partition walls, in interchangeable sections so that the floor plans of any suite of offices could be changed overnight, were installed. Not only functional, they were made to be beautiful too, for they did not look like steel at all, but rather the choicest grained walnut, with panels, moldings, and doors as finely proportioned and fitted as the best workmanship of skilled cabinet makers. This was done by a photographic reproduction process.

Murray Radiator supplied copper convection radiators placed in recesses in the walls under the windows and enclosed behind ornamental grills with direct control supply valves, enabling any tenant to have the amount of heat to satisfy his personal wants. A ventilating system utilizing huge fans throughout the building, from the basement to the 74th floor, washed the air by drawing in six tons of fresh air per hour and expelling 5½ tons of vitiated air per minute. Two Carrier supplied air conditioning units supplied tempered air to the basement subway corridor and shops at this level, the second and third floors, and all interior space located below ground. An automatic centrifugal refrigerating machine cooled air in hot weather. The building supplied its own drinking water to all levels through a plant that treated the water in the basement. Much attention was paid to soundproofing, and the building was the first to conform to brand-new city fire codes; it was fully sprinklered to the fourth floor.

It had a centralized vacuum system on all levels, which made daily office and corridor cleaning much quicker and more efficient. Waste was taken care of in the basement by a 19-foot-long, 8-foot-wide, and 9-foot-high disposal unit called the Destructor. Its normal capacity was 800 pounds of rubbish per hour, though it could handle up to 1,120 pounds under unusual conditions, such as when new tenants were moving in.

Underground, direct connections were emplaced between the building and nearby subways, Grand Central Station, four large hotels, and fifteen office buildings, to eliminate congestion and speed up ingress and egress.

Note was duly made of the Chrysler Building's "firsts," such as Van Alen's use of hollow steel construction, steel roofing, and windows flush with the exterior walls, rather than set in behind deep reveals. The Chrysler Building Corporation sang the praises of those longer-than-ever elevator rides at every opportunity too, and both the building trades and the public were made well aware of the innovations in working methods employed during construction.

Another important Chrysler Building innovation didn't make its influence felt until modern times. Originally, the dome of the building was to be illuminated with floodlights, some located in trenches dug into the tops of the gargoyles, though this didn't happen right away. In a letter to the *Times* on January 2, 1931, a Phillip Tapley complained that he had been waiting for lights to be beamed upward to the dome ever since it had been completed. "Surely the designers can visualize the grandeur this tower would present if lights from the base of the silver dome were focused on all sides of the tower." This was during the Depression however, so it took a bit of time to get it done. Later on, and until the 1950s, the triangles of the dome were illuminated from within by 50-watt incandescent bulbs. Then for 25 years there was nothing.

According to Jack Chrysler, Jr., as Jack Kent Cooke, the new owner in 1979, was announcing plans for sprucing things up in the building, Walter Chrysler, Jr. told him about the dome lights, including the location of the switches. Amazingly, when they were turned on, a good many still worked. Cooke was so taken with this idea that he replaced the incandescent lights with fluorescents, creating a stunning visual effect visible for many miles around. This started a trend which spread throughout Manhattan and then to other great cities in the U.S., many of which have dazzling illuminated night skylines today. Tapley was prophetic when he concluded his letter with the comment, "I am sure this addition will help to make New York City all the more impressive."

On December 10, 1929, the *New York Times* reported that 28 real estate men ascended to the 67th floor of the tower by elevator, then walked to the 71st floor to inspect the new skyscraper. Howard Hay of the Chrysler Building led Fenimore C. Goode, Robert F. Leigh, and 25 members of the rental department of Brown, Wheelock, Harris, Vought & Company on the one-hour informational tour, during which they enjoyed the view from the highest point on the Manhattan skyline. It was reported that no one took advantage of the opportunity to climb the vertex.

Occupancy was scheduled for May 1, 1930, the traditional day on which new leases were signed in Manhattan, but it was reported that people actually began moving in on April 1st. Apparently, some were even installed as early as March 15th. So the building was actually habitable far in advance of its 18-month completion schedule.

The official grand opening occurred on May 27, 1930. A formal ceremony was held in the lobby, in conjunction with the annual meeting of the Forty-Second Street Property Owners and Merchants Association. Governor Alfred E. Smith, among many other dignitaries, attended. Before a very fancy luncheon at the Commodore Hotel across the street, Mr. Chrysler accepted the great ceiling mural from Edward Trumbull, and also a bronze plaque from George W. Sweeney, president of the Merchants' Association. It reads: "In Recognition Of His Contribution To Civic Advancement Through The Erection Of This Magnificent Building, This Tablet Was Presented To WALTER P. CHRYSLER By The Forty-Second Street Property Owners And Merchants Association, May, 1930." He was enormously proud of this honor, and the plaque hangs in the lobby to this day.

In actuality though, the building was not finished. Several of the tower floors were not ready until the end of July. As things were completed, they were opened up.

The much heralded Cloud Club was inaugurated at a luncheon on Bastille Day, the fourteenth of July, 1930. It was an exclusive midtown luncheon club, meant to serve a membership of the city's, and the world's, top leaders in business, politics, sports, and the arts. Built on three stories, with a median height of 733 feet from the ground, and offering a four-sided view of the New York metropolitan area second to none, the Cloud Club was one of the most impressive semi-private spaces in the city. It was styled in a combination of classical, Tudor, and German Expressionistic decor.

A special express elevator opened onto a beautiful reception lobby, tastefully carpeted and featuring lattice grilled doors, a coffered ceiling, and a wide, handsome stairway leading up to the sixty-seventh floor. A library lounge, office, grill room, and oyster bar were found on the lowest level too, along with a ticker room and three private dining rooms. There was an abundance of rich wood panelling and thickly upholstered chairs and settees in the various lounges, along with sleek-looking modernistic chairs in the various dining rooms.

The next level featured the main dining room, held up by four square blue marble columns, cornered in aluminum strips and topped by large lighting fixtures, featuring big lozenge-shaped glass panels, rounded on top and chevron-shaped at the bottom, and separated by semicircular, fluted illuminated glass columns. Shirred curtains and huge high drapes with sideways dart-shaped patterns graced the windows. Tremendous arches began at the floor and swept up and over the ceiling. These were pale blue, and stuccoed with puffy white clouds, angling their way to the windows, where they met the real clouds of the Manhattan skyline. They also blended in with the clouds in the huge, double-height framed painting of New York harbor by Gardner Hale, which dominated the space. This extraordinarily ebullient work showed a forest of skyscrapers rising like needles from the rock of lower Manhattan, ringed by huge ocean liners and crowned by colorful, swooping airplanes overhead. The total effect was to make one think that the dome had been lifted from the building, leaving the diners in the open air under the canopy of heaven. Jack Chrysler, Jr., himself a world record holder for jet speed, remembered dining with the likes of Juan Trippe, of Pan Am, and Bob Six, of Continental Airlines, in this room, and noted that it was always a favorite of the great figures of aviation. He imagined that they simply felt at home in this blue sky aerie.

On this level, too, was Chrysler's private dining room, an intimate space that was a true stunner, for its walls were hung in full with blue silvered mirrors depicting, in black figuring, sturdy examples of all the kinds of workers involved in building automobiles, from burly laborers to intense scientists and draughtsmen. The images are simple and refreshing, and the materials lend a quiet dignity, nobly set off and outlined, to these people. They were Chrysler's men, the kind of men he came from, who made him what he was. It is very touching not only that he wanted to be reminded of them every noontime as he took his meals, but also that he was proud to display them to the rich and powerful of the world as they joined him in breaking bread. He had become a very big man, but he never wore a high hat on a swelled head.

The sixty-eighth floor had a gymnasium, shower and dressing rooms, a barber shop, and rest rooms. Special note must be made of the men's room, of all things. Tracie Rozhon described "one of the great lavatories of all time, this tiny-tiled gray, black, blue and white men's room, with its seven pure white porcelain pedestal sinks, its narrow chrome framed mirrors and its thick swirled marble partitions. (The much smaller women's room is great, but, alas, not as great—a sign of the time.)" (Actually, it was a sign of the fact that this was a men's club, with women only occasional visitors.) According to Jack Chrysler, Jr., Mr. Chrysler would say that his favorite thing about the building was the spectacular view from this men's room window, thought by many to be one of the great views in New York.

One other important thing about this club is that it was a speakeasy, like a lot of clubs and restaurants in the city then. Members had their own private "lockers" there in one of the rooms, behind wood panels encrypted with secret code letters and numbers identifying their rich and powerful owners. There were cedar cigar humidors too.

The club went a long way toward reaching its goal of 300 resident members and 200 non-resident members when it opened, and it was able to accommodate 200 member guests on a daily basis. The main dining room alone could accommodate 175 persons.

If one was elected to membership, the initial fee was $200, plus an annual membership of $300 for resident members; non-residents paid $150. There were 2,000 shares in the club available, with a par value of $100 each. The 300 resident members were expected to purchase one of these shares at the subsidized price of $800 upon joining. They were purchased back upon the death of a member. Members had unlimited privileges.

Harold E. Talbott, Jr., international polo player and president of the club, and William F. Cutler, vice president, presided over the opening luncheon, which was attended by 250 members and guests. Among those present were such noted club directors as Arthur V. Davis, Edward F. Hutton, Messmore Kendall, Condé Nast, Joseph R. Terbell, and Cornelius V. Whitney. Gene Tunney, the retired heavyweight boxing champ who was strikingly photographed in 1929 with a Chrysler Imperial roadster, was among the guests.

On Monday, August 4, 1930, the Observation Platform of the building, on the seventy-first floor, opened. It was operated as a concession by the Chrysler Tower Corporation, by arrangement with the Chrysler Building Corporation. For fifty cents patrons got a ride on those fabulous elevators along with a chance to see the highest view then available in New York. The triangular windows of this floor were framed by sunburst spires that reached up into the cerulean blue ceiling, from which hung small crystal planet lighting fixtures. Right by the elevators, flanked by a drawing of Mrs. White's goat farm on one side and a picture of the four-story structures replaced by the Chrysler Building on the other, stood a glass case containing the tools Chrysler had fashioned himself as a young man in Kansas almost forty years before. Above it an image of the Chrysler Building rose like a rocket.

So Walter P. Chrysler's humble mechanical beginnings were now ensconced in his great architectural monument, for all to see and ponder. There was much meaning in the history that created this scene; Chrysler himself thought you could learn a lot more by gazing into his toolbox than you could by looking at the surrounding view lavishly laid out beyond the tower windows. For in that box were what Chrysler thought were mankind's greatest achievement: tools, which man could use to create the glories of the world.

          ✧   ✧   ✧

The building was quite a commercial success. Occupancy was gratifyingly high, despite the fact that the Depression's icy grip was beginning to be felt in the spring of 1930. On June 15, 1930, the *New York Times* reported that it was 65 percent rented. The Texas Corporation, later known as Texaco, was the anchor tenant, occupying the entire sixteenth through nineteenth floors, or some 200,000 square feet, as it would for decades to come. The tenancy lasted despite a bumpy patch in the early days. In late July, 1931, the W. P. Chrysler Building Corporation had to sue the Texas Company for $48,583 in rent due the previous July 1st as a prorated part of an annual $583,000 yearly rent, which commenced on May 1, 1930. The issue was shortly resolved, and the Texaco-Chrysler Building relationship continued on its long road. The reason for it was a payback to Chrysler, who was so instrumental in the development of no knock Ethyl gas, which made the Texas Corporation's fortune.

The Chrysler Corporation had its headquarters in the building as a rent-paying tenant occupying considerable space, and for a number of years the very jazzy-looking two-story Chrysler International Salon, showcasing the company's products, was at street level. Walter Chrysler himself occupied a magnificent office on the fifty-sixth floor of the building. It was extremely rich-looking, impeccably decorated in the High Renaissance style that he much favored. The coffered ceilings were intricately carved with floral motifs, and the heavy marble-framed doors featured beautifully painted architectural scenic panels, one of which showed the main entrance to the Chrysler Building. Mirrors, a small set of built-in library shelves, and a stunning portrait of Della adorned the walls; crown-like bronze chandeliers hung from the beams. Luxurious carpeting covered the floor, and a big, comfortable sofa and lounge chair upholstered in royal blue velvet with gold patterns awaited their occupants. Two Hamlet chairs faced his desk, which was an elaborately carved affair inlaid with precious woods. He sat in a capacious and sturdy open-armed leather chair with nailhead trim, and a large leather lounge chair, similarly trimmed, sat to his left. The upper part of the mullioned windows showed stained-glass heraldic motifs, apparently depicting some of the crests associated with his family. Though its style was decidedly heavy by today's standards, this office was the nec plus ultra of luxury and chic in its day.

Chrysler purportedly had a duplex apartment above this office on the fifty-eighth and fifty-ninth floors, very grandly appointed. Though its existence was widely reported in the newspapers, information on it is very sketchy, and there seem to be no surviving pictures of it. Apparently he wanted his private existence in the building to remain private.

Walter Chrysler, Jr. maintained a huge fifty-seventh-floor office there for his Cheshire House publishing company, and later had a personal one for himself. Jack Chrysler, Sr., associated in a venture capital partnership with Fred Zeder, Jr., also had an office in the building.

Other tenants of extraordinary stature rented in the Chrysler Building. In addition to the Chrysler Corporation and Texaco, which created modern state-by-state maps and practically invented the credit card there, Henry Luce created and built his Time, Inc., empire, resting on the foundations of *Time, Life,* and *Fortune* magazines, in the Chrysler Building. In 1930 the Tom Thumb Golf Company created a new type of roadside entertainment called miniature golf there, inventing an important national industry so strong that some thought it would singlehandedly lift America out of the Great Depression. Margaret Bourke-White, who made spectacular photographs of the building, printed up her striking Depression-era prints here. And then there was James Agee.

David Michaelis spoke of "the fiftieth floor where, late at night, James Agee, sweating over *Fortune* assignments on butter, streamlining, roadside foods, orchids, unemployment, machine-made rugs, cockfights, and quinine—feeling "nausea at the sight of this symbol $ . . ."—played Beethoven's Ninth Symphony on a phonograph at top volume while plotting ways to murder Henry Luce." A famous incident involved his office's "window ledge, from which, in October, 1934, the despairing Agee, ambivalent about suicide, dangled 544 feet above the sidewalk before changing his mind when a colleague entered the office, stunned to see the writer's hands 'clinging to the outside window sill.' "

The bloom on the rose of being the world's tallest building did not last long, for less than two months after Walter Chrysler's "topless tower of Ilium" was capped, Governror Alfred E. Smith announced a new commercial building to be built on the site of the old Waldorf Astoria at 34th Street and Fifth Avenue. This was to be the Empire State Building, a considerably larger structure that would rise to a height of 102 stories, crowned by, of all things, a dirigible mast. Governor Smith and his backers, who included John J. Raskob of General Motors fame, wanted to be sure they would have the world's tallest building, and pushed the architects Shreve, Lamb & Harmon to raise it from its initial 65 stories to 80 and then 85 stories, before they got the dirigible mast brainstorm, which brought it up to 1,250 feet. Soon after the November 23, 1929, announcement of the building, photos were published of Governor Smith showing diagrams of the mast to the Undersecretary of Aviation in Washington, in an effort to convince him that such a structure, and its proposed use, was safe. The mast was never used for its intended purpose however, for the thought of the potential disaster that could be caused by a mammoth helium-filled balloon either exploding or pulling loose some part of the building in gale force winds was too horrible to contemplate. Due to its height, it became a popular radio, and later a television, transmitter.

The Empire State Building certainly offered an alternative to the Chrysler Building, for it was as simple in its lines as the Chrysler Building was rococo. A staggering construction achievement by the Starrett Brothers, it was rushed through from the first drawings to completion on May 1, 1931, in a mere eighteen months, at a cost of a little over $26 million. But unlike the $14 million Chrysler Building, it was an enormous financial flop, and remained so for decades to come. By the time it opened, a year after the Chrysler Building, the country had fallen precipitously into Depression, and its initial occupancy rate was only 23 percent, earning it the sobriquet "Empty State Building." Governor Franklin D. Roosevelt may have brought his dapper cheer to the observation deck, and the King of Siam may have brought his entourage, but paying customers were few. In 1935, when Mr. Chrysler claimed his building was 70 percent full, the lights were turned on in vacant offices in the Empire State Building to reduce the morguelike aura of a largely dark facade. In future years, the building would once change hands for just a few million dollars, as owners were eager to get out from under the albatross-like burden of its enormous upkeep. By contrast, the balance of the $7.5 million mortgage leasehold bonds on the Chrysler Building, dating from 1928 and due October 1, 1948, were called April 1, 1937, 11½ years ahead of schedule.

In addition to losing its height record, there were controversies that swirled around the new Chrysler Building. A major dispute arose between Walter Chrysler and William Van Alen for payment of the latter's services. Just three weeks after the building's opening, Van Alen sued the W. P. Chrysler Building Corporation, claiming that $725,500 of his $865,000 fee, representing 6 percent of the building's $14 million-plus cost, remained unpaid. He named Cooper Union, owner-in-fee of the property, and Senator Reynolds' Reylex Corporation, whose contract with Van Alen Chrysler had assumed, as co-defendants.

When he was retained as architect for the building by Chrysler, no new specific agreement for payment was made, despite the fact that Van Alen was drawing plans for an altogether different type of structure from the one planned by Reynolds. Van Alen asked for the 6 percent fee established by the American Institute of Architects (many then charged 10 percent), but Chrysler declined to pay more than $175,000. Van Alen had by this point, June 17, 1930, received about $140,000 from Chrysler and Reynolds.

He placed a mechanic's lien on the building for the $725,500, which was lifted on August 11 by the posting of a $770,000 bond by the National Surety Company. Settlement, on undisclosed terms, came a year later, on

August 21, 1931. Through the course of negotiations it was revealed that Chrysler had paid Van Alen the $34,500 still due him from the Reylex group and an additional $74,000 when the dispute arose. Chrysler had asserted that Van Alen had agreed to work for $8,000 a week. The ruckus caused *The American Architect*, in the same September, 1930, issue in which it analyzed and extolled the new Chrysler Building, to publish an article by lawyer Clinton H. Blake entitled, "What to Put in a Contract to Keep Out of Trouble with Clients." In it Blake spoke of the importance of written contracts with clients, despite the fact that most architects then proceeded without them, either out of fear of upsetting clients, reluctance to overturn longstanding practice, or a desire not to seem somehow unprofessional and cheapen the architect's professional status. The article published a copy of the A.I.A.'s recommended form of contract, and urged architects to use it, to prevent the sort of mess that Van Alen had gotten into with Chrysler.

However, it appears there may have been another reason for the problems between the two men. According to an article by Joseph Pell Lombardi, James E. Gambara said the reason Chrysler didn't want to pay up was because he was well aware that Van Alen, who was doing a lot of supervising of the project, was taking bribes right and left from the various contractors at work on the building. Though Van Alen effectively won his suit, the resulting publicity may have damaged his reputation, for though he lived another quarter of a century, he never again had another project even remotely as expensive or important as the Chrysler Building.

Later on, in August 1939, Fred B. Rogers, vice president of the W. P. Chrysler Building Corporation from its inception, brought suit against Walter Chrysler for summarily dismissing him from what he claimed was supposed to be a lifetime job managing the Chrysler Building. He said he was hired by Chrysler in 1928 to acquire the site and erect the building, and was to be paid $30,000 per annum on a lifetime basis, a sum modified to $15,000 in 1932. He was seeking $300,000 in damages, which represented $15,000 for the next 20 years, his lifetime expectancy (he was then 51). According to the suit, Mr. Chrysler, then disabled for more than a year, notified him on June 6th of his impending dismissal on October 1st, relying on advice from his children, who claimed that the two men had mutually agreed on the termination of Rogers's agreement. There is no published record of how this suit turned out.

A far bigger controversy arose over the subject of taxes. Due to the tax-free status of Cooper Union (owner of the land under the building), which derived from an 1859 statute which granted this status so that the Union could use these funds for its educational and charitable purposes, both that organization and the W. P. Chrysler Building Corporation claimed that no taxes on it were due to the city of New York. Needless to say, the city saw the matter quite differently.

The lease for the land signed by the W. P. Chrysler Building Corporation on October 18, 1928, called for a complicated step deal. The corporation and Cooper Union, clearly assuming that the new building would enjoy the Union's tax-exempt status, agreed that the Union would be paid ground rent and tax equivalent fees of $119,000 in 1928 and 1929, $26,000 in 1930, and $36,000 in 1931 and 1932; for the following ten years the sum would rise to $265,500, and then $330,000 for the eleven-year balance of the lease through 1953. Thereafter, two consecutive twenty-six year renewals through 1995 provided for rent at 5 percent of reassessed land value. In addition, the corporation agreed to pay the Union an amount equal to the tax on 4/5 of the assessed value of the land, in lieu of paying city taxes on 100 percent of the assessed value of the land.

The city began an attempt to collect taxes on the building by levying a $12.5 million claim on it in October 1930, for the 1931 tax year; they argued that the Cooper Union land was tax exempt, but not the building erected on it, since the building did not belong to them. Furthermore, since Cooper Union was being paid monies in lieu of tax, the city claimed that it was unlawfully collecting taxes. The Union claimed that, under a 1904 New York Supreme Court ruling, all its properties, and anything on them, were exempt. This plot of land was deeded to the Union in 1902 from Peter Cooper's son, Edward, and daughter, Mrs. Sarah Hewitt, and a city attempt to collect taxes on it in 1903 failed. So the Union felt it had a good case. The whole business went to court, where it remained for six years.

This case was widely followed because it dealt with the whole issue of tax exempt properties. Somewhere between 20 and 25 percent of all city properties were tax exempt, amounting to some $5,118,884,005 in tax year 1930. But of that figure only $878,001,334 belonged to churches, hospitals, and other philanthropic organizations like Cooper Union. A nearly equal amount was attributable to exemptions to relieve a public housing crisis. The bulk of the exemptions, some 65%, were for public property, such as government buildings, prisons, schools, parks, and playgrounds, which clearly promoted the public good of the community. True, the charity-owned properties used police, fire, and other services, but the idea, then as now, was that they were providing services privately to promote the public good, and deserved their tax breaks.

A ruling by State Supreme Court Justice Phoenix Ingraham in January 1934 held that the city had the right to collect $326,400 in taxes on the building and the land underneath it for the 1931 tax year. He held that no part of the land or property was used for the purposes of the Union, and hence it was completely taxable, though he acknowledged that the net proceeds from the property were appropriated for the uses of the Union. Since this ruling would affect 1932 and 1933 taxes as well, the city would stand to collect some $1 million if the ruling were to be affirmed.

After Justice Ingraham's ruling, the city moved to impose taxes on land

and buildings held by a large number of educational and charitable institutions. Cooper Union took its case into Appellate Court in April, 1936, and many eyes were focused on the outcome, for it was sure to affect the tax situation of many other similar institutions. John W. Davis represented the Union.

On May 1, 1936, Justice John V. McAvoy ruled in favor of the Union. Assistant Corporation Counsel William C. Chanler had argued that the 1859 statute had exempted only property given to the Union by Cooper directly, and not this piece, given by his children. Justice McAvoy noted first that the 1859 statute stated that all land deeded to Cooper Union by Peter Cooper, "including all endowments made to it, shall not, nor shall any part thereof, be subject to taxation while the same shall be appropriated to the uses, interests and purposes hereby and in the same deed provided for."

Next he disagreed with the city that the 1859 statute did not survive the General Tax Law of 1896. This law exempted from taxation real estate of corporations or organizations organized for religious, charitable, and kindred purposes when such property was "used exclusively for carrying out one or more of such purposes."

Justice McAvoy ruled: "Concededly the property herein involved is not used exclusively for carrying out thereupon the corporate purposes of Cooper Union and is not within the exemption granted by the Tax Law. It has been held that the legislature intended by the passage of the General Tax Law to repeal prior general laws which also dealt with the subject of general taxation. It has been pointed out, however, that a distinction must be drawn between general laws and special acts on the subject of exemption. The General Tax Law does not specifically repeal the exemption granted to the Cooper Union and such repeal will not be implied."

Thus ended this dispute, with a general sigh of relief heard not only from Cooper Union and the W. P. Chrysler Building Corporation, but from not-for-profit institutions citywide.

It didn't affect Walter Chrysler that much. "I don't own a penny of it," he said. "Such matters are now problems for my son, Walter. He is running the building. He is president.

"When he was ready to go to work, I said, 'You better learn something about the building. It's yours, not mine. If you don't pay attention to it . . .'

" 'What do you think I ought to do, Dad?'

" 'Get down in the basement and learn what the other fellow's got to do. Go and scrub a few floors. Clean some offices. That way you can begin to see through the glasses of other people as well as your own.' He did these things too, and then proceeded though various other jobs until he was well able to run the building." Walter Junior would have learned his lessons among a Chrysler Building staff of 500 persons, 150 of whom alone were cleaning people who prepared the building at night for the next day's business.

It was characteristic of the man that he would want his son to start to understand his business by learning the work of that business with his own hands, and gaining respect for people who worked in that way. Boyden Sparkes reminisced about him twelve years after his death: "He never let himself forget how it felt to be dressed in overalls with only a broom and cleaning rag for tools. 'I've been a nut about that for years,' he said.

" 'What?' "

" 'Taking pains to make any workman I come across know I don't think I'm any better than he is. Unless I do, he will. Watch me leave here some night. I find things to say. 'It's a bad day,' or 'kind of cold out,' or something. I speak coming and I speak going. If the young man at the information desk on the ground floor has his back turned, I make a point of it; He's got to speak to me. I say: 'Good night, Son.' Now they all speak to me as soon as they see me!' "

So there it was, the Chrysler Building, from first to last. Not three months after his acquisition of Dodge Brothers, barely taking a breath, he began this huge project. "I had a lot of fun when it was being built," he said.

In later years he was to judge that his purchase of Dodge was the best thing he ever did, and in terms of his business life that was true. But the greatest thing he ever did was the erection of this building. Whether, in a hundred years, it is still preserved, as properly it should be, or even if it disappears, it will always remain in the collective memory as the avatar of an age. Few people can say they contributed that to the world.

25

1929: The Crash

Running Off a Cliff

"Early in 1929 it had seemed to me that I could feel winds of disaster blowing," said Walter Chrysler. "I had great responsibility as a trustee. In my half year of retirement from the automobile business after leaving General Motors and selling my stock to du Pont and Durant, I had given everything I owned to my wife and children. "I put it all into trusts which were made irrevocable. So, when I had gone to work for the bankers in the Willys-Overland situation I had been a man without money. Of course, I knew that if the worst came to the worst my wife would not let me go hungry nor want for clothing. But it was not my money. I never used it, but I did have a voice in its investment. So, during 1929 I was concerned with selling off their higher priced stocks, such as Steel at $152. In consequence, a lot of their money had taken the shape of cash in the banks. About the stuff I owned myself that year I was something less than smart."

In other words, Walter Chrysler worked for money during the 1920s because he had to. He was about the business of empire building, but he had decided that he would not put his loved ones at risk in order to achieve his goals. He made big dollars with his labor, in fact some $2,000,000 in cash alone between 1920 and 1924, according to his own handwritten record. With this earned money, he recklessly took every business risk in the world and won, devil take the hindmost. The result was that he personally was as big as the 1920s were big, and stumbled when they stumbled. But his wife and children were never less than millionaires from 1920 until the days of their deaths.

In 1929 American prosperity was quite visible. The year before, Herbert C. Hoover, a great man in many ways but an unfortunate President, got

Walter and Della Chrysler relax in Palm Beach, FL, late 1920s. (*Courtesy Frank B. Rhodes*)

himself elected by famously promising Americans "a chicken in every pot." Many had one, too, cooking in a modern kitchen that was part of a home that also contained indoor plumbing in a sanitary tile-and-porcelain bathroom, a washing machine, vacuum cleaner, telephone, sewing machine, and radio. Attached to almost every home built in the 1920s was a garage, and inside of it was a Chevy, flivver, Buick, Essex, or Dodge. If you couldn't buy a new car, you got a used one; for $25, $10, or as little as $5, even Junior could buy an old jalopy to fix up and parade around town, girlfriends and buddies in tow. Factories were grinding out reasonably priced mass-produced goods, people were working, and cheap credit was widely available to keep the whole of American enterprise afloat.

The problem was that not everybody was sharing in this prosperity. Farmers and mineworkers, for instance, were not doing well at all. Their products were cheap for the city dwellers, but that did them no good at all. Then too, though the population was growing, it was certainly not exploding, which meant that after first-time buyers of novelties such as radios and cars were reached, industry had to strain harder and harder to make both new and replacement sales in order to continue to expand. Volume and expan-

H.Firestone   J.Rosenwald Thomas Edison Sir Thomas Lipton Chas.Schwab   Henry Ford W.P.Chrysler   Geo.Eastman   T.A.Wilson

Dinner in honor of Sir Thomas Lipton, 1928. (*Courtesy Frank B. Rhodes*)

sion were the underpinnings of the mass production society, since mass production necessitated mass markets, and only growth was progress in such an atmosphere. But with absolute numbers of customers limited, sooner or later the realities of the mass market would have to come into conflict with the exigencies of mass production, and result in a terrible crisis. It was like Lucy Ricardo and Ethel Mertz trying to get nuclear warheads off their speeded-up assembly line—where would they stack them? And by extention, once stacked, what would the company do with them? As long as that speeded-up line continued to spit them out, sooner or later there was bound to be a disastrous explosion.

The trouble was, nobody saw it coming. Everyone was sure there would be some way of keeping the whole shebang going. Based on optimism at first, and then on pure speculation, the stock market kept going up and up to vertiginous heights. Then, like the sudden appearance of the vertex on the Chrysler Building, just when you thought it couldn't go up anymore, the whole thing spurted up to undreamed-of levels. It wasn't stopping, so people seemed to believe it *couldn't* stop. Sure, there were setbacks, like the sudden scary break in the first week of December 1928, or another in March 1929, but these were seen as temporary pauses in the stock market's inexorable upward climb. Both times the market recovered and went on to new record highs.

Walter Chrysler, like many of the other big auto men, was playing the market for all it was worth. At its peak in 1928, the Maxwell stock he bought in the early twenties at about $16 a share was worth $563 a share in converted and split Chrysler stock, and that was just what he made on stock he had bought and held in his own business.

Wall Street ballooned in the 1920s through the manipulations of vast investment pools. The biggest operator with pooled money, the greatest

President Hoover—
"Looks at all Three!"

Ford   Chevrolet   Plymouth w 3938

Unique photograph of Edsel Ford, Alfred P. Sloan, and Walter Chrysler, taken while visiting President Hoover in Washington, 1929. (*Courtesy Frank B. Rhodes*)

plunger on Wall Street, was Billy Durant. Through the successful launching of both Durant Motors and its stock, Durant himself had come back in a big way from the financial and stock market disaster that caused him to lose control of General Motors for the second time at the end of 1920. By 1924 he was in the chips again, and now devoted himself to wheeling and dealing on Wall Street. It was his main interest in life; indeed, one of the reasons Durant Motors didn't prosper after its impressive first couple of years was that Durant was spending more time worrying about his company's finances than he was about its products and their promotion.

"During the peak of his operations, Durant worked through fifteen brokers, contacting them at all hours of the day and night and from any part of the world he happened to be in. His calls from Europe alone cost over $20,000 a week. By 1928 he was handling more than ten million shares of stock, representing over a billion dollars. That year Durant paid one broker alone over $4 million in commissions," wrote Dana L. Thomas in *The Plungers and the Peacocks*.

Heavyweight boxing champion Jack Dempsey in his 1930 Chrysler Imperial Roadster. (*Courtesy DaimlerChrysler Corporate Historical Collection*)

In this book, Thomas pictured Durant's operations this way: "Durant acted as a commanding general, supervising a vast chain of command that passed through corps of captains and lieutenants, who gave orders to a battery of stock specialists, who in turn carried out the actual trading on the floor." Sometimes they pushed up a stock when you thought they would sell, or dumped it just when it seemed right for a buy, just to dazzle and keep people off guard. Through all this maneuvering they managed to accumulate more and more stock for themselves.

"It was with such talent as this that Durant and his associates manipulated the great bull market. They played on it like an artist on a pipe organ, pulling out the stops here, pushing them in there, providing a caressing legato here and a booming crescendo there. They had a whole society under the touch of their fingers." In addition to Durant's own money, $2 billion of other people's money was invested in stocks on his recommendation by individual members of his consortium, this at a time when the total capitalization of the market was just under $90 billion. "Not just a few speculators but a whole nation responded to their tunes."

The seven Fisher Brothers, who reportedly were paid a total of some $200 million dollars by the time they sold out the last of their body-building concern to GM, plowed heavily into the stock market and joined in Durant's pools. So did Arthur W. Cutten, the virtuoso commodities trader from Chicago. Among many others, John J. Raskob of General Motors came along from time to time, as did Michael J. Meehan, who started out as the manager of McBride's theater ticket agency in New York City. Together they looked over moribund companies such as International Nickel, American Smelters, and Baldwin Locomotive, found them ripe for manipulation, and bulled up their stock by hundreds of points.

The run in Baldwin Locomotive stock epitomized the whole situation, according to Thomas. "The stock had taken a ride to the amazement of thousands of petty speculators who eagerly followed the price climb in the newspapers. Although the company failed to earn any dividends or show profits, this fantastic ride-up—this something for nothing—whetted the appetite of the average American. He wanted to get into action like this. This run up of a stock didn't have to have any relationship to the earnings prospects of a company, he concluded from the Baldwin experience. Run ups like this awakened the greed in many an honest breast."

Though there surely were other occasions, the one time we know Walter Chrysler was involved with the Durant pool was during the manipulation of RCA stock in the spring of 1928. Radio was an exciting phenomenon to Americans in the 1920s, much like the Internet is today. Everyone was fascinated by the prospect of broadcasts coming through the air into their own homes. RCA, the leading manufacturer of radio sets and the parent company of NBC, was first listed on the Big Board in 1924. "It was a company that was still suffering its growing pains," said Thomas. "Its promise was far greater than its performance, since it had not yet paid a dividend. At from $40 to $50, the range in which the stock hovered, it was fully priced; in fact, its earnings had been discounted for years into the future."

Mike Meehan, however, was totally sold on the promise of Radio, and ballyhooed it to the skies. It didn't budge until the Durant crowd and others started to take a close look at it in 1927. Most of the issued shares were held by such big companies as General Electric and Westinghouse, so that the actual number of shares available for daily trading was a relatively modest 400,000. This fact and the company's glamorous name made it ideal for exploitation.

The RCA pool Durant organized consisted consisted of himself, the Fisher Brothers, John J. Raskob, Charles Schwab, Percy Rockefeller, Herbert Bayard Swope, Mrs. David Sarnoff (her husband was the founder of RCA), and Walter Chrysler. As they, along with Arthur W. Cutten, began accumulating radio stock, the bears, noting that the company's earnings weren't rising and weren't likely to, began to build up a large short interest in the stock, betting that they would make money on it when it fell, as they were convinced it would. When this happened, the Durant pool bought up whatever became available, forcing the shorts to buy to cover their positions. The public, fascinated by the daily newspaper reports of the stock's rise, jumped in and started a wild frenzy of trading in the company's shares. "Radio stock was being exchanged at the rate of 500,000 shares a day although there were only 400,000 shares officially available."

In a ten-day period in March 1928, the bull pool forced the stock into a technical corner, which meant that though there were more shares held, the floating supply had dried up. (Real corners, such as those that occurred earlier in the 1920s when all the stock of the Stutz Motor Company and Piggly Wiggly grocery chain dried up, were much more serious affairs.) Beginning on March 12, when the trap was sprung, pandemonium broke out on the floor of the stock exchange, with traders pummeling Mike Meehan and ripping his clothes to shreds as they frantically sought advice on what to do about their RCA stock. When the trap was broken four days later, the stock had risen 61 points, and the Durant pool, which had put up $400,000 ten days earlier, walked away with a profit of $145,855.

They were just out of the market temporarily, however. They continued running the stock up and up with their artificial buying and selling for the rest of 1928 and well into 1929. At its peak, after a split, it went for $570 a share. A few weeks later the bubble burst, and knowledgeable insiders who had quietly gotten out at the top could buy the stock for $300 less.

In such an atmosphere the end was nigh, and Billy Durant, among a few others, recognized it. The tipoff was an action of the Federal Reserve in February 1929, which at that time tried to throw cold water on rampant stock speculation by asking its member banks to stop diverting their funds to brokers carrying loans on securities. The Fed had good reason to make this request. At the beginning of 1929 brokers had loaned out some $6 billion to about 600,000 margin customers, a figure that would increase by $250 million in January alone, and rise to $8.5 billion late in the year. At a cost of 3 percent, the money was cheap for the brokers, and made it possible for their high-flying customers, like Durant, to expand their holdings. Indeed, Durant's market speculations were based on the unlimited use of credit and the promise that it would always be there. He knew people wouldn't buy the stocks he was manipulating without the availability of cheap credit, and he was willing to fight tooth and nail to make sure it wasn't going to disappear.

On April 3, 1929, his concern became so great that he went to see the recently inaugurated President Hoover to discuss the matter with him. His visit was made secretly, under cover of night, so as not to alarm any of the multitudes of people who relied on him for guidance. Thomas recounts the conversation: "There was no distinction, he argued, between credit extended for stocks and credit used to boost other types of business. And if the Federal Resrve Board wanted to curtail security credit, it might just as well compel all business to function on cash. The financial health of the nation was based on credit. The huge volume of checks issued in the United States represented an employment of credit. The Federal Reserve Board in its tightening of security loans was killing the goose that laid the golden egg."

Hoover listened, as "the man who founded General Motors and who represented powerful investment forces was a man entitled to a thorough hearing." But he was not convinced, and the Federal Reserve continued on its course.

When he saw this was the case, Durant decided to get out of the market. This wasn't easy, as he had some $4 billion worth of stocks to liquidate, and he knew that he could create a panic by selling too publicly and too rapidly, which would undercut his own position. "The most delicate maneuver in the art of speculation is the unloading of heavy holdings without collapsing the price of the market. Somehow or other, the stock must be unloaded quietly and skillfully in stages—unloaded in such a way that no suspicions are awakened and no panic ensues. Indeed, the essence of success is that large numbers of outsiders must continue to be bullish enough to take over the stock at a high price," as Thomas reminds us.

To accomplish this, in the spring of 1929 Billy Durant turned to John J. Raskob. As the chairman of the Democratic Party, Raskob had attracted national attention in 1928 by running Alfred E. Smith's campaign for the presidency of the United States. He was also a big-time speculator who owned a great deal of stock in a large number of corporations, and with Durant worried, he launched a drive to create the right atmosphere for the large-scale unloading of stock. Thomas writes: "As the Durant group began quietly to get out from under, Raskob went around the country making speeches urging Americans to get deeper and deeper into the market, tossing out optimistic prognostications about the future of stocks as casually as a bridesmaid tossing out nosegays. . . . Raskob spoke on and on, and the Durant group stepped up its unloading operations. The evidence strongly suggests that Durant himself had completed the final stage of his liquidation by [the end of] May, 1929."

What he did next was utterly characteristic of Billy Durant. Like many a smile-and-a-shoeshine, wing-and-a-prayer salesman, he finally outsmarted himself. Out of the market when the crash wiped out $20 billion worth of securities in October 1929, he got back in a short while later, believing that stocks had fallen to bargain levels.

He dove in off the high board, heavily margining his purchases, waiting for what he thought would be the "inevitable" rally to occur. But the market had a mind of its own. After the "dead cat bounce" that usually follows a crash, it continued to sink, with occasional sucker rallies, until it reached a low in July 1932 that was 89 percent off its 1929 peak. Durant was long gone from Wall Street by then, having been sold out precipitously in 1929 and 1930 by the same brokers who had made money off him for the previous decade. He took what money was left and decided to concentrate on his ailing car business, Durant Motors, which by now had shrunk to a single brand, the Durant.

In 1929 he hired four of the former top Dodge Brothers executives, including Frederick Haynes, who had been displaced in the Chrysler merger.

They were supposed to reorganize it into a vital new enterprise, but they turned out to be undertakers for the company rather than saviors. Durant let three of them go in the summer of 1930, and struggled along with his customary brave face until the spring of 1931, when the receivers began closing in to seize and sell off what they could. Production continued through the 1931 model year, with a few warmed-over 1932 prototypes cobbled together the following January, after which the firm gave up. The company was liquidated in 1933.

But it was really over years before. At the end of 1930 Durant had admitted to John Thomas Smith, an old friend from the General Motors days, "I'm wiped out." From there, he slid downhill until he was forced into bankruptcy on February 8, 1936, listing debts of $914,000 and assets of $250, which represented the clothes on his back. When he was at the top of his game, he had said, "Money? What is money? It is only loaned to a man. He comes into the world with nothing and he leaves with nothing."

Walter Chrysler did not go broke. Time and again he was willing to bet everything he had in life, but on his business, the thing he worked hard to build and expand, not on a chimera like the stock market of the late twenties. Certainly he invested large sums of money in it, but as a dabbler, quick in and quick out. Compared to Durant and the Fishers, he was a relatively small-time operator. He had a great deal of Chrysler stock, and indeed was the largest individual holder of it, doing very well as it went up over 2,000 percent in value. But this was in the nature of a holding in his own business, something that he acquired and held through the years. Even when the world went to hell in a handbasket and Chrysler stock dropped to as low as $5 a share in 1932, he still held it, and lived to see his faith in his own enterprise justified when it recovered with the rest of the economy later on in the 1930s.

＊   ＊   ＊

In the late 1920s Walter Chrysler led a handsome life. There were golfing and fishing on Long Island, fancy parties in Palm Beach, costume balls and other opulent affairs in New York, and attendance at boxing and other sporting events, the theater, and the opera.

Every year he sailed to Europe, too, soaking up the cultural sights and, in the time-honored tradition of rich Americans, buying up artworks and antiques to ship back to his home in King's Point. He and Della, who accompanied him on these trips, brought back Italian, French, Spanish, and English furniture and tapestries (including Gobelins) of the Gothic, Renaissance, and Baroque periods, and sixteenth-, seventeenth-, and eighteenth-century velvets, damasks, embroideries, and brocades. There were Limoges,

Bavarian, Lenox, and Venetian-glass table services, and an extraordinary collection of Italian vestments, altar coverings, and papal hangings from the late Renaissance and baroque periods. Sculpture and painting did not escape their purview, either, and works ranging from a Gothic polychromed limestone statue to a Bellini and Van Dyck's "The Madonna in Glory" found their way across the ocean to the Chryslers' home. In 1929, when Della, Thelma, Bernice, and Walter Junior went on an extended trip to the Orient, beautiful Chinese porcelains and pottery pieces made the journey back home with them to the States. Meanwhile, back at home, Walter Senior continued to haunt the Fourth Avenue Saturday rug auctions, picking up his Kirman Millefleurs Oriental Carpets and Ghiordes Prayer Rugs.

Of the four Chrysler children, only Jack would not develop an abiding interest in art. Walter Junior, who bought his first painting, a small Renoir for which he paid $350, at the age of fourteen, became one of the greatest American art collectors of the twentieth century, estimating late in life that he had owned some twenty-five thousand works at one time or another. "With great works of art your mind is like a camera; it takes that picture with you forever," he commented. His tastes in collecting were catholic and eclectic, two traits that once upon a time were considered démodé, but now, in our present age of collage, are thought of as the height of perspicacity and chic.

Walter Junior said that Della influenced her children to understand and appreciate art; "Dad was too busy," said Bernice. With her husband, Colonel Edgar W. Garbisch, Bernice was to amass one of the country's great collections of American furniture and American Primitive Paintings. As we have seen, Thelma was also an art collector, and the Dior gowns she collected can also be recognized as works of wearable art.

❖   ❖   ❖

Though Walter Chrysler's life was charmed in many ways, it was not without problems. The most serious involved Walter Junior's health. In 1926, at the age of seventeen, Walter Junior had a severe hemorrhage resulting from a bleeding ulcer, and had to be brought back from the Hotchkiss School in Connecticut to New York in an ambulance for treatment. Later, in 1929, after taking a year off to travel around the world, he entered Dartmouth College, where he was stricken with a sudden case of severe appendicitis at the school on November 9, 1930, and had to have an emergency operation. Apparently it was a serious situation, as Della immediately was driven to be with her son at Hanover, New Hampshire, and Walter Senior, Thelma, and Bernice raced up there from Cambridge, Maryland, in Chrysler's private railroad car, called the Ideal. All tracks to New Hampshire were cleared for Chrysler's car, which left Penn Station only four minutes after it arrived.

The party arrived to find to their relief that the operation had gone smoothly and no complications developed, though Walter Junior was to be plagued with digestive problems for the rest of his life.

In August 1925 a bizarre incident involving Mr. Chrysler and tax-related graft hit the papers. Apparently a man named John J. Hughes, a clerk in the office of the North Hempstead, Long Island, Board of Assessors, conspired with John Brown, the chief clerk of the same office, to get Walter Chrysler's Long Island property assessment reduced over time from $272,000 to $122,000, when in fact it should have been raised to $279,000. This resulted in a savings of some $10,000. Hughes had approached Chrysler's secretary, Richard B. McClean, saying he could get the assessment reduced, and though McClean never told Chrysler, he agreed to pay Hughes one-half of the savings, or some $5,000. Eventually neighbors complained that Chrysler was paying less than they were, so town assessors investigated and discovered that assessments against Chrysler had been either reduced or erased. Suspicions were aroused when another clerk in the assessor's office, Clarence Heifer, discovered Brown with the field book before him one morning, and notified township attorney Seward Poor, who conducted the investigation. Chrysler was exonerated, but Brown and Hughes both went to prison.

Three years later Chrysler got into a wrangle with Great Neck town officials over the public beach adjacent to his mansion at King's Point. Chrysler didn't like the fact that local townspeople and day trippers had access to land that was within sight and earshot of his own property. "If Chrysler jumped off his own pier, he would land on the municipal beach," said fireman Malcolm Neilson. So he tried to obtain the property by offering to trade it to the town for a nearby eight-acre estate and mansion on the Sound that he had bought from actress Olga Petrova.

At first he offered to sweeten the deal with $85,000 in cash, and when that was refused, he proffered $15,000 in cash and in addition offered to build two swimming pools and a bath house on the property, plus a long pier that would stretch out into the water; he even offered to take all risk on a possible defective title and to take over the park district's lease on that part of the park owned by the town. The Park Commission turned him down on the advice of their attorneys, who said they could not legally turn over public property to an individual, no matter how attractive the offer.

Chrysler did not walk away from this negotiation a happy man, because he wanted to make a family compound around the mansion by owning all the surrounding property. He gave Thelma and her husband a house on one side of him, and eventually Bernice and her husband would have one nearby. When the Park Commission turned down his offer, he took Madame Petrova's property, less than a half mile from his own, and gave it to his son Jack.

But nearby public beach or no, family films from that era depict the Chrysler children and their friends having a glorious time laughing, drinking cocktails, and racing all over the Sound in polished mahogany speedboats. There was privacy enough for their good times.

Speaking of drinking, the *New York Times* of February 15, 1929, reported, in an indirect way, that Walter Chrysler seemed to be enjoying that pastime himself. "Liquor Is Seized from Chrysler Valet," the headline said; "83 Bottles Taken by Customs Officials on Party's Arrival in Hawaii." The article detailed the situation: "Customs officials seized 83 bottles of choice liquors said to be the property of Walter Chrysler, the motorcar manufacturer, upon his arrival yesterday on the liner *Malolo* with members of his family for two week's vacation. The attention of officers was attracted to Mr. Chrysler's valet, who was carrying off the liner some hand luggage from which a strong odor of whiskey emanated. Asked whether the bags contained liquor, the valet replied in the affirmative and the seizure followed." Of course, at this time Prohibition was the law of the land, and the possession of alcohol was a serious offense. The customs collector, Jeannette Hyde, said that if the owner didn't appear in person to pay the fine of $5 a bottle, she would have to turn over the case to the United States Attorney. It got straightened out.

All his life Chrysler was a hard-drinking, cigar-smoking, big-eating man who loved a laugh, a joke, and a good time, and success had not dampened any of his appetites. Needless to say, by the late twenties he was an anti-Prohibitionist, along with his good friend John J. Raskob. Aside from his own enjoyment of booze, he thought that Prohibition fostered crime and left the public vulnerable to sicknesses caused by bootleg liquor produced under unregulated, unsanitary conditions. By the early thirties he was very much on the bandwagon against it.

It must be said that Walter Chrysler had quite an eye for the ladies, too. One day he was met by a gaggle of reporters at Penn Station in New York upon his arrival from Detroit. The reporters asked him if it was true that he had a woman in his compartment during his overnight train ride. "Absolutely not!" he thundered as he strode briskly away from them down the platform. As he did, he turned to a close personal associate walking beside him and said with a wink, "I had two."

Della was tight-lipped. If she knew about such things, she never said anything. She spent her time looking after her children, pursuing her interests in the arts, and being a dutiful wife to her husband. Now that he was rich beyond all their dreams, she had the freedom to do and acquire anything she desired. Materially, Walt made up to her for all the hardships and deprivations of the young days of their marriage, and perhaps this was a decent settlement to her for the absences and high living of his that she had to endure now. Her photographs from these times show a woman who was beautiful but somber of mien; whatever her sorrows were, she did not parade them publicly. The loss of a $5,000 monogrammed platinum-and-diamond cigarette case from Walt at a dinner in Palm Beach was the only unfortunate circumstance in her life that ever appeared in print.

❖   ❖   ❖

Chrysler was both a creator and victim of the prosperity consciousness of the 1920s that eventually brought everyone to financial ruin. Most of the new stock market wealth was going to the top 5 percent of the nation's households, and it was all on paper anyway. These people felt rich and spent money on the things that went with that feeling, including expensive cars, big houses, jewelry, and all sorts of good times. Those among the other 95 percent who were close enough to these wealth leaders to have some of it rub off on them felt prosperous, too, and along with them, they upgraded their living circumstances with everything from new cars and clothes to better furniture and newfangled contraptions such as radios and electric refrigerators. "There is no place in this country for the timidity that hoards its possessions," Walter Chrysler was quoted as saying in a 1928 *Chicago Tribune* editorial. "Our present progress is but a beginning. We have but culled the first fruits." Beneath this apparent prosperity was large-scale industrial employment and cheap, easy credit. America seemed to be as strong a structure as Chrysler's new skyscraper, moving ever upward on a frame of solid steel. America was rising far and fast, all right, but upon close examination, it was really doing so on a framework made out of pot metal. It couldn't last.

Walter Chrysler, like Sloan, Willys, and so many others during this period, was a dyed-in-the-wool all-American booster. His public pronouncements from 1923 to 1930 and beyond are full of encomiums to modern business practice, and certainty that American economic expansion would continue no matter what temporary setbacks might crop up. "We should feel with confidence that our prosperity is continuous," Chrysler said in 1928. "There is no good reason why there should be any change."

He felt that the astute businessman had to be alert, hawklike, ready to move ahead and pounce on any possibilities for advancement as soon as he spotted them. Things were changing much faster than ever before, and the businessman who wanted to survive and prosper had to be prepared to change with them. "The American people are so progressive—they move so swiftly—that the manufacturer who was on the crest of the wave a year ago, unless he keeps pace with the progression of progress, may become old fashioned in twelve months' time," he told *Printer's Ink* in 1927. "Prosperity is available to the alert and the aggressive. The timid hang back. But those with courage will march on and will enjoy the fruits of industry."

Others, like David Beecroft, former president of the Society of Automotive Engineers, pointed out the importance of the automobile's role in this ever-expanding prosperity. In a superb article in the *New York Times* on January 6, 1924, Beecroft stated the case for the eminence of the motorcar's position in American society, calling auto transportation "the great humanizer of mass population." By bringing together peoples of all regions of the country, he thought the automobile forged a much stronger patriotism than we had ever known before. "Nothing builds patriotism so much as familiarity," he said. He also pointed out the tremendous economic advantages the motorcar was bringing to everyone in America, and like everyone else in the car business, he saw no reason it would not continue to do so indefinitely. "The saturation point of the motor vehicle will be reached when the saturation point of transportation is reached. The two are coincident. Man has not yet correctly set his slide rule to determine this period of transportation, for he has not yet completely comprehended the necessity for individual transportation in the fullness of its usefulness."

Observers had been worrying about a "saturation point" in motor car production since the days of World War I. "Remember that when the one millionth car was registered in 1913 the saturation point was hailed as close at hand!" laughed Walter Chrysler in 1927. But Chrysler and Beecroft, among others, thought that it would not come anytime soon. In July 1924 he said in *Bankers Magazine*, "The automobile business has grown with amazing rapidity, but it is going to continue to grow. First, increase in income means an increased number of car buyers. Others whose income has not increased will buy cars by getting along with less in other lines. Present owners of cars are buying second and third cars. It is getting increasingly common for families to have more than one car. Finally there is the replacement business, that is the business of replacing the entire car." After quoting supportive statistics, he asked, "How can there be any saturation point when the number of complete cars replaced exceeds the increase in production each year?"

In the beginning of 1926 he was not the least bit worried about the industry having too much production capacity. "In the automobile industry as in all industries we have the survival of the fittest," he said. Surveys had shown him that untrammeled production had been replaced by demand production based on quality, and that big production was still there for the responsive manufacturer who concentrated on improving the product. On December 22 he pronounced: "The great diffusion of wealth in this country, together with labor well employed and wages rising, promises a continuation of good times."

To counter continuing worries about saturation, in November 1926 he had told *Nation's Business*, "It has been seen that the business of manufacturing automobiles has as much to fear from a saturation point as has the clothing business or the shoe business or any other industry which produces a commodity which wears out or is capable of improvement." In August 1927 he told *Business* that prophets of saturation "are like the youth who rejected the saleswoman's suggestion of a book as a birthday gift to the youth's best girl by saying, 'No, she's already got a book.'"

His statements about the importance of replacement business in the car industry were true, but unfortunately neither he nor anyone else at that time recognized that there was a vast difference between clothing and shoes, on the one hand, and automobiles, on the other. All wear out, but the former are considered nondurable consumer goods, which need to be replaced quickly, while cars are durables, meant to last three years or more. If he and others had been able to understand this principle clearly, they might have understood long before 1929 that the saturation point was nigh.

In fact, the only saturation danger Chrysler saw ahead was "street and highway saturation and the lack of parking facilities. The argument has been advanced that one of the greatest obstacles faced by the automotive industry today is the fact that many people who can afford motor cars get along without them rather than subject themselves to the discomforts of driving in congested traffic." He had many ideas for improvements in this area, from urging the construction of ramp garages and wider streets to suggesting greater use of traffic signals, valet parking, and unloading trucks underground or through side doors of vehicles parallel-parked on the street.

In January 1927 he foresaw 30 million cars on the road, and despite the increase in their sheer numbers he wasn't concerned about traffic's ability to hinder growth; he felt sure that adequate roads would be built. "Knowing that the automobile is a creator of economic wealth, and an instrument in simultaneous prosperity, cities will continue to adapt themselves to the requirments of motor vehicular traffic," he said.

Chrysler's 1927 comments on prosperity in general and the automobile business in particular were almost word for word what he said in 1926. The big change was that now he was pushing a new element of auto industry prosperity, the export market. As early as October 24, 1925, as he sailed off for Europe with Lawrence P. Fisher aboard the *Berengaria*, Chrysler was boasting of hundreds of car agencies for his new Chrysler line throughout Europe and the British Isles, claiming 10,000 sales in 1925, and predicting a further 25,000 in 1926.

Two years later, returning to the United States aboard the *Majestic* after attending the Paris and London car shows and studying business conditions abroad, he was very optimistic about car prospects in Europe, especially in Germany, where he had a factory assembling 40 cars a day. He had plants in England and Belgium, too, and was decorated by Leopold, King of the Belgians, in 1929 for his services to that country. (In that year also, GM and Ford got into foreign production in a big way, with GM buying out

Opel, which made 45 percent of all German production, for $32 million, and the organization of Ford of Britain and German Ford.)

On February 12, 1928, the *New York Times* could head an article, "Walter P. Chrysler and Other Executives Look for Business of One Million Cars in Near Future," with the subhead "American Motor Industry Expanding Export Trade." Noting that both domestic and foreign auto sales were up 20 percent in 1927, the article said that other executives agreed with Chrysler's sales estimate. There followed Chrysler's full assessment of the British and European situation, based on his own extensive on-the-spot study. He felt that building good roads was key to the increase of car sales abroad, and despite the fact that duties made American cars fairly expensive overseas, he thought they were selling well, even in competition with local makes.

He noted that not all European markets were equally good, however. Though there was only one car for every 325 citizens in Italy, that country's high tariffs did not make it a good market for American cars. But Germany, with one car for each 196 residents, was thought to be the best market in Europe, based on need and the absence of restrictive tariffs. The best foreign market of all for American cars, however, was not in Europe but in Australia, where the market absorbed all the autos it was sent.

Two months later, sounding exactly like David Beecroft four years earlier, Chrysler opined, "No one can place a limit on the number of motor cars which this country and the world will eventually consume annually. We are giving greater value than ever before for the dollar, and the public is responding with larger orders than ever before." The only real difference from 1924 was that in the intervening time the prospects of the foreign market had been added into the mix of circumstances that were expected to keep the American car business booming.

It wasn't that Chrysler never heard any prophets of doom during these years; it was just that he simply didn't believe them. As he said in *Printers' Ink Monthly* in January 1928, "For years I have heard the cry of the pessimist, I have heard the prophecies of economic depression. I have listened to men argue that because of the law of economic cycles we were bound to have troublesome times. Business was bound to experience a setback. And my associates and I have looked ahead and we failed to see any reason for change. We could find no economic justification for cycles of depression. All the indications we could see were that times were good and would continue good."

In early 1927 Theodore F. MacManus perspicaciously had noted that a twelve-, twenty-four-, or at most thirty-six-month perspective "has been almost the extreme limit of extraordinary fore vision" in the automobile industry. As far as foreseeing the end of prosperity was concerned, he was right on the money about the auto executives of the day. Absolutely nobody, including Chrysler, could look past the next couple of years to see disaster's approach. This man, who was so sensitive to the necessity of detecting the slightest change in his own marketplace, was then deaf to the voices that spoke of coming vast changes in general business conditions. He was not unique in holding such ideas, but he did stand out even among most of the other Pollyannas by becoming one of the leading spokesmen for such soon-to-be-discredited views.

Chrysler's paean to unlimited prosperity in the New York Times on January 2, 1929, was unfettered in its optimism. "All signs favorable," "Most lines to be better than at present," "Unprecedented prosperity," and "Good times will be experienced not only by the great majority of the inhabitants of the U.S., but by those of almost every other country in the world that is at peace" were some of the Walter Chrysler quotes from this article. As for foreign lands, "Other governments are beginning to take intelligent notice of the growth of motoring among their peoples. They are encouraging this factor of prosperity and civilization by creating new highways and by many other means as well. [As Chrysler had said in 1927, "Better living, working and social conditions, as a whole, are available to people who own automobiles."] During the next decade vast territories in South America, Africa, Australia, Asia and elsewhere will be developed to a higher state of agricultural and industrial activity. I believe 1929 will witness notable progress in this direction largely through the importation of motorcars and the creation of new highways through jungles, plains and deserts." The polar ice caps were about the only areas left out.

His New Year's prediction of a 4.75-million-car year for the U.S. auto industry certainly wasn't crazy, and in fact turned out to be low by 750,000 units. (Alfred P. Sloan didn't think there would be a 5.5 million car year for another three or four years.) On the same day he made that forecast, John North Willys noted that over 810,000 cars had been exported in 1928, and Chrysler's prediction that a million would be exported in 1929 turned out to be overly optimistic by just a few thousand.

On that day, too, Roy Chapin of Hudson pointed out that the mileage of paved roads in the United States had doubled between 1921 and 1929, without so much as a breath of scandal involved in their construction (as opposed to the horrific boondoggles involved in the building of our railroad system). The American public had willingly paid out more than $10 billion for these roads, or enough to defray the total cost of our involvement in World War I, excluding foreign loans. "There has never been a public works improvement in the world's history which has even remotely approached this expenditure of public funds," he said. With no cessation of the growth in the number of cars, demand for new roads was continuing unabated, though over half of the 6.5 million miles of roads in the world were in the United States already. Such was the growth of the U.S. automobile industry and the change it had wrought in the movement of people.

Things were so good that Walter Chrysler, on the dais with Alfred P.

Sloan at a luncheon given in April 1929 for the German Tax Commission, could say, "The major effort is not competition between companies or between nations. We are united in an effort of encouraging motor transportation through better highways and more reasonable taxation to bring about a greater use of motor transport, which will provide business enough for all."

Chrysler's ultimate good-times statement came in an article called "Here Comes Prosperity!" Its first paragraph read: "A new era of prosperity which will sweep the world and revolutionize modes of living is rapidly approaching. The next ten years will witness a decided change in business and industrial progress and will bring with it a new plane of living approximating that now existing throughout the United States." This piece appeared in a student magazine called *The Dragon*. The date was August 1929.

The whole affair was like a freight train running off a cliff. Whenever you hear such statements of unbridled optimism at a business peak, you can be absolutely sure disaster is imminent, and never was it more so than in 1929. Problems began developing in the stock market in September 1929, which took sickening dives during the following month, culminating in the infamous stock market crash of October 29, 1929, the single worst day in U.S. financial history. Sloan, retuning from yet another European trip aboard the *Mauretania* on October 26, said that the slump on Wall Street had to come sooner or later; in his view, it was a healthy thing that might as well be gotten over with. Willys, returning on the twenty-eighth aboard the *Leviathan*, thought motor companies were well enough financed to recover any stock market losses in capitalization. History does not record his feelings the next day, when the market hit a brick wall.

Two days later Ford cut prices by $15 to $25 throughout his entire line, giving pause to everyone in the industry, no matter what their public statements about continuing prosperity. On November 2 Sloan called the stock market "a mystery," saying he couldn't understand the crash with business conditions so good.

On November 21 Walter Chrysler, whistling past the graveyard, said, "Motor car production has been, with normal variations, consistently upward for the last 30 years. Adjustment of automobile production to temporary economic conditions from time to time simply accords with good industrial practice. The industry's long term outlook is healthier for these adjustments."

The following December 17, Sloan, whistling even louder, was predicting a 13 percent increase in production during 1930. He based this on the replacement rate he was sure would be determined by the wearing out of cars produced five, six, and seven years previously. But the article following his statement noted that although car production for the first eleven months of 1929 was over 5.2 million units and all manufacturers had big increases through September, there had been a decline in October, and a steep decline in November. As recently as August, 516,000 cars were turned out, but only 119,000 in December. Output was usually lower in that month, but December 1929 produced fewer than half as many cars as December 1928, and was the poorest December since 1921. The chill wind of reality was beginning to blow through the promised land.

In fact, that wind was already being felt as early as May 1929 in the automobile industry. Dealers were having a tough time getting rid of the cars the manufacturers were sending them, though poor sales were blamed on a late spring and bad weather. When sales didn't perk up in June, the explanation was continued bad weather; by July, it was prolonged bad weather. Though industry production for the year would wind up over a million units higher than in 1928, profits for all but GM, Ford, and Packard declined from 1928, and for all but GM, Ford, Packard, and Nash, they were considerably lower than they were in 1925, a year of far lower production.

Another way of looking at the situation is to note that if the industry had continued to produce at the overheated rate of early 1929, it would have churned out seven million cars. As Edward D. Kennedy wrote, "Since the automobile dealer was already handling a larger number of used cars than of new cars, the sale of 7,000,000 new cars in 1929 would require the sale of at least 8,000,000 used cars, or 15,000,000 cars in all. No matter how many chickens there might be in every pot, there was nothing to indicate that the American people could buy 15,000,000 automobiles in any year under any circumstances."

Kennedy summed it all up this way: "The creation of wealth was proceeding so much more rapidly than the distribution of wealth that the output of the producer was becoming too great for the income of the purchaser. . . . By the final weeks of 1929, the auto makers had ceased to worry about the saturation point. The delicate equilibrium between new car production on the one hand and on the other trade ins, installment sales, exports and scrapped cars had been irrevocably upset. For all the calculations had depended upon a steadily increasing consumer purchasing power; that is, upon the continuance of the prosperity of the period and the resulting ability and willingness of the public to buy. But by mid 1929 the prosperity of the 1920's was over, and at no time in the 1930's was a similar prosperity to return."

❧   ❧   ❧

Among the thousands of pieces of Americana at the Henry Ford Museum in Dearborn, there is a huge painting entitled "America's Tribute To Thomas Alva Edison By Leaders Of Industry, Science, Literature And Art, On The

Fiftieth Anniversary Of His Invention Of The Incandescent Lamp". This was a spectacular affair put together by Edison's great friend and disciple, Henry Ford. It took place on October 21, 1929, and was the last great moment of the 1920s.

A committee to sponsor what was called Light's Golden Jubilee had been formed the previous June, with President Herbert Clark Hoover as its honorary chairman. Walter Chrysler and Dr. William J. Mayo were prominently named as members of the general committee sponsoring the event. Ford also chose this date as the official opening of Greenfield Village and the Henry Ford Museum, in order to get the maximum possible coverage for the inauguration of his grand new project.

President Hoover himself travelled from Washington for the event, which was packed with newspaper reporters and newsreel cameras. The painting in the museum shows hundreds of gowned and bejewelled ladies and tuxedoed men sitting at dinner tables in the replica of Independence Hall Ford had constructed for his museum. A guide to the figures in the painting reveals the presence of such notables as Madame Curie, Orville Wright, Will Rogers, Charles C. Kellogg, George Eastman, Jane Addams, Cyrus S. Eaton, Henry Morganthau, Otto H. Kahn, Charles Dana Gibson, Russell Doubleday, Adolph S. Ochs, H. M. Doubleday, Harvey S. Firestone, George T. Peabody, and such automobile figures as Ransom E. Olds, Charles W. Nash, Alvin Macauley, Howard E. Coffin, Henry B. Joy, and Charles B. King, in addition to Henry, Edsel, William and Benson Ford, President Hoover, and Walter Chrysler. The public was invited too, as tens of millions of people across America listened to this event on their radios.

Robert Lacey describes the climax of the affair. "The centerpiece of the entire evening was the moment when Thomas Edison, now old, frail, and overcome with emotion went out into Greenfield Village with Henry Ford and President Hoover to fumble through a reenactment of his famous discovery in his reconstructed Menlo Park laboratory. Until this moment, the hundreds of dinner jacketed guests in the replica of Independence Hall had been sitting in candlelit obscurity. The millions across America, listening to the broadcast ceremony, had followed Henry Ford's suggestion to switch off their own lights at home, and when Edison's carbonised fibre first broke into a tenuous glow, the word went forth. Henry Ford did not say it in so many words, but he might as well have done: 'Let there be light!'—and the switches were thrown."

It was a moment of great sentimental outpouring for Thomas Edison, the greatest inventor that America, and possibly the world, had ever known. It was also a moment of great pride in his achievement, which was America's achievement in the 20th Century: progress in the material aspects of the human condition through the invention and widespread distribution of machine technology. Countless drudgeries had been relieved, countless lives of ignorance, isolation, and grinding poverty had been opened up by the work of Edison and other great men of the previous fifty years, some of them sitting in the banquet room with him on that historic night.

One of them was his host, Henry Ford, who had changed the transportation of humanity from a matter of straining flesh and blood to one of steel, rubber, and internal combustion. Another, Herbert Hoover, was responsible for one of the greatest engineering projects of the 20th century, the saving of millions of Russians from starvation during the brutal winter of 1921. Thirty-five years later, Edison and Hoover would be voted the greatest engineers of the 20th century.

Hoover once made a statement that epitomized the calling of these engineers, great benfactors of humanity whose effects are with us every minute of every day of our lives:

"It is a great profession. There is the fascination of watching a figment of the imagination emerge through the aid of science to a plan on paper. Then it moves to realization in stone or metal or energy. Then it brings jobs and homes to men. Then it elevates the standards of living and adds to the comforts of life. That is the engineer's high privilege."

That night, the greatest of Henry Ford's life, took place just eight days before the stock market crashed. When the lights went on in the banquet hall, the men, like Walter Chrysler, who had created the age everyone was happy to live in, could smile and toast one another in triumph over their accomplishments; but though they did not know it, they also were raising their glasses in valediction, for the world they had built was soon to be swept into the dustbin of history.

◪ 26 ◪

The Great Depression Hits the Automobile Industry

Never face the facts
Ruth Gordon

A good many of the top motor company executives were so confident of their positions and success in 1929 that their companies were pretty much allowed to run on auto pilot. It seemed that most of the these men's public pronouncements were made as they embarked on or disembarked from one or another of the great ocean liners plying their way across the Atlantic from spring to fall. No one's mind seemed to be on his business, until events late in the year caught all of them up short.

Alfred Sloan was enjoying his $1.5 million yacht the *Rene* and Billy Durant was worrying about the stock market. John North Willys, a staunch Republican supporter of Herbert Hoover, sold out his holdings in Willys-Overland to a group of Toledo businessman for $25 million in anticipation an ambassadorial appointment, which turned out to be to Poland. Walter Chrysler was bustling around watching the construction of his new Chrysler Building.

During 1929, Chrysler offered down-draft carburetion and rust-proof bodies and fenders for the first time, car radios became widely available, Harley Earl's "pregnant" Buick flopped in the marketplace, and the extraordinarily beautiful front wheel drive L-29 Cord was introduced. But on the whole it was not a year for notable advances in automobile history. The most striking thing about 1929 was the number of cars and trucks built and sold to the public, over five million, for the first time. In fact the final total of 5,651,000 was over a million more than in 1928, the previous record holder for production. So perhaps it was not hard to understand how industry leaders could be lulled into a certain kind of complacency, at least until unsold cars began stacking up like cordwood on dealers' lots in May.

Around that time the wake-up call from the marketplace began to be heard, despite public pronouncements of unabated prosperity. Production

A. R. ERSKINE   C. W. NASH   F. J. HAYNES
W. P. CHRYSLER   ROY D. CHAPIN   PRESIDENT HOOVER   ALVAN MACAULEY   JOHN N. WILLYS

Walter Chrysler and other top executives visit President Hoover at the White House, 1930. (*Courtesy Frank B. Rhodes*)

schedules were cut, at first just a bit, and then more and more severely, until by December less than half the December, 1928, total of cars was turned out; this was the poorest showing for the month since 1921. The deteriorating situation was in part masked by the success of Ford, who after a year of being stymied by problems in getting mass production of the Model A up to speed, managed to turn out just under 2 million of these wildly popular cars in 1929. If the industry as a whole had continued to turn out cars as quickly as it did in the beginning of 1929, it would have produced some 7 million vehicles, a figure which shows in another way how severe production cutbacks were in the latter half of that year.

Competition was getting tougher too. Throughout the 1920s the prices of cars were going lower and lower, and the product value given at these lower prices was constantly on the upgrade, placing a tighter and tighter squeeze on manufacturers' profits. Increasingly, volume was becoming essential to making money in the auto business. When Ford didn't have production he lost money in buckets; it is estimated that the shutdown of the Model T cost him some $43 million in 1927, and the troubled startup of the Model A, of which only 819,000 were produced in 1928, cost another $72 million that year. But when his assembly lines were running at full tilt in 1929, he made a profit of $92 million.

Mickey Rooney and his 1931 Chrysler sedan. (*Courtesy DaimlerChrysler Corporate Collection*)

Volume wasn't everything, however. General Motors, on much greater volume than Ford's in 1927 and 1928, and even on similar volume in 1929, made a great deal more money than Ford, owing to the fact that around a third of its cars sold in much higher and more profitable price categories. Selling 250,000 Buicks was worth as much to GM as selling two to three times as many Chevrolets, which in any case were more expensive and more profitable than Fords. Thus, in 1928 GM showed a profit of $276 million, higher than that made by any other company before World War II, and in 1929, dipping slightly on somewhat higher volume, it earned $248 million.

Virtually all others in the marketplace were single-line manufacturers until Chrysler formed his multi-line company in 1928, and with rare exceptions, they all did less and less well as the decade progressed, despite production increases (with fluctuations) during this period. Kennedy's comparison between the 1925 and 1929 profits of the major independents shows that only Nash and Packard improved their positions.

Nash was such a good and efficient manager that he always made money, even in the worst years of the Depression, until continual shrinkage in volume finally pushed him briefly into the red in 1935. Packard was the premier luxury car manufacturer between the two World Wars, blessed with a superb product, a fiercely loyal clientele, and astute management, headed by former Burroughs Adding Machine general manager Alvan Macaulay. Packard brought out a Six for 1924, enabling it to be sold for the previously unheard-of low price (for prestigious Packard) of as little as $2,585; by

Publicity stunt to show the strength of the 1931 Chrysler's roof. (*Courtesy DaimlerChrysler Corporate Collection*)

1928, the price of the phaeton had dropped to as low as $1,985, a figure which did not go up when Packard became an all eight-cylinder line for 1929. Essentially, the company was offering its cachet to some buyers at the upper end of the middle-price field. No wonder sales jumped from the 25,000 to the 50,000 level, and profits soared to a peak of $25 million for 1929, a fantastic return for the company's investors.

In 1925, some of the independent manufacturers achieved volume and made money. Dodge Brothers, under Frederick Haynes, produced 331,000 cars and showed a $28 million profit. But like the Model T, Dodge Brothers' models were becoming moribund, and the company, lacking new product ideas, was poised for the slide that inevitably came. Roy Chapin at Hudson revolutionized the industry by cutting the price on his Essex Coach to $895, $5 under the price of his touring car, and created a sales sensation. Immediately, 80 percent of his volume was in the closed model, and sales

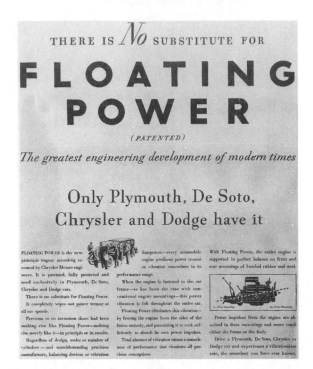

Ad for Floating Power, one of many important mechanical improvements that helped boost sales of the corporation's cars in the early 1930s. (*Courtesy DaimlerChrysler Corporate Collection*)

soared into the stratosphere. He produced 269,000 cars in 1925, and earned a profit of over $21 million. But it was the idea as much as the car that was responsible, and as competitors rushed in to match Chapin's cuts, Hudson's profits were squeezed. Willys moved 214,000 cars that year, and for once made a respectable profit of $53 per car. But thereafter his relentless pursuit of volume at the expense of profit led to declining fortunes for his company. A 50% rise in volume by 1928 led to profits of just $20 per car, and a 20% decline in volume the following year meant no profits at all.

Probably because of Henry Ford's monolithic policies and his inability to diversify his product line, there was room for a third major company in the auto industry in the late 1920s. The bill was filled by Chrysler because he was the only one to create a company with both volume and diversity.

It might have been Studebaker that filled the bill in 1923, if that company had been able to effect the merger with Maxwell-Chalmers, thus gaining control of that company's new ZSB product. But that didn't work out, and Studebaker's head, Albert R. Erskine, though an able executive who proved capable of keeping his company a profit-making volume producer of over

$1,000 cars, nevertheless could not expand into other areas of the car market. His low-priced Erskine car was a big flop, never selling more than 23,000 cars a year in the big prosperity era. And his acquisition of Pierce-Arrow in 1928 was the wrong purchase at the wrong time.

If it were only a matter of volume, two other companies would have qualified. Willys was up to 314,000 cars in 1928, and Hudson's volume was 300,000 in 1929. But Willys, who never could make a reliable profit no matter what his production, based his company's output on the cheap, light-weight Whippet Fours and Sixes that were hopelessly outclassed by the Model A and the Chevrolet International Sixes of 1929. Unlike Chrysler with his terrific new Plymouths, Willys didn't have any new low-priced miracles up his sleeve. Neither did Chapin, who had spent a mint expanding Hudson production capacity in 1926, only to find it useful for just three years before the roof fell in.

Dodge Brothers had volume and profits too under the caretaker management of Haynes, who was running things for the widows. But the management menagerie of Dillon, Read, Wilmer, Haynes, and the Graham Brothers who took over after the widows sold out in 1925, couldn't seem to put a foot right, and the company was a shadow of its former self by the time it was ripe for Chrysler's takeover in 1928. Clearly, it was the original ideas and product of the Dodge Brothers themselves that had made and sustained their company through its first decade. The same thing happened to the Dodge Brothers' cars that happened to the Model T after that, but the Ford Motor Company still had one asset that Dodge Brothers did not: its founder. Pigheaded, autocratic, and slow to respond, when it came down to it, Henry Ford had the personal, financial, and managerial resources to rebuild his company with the sensational new Model A.

So in the end, it was Walter Chrysler who pulled away from the pack. He fielded the products, raised the money, built and acquired the production capacity, and though he was the unquestioned leader of his company, he assembled the best men he could find to run it and gave them their heads.

It was just in time. Everything was put in place only 15 months before the crash that almost wiped the Big Three clean of competitors in the Great Depression. Alone among the late 1920s independents, Walter Chrysler knew that his vast production capacity had to produce something, and knew that the something would be the ultimate fruit of the mass production process that had worked its way through the industry during the previous decade: large numbers of high-quality, low-cost cars.

In 1928, he didn't know the Depression was coming, and he didn't bring out the Plymouth to prepare for that event. He brought it out because he wanted to be a major player in the low-priced market, competing with Henry Ford by using Ford's own well-tested methods of mass-market success. However, it so happened that by 1929 the bottom was about to fall

"Look at All Three," one of the most famous ads in history, devised by Sterling Getchell and J. V. Tarleton in 1932. Through this stroke of advertising genius, the public now thought of Plymouth along with Ford and Chevrolet as the low-priced three. (*Courtesy DaimlerChrysler Corporate Collection*)

out of the American economy, and the car business with it. This played perfectly to Chrysler's situation. As Kennedy astutely noted, "Chrysler made an opportunity out of what might have been a disaster. By making a much better Plymouth at a much lower price, he came out of the Depression in much better condition than he had entered it. Indeed, Chrysler was the only man in auto history (and one of the few men in industrial history as a whole) who was able to make outstanding progress against the trend of the times."

In the beginning of 1930, no one was sure if the industry only had a flat tire or if the wheels were coming off. Sales were down considerably from the previous year, but many thought this might just be a "breather" from the relentless upward push of production and sales in the last few years.

Custom 1932 Chrysler Imperial Roadster designed for Walter Chrysler, Jr. Fred Zeder and Barney Oldfield are seen in it on the day it was completed. Attributed to custom coach builder LeBaron, it was actually the work of talented young designer Herb Weissinger. (*Courtesy DaimlerChrysler Corporate Historical Collection*)

Some manufacturers, such as Nash, Packard, and Studebaker, raised their prices in an effort to keep profits up, which certainly didn't help their volume. In the low-price category, however, a number of producers made cuts, following Henry Ford's lead at the end of the previous year. Chevrolet knocked off $30 from its coupe, Willys cut $50, and Chrysler made the biggest gesture of all, bringing the Plymouth down by $70, all the way to $590. It now cost just $25 more than the Chevy, and was evidence of Chrysler's determination to move the Plymouth into the low-price, high-volume category.

To that end, Chrysler made a brilliant marketing move on March 7, 1930. He announced that henceforward all Dodge, DeSoto, and Chrysler dealers would carry the Plymouth line, thus expanding the number of Plymouth dealers overnight to ten thousand, and giving dealers of the corporation's higher-priced lines a price leader to help get them through the bad times. He also created a separate Plymouth division of the Chrysler Corporation, headed by Fred L. Rockelman, a former Ford mechanic who had been with Henry Ford since 1903, rising to general sales manager in 1927. He was let go in March 1930 because he disagreed with the cavalier treatment Ford dealers were getting at the hands of Henry Ford's right-hand man, "Cast Iron Charlie" Sorensen. The minute Rockelman became available, Chrysler eagerly scooped him up.

1932–33 Chrysler Custom Imperial Limousine designed for Walter Chrysler. It too was the work of Herb Weissinger. (*Courtesy DaimlerChrysler Corporate Historical Collection*)

In addition, Chrysler added a 62-horsepower Chrysler Six, ranging in price from just $795 to $845, to his lineup. It competed directly with the DeSoto Six and was priced not too much above the Dodge Six; however, both those lines were shored up with the introduction of new eight-cylinder cars.

Despite the price cut, Plymouth sales sank to 67,000 units. But even though the other lines shrank in volume, too, the new combination franchises kept dealers afloat. The corporation as a whole suffered a startling earnings slippage, however. In the first quarter it made only $200,000, off by $8 million from 1929, and in the rest of the year it earned just another $34,000. That was $21,668,000 less than in 1929; on a volume of 267,000 cars, 60 percent of its 1929 volume, this amounted to a profit of 89 cents per car. One does have to take into consideration that Chrysler was paying off $3 million a year on its Dodge bonds, and had the largest writeoffs for depreciation in the industry outside of Ford and GM, but even so, this was quite a turnaround in fortunes. Many other companies fell into the deficit column, but despite large drops in volume, which saw total passenger car production fall from 4.8 million to 3 million units, GM, Ford, Nash, and Packard still made hefty profits on the year. But Walter Chrysler and his organization weren't standing still, and they were about to improve their company's fortunes dramatically.

Essentially, what Chrysler did harkened back to the statement he made at the introduction of the Plymouth in 1928: "Give the public something better and the public will buy." He insisted throughout 1930 that the industry was going through a period of cleaning piled-up inventories from its houses, bringing production and sales into an equilibrium sharply broken on the upside in the previous two years. Smart manufacturers, he said, were using this slack time to develop better products than ever before to

Special composite photograph of Byron Foy showing 1933 DeSoto to Walter Chrysler, processed to look as if this event was taking place on the observation deck of the Chrysler Building. (*Courtesy DaimlerChrysler Corporate Historical Collection*)

offer to the public. When the public saw these products and realized that they were to receive much more for their money than previously, surely they would throng the showrooms, ready to buy.

What he gave the public was the new "Floating Power" Plymouth, introduced to the public on July 5, 1931. The simplest way of describing Floating Power was to say that it amounted to rubber engine mounts, but that would be like saying that a Gainsborough portrait amounted to canvas and paint.

Cars had used rubber engine mounts since Nash pioneered them in 1922, and they had been part of Chryslers since the early days, but they were relatively crude, and Floating Power was a big advance.

Fred Zeder, Jr. explained that the genesis of Floating Power came about through the friendship between Fred Zeder, Sr. and the Mayo Brothers, physicians who founded and operated the famed Mayo Clinic in Rochester, Minnesota. Zeder first went to the Mayo Clinic at the suggestion of Walter

Silent-film star Clara Bow and her husband, future Nevada Governor Rex Bell in a publicity shot with their DeSoto sedan. (*Courtesy DaimlerChrysler Historical Collection*)

Chrysler, to receive treatment for ulcers. While taking a milk cure, he became close friends with both Charles and William Mayo. Fred Zeder, Jr. wrote: "Not only was he impressed with the efficient way they operated their business, but he was also absolutely fascinated with the mechanics of the human body. He often drew parallels to how 'God's design' of the human body compared to 'the crude mechanical structures' man was capable of. The suspension system for internal organs and the electrical impulses to the nervous system—the wiring diagram to the brain—were things he related to automobile design.

"Dad spent so much time at Mayo following 'Drs. Will and Charlie' around that the staff of the hospital thought he was also an M.D. He observed hundreds of operations, scrubbed and gowned, alongside the real doctors.

"He studied how cartilage between the bones acted as a shock absorber and how the heart was designed as an efficient long lasting fuel pump. Watching the human heart in open heart surgery started him thinking about how the engines in cars were mounted to the chassis. The beating heart was, as he noted, suspended by arteries and veins and the aorta—all this plumbing—to allow dynamic balance for an harmonic oscillation. Two main concepts then occurred to him that were translated into the engineering of Chrysler cars.

"First, he recognized that the engine of a car was traditionally mounted in the chassis at back and front on the bottom, causing it to shake from side to side. So they changed the design to mount the engine toward the top in the front and at the bottom in the back. Next, from the lesson of the cartilage between bones, they installed rubber mounts on the engine brackets. They called this 'Floating Power,' and it became a big sales feature—also much copied by other companies."

Floating Power was developed over a five-year period, during which over a thousand different engine-mounting ideas were evaluated. Owen Skelton was in the main responsible for the program. As Jim Benjaminson explains it, "Skelton found that by mounting the engine following its own mass, or center of gravity, then mounting it in rubber, most of the vibration passed on to the car's frame and body—and passengers—could be eliminated." Results were amazing. "Try watching an early Plymouth, preferably a four-cylinder PA or a PB series, as it sits at idle," said Arch Brown in *Cars & Parts*. "The engine will rock alarmingly, yet none of theis reaction is transmitted to the passenger compartment."

Benjamin continues, "The front engine mount was located up high, just underneath the water pump, with the mounts low at the rear of the engine—transmission. Special 1-inch-thick rubber blocks bonded to steel upper and lower halves formed the mounts. These 'rubber sandwiches' made no metal to metal contact between the engine and frame.

"To prove the strength of the rubber to metal bonding process Chrysler engineers attached a rear motor mount to a loaded 30 ton railroad freight car, hooked one end of a cable to the motor mount and the other to a tractor and proceeded to pull the freight car about, without any apparent damage to the rubber or its bonding." In another demonstration, photographs were taken as a Plymouth was lifted off the ground using a single rubber motor mount.

Vibration was one of the worst problems of engines at that time, especially four-cylinder engines, because they had an inherent imbalance of torque reaction. Anyone who has ever ridden in a Model A will remember all the shaking he experienced. Greater smoothness was one of the things Chevrolet had been touting since the introduction of its new Six in 1929, when it advertised "A Six for the Price of a Four." But with its Floating Power system, Chrysler now had an enormous advantage in smoothness over its competition. To promote it, the company dispatched a fleet of its new Plymouths to major cities around the United States and asked the local mayors to take a ride in one of them, blindfolded. Was the car a Four, a Six, or an Eight? Most guessed eight cylinders, and Chrysler began advertising the Plymouth as having "The Smoothness of an Eight—the Economy of a Four." Chrysler himself trumpeted Floating Power as the auto industry's "fourth milestone," after the self-starter, enclosed body, and four-wheel brakes.

But it wasn't the only important innovation offered by the new

First Lady Eleanor Roosevelt sits smiling at the wheel of her 1933 Plymouth Roadster, one of several Plymouths that were specially made for her. (*Courtesy DaimlerChrysler Corporate Historical Collection*)

Plymouth, known as the Model PA. It had an "Easy Shift" transmission, in which second and third gears were in constant mesh, allowing upshifts or downshifts at any speed without double clutching. It also was the only low-priced car to feature the most popular of all contemporary auto fads, Free Wheeling, which had been pioneered by Studebaker. With Free Wheeling you never had to use the clutch unless you were shifting into low or reverse. Also, it allowed the driver to disengage the driveshaft by removing his foot from the accelerator, once under way. This made the engine slow to idle speed while the car coasted under its own power; to reengage, all you had to do was press on the accelerator once more. Though very popular for a few seasons, Free Wheeling raised safety concerns that led to its demise, because when a car was in Free Wheeling mode, the engine's braking functions were out of commission, placing an extra strain on the brakes. (There was a knob on the dashboard that allowed the driver to cut out the system completely.)

Plymouth's revised engine put out 56 horsepower, as opposed to Chevrolet's 50 and Ford's 40. Oliver Clark's body design gave the car the longest, lowest profile in the low-priced field. The PA was the first Plymouth to have a radiator grille, which consisted of vertical bars surrounded by a gently sloping shell topped by a beautifully detailed flying-lady ornament designed by Herbert V. Henderson, head of Chrysler's tiny Art & Colour Section from

Walter Chrysler and Byron Foy at the groundbreaking for a new DeSoto plant in Detroit, 1933. (*Courtesy Frank B. Rhodes*)

its inception in 1928. Viewed from the front, the radiator resembled a stylized harp. Forward placement of the radiator necessitated an elongated hood, which emphasized the Plymouth's big-car look, especially in comparison to the rather stubby-looking Model A. Broadcloth upholstery, an elegant, indirectly lighted round instrument cluster trimmed in walnut and chrome, and an oval rear window all reinforced the atmosphere of chic luxury the car exuded. Basically the new Plymouth body was another version of the DeSoto SA and Chrysler CM Sixes introduced six months previously, and it was advertised as "The Most Beautiful Low Priced Car in the World" with justification. At prices ranging from $535 to $645, this new Plymouth PA was a very good value and, though still more expensive than the Ford, it was comparably priced to the Chevrolet, and a formidable competitor indeed.

According to a legend that seems to be true, Chrysler was so proud of the new PA that he brought one of the first ones off the line to show to Henry and Edsel Ford. According to Charles E. Sorensen, Ford's right-hand man, this happened on May 10, 1932, at Sorensen's invitation; he and

GREAT WORK, BOYS.... YOU'VE BUILT THE CAR THAT MILLIONS CAN AFFORD TO OWN ! WE HAVE NOW PUT DODGE IN A DOMINANT PLACE IN THE VOLUME MARKET.

Mr. Chrysler congratulating Fred M. Zeder and K. T. Keller

Fred Zeder, Walter Chrysler, and K. T. Keller, who succeeded Chrysler as president of the Chrysler Corporation in 1935, in one of the highly effective company ads featuring dialogue in cartoon-style balloons. This one is for Dodge. (*Courtesy DaimlerChrysler Corporate Historical Collection*)

Chrysler had been friends since the start of Chrysler's automobile career. (Sorensen's 1932 date seems curiously retarded by a year, but a *Detroit Free Press* article of July 10, 1932, refers to this incident as a recent event, so either it took a year for Chrysler to make his visit or it took a year for the incident to be reported, though the latter seems more likely; in any case, Sorensen's coauthor copied the date from the paper decades later.)

After driving over to the River Rouge plant in his new car, Chrysler was greeted by the Fords and given a tour of their engineering laboratory. Then, eyes twinkling, Chrysler called them over to the window and said, "I have something I want to show you." After inspecting the car, they were given a demonstration ride, and when it was over, Chrysler presented the car to his astonished hosts and took a taxi back to his office.

Sorensen looked it over and admired the fact that the noise and vibration of this car were much less than usual because of its novel rubber suspension. He noted that there was lots of movement in the engine at idle, but that it settled down under a load. When he discussed it with Henry Ford, however, the old man said he didn't like it, and that was that.

But Sorensen told Chrysler that Floating Power was a step in the right direction. Fully developed, "it would smooth out all noises and would adapt itself to axles and springs and steering gear mounts, which would stop the transfer of road noises into the body." In writing his memoirs, Sorensen said, "Today, whenever mechanical noises appear, rubber is used to eliminate them, in refrigerators, radios and TV's, in addition to cars. We can thank Walter Chrysler for a quieter way of life."

The car was heavily promoted to a public weary of the Depression and eager for sensations of any kind to lift them out of the doldrums. At one point a stock blue Plymouth PA sedan was pulled off the line in Detroit and shipped to San Francisco, where 57-year-old Louis B. Miller and Louis Pribeck set off to establish a new round-trip transcontinental driving record. They succeeded, covering the 6,287 miles to New York and back in five days, twelve hours, and nine minutes, at an average speed of 47.52 miles per hour. In doing so, they overtook the record of famed race car driver "Cannonball" Baker who took 25 hours longer to complete his trip in a much more powerful and expensive Franklin, on the shorter Los Angeles-New York southern route. At the completion of the record-breaking run, the car was sent off on a 5,000-mile promotional tour.

That August, Washington, D.C. had a "Floating Power week," during which families were treated to airplane rides over the city, night or day, provided the fathers would take a demonstration ride in a new Plymouth and buy one $3 ticket. Plane rides were given at twenty-minute intervals, with a grand finale planned for Saturday, August 23, featuring a special fireworks display and nighttime parachute jump. The promotion was so successful that an army cavalry unit had to be called out to clear the streets on Saturday night, and when the parachutist's chute at first did not open, and he was blown off course and disappeared for forty minutes, the dealer promotion became a front-page event in the Sunday papers. It was a publicist's dream, the kind of press attention that cannot be bought. So also, later, were the photos of President Roosevelt tooling around the Little White House in Warm Springs, Georgia, in his Plymouth PA phaeton.

In creating the new Plymouth, Chrysler did exactly what he said he would, spending $2.5 million in the face of declining sales and a worsening business climate to give his customers a car value so special that they couldn't say no to it. He promised to continue to spend millions more on his low-priced car program in the future. Referring to Floating Power, Chrysler said, "We're betting our money on a mechanical improvement that will be as revolutionary as was the self starter. It's not gambling, because the innovation represents four years of developments, refinements and tests." Spreading around the credit, as was his invariable wont, he continued, "The

Chrysler Corporation is able to take this bold step forward while others are singing the 'Depression blues' because there are associated with me some men who have met the economic problems of the land in the last year with raised fists—fighting rather than moaning."

And the customers came. Plymouth sales rose from 67,000 in 1930 to 94,000 in 1931, in the teeth of the Depression. True, this figure didn't come anywhere near Chevrolet's 623,000 or Ford's 541,000. But Chevrolet was off by more than 25 percent and Ford was off by more than 50 percent from 1930 sales, while Plymouth was up by 40 percent in this very bad year for the auto business.

The Chrysler and Imperial lines for 1931 were revamped, too. Walter Chrysler had been very impressed with the 1929 Cord L-29, the longest, lowest, and most rakish car ever introduced to the American market. It was designed by Alan Leamy, a twenty-seven-year-old who was responsible for the elegantly refurbished 1929 Auburn line.

Leamy belived that automobile design had been heavily influenced by the horse-drawn vehicles that cars had replaced, with most changes in appearance due to engineering advances. He, however, was a great admirer of low-slung European models such as the Isotta-Fraschini and Hispano-Suiza, and believed that beauty for its own sake could be used to make cars appealing to the public, especially to women. Errett Lobban Cord, who resurrected the fortunes of Auburn in the mid-twenties, had great faith in the young man's ideas and put him to work on the Cord, and probably also on the Duesenberg Model J, as soon as he was finished with his work on the Auburn.

The novelty of front-wheel drive allowed the Cord to be built very low to the ground, which gave Leamy the opportunity to display his design ideas on the new car. Every inch of it, from curving front bumper to curving rear bumper, was "designed," rather than just added on to the rest of the car in a more or less utilitarian and haphazard fashion. In its first year on the market, the L-29 won thirty-three awards for design excellence.

Legend has it that Chrysler saw one of these new cars in late 1929, purchased it immediately, and had his design staff go over it from stem to stern. Practically on sight he decided that since this Cord was the most beautiful of cars, he wanted his own senior lines to bear a close resemblance to it. One of the main designers of the new Chryslers and Imperials was a twenty-two-year-old native of Kentucky named Herbert Florian Weissinger. When he began to make Chrysler design-study drawings based on the Cord front ends, Herbert Henderson asked him to refine them into a design for the new Chryslers. He did so, but he wanted to take the Chrysler-Cord resemblance one step further.

Weissinger proposed both front-wheel drive and a rear engine to Fred Zeder, who wouldn't even discuss either one. What Weissinger wanted, of course, was the lowness that only front-wheel drive or rear-engine placement could give him. Walter Chrysler ended up hiring C. W. Van Ranst, chief engineer of the L-29 Cord, and gave him orders to duplicate the Cord design on a rear-wheel-drive chassis for the new Imperial. So Weissinger didn't get exactly what he wanted, but Van Ranst's adaptation did allow him to have a great deal of freedom with the Imperial.

For the regular Chrysler cars he provided wide, low-looking bodies, using, on the six, sheet metal and chassis that were interchangeable with DeSoto's. The most prominent feature on the cars was a wide, slightly inclined split-V painted radiator, surrounded by a thick chromium shell. The process was a great advance for Chrysler, which had always been far more interested in engineering than styling. Notes Michael Lamm, "The 1931 Chrysler gave [Art & Colour] its first major role in the styling of an entire automobile. It was also the first time that the corporation designed a chassis to fit a new series of bodies rather than the other way around."

With the new Imperial CG models, the Cord resemblance really was displayed to brilliant advantage. A 145-inch wheelbase permitted the car to display a long hood, sweeping fenders with chrome slashes on the rear set, a slanting split windshield, and a mesh V-shaped grille, topped by a leaping-gazelle ornament and fronted by swooping double-arched fenders. All these features contributed to a total design considered by many to be the apex of classical automobile styling. Regular bodies were turned out by Briggs, with four semicustoms by LeBaron and full customs by Waterhouse, Locke, Dietrich, and Murphy also offered. (Hugo Pfau, a former LeBaron designer, and Ralph Roberts, a Briggs designer and Briggs' LeBaron division vice president, both said that the LeBaron studios acted as styling consultants for the standard 1931 to 1933 Imperials, which accounted, in part, for their racy appearance.) A brand-new 125-horsepower, nine-bearing, 384.8-cubic-inch straight-eight engine, which could put out 135 horsepower with the Red Head high-compression feature, completed the package. Even at prices ranging upward from $2,745, some 3,228 Imperials were sold during this year, which was quite a respectable figure in the midst of the Depression.

The Imperial body design was so impressive that Auburn, which had been planning a family resemblance to the beautiful Cord front end, went back to work and devised an upright, flat grille for its new line of cars, so as not to look like an Imperial copycat. And the GM board, upon seeing the new Imperial with its recessed V grille, put a great deal of pressure on Harley Earl to go to his drawing board and come up with something equally impressive for the Cadillac, which he wasn't able to do until 1933.

The rest of the Chrysler line consisted of a 116.5-inch-wheelbase 65-horsepower six starting at $885, and a new eight, first rated at 80, then 88, and in a deluxe version 100 horsepower; this car sat on a 124-inch wheelbase and started at $1,545. As expected, the six outsold the eights by more than six to one.

Several stock car records for the new engines created a lot of excitement that year. Race car drivers Harry Hartz and Billy Arnold set twelve new AAA Class B stock car records at Daytona Beach, running an Imperial roadster at up to 90.4 miles per hour and an Imperial sedan at up to 90.3 miles per hour. In August of 1931 a stock Chrysler eight won the Belgian Grand Prix at an average speed of 62.5 miles per hour. Such records, and sales to prominent celebrities including Mickey Rooney, Myrna Loy, and Al Smith, certainly got Chrysler cars noticed. Though total 1931 sales of 52,819 were down by 8,000 from the previous year, they were still quite respectable, considering general business conditions.

In 1931 also, the Chrysler Corporation was enjoying the profits of its Amplex Division, which had been created the previous year. It was formed to handle the sales of all Chrysler products other than finished passenger cars and trucks. There were three main products handled by this division: Chrysler marine engines, Chrysler industrial engines, and perhaps most important, Oilite self-lubricating bearings, which were a revolutionary new product.

As Arthur Swigert, Jr., tells us in his illuminating book, *The Story Of Superfinish*, the importance of lubrication on moving surfaces has been known since ancient times. In 450 B.C., Herodotus wrote a detailed description of petroleum oils and early lubrication. In 60 A.D., Pliny the Elder compiled a complete list of vegetable oils then in use. Even earlier, beef or mutton tallow was used on axles in chariot races.

In modern times Isaac Newton was given credit for laying the foundation of modern lubrication theory, based on the fundamental law of the viscous resistance of a fluid. This states that the shearing stress at any point in a fluid is proportional to the rate of shear. In 1687, he said that lubrication was a mechanical action, thus governed by his newly expounded laws of motion. This is illustrated by two lubed parallel surfaces, one static, one moving at a constant velocity. The law Newton applied stated that the resisting force per unit area is proportional to the velocity gradient, or the velocity divided by the distance between two surfaces. The resultant constant of proportionality was later termed viscosity.

Two hundred years later Osborne Reynolds, combining his ideas with the results of research conducted by Beauchamp Tower, wrote a paper for the Royal Society of Engineers including mathematical introductions to the theory of lubrication, as believed at that time. It was the first recognized treatise on the theoretical reasons for fluids' diminishing friction. The discovery of constant oil pressure buildup in a mechanical operation in Tower's experiments was a turning point in the history of lubrication.

Bearings are designed to produce only one major result: to carry loads with maximum efficiency. To accomplish this, wear must be minimized or eliminated to the greatest possible degree, requiring adequate lubrication, which is a matter of correctly determined viscosity. The development of proper fluids and their delivery systems was one of the major issues in the creation of the modern motor car, and Oilite bearings were a significant advance.

Oilite bearings were self-lubricating. As developed by Chrysler research under Carl Breer, they consisted of finely powdered tin, copper, and graphite in various proportions that were formed in molds under high pressures, heat-treated, sized, and impregnated in an oil bath in which the bearing material absorbed up to 30 percent of its own volume in oil. Under pressure or heat this oil was exuded, then was absorbed again when the load was released. This property could be varied to suit many applications, and resulted in low-cost production of no-maintenance bearings for use in water pumps, spring shackles, and the like. They were also useful in such items as fuel filters. In addition to their placement in Chrysler products, some half a million Oilite bearings were sold to outside manufacturers in 1930, a figure that quintupled in 1931. When Super Oilite was introduced in 1932, sales rose to 7 million units, and soared to 18 million in 1933. Altogether Oilite and Amplex were significant profit centers for the Chrysler Corporation throughout this period.

Indeed, just about the only thing that didn't work out too well for Chrysler in 1931 was a new four-speed, dual range transmission for the Imperials, which turned out to be balky and not nearly as smooth as GM's Syncromesh transmission. It didn't last long.

Investors in Chrysler were well rewarded for their confidence in the company in 1931. The corporation's sales actually went up in 1931 to 272,000 cars, compared to the 1930 total of 269,000. Though this was only an increase of 3,000 units, profits rose from $234,000 to $1,468,000, which was a strong testament to Walter Chrysler's managerial skills. In addition to fielding new products that caught the public's fancy, he cast a ruthless eye on expenses and cut wherever he could. On July 3, 1930, he decreased all salaries, including his own, by 10 percent, so that hourly workers whose time had been cut back would not be the only ones bearing the burden of hard times. A statement given out on that day was vindicated by the 1931 annual report: "The Chrysler organization is determined to operate its business on a profitable basis under whatever conditions may exist, and the readiness to make all necessary sacrifices, as indicated by this move, is a factor of strength which is bound to be reflected in the ultimate success of the company and its continued progress in the automobile industry."

But things in the automobile industry in general were not going well. Sales were diving all over the place. Popular makes such as Hudson and Willys had seen their deliveries plummet from 1929s 300,000 and 257,000, respectively, to 113,000 and 80,000 in 1930. This was approximately a two-thirds drop in just one year. By 1931, Hudson volume was cut in half again, to 58,600, and Willys-Overland sales collapsed by more than two-thirds, to

26,444. On top of a $7.5 million loss in 1930, Willys dropped a sickening $14.6 million the following year, and had only $1 million in the bank by year's end. Even Ford, with his volume cut nearly in half in 1931, went from a $42 million profit in 1930 to a $37 million loss, by far the largest in the industry, in 1931. Starting in 1929, such famous old names as Chandler and Locomobile had gone out of business, and by 1931 other equally well-known makes including Gardner, Moon, Kissel, and Jordan had joined them in oblivion, with Durant and Peerless soon to follow.

Some companies were still showing a profit in 1931, but very few. In addition to Chrysler, Nash and Studebaker continued to make money, despite significantly lower volume. And Auburn, which featured 98-horsepower straight-eight engines and astonishingly beautiful Cord-influenced bodies, saw its sales increase by 162 percent to their highest level ever, at 29,536 units! Though its triumph would be brief, this company did well that year despite sluggish sales of the Cord and the very expensive Duesenberg. The profit leader, of course, by a vast margin was GM, which made $94.6 million; but even this figure was more than a 50 percent decline from 1930, despite the fact that its unit volume was down only about 10 percent.

The 1920–21 depression had been an inventory depression; this one was a credit depression. But in the beginning the Great Depression could also be said to be a psychological depression on the part of the American public as much as anything else. Susan Estabrook Kennedy shows that the sum of all wages and salaries in America dropped from $51 billion in 1929 to $47 billion in 1930, a difference of 8 percent (farmer cash income dropped 15 percent, to $8.5 billion). But expenditures on new automobiles, one of the hardest-hit industries, dropped by a third, from roughly $3 billion to $2 billion. "The automobile manufacturer was particularly the victim of the 1930 state of mind—a state of mind governed by anxiety instead of optimism," Kennedy says. "The inflation of the 1920s had been primarily a credit inflation, and a credit inflation is always founded upon confidence in the future. During the 1920s millions of persons traded in automobiles that were one, two or three years old and that were still in excellent working condition. Their trade in allowances covered the cash payment on the new car, and they did not mind meeting the remaining monthly payments for a year. But they did not feel the same way in 1930. An automobile is not, strictly speaking, a necessity of life. A *new* automobile is not a necessity of life even to the confirmed motorist. Unemployment was rapidly increasing. The old feeling of an ever growing personal income had entirely disappeared; even the sense of being secure in a job was rapidly vanishing. Few people needed a new car, and in 1930 few people were buying things they did not need. The status of the automobile as 'durable' consumer's goods had finally caught up with the automobile manufacturer."

In 1932 things got a lot worse, but Walter Chrysler kept on with his program of impressing the public with terrific new values in what was now known as "the amazing Plymouth." This shored up his participation in the only field with any vigor left at all in the automobile business—the low-priced market. In addition, he was preparing his company for booming prosperity when the Depression abated and prosperity returned, as he was sure it would. His motto was to have faith in the future and act on it.

Everyone knew that Walter Chrysler was planning an all-new Plymouth for 1933, and they assumed that the replacement for the PA model would be just an interim car. But, as Jim Benjaminson says, "Walter Chrysler's interim car would be the zenith of four cylinder Plymouths."

The PB model was practically an all-new car, with a 112-inch wheelbase, smaller wheels, larger tires, a 65-horsepower engine, centrifuse brake drums, a silent second transmission with an $8 optional automatic clutch, Free Wheeling, and, of course, Floating Power. Ten models were offered at prices starting as low as $495 and reaching up to $785 for the stunning two-door convertible sedan. Production started on February 4, 1932, and lasted only until September 27, during which time some 81,010 cars were produced.

One of the most famous of all Walter Chrysler stories is connected to the promotion of this car. It involves the ideas of a thirty-one-year-old advertising whiz kid named J. Sterling Getchell and his twenty-nine-year-old partner J. V. Tarleton, who had acquired the DeSoto account in 1931. When Byron Foy invited Getchell to see the dealer preview of the new Plymouth on Long Island in March 1932, he was distinctly unimpressed by the advertising campaign that was supposed to accompany the car's introduction. "It was simply the same old Detroit formula stuff with not a kick in a carload," said Tarleton. The two men persuaded Foy to allow them to come up with a better approach, all at their own risk and on their own responsibility.

It would not be an easy job, since the car was to hit the showrooms the same week as Henry Ford's long-rumored and much-discussed Ford V-8. To get attention, Getchell at first wanted Walter Chrysler's old friend Arthur Brisbane, the famous Hearst editor and publisher, to write a series of ads extolling the virtues of his friend's new car. Brisbane was willing, but he thought the ads would be more effective if Chrysler himself appeared in the ads. He sent Getchell a crude layout of a proposed ad with a picture of Chrysler's head pasted over a photograph of evangelist Billy Sunday, in a theatrical pose, with Chrysler inviting people to come in and see his new Plymouth. Getchell immediately recognized the worth of the idea and he and Tarleton began composing a series of ads showing Chrysler and his new PB Plymouth.

The problem was that they didn't have any suitable pictures of Chrysler, and just pasting his head on photos of posed models didn't work very well at all. DeSoto's general manager, Ray Peed, saved the day by suggesting that Walter Chrysler himself pose for the project. "If you can get a photographer, I'll get Mr. Chrysler," Peed said. True to his word, Peed called him up, interrupting his dinner, and got him to agree to come down to the Chrysler showroom in the Chrysler Building and pose. At 10 P.M. he arrived, and faced the photographer and his battery of cameras and lights.

Tarleton described what happened: "As far as I know Mr. Chrysler had never had the experience of being pushed around by a commercial photographer before under a battery of very, very hot kleig lights. We were afraid he would put on his hat and go home any minute, but as time went on it was obvious that the boss was enjoying himself tremendously. We kept him there until midnight and sent our photographer packing with some 50 negatives, which he developed and printed overnight.

"The following day, using these pictures, we laid out and pasted up six full newspaper ads and that evening took them up to Mr. Foy's apartment after dinner and spread them on his library floor. One of these ads showed a large picture of Mr. Chrysler in a very informal pose with his foot on the bumper of the new Plymouth. The headline of the ad had originally read, 'Look At All Three Low-Priced Cars Before You Buy.' In the process of making the layout, the writer had boiled this down to four big words, 'Look At All Three.'

"Mr. Foy's first inclination was to eliminate this advertisement from the series because it didn't seem a good idea to invite inspection of our competitors' products. It was finally decided, however, to submit three of the ads, including this one, to Mr. Chrysler the following day."

Within ten minutes Walter Chrysler decided to run the ads. His advertising staff objected, however, because Getchell didn't have the Plymouth account. "Finally Chrysler put an end to the discussion, slamming his fist on the desk and saying, 'I don't give a goddamn how you do it, but I want to run these ads.'"

Tarleton continued: "The day 'Look At All Three' was published in newspapers all over the country the reaction was unmistakable. Chrysler Corporation dealers reported that their doors started swinging early in the morning and didn't stop until late at night. Opinions on this point may differ, but I believe that essentially it was the sportsmanship of this appeal and the forthright tone of the copy that captured the public's imagination."

Getchell's firm was paid for its expenses on this ad, but nothing more, as Lee Andersen & Company of Detroit had the Plymouth account. After the ads ran, Chrysler asked the men up to his office and asked what sort of payment they wanted for their work. "We said, 'Nothing—except the Plymouth account.' Mr. Chrysler asked us how we would like a nice 30-day European vacation with our wives and all expenses paid. We said, 'No thanks, Boss.' He said, 'How would you like to each have a custom Chrysler Imperial with a LeBaron body and your initials in gold on the doors?' We said, 'No thanks, Boss.' Then we went downstairs and kicked each other for a while. P.S., four months later, we got the job."

Many people think that "Look At All Three" was a campaign, but it was just one ad in a whole series. Another one of these striking ads featured a forceful picture of Chrysler under a banner proclaiming, "Two Years Ago I'd Have Said It Couldn't Be Done," and a third depicted a visionary Chrysler across from a photo of Zeder, Skelton, and Breer beneath the legend "In 1929 I Couldn't Have Built This Car." But it was "Look At All Three" that decades later was praised as among the one hundred greatest advertisements in American history in a book by Julian Watkins. Though the term "Big Three" had been in use since 1928 to describe General Motors, Ford, and Chrysler, this ad did more than anything else to cement that term in the minds of the public.

The very modestly priced DeSoto, now offered only as a six, was attractively restyled for 1932 with a rounded grille copied from Miller race cars of the period; however, Dodge Sixes and Eights carried over what now looked like very old-fashioned styling into the same year. The beautiful Chryslers were not much changed, though they now had V-type radiators and, on sedans, split-V windshields as well, in addition to redesigned instrument panels. Like all Chrysler products, they featured Floating Power.

The Imperials were now designated CH in the regular series and CL in the custom, and in the regular series featured the same changes found in the lower-priced Chryslers. The CL series, which featured bodies solely by LeBaron, were made even more beautiful than the semicustoms and customs of the previous year. Five ventilation doors replaced louvers in both sides of the hood, which stretched past the cowl in an unbroken line almost to the windshield. These styling touches were cleverly arranged to disguise the fact that Walter Chrysler had decided not to spend the money to develop the twelve- and sixteen-cylinder engines now sported by such Imperial competitors as Cadillac, Packard, Lincoln, Pierce-Arrow, and Marmon. The back of the much-admired CL four-door convertibles, where the folded tops rested, dipped below the belt line on the sides of the car, creating one of the most beautiful styling effects ever seen on an American automobile. Other distinguishing features found on all CL models were larger tires and, inside, a walnut dashboard with an engine-turned instrument panel and twin glove boxes.

Two notable custom Imperials were turned out in 1932. One was built especially for Walter Chrysler, Sr. It was a Custom Eight CL Landau Formal Sedan, featuring a padded top with landau irons, which flowed forward and upward into the line of beautifully arched suicide doors. It also displayed Graham-style fully skirted front fenders, a feature that never appeared on classic Imperials except for another special, this one a phaeton built for Ralph Roberts in 1933. Chrysler's CL, now on display at the Henry Ford Museum in Dearborn, had an engine replacement in 1937, and from time to time other new features were installed on the car. The body had gold-plated fittings and was painted an extraordinary shade of brilliant carmine red, said to have been chosen by Chrysler himself to match a color in his favorite Ming vase. All in all it made quite an appearance, and thereby hangs a tale. When the car was completed, he had his chauffeur drive it round to the house on Long Island to show it to Della. She came outside, walked around it in total silence, and gave it her complete scrutiny. When she finished, she turned to the chauffeur and said, "Tell Mr. Chrysler I'm not going to ride around in a whorehouse on wheels." And that was that.

The other special was a glamorous 160-horsepower low-slung speedster for Walter Chrysler, Jr. with a cut-down raked windshield and an aluminum body sprouting all-steel pontoon fenders front and rear. Its disappearing top folded down into a leather-lined compartment that also accepted the side curtains, and its spare tire, held in by side-mount brackets on a trolley base, slid out of the trunk compartment on track rails. The bechromed front-end ensemble was enhanced by quadruple trumpet horns. Bodywork on both cars is credited to LeBaron, but Chrysler historian Don Butler informs us that these cars were actually the work of the extraordinarily talented young designer Herb Weissinger, who supervised their construction in Chrysler's custom body shop. There are photos of Barney Oldfield and Fred Zeder sitting in the speedster the day it was completed in May 1932 (though Walter's car is now black, the photo shows that it was originally gray). Apparently another car just like it was built for Jack Chrysler.

Al Nippert, who later owned the car, told Beverly Rae Kimes, "Obviously, this speedster was used to try out a lot of new ideas because many of the mechanical parts are marked 'experimental'—the gas pedal starting, the anti-stall restart system, the generator, the automatic choke with flood gas charge dump button on the dash, the pendulum control valve that disengages the clutch in a panic stop, etc."

Though these roadsters were special designs, they reinforce the view of Richard Burns Carson, who says in his book *The Olympian Cars,* "The Chrysler Imperial was a veritable rolling laboratory of advanced ideas that would later appear on the corporation's cheaper products. Such examples of Chrysler's many contributions to automotive progress as four-wheel hydraulic brakes, downdraft carburetion, overdrive transmissions, semi-unitary body construction and airflow design typically debuted on the firm's most expensive line." Just as tellingly, Warren H. Erb adds mention of one-piece curved-glass windshields, fluid drive, air conditioning, and disc brakes. This was in direct contrast to other luxury car makers, whose senior products were expressions of the most tried-and-true automotive ideas of the time, "and it stems from Chrysler's belief that his Imperial customers deserved the best and most modern automobiles possible."

But no matter how good the cars, nothing above the low-price level was selling. Dodge moved about 30,000 cars in 1932, DeSoto about 27,000, and Chrysler roughly 25,000. Even those glorious Imperials, with CH prices cut by $1,000, or more than 35 percent below 1931 levels, saw sales plunge by 50 percent to 1,622.

Everybody else was in the same boat, with sales sinking to levels little more than half that of 1931, already a severely depressed year. From 2,038,000 cars in 1931, the industry turned out only 1,170,000 cars in 1932. It was now selling about 25 percent of what it had sold in 1929.

This was a great pity, for the industry was making much better cars in 1932, at prices that averaged $100 less than they had in 1929. With price cuts, manufacturers competing with Ford were actually selling their cars at the same level as his for the first time. Fords, Chevrolets, Plymouths, and Terraplanes could all be bought for under $500. But the customer had disappeared from the marketplace, no matter what the price of the goods. Nonfarm workers had only 60 percent of the income they had had in 1929, and farmers did even worse, at only 44 percent of already depressed 1929 levels. All told, Americans were earning $26 billion less than in 1929, with 25 percent of all workers unemployed. Per capita income had been cut in half, from $600 to $300, so that a family of four earning $2,400 in 1929 had to get by on $1,200 in 1932, provided it was getting by at all.

The irony of all this is that 1932 is considered the zenith of the classic automobile era, a time when the most beautiful of all American cars were produced. Many of the designers and craftsmen who had worked for custom coach builders of the twenties and thirties were now employed by the remaining car manufacturers, whose products were reflecting ideas of grace and beauty previously unavailable to the masses. In the description of future Chrysler head designer Virgil Exner, Jr., what had been true of Packards, Cords, and Pierce-Arrows in 1930 was true in 1932 of Auburns, DeSotos, Buicks, and Grahams: "The main elements of design were high bodies, long wheelbases, long hoods, huge tires and wire wheels, narrow-coupled cabs, long flowing clamshell fenders, distinctively styled radiator shells for each make, and short trunks or turtle decks. And the designs exuded beautiful continuity. . . . They had gotten away from the very straight, flat surfaces and gotten into contouring, which combined a flow of finely tuned curves with very artful, mechanical details. . . . The mechanical detail was very nice and they made it nicer in door handles, and hood latches, and window frames, and spare tire covers, and taillights, and headlights: all of the mechanical elements that were for the most part separate on automobiles as opposed to built in, like today."

Auburn came out with a beautiful new car with a fine Continental

V-12 engine selling for the incredibly low price of $975 to $1,275, yet only 5,000 of them moved out of the showrooms. The company's total sales of 11,646 were off a whopping 60 percent from the previous year, and after making money in 1931, it posted a $1 million loss, part of which was due to the total collapse of Cord sales. The last 157 of the L-29's were sold in 1932.

Graham came out with an extraordinary new design in the Blue Streak Eight, curvily styled by Amos Northrup, with detailing by Ray Dietrich; it was the first car to feature skirted fenders, a development widely considered the harbinger of modern streamlined styling. Total production of all Graham models came to just a shade under 13,000 in 1932, down from 77,000 in 1929, 33,000 in 1930, and 21,000 in 1931. Even though the Blue Streak, which accounted for most of the company's sales, was the only eight to show a sales increase in 1932, the picture at Graham was bleak. The death of the brilliant forty-five-year-old Ray Graham, so despondent over the Depression that he suddenly jumped into the water and drowned himself during a swimming outing in August, only added to the company's woes.

Hupmobile fielded a beauty that year, too, in its F and I series eights, on which Amos Northrup assisted Raymond Loewy. These had cycle fenders on the front of the car. In Karl S. Zahm's description: "Instead of sweeping gradually rearward as on most cars, these front fenders curved smartly around the wheels, then abruptly reversed to meet the running boards. The rear fenders were similarly curved at the base, thereby mating with the running boards in an unbroken line. As a final touch, the outer edge of the running boards were streamlined to conform to the body contours." This exposed much more of the body than usual, and contributed to a much longer, more impressive-looking car. Despite offering such a striking car at value prices, sales nosedived from 17,000 in 1931 to 10,000 in this year, a level only one-sixth as high as it had been in the company's peak year, 1928.

These results were utterly typical of the times. An attractively restyled Pontiac, featuring both six- and eight-cylinder models, was *fourth* in the industry with sales of only 48,789. Buick's extensive and elegant model range sold just 47,717 units, with a soup-to-nuts Studebaker-Rockne lineup not far behind at 45,227; Hudson-Essex-Terraplane weighed in with sales of just under 42,000 cars. After the low-priced three, these were the industry's big sellers. The chic little Oldsmobile moved just 22,000 vehicles, and Willys a paltry 21,000. Packard, with its eights and brand-new twelves, managed to outsell all other luxury cars *combined* with sales of 16,613, a figure that would have been appalling three years before. Now that number was gigantic, compared with 3,384 Lincolns, 2,200 Pierce-Arrows, and a sickeningly small 720 Marmons and 127 Stutzes. Reo put out six-cylinder Flying Clouds and gorgeous eight-cylinder Royales, the latter designed by the ubiquitous Amos Northrup (assisted by Julio Andrade); nevertheless, its sales were almost cut in half to 3,623, causing a $2.5 million loss on top of a $3 million one in 1931. Even smart LeBaron styling couldn't pull up sales of America's only air-cooled car, the Franklin, above 1,862 units, just 13 percent of what they had been in 1929. Chevrolet, the industry leader, sold a mere 319,000 cars, and Ford sales, even with the new V-8 and fresh styling, amounted to just 300,000 (partly due, it must be admitted, to Ford's usual problems getting production of his new model up to speed).

Truly, nothing could have been worse than 1932 conditions. Every company making automobiles in the United States lost money, with two exceptions. Losses ranged all the way up to the gigantic sum of $70,900,000, rung up by Ford. Henry Ford had by now proved that he was the mass-production genius of one product, the Model T. Though the Models A and B and the V-8's that succeeded it were fine cars that sold very well, Ford's process of designing and producing them was arduous and protracted, at a time when the same processes at competitors such as GM and Chrysler were for the most part swift and assured. Perhaps we would do well to remember that the original mass-production process took years for Ford and his associates to develop and perfect, and though Ford was able to come up with strikingly fine new products to replace the Model T, he never was able to initiate them as swiftly and smoothly as more flexible production minds such as William S. Knudsen's at General Motors and Walter Chrysler's at his own firm.

The two exceptions to the losses in 1932 were telling. General Motors produced 450,000 cars, yet earned the minuscule profit of $164,979, down from $94,800,000 in 1931. The company that a few years previously had earned the largest profit of any firm in history had now become unable to earn any money at all. In one of the great industrial triumphs of the era, Charles W. Nash was able to wring a profit of $1,029,552 from production of a mere 17,696 cars. Through superb management and cost control, and the ingenious timing of his introduction of a beautiful new line of cars in the spring of 1932, the only automobile leader to rise from a background of abject 19th-century rural poverty was able to turn a profit six times as large as General Motors' on a volume only 4 percent as large. Clearly, when only the biggest of the behemoths and a tiny anomaly in an industry can make money, something is radically wrong. It was beginning to look as if the automobile industry might not survive in any recognizable form at all.

By the end of 1932 people were very frightened. They were wondering if capitalism was falling apart underneath their feet, plunging them into bolshevism, or worse, into some hideous unknown anarchy. Large numbers of people continued to go to their jobs at companies that could no longer pay them, hoping that their efforts would help to pull them and their employers through this bleakest of times.

The fortunes of Willys-Overland were so depressed that John North

Willys gave up his post as ambassador to Poland in June of 1932 and returned to Toledo to manage his company. The Willys-Overland stock he'd sold out at $32 a share a few years before was now worth $1.13. Though Willys himself undoubtedly remained a wealthy man, he felt a great sense of responsibility to the company he founded and to the city of Toledo, which had done so much to help him make his fortune, and so, after President Hoover personally requested him to do so, he rolled up his sleeves and went to work to help save his firm. At Studebaker, deficits were piling up for the first time, and its president, Albert R. Erskine, was frantically trying to shore up the company's finances. Durant sold his last cars, and his firm was dissolving. In Cleveland, the Peerless factories lay idle, awaiting their eventual transformation into the Carling brewery.

Henry Ford, who had bravely raised his daily wage to $7 after the crash at the end of 1929, reduced it to $6 by the end of 1931, and within a year he scaled it back to just $4. The number of Ford employees fell from 101,000 in 1929 to 56,000 in 1932. Robert Lacey recounts perhaps the grimmest fact of this period in Ford history: "As business continued to wilt, the company was forced to resort to the most demeaning expedient of all. If you had a few hundred dollars of life savings to put down, or a rich relative in need of a new car, you could obtain a job at the Rouge in exchange for the purchase of a new Ford. To maintain his sales, the world's greatest capitalist had been reduced to barter."

Just west of Ford headquarters in Dearborn lay the community of Inkster, at this point of the Depression a miserable shantytown primarily inhabited by the blacks who once had jobs in Ford's foundry and now were unemployed. Inkster was at the bottom of the barrel, with no bank, no electric power, and no police. Almost all its people were in debt, and hunger was widespread; most of Inkster's children suffered from rickets.

It was not to remain so, due to yet another of Henry Ford's brainstorms. Lacey relates: "In November, 1931, Henry Ford moved in. For more than a decade he had been operating supermarketlike commissaries for his workers at Highland Park and the Rouge, and now he set up a similar store in Inkster to sell food and clothing at near wholesale prices. He reopened the school. He provided seeds for men to cultivate in their gardens. He purchased sewing machines for the women and had dressmaking classes organised for them. Within a matter of months the village of Inkster was back on its feet again, glowing with paid for electricity and a certain self respect, since the community was paying for its revival with its own hard work."

It wasn't subsidized charity, for Henry Ford didn't believe in that. His idea was that men should be helped to stand on their own two feet. To that end, he offered the village men jobs at the Rouge for which they were paid but $1 per day, with the other $3 of his standard Ford wage going to finance the revival of community services (the work of cleaning up the town was also given out on the same dollar-a-day basis) and paying inhabitants' documented debts.

This exercise in paternalism worked well for Inkster, but something seemed wrong about the whole thing. Ford was putting people to work, but they were working in gardens and cleaning up backyards and roads. When Anne O'Hare McCormick came to visit Dearborn and Detroit on behalf of the *New York Times* in the spring of 1932, she found them a sorry sight, and put her finger on what was wrong. Mass production might be great for the people in prosperous times, but when production slowed down, all it led to was mass idleness. The value of Fordism to society was now drawn into question. "Something has happened to Ford," McCormick wrote, "and perhaps through him to the America he represents."

When even paternalism dried up people truly saw the void gaping in front of them. On July 28, 1932, a badly trained U.S Army attacked and destroyed an encampment of World War I veterans. They had come to Washington to request that the government give them early payment of the $500 bonus due every veteran in 1945 under the Adjusted Compensation Act of 1924. The veterans had been camped out in what became known as 'Hooverville' shanties in the shadow of the White House as they awaited disposition of their request. Trouble began with the shooting of a vet named Hrushka, and increased with the shootings of three others. President Hoover told Secretary of War Patrick J. Hurley to use troops to deal with the situation. Dwight D. Eisenhower said that the soldiers should not be in uniform, as this was just a street brawl. But Douglas MacArthur ordered him and everyone else into uniform saying, "There is an incipient revolution in the air." Hoover issued a communiqué stating that the troops will "put an end to rioting and defiance of civil authority." A few minutes later the White House said the men who clashed with the police "were entirely of the communist element." Major George S. Patton led troops of the 3rd Cavalry on the veterans, brandishing swords as they advanced.

With incredibly bad timing, the cavalry advanced on a parade of veterans on Pennsylvania Avenue at 4:45 P.M., just as 20,000 office workers lined the streets to watch the event. The cavalry gas bombed the marchers, to the horror and confusion of all, veterans and onlookers alike.

By 9:00 P.M. most of the veterans were out of Washington on the other side of the Anacostia River, and Hoover ordered the military proceedings to stop. But in a brazen act of disobedience, MacArthur countermanded Hoover's order, and at 10:14 P.M., he began gassing the remaining shantytown settlers and torching their pathetic tents and shacks. At 11:15 P.M. Patton led his cavalry men in a final destructive charge.

Among the ragged bonus marchers routed by this charge was Joseph T. Angelino, who on September 26, 1918, won the Distinguished Service

Cross in the Argonne Forest in France for saving the life of a young officer named George S. Patton, Jr. This was the supreme irony of an action that remains one of the darkest in American history. In this Depression, even the memory of patriotism and valor was being scorched from the earth. The words of Bertolt Brecht and Kurt Weill's 1930 *The Rise and Fall of the City of Mahagonny* come to mind: "We only built this Mahagonny because life is so evil. There is no unity. There is no friendship. And there is nothing for man to rely upon."

Walter Chrysler did as much as he could according to the lights of the time, which revolved around ideas of private charity. He organized a clothing drive to help Depression victims through the company's welfare department in the winter of 1930. Anticipating a much larger need the following year, he expanded it greatly and started it much earlier, even writing to Nicholas Kelley as early as September 9 for contributions. The Chrysler Industrial Association (CIA), of which every Chrysler official and employee was a member, went to the welfare departments of the cities of Detroit, Hamtramck, and Highland Park in 1930 to request notification if any Chrysler employee should apply for relief. The CIA wanted to be sure that the needs of every Chrysler employee were taken care of privately by the association, in order, as CIA head Charles Winegar put it, "to spare our fellow workers the humiliation of becoming public charges." Eighteen hundred families were helped during the winter of 1932, and during the fall of 1933, as many as twenty-six hundred families were given full or partial relief by the CIA, which laid out $314,817 for this purpose through its mutual aid division. The men could come in themselves, or families too proud to do so could be recommended by others aware of their need; all were encouraged to speak freely of their situations, for the object was to provide immediate relief. In addition to this, the association, which was not under the control of the Chrysler Corporation, spent $12,000 on 3,000 Christmas baskets and delivered toys to 2,600 children at Christmas, 1933. Furthermore, it dispensed 3,000 loads of coal and 837 loads of wood to laid-off workers in 1933 alone, and distributed a great quantity of shoes and clothing to their children, to ensure that they could continue their schooling without interruption. On days of extreme cold during these years, the CIA provided hot soup and coffee during the noon hour to men in line looking for employment, whether they were ex-Chrysler men or not.

Of course the work of such an organization would be considered an example of an outmoded paternalistic approach to relief today, in the mold of Ford's Sociological Department. But in February of 1934, before any notion of national welfare underpinning the social fabric of the United States had taken hold, it meant a great deal for Charles Winegar to be able to say, "To my knowledge, I know of no Chrysler Corporation employee who has been on the public welfare."

In terms of helping people by giving them the dignity of work, it can be said that Walter Chrysler did more than anyone else in Detroit. Due to rising corporate sales in every year but 1932, Chrysler gave more consistent employment to auto workers than anyone else during the Depression, especially during the desperate, uncertain year of 1933, when his sales more than doubled those of 1932. It was the best thing he knew how to do for his workers and his industry. "When men are not employed, they cease to be buyers of anything but the bare necessities," he had said in 1931.

The backbone of everything was the amazing Plymouth. It was squarely situated in that segment of the market where 85 percent of all sales were taking place, and Chrysler poured all his resources into it. As each succeeding Plymouth model reached the market, it delivered more and more for the corporation.

In promoting the Plymouth Walter Chrysler managed to do a good turn for an old friend, Florenz Ziegfeld, the famed producer of the *Ziegfeld Follies*, who, by 1932, had fallen on hard economic times and was, in addition, dying. To help out, Chrysler sponsored a *Ziegfeld Follies of the Air* Sunday night radio program that set a new record for sponsor costs: $20,000 went to the Columbia radio network, $7,000 was paid to the top talents who performed, and another $5,000 was paid to Ziegfeld himself. Throughout each broadcast, the announcer asked the audience "to accept Mr. Chrysler's personal invitation to inspect the good value of the Plymouth."

Though Chrysler showed a substantial deficit of $11,254,000 in 1932, his production record was by far the best of the year. His total output of 222,000 cars was greater than that of all other independent companies combined; none of the other independents produced as many as 50,000 vehicles. Walter Chrysler himself pointed out that in 1932 his company captured 17.4 percent of the total passenger car market, as opposed to 12 percent in 1931 (it was 6.3 percent in booming 1929). And in a market where sales of all makes were 57.5 percent of what they had been in 1931, Chrysler sold 83.7 percent of his 1931 volume. Plymouth alone climbed to 118.6 percent of its 1931 registrations, and was the only make in the industry to show an increase in volume over the previous year.

Chrysler's stock bottomed out at $5 this year, but a look at the facts behind the figures gave investors good reason to hang on. After dropping the quarterly dividend from 75 cents to 25 cents per share in late 1930, the board continued to pay out dividends, even in the straitened circumstances of 1932; in that year alone, it authorized payment of $4,390,000 to shareholders. Second, it bought up and retired $2,080,000 of the Dodge Brothers gold bonds. And last, it spent some $9 million investing in new products, primarily the spectacular new 1933 Plymouth six, which would be mainly responsible for leading the Chrysler Corporation to overtake Ford as the second-biggest automobile producer in the United States. Without these items the company would actually have earned $4.2 million on the year. And it had $43 million in cash and securities at year's end.

Walter Chrysler had carefully noted the factors that would one day lead to the return of automobile prosperity. The gasoline business was doing very well through the Depression, which meant that people were using their cars. This meant the cars were going to wear out sooner rather than later. And now at last more cars were being junked than were being built, so it stood to reason that after a few years of this, new cars would have to be bought to replace them. He had said, "Even those people who have lost their paper profits in Wall Street have an amazing amount of money left. The secret of good times is in the hands of the public. It is up to them to end the Depression."

In January 1932 Chrysler had seen "a rising tide of busines" for the coming year. For the auto business, he envisioned a 10 percent rise in sales during 1932. He urged every man in business to refuse to be influenced by those who tried to discourage him, to forget past reverses and by his own example to "instill a spirit of courage and enthusiasm."

Of course, the opposite happened, with sales off by 40 percent during the year. But Chrysler never let up, either in his words or his company's policies, which produced the products that would lead the Chrysler Corporation out of the wilderness, stronger than ever before.

It wasn't easy. Walter Chrysler pinned most of his hopes on the new Plymouth PC six-cylinder car, the first ever for that marque. He personally thought that a four was the ideal engine for a low-priced car, but with Chevrolet sporting a six since 1929 and Ford now powered by a V-8, the handwriting was on the wall. If that was what the public wanted, he would give it to them. "Chrysler Shoots the Works," headlined *Automotive News*. "Puts Millions in New Equipment to Squeeze the Last Nickel Out of Costs So that Buyers Would Be Sure to 'Look at All Three.' "

Production of the PB model stopped on September 27, 1932. As Jim Benjaminson describes it, a few days later Plymouth's "huge Lynch Road plant had been stripped bare—its production lines, machine shops and even its vaunted system of conveyors ripped out. Up and down the plant new machine tools replaced what had been considered just a few short years earlier the last word in automobile assembly plants. Other parts of the half mile long plant were revamped to make materials handling more efficient, including in the paint shop and chrome plating departments. Nothing in the plant was left untouched. Forty-five days and nine-million dollars later Lynch Road would be back on line." Car production was ready to roll on November 11th.

The new six-cylinder Plymouth to be produced at the Lynch Road facility was smaller internally than the four it replaced, but it put out more horsepower, rated at 70 as opposed to the former 65; with the Red Head

6.5-to-1 compression ratio feature, horsepower went up to 76. This basic
engine was so sturdy and reliable that it remained in production from 1932
until the end of the 1959 model year (Dodge trucks used it into the 1960s),
and more than 400,000 of them were sold for other industrial uses—truly
an extraordinary run for any power plant. Otherwise, mechanically the PC
was very up-to-date, featuring downdraft carburetion, Floating Power, Free
Wheeling, automatic clutch, silent second gear, and hydraulic brakes. The
body had a Safety Glass windshield, and Safety Steel construction, too, as
had all Chrysler Corporation products since 1930. This meant that bodies
were built from only four major body stampings, which were flash-welded
into one continuous whole. Most manufacturers then either used composite
construction, in which steel panels were nailed onto a wooden form, or else
a type of all-steel construction in which steel panels were welded onto a
steel frame; the result of the latter was a body made of approximately eight
hundred to nine hundred steel pieces welded together, which was neither
as sturdy as Chrysler's product nor as speedy and inexpensive to manufacture. Many advanced Plymouth features, such as hydraulic brakes, full-
pressure oil system, and aluminum pistons, took years, sometimes decades,
to appear on rival Ford and Chevrolet products. No wonder Plymouth sales
increased when customers really "looked at all three."

No matter how strong and up-to-the-minute mechanically the PC was,
however, the appearance of its body was another matter. Everyone expected
the car to be greeted with open arms, but when they got a look at it, both
dealers and the public strongly disapproved. After spending several years
trying to make the Plymouth look longer, Chrysler stylists had now cut the
car's wheelbase by 5 inches to 112 inches, and on top of that came up with
a front end and hood treatment that made the car look short and stubby.
It had a thick, slanted chrome-plated radiator shell and a hood with sloping
side louvers that were decidedly out of sync with the body's forward-
opening suicide doors. All in all, it looked more like a four-cylinder car than
the actual 1932 four-cylinder car ever did. To make matters worse, the front
end was too short to allow the fitting of optional fender-mounted spare
tires, and dealers complained loudly.

But the November introduction of the car was so well hyped that enough
customers came in to buy cars to get sales momentum going on the new
vehicle while the company scrambled to fix the situation. Even before the
official introduction, a single attractive but uninformative brochure mailed
out to dealers managed to drum up 20,000 advance orders.

The Plymouth PC six-cylinder car made its debut on a nationwide Columbia Broadcasting System (CBS) radio hookup at 1 P.M. on Tuesday, November 1, 1932. In all the history of the motor car, there had never been
anything like this announcement, which amounted to the first international
radio business conference, according to William S. Paley, the president of

CBS. The whole thing was cooked up by Joe Frazer, and it was very cleverly done.

The day before the broadcast, Plymouth purchased ads in sixty major newspapers "apologizing" to the public for taking up an hour and a half of radio time to tell 7,232 dealers about Walter P. Chrysler's new Plymouth. Master of ceremonies Lowell Thomas headed a company of forty, which included such "actors" as Walter Chrysler, B. E. Hutchinson, Fred Zeder, Plymouth sales manager Harry G. Moock, and race car drivers Barney Old-field and Billy Arnold playing themselves in the drama of the new car's presentation, aided and abetted by professional actors and "real-life" people playing bits. Supernumeraries and a seventeen-piece orchestra filled out the presentation, giving it color and excitement.

Dealer meetings were scheduled in twenty-five major cities in the United States and Canada. Perhaps twenty thousand individuals were in attendance at the various locations. The exact same program was carried out at each meeting, perfectly synchronized with the broadcast from New York. In addition to amplifiers in the auditoriums, which delivered the broadcast to each of the twenty-five audiences, there were stage effects, including a car wrapped and tied in a package to be broken open on cue from Western Union time clocks. Each city had its own synchronized master of ceremonies who spoke from a standardized script that led up to various breakovers from radio to the personal and direct features of the program. Dealers who were too far away to attend one of the big-city meetings could still hear the presentation on radio, even if they didn't get to see the car. Later, they could see a detailed sound film about it, which was shown at the meetings as a supplement to the broadcast.

Buoyed by those preannouncement orders, sales started off briskly, with fourth-quarter Plymouth production up by 137 percent and January 1933 sales up by 242 percent over the previous year. But nobody was kidding themselves, and drastic action was taken. On December 16 Plymouth prices were cut between $20 and $30, bringing them as low as $495 for the business coupe. By January the wheelbase had been stretched by an inch so the spares could fit into the front fenders. As expected, sales of the rather unattractive car now began to nosedive, and the company rushed frantically to bring out a new Plymouth model in time for the spring selling season.

Clearly, the car had to be made longer. In order to save time and money, it was decided to use the frame from the 111-inch-wheelbase Dodge DP model, stretching it by an inch to equal Plymouth's 1932 wheelbase. It would be too expensive to make another body, so the increased length was going to come in the area forward of the cowl.

This time the stylists got it right. The chrome grille was now vertical, and surrounded by a painted shell with a chrome-plated rim and bullet-shaped chrome headlights. Louvers in the elongated hood were also straightened, and new longer, flowing fenders easily accepted side-mounted spares. Prices were the same as those for the PC. Everyone was delighted with this new model, called the PD, and sales took off like a rocket from the time of its introduction in March 1933. Thus for very little money, but with a lot of quick thinking and ingenuity, Chrysler turned the replacement of a foundering model into a triumph. Later Carl Breer was to say it was possible only because in those days "we couldn't afford to think about things. We just did it."

For competitive reasons, the company decided to keep selling the short-wheelbase model, but this too was transformed, into the PCXX Standard, whose styling was modified to reflect the PD changes. With prices slashed to as low as $445, this car made Plymouth directly competitive with Ford and Chevrolet for the first time. It sold about as well as the original PC.

When it was all over, 1933 Plymouth sales of all models rose to 255,564 cars, more than double the 1932 total. The most prominent buyer was First Lady Eleanor Roosevelt, who purchased one of 4,596 PD convertible coupes made that year. Evidently quite a Plymouth fancier, the previous year she had had an elegant little Plymouth Town Car, complete with coach lights, built to her specifications.

Dodge finally modernized the lines of its cars in 1933, creating attractive all-new Model DP Sixes and DO Eights. Though the sixes were a bit smaller and less powerful than the previous year's models, new styling and price drops of $200 or more on these cars made them very appealing to the public, and sales more than tripled 1932 totals. (One bold Dodge ad said, " 'But you are asking for a miracle!' said Dodge engineers. 'Then give me one!' Walter Chrysler replied. And so the new Dodge was born — A 'Miracle Car' if there ever was one! $595 and up—Only the combined creative genius of Walter P. Chrysler and the Dodge organization could have built the big new Dodge Six at such a price.")

Though DeSoto was even prettier than in 1932, with front fenders that reached down to the bumper and a cleaner, more rounded grille, it was now priced above the Dodge, and sales went even lower, to 22,736. (Ads emphasized smartness at a low price, and some depicted Clara Bow and her husband, Rex Bell, frolicking in the snow nearby their new DeSoto sedan; others pictured the famous diva Ernestine Schumann Heinke in her '33 DeSoto.)

Chrysler models, too, were curvier and more stylish, but sales remained anemic, around the 30,000 level. There was an all-new downsized Imperial, which now could be had for as little as $1,275; this was accomplished by rebadging the previous 108-horsepower, 126-inch-wheelbase Chrysler CP Eight into an Imperial CQ, at a price just a few dollars higher than that of the Buick Series 60. With this clever bit of sleight of hand, Imperial saw its sales revive to near the 4,000-unit level. (Elegantly illustrated Chrysler ads were signed by Walter P. himself, under the legend "Chrysler engineers create for 1933 the finest cars ever to bear my name.")

By the time the year was over, not only had the Chrysler Corporation's sales more than doubled, it also became the only firm to produce a greater number of vehicles than it had in 1929. With a grand total of slightly more than 450,000, it now had 25 percent of the market, and for the first time in history, Chrysler replaced Ford as the number-two producer of vehicles in the United States. It also made a $12 million profit, completely wiping out the previous year's deficit.

Part of this success came from managing the company well and producing good products, but part of it came from steely, determined, undaunted optimism. The majority of Americans were scared and hopeless in 1933, with a sickening feeling about both the country's future and their own. But Chrysler was an unbounded enthusiast and put his company's resources behind his optimistic ideas. At the time of the Plymouth introduction in November 1932 he described his expenditure on it as "a $9 million bet on the economic future of America." Even though he was losing money, he wouldn't even cut his dividend. This is what he said:

"It's a time of opportunity! It's the biggest chance a man ever had. It's a time to get out and do things—and keep doing them. And that doesn't mean the big fellow alone—it means everyone, the worker, the office man, everyone—whether he's got a job or not. . . . If he'll get out and dig for chances. Find them. Use them.

"It's a time for courage! A time for enthusiasm and imagination. It's a time to work and think, to tighten our belts the way the Indians did in famine, to drive through for the good times we know are ahead. It's silly to doubt a country like this. We're in a deluge. But we've got men left—Chrysler Corporation has men—tireless, working, driving, thinking, planning men. We can buy now at prices we could never buy at before. We can build better and sell lower. It's the biggest chance we ever had. We're making the most of it.

"Every man's got to do the best he can. Common sense tells us that this country is coming through. But courage tells us, whether we have a job or not, that the big chances are here today, bigger than before, and we've got to work and sweat to find them. I'm not a prophet. I don't pretend to say when bad times will end. They may be over right now. But we can't worry about that. There's a job to be done today."

Indeed there was. Part of the job was for people to turn themselves into Walter Chrysler, to convince themselves that things really would get better. Chrysler, one of the people the American system had most rewarded, was doing his civic and moral duty, trying to stand like a beacon of courage and strength before the public. He and his family still were very wealthy, but he was not about to desert the millions of people, both employees and the public at large, who had made him what he was.

However, this was November 1932, and the end of bad times was still a
long way off. Before they were to disappear at last, Walter Chrysler and
everybody else was going to pass through the darkest economic moment
this country has ever seen, the banking crisis of 1933. Simply put, in February and March of that year the banking system of the United States
completely shut down, and for ten terrifying days no one knew if it would
ever reopen, or whether the country would be the same if it did. This crisis
was born in Detroit, and spread its paralyzing menace through the rest of
the country. At the end of it Detroit, once the grandest of American boom
towns, would be changed forever.

❧   ❧   ❧

The banking system of the United States had serious flaws which only this
crisis exposed to full public view. The nub of the matter was this: "The
history of banking in the United States reveals constant resistance to both
unification and controls," said Susan Estabrook Kennedy in her excellent
overview of the situation, *The Banking Crisis of 1933.*

The country had a dual banking system of both state-chartered and
nationally chartered banks. "Each state had institutions answerable separately to the state banking commissioner and to the federal Comptroller of
the Currency, with no uniformity of rules except for the national banks.
The coming of the Federal Reserve System in 1914 did not supersede this
complex structure, and, in fact, added to its diversity, for the System exer-
cized only limited powers over the national banks and such state institutions
as chose to join it.

"Those among the framers of the Federal Reserve Act who hoped for
centralization of banking were thwarted by the defenders of the small, independent bank; the latter continued to resist measures that would allow
larger and stronger banks to establish branches where they would compete
with the local unitary banks. In the same way, the directing Board of the
Federal Reserve System quickly became the instrument of the 12 Reserve
banks and their members rather than a strong, controlling body. Thus, the
Federal Reserve Board could only hope that the member banks would respond to its requests and influences; so long as those banks met the minimum requirements of capitalization and reserves to remain in the System
and passed periodic audits of their accounts, they could operate with relatively little attention paid to Board proposals."

The problems of this loose-jointed system are self evident, but the whole
situation was complicated by Federal Reserve policies that were "intended
to assist European countries in sustaining or restoring their monetary standards." Instead, they "created easy money at low interest rates which encouraged member banks to borrow from the Reserve in order to lend to
their customers at only slightly higher rates." As business continued to

expand throughout the 1920s, so did bank resources, and more and more the directors of these institutions sought out the huge profits that could be found by backing mortgage loans and advancing money to stock market speculators. Thus, with the unintended help of the Federal Reserve, banks helped to bull up the markets of both these types of investments to previously undreamed-of levels. It took until 1929 for the Reserve to become concerned about credit-driven investment excesses, but the weakness of its powers and sanctions meant that almost nobody paid any attention to it until the stock market crashed that October.

Before 1929 bank failures were generally confined to small institutions that did not participate in the Federal Reserve System and resisted consolidation moves. Many of these banks were located in farming areas, due to the postwar agricultural depression that persisted despite the nation's general prosperity. But beginning in 1930 banks that were awash in loans paid out to various kinds of speculators who could not repay them began to go down with increasing frequency. Frightened into a newfound respect for liquidity, larger and more stable banks raised their rates and dried up credit, just when legitimate businesspeople and smaller banks needed it most. Neither the National Credit Corporation nor the Reconstruction Finance Corporation (RFC), which replaced it in 1932, managed to convince conservative bank directors to fight contraction and save banks, railroads, and industrial corporations.

In 1921 the United States had more than 31,000 banks. After eight years of unprecedented prosperity, 25,000 much richer institutions were left. By 1933, 7,000 more banks had disappeared, and the whole banking system was in a state of collapse. To give a sense of how bad things had become so quickly, one need only look at this statistic: from 1865 to 1929, 8,599 commercial banks, representing $2,506,045,000 worth of deposits, failed. But from January 1, 1930, to March 15, 1933, 5,790 banks with $3,456,708,000 suspended operations. In other words, in just three years and two months, nearly 50 percent more damage was done to United States banks and their depositors than in the previous six and a half decades.

The first wave of postcrash bank failures hit Kentucky, Arkansas, Tennessee, and North Carolina in late 1930, followed by a second one that began in mid-1931 and lasted through February 1932. This one started in Chicago, spreading to Ohio and other midwestern states before jumping into Pennsylvania, New York, and New England. The RFC kept things going without any major disasters until November 1932, when Nevada had to declare a banking holiday to save a group of banks holding 80 percent of the state's assets. Things got progressively worse through December 1932 and into the first six weeks of 1933, when especially large amounts of deposits were stuck in suspended banks in southern New Jersey, Iowa, California, Tennessee, Illinois, Missouri, Nevada, and Washington, D.C. But nothing approached what happened in Michigan starting in mid-February of that year.

Detroit was America's biggest boom town, with a 1930 population of 1,568,602, up from just 285,704 thirty years before. Other auto towns, including Flint, Highland Park, Royal Oak, Dearborn, Grand Rapids, and Lansing, also participated in the population explosion fueled by the state's signature industry. By 1927, 56 percent of Detroit's economy was based on auto manufacturing, most of which was exported from the city. This meant that Detroit was dependent on the national economy, since it consumed less of its own products than any other city in the country. Until 1927 the city was also dependent on other cities for commercial banking facilities.

In June of that year, a banking group obtained a Michigan charter for a combination bank, investment affiliate, and trust company to be called the Guardian Detroit Bank. Two years later the organization increased its capital and set up the Guardian Detroit Group, Inc., which began acquiring shares in other area banks to form a statewide association of strong banks, in an effort to form an institution large enough to handle Detroit's banking business at home rather than sending it to New York or Chicago. To that end, Guardian Detroit and another holding company, the Union Commerce Corporation of Detroit, acquired all or most of the capital stock of twenty-three banks and trust companies, merging into the Guardian Detroit Union Group, Inc., in December 1929. This new institution immediately took over eight more banks. Ford interests dominated Guardian, with Edsel Ford and his brother-in-law Ernest C. Kanzler, head of Ford's Universal Credit Corporation, two of the institution's cofounders.

A much larger Detroit combination, the Detroit Bankers Company, was founded early in 1930 and centered around the First National Bank of Detroit, which had 76 directors and 194 branches, making it the third-largest separate bank outside of New York City. By the time it was done with its acquisitions, Detroit Bankers had forty banks in its organization. Its 120 voting shares were controlled by twelve men who had each put up $1,000 for ten shares. Two-and-a-half million non-voting shares were sold to the public for $20 apiece.

Both organizations, skirting the outer limits of legality, threw caution to the winds in their lending practices, getting involved in the stock market craze of the late 1920s and imprudent real estate speculation in Detroit and other Michigan cities. Through the Depression years they also drained bank assets to pay ludicrously high dividend rates. One Guardian bank paid out nearly 25 percent of its capital to help support the 1931 dividend. Another had questionable loans amounting to $1.3 million more than the entire capital of that bank. By 1933 laid-off auto workers couldn't even pay the interest on their mortgages, and there was no use foreclosing on their properties either, because no market for them existed. In this fashion, 72 percent of all Guardian assets were immobilized by February 1933.

Detroit Bankers pressed its constituents for funds to pay out a 17 percent dividend no matter how bad business was. By the time 1932 was done, Alfred P. Leyburn, the chief national bank examiner, said the condition of Detroit Bankers' core institution, the First National Bank of Detroit, "was not rotten—it was putrid."

Though the public was unaware of it, by January 15, 1933, the assets of the Guardian group had so far deteriorated that board chairman Kanzler said privately, "We have to get considerably more money, or the whole group is going to collapse." He tried to drum up support for a new RFC loan, claiming that Henry Ford would not remove his $7.5 million deposits with Guardian, thus reducing its $14 million deficit to $6.5 million.

When John Keown McKee, the RFC's chief examiner in charge of reorganizations, went to Detroit to look for good collateral for a Guardian loan, he found that its portfolio of $88 million in face-value real estate equities was worth $17 million in loan value. He suggested a new mortgage company be formed with capital of $5 million, to take over the assets of shaky Guardian banks whose mortgage loans exceeded 50 percent of their portfolios. Then all assets could be totted up for collateral to pledge against a $47 million loan from the RFC, which would be granted in addition to a previously authorized $18 million loan, for a total of $65 million.

Ten days later, after a dozen examiners worked night and day to find usable assets, McKee stated at a February 6 RFC meeting that major Guardian component Union Guardian Trust Company was insolvent, with only $7.9 million in loan assets standing against $20.5 million in depositors' liabilities. He then proposed the $5 million new mortgage company idea, but stated that Guardian's total collateral would support a total loan of only $35 million, not the $65 million required to save the situation. Even with the $7.5 million Ford subordination, which now was doubtful, there weren't enough assets available.

After much pulling and hauling, the RFC agreed to make the loan, provided Guardian could raise $5 million in capital for the new bank and find enough local cash and deposit subordination to reduce its liabilities to the point where its assets would support this loan.

When James Couzens, the former Ford partner who was now the senior Senator from Michigan, heard about the RFC loan, he was adamantly opposed to it unless Guardian could provide full security.

Attention shifted to Henry Ford, for unless he agreed to freeze his Guardian deposits, other large depositors would surely not do the same and insure sufficient reserves to meet the demands of smaller depositors.

President Hoover called a White House meeting with several key financial men and both Michigan senators on February 9 to discuss the situation. Senator Vandenberg said that "all present agreed that the trust company

would have to be supported by voluntary contributions to merit RFC aid."
Nobody disagreed with Charles Miller when he spoke out against the loan,
or with Couzens when he demanded that any loan have absolute security.
Hoover had already obtained an agreement from Henry Ford to freeze his
$7.5 million, plus a further agreement from Alfred P. Sloan and Walter
Chrysler for GM and Chrysler to each deposit $1 million with the Guardian
to help back the RFC loan. But when Hoover asked Couzens for $1 million
also, he blew up and said the Guardian was Ford's responsibility, not the
government's. Besides, he later told Arthur Krock of the *New York Times*, he
knew Henry Ford to be a miser who wouldn't put up any money if he knew
Couzens were going to do so.

Hoover was baffled by this lack of cooperation, and sent everybody back
to Detroit to sort things out. Because of the Lincoln's Birthday holiday, it
would be a long weekend, and the parties to this situation would have until
the start of business at 9 A.M. on Tuesday, February 14, to sort things out.

When Hoover's men, undersecretary of the treasury Arthur Ballantine,
and former Hudson auto entrepreneur and now Secretary of Commerce
Roy Chapin arrived in Detroit, they found what chief bank examiner Leyburn called "a hell of a mess." For two days they dithered around trying to
raise the capital necessary for Guardian's salvation, to no avail. Finally they
came to the conclusion that the mortgage company plan was the only solution. The RFC agreed, urging McKee to agree to it if local money could
be drawn into it. At a breakfast meeting in Washington with Herbert Hoover
on Sunday, Sloan and Chrysler renewed their million-dollar pledges, fearing
that suspension of Union Guardian might start a general panic. But when
Chrysler and Donaldson Brown, chairman of the General Motors finance
committee, arrived in Detroit along with representatives and officials of major New York banks that had an interest in these proceedings, both Chrysler
and GM took a hard stand and agreed to support their million-dollar pledges
only if they were given full security. When they were not, Chrysler scaled
back to $274,000 and GM to $619,000. So things were now sliding backward. When both parties made even this reduced loan participation contingent on Edsel Ford's provision of new capital, it became clear that the whole
affair depended on Henry Ford, for everyone knew that Edsel was only a
stand-in for his father.

Until Saturday no one had informed the Detroit Bankers group of the
desperate situation at Guardian. Finally on that day Leyburn and the Guardian officers told president Wilson W. Mills of the First National Bank that
Union Guardian would probably fail, bringing the Guardian National Bank
of Commerce down with it. Mills, fearing terrific runs on his bank, asked
the RFC for a $100 million loan to bring his firm up to 40% liquidity. But
though his bank had plenty of assets and the RFC examiners recommended
the loan, the RFC board refused it without explaining its action.

On Monday, an increasingly desperate Herbert Hoover urged the RFC to cooperate with the loan, in the face of continued criticism from Couzens. Hoover thought the loan involved insignificant amounts of money when compared to the problems a Detroit banking collapse might unleash. He called Henry Ford, who agreed to see Chapin and Ballantine to discuss subordination, but nothing more.

When the two men showed up at Ford's offices, they first encountered Edsel, who said he couldn't understand government restrictions that prevented the RFC from saving the situation by loaning out the required sums, since it had prevously loaned out much more.

Things got a lot worse when the men saw old Henry. He said he would be happy to discuss the situation, but not to cooperate. If he had ever given that impression, well, either he hadn't fully understood things, or he had changed his mind. Not only would he not cooperate, but if the RFC did not make its loan promptly, he would draw his own funds and those of his company out of Detroit Bankers banks as well as Guardian banks the very next day. With $65 million in Detroit banks, he could indeed have ruined them all. The government men were alarmed when they heard this, and they had good reason to be, for during the panic of 1914 Ford had drawn out all of his funds out of his own banks. Why wouldn't he do it again?

Ford authorized Ballantine to tell his position to the RFC. Ballantine and Chapin pleaded that three million people would suffer if he did this, that he "would almost certainly bring down the whole banking structure of the country and lead . . . very likely to to the failure of very many manufacturing and business institutions as well." But Ford countered that he could not understand how the government could let such a disaster occur for the sake of a few millions. He refused to believe that the government was unable to act without Ford's subordination of his accounts. Ballantine and Chapin didn't understand what was going on in Ford's mind. In fact, Ford thought the whole affair was a scheme among the Treasury, his competitors, and "the people in back of them" (by which he meant his longtime bugaboo, the investment bankers of Wall Street) to gain control of the nation's banking system by ruining Henry Ford and his business.

Would everything be ruined? In one of modern history's more striking statements, Henry Ford, soon to be seventy, said, "All right, let the crash come. Everything will go down the chute. But I feel young. I can build again."

When the men left Ford and reported the results of the meeting to assembled officials back at Guardian headquarters, both Chrysler and GM pulled out of the deal, and it became apparent that there was now no alternative to a general banking moratorium in the state of Michigan. Even when they called Ford in a last-ditch effort to tell him that many banks would have to operate on a clearing-certificate basis that would stifle the automobile business, the old man refused to budge. Not only that, but at lunch he told Mills of First National of his threat to take his money out of that bank, and that night when Couzens let Ford know through an intermediary that he would put up half the collateral for an RFC loan if Ford would do likewise, Ford again said no.

At 1:32 A.M. the next day, after much discussion of the legality of the matter, Governor William A. Comstock signed the proclamation for a bank holiday, to commence that morning and continue through the following Tuesday, February 21. By this action he closed 550 national and state banks, holding deposits of $1.5 billion belonging to 900,000 customers.

Hoover, who thought his conversation with Ford had saved the day, was taken by surprise, and not at all happy. But he never really had come up with a viable alternative plan to the local rescue idea. In fact, as a lame duck president, he refused to sign any major legislation without Franklin Roosevelt's signature as well, and Roosevelt, wanting to be a new broom when he took office, refused to sign anything or even let his intentions be known in this and other areas of government policy.

The nation was shocked, and the Michigan closings had a domino effect that led other states to shut down their banking systems as well. Indiana went down on February 23 and Maryland two days later, followed by Arkansas on the twenty-seventh and Ohio on the twenty-eighth. On March 1 Tennessee, Kentucky, Nevada, and Alabama closed, as did Louisiana, California, Mississippi, Oregon, and Arizona the next day. Governor Lehman closed the banks in New York on March 3, and Illinois followed immediately thereafter. By Inauguration Day, March 4, bank holidays had occurred in thirty-four states, and very few banks anywhere were still open.

In Michigan, efforts to get banks reopened and deposits freed up, even in part, were thwarted by legal technicalities at every turn. Big corporations with large deposits in other states trucked in money by heavily guarded armored cars to meet their payrolls and other obligations. Walter Chrysler rented a closed bank building and staffed it with tellers from failed banks, who paid out trucked-in money from other states to employees and vendors. Lines surrounded the building for blocks.

Detroit was almost totally without money, and people were very scared. There was a food panic in the city, as anyone with cash rushed to buy up any supplies that hadn't already been cleaned out of the grocery stores. But then even dollar bills dried up, as anyone who had any secreted them away. Nicholas Kelley, who was in the city trying to help resolve the crisis, later recalled: "I was staying at the Detroit Club, where you had always been able to get meals. All you could buy then however, was breakfast. You had to go out for the other meals. People had to sit on their porch with money in their hands to get milk from the passing milkwagons. It was like a deceased city. There was no credit at all."

Finally the city, which had defaulted on its bonds, issued $42 million in scrip, to be redeemed when cash became available again, so that the city could function.

By now Couzens was becoming a pariah for what he had done to his state, and in so doing, he took some of the heat off the Fords. They even became popular heroes for a short time when they proposed to take over not only Guardian but most of Detroit's other closed banks as well, putting up $8.25 million in new capital to do so. Three thousand demonstrators chanted "Bank with Hank" outside Dearborn Town Hall on one occasion. But in short order their proposal fizzled as it became apparent that the Fords were just trying to get away with what they had accused the "New York bankers" of attempting: a cheap takeover of Detroit's entire banking system.

At last, on March 6, two days after he was inaugurated President, Franklin Roosevelt declared a national banking moratorium, using the exact same tool people from Hoover's administration had offered the former president earlier: a proclamation under the Trading-With-The-Enemy Act of 1917 temporarily suspending banking activities and all gold dealings. Hoover had feared that this action might be invalid, but Roosevelt seized upon it. As Susan Estabrook Kennedy says, "Roosevelt became the voice and spirit of hope on March 4, 5 and 6, willingly taking up a policy prepared by and for the old order but transforming it into his own optimistic instrument to rescue the banking system." He showed the people that he wanted to preserve the existing system and reject radical solutions, and gave them "a triumphant belief that the economic paralysis of three and a half years had been conquered. Insofar as the banking crisis offered a keynote to the New Deal, it was this: the end of the era of drift and the beginning of hope under new and vigorous leadership."

Around the country, people seemed relieved that something was finally being done to end the panic that had seized the nation. Over the next few days Ogden Mills, a former Secretary of the Treasury, put together a plan dividing banks into three classes: sound banks, which would immediately reopen; unsound banks, which would remain closed and be liquidated; and questionable banks, which might be rehabilitated and later reopened.

On March 12 Roosevelt reassured the nation that banks would be reopened over the next three days—totally sound ones immediately, others as they became safe. But all would have enough cash on hand to meet any demands presented to them. When they began to reopen the next day, they took in more money than they paid out. "The banking crisis was over; the hoarding peril had been reversed," says Kennedy. And with surprising efficiency, too.

The banking crisis of 1933 finally allowed banking reform advocate Senator Carter Glass to gather enough support to pass the Glass-Steagall Act through Congress. Though watered down from what he wanted, the act did provide for major banking reforms on a broad scale. The most important provisions were the establishment of the Federal Deposit Insurance Corporation to protect bank depositors' assets and the permanent separation of investment affiliates from commercial banks.

Detroit got out of the hole by finally establishing a new banking institution, the National Bank of Detroit, organized by General Motors and enthusiastically supported by Chrysler, which became one of its major stockholders. The Guardian Group and the Detroit Bankers Group were finally liquidated because not enough local money could be found to support their reopening. A receiver was appointed on March 31, 1933, and NBD bought up their quick assets the following month, thus ending for good any possibility of their ever reopening.

What is less widely known however, is that with one exception, no depositor lost money on their demise. First National Detroit repaid its depositors in full by 1940, and two years later even threw in 7.6 percent interest, despite the facts that it had not been allowed to do any banking business after February 13, 1933, and that its receiver took $15.4 million in expenses. Guardian took twenty-two years to pay off 89.5 percent of its depositors, with only a $9 million loss going to Ford interests. In fact, the receivers of both banks eventually declared that they were solvent at the time of closing, as did a grand jury. Thirty-six years later, RFC examiner Howard Stoddart told a joint committee of the Michigan state legislature that the two banks "should never have been placed in receivership. With the same assistance as provided to other banks of similar size and importance, they could have been saved and not forced to close their doors."

Both banks were technically and legally insolvent in early 1933, because their capital was impaired and they could not pay off their depositors. But a case could be made for their soundness, especially that of the First National Bank—Detroit. Altogether, these major Detroit institutions, controlling some $700 million, were allowed to collapse for want of $10 million or so. What happened?

The answer lies in a tale of snobbery, pretentiousness, cunning, hatred, and the sweetest of all cold dishes, revenge, that would need a Balzac for its true chronicler.

Donald Finlay Davis's *Conspicuous Production: Automobile Elites in Detroit, 1899–1933* gives a brilliant, basically Marxist, overview of the situation that led to the downfall of old Detroit. Through detailed analysis, he shows that the kinds of cars produced by Detroit's manufacturers were determined by the social class of the principals in the companies. They produced cars for other people like themselves, either as they were when they started out in business if they were wealthy, or as they imagined they had become after they achieved success if they were not.

In the beginning of the auto business, elite cars were produced in the East by wealthy men for wealthy people; since their markets were so limited, most of them did not last in the marketplace. In the Midwest, since money and social standing were less, middle-class people such as Robert C. Hupp and Ransom E. Olds produced mid-priced cars that reached a wider public and survived in the marketplace as long as their companies stuck to their initial positions. But Davis shows that almost all firms eventually indulged in the prestige behavior of building bigger, more expensive cars, no matter where they started out on the price and class scale. In almost all cases, sooner or later this led to trouble.

Contrary to common belief, the capital for these firms was supplied in large part by scions of wealthy old-line Detroit families, who had mostly made their money in railroads, stoves, land, or lumber fifty years before entering the car business.

At first things went well, but when the boards of these companies decided to produce the sort of luxury cars that they themselves would like to drive to bespeak their social standing, things changed considerably. As in the East, the market just wasn't there, except for Packard, the one company able to earn big profits producing first-class luxury cars. Perhaps the best example of what went wrong was the Oldsmobile. When the company produced $650 Curved Dash runabouts, it was a big success. But when backer Frederick Smith insisted on turning out huge, expensive luxury models instead, Ransom Olds left the company to found middle-class REO and Oldsmobile lost money in buckets. By the time Durant bought it in 1908, the company was sold for practically all stock to GM.

In the period 1908 to 1910 the most curious thing of all happened. The old-line Detroit families sold out their interests in the auto firms, practically abandoning this burgeoning business to the control of outside bankers and decidedly middle-class men such as Walter Flanders and Billy Durant. It seems that when they realized that the car business was going in the direction of lower-priced vehicles aimed at the masses, they simply didn't want to be associated with firms that produced them. Furthermore, as more and more capital was required to float auto firms, they didn't want to face the inevitable fact that they would have to share control of companies that they were used to dominating. If they were not going to be able to be in the car business and run things their way, then they wanted to be out completely. Characteristically, GM stock paid out for the acquisition of Oldsmobile was quickly jettisoned by Smith and the other backers of the firm. They were relieved to be out of it, and had no interest in the new auto conglomerate that had rescued them.

And then there was Henry Ford. After two conspicuous failures, he started up the Ford Motor Company with just $28,000 in paid-in capital in 1903, partly raised from the likes of a coal dealer, the Dodges, and even a maiden lady schoolteacher. Alone among the early manufacturers, his dream was to produce a car for the masses, and when "conspicuous production" of luxury vehicles raised its head in his company, he got rid of both the vehicles and the people who supported them. He of course made a great deal of money in the car business, and there was no question about the fact that he was producing a utilitarian car for the common man.

Now, Henry Ford did not come from the working classes. His family were landed farmers of the middle class, but down to the bottom of his soul he was a midwestern agrarian populist. Even when he became the world's richest, most successful businessman, he didn't in any way think of himself as "rich," but as just an ordinary man who did extraordinarily well giving the public a product that immensely improved the quality of their daily lives "I do not want the things that money can buy," he said in 1915. "I want to live a life, to make the world a little better for having lived in it." Just like the rich and the middle-class manufacturers, he thought he was producing a car for people "just like himself."

For this reason, the elites of Detroit took every opportunity to belittle and even ostracize him from their community. Henry Ford, whose nature was paranoid to begin with, in turn nurtured long and deep-seated grudges against these people. He never, ever forgot a slight, and when his time came, he repaid every one of them a hundredfold.

Henry Leland's ideas caused Ford to be fired from the Henry Ford Company in 1903, before it transformed itself into Cadillac. In early 1922, he bought out the Leland's new Lincoln car company, a prestige manufactory which had gone bankrupt due to its unfortunate entry into the marketplace during the Depression of 1920–21. Within three months Henry Leland and his son Wilfred were out on the street.

In 1903 also, Ford applied to the Association of Licensed Automobile Manufacturers (ALAM) for the right to manufacture cars under the Selden patent. He was turned down on the basis that his car was an "assembled," rather than a manufactured, vehicle. Eight years later, after the expense of a fortune in legal fees, he broke any meaningful validity of the patent in court.

Three years after that, Ford horrified the rest of the auto industry by proclaiming the Five Dollar Day. They thought it was a populist stunt, a gesture from a wealthy demagogue to the masses. Though of course Ford turned out to be doing U.S. manufacturing a great favor, the Detroit rich didn't realize it at the time, and privately snubbed and spoke against him, which gnawed away at his sense of pride.

Henry Ford was roundly ridiculed for his pacifism prior to America's entry into World War I, especially after he got a draft exemption for his son Edsel. People like the patrician Henry B. Joy strongly criticized him in the public presses. When he ran for the Senate in 1918 against old-line Grosse Pointe Packard executive Truman H. Newberry, he lost by a very small margin, with people like Roy Chapin of Hudson impugning the patriotism of the Fords in opposing Henry's election. Members of the Detroit Club went so far as to affix bumper stickers proclaiming "my son is not a slacker" to their cars. Top executives of Packard, Paige-Detroit, Maxwell, Hupp, and GM, as well as Hudson, came out against Ford in the effort to defeat him. As soon as the election was over, Ford immediately began waging a vendetta against Newberry, accusing him of winning the election by overspending the legal limits with money provided by an "influential gang of Jews." It took him four years, but he finally hounded Newberry from office. Not only that, but he managed to get ex-Fordite James Couzens appointed to fill out his term, and got his own candidate, Woodbridge Ferris, elected to Michigan's other senate seat. Once back in Grosse Pointe, Newberry conducted a social vendetta of enormous proportions against Ford, making him feel even more cut off from the Detroit business community than ever. And old Henry never forgot or forgave any of this.

James Couzens too, who became vastly wealthy after being bought out of his Ford stock by Henry Ford, suffered Detroit's opprobrium for his populist views. He had been a vital part of the decision to implement the Five Dollar Day, and was an outspoken advocate for wage justice for workers, which cost him dearly among the wealthy set in Detroit. In December, 1914, he severely criticized the Board of Commerce for not dealing with the city's unemployment problems, and a year after that, he castigated S. S. Kresge for fundraising for a rescue home for unfortunate girls, saying: "I think you can do much more for girls and women by paying them better wages than you can by subscribing $1,000 to rescue them after they have gotten into trouble." Kresge never forgave him, and took every opportunity to put stumbling blocks in his path.

When Couzens became Detroit's police commissioner in 1916, he was ridiculed for an ineffective anti-vice campaign. Later, as mayor, Detroit's top men rallied against him to oppose his plan for municipal ownership of the city's surface rail system, to no avail.

During his fourteen years in the Senate, he seemed to take special pleasure in embarrassing and attacking his foes in the auto industry. He accused the Lelands of war profiteering in 1923, and called on the government to investigate them for tax fraud. Two years later he accused two of Hupmobile's founders, Edwin Denby and J. Walter Drake, of influence peddling to a Detroit capitalist. And in that same year, Couzens and Ferris managed the defeat of the nomination of Charles B. Warren for U.S. attorney general, the first time any cabinet nomination had gone down to defeat since 1868. Though a distinguished former ambassador to Mexico and Japan and a longtime prominent member of the Republican national committee, he was a wealthy Detroiter who had invested in E-M-F, Lozier and Paige, and represented the values of Detroit's Republican business establishment. Couzens was determined to send a message back home by defeating him, and so he did.

Of Ford and Couzens, Davis says: "Whatever the issue—charity work, banking, labor relations, national politics, or war and peace—they seemed unerringly to take a position offensive to the limousine set. It is therefore tempting to regard Ford and Couzens as the architects of their own exclusion, to say that they declined to make the concessions necessary to gain admission to Detroit's upper class and thus earned for themselves social opprobrium and for Couzens the epithet 'scab millionaire.' Years later, Couzens explained, 'They (the upper class) hate me because I won't conform. I'm still a poor man as far as they are concerned.' "

Thus both of these men had decades in which to nurture grudges against the elites of Detroit, and when the time came for those elites to seek their aid in 1933, Ford and Couzens had absolutely no reason to save any of the people who had spent decades treating them as pariahs. No matter what he said about his willingness to offer help, it must have gladdened Henry Ford's heart to turn down Roy Chapin, a man who had denigrated him for decades, and Arthur Ballantine, a New York banker of the sort Ford despised, when they came groveling on that fateful February day in 1933 to ask his aid in saving old-line Detroit. Equal joy must also have resided in the breast of James Couzens, first as he did everything in his power to thwart the RFC rescue, and then later as he presented evidence to a federal grand jury that led to the criminal indictments of twenty-eight prominent Detroit bankers in the summer of 1934. As he purportedly said to *Detroit Free Press* editor Malcolm Bingay, "I'll never rest until every one of the sons of bitches are behind prison bars where I can walk up and down in front of them and laugh at them."

So, having long ago sold off their ownership of the Detroit auto business and systematically alienated the two Detroit auto men who were rich enough to help them, where else could Detroit's leaders turn?

General Motors? It was now the biggest auto company in the world, having grown to that size by expanding its production of low-priced cars, while at the same time giving buyers fine cars in all other price ranges as well. It had been founded by Billy Durant, a man whose background was not that dissimilar from Ford's own. But almost from the beginning, GM was under the control of the eastern banking establishment. After Durant's second ouster from GM in 1920, the du Pont interests became its largest shareholders, and Pierre du Pont gave the company its guiding vision. Together with the management genius of Alfred P. Sloan, du Pont turned GM into the model of the decentralized, vertically integrated modern corporation. Its beautiful headquarters was in Detroit, and many of its cars were produced there, but its soul was a banker's soul that lived in Wall Street. Thus GM had no reason to help out the Detroit old guard; it could do quite well without them.

What about Chrysler? He was a true "man of the people" who had risen from the ranks of the working classes, though unlike Ford, he held no animosity toward the rich. In a way, he does not match Davis's picture for lasting auto success, having got into the car business "too late" manufacturing a prestige type of vehicle, the Chrysler. But, like Ford, he knew that his ultimate salvation would be in the mass production of a high-quality, low-priced vehicle, and so he began his Plymouth program almost as soon as he got over the Chrysler Corporation's birth pangs. At the same time, he filled in all the price steps up to the superluxury level just like GM, while adopting a version of their decentralized management. But though he may have run his company, he never confused it with himself, like Henry Ford.

As far as Detroit was concerned, however, Chrysler too was an absentee manager. From start to finish, Chrysler as a car manufacturer was a creature of bankers, and most of them were from the East. He ran Willys and Maxwell from New York, and later did the same with the Chrysler Corporation. After selling his house in Flint to Albert Champion in 1921, he never again owned a residence in Michigan, living either in New York and Maryland or "chez Pullman" as he commuted back and forth from New York to Detroit, arriving on Sunday night in the Motor City and leaving on Friday. (According to Eugene Weiss, there is evidence that he had apartments built into the fifth floor of the 1928 Highland Park body building that eventually became the Chrysler Corporation's general office building. He stayed there, and in the crisis times of the '30s often complained if his top officers didn't stay with him on weeknights.)

Though not known for his larger eleemosynary instincts, Walter Chrysler was civic-minded, a booster, and very concerned with the welfare of his workmen. But he and his corporation had no reason to be the financial saviors of Detroit's elites. Chrysler, both the corporation and the man, belonged to another setting almost entirely. He tried to help out in the beginning, but when no one in Detroit was willing to cooperate, he supported the General Motors bank plan with vigor.

Perhaps it would have been different if Detroit's leading families had been smart enough to co-opt the leadership and money of the industry's mass market companies. Perhaps the 1933 crisis would have come to a happier conclusion if Detroit itself had been a Federal Reserve banking center with financial autonomy, instead of just a satellite of Chicago. Perhaps cooperation among Detroit's leading families as they dealt with the GM and Chrysler interests could have saved its two big banking groups, instead of forcing these companies to abandon them in favor of a new institution. But by the middle of March 1933, Detroit was exposed to all the world for what it really was: a provincial one-industry ex-boom town, dependent for its business on the rest of the country, and dependent for its finances on large institutions in the real centers of financial power, located elsewhere. As for its leaders, they had shown themselves to be pretentious, shallow snobs, oblivious to anybody's welfare but their own over a long period of time; a sort of version of Lillian Hellman's *Little Foxes*. It came as no surprise that anybody who was able to help them, whether in Detroit or not, would not lift a finger on their behalf. Nobody cared about them or what they stood for.

It took Detroit a long, long time to recover from the disaster of 1933. Depositors got back their money for the most part, but not so the bank owners and bank stockholders, most of them from Grosse Pointe, who had the double liability of making all losses good from their own personal funds. Looking for a scapegoat for their woes, they found him in James Couzens, who was completely ostracized for not representing the interests of Detroit, of which he was a former mayor, in Washington.

Investment in the city dried up for a long, long time. The skeletons of huge uncompleted buildings haunted the cityscape for decades, and large tracts of land intended for housing lie empty and weed-covered even now, sixty-five years later. Detroit became a gigantic and failed place.

Albert Erskine was let go when Studebaker went into receivership in the spring of 1933, and he shot himself three months later. John North Willys gave up his post as Ambassador to Poland to try to save his company, only to see it too go bankrupt in 1933. It survived, but Willys's efforts exhausted him, and he died in 1935, at the age of sixty-two. The next year Roy Chapin, who went back to help Hudson after his stint as Secretary of Commerce, died prematurely too, at age fifty-six.

The last vestiges of Durant's automobile involvement ended in 1933, and though he didn't die, he had perhaps an equally awful fate: William C. Durant, perhaps the highest of all high flyers in the 1920s, was flat broke by 1936.

But Walter Chrysler's story was not Detroit's, and for him and his corporation, greater prosperity than ever was yet to come, along with one of the most important advances in the history of motorized transportation.

27

Streamlining
and the Airflow Car

What a piece of work is man!. . . . . In form and mov-
ing, how express and admirable!
Hamlet
William Shakespeare

Did you ever see a rectangular swan gliding across a
pond? So why put a box on wheels and shove it
through the air at high speeds?
Paul Jaray

In the beginning was the idea. Material and mechanical advancements
for mankind, like all others, begin with someone imagining them, and
then figuring out how to bring them into the realm of the practical and
real. What is a man? What does he want? What is good for him? Can it be
created? How can it be done?

The first automobiles were expensive, uncomfortable machines that,
though simple, were very difficult to drive. It could be said that the subsequent history of the automobile was a constant, Herculean labor to make
it cheaper, more comfortable, and easier to drive; in consequence, it became
a far more complex and finely engineered machine.

Though the original 1924 Chrysler was the first mass-produced automobile that was fully engineered and felt modern to drive, the 1934 Chrysler
Airflow was equally revolutionary: It was the first mass-produced automobile that was streamlined and felt modern to ride in.

It was aerodynamic, and people said it was born in a wind tunnel, which
to a certain extent it was. But its birth came not only from the study of
wind currents, but also from the study of the human body, and in particular, the walking man. In a sense, its real birthplace was the Mayo Clinic.

During Fred Zeder's "sippie" milk diet cure for ulcers at the Mayo Clinic
during the late '20s he became quite close to the Mayo brothers, "Dr. Will

Publicity photograph showing the 1934 Chrysler Airflow next to a streamlined locomotive to emphasize the similarity between these two streamlined
technological marvels. (*Courtesy DaimlerChrysler Corporate Historical
Collection*)

and Dr. Charlie," and was impressed by the efficient manner in which they
operated their business. But he was even more impressed by the scientific
method by which they conducted their investigations of the human body,
and saw a useful parallel between medical science and engineering. He
quickly began to realize that he could apply the methods he was learning
here to the conduct and improvement of his own business. Eventually he,
Breer, and Skelton patterned Chrysler Engineering directly on the Mayo
Clinic. Scientific inquiry would lead them to a controlled, though creative,
flexible and self renewing, adaptive process of evolution.

Among the results was the development of Floating Power. Later, Carl
Breer's study of the moving human body would lead to perhaps the most
important of the many contributions of the extraordinarily influential Airflow car: previously undreamed-of passenger comfort.

Under the heading, "Human Comfort Range," Carl Breer, in notes for his
autobiography, considered the development of transportation for man, and

Airflow publicity shot emphasizing the sturdiness of the car's body. The car was pushed off a cliff, and when it reached the bottom, all the doors opened, and it was started up and driven away. (*Courtesy DaimlerChrysler Corporate Historical Collection*)

showed the kind of thinking which led to the innovations in the design of the Chrysler Airflow.

"Let us now consider the cave man. When we look at the human being structurally we see one of nature's most wonderful pieces of mechanism, consisting of levers of bone which are directed in operation by senses, and operated by sheer muscular strength. His legs are used mainly to move from place to place. His hands, more refined, with multiple levers in the form of fingers, are useful in doing mechanical work in his all-around environment.

"We can experience the thrill primitive man experienced when he discovered that by means of the club he could pry things loose and do many things that without this lever he could not accomplish. Think also of the thrill of discovering that if he built this lever in a continuous form about a pivot he had a wheel. What a revelation! Today we mark this accomplishment one of the important points in the advancement of civilization.

"When we think in terms of what caused us to develop the motor car,

The Star Car, a 1935 prototype of a proposed radial-engined small car for the corporation. It was never put into production, but Ferdinand Porsche may well have seen it during a visit to Detroit, and there has been much speculation on its possible influence on the Volkswagen Beetle, which greatly resembles this car. (*Courtesy DaimlerChrysler Corporate Historical Collection*)

we return to our human desire to move about in a more efficient manner— on water by dugout, and more importantly on land by foot and animal. Since the horse, which became man's main means of land transportation in recent times, was not dependable and did not fully satisfy his wants, man made a machine to substitute for the horse. . . . . . .

"Briefly we may now outline the development of the automobile of the day. It was first necessary to make it run. Second, it was necessary to make the mechanism endure. Third, to make it quiet, and last, and all important, to make it a comfortable and efficient companion.

"Before we reached this latter stage we awakened to the fact that we had been selling automobiles to human beings and, in effect, had been saying, 'Here is our car; drive it and you will like it! Then ride in it, and if it jolts you around, you will soon adapt yourself to its inequalities. It's the great new way to get from here to there!'

"Then suddenly we awakened to the fact that our thinking was all wrong; the human being was the relatively fixed entity and the automobile must be carefully adjusted to suit man's comfort.

"We reverted our thinking back to the evolution of the cave man and life. We thought in terms of this early man walking from place to place for many generations and we discovered that during this period nature built up a most efficient human machine in proper balance in every respect. This beautiful mechanism is a structure of mechanics that we all admire and respect. Thermodynamically, mechanically, dynamically, and in every way, it is perfect, and we forever continue to marvel about it! So with due consideration, we studied nature's own action."

In essence then, at Chrysler Engineering the study of man's structure and movements became the centerpiece of the effort to move man better on land and through the air.

The Airflow car burst upon the public consciousness as an astonishment, a revelation, in early 1934. Never before had anything like it been offered to the general run of buyers. For the first time, this newfangled idea of "streamlining" was being brought to them. But like all things new under the sun, it had been in the air for a long time, and represented the culmination of years of investigation, not only by Chrysler but by many others as well.

Streamlining has to do with the movement of a fluid, whether gas or liquid, as it passes over an object moving through it. The bigger and squarer the object, the more energy is required to move it along. Even in ancient days people realized that tapered shapes were easier to move than boxier ones. Man first applied streamlining to boats, whether just long slim primitive dugout logs or the magnificent vessels of the Phoenicians, Egyptians, Greeks, and Romans.

It was Isaac Newton who provided the basis for a scientific understanding of streamlining, and hence more efficient moving vehicles, in his law of fluid dynamics. This stated that the resistance of a fluid, whether liquid or gas, to a solid body varied directly in proportion to the square of the body's velocity, the square of its surface area, and the density of the fluid. Clearly, the less area the frontal surface of a moving object presented to the wind or a liquid, the less energy would be required to move it.

As Howard S. Irwin further explains, "Streamlining as a principle of design had its roots in hydrodynamics and aerodynamics. In the 19th century the Scottish physicist William J. M. Rankine determined that the motion of fluids has two forms: laminar flow and turbulent flow. Laminar flow can be visualized as a series of parallel layers in a moving fluid, each with its own velocity and direction without disturbance in its forward motion. Turbulent flow is characterized by eddies or vortexes and can be visualized as a tumbling of the fluid caused by a solid body. The turbulence creates a partial vacuum behind the body, which in turn causes drag and impedes the body's forward progress. When a body immersed in a flow does not cause turbulence, it is said to be streamlined."

The actual term "streamlining" was invented by D'Arcy Wentworth Thompson in his classic 1917 treatise on growth and form. In it, he mathematically analyzed the shape of a bird's egg by applying the principle of least action, which states that a fluid medium tends to impress its "stream lines" on a deformable body until the body yields and offers a minimum of resistance. Snowdrifts, sand dunes, and lamp flames, he noted, similarly illustrate eddy curves that have been imposed by moving air facilitating its own flow. He concluded that this principle brought about the shape of a bird's egg over time, and deduced that it must also have come into play in the evolution of the body form of a fish or a bird.

Long before this these ideas had been applied to mechanical locomotion. In 1804 Sir George Cayley proposed that a dirigible should take the "form approaching to that of a very long spheroid" after studying the forms of the trout and the porpoise; he also concluded that the shapes of these creatures, split lengthwise, would create two ideal ship's hulls. By 1827, an Englishman named Medhurst proposed a rail car tapered at both ends to reduce wind resistance, and in 1865 a patent for a similar design was granted to the Reverend Samuel R. Calthrop of Roxbury, Massachusetts. Calthrop's patent foreshadowed practically every modern principle of the streamline train, including fairing of the undergear and articulation of the cars with flexible covering. It was never built, however.

In 1871 the first, or one of the first, wind tunnels was built in Britain by F. H. Wenham and John Browning, to experiment with aircraft wing shapes. Ludwig Mach tested both laminar and turbulent airflow of various objects by means of silk threads, cigarette smoke, and glowing particles of iron recorded on a photographic plate. In the 1890s Etienne-Jules Marey in France analyzed the aerodynamics of birds in flight, and used smoke streams in a simple tunnel to study airflow around various shapes. In the same year, airflow around a railroad train was checked in a tunnel. Ten years later, Orville and Wilbur Wright designed and built a six-foot-long wind tunnel in Dayton, Ohio, where they conducted airfoil tests from September through December, 1901, on more than 150 wing profile models. Later, as the aircraft industry developed, larger wind tunnels with better instruments were built in a variety of countries; some of these tunnels were available for automotive research.

The very first streamlined automobile was Charles Jeantaud's La Jamais Content, an 1899 electric car that set a land speed record of 65.9 miles per hour. Other striking streamlined cars appeared in the years that followed, like Louis Ross's Stanley Steamer–based Wogglebug racer of 1905 and the record-holding Stanley Steamer Rocket racer of 1906, both of which were astonishingly quick and fast. The Rocket reached 121.57 miles per hour in 1906 and 132 miles per hour a year later, and was the fastest object then known to man.

Shaped like an inverted boat hull bordered by huge outboard wire wheels, it had a full-length flat underpan and enclosed front and rear suspensions; the engine was placed behind the driver, who sat very low on the floor.

James J. Flink describes the abrupt conclusion to its record-breaking run; When the car hit a gully at 132 miles per hour, "It became airborne and flew a hundred feet at a height of fifteen feet before it crashed. The driver escaped with few injuries, and an aerodynamic principle was demonstrated: automobile aerodynamics not only is complicated but it is very different from airplane aerodynamics. To reduce drag without preventing lift can be disastrous."

By 1913 wind tunnel experiments had produced a large assortment of aerodynamically improved forms derived from the three basic streamline shapes of the day: airship, torpedo, and teardrop. They were more or less aerodynamically successful, but none was practical because of their inefficient use of overall space.

Meanwhile proposals for streamlined bodies were popping up everywhere. J. J. Ide's streamlined auto body sketches appeared in *The Automobile* in 1913. They were on the right track in a primitive sort of way, except for the fact that they were backward, a common mistake of the time. The January 11, 1913, edition of *Scientific American* contained a startling artist's conception of the "car of the future," which featured a cigar-shaped body, fully rounded in cross section, front ended by a bluntly rounded nose and rear ended by a tapering tail. The artist even imagined a then technically impossible curved windshield built into that rounded nose.

This was all just on paper, though. In 1914 a real streamliner came into being. Count Marco Ricotti worked with the famed coachmaker Castagna to design a teardrop-shaped auto body that was then placed on an Alfa Romeo chassis with a motor that ranged between 40 and 60 horsepower. The vehicle was positively weird looking, but it was aerodynamically correct; the mechanics were wrong however, and the car was slower than the standard Alfa model.

In 1921 Edmund Rumpler, an aircraft designer and builder, created an aerodynamic car he called a Tropfcnwagen, or "teardrop car." It was a rear-engine, vertical airfoil mounted on wheels, with such features as disc wheels, an enclosed rear-mounted radiator, and airfoil fenders, all of which reduced its drag. Rumpler's design was intuitive rather than scientific, based on his experience with aircraft. He had tested it at Gustave Eiffel's French research institute, however, and when it was formally tested by Wolfgang Klemperer in the wind tunnel of the Zepplin airship works, it was shown to have a drag coefficient of .54, which was quite good for its day, but not really extraordinary in any absolute sense. The reason for this was that it had two-dimensional, or horizontal, streamlining only. For streamlining to work truly it must be a totality.

Richard Burns Carson pointed out that there are really three types of streamlining: (1) visual streamlining, which unifies otherwise uncoordinated elements of a design; (2) aerodynamic streamlining, which "organizes the invisible air currents passing around the car's outer features into larger, smoother, and less turbulent ones—aerodynamic streamlining seeks reduced air drag and wind noise and increased stability at speed as its goals and uses scientific tools in achieving them (coefficients of air drag range from .05 for an airfoil and .10 for a sphere to 1.25 for a barn door flying flat side first and 1.35 for a parachute); (3) structural streamlining, which is independent of the other two, and is concerned with inner structure rather than outer form, transforming distinct component frameworks into supporting aspects of a larger framework, thereby eliminating duplication of structural rigidity throughout the car."

The end result of the last of these was the unitized body frame, in which each element lent its strength to the others. Aerodynamic streamlining had quite a vogue in the mid-1930s, but it took more than fifty years for the benefits of its influence to become pervasive in the auto industry. But the most superficial of the three, visual streamlining, turned into an immediate hit, and appeared on many other items besides cars. By the late thirties everything from radios to buildings to waffle irons had some sort of streamlining slapped onto their exteriors, for no useful reason whatsoever. The public thought these items looked good and seemed modern somehow, and what the public wanted, it got. But purists were horrified. The December, 1942, number of the *Bulletin, Museum of Modern Art*, showed a picture of a streamlined toaster under the heading, "All Change Is Not Progress." The text read, "Toaster of 1940 which is streamlined as if it were intended to hurtle through the air at 200 miles an hour (an unhappy use for a breakfast utensil), and ornamented with trivial loops, bandings and flutings. This object has never been exhibited by the Museum."

The purist of the pure was Paul Jaray, the Hammurabi of streamlining. He was the man who figured it out and codified it, and though he is little known today, and profited not at all from his discovery in his own time, he is nevertheless the great figure in the field.

Jaray was born in Vienna on March 11, 1889, into a Hungarian family of businessmen and artists. He was educated at the German Technical College of Prague, where he assisted Dr. R. Doerfl, a pioneer in the study of aerodynamics who introduced this new science to Jaray. He found no work in this nascent field upon graduation in 1910, and took jobs at the Prague engineering firm E.A.G., and later consulted with Austro-Daimler in Weiner-Neustadt. By 1914 he at last began work in aerodynamics at Flugzeugbau Friedrichshafen, a Zeppelin subsidiary, where he was set to work on aircraft. Successful as he was with the FF17 and FF21, he lost interest in airplanes quickly, and went to work on the LZ 38 airship at Luftschiffbau, where he ran into a great deal of frustration. "I wanted a wind tunnel but they dragged it out and dragged it out. Those first Zeppelins were all done mathematically," he said.

In 1916 he finally got his first wind tunnel, and a year later designed and built the largest one in Germany with colleagues Max Munk and Paul Schoenfeld. The exigencies of the war put him to work on airplanes once again, and though he designed two beautiful and useful aircraft, the Zepp I and the Zepp II, the Treaty of Versailles put Germany and Jaray out of the airplane business.

By the end of World War I he had begun to amass some of his many patents, most concerned with drag reduction or structural advantage ideas relating to airships. He was earning very little however, and by 1921 he began applying his talents to the automotive field, obtaining his first auto patent in that year and also presenting Zeppelin with a design for a stream-lined car body.

Early in 1922 Klemperer began methodical testing of 1:10 scale models (they worked just as well as full-sized models) of Jaray's designs and con-ventional designs in a wind tunnel, devising an ingenious way of suspend-ing the models on wires on their sides above stretched, doped linen so that the wheels barely touched the linen; this way he eliminated any chance for the models to press the "road" out of shape and influence the measure-ments. (Rolling resistance, resulting from mechanical losses in the drive train and wheels, and friction between the tires and the road, affects mea-surements of aerodynamic drive.) A Pitot tube measured the windspeed, with the drag of the wires and hanging devices deducted from the results.

The results, published in the *Zietschrift fur Flugtechnick und Motorlufts-chiffahrt (Magazine of Flight Technology and Airship Travel)* on July 31, 1922, showed that Jaray's model, with its enclosed bottom, rounded windscreen and airfoil shaped body, was far superior to the others, which were standard open and closed bodies of the day. The Jaray model had a cd of only .28, an astoundingly low figure which was shown to be even lower at .245 when the model was retested in Stuttgart's far more eficient wind tunnel in 1939.

Jaray concluded that the ideal aerodynamic form for a car was that of the upper half of a streamlined body of revolution, such as those he had previously developed for airship use. It was in fact half a dirigible with a flat bottom and air deflected up from the tail. This would be best utilized in a three-wheeled vehicle with the engine at the rear, but since, practically speaking, cars were four-wheeled vehicles with motors in front, modifica-tions had to be made. A separate vertical airfoil to house passengers, tapered downward toward the rear and narrower than the main hull, had to be placed atop the basic airfoil form. It had to be tapered in the vertical plane, as the basic shell was tapered in the horizontal plane, to guide the airflow up and over the car and down at the rear so that the least air disturbance would be created. In order that air could be permitted to resume its former shape as quickly as possible after passing over a vehicle, it was best that it not be forced to the side of or under the car to any greater extent than was absolutely necessary. Jaray's shape proved to be as close to the ideal as possible in any practical sense.

The importance of his findings was expressed by Jerry Sloniger in his *Automobile Quarterly* article, 'The Slippery Shapes of Paul Jaray': "Prior to 1922, various flow advocates had aerodynamically shaped separate parts of a car but accomplished little because the combination of faired sections moving in loose formation created eddies. Jaray now contended that, 'It was the overall concept that mattered. All cars should be enclosed on the bottom, but that alone wouldn't make sense if nothing else was done. You can't change lights and say it is better. We didn't put door handles on my cars, for instance. Only a hole and you kept the key in your pocket. But for somebody to say, 'okay, no handles,' well, that wouldn't mean the car was streamlined.' "

The first Jaray-designed car was built on a 2-liter Ley T6 chassis at the Zeppelin works in 1922. It was a very strange-looking vehicle, both very narrow and very high, and it proved to Jaray that existing chassis were not really suitable to his designs, but it demonstrated great fuel economy and hill-climbing ability when compared to a standard-bodied Ley model.

Jaray left his job at Zeppelin in 1923 and moved to Switzerland, where he set up the Jaray Stream-Line Carriage Body Company in Zurich, through which he hoped to expand his growing portfolio of automobile patents. His next project was a Ley racer, so well proportioned that it managed a speed of 80 miles per hour from a 26-horsepower engine, attracting widespread attention through its many racing victories.

On August 19, 1927, after five years of proceedings, he was granted a U.S. patent on streamlining, and established the Jaray Streamline Corporation in New York. Over the next few years he amassed a number of patents relating to automobiles, all on various aspects of streamlining. "You could choose as if from a menu," he said of them. Despite the efforts of Lowell H. Brown, a Jaray vice president and investor who tirelessly promoted the benefits of Jaray's ideas in the United States, his licenses didn't sell. The big manufacturers, both here and in Europe, either sidestepped his patents or waited them out, and Jaray couldn't afford to launch big legal battles against them when they did these things.

Nor did Jaray, who readily admitted he wasn't much of a businessman, fare that much better in Europe, and he became bitter about his lack of financial success. Many companies, such as Fiat, Alfa Romeo, Maybach, Mercedes, Audi, Steyr, Adler, Peugeot, Singer, Skoda, Tatra, Apollo, Hanomag, Jawa, and Wikov built one or two prototypes, but nothing more. Tatra was the sole, and very notable exception, eventually building a Jaray-inspired streamliner for over 40 years in Czechoslovakia. Eventually Jaray turned his attention to other areas of engineering, working on everything from airport snow removal to mufflers, vacuum cleaners and torpedo and hydrofoil boats.

Serious research on aerodynamics in the United States began in 1926, when the Daniel Guggenheim Fund for the Promotion of Aeronautics was established on January 26 with a grant of $2.5 million. This money, and more that followed, enabled several U.S. universities to build experimental wind tunnels, which became available to automobile as well as aircraft researchers.

By the early 1930s, when streamlining was everywhere "in the air," a number of streamliners began to appear, causing much notice and comment, but little follow through. Still, several were quite striking and had wide influence on the automotive community.

R. Buckminster Fuller, who later became world famous for his invention of the geodesic dome, in collaboration with noted yacht racing designer W. Starling Burgess, created the futuristic Dymaxion, virtually a three-wheeled balsa and Duralumin airplane fuselage, in 1933. Tested at the Locomobile Speedway in Bridgeport, Connecticut on July 12, 1933, it did 120 mph. Weighing only 1,850 pounds, this rear-engine vehicle got 40 miles from a gallon of gas. Fuller built two more examples, despite the fact that two Gulf Company officials were killed in a later test. Though widely seen and demonstrated, the Dymaxion was too far out for the general public, and never received production financing.

The Dymaxion was powered by a Ford V-8, as were two other streamliners, Wellington Miller's Arrowhead Tear Drop and William B. Stout's Stout Scarab. Stout had built the all-metal Stout Tri-Motor airplane for Ford, and naturally turned to Ford to power his car. This seven-passenger car, streamlined without being really aerodynamic, was aluminum-bodied and replaced the conventional chassis with a rigid alloy tubing structure. Its seats could be converted into a bed, predating a similar arrangement in Nashes by quite some time. Stout, who premiered his car in 1935, expected to build 100 cars at $5,000 each, but here too financing did not materialize.

The Stout Scarab was a heavily reworked version of the amazing 1931 Sterkenberg streamliner, which was the work of legendary Dutch designer John Tjaarda. Both the man and his car figure heavily in the later history of American streamlining.

But streamlining in any real and popular sense first came to the American car-buying public through the work of the least heralded of all the designers of the classic age of car design, Amos E. Northrup. He was the head of all production body design for the Murray Body Corporation of America, whose clients included many of the struggling independent manufacturers who could not afford to maintain their own body design divisions, as General Motors and Chrysler were beginning to do in 1928. These companies were locked in a desperate struggle with the majors to remain competitive, and thus hired the services of companies such as Murray, Briggs, Budd, and Hayes, which maintained stables of first-rate designers available to all comers. In order to look like industry leaders, even though they were on a tight budget, these companies often took chances on advanced design ideas that left the majors struggling to keep up.

Amos Northrup first came to prominence through his design for the elegant and meticulously built Wills Sainte Claire of the early and mid-1920s. Next he achieved a great deal of notice for his slim and graceful Hupmobile Century Six and Eight of 1928, which led to that company's peak period of popularity. These cars bore a distinct resemblance to Harley Earl's sensational 1927 LaSalle. But at prices that topped out where the LaSalle's began, Hupmobiles sold at a rate five times greater, causing the company to push its plant capacity to the limit with overtime work. Hupmobile even bought out the Chandler-Cleveland Motors Corporation, maker of Chandlers, just to get greater production capacity. (To no avail; a fickle public bought just 50,579 Hupmobiles in 1929, half of the 100,000 the company expected to sell, and off 23 percent from the 1928 all-time production high of 65,862 cars.) After the Hupmobile job came the smart and sexy Willys "plaidside" roadster of 1929, which sold like hotcakes for the Willys-Overland Company.

In September of 1930 REO announced for the 1931 model year the finest car it had ever attempted to build. This was the Royale, clearly named after the gigantic Bugatti Royale, perhaps the largest and most expensive car of all time. The stunningly beautiful REO Royale was developed from a concept created by Fabio Segardi, who had designed the first REO Flying Cloud, a highly successful car that first came out in 1927, and his staff. However, the actual design was the work of Amos Northrup, who was assisted by a young designer named Julio Andrade, later to work for Harley Earl at General Motors.

The Royale was the first production car to offer aerodynamic styling to the American public. Its design flowed from the idea that if you simply rounded off the edges of a square box, aerodynamic efficiency increased enormously. As Karl S. Zahm describes it, "The Royale owed its beauty to lines that flowed in a symmetrical, unbroken sweep from a V-shaped radiator to to a sleek 'beaver' tail. Tested extensively in a wind tunnel, the shape achieved a new standard of excellence in the growing movement toward streamlined styling. . . . Northrup's fondness for well-rounded curves was evident in the wing-like, rolled-edge front fenders, an industry first. Gone was the bolt-upright style of the past, the blocky roofline with an external sun visor up front and an abrupt, near vertical drop at the rear. Clearly, this was styling like no other, for it owed little to the past. Indeed, the Royale was a harbinger of the future, and its graceful bodywork would be a catalyst for designers throughout the industry in the years ahead."

The REO Royale, though as well engineered as it was beautiful, never succeeded in the marketplace, through no fault of its own. Conceived in 1929, before the Depression hit, it was brought to completion due to pressure from many of the company's dealers, who felt that to keep up with competition from other cars in its class a luxury car was needed to draw attention to the rest of the REO line. The management of Murray Body, which had just completed a plant with capacity for 900 bodies a day and needed business to keep it humming, wanted it also. Perhaps too, REO management, in common with those of other companies such as Pierce-Arrow, Auburn, and Franklin, thought the Depression would be a short one, and assumed that customers would be found for their exciting new offerings. Few remember today that it wasn't until 1931 that many people realized how bad things might get, and for how long.

By common consensus, Amos Northrup's masterpiece is acknowledged to be the 1932 Graham Blue Streak Eight, which stole a march on the giants of the industry "by suddenly, in one stroke, making all of their styling obsolete," according to Strother MacMinn and Michael Lamm. "In this design Northrup abandoned the practice of refining and assembling traditional parts, and instead conceived the entire car as a coherent, carefully sculptured shell to cover its components." Graham expert Jeffrey I. Godshall called it "a car of such trend-setting appearance that it served as a blueprint for the future, sending rival automakers into overtime scrambling to catch up."

Every aspect of the Blue Streak's body was rounded and smoothed, with any unsightly chassis parts concealed. The windshield, whether one-piece, as on the sedan and coupe, or two-piece, as on the convertible, was sharply raked, a design element echoed in the backward slanting hood louvers and stylishly sloped V-shaped radiator grille, whose vertical chromium bars were tapered toward the bottom. The car had no separate radiator shell, and the hood went all the way up to the radiator surround molding. This was possible because the radiator cap, as on the REO Royale, was located under the hood. Since there was no radiator cap, there was no need for a radiator cap ornament either, though customer complaints later forced the company to offer a flying goddess hood ornament typical of the times. To reinforce the notion of the unity of the design, headlamp shells and even body frames were painted to match the body colors of the cars, and a unique "banjo" frame kick-up surrounding the rear axle and outboard springing allowed the height of the car to be lowered by several inches, giving the car a sleek, road hugging look. "Pearl essence finish," a crystalline paint made from a certain type of fish-scale lacquer compound, gave colored Graham bodies a striking appearance that set off their low rounded curves from all the squared-off, upright, mostly black auto bodies of other cars of the day.

But more than anything else, what made every other manufacturer's cars seem suddenly obsolete were the Graham's fenders. For the first time they cascaded all the way down to the bumpers to conceal axles and frames. The often road- and weather-dirtied undercarriage of the automobile was now hidden from side view by vertical valance panels or skirts. Contributing to the sleek wholeness of the car's design, these fenders were smooth one-piece units without any distracting detail, and edges that were gently rolled inward. Completely taken unawares, all other manufacturers scrambled to incorporate these new-style fenders into their products for the 1933 model year. But no one's styles were as graceful as Graham's, because Graham's bespoke an entire design concept, rather than a hastily added styling gimmick.

These new Grahams caused quite a sensation with the general public. All in all some 4.2 million Blue Streaks were sold. Unfortunately for Graham however, these were only model cars manufactured by Tootsietoy. Real Graham production nosedived from 20,428 in 1931 to 12,967 in 1932 as the Depression worsened. The Blue Streak, which debuted on December 8, 1931 in 21 body styles, accounted for most of these sales, and Graham had the distinction of producing the only Eight whose sales improved in 1932, doubling the 1931 total. 1933 sales fell again, to 10,967, though the well-run company could boast of a profit of $67,000 that year, despite a declining number of customers. After that the scrappy little company increased sales by offering the public such novelties as supercharged engines and windshield defrosters, and through the 1937 model year at least, it showed promise of carving out a niche for itself among the independents. But Amos Northrup's Art Moderne "Sharknose" Graham of 1938–40, which was too radical for the public, and the Graham Hollywood of 1940–41, a redone version of the 1936–37 Cord, which, like its original, proved too complicated and expensive to produce, eventually led the company on a path away from automobile production in the postwar years (though its automobile operations formed the basis of the Kaiser-Frazer Corporation).

Far more radical than any Northrup design was Philip Wright's truly futuristic Pierce Silver Arrow V-12 of 1933, a car so radically streamlined that though Pierce literature proclaimed, "It gives you in 1933 the car of 1940," in truth it gave you the car of 1950. Everything—running boards, spare tires, radiators, and headlights—were faired into or concealed by flowing sheet metal that swept along into pontoon rear fenders and a radically tapered fastback tail. People were simply thunderstruck by its appearance at the Chicago World's Fair in the summer of 1933, but unfortunately its $10,000 price tag put it beyond the reach of all but the wealthiest plutocrats.

As for Northrup, he went on to design the little Willys 77 of 1933, which, though not very attractive, offered Floating Power engine mounts (a gift from Walter Chrysler to the embattled John North Willys) and a peppy little

48-horsepower engine for a price as low as $335, managing to pull the company out of bankruptcy. He also styled the rather stodgy Hupmobile 417/W and 517/W, which functioned as low-priced companions to the beautiful Hupmobile Aerodynamic cars of 1934–35. While working on the Graham Sharknose in early 1936, Northrup slipped on the ice near his home in Ferndale, Michigan, sustaining head injuries that led to his death. Called "the Mozart of automobile design" by MacMinn and Lamm "because of the significance of his contributions," it was his "adjustment to the prevailing classic style that alerted the public to more radical things to come."

❦   ❦   ❦

For the American public, the radical thing that came was the Airflow from Chrysler. Like the Graham Blue Streak, it was a unified design, rather than an assemblage of disparately designed parts. But Chrysler went much further than Graham. The Airflow was a total concept design, worked on from the ground up in utter secrecy over a period of six years. Walter Chrysler himself famously called it "the first real motor car since the invention of the automobile," and in a sense he was right.

Until the Airflow, all cars were really variations of horse-and-buggy transportation, with passengers sitting in a wagon behind a motor that provided movement power. Even the Blue Streaks and Royales, as beautifully novel as they were, did not flout the long-established conventions of automobile appearance. But the creators of the Airflow did something never before attempted. The body of the car was designed around the engineering of the car, and the engineering was considered as if it were something brand-new. New layouts and structures were used, and new forms and materials too, giving the drivers and passengers of Airflow cars a new experience of automobiling. It jumped far ahead of its predecessors and competition with an array of novel features, and as Howard Irwin says, it posed a daring question to the car-buying public: "Is honest functional design in an automobile beautiful, even when it breaks completely with tradition?" The achievement of the Airflow was remarkable, and had an influence on the progress of the automobile that lasts to this very day. But the public's reaction to it in 1934 cast a shadow of equal reach and duration over that progress.

The Airflow began with one of the best-known stories in the history of the automobile. One evening in the fall of 1927 Carl Breer was driving from Highland Park to his summer home at Gratiot Beach in Port Huron, a distance of some 60 miles, when he saw a flock of a dozen or so geese flying low in perfect formation through the sky. This seemed strange to him because it was too early for them to be winging their way southward on their annual migration. On closer inspection however, he realized that they were not geese at all but a formation of Republic Army planes making their way back to Selfridge Field near Mount Clemens. As he rolled along he was impressed by the ability of the planes to stay in the air at a low speed, and wondered whether the ground speed at which he was traveling would cause the wind to lift his car's front end and give him reduced steering control or, on the contrary, if it would cause downward pressure that would overload the tires. He stuck his arm out the window and noticed the surprising amount of lift his forearm got as it cut through the moving current of air. When he angled it farther out from the elbow the back pressure bucked the air enough to make him feel the car slow down and pull to the side. This was a lot of fun, but it also set him to thinking.

The following Monday he spoke to Bill Earnshaw, a Dayton engineer of independent means who was fascinated by research and who had come to Chrysler without portfolio just the week before. Breer set him to the task of finding out whether the air lift or downward pressure problems his Saturday experience raised had any scientific basis in fact. The answer was no, but Earnshaw did find a great deal of head-on wind resistance. Earnshaw knew Wilbur Wright back in Dayton, and went to discuss this situation with him. After conferring with Wright, Earnshaw set up some simple blower experiments in a corner of the Chrysler service parts plant in Dayton that dramatically illustrated the better effects of air currents on curved, as opposed to square, forms.

The results so impressed Breer that he determined to have his own wind tunnel, though he stipulated that the cost had to be reasonable. In a few months, with the help and advice of Wilbur Wright, Earnshaw managed to build inexpensively a 40-foot-by-30-foot aerodynamic lab with a 35-horsepower engine powering a wind tunnel with a thirty-foot-by-twenty-foot throat. There was also space and equipment to build variously shaped small wooden models.

After testing two regular models, Breer got the idea of testing the cars running backward; to his astonishment, the air drag was 30 percent less. "Our laboratory was on the fourth floor of the engineering building," he said, "and as I looked out of the window at all the cars outdoors, I called the boys over and remarked, 'Just think how dumb we have been, when you look at these cars and realize that they are all running in the wrong direction!' This impression would not leave us. It just seemed that suddenly we discovered that we were thrillingly living in another world, and that in our everyday life the automobiles around us as designed were telling us that the basis of design was all wrong! This discovery touched off more enthusiasm and the more we thought of it the more we thought something should be done about it! This astounding enlightenment was the motivating force that started the all-important design of the Airflow series."

The engineers saw that in conventional cars the cross section of the body over the rear wheels was the largest, and that this was very bad placement. Wind tunnel tests told them that the spheroid zeppelin shape, blunt at the front and tapered toward the rear, was best. The first thing they had to do was get the rear seat off its time-honored buckboard position over the rear axle. Breer called in Oliver Clark, the head of the Body and Styling Division, to effect the solution. He brought the rear seat some 20 inches ahead of the rear axle and down lower into the frame, on the same level as the front seat. They figured out the correct driver leg room, located the floorboard and dash, and placed the front wheels as close to these items as possible, with minimum wheel clearance. Now they had established their wheelbase, which was shorter than before, a state of affairs contrary to what would have been predicted.

Next they needed to figure out where to put the engine. They considered placing it in the rear of the car, which aerodynamically would have been a good idea. But it would have created too many problems with weight distribution, and meant that production facilities would have to have been torn up completely, at great expense, to accommodate such a layout. Previous Chrysler engines had always been located to the rear of the front axle, which in this new setup would not have been practical. Placing them in front of the front axle was out of the question, so the only option was to place them above the front axle. This was accomplished by altering the shape of the engine underpans and placing the engine at an increased upward angle.

The next decision was to determine the shape of the body. Oliver Clark said, "When Mr. Chrysler told us to produce in 1934 the best body ever built for Chrysler's tenth anniversary, we told him that could only be done by throwing all traditions to the winds and forgetting the milk wagon and buggy eras of transportation." And so they did.

Clark and his team marked out passenger headroom and drew a parabola around the front end of the car and up over the top, with the highest point over the front seat passengers. For the sake of streamlining, it tapered gradually from the front down to the rear, leaving enough headroom for rear seat passengers. The forward oval was notched in for a windshield close to the driver and a hood line that cascaded down over the hood and front wheels to the bumpers (research had shown that curving the fender down to the wheel caused less air disturbance). Since the centerline of the horizontal axis of the blimp form, from which the Airflow was derived, passed through the wheel centers, nothing below this needed to be of any concern. Of course, the lower and narrower the back, the more streamlined the car would have been, and originally they designed a car with a three-passenger front seat and a two-passenger rear, exactly the reverse of the prevalent arrangement then. But Walter Chrysler himself eventually nixed this, feeling that a two-passenger rear seat would limit the sales appeal of the car, and his sales department backed him up. So modifications were effected, and the Airflow sedan became a six-passenger car. (However, this was not considered necessary with the coupe, which as a result had a far more beautiful, deeply slanted rear end.)

Following the Airflow's "fashion by function" philosophy, Breer worked with Herv Sherts of Pittsburgh Plate Glass to create the industry's first curved one-piece windshield for the car. In the end, it proved so costly and so prone to breakage during installation that it was used only on the gigantic, wildly expensive CW Airflow models (power windows were also pioneered on this model). Regular Airflows had V-shaped two-piece windshields so deeply slanted that the driver's line of vision was forward of the side A posts for the first time. Their 52.25-square-inch area was 25 percent larger than Cadillac's. (The windshields were cleaned off by two-piece windshield wipers, another industry first.)

Ornamentation was kept to a minimum on the body, whose most striking feature was its front end. The hood was short and deeply sloped, giving the driver an excellent, clear perspective on the road ahead for the very first time in American motoring. There was no bolt-upright radiator prow on the car, just a waterfall of chromium bars cascading down from an inverted V on top of the hood. Another Airflow first was that the hood was all in one piece, opening from the back end near the windshield. Headlights were positioned in chromium bezels flush with the fenders, which were attached directly to the hood without any space in between.

Now came the question of how to build it. Body structure had been developing slowly over the history of the automobile, from the early days of motorized buggies with all-wooden bodies. As cars began to attain greater speed around the turn of the century, veneered wooden bodies were replaced by light-gauge steel panels attached to wooden frames, because the steel panels carried paint better and gave much greater resistance to weather and the dust and stones that were pervasive hazards of early motoring. Even though the steel panels became more attractively curved through advances in steel stamping, the basic steel-on-wood-frame body structure continued for decades, even after the introduction and eventual prominence of the closed car.

As Oliver Clark explained it at the time, "The great difficulty with the so-called composite body lies in the fact that wood and steel do not work well together, as no one has ever yet found a satisfactory method of permanently joining these materials. Wood and steel are subject to different laws of expansion and contraction. Their periods of deterioration vary, and vibration loosens the nails and screws by which the two are joined. Consequently a composite construction of wood and steel is no stronger than its joints."

In the early 1920s, when the first all-steel bodies were made, a significant advancement came about, for now body panels could be welded to the frames, eliminating the wood screws, nails, and glue formerly used to hold bodies together. The difficulty with these bodies was that they were made from 800 to 900 small pieces welded together, which created substantial manufacturing difficulties. Furthermore, they were noisy, because the steel panels were flat drumhead-like vibrating surfaces. For this reason the public thought of these vehicles as tinny, and since only mass manufacturers of low-priced vehicles could afford the tools to produce them, all steel cars were also thought of as cheap.

When Chrysler acquired Dodge, it acquired all-steel bodies with it, and in 1929 the company set out to solve their inherent problems. Vibration was reduced by putting greater formation and stretch into the steel panels and lining them with acoustical materials. Later, so-called mono-piece bodies were created by making the stampings larger and fewer, reducing their number to four, which were then flash-welded into one continuous whole.

For the Airflow, Clark decided on a revolutionary concept. Steel reinforced with steel was his guiding principle—this was "the best and most economical building material, and only with it could we produce a homogeneous structure of proven worth."

After looking at an assemblage of the best American cars then built, he came to the conclusion that "they were constructed of a chassis with a rigid frame, on which was set a body, as a howdah is strapped to an elephant's back. In a howdah the occupants ride for protection from the jungle tiger, but beyond that all the howdah does is to increase the load on the elephant's back. In a perfect engineering structure every part should have a useful duty to perform. Consequently, in our new Chrysler and DeSoto automobiles for 1934 we decided actually to make the body do some work, and thereby increase the strength of the structure and at the same time lighten the total weight. We therefore built trusses like the sides of a bridge into the body and we have put our passengers inside the steel frame work." The resulting body had forty times the torsional rigidity of previous models, and in a famous publicity film one of these cars was driven off a 110-foot cliff in Pennsylvania, then started up and driven away; amazingly, even after this huge blow to the body, the doors opened and closed without difficulty.

But the primary consideration in all of this was passenger comfort. As this intent was uppermost in the minds of its creators, so its actualization was the crown of its builders. In fact, whenever Airflow customers seemed reluctant to consider these cars in the showroom, salesmen were urged to try anything to get them to go for a drive in one of them. This tactic closed many a sale, as amazed drivers and passengers often bought one on the spot upon alighting from the car.

The experience of motoring in an Airflow was called "Floating Ride," clearly drawing on the fame of the Floating Power rubber engine mounts introduced by Chrysler three years earlier. It has come down to us as the "boulevard ride" still to be found in the Lincoln Town Cars and Cadillac DeVilles of today.

The way it was brought about was this. After studying "nature's own action" with regard to man's construction and movement, Carl Breer had concluded that there was a "human comfort range." "We realize over a period of evolutionary time that man has established a comfortable stride without fatigue. Specifically, we find this to be around 2 ½ to 3 miles per hour. In terms of engineering we think of it as 80 to 100 step cycles or rhythms per minute. Let us call this the human comfort range. We notice further that our heart, the kidneys, the liver, etc., are all suspended in the body cavity by means of muscular cords. Nature has established a natural rhythm at which the whole human mechanism seems to relax in comfort."

Breer discovered that most American cars functioned at a springing rate of about 120 rhythms per minute, and that some European models had a periodicity of 135 per minute. This was due to the short springs commonly used on these heavy-framed, engine-behind-the-axle vehicles. No wonder passengers felt fatigued after spending even moderate amounts of time in such cars. The Airflow reduced periodicity from 120 cycles to just 90, in large measure due to much longer springs, in addition to reconfiguring the placement of engine and seats. The improvement was more accurately expressed by comparing the cube of these numbers—in other words, the rate of improvement was 25 to 1. Anyone who rode in one of these cars felt the difference between it and all others immediately.

Redistribution of weight, via a reconfiguration of the placement of engine and seats, was just as important as longer springing in creating the Floating Ride. It involved moving weight factors in the car farther away from the center of mass, noticeably increasing the the moment of inertia, slowing down forward and aft oscillation, and bringing the points of the center of percussion closer to the front and rear axle centers. This meant that any upward force on either the front or rear wheels would cause the body to pivot around the axle at the opposite end of the car, reducing the pitching and bouncing that had been the bane of automobile riders since the beginning.

The law of the center of percussion, first published in *Pemberton's View of Newton's Philosophy* in 1728, was never applied to automobiles before, and was a real discovery for Breer and his team. By redistributing the Airflow's weight, they were able to make the center of percussion fall at the same point as the center of oscillation, and this established the car's much smoother than ever ride. Just as a properly designed hammer held at the center of oscillation produces no sting when hit at the center of percussion, so a car in which these forces fall at the same point will produce no unpleasant jostling when going over bumps.

Until the Airflow, the commonly accepted wisdom was that the longer the wheelbase, the better the ride, but from now on this would no longer be so. The Airflow clearly demonstrated that in the scientifically designed modern car comfort was a matter of proper placement of elements and distribution of weight, all determined by the laws of physics. This was truly new, and the public benefited from it in a big way.

The DeSoto version of the Airflow rode on a 116-inch wheelbase, and came equipped with a 241.5-cubic-inch 100-horsepower six-cylinder engine. The Chrysler Airflow came in four straight-eight versions, the 121-inch-wheelbase CU with a 299-cubic-inch engine rated at 122 horsepower, the 123-inch-wheelbase CV, and 137.5-inch-wheelbase CX with a 323.5-cubic-inch engine rated at 130 horsepower, and the huge 146.5-inch-wheelbase CW, powered by a 384.84-cubic-inch engine rated at 145 horsepower. Bohn-alite aluminum cylinder heads were featured in the engines, and pistons made from anodized aluminum alloys were used after 1934. An export version of the Airflow was actually a DeSoto six with Chrysler badging.

Coupled to the eights, as an option on the base model and standard on the others, was the first automatic overdrive transmission. This system was developed from the clutch invention of a West Coast man named Keller, and therefore it was referred to at Chrysler as the Keller clutch. It was in full form the invention of Howard Barnes of Warner Gear, which supplied it to Chrysler. What was special about it was that it was so uncomplicated for the driver to use. The fourth, or "overdrive," gear was independent of the other three, hence making it possible for the driver to use the well-established three-speed H gearshift pattern while still getting the benefits of overdrive. A lot of experimental work went into developing it, but the driver's instructions were easy. When a speed of 38 mph or more was reached, the driver released the clutch by pushing the clutch pedal with the left foot and closed off the throttle by removing the right foot from the accelerator. The clutch slowed down to the point whereby a pawl would lock out the fourth gear, actually a planetary gear set unconnected to the other three. At this point, the basic three gears would not, as usual, be running through the slow and quiet planetary gear set, and hence none of them would be engaged. This meant the car was running in direct drive, and the engine would be making the least number of turns per mile. The practical consequence of all this was that when the car traveled at a fast speed its engine speed was lower than it would have been if the gears were engaged. The Airflow was therfore able to ride along at high speeds with much less engine noise and effort than other cars. A salesman's bulletin claimed that at an engine speed of 3400 rpm a 1934 Cadillac could do only 68 miles per hour, while an Imperial Airflow could do over 100 miles per hour, which was an impressive statistic. It also decreased gasoline consumption by a considerable margin, which meant something to everyone in those late Depression days.

The interior of the car was another leap forward. Moving the position of the rear seat forward and down into the frame widened the whole passenger compartment. The rear seat had always accommodated three passengers, and its position over the rear axle had always been the widest point of the car. But now the location of the front seat was the widest point of the car, meaning that for the first time the front seat could comfortably handle three people, and therefore, the six-passenger, two-seat sedan was born. Lowering the seating position gave extra headroom, too, and moving the engine forward meant more legroom than ever before.

Clearly showing the influence of modern furniture design, the front seat was not flush with the floor, but rather was raised off it by several inches. This allowed air to circulate freely undearneath the seats, giving much better heating and ventilation in cold weather and warm. Also, these seats had highly polished chrome-plated seamless steel tubular frames, attached to the specially upholstered seat backs with brackets. This permitted frames to stand free of the edges of the leather-trimmed Bedford cord seat cushions, giving them an ultrasophisticated Art Moderne armchair look. Even the rear seats had curved chrome siderails, topped by soft leather upholstered armrests and ash receivers.

Such seating was something brand-new in car interiors, and essentially caused Chrysler to go into the furniture business to produce them. Chrysler bought all-new machinery to manufacture the chrome tubing for the seating, hiring and training a new crew of workers right off the streets during the start-up period. Operators for cutting, bending, polishing, punch press operations, welding, and plating were all needed. (Plating alone involved copper plating, nickel plating, nickel buffing, and chromium plating.) There was no other way the situation could be handled.

That wasn't all that was new inside. Above the passengers, headliners were no longer made of soft woven cloth; instead, hard surfaces were molded out of smooth Bakelite or Formica, held in place by molding strips. Underfoot in the front passenger compartment the flooring material was made of marbleized rubber, both attractive and durable. And for the first time, passengers did not have to step up from the running board to the floor of the passenger compartment, as they were flush with each other. Intriguingly, by the flick of a little lock, front passengers could lower both the side windows and the vent windows simultaneously, creating the look and feel of a car of the 1980s or 1990s.

Buyers also got an important safety feature on their Airflows. For the first time, these cars were equipped with inner-tube tires, which greatly increased stability in case of a blowout on the road. Airflow Imperials also had an overflow dam in the gas tank that held three gallons of gas in reserve. If you ran out of gas on the road, all you had to do was pull a knob on the instrument panel, and extra gas was released so you could go on your way.

The Airflow was developed by Carl Breer and his staff over a period of six years, but it never would have seen production without its eminence grise, Walter Chrysler. It was he who finally decided that this automobile was the car of the future, and gave his wholehearted support to its actualization. Several things convinced him to go ahead with it.

One was the work of Norman Bel Geddes, a theatrical designer renowned for his Art Deco designs for such famous 1920s musicals as *Lady, Be Good!*, *Fifty Million Frenchmen,* and the *Ziegfeld Follies of 1925*. In November, 1932, he published an article with illustrations on streamlining in *Horizons* which had an enormous impact on the public consciousness.

Geddes became interested in streamlining both through his sailing experiences, which taught him about currents, eddies and waves, and Le Corbusier's 1920s book *Towards A New Architecture*, which compared the evolution of the automobile form to the development of Greek architecture, which culminated in the perfection of the Parthenon. Le Corbusier was convinced that the teardrop was the perfect automobile form, and Geddes paid close attention. After setting his staff to the investigation of streamlining, Geddes tested models of various streamlined shapes in the water and the wind tunnel, and his *Horizons* article was the result.

After giving a simplified layman's description of streamlining, he showed illustrations of trains, boats, planes, cars, and buses which used this principle as their guiding force. Some were amazingly prescient, like the ovoid oceanliner that looks remarkably like the sleek cruise ships of today or the mammoth flying wing airliner which prefigured the stealth bomber of the present. All were astonishing, and very widely reproduced to give the public a sense of what was coming to them tomorrow.

Though critics as diverse as Lewis Mumford and Frank Lloyd Wright denounced Geddes's article as superficial and simplistic (one said he offered a vision of the future "in which everything that moved through the water or air or under the sea was somehow manipulated into the shape of a catfish"), he nevertheless crystallized for the public the diverse forces of streamlining which had been in the air for some time.

Engineers had been talking of the streamlined teardrop shape as the perfect vehicle form for years, and building models and even full-sized versions of cars that embodied this idea. They were confident that this would become the standard auto shape of the future. H. T. Woolson of Chrysler, at a meeting of the Society of Automotive Engineers in January 1931, said the teardrop "might not at first appeal to the public, but, if it is fundamentally correct, it will grow in favor and be acceptable." The trouble was that no matter how many such models were tested in wind tunnels, auto executives remained reluctant to produce them, due to the enormous costs involved in retooling for them and the considerable uncertainty as to whether or not the public would accept them.

Walter Chrysler was the exception. Closely following discussion of the teardrop car in the industry, he didn't want to miss out on its development. In a letter to Carl Breer on August 19, 1931, he said, "The way things are going it looks as if they are going to be up and doing something like this within the next twelve or eighteen months in some way or other." Referring to Breer's own version of this sort of car, then languishing, he admonished, "We don't want this to lie dormant and it might be well for you to get this car back upstairs and get our wind tunnel going again." The *Horizons* article 15 months later would put the final seal on this process of inquiry and design.

Beginning in 1927, Carl Breer had been building wooden models, some fifty in all, of streamlined designs to be tested in the wind tunnel. This program lasted into 1931. Recently discovered microfilm of company correspondence and meeting notes shows that Chrysler had decided to proceed with the Airflow program at least as early as April 1932. Some $25,000 was appropriated for development of what the company internally called the RD 124 model, referred to as such so that no outsiders would know what it was all about. Two sedans and one coupe were to be constructed, with the hope that they could be shown to Chrysler as early as late August 1932. In fact, by July 5 it was decided that the car, at that point to be a DeSoto only, was to be in the hands of dealers and distributors and exhibited at the 1933 Auto Show by the following January. As late as November 17, 1932, it was hoped that at least one car would be completed by January 15, 1933. In addition to Zeder, Skelton, and Breer, A. Griswold ("Gid") Herresh off was importantly involved in its engineering.

All sorts of delays ensued, and the project was pushed back. Though a car was run as early as August 22, 1932, it took until December 1932 before the first running prototype was ready to be exhibited to Chrysler. This was known as the Trifon Special, after Demitrion Trifon, a driver and mechanic who had worked on the car. It was registered in his name as a built-up special in order to throw any possible industrial spies off the trail.

No testing was done in the Detroit area, either night or day, because Chrysler wanted to be absolutely sure that no one would know about the car. Instead, the company worked out a deal with the Struble family, who had a large farm on the Au Sable River 200 miles north of Detroit, just north of Grayling. Harking back to the days when Walter Chrysler worked on that Locomobile in the barn in Oelwein, Iowa, ZSB and Herreshoff set up a small garage and workshop behind the Strubles's farmhouse where they could work on the new car. The very first one went up to Grayling in the back of a trailer under cover of darkness. When all the top Chrysler engineers went for a ride in it they were astonished, for only then did they realize the totally new tension-free type of ride they had created—even without independent suspension, which was yet to be introduced on American cars.

Imbued with a great sense of confidence, ZSB then asked Walter Chrysler to come up to Grayling for a test drive. After a good home-cooked dinner from Mrs. Struble's kitchen, he went on a test drive that lasted for several hours. He came back bursting with enthusiasm for the new model, giving it his wholehearted approval.

It wasn't enough at first. The company's business managers and marketing people weren't convinced that this car would sell, and only gave in after Chrysler sent them a copy of the *Horizons* magazine in which Geddes's article had appeared. Later Fred Zeder said that this article was "entirely responsible" for giving the firm the courage to proceed with the Airflow.

As was his wont, Walter Chrysler paid close attention to the Airflow's development from then on. It was he who insisted on the full-width backseat, for marketing reasons. He also made another change, this time in the car's appearance, when he was shown the first all-metal sample car near the production date. After pronouncing the car "fine," he sat down and looked at it from the front on a diagonal, and proclaimed, "Too damn much overhang at the front end." This caused a certain amount of consternation among the engineers, who were dealing with a somewhat stubby front end that barely had enough room for the headlight housings. But Chrysler was the boss, so they did a big tear up and shaved an inch-and-a-half from the front.

But the Airflow had one very large problem that Walter Chrysler actually made worse. It was a brand-new car from the ground up, and like any pioneers, its developers were constantly dealing with problems they didn't know were there until they encountered them. Seeing a Cadillac aerodynamic design, and hearing rumors from his own spies that rival General Motors was about to bring out an aero car called the Albanita, Walter Chrysler became impatient to get the car on the market, and in the fall of 1933 he rushed it into production. It didn't make the January 1933 New York Auto Show, as planned, but he was bound and determined that it would show up at the one in January 1934. It did, but that decision was probably its undoing.

❧   ❧   ❧

At the end of 1933, the Chrysler Corporation was flying high. It had turned a 1932 loss of $11 million into a 1933 profit of $12 million, and was the only company to produce more cars that year than it had in 1929. True, it was only 691 units more, but no other manufacturer came near matching that performance. Market penetration for the company reached 25.8 percent, an all-time high, up from a mere 5.7 percent in 1928, when Chrysler took over Dodge Brothers and brought out the Plymouth and DeSoto. This meant that while all other manufacturers languished during the worst depression in the country's history, Chrysler held its own and, by comparison, leaped ahead of the competition. No wonder *Auto Topics* devoted its entire December 30, 1933, issue to Chrysler, dubbing it "A Century of Progress in Ten Years," echoing the "Century of Progress" theme of the 1933 Chicago World's Fair. Having watched the development of aero cars for years now, and having waited for his own stunning aero to reach the market for almost two years, Walter Chrysler was sure he would crown his own car career with the Airflow, changing the course of automobile history forever.

It didn't turn out that way, however, mostly because he forgot the most important lesson any production man needs to remember: Don't produce it until it is ready.

Advertising was ready. For years Chrysler had been winning sales with what Richard H. Stout called "slam-bang advertising, hammering themes over and over, carrying their messages to a bemused public who absorbed and eventually found themselves accepting the messages. Fortunately, Chrysler had the goods to back up what they claimed." For example, Chrysler launched a saturation campaign for *patented* Floating Power in January 1932 as if it were the greatest thing since self-starters and electric lights— how could any modern car be without it? Well, when you rode in a car that had it, you immediately realized it *was* a good thing, so why shouldn't Chrysler trumpet it to the winds?

By April 1932, when Walter Chrysler leaned forward on the bumper of his new Plymouth and urged buyers to "Look At All Three" in magazine ads, people believed that Plymouth was now in the same charmed circle as Chevrolet and Ford in the low-priced field; through Walter Chrysler's half decade of effort, it actually was in that league, so why not say so in the loudest voice possible? In a sort of comic-book style, real people were depicted in photo sequences chatting about Chrysler products, their words spelled out in dialogue balloons above their heads. "Won't it crash?" said one man in a Dodge ad. "Not a chance—with its monopiece steel body and bridge type frame," replied his friend. "A Safety Steel body saved my life!" proclaimed a nurse in a 1933 Plymouth ad. "My car rolled over five times— with ME inside!" race car driver Billy Mitchell testified. Andy Warhol and Roy Lichtenstein would have loved it. Such advertising got the manufacturer's message to the public in the most direct way possible, and the public responded, buying Chrysler's cars in record numbers.

Celebrity ads also began about this time. There were famous writers' accounts of famous people's reactions to new Chrysler products; Heywood Broun, Irvin S. Cobb, and others were pressed into service, the thinking being that some people would be attracted by the writers, others by the celebrities themselves. "Helen Hayes Buys New Plymouth; 'Snappiest Car on the Road,' Says Lovely Actress," reported Grantland Rice in one ad. "I Go Riding with Kate Smith in Her New Plymouth—and How She Can Drive!" another proclaimed. Throughout the 1930s all sorts of stars, from Deanna Durbin, Joan Bennett, and Tyrone Power to George Jessel and Major Bowes, were seen in print ads endorsing Chrysler products. Other ad series featured the encomiums of editorial writers, scientists, beauty contest winners, and debutantes.

For five weeks before the Airflow's debut, a high-intensity suspense campaign was launched in the press. "A New Kind Of Car That Literally Bores a Hole Through The Air!" and "Coming: The Airflow DeSoto!" screamed the first ads. For five weeks the campaign intensified, until finally Walter Chrysler, photographed smiling and emphatically pounding one fist into the other in his Chrysler Building aerie, described the new Airflow in an interview-style ad, echoing the very first ones for the Chrysler car ten years before. Asking, the public, "How would you like . . . ?" followed by a long list of improvements every motorist would desire, he then explained how ZSB's research was now making these things a reality in the new Airflow. He finished up with, "We had the horse and buggy—we had the automobile— *now* we have the motor car—the first *real* motor car in history—the new Airflow Chrysler. I'm proud to present it on the tenth anniversary of the first Chrysler car—I sincerely believe that like the original Chrysler, it will bring about a whole new trend in personal transportation."

During the end of 1933, all sorts of celebrities were brought up to Grayling for Airflow test drives with Tobe Couture, then photographed with the cars and asked for publicity comments. Ernest Hemingway, Jimmy Doolittle, and Alexander Woolcott were just a few of the many notables who made the trek and whose endorsements were later used for the cars. Woolcott was photographed staring bemusedly at an Airflow model in a small wind tunnel, and later, reading a book undisturbed in the backseat of an Airflow traveling at a high rate of speed down the highway. He expressed due astonishment at this automotive feat.

Show models of both the DeSoto and Chrysler Airflows were produced and delivered to the auto show in time for the opening on January 6, 1934, where they got center stage—Walter Chrysler saw to that. When he heard that Buckminster Fuller's Dymaxion was to be the featured car in the show, despite having been shown six months earlier, he got it banned. Undeterred, Fuller simply set up shop outside and got a lot of attention anyway.

But not like the Airflows. They caused an unbelievable sensation. "Fashion By Function" and "Born In A Wind Tunnel" were the themes, with huge displays telling and showing the revolutionary features of the new cars to the public. People crowded about, and salesmen wrote orders by the thousands in the greatest order-writing frenzy the auto show had ever seen. Even the fact that the extra expense of engineering and building the new cars added $200 to their cost didn't faze buyers at first, though a $995 DeSoto Airflow and a $1,345-and-up Chrysler Airflow were pretty dear when, say, a Pontiac Eight could be had for $765 or a top-of-the-line Hudson for $1,050.

The problem was, there were no cars to deliver. With all the work that had gone into designing the Airflow over the years, production was way, way behind. Part of the problem was that there were so many new features built into the cars, each one of which had to be figured out and laid out from a production standpoint. Problems popped up over and over again, and delays piled up on top of one another.

Nobody thought about it beforehand, but as we have seen, a mini furniture factory had to be designed, built, and manned to produce those gorgeous chrome-lined seats. Then there were the curved windshields. They were so hard to install that four were broken for every one that was put into place, which was the main reason that they were only offered on the $5,145 CW series (and why so few of the 100 or so CWs produced survived—the windshields leaked, and after a few years you couldn't find replacements). Then there was the matter of those all new bridge-type truss frames. As Stout tells us, "Manufacturing and engineering had an unexpected and serious problem. Welding the semiframe to the unit body unexpectedly required turning the car upside down on the assembly line, an unhappy and costly development." Fred Breer noted that turning the frame over on the engine put a terrible strain on the engine, which didn't help matters one bit.

Supplier strikes caused further production delays, and the head of the Chrysler Division was fit to be tied. Finally, in April 1934, Airflows began trickling down the DeSoto and Chrysler assembly lines. But to make matters even worse than ever, the workers didn't know how to build them. Fred Breer explained: "When they finally came down the line in April, because of the unique production problems, the first two or three thousand had a lot of problems. All the letters that came back from dealers and customers were sent to my father, and I can remember him bringing them home and reading them to me. Some of the problems were unbelievable, like engines breaking loose at 80 mph. Really. The workmen just didn't know how to build the car properly, and by that time the public—and the dealers particularly—had become disillusioned with the Airflow. Initially, it was nondelivery, and then it was service troubles with the first ones."

When you introduce a radically new product, especially in a fast-moving, style-conscious field, as the automobile business had become by the mid-1930s, momentum is everything. By the spring of 1934 the Airflow had clearly lost it—partly because of production and initial quality problems, to be sure, but also because of a symbiosis between a basically conservative car-buying public and the the Chrysler Corporation's competition, which did everything to discredit the car.

At its debut, people stared at the Airflow and didn't quite know what to make of it. The major problem was the hood. It was short and stubby, a look that flew in the face of contemporary notions of automobile beauty, which emphasized long wheelbases, long hoods from which sensuously curving fenders flowed, and goddess-crowned upright prows adorned with bullet-shaped headlights. The more a car strove for length and verticality, the more value it was perceived to embody. But here was Chrysler saying, "Forget all that. Value is expressed in a new kind of design. And it looks different, too." However, a lack of well-built Airflows on the street for people to ride in and talk about gave the public time to think. And the more they thought about it, the less they liked the looks of this radically new car.

The majority of people in 1934, and a good many even today, found that the front end of the Airflow was simply ugly. As Paul Carroll Wilson bluntly put it, "For them it had a rhinocerine ungainliness which automatically consigned it to the outer darkness of motordom. The Airflow had the lumbering, stupid look of some early touring cars, such as the 1906 Grout. It was similarly criticized as looking clumsy and out of balance. The round blandness of the front also robbed it of the distinctive 'expression' formed on most cars by the relations of hood, fenders and lights. It had some of the same grotesque anonymity as a human face covered by a nylon stocking." Others thought its close-set headlights and cascading waterfall front made it look like a basset hound.

Wilson's analysis thirty years after the fact may seen unduly harsh, but even contemporary press accounts of the Airflow showed there was a problem. Hesitation and faint praise are their hallmarks. A scribe in the January 1934 edition of *Motor* said: "At first glance, these cars will look strange to most people, but the writer finds that after you have looked at them for two or three days you become accustomed to them and sooner or later you begin to admire them. Finally you are quite likely to come around to the viewpoint that these cars look right and that conventional cars look strange." *Scientific American* in February 1934 rather meekly hoped that the "streamlined car may, in a very short time, be quite as pleasing to the eye as a conventional car." Even when Chrysler enlisted the aid of *Harper's Bazaar* fashion artist Carolyn Edmundson to promote the car, she noted "that you surely are going to gasp when you first see it," before burbling that surprise would quickly yield to delight and profound admiration at "the realization that here is an authentic new style . . . one of those sweeping advancements that is going to initiate a whole new school of design."

The public could be and was more blunt. In a letter to Carl Breer of June 20, 1934, Chrysler employee Jack Whitaker reported some of the reactions to the Airflow at the Century of Progress exhibition in Chicago. Though many were favorable and a few more were of the maybe-it'll-grow-on-me variety, the most pungent reactions were condemnations. A. J. Hoersting of Dayton, Ohio, said, "I don't like it. It looks like a bathtub. I rode in one and the kids all shouted, 'Get a can opener.'" Charles Pretschold of Chicago scolded, "Frankly, Mr. Whitaker, you may be technically correct but it still looks like hell to me."

Whitaker was shortly to suggest that the best way to sell the car was to get people to ride in one of them and overcome their resistance to its looks. He also thought the looks could be improved with specially colored "flash" two-tone paint jobs. "We are trying to paint this car of tomorrow with the colors of 1930," he said. "I contend that a stylist harmonizing a two-tone color design for our Airflow cars could do much in stressing the beautiful characteristics of this car and minimizing the unbeautiful (from the public's point of view) and unfamiliar design around the nose." Fred Zeder considered this idea, but nothing came of it.

Chrysler caught on to its front-end problem quickly. Only four days after the opening of the auto show on January 6, Fred Breer had a conference with Norman Bel Geddes at which he hired his design firm to work on the Airflow. Nothing could be done to the very first cars off the line, but before the model year was out the thirty-nine slender vertical bars of the Chrysler Airflow grille had been reduced to twenty-one thicker ones, with an eye to broadening out the front end of the car and softening its tinsel-on-a-Christmas-tree look. By 1935 Airflows sported a far more conventional V-shaped, horizontal grille that entended forward from the hood and did not curve back onto it. For 1936 and 1937 it got a hump-backed built-in trunk and a front end indistinguishable from others of the division's cars. But by the time the appearance improvements were brought into the marketplace, both word of mouth on the poor quality of the first cars and a giant smear campaign on the part of General Motors had damaged the car's reputation.

Typical of the complaints was an August 25, 1934, letter to J. W. Frazer, head of the Chrysler Sales Corporation from Charles W. Berg of Philadelphia. Berg, who owned a company that manufactured special oils and chemicals, was a great Chrysler enthusiast, having bought a dozen of the cars and sold "twice that many to my friends" over the years. Though J. W. Frazer, head of the Chrysler Sales Corporation, had asked him to jot down his reactions to his new Airflow, Berg sent his overwhelmingly negative letter to Walter Chrysler, since they were personal friends and he did not want to upset the morale of Chrysler's workers.

"Frankly, I am absolutely disgusted with my new Airflow," he began. "A driver sits in one of these Airflows like a dog sits in a dog crate. You can not see out of them." After going on about his problems with line of vision, fogged-up windshield, and windshield glare at night from the nickel-plated dashboard guages, he sums up with: "It seems that everything short of painting the windows has been done in the Airflow to prevent a man seeing where he is going." Then he complains that "it is the most dangerous automobile on a slippery street that has ever been built" since "your center of balance is entirely too far forward, and unless you balance up this weight, nothing on earth will keep this car from being the most dangerous one on the road." His conclusion is that "the Airflow is like the cow that gives the proverbial large pail of good milk, and then kicks it over." Though Chrysler thought Berg was "quite a character," he also thought attention should be paid to his complaints. How much attention can be shown by the fact that eventually Tobe Couture was sent down to Philadelphia to deal with this situation.

Two months later no less a personage than Charles Lindbergh questioned whether the hood latch on his new DeSoto Airflow coupe was of sufficient strength to keep the hood buckled to the car at high speeds, and had to be assured by a response from Carl Breer that it was.

❖   ❖   ❖

General Motors had a lot at stake in combating the Airflow, which had caught it flat-footed, featuring 1934 models that were for the most part just warmed-over 1933 models. Their biggest problem was with the all-steel frame, heavily touted by Chrysler. By now people were coming to realize the inherent superiority of the all-steel frame, but the plain fact of the matter was that for General Motors to introduce it into its products would take millions of dollars' worth of reengineering and retooling, and many years' time. Ominously, the General Motors exhibit at the Chicago World's Fair, which featured an actual moving assembly line, clearly showed the wooden frames of Fisher bodies, while across the street at the Chrysler exhibit race-car driver Harry Hartz and his team were flipping all steel-frame Airflows in a sand pit every hour and driving them away.

GM (and others) countered Chrysler's drum beating for the all-steel frame by starting a campaign against all-steel construction, proclaiming, "Steel is not enough." George Trautvetter of Budd (which built the Airflow bodies) recalled: "They demonstrated this theory by the use of a very light-gauge piece of steel tubing to show how easy it was to bend. They then inserted a dowel into a similar steel tube and, of course, it couldn't be bent. This demonstration and slogan soon stopped, though, when they were asked if tubing with wooden inserts were used in any of their bodies," which of course it wasn't.

GM didn't languish for long, however. In 1935 it brought out the one-piece steel turret top, which revolutionized car construction and swept up the attention of the public. They didn't even notice that though the top was all steel, the body beneath it still had a wooden frame. What a great subterfuge!

But Harley Earl and his designers had also learned something else. Ralph Roberts, chief designer for Briggs and thus important in the design of Ford products, noted in *Automotive Industries* in 1932 that the pure torpedo shape was not ideal for car bodies, because they were subject to crosswinds. Furthermore, wind tunnel experiments in Stuttgart that same year conducted

by Wunibald Kamm and Reinhard Koenig-Faschenfeld proved that alterations in the pure torpedo form actually improved efficiency in head-on aerodynamics. If you lopped off the tail, the torpedo lost nothing in efficiency,
and if you extended the rear in a higher and less sloping roof, drag was
actually reduced. Two years later, in a widely read study published as a
three-part series in *Automotive Industries*, Frenchman Jean Andreau said that
changing the profile of the car to a torpedo shape would not materially
reduce air resistance. Instead, he suggested that "development work on the
fenders, running boards and headlight lamps seems much more promising."
This is exactly the path that the auto industry, including GM, followed.

They realized that Airflow-type streamlining wasn't really desirable or
correct. In the first place, the only way in which the car was streamlined
in any important sense was vertically. Furthermore, even though it had all-
steel construction, the three major body panels were hung on its steel truss
frame just as they were on wooden frames in the old-fashioned composite
body construction. As C. Edson Armi says, the Airflow did not take advantage of "a new aesthetic made possible by all-steel, large-die modelling."
Indeed the back panel, interchangeable on all Airflows, was practically flat,
while the front panel, the only part actually assembled by Chrysler, required
every trick in the master welder's repertory because it was such a complex
structure involving the joining of a multiplicity of small pieces. Built-up, or
"filled-in," pieces separated the fenders and hood in the front and the fenders
and side panels in the rear, and the fenders themselves lacked the round-
edness of those found on other makes. Furthermore, their bottom edges
bent out in a concave manner, and stringy ridges lined fender edges and
surfaces between infill panels. So just as the Airflow was coming out, its
torpedo shape was shown to be less than ideal, on one hand, and on the
other, the articulation of its parts was shown to be far less advanced than
those of carmakers who only streamlined individual parts in their styling
efforts.

As famed stylist Bill Mitchell of GM said, once GM's stylists realized there
wasn't one single shape that was really aerodynamic to the exclusion of all
others, it gave them a great sense of liberty, and "we did as we damned
pleased. . . . We didn't worry about it because some of the aerodynamic
things right away showed it made the car look like hell." Sidestepping full-
blown aerodynamics altogether, they eventually combined certain streamlined features with the advantages of all-steel construction to give their cars
the kind of flowing, integrated look epitomized by the landmark Cadillac
60 Specials of 1938–41.

Chrysler did have a go at considering the full rear-engine aerodynamic
car before he decided on the compromises of the Airflow. Still dazzled by
the theories of Norman Bel Geddes, Chrysler saw him present and defend
such designs in October 1933. By mid-November, after Geddes's aerodynam-

ics expert Roger Nowland refuted Chrysler's and his top engineers' objections to rear-engine cars, Chrysler went so far as to give him a tentative agreement for the production of such a vehicle. But by early 1934, when the disaster of the Airflow's appearance was fully apparent, Chrysler let Geddes know through Carl Breer that he wouldn't even consider such a car until the Airflow restyling was done. On his own authority Breer let Geddes keep working on a 1935 or 1936 design embodying "ideal streamlining, letting engine space come where it may." But just one week later Walter Chrysler told him to downpedal it, and in the end he couldn't even talk Chrysler out of the aerodynamically incorrect V-shaped radiator in the 1935 Airflow restyling, much less convince him to produce a rear-engine teardrop car. Geddes's "perfect" streamline design got no further than the quarter-size model stage of development.

As if calamity were determined to field its worst blows against the Airflow, the Jaray Streamline Corporation of America filed a highly publicized patent infringement lawsuit against Chrysler on May 24, 1935. The suit made Carl Breer mad as a hornet, because he claimed, and it seemed to be so, that the Airflow car had been developed through his own aerodynamic research at Chrysler. However, it was impossible for anyone in Detroit not to know of Jaray's work, as it was so highly publicized in all sorts of automotive and scientific journals for years before the Airflow's debut. Jaray's work, and that of many others involved in streamlining, was also frequently, sometimes heatedly, discussed at meetings of the Society of Automotive Engineers, of which many Chrysler engineering employees were members. Furthermore, Lowell H. Brown had sent letters to both B. E. Hutchinson and O. R. Skelton on March 15, 1933, in which he enclosed a detailed article written by Jaray entitled "The Effect of Streamlining on Comfort" and said he hoped "this article will interest you and will help you in the study of our patent." The files at Chrysler also yield another detailed article received by the company on June 26, 1932; this one was called, "The Stream-Line Body, Jaray's System." It was published by the Stream-Line body company of Zurich. So it is inconceivable that the Chrysler Corporation was unaware of Jaray's work and patent as the Airflow was developed.

Perhaps Carl Breer viewed the Jaray patent as Henry Ford viewed the Selden automobile patent twenty-five years previously, as something too general to be recognized. At any rate, the Chrysler Corporation spent $25,000 defending itself against the suit, in part on elaborate charts and models and in part on the services of Walter T. Fishleigh of Detroit, an independent engineer, streamlining expert, and patent expert. It lost in two ways. All those charts showed that the car wasn't truly streamlined in a pure sense, and furthermore Fishleigh advised that the Airflow truly did infringe on the Jaray patent, and so the company would have to "pay the two dollars," as the old vaudeville sketch had it, after all.

Chrysler paid $5,000 for a Jaray license, plus another $300 to cover Airflows already exported. It also agreed to pay substantial royalties if the company were to build Airflows in large numbers. But by this time sales of the Airflow were faltering badly, and in the end, $5,300 was all the Jaray group realized out of its suit. By the time they paid for their attorneys, nothing was left.

Pierce-Arrow admitted patent infringement, too, and promised to pay up if more than the original five Silver Arrows were built; then Studebaker, which owned it, went broke, and that was that. Willys-Overland also went broke before Jaray could press its claim on the Model's 77, and though Jaray thought it would have a good claim against Ford on the Lincoln Zephyr, it couldn't afford to press its suit. In the end, Paul Jaray exercised his option with the U.S. Jaray branch to reclaim his own patent, and left the American scene.

The Airflow went on to win styling awards in Monaco, where it garnered the Grand Prix and Premier Prix in the Concours d'Elegance in both 1934 and 1935. The car also made a clean sweep of every closed stock car record in its class, managing an average speed of 86.2 miles per hour for 1 mile, 80.9 for 100 miles, 76.2 for 500 miles, and 74.7 for 1,000 miles. And it was impressive on the economy front, too, averaging 21.4 miles per gallon on a 3,114-mile run from New York to San Francisco, with a total fuel cost of just $33.06.

The Chrysler Airflow set impressive speed records in the U.S. too. A stock Imperial CV Coupe driven by race-car driver Harry Hartz established no fewer than 72 stock car speed records during a one-day trial run at the Bonneville Flats at the Great Salt Desert in Utah. Thirty-five of these records were in the Unlimited Stock Car class, which included cars of any engine displacement. These records, set in 110-degree heat, included 95.7 miles per hour for a measured mile and 84.43 mph for 2026 miles over 24 hours, and lasted until Johnny Mantz and his team broke them in a Ford in 1957. One week later Hartz also managed to get a very fine 18.152 mpg in the same car on a transcontinental run from Los Angeles to New York, amazing for an eight-cylinder car of this size and weight in those days. But no matter how impressive these records were, it didn't seem to matter.

By the summer of 1934 it was apparent that the Airflows just weren't selling, no matter what anyone said or did to promote them. DeSoto, which was originally scheduled to be the only make producing the Airflow, saw its sales drop from 22,736 in 1933 to 13,940 in 1934, a disaster that almost put it under. The Chrysler division unloaded just 11,292 of its Airflows, and was saved from a similar disaster only by the fact that it also fielded a thoroughly conventional six-cylinder model that year that outsold the Airflow by a seven-to-one margin. Despite some attractive redesigning of the front end, Airflow production of both makes sank like a stone in ensuing years, with DeSoto registering 6,797 in 1935 and 5,000 in 1936, its last year, while Chrysler registered 7,751 in 1935, 6,275 in 1936, and 4,600 in 1937, the year of its swan song. In all, just 55,155 were produced in all forms during its four model years.

The Chrysler Corporation lost a fortune on the Airflow, though it never revealed just how much of a fortune. It did not ruin the company, however, because its other products, led by "the amazing Plymouth," sold by the trainload. It did, however, become known as the biggest failure in American automotive history until the advent of the Edsel twenty-five years later. Unlike the Edsel, though, it was recognized as a landmark vehicle from the beginning, its influence and daring never doubted. For when the Airflow came out, suddenly all other cars, still styled according to the "classic" look epitomized by cars of the 1932 season, seemed old fashioned. By decade's end fastbacks, concealed trunks and running boards, integrated head- and taillights, and fenders faired into hoods and trunks were the norm—most of them features pioneered by the Airflow. And nobody sat over the rear axles anymore. Even fifteen years later, fastback Buick Specials, "pregnant elephant" Packards, and Nash Airflytes, the most streamlined production cars ever made in America, showed the influence of the Airflow.

It is interesting to note that other pioneering attempts at streamlining did not fare too well in the marketplace, either. The Graham Blue Streak Eight and its successors through 1935 never sold as many as 8,000 units in a single year. Raymond Loewy's (assisted by Amos Northrup's) beautiful Hupmobile Aerodynamic series of 1934–35, with its faired-in headlights and three-piece Jaray-inspired windshield didn't burn up the world, either, with sales of fewer than 5,000 units a year. The REO Royale's sales were just 2,736 in the 1931 model year, by far the best of the three of this car's existence.

In an irony of fate, both Graham and Hupp were eventually ruined as car producers in 1940 by the same problem that did in the Airflow. In a joint arrangement, they were producing slightly redesigned versions of Gordon Buehrig's manificent 1936–37 Cord 810 and 812 series cars. But nobody seems to have recalled that these cars were financial disasters for Cord. It wasn't that these Cords weren't beautiful or desired (at their New York Auto Show debut people were standing on top of each other to see them); rather it was that they were rushed into production, just like the Airflow. By the time Cord dealt with the car's production problems, they were terribly delayed and too expensive to compete in the upper-middle price class, and it was too late to stem a rising tide of financial disaster for the company.

One of the production problems was the Cord's all-steel top, which had to be welded from seven separate pieces, since parent company Auburn couldn't afford a press large enough to stamp it in one piece. As with Cord in 1936, the new Hupmobile Skylark stole the 1940 auto show, but when the Hayes Body Company had to deal with the Cord dies, it had exactly the same problem Cord had, which led to a loss of $580 per unit on a car that sold for $895 to $1075. Hasty arrangements with Graham, allowing that company to produce its own version of the Cord, called the Hollywood, while at the same time building the Hupp Skylark fared no better, and both companies left the car business in the 1941 model year.

There was, however, one American streamliner that was successful in the 1930s, and that was the beautiful Lincoln Zephyr. Few today remember that its debut was almost as shaky as the Airflow's. Sales of 14,994 units in 1936 topped the Chrysler Airflow's 1934 total by just 3,700, and like the Airflow, the Zephyrs were plagued with design and quality problems. But there was one quality that the public immediately recognized in the Zephyr that they did not see in the Airflow: beauty.

The Lincoln Zephyr grew out of the work of an inventive young Dutch designer named John Tjaarda. His early experience was as an engineer at the Fokker aircraft firm before beginning a career designing car bodies in America, first at Locke and Company custom coach builders, then at Due- senberg, then at GM's Art and Colour section. As early as 1926 he began work on his own series of streamliners, which he called Sterkenbergs, a name derived from the family estate of the Tjaarda Van Sterkenberg family in Friesland, North Holland. By 1931 he had designed a very impressive- looking four-door fastback Sterkenberg, which featured a unit body/frame (a setup pioneered by the Lancia Lambda in 1921), seating between the axles, and an automatic transmission. But despite much publicity in *Auto- motive Industries* and elsewhere, no one came forward with the financing to put this high-priced car into production in those hard times.

The Sterkenberg caught the attention of Edsel Ford, however, who was desperately looking for new ideas to help his company out of the Depression. By then, in 1932, Tjaarda was working for Briggs, which was a Ford client, and so Edsel set him up in a special design department there to work on adapting his design ideas to standard production. Tjaarda's son Tom, a well-known car designer in his own right (responsible for the 1970s Pantera, among others) said of this situation, "It was to be a very happy period for my father and he gave just as much credit to Edsel Ford for the development and realization of the Zephyr as he did to himself. Without the foresight-edness and taste of Edsel Ford, my father often told me, my father's work would have gone unnoticed."

He began work on a 125-inch-wheelbase car that featured automatic transmission and an 80-horsepower all-aluminum rear-mounted engine that weighed only 300 pounds and was capable of speeds of up to 110 miles per hour. Its lightweight design meant that the whole car weighed in at a mere 2,500 pounds.

Crucial to it was its semi-monocoque construction, quite a novelty in car design then. Tjaarda employed what he called "guessomatics" in figuring out the various stresses that came into play in designing such a structure, because he felt that it was impossible to test these things then on a purely mathematical basis. His aerodynamics teacher, Professor Alexander Klemin of England, always complained that this approach was sloppy. But years later, when Klemin was working on the Airflow in another secret design studio at Briggs, it would turn out that the fruits of his labors would be overengineered in comparison to the Zephyr. "My father's experience in aviation helped him to sharpen his instinct to see just by looking at the structure and understanding the materials he was working with which members were overstressed or understressed," said Tom Tjaarda. "The result was an extremely light and vibration-free automobile."

While the prototype was being displayed around the country from October 1933 on, most notably at the Chicago World's Fair in 1934, two other front-engine versions were being tested on racetracks at the Ford River Rouge plant and turned out to be perfectly balanced. Tjaarda said, "Fundamentally those early Zephyrs were the first cars in which a stress analysis, the same as applied to aircraft, definitely proved the advantage of unit body construction. Stiffness of the structure was accomplished by bracing at the spots where the lightest bracing would be most effective. Therefore, large, rounded corners were used in the door openings. The enormous strength of glass was used for bracing the roof by making the windshield and rear window a part of the structure."

The public gave the cars 80 percent approval ratings but, predictably, didn't like the rear engine. Independent four-wheel suspension and hydraulic brakes were planned, but old Henry liked the old-fashioned transverse leaf springs, solid axles, and mechanical brakes he had always insisted on, so the new Zephyr was going to be behind the times mechanically in a lot of respects.

It did, however, get an all new V-12, which shared many features with the Ford V-8, and performed rather like it in many respects. This engine turned out to be the Zephyr's Achilles' heel, causing a lot of problems that led to a reputation for poor quality. Chief among them were inadequate crankcase ventilation, which caused rapid sludge buildup in low-rpm running, aggravated by poor oil flow. Overheating, bore warp, and ring wear were caused by water passages that were too small. Improvements such as hydraulic valve lifters and cast iron heads eventually helped, but it was years before all the problems were worked out, which led to a general reputation for lack of engine reliability in the Zephyrs.

When the snub-nosed Airflow received such negative reactions in the marketplace, twenty-six-year-old Eugene T. "Bob" Gregorie of Ford's design section set about changing the similarly shaped Zephyr prototype's front end to a graceful, V-shaped prow-like design with delicate horizontal bars.

Pontoon fenders with faired-in headlights and a rearward-flowing body reminiscent of the Pierce Silver Arrow gave the car a pleasant sense of forward motion even when it was at rest. Attractive interiors, featuring Airflow-type chromed front seat frames, completed the picture.

The production car weighed in at 3,300 pounds, 940 less than a comparable Airflow, but according to Tim Howley, "it was much stiffer, and in crash tests could sustain almost twice the impact loads of conventional body-on-frame cars. So it turned out that the Airflow had been built twice as strong—and heavy—as it needed to be." At .045, the Zephyr also had a lower coefficient of drag, compared to the Airflow's .050 to .053.

The public obviously went for the Lincoln Zephyr in a big way, as sales doubled to 29,997 the following year. Though that was its all-time high, it nevertheless sold at a steady pace for a dozen years, racking up sales of 130,000 units before World War II and 42,000 after. If it hadn't been for the advent of the V-8 Mercury in 1939, offering good performance and similar looks at a much lower price, the Zephyr probably would have sold even better. But the fact remains that despite its problems, it was a big success for Ford. And the reason was plainly and simply the way it looked.

For Chrysler, this meant that never again would engineers determine the shape of a car. Conventional but increasingly attractive designs throughout the thirties would be the hallmark of Chrysler products, thanks to the supervision of Ray Dietrich, personally hired by Walter Chrysler to supervise styling. Most of Chrysler's cars may not have been eye-catching, but they were unobtrusive and made a conservative public feel comfortable. They sold profitably and well.

The story of streamlining in the 1930s wouldn't be complete without the mention of one other success, the Czechoslovakian Tatra 77 and its successors. Developed by the great aerodynamicist Hans Ledwinka and styled by Erich Ubelacker, it was the only Jaray concept car to be produced in any quantity, though in fact fewer than 750 were made before World War II. A rear-engine, fin-backed streamliner of striking proportions, it was introduced to the press on March 5, 1934, and, much modified over the years, it remained in production on and off for the next forty years.

A great deal has been published about the effect the Tatra, the Lincoln Zephyr, and the Chrysler Airflow had on the design of Ferdinand Porsche's Volkswagen, the most popular car ever made and one of the most notable artifacts in the history of machine civilization. This tiny, cheap, rear-engine, streamlined car certainly did not pop full blown out of the head of Dr. Porsche, and clearly there was a lot of cross-pollination going on among him and the designers of the above-mentioned vehicles.

Porsche's first VW prototypes were almost identical to Tatra prototypes that preceded them. He acknowledged his debt to Ledwinka by saying, "Well, sometimes I looked over his shoulder and sometimes he looked over mine." Adolf Hitler, the originator of the VW idea, was a great admirer of Ledwinka's Tatras, and once robustly proclaimed, "Das ist der Wagen für meine Strassen!", after studying them at the Berlin Auto Show. Ledwinka's son Erich even claimed that the basic specifications for the VW were laid out by Hitler and his father, and then passed on to Porsche to put into practice. Indeed, Tatra claimed patent infringement on some of the VW design elements, and after the war collected 3 million deutsch marks, in part to hush up Ledwinka's contributions to the VW legend.

Dr. Porsche himself visited Detroit twice in 1936, ostensibly to study race-car design but actually to pick up knowledge of mass production techniques that would be required to turn out Hitler's "people's car" in vast numbers at his desired retail price of $250. Hitler, a great admirer of Henry Ford (he read his *My Life and Work* and kept his picture on the wall of his room), had promised "to do my best to put [Ford's] theories into practice in Germany. I have come to the conclusion that the motorcar, instead of being a class dividing element, can be the instrument for uniting the different classes." So it was Porsche's job to find out how to do it.

While in the States he purchased mass-production tooling equipment and convinced two German-born Ford mass-production experts, Frederick Kuntze and Hans Meyr, to return to Germany to help him set up assembly lines.

The red carpet was laid out for Porsche in Detroit, according to Tom Tjaarda, and he took advantage of the universal hospitality shown him to visit all the major car firms in order to see what they were up to. Certainly he was familiar with both the Airflow and the Zephyr, which had been on the market for some time. But at Briggs he also saw the rear-drive Zephyr prototype. At Chrysler he may have seen the Star Car no. 2, a small front-drive prototype styled by Ted Pietsch, working under research engineer R. K. (Ken) Lee, which featured a five-cylinder radial water cooled engine. The Zephyr prototype bore a resemblance to the VW, but the Star Car looked amazingly like it, in regard to its roofline, door profile, and particularly its front end. However, no one has ever proved that Porsche copied the Star Car's looks for his new VW. Indeed, the front parts of the secret 1933 Mercedes Benz Type M23D, the 1934 Mercedes Benz type 150 sports sedan, and the 1933–34 Nsu Volksauto, designed by Porsche, also resemble the VW. So it's possible that this look was just "in the air," close resemblances to the Star Car notwithstanding.

Several foreign companies made their own versions of the Airflow. Toyota's first mass-produced cars, the AA and AB series of 1937, were close copies of the Airflow, as was the Volvo PV 36 Carioca of 1935–36. But the most successful version of the Airflow ever produced was the Peugeot 402/302/202 series, produced from 1935 to 1940 under a Chrysler license; over 75,000 of the 402 series alone were produced.

But for Walter Chrysler the Airflow was his first, biggest, and only flop. True, history would eventually give it a high place in the automotive pantheon. In 1953 the British magazine *Autocar* said, "Squarely, pugnaciously as a rock in the seas of memory, stands the Chrysler Airflow, a production car which can still be mistaken for a contemporary model although it appeared twenty years ago. It was indeed the egg which preceded the chicken of modern style.

"Today, after twenty years, the Airflow is beginning to collect the tributes it should have had in 1934."

But people live in the present, not in history, and the Airflow was quite a blow to such a man as Walter Chrysler, who never lived to see these tributes.

It was not for nothing that when he wrote his autobiography in 1936 he never mentioned either the Airflow nor DeSoto, the division that spawned it.

◨ 28 ◪

Labor and the Strike of 1937

I sing a song with Hammer and Heat,
For shaping metal is he-man's meat,
A job for sinew and muscle and bone,
A job for a Man and a Day!

The Hammer Man into Moloch's maw,
Spits the contempt of a fighting trade;
Hurls white steel beneath crunching jaw,
Holds it there with his devils's claw,
There where the guts of a car are made.

So here's to brawn and sinew and sweat,
The Soul of the Man that you are!
Victor Shipway, Plymouth
The Hammer Man

There is a time when the operation of the machine
becomes so odious, makes you so sick at heart, that you
can't take part; and you've got to put your bodies
upon the gears and upon the wheels, upon the levers,
upon all the apparatus, and you've got to make it stop.
And you've got to indicate to the people who run it,
to the people who own it, that unless you're free,
the machine will be prevented from working at all.
Mario Savio

Our problem is not just how big business functions
but how the large corporation functions in America's
free society. This is a new problem—it hardly existed
before 1929 and was totally unknown before 1914.
Peter F. Drucker
The Concept of the Corporation

In Spain there was revolution. . . . Here there were
disturbances of labor, sometimes pretty violent, in
otherwise peaceful cities such as Chicago, Cleveland,
Saint Louis. . . . This is the social background of
our story.
Tennessee Williams
The Glass Menagerie

Ed Sheard, who was hired as a designer in the then still quite new Art
& Colour department at Chrysler in 1929, had this to say about Walter
Chrysler the man: "Walter Chrysler—by golly, he was the most wonderful
man with the people working for him. They don't come like that anymore.

"They had a meeting one day—he and Zeder, Breer, all the vice presi-
dents. . . . it was about 12:30 and lunchtime, and Mr. Zeder said, 'Well, Mr.
Chrysler, it's time for lunch. Where should we go—down to the Book
Cadillac?'

"Mr. Chrysler said, 'No, we're going right there,' and he pointed down
to the cafeteria, where all these workmen in their greasy overalls were sitting. And it *was* a dirty place at that time. He said, 'We're going to eat
there.'

Walter Chrysler (standing second from the left) visits the men on a Plymouth assembly line in Detroit in the mid-thirties. (*Courtesy DaimlerChrysler
Corporate Historical Collection*)

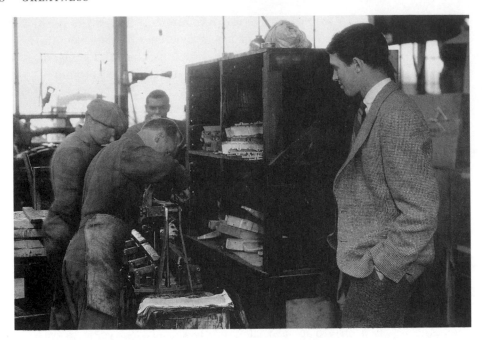

Actor James Stewart visits a Chrysler Corporation assembly line in Van Nuys, CA, 1936. (*Courtesy Frank B. Rhodes*)

"So, we let them go down first, and in two, three minutes we followed them, because we didn't have time to go down to Woodward Avenue to eat. Mr. Chrysler was in line with his tray. The cafeteria had like picnic benches at that time, and here were five men in overalls sitting at his table. Mr. Chrysler walked over with his tray, and he said, 'Hello, boys, I'm Walter Chrysler. Do you mind if I sit down?'

"We could hear everything that was going on, because we were sitting at the next table. He said, 'How's your work going? What do you do? What do *you* do?' and he said, 'If there are any complaints, now, you let me know, because I'd like to hear about them.' And that's the type of man he was."

Indeed so, and it was eventually to stand him in good stead with his own workers. An Alfred P. Sloan might have broken bread with various levels of General Motors satraps, and Henry Ford with any number of ill-defined Ford executives, but only Walter Chrysler would sit at a cafeteria table with his own greasy line workers, genuinely interested in their lives and efforts in his company's behalf. No matter how high he rose, and he rose to the summit as an automobile executive, he could look these men straight in the eye, because he always saw himself as one of them. And his men knew it.

As a result of this, and his company's assiduously displayed sensitivity to its workers' needs throughout the Depression, he held far greater respect from the workingman than his counterparts at GM and Ford during the tremendous labor strife of early 1937. His men didn't really want to strike against him, and when they were persuaded that they had to, their leaders, such illustrious union opponents as Richard Frankensteen and the great John L. Lewis, finished negotiations with Chrysler with high regard for his integrity and abilities. Though he came to the negotiating table accompanied by phalanxes of lawyers and executives, it was his work and word that really mattered. Absent him, the Chrysler sit-down strike of 1937 might have turned into a protracted and dangerous situation for a nation that uneasily felt itself just then on the brink of a possibly disastrous breakdown of its understanding of the relationship between labor and property. It seems clear that without the functioning symbol of Walter Chrysler, the essentially amicable everybody-wins settlement of the Chrysler labor dispute would not have been possible.

The trouble with much writing about the problems of industrial organized labor in the mid-1930s is that insufficient emphasis is placed on the fact that both the unions and management had to make things up as they went along. Fordism, as mass production theory and fact, had been worked out by the mid-1910s and penetrated a majority of large manufacturing industries in the subsequent decade. (Indeed, it is to Henry Ford's eternal credit that unlike, say, Robert Fulton, he never tried to patent his achievement or in any other way profit by it from others, or restrict universal access to knowledge and implementation of it. He promulgated his system, as much as a St. Paul or a Karl Marx did Christianity or Communism, for what he saw to be the good of mankind.)

In the auto business, giants such as General Motors, Studebaker, Willys, and Maxwell scrambled quickly to adapt to it. Smaller manufacturers, who were either shortsighted or unable to afford the production costs of tooling for mass production, were essentially manufacturers of assembled parts, and all, even efficient ones like Stutz, eventually fell by the wayside. So while automobiles proliferated, the number of manufacturers of those goods concentrated down to just a few, through either merger or bankruptcy.

Ownership of the original companies came from founders and venture capitalists who, at least initially, often had much to do with running them. But the surviving mass production companies were owned by financial syndicalists and stockholders, who had little or nothing to do with management of them, except in the area of finance and profit. The companies themselves increasingly were run by professional managers in a decentralized, multidivisional structure worked out through the 1920s by Alfred P. Sloan and his associates, based in no small measure on certain structural developments previously devised by du Pont, then General Motors' largest stockholder, and elsewhere at General Electric. (Also, as Peter Drucker points out, though there is no evidence of direct influence in this regard, this type of structure closely resembles those of two of the most successful organizations in the world history, the Catholic Church down through the centuries, and the modern army, as first developed by the Prussian General Staff from 1800 to 1870.)

But these people had their hands full with laying out the systems of mass production, distribution, and consumption. They did not concern themselves much with what the laborers thought about it, and truth to tell, neither did the laborers themselves. For these were new kinds of laborers, both unskilled and highly paid, enjoying far, far more of the fruits of labor than any other workers in history. Both managers and workers expected factory laborers to work, and work hard. But now all were caught up in what all that hard work brought into their lives. By the end of the 1920s an average auto worker annually earned three times the cost of a Ford Model A, had a nicely furnished city home, wore attractive store-bought clothes, ate out in restaurants, and was lavishly and inexpensively entertained in movie palaces of what were to him a sort of stupendous splendor previously accessible only to the fabled and wealthy. If he didn't like his job at Ford, no matter—he could easily get one at Packard or Hudson, or get involved in lucrative work making iceboxes or radios. If he found assembly-line work demoralizing or dehumanizing, stressful or unhealthful, life in general was prosperous, and other kinds of work were available to him. In other words, he wasn't tied to the assembly line or any particular firm. There were manifold possibilities of a good life for him.

True, auto factories were mostly not models of cleanliness, safety, and good ventilation, and working conditions were often unpleasant, especially in places like the foundries. But these plants were far from Blake's "dark, Satanic mills" of the early days of the industrial revolution. It was also true that work was usually seasonal—there were often employment lags in the summer and early fall—and hiring and firing and job assignments were at the mercy of often arbitrary, inefficient, or corruptible foremen who were not loath to play favorites. But for the most part, people who wanted jobs could get them, and do well at them, so why should there be labor strife? And really, there wasn't. The sort of conditions that produced the 1926 General Strike in Britain, where workers saw their relationship to management quite differently, seemed far from our shores.

At first, of course, auto workers were dismayed by the layoffs at the beginning of the Depression, but like everyone else, they believed that the downturn would be over quickly, as soon as problems of oversupply and slackening demand were adjusted. Many remembered the Depression of 1920–21 and took comfort from the fact that its ill effects on employment had not been all that long-lived. Bad times might bite for a while, but they wouldn't last. Through the spring, perhaps even the autumn, of 1930, no one had realized what was really happening; even the stock market was going up, creating a bear trap for unwary optimists, of whom Billy Durant was just one of many.

By 1932, however, things had become quite desperate. In 1930 the proportion of workers laid off at Chrysler, for periods ranging anywhere from one shift to many months, was 49.2 percent; by 1932 that figure had risen to 86.2 percent. It meant that there was just a skeleton crew of permanent employees at this giant corporation. Average weekly wages had fallen from $35.14 in 1928 to a miserable $20 that year. And things were better at Chrysler than elsewhere, for thanks to the ever-increasing sales of the Plymouth, the collapse in sales of the company's other lines did not bring Chrysler to the kind of structural crisis faced by so many others who could not maintain the minimum number of sales to sustain a large auto firm, which Kennedy put at 200,000. Indeed, most of Chrysler's $11 million loss for 1932 represented an investment in a much-improved Plymouth, which practically doubled corporate sales in 1933, to a level above even 1929's record pace. The result was that Chrysler provided more steady employment than either GM or Ford during the depths of the Depression, especially in 1933. But even the best employment situation in Detroit was abysmal.

What to do? Nobody seemed to know, and people became increasingly frightened. The American worker labored under a system of practically unfettered capitalism and placed his faith in that system to give him work, livelihood, and a sense of community and identity. The United States wasn't England, where the state managed enterprises, or the Continent, where giant combinations of family cartels did the same. Answers and solutions had to come from the institutions that controlled and owned the places that created work and wealth: the corporations.

The corporations were not prepared to deal with these problems. Their only stroke of real good luck, and the country's, too, was that the labor movement in the United States in the 1930s was not an independent working-class creation, but rather an essentially parochial effort that dealt with issues of employment, pay, and working conditions. It was a response to the conditions of big business, not an attempt to take over its management and ownership. Laborers just wanted to have an important say in the conditions under which they worked for a corporation, and to feel that they were participating in any security and financial success it achieved. In effect, the workers wanted big business to work for them too, just as it worked for itself.

None of the Big Three in the automobile business, nor anyone else, either, had ever had any reason to think any of this through. The only major labor upheaval in the auto industry had been in Toledo in 1919, when Willys-Overland had ham-handedly tried to cut workers' wages down to "normal" pre–World War I levels, and that was ancient history by the early thirties. Besides, this action didn't work, and by common consensus it was a foolish notion. There were no long-lasting effects on the national consciousness.

The companies were mainly concerned with their management styles. GM was the *nec plus ultra* of federalism; Ford was an absolute monarchy: Chrysler fell somewhere between the two. Walter Chrysler had not seen the need for a decentralized corporate structure, yet he had stockholders to answer to and genuinely believed in giving the brilliant team of men he had assembled around him real power to run their parts of the company. The main decisions were made in lively conference around the boardroom table, with Walter Chrysler the point of last reference as to the company's direction. But in none of these corporations' systems was labor discussed as other than an economic unit whose concerns should be dealt with in a paternalistic manner. Labor was managed by foremen and plant managers in varying combinations.

In the atmosphere of the early 1930s all sorts of long-identified workers' concerns about money, working conditions, and job security began to fester, pulled down into the vortex of the Depression. Communist agitation was behind some of it. The Party had not caught on in the United States in properous times, and indeed the majority of Americans thought of it as a menace to their way of life. But when the populace, especially working people, saw the capitalist system going increasingly sour, many were drawn to Communist ideas.

In Detroit the Communists began organizing demonstrations in front of some of the auto plants, using distressed conditions to highlight the miserable situation of the unemployed. These demonstrations were often dramatic, but were conducted in an orderly fashion. All that changed, however, on March 7, 1932, the day of the Ford Hunger March in Detroit and Dearborn.

In Robert Lacey's account, the Communists had organized a crowd of some three thousand unemployed workers to march through Detroit to the gates of the River Rouge plant in Dearborn. They had no permit for the march, but the Detroit police just let them pass. In Dearborn, however, forty policemen under Chief Carl Brooks, former head of the Ford plant police at Highland Park, fired tear gas into the crowd when they refused to turn back. A melee ensued. The workers broke up into small groups and continued to march on the plant. The police were in hot pursuit, brandishing rubber truncheons against them, the marchers fighting back with anything they found to hand, from stones to fence posts. Newspaper reports were unanimous that the marchers had not brought weapons with them. Fire trucks in Miller Road waited to spray the marchers, and Ford Servicemen waiting on an overpass doused them with freezing water.

At the gates to the plant Henry Ford's personal henchmen, led by the thuglike but effective and personally brave Harry Bennett, confronted the leaders of the march. He began arguing with Joseph York, a nineteen-year-old organizer of the Young Communist League, and seeing this, the mob began to menace Bennett. Suddenly a piece of slag hit Bennett on the side of the head; bleeding profusely from his wound, he grabbed York, and the two men began wrestling on the ground. When York got up, he was mowed down by a hail of bullets from a machine gun and fell dead atop the prostrate Bennett. Three others died in the same fusillade. Twenty more were wounded in the riot that followed.

Though the Dearborn police and Ford Service Department personnel did their level best to seize film from all the photograpers present at the scene, going so far as to shoot a camera from a *New York Times* photographer's hand, and also threatened and drove away reporters from the scene, the story was on every front page in the country the next day.

The accounts of this event were a devastating blow to the reputation of Henry Ford, until now thought to be the Workingman's Friend. America had come asking for help in frayed trousers, cracked shoes, and with belts tightened over hollow bellies, John Dos Passos wrote, "and all they could think of at Ford's was machine guns." "The legend of high wages, good conditions and contented workers was riddled by the bullets which killed four unemployed workers," wrote pamphleteer Robert L. Cruden. In New York, the *Herald Tribune* cried, "The Dearborn Police are to be condemned for using guns against an unarmed crowd, for viciously bad judgement and for the killing of four men. Such action must arouse resentment among the unemployed everywhere and accentuate class antagonisms so alien to our American life." Shortly Upton Sinclair, who had idolized Ford at the time of the Five Dollar Day, excoriated him in a novella called *The Flivver King*, in which he said that now, after the River Rouge massacre, you could truly say that Ford cars came in any color, so long as it was "Fresh Human Blood."

On March 11 a four-mile funeral procession wound through the streets of Detroit, with fifteen thousand marchers following the red-flag-draped coffins of York and the other three fallen marchers. Red banners and armbands were everywhere, and the "Internationale" and funeral march of the 1905 Russian revolutionaries played as the coffins were lowered into the ground.

March 7, 1932 was one of the saddest days in the history of American labor, and laid bare for all to see the sorry plight of once-glorious American capitalism. If this is what things with Henry Ford had come to, what could people believe in anymore? And what would come next? By the summer of 1932 it would be the veterans' Bonus March on Washington, which ended with the government doing to this sorry, bedraggled lot of some of the nation's greatest World War I heroes exactly what Ford had just done to its own workers.

It would be no surprise that Norman Thomas's Socialist Party ticket in the 1932 presidential election polled 881,000 votes, up from 267,000 in 1928. Even the dreaded Communists more than doubled their votes, from 49,000 to 103,000. A million votes for Socialism and Communism—that's what America had come to in 1932.

What with red banners unfurled at their gates and Communist workers dying at their portals, the big car companies were increasingly afraid of their labor situation. Ford, of course, had always had its Service Department, which, headed by Harry Bennett, had turned into an internal police force and spy ring populated by toughs he personally recruited. After the Hunger March disaster, Bennett's department used pictures from the York funeral and information gleaned from the plant to identify anyone in its employ thought to be one of the marchers or their sympathizers; once picked out, they were let go. But much more than this, Ford's spies made detailed reports on the activities of any employee who deviated in any way from the uninterrupted floor work pattern. Too many trips to the bathroom could easily get you fired.

When Charles Chaplin's assembly-line satire *Modern Times* opened in 1936, there was a scene in which the Boss, spying on Charlie through a television screen in the men's room, tells him to stop malingering and get back to work. Blue-collar workers in Pittsburgh didn't laugh at the sequence in which Charlie gets a five-minute break and his hands can't stop twisting in the repetitive movement of his job long enough for him to drink a glass of water. It was simply too close to reality. Several years before making his film, Chaplin had been shown around the River Rouge plant personally by the Fords, and paid close attention to what he saw. As Celine said in *Journey to the End of Night*, for the Ford worker, "Life outside you must be put away; it must be turned into steel, into something useful."

But lest anyone think that Ford was unique, that notion is easily dispelled. Standing company armies had been around for fifty years in the railroad, steel, and mining industries. As William Manchester says in *The Glory and the Dream*, by 1932 "Aggressive industrialists were convinced that in confronting labor organizers they were confronting the devil himself, and didn't mean to lose. Robert LaFollette's Civil Liberties Committee discovered in December, 1934, that more than 2,500 employers were employing strike-breaking companies."

The largest were Pearl Burgoff Services and the Pinkerton National Detective Agency; the latter was much favored by the auto industry and earned some $2 million between 1933 and 1936. Writes William Manchester, "Each maintained a small army which was ready to move into struck jobs carrying machine pistols, gas guns and clubs. Both also infiltrated workmen's ranks as undercover agents. When a senator asked Herman L. Weckler, a vice-president of the Chrysler Corporation in charge of dealing with labor issues, why he hired spies, he replied, 'We must do it to obtain the information we need in dealing with our employees.'" In other industries it was much worse. At Pittsburgh Coal machine guns were trained on workers in the pits. Company chairman Richard B. Mellon told LaFollette's committee, "You cannot run the mines without them."

One problem labor had at this juncture was a huge vacuum in leadership. American industrialists had successfully kept organized labor out of their plants all along, with the open shop the order of the day. Only 4.5 million workers, representing just 22 percent of the workforce, were organized in 1926. And these were skilled workers only, which was the real root of the problem. Until the 1930s came along, says Alfred Chandler, "craft unions had some success in organizing the workers in such labor intensive skilled trades as cigar, garment, hat and stove making, shipbuilding and coal mining—trades in which modern enterprise rarely flourished. They organized the workers in the shops of small, single unit, owner managed firms into local, city and state unions. These regional organizations were represented in a national union which was, in turn, loosely affiliated with other craft unions in the American Federation of Labor."

In the automobile factories the AFL was generally accepted as labor's spokesman, but its attempts to organize foundered on the factionalism among various craft unions such as those of the upholsterers, blacksmiths, and painters, all of whom fiercely competed with one another for members and influence. And none of them wanted the assembly-linemen, who were viewed with contempt for their lack of skills and with jealousy for their high pay. They were also looked down upon because their ranks included many blacks, who did the jobs nobody else wanted in places like the foundries or the paint shops, or recent immigrants from southern and eastern Europe who spoke little or no English. In 1928 at Dodge alone some fifty-seven nationalities were represented in its workforce; in 1930 42 percent of all auto workers in Detroit were foreign-born.

By 1932 the AFL represented a still weak 6 percent of the workforce, but bad times meant they were losing seven thousand members a week. No wonder, says Manchester, since they were so servile to management as even to oppose the establishment of national unemployment insurance that year. (Wisconsin's Governor La Follette signed the nation's first unemployment insurance bill into law on January 8, 1932, after a ten-year struggle in the state legislature; Great Britain had had a compulsory national system since 1911.)

With the coming of the New Deal after the elections of 1932, there began to be room for optimism in the precincts of the labor movement. Franklin D. Roosevelt of course was seen to be very pro-labor, and as soon as he came to power in March 1933 he began to formulate recovery plans for the nation that would include the working man along with everyone else. His main legislative tool was the National Recovery Act of June 1933, whose

Section 7A dealt with certain rights of labor—specifically, the right to organize and bargain collectively with employers through representatives of labor's own choosing. The AFL felt emboldened by this to restart organizing efforts in the auto industry, and a strike was organized in March 1935, both at Buick and Fisher Body in Flint, and at Hudson in Detroit.

In January 1933 there had already been a spontaneous laying down of tools by workers at the notorious Briggs body plant, whose 10 cent-an-hour wages and appalling working conditions had proven too much for its employees to bear; this strike would prove to be prescient in terms of the automobile business, though no one knew it at the time.

The Roosevelt administration found the prospect of such previously unknown strikes in the auto industry alarming, for cooperation between business and management was its keynote for the New Deal. Something had to be done, and in the spring of 1934 Roosevelt asked the AFL leadership to come to the White House for talks. The AFL leaders agreed to halt strikes in return for the establishment of an Automobile Labor Board, which would supposedly keep an eye on their interests and also establish a system of workers' voting rights, which appeared to offer a chance for the unions to gain recognition in the auto plants.

What this set up was a convoluted system of competing proportional representation in the car plants among various outside unions, unaffiliated workers, and most significant of all, company-run unions. The system proved to be confusing and led to a good deal of factionalism and disagreement, both on the factory floor and between labor and management. The companies favored their own unions, of course, and no one really knew who was authorized to speak for whom. Though some of the company unions, such as the one at Chrysler, weren't half bad, eventually the whole system collapsed under its own weight, as unskilled auto laborers came to believe that the craft-dominated AFL had been snookered into this arrangement, or worse, had sold out to the employers.

Walter Chrysler got on the labor bandwagon rather early. His plants were paternalistically run by foremen who maintained strict discipline, but among things he inherited from the Dodge Brothers in 1928 were certain labor benefits that had been given to its workers through the years. There was a welfare department for small loans, group life insurance, legal advice for workers, and even organized dances. The Chrysler Corporation examined these practices, as well as others it had initiated on its own workers' behalf, and instituted new policies that eventually evolved into the Chrysler Industrial Association, a One Big Happy Family-type institution modeled on a similar program that had been in effect at General Motors since the mid-1920s.

The Chrysler Corporation had put out an attractive booklet, complete with a statement from the boss, detailing all the benefits of the CIA. After studying eighty corporate programs, Chrysler instituted an insurance policy providing death, sickness, and accident benefits underwritten by Aetna. Employees paid for it, with costs and benefits keyed to their wages. The CIA also supported a "Good Cheer Fund," to cover the needs of temporarily distressed families and individuals. This fund paid for hospitalization, surgery, and a variety of other sorts of medical expenses, as well as legal expenses, food and clothing, and even family counseling. Any employee could apply for aid or identify candidates for it. Neither the corporation nor the employees paid directly for this fund. Monies came from the receipts of thirty or so small stores placed around the plants to sell convenience items to the workers, and were invested by the corporation treasurer in high-grade securities.

Recreational and sporting activities were cleared through and coordinated by the CIA, which also held employee roundtable discussions and gave courses that could lead to better positions. The Chrysler Management Trust invested company profits in corporation stock for the benefit of ninety key men, while a stock bonus plan covered four hundred department heads and other supervisory personnel. For employees earning less than $5,000 per annum, the company had a savings and investment plan under which the company added 50 percent to any employee's contribution and bought stock for the person with the total. Within a year after this latter plan was inaugurated in July 1929, over 3,700 employees had some $215,000 invested in it.

Much touted was an annual two-week educational tour taken by five hundred "especially deserving sons" of employees. Every boy paid in $15, which he was supposed to have earned himself, with the company supplying the balance of the cost. The tour went to cities and historical sights that reflected our national heritage, such as Gettysburg, Mount Vernon, and Washington, D.C., or inspired admiration of our patriotic national virtues, such as Annapolis and West Point. They always ended up with a visit to the Chrysler Building in New York City, where the boys could gaze in admiration at those tools handmade by another Chrysler boy, Walter P. himself, so many years before.

In June of 1934 Chrysler inaugurated the *Chrysler Motors Magazine*, a monthly publication distributed to all the seventy-five thousand workers in "the Chrysler family." A combination house organ, newsletter, and propaganda pamphlet, it detailed past glories and future events the company or its employees might be involved in, mixed in with folksy columns, short stories, recipes, letters, and even poems. In the first edition you could learn how to bake brown betty, how to prevent whooping cough with a new serum, and all about the good deeds of the T. C. Motors Girls' Club. Doc Cooper's "Hard Boiled Sermons for Robust Sinners" offered such nuggets as "When a man loses his goat, he generally becomes one" and "The first sign of anger is usually the first sign of defeat."

But the biggest item of all was a lavish report on the most spectacular of all the Chrysler employees' extracurricular activities, the company-sponsored 185-voice all-male choir, established in late 1933. "Giant Chrysler Motors Choir Attracts Nationwide Attention in Concert over 85 Station Radio Hook Up," blazed the headline. This spectacular event, the third public concert of the choir made up entirely of shopmen, was broadcast over the Columbia radio network on May 1, 1934. Arranged in rows before a setting of potted palms, the singers were attired in tuxedos, black ties, and white boutonnieres. Before the broadcast began, the choristers sang Handel's "Let Their Celestial Concerts," Purcell's "Passing By," and Coleridge-Taylor's "Lee Shore" before violinist Emily Adams soloed in Lalo's "Symphony Espagnole." Then at nine-thirty a hush fell over the audience as the choir began its broadcast performance with "Oft in the Stilly Night," followed by a fortissimo "Triumph, Thanksgiving" by Rachmaninoff, Sullivan's "The Lost Chord," Laurent De Rille's "The Martyrs of the Arena," and several solos essayed by the Messrs. Herbert, Webster, Hooper, and Paterson to close out the first half. The second half was dedicated to popular fare, and included a rendition of "Home on the Range" that so pleased the audience that it had to be repeated. "The Pilgrim's Chorus" from Wagner's *Tannhauser* concluded the proceedings.

Much moved, Walter Chrysler himself made his way to the stage, where the boys were waiting to have their picture taken with him. They gave him a rousing welcome. Stepping up to the microphone, he said: "Men, this is one of the greatest thrills of my life. It is indeed beyond my expression of appreciation to think that this was done entirely on your own. You were not asked to do this but are doing it because you like it. That is why you are doing it so well. It shows the human side of the thing in our organization. I am excited! You boys have shown tonight a new power that unites us all."

No matter how popular or good these programs seemed, they were still icing on the cake. The bottom-line issues for the workers were wages, plant conditions, and the right to organize and bargain collectively. The biggest problem for Chrysler workers was who was going to represent them.

As stated previously, the AFL was of little use. Weak and hopelessly inept at organizing, the carriage- and wagon-makers' union of the AFL, even as early as 1930, had deteriorated into a minuscule organization whose sole function was as a base for Communist organizers, according to John B. Rae. The workers were not interested in the very left-wing Industrial Workers of the World, either. By 1932 the Communists had gained firm control of the Auto Workers Union, built on the remnants of the old carriage- and wagon-makers' union, and it was these people's demonstration which precipitated the ghastly massacre at Ford's River Rouge plant in that year. Despite desperation, most people were frightened by the specter of Communism, and after the funeral of the fallen in that incident, this movement went nowhere.

As Rae says, "By early 1933, there were sporadic strikes in the automobile industry. Spontaneous, almost purposeless expressions of discontent, they were probably a blind response to a feeling that with the election of a new president, things should be changing. Significantly, the strikes were in the parts plants, not the auto plants. The worst were at Briggs, which manufactured bodies for Ford [and others, including Chrysler]; they achieved nothing."

The spring of 1933, after Roosevelt's inauguration and the banking crisis had passed, brought the National Industrial Recovery Act, or NIRA. Under NIRA, every industry was to establish a code by which its participants were supposed to act; adherents were allowed to display its symbol, the Blue Eagle. Essentially, it was a form of legalized price fixing, that gave no advantage to the automobile manufacturers, who operated on a competitive basis and got no advantage from maintaining prices. The industry hated it, perhaps most of all because of its infamous section 7a, which gave labor the right to organize and bargain collectively with employers through representatives of its own choosing. The manufacturers complained loudly and long that the act compelled the closed shop, which was completely untrue. (Ford wouldn't subscribe to the NIRA code at all, referring to the Blue Eagle as the "Blue Buzzard.") But the act did compel the establishment of an auto industry code, and by August one was established. Immediately thereafter, just about everybody, including Chrysler, had a company union, mostly as an attempt to avoid the spirit of collective bargaining by adhering to its letter. Adherence to NIRA was widely perceived throughout the land as the patriotic thing to do.

In order to help with establishment of the code, Walter Chrysler sent Nicholas Kelley and Herman L. Weckler to Washington. (Weckler had worked with Walter Chrysler at ALCO, and subsequently at Buick, before joining him at the Chrysler Corporation.) Completely at sea, they decided to sit in on hearings for codes for other industries, such as the textile industry, at great length. After this, there were meetings in New York, Detroit, and Washington on the proposed automobile code. The industry didn't really want one at all, but the government made it plain that if the industry didn't devise one, the government would. By July 25, 1933, a code had been prepared and submitted to the board and members of the National Automobile Chamber of Commerce. On July 28, after eight drafts, it was finally submitted to the man who was in charge of administering the entire NIRA, General Hugh S. Johnson, at a huge meeting of the twelve major manufacturers, minus Henry Ford, at the General Motors building.

The code, with its scale of wages and hours adjusted for men and women in different jobs and in different cities, was perfectly agreeable to the manufacturers. (Through December 31, 1933, thirty-five hours a week were guaranteed to laborers and forty hours to white-collar workers, at salaries ranging from 35 cents to 43 cents an hour.) They were even willing to swallow the dreaded Section 7a. But there was one big problem, and that was Henry Ford.

Everyone was concerned that Ford would have a competitive advantage because he paid lower wages than the others and might take advantage of his position as a nonadherent to the code to embarrass the other manufacturers in some way. Walter Chrysler told Johnson, "We want every advantage and disadvantage equally. If that baby (Ford) should go to 30 hours a week and $1 an hour and he signs that clause 7a it will put us in a hell of a position." (He knew the 30-hour-a-week guarantee was just as important to the workers as the $1 an hour, for they preferred more workers to be employed for fewer hours to spread the work around.)

Johnson, a crusty World War I veteran whose nickname was "Ironpants," assured all that Ford wouldn't upset the industry's price structure, and blustered that neither Ford nor anybody else would want to go out and sell products without the Blue Eagle. (Which is just what Ford did, loudly proclaiming his position in full-page ads; Johnson bluffed that the government wouldn't buy his cars, but Ford shot back that Johnson's "daily expression of opinion is not the law," which Johnson was finally forced to admit when Comptroller McCarl said that Ford could not be prevented from getting government orders. In the end Ford didn't cause the industry any troubles, and was able to function very well without a union shop until he was forced into having one in June 1941.)

Later in the meeting, the industry twice its read position on Section 7a, which was that it did not compel union representation, and Johnson replied, "100 percent," a remark he was later to regret. Asserting a strong position, Chrysler said that his company had "fired a fellow who was going around and agitating," and would continue to dismiss such employees. Johnson did not object to this. In the end, the code was agreed to by Kelley, Weckler, Keller, and top men from the other companies, such as William S. Knudsen of Chevrolet. Then Johnson took the plan to Washington, D.C., where it was cleared with the help of Donald R. Richberg, general counsel of the National Recovery Administration (NRA).

Chrysler was then in the forefront of dealing with the union situation the new code raised. "I am proposing a plan of employee representation in our plants," he said in a letter addressed to his workers. Many other large companies had representation plans at that time. He had studied a similar plan at the International Harvester Company, which had worked very well. Chrysler's plan was presented not to the employees as a group or in groups, but as individuals. They could choose to be affiliated with the new company union or with any other union they wanted to be a part of. Only Chrysler and a few other firms which followed its plan allowed employees to vote on whether or not they wanted to accept the new employee representation plan submitted to them; 86 percent of Chrysler workers accepted the company plan, and 90 percent of Dodge workers did the same. Chrysler crowed loudly about this, but in reality the workers had little alternative, as no outside auto workers' union amounted to a hill of beans in 1933. Besides, the company union charged no dues, which meant a lot to the deprived workers of that time.

Under this plan, the company's plants were separated into districts, whose workers elected representatives. These representatives appointed officers and committees, with whom company representatives communicated. These company representatives also were in touch with officials from the outside unions. There was an overall joint council at the top of this structure. "Any employee who feels he is not being given a square deal may take up his grievance with his representative, and through regular procedures, to joint council and management," the workers were told.

"Chrysler had great hopes for this plan," Nicholas Kelley recalled. "He thought it was desirable to have a way of knowing what the workers had in mind, and what was going on, so that management could meet their demands." It sounded plausible, but it didn't work out that well in reality. Sidney Fine says the trouble was precisely this joint council plan, which had a reputation of intransigence in dealing with Chrysler workers. One employee bitterly remarked, "Company unions could obtain such marginal benefits as larger milk bottles for lunch and cleaner factory windows, but on really important issues their complaisance was a farce."

More needed to be done to straighten out the automobile code under NIRA. A threatened large-scale auto strike in February 1934 caused General Johnson to call industry and labor representatives down to Washington to hash things out. Lack of job security, uneven employment, arbitrary hiring practices, and many shop-floor issues, among other items, had caused widespread dissatisfaction in the plants. For instance, speedups on the line were a big cause of worker concern. In 1933 Chrysler worker John Palm had complained to General Johnson that in the previous two years his company had insisted on more and more production to be achieved by fewer and fewer men, with the result that the plant had "become a racetrack." Both company and union people went to meetings with President Roosevelt and Secretary of Labor Frances Perkins.

Walter Chrysler was present at a crucial gathering to decide whether or not there should be an election held in the plants to decide if all the workers should be represented by a union, an idea that was anathema to the companies. They were trying very hard to talk the President out of this idea. The meeting took place in the Oval Office, with Charles Nash doing most of the talking, abetted by Chrysler and his old nemesis John Thomas Smith of General Motors. Somehow they prevailed. Walter Chrysler told Kelley he knew the exact moment the President had changed his mind. "That was characteristic of Chrysler," Kelley said. "He had what I call intuition, very delicate intuition, like that of a woman's. When he said that the President had changed his mind, I think he was the only one in the room who knew when he did that. . . . That is the way Chrysler was. He knew what people were going to do."

What came out of this meeting was the establishment of an Automobile Labor Board, consisting of Kelley; Richard L. Byrd, representing the AFL; and Dr. Leo Wolman, an expert on vertical unions, as the chairman, representing the government. Kelley and Thomas J. Ross, a Chrysler public-relations man, wrote up what was to be called the "Roosevelt Agreement" on a Saturday night, immediately after it was settled. In addition to the establishment of the board, it covered details of union negotiations, reinstatement of laid-off union organizers, and layoffs in accordance with seniority and family obligations. Roosevelt touched it up a little and signed it.

Previously Chrysler had warned Kelley, "Now don't get caught. Don't get caught by the government," but once he realized this board was the industry's salvation from outside unionism, his tune changed completely. "Chrysler had come rushing in that Saturday evening, and had told me he wanted me to do it. I said, 'If you want me to I will. But are the other people willing?' Chrysler said, 'They have to be.' And he stood by me all the way through."

The Automobile Labor Board worked very hard to adjudicate cases brought to it during the fourteen months of its existence. Kelley's firm was reimbursed $25,000 for the loss of his services, and both Byrd and Dr. Wolman received per diems of somewhere between $15 and $25. Byrd had a hard time of it financially. He was just a workingman with a workingman's resources, and the AFL loudly proclaimed that it was giving him some financial help to make it possible for him to do his job. Though he was apparently well liked, and Roosevelt's choice for labor's representative on the board, he was not particularly bright, nor was he experienced as an administrator. He was an honest man, however, and, like the other two, strove mightily to be fair minded in doing his job. According to Kelley, he and Wolman tried very hard to be sure Byrd understood all the cases, and helped to make sure any objections he had were clearly understood. Kelley always wrote up the opinions. In all there were some 244 cases.

Nobody was too happy with the way the board functioned. Kelley said he and Wolman always agreed, and many felt that Byrd was too influenced by them. Then, too, Byrd was often criticized for the very qualities that made Roosevelt and Perkins want him for the job in the first place. He was young and idealistic, and not too well versed in the traditional ways of the old-line AFL bosses, often finding himself severely criticized for disagreeing with them. Kelley thought he was often not solid enough in his own opinions to avoid being swayed by the emotion of a given situation, which could cause difficulties.

Still, in the beginning one or sometimes even all three often went onto the sites of various disputes to determine what physical or managerial conditions caused the problems; later, after secretaries had been trained, they were often sent out to hold the hearings and make full stenographic records of the proceedings, after which the board would render a decision. By holding their hearings in these places, they also had instant and complete access to plant records, on which they relied heavily in their decisionmaking. Most of the cases the board heard were over matters of discharge, and Kelley was proud of the fact that their decisions resulted in the reinstatement of over two thousand workers over the board's lifetime. After the board was disbanded, whenever scholars came to argue with him over the decisions made, Kelley invariably had an assistant bring out the boxes containing the voluminous papers on all 244 decisions, and would tell his interlocutor that the real test of the decisions was to read the records to see if the decisions were fair.

As for Chrysler, Kelley told him "that what I was doing was to call the shots as I saw them. If I thought people should be reinstated I ruled that way, even in a case involving Chrysler. Chrysler told me that was all right with him. He also told Knudsen that; that he was going to stand for it in his own plant, and would back me up."

Kelley spoke of the funniest case, involving an old fellow at Hudson, which devolved on the issue of what constituted a break in employment. If a man was fired, then his seniority only went back to the last time he was hired. The man in question was a trimmer, a department in which there always seemed to be a lot of trouble. He had been hired a long time before, been discharged, hired back, went to work elsewhere, and returned to Hudson. He was claiming the earliest date for seniority.

The man was asked if he could remember the first discharge.

" 'No, I don't remember,' he said.

" 'Are you sure now?' the Board asked. 'Here it is on your card. You must have known when you were discharged. Do you remember what it was all about?'

"Then a wonderful light came into his eyes. I can still see the look on the fellow's face. 'Oh, I remember. That's the time I let the foreman have the packhammer on the head.'

"He had hit the foreman with the hammer. Then he was satisfied. He knew he couldn't hold out, that he didn't have the seniority."

One other important thing the NRA accomplished in early 1935 was to hold elections in each plant in which workers for the first time could vote for an unaffiliated slate, instead of either the company unions or outside unions. This was a great success with the workers, who overwhelmingly voted this way in the days before any union was strong enough to gain a major adherence from the workers. It showed very clearly that workers, given the chance, certainly preferred not to be represented by company unions.

In the end, NIRA and the Automobile Labor Board proved to be unsatisfactory in addressing the concerns and aspirations of American automobile workers. These people had been profoundly shaken by the depradations of the Depression, and desperately felt the need to have some kind of guarantee of employment, good living wages, and decent working conditions, as the industry and the nation came back to prosperity. As Richard Byrd said in the autumn of 1934, "The homes of my neighbors are hovels; there are rooms without carpets, walls without wallpaper, no modern conveniences; and their children are undernourished." Partly through union agitation, some of it Communist, partly through powerful and successful labor organizing, partly through a perception that the NRA and the company unions it spawned didn't do enough to make things better for the workers, and partly through the Wagner Act, which superseded NIRA in 1935, American auto workers finally focused on the need for, and right to, collective bargaining under the auspices of a single outside agent. The method by which they got it was imported from Europe, lock, stock, and barrel.

The sit-down strike originated in Wales and Hungary in 1934, when mine workers refused to come to the top until their wages were raised. It took some time for it to reach the American automobile industry, where the first instance of it was recorded in December 1935, when some men who belonged to the Mechanics Educational Society and to the Association of Auto Workers of America went out on strike against parts maker Motor Products, Inc. These were not UAW workers, but UAW workers at the plant struck in sympathy with the others, staying in the plant and refusing to work. The affair was quickly settled and little noticed, but it was the beginning of something that would turn out to be very big.

Reluctantly and out of necessity, in August 1935 the AFL had issued a charter to the UAW, which was organized on an industrial union principle, rather than like a craft union. The AFL had finally realized that there were tremendous opportunities it could no longer ignore in autos, rubber, steel, and other such nonunionized industries. But only workers who were not eligible to join the AFL craft unions could join the UAW, which meant that the AFL was primarily just protecting its existing jurisdictions; the typical auto worker had little benefit from this arrangement, and less to say about it. In the autumn of 1935 there was a famous incident in Atlantic City in which John L. Lewis was infuriated by the condescension of the head of the carpenters' union and punched the fellow in the face. Lewis then headed a walkout of mass production workers from the AFL and formed the Committee for Industrial Organization (CIO) to represent them.

In April of the following year the UAW, which had already been distancing itself from the AFL, separated from it and joined the CIO. After all, the previous year a non-AFL union, the Associated Auto Workers of America, beat out a company union in an election at Hudson, showing that an outside union could successfully organize auto workers; this was a graphic illustration to the UAW men of the inadequacy of their own union's organizing efforts. In addition to John L. Lewis, the new CIO was formed by Sidney Hillman and David Dubinsky, and by joining it, the UAW signaled that it was identifying itself with an organization committed to the industrial, rather than the craft, type of union. It brought along with it talented and aggressive newcomers to the labor movement, such as Homer Martin and the Reuther brothers, Walter and Victor. Within a short time most of the independent auto workers' unions joined the CIO also.

One of these unions was the AIWA, the Automotive Industrial Workers Association, which had developed out of the Automobile Labor Board bargaining agency at the Dodge Main plant, and then spread and grew in the rest of the Chrysler Corporation factories. The workers in this union, which numbered twenty-four thousand by the fall of 1935, were greatly influenced by the populist "radio priest" demagogue, Father Charles E. Coughlin; many union members thought of him as their advisor and supporter, who did "more toward educating the working class than any other living man"; indeed, so great was his influence on AIWA that it became known as "Coughlin's union," and it turned into quite a handful for Chrysler to deal with. One of its major officials was Richard T. Frankensteen, a big, burly, and very capable organizer who proved to be both an ambitious and pragmatic labor politician.

Frankensteen, who earned 49 cents an hour at Chrysler, was no better off than any other typical Chrysler worker; when his child was born, he had to borrow money for the delivery. He read the statements from Walter Chrysler posted around the plant, which said "Our door is always open. Come in and present your problems. We will discuss any matter with you." So one day he decided to do just that. He submitted a statement on living costs to the Works Council with a request for better pay. Chrysler's vice president in charge of labor relations rebuffed him. "We don't control the price of butter, Mr. Frankensteen," he said. "We have nothing to do with the question of whether your wife is as frugal as another man's wife. We don't control the level of rents. All we can say to you is that we pay a competitive going rate—and if we paid more, we'd be out of business." As Allan Nevins and Frank Ernest Hill report, "To Frankensteen, this was a revelation. 'It made plain to me that the only answer was to organize,' he said later. 'We workers had to take care of the competitors.' Industry alone would not put a stop to competitive wage cutting. . . . Henry Ford, Walter P. Chrysler and Alfred P. Sloan were not yet ready to match the enlightened attitudes taken by Myron Taylor and Thomas W. Lamont in the steel industry."

Frankensteen was right that the companies and the workers were on a collision course—not just over wages, but over the larger right of workers to organize independently and bargain collectively with their employers. Edward D. Kennedy, writing in 1941, gives an excellent analysis of the essence of the conflict between management and labor in the '30s: "There is involved not merely a matter of wages but a matter of authority. The employer of mass labor feels that his control over labor is lost when labor organizes. He would rather grant a 10 percent increase as a gift than be forced to concede a 5 percent increase as the result of a strike, or the threat of a strike. He is not accustomed to deal with labor as an equal; he is accustomed to deal with it as an inferior. Labor is to him a commodity, just as coal and steel are commodities. He buys it (as he buys coal and steel) at the prevailing market price and he uses it (as he uses coal and steel) strictly as his needs at the moment may dictate. He does not consciously abuse his labor any more than he consciously abuses his machinery, and in times of prosperity he will often invest in a gymnasium, an athletic field, and similar sociological amenities. But he does not like—and if possible he will not permit—any conflict of will between himself and his workers."

In May of 1935, NIRA was declared unconstitutional in the *Schechter Poultry* decision handed down by the U.S. Supreme Court. Schechter successfully argued that it was strictly an intrastate corporation, and that NIRA, in attempting to regulate its affairs, was illegally attempting to regulate intrastate commerce, when NIRA's sole province was interstate commerce. Therefore the NRA, and the Automobile Labor Board with it, was out of business. Kelley and his partners immediately shut down, making a final report on their affairs to the government on August 6, 1935. Nobody paid much attention to the report, since most people were glad to get rid of the board.

Hard upon the Supreme Court decision came the passage of the Wagner-Connery National Labor Relations Act, which Roosevelt signed into law in July 1935. This was much stronger than NIRA had been, and emboldened the ever more powerful unions to become much more aggressive in seeking their rights to worker representation than they had ever been before.

The Wagner Act restated the collective bargaining principles of the NRA, but what made it significant was that it made those principles much more difficult to evade. It stated that employers must not interfere with, restrain, or coerce attempts at organization, nor should they dominate, interfere with, or support a union; they must also not discriminate among union and nonunion men, and they must not refuse to bargain collectively. All employees had the right to self-organization, collective bargaining, and other activities for their mutual aid and protection. There were stiff penalties for violations such as the measures GM and Chrysler had taken to cripple free organization of company unions, including discrimination against those who did so. (Walter Chrysler and his counterparts at GM made no secret of their dislike of and attempts to get rid of anyone they thought of as a troublemaking union organizer; one of the most controversial cases the ALB dealt with involved a man named Cook, an AFL man who had been dismissed from GM as a big troublemaker for his organizing activities; his dismissal was upheld, much to the dismay of the union.) Open-shop attitudes and practices were also outlawed, and a three-man National Labor Relations Board with almost dictatorial powers was established; its first members were Joseph Warren Madden, John Michael Carmody, and Edwin S. Smith. To be sure, the act still had problems, such as an absence of a definition of collective bargaining (for instance, did the bill compel the signing of a contract between employer and employee or not?), but still, it left labor in a much stronger position.

After a raft of strikes over various issues in the auto, auto parts, and related industries in the period from 1933 through late 1936, particularly in such cities as Detroit, Flint, Toledo, and Akron, things began coming to a head over the central issue of labor representation. February 1936 saw brief sit-down strikes at the Firestone, Goodyear, and Goodrich tire plants in Akron. After a big and contentious strike the following month, Goodyear began putting on nonunion men at its plant in Gadsden, Alabama, rather than adding new union men in Akron. In the summer, terrible trouble erupted in Gadsden when union organizers were cornered in a building there and beaten up.

On November 27 twelve hundred workers sat down for a week at the Midland Steel Products Company, which made frames for Chrysler, Briggs, and Lincoln Zephyr. They got union recognition, and half of a requested 20 percent pay increase, but in the process they idled fifty-three thousand other workers who wouldn't work on substitute frames, thus demonstrating true worker solidarity.

The glass industry produced so much glass for cars that it was practically an automobile industry subsidiary, and when the Pittsburgh Plate Glass Company went out on strike on October 24, later joined in a sympathetic strike by Libby-Owens-Ford on December 2 after Chrysler switched its business to the latter company, it meant that 85 to 93 percent of plate glass production in the United States was off line, a very serious affair that was finally settled on December 15.

Workers at the Aluminum Company of America in Detroit sat down in December over the usual issues of pay and union recognition, but management refused to negotiate with them until the plant was evacuated.

As an extreme measure, workers at Bendix also held a sit-down strike in an attempt to organize in December. Workers there had petitioned the NLRB for a labor union election, but Vincent Bendix, who didn't want one, went to court and got a federal judge to declare the Wagner Act "unconstitutional in its entirety" and prevent the election. Clearly, the pot was boiling over.

The lid flew off in the last week of December 1936. Homer Martin sent

William Knudsen a telegram in which he alleged that GM was discharging union men and discriminating against them in other ways also. Knudsen wired back that Martin should take up these matters with individual plant managers. That did it. On December 28, 1936, workmen in the Fisher Body Plant no. 1 in Cleveland spontaneously sat down and ignored the steel skeletons on the assembly belt. The larger issues here had to do with speedups on the assembly line and sweatshop conditions. Like a prairie fire, on December 30 the strike spread to Fisher Body Plant no. 2 in Flint, where ostensibly the issue was the demotion of two inspectors who were wearing union buttons; actually it was because the union had gotten wind of the company's determination to move body-stamping equipment out of the plant during the night. From there it went to other GM plants in Pontiac, Atlanta, Kansas City, and Detroit until some 74,000 men were idled in twenty plants; by mid-January 115,000 workers were either on strike or idled.

The biggest company in the world's highest-profile industry had been struck and crippled, and its plants had been seized. Workers everywhere were electrified, and many were encouraged to follow suit. The heady atmosphere of those days is well described in William Manchester's account of a sit-down strike at Firestone: "To some it seemed almost miraculous. In Akron, for example, the men struck Firestone Plant #1 at 2:00 A.M. on January 29th. A puzzled foreman watched as a tire builder at the end of the belt moved three paces to the master safety switch. At this signal, with the perfect sychronized rhythm mass production had taught them, all the other tire builders stepped back. The switch was pulled, and a great hush fell over the plant. Into this silence a man cried, 'We done it! By God, we stopped the belt! By God, we done it!' A worker beside him broke into tears."

The whole business was not as spontaneous as it appeared to be. Rae points out that at GM, sit-down-strike leaders were imported from Europe, where they had had similar experiences, to ensure that replacement workers would not disrupt the strike action.

John L. Lewis stood squarely behind these sit-downs, because he realized that if he didn't lead these workers, he would lose them. Father Coughlin called him a Communist.

On January 2 Judge Edwin T. Black issued an injunction against the Flint strikers, but this proved to be quite an embarrassment when it turned out that Black had a conflict of interest, due to the fact that he owned almost $220,000 worth of GM shares. GM abruptly gave up its injunction tactic for a month.

By mid-January the union had formulated its demands. The UAW asked for a thirty-hour week, an agreement between management and labor on production speed, a national rather than plant-by-plant agreement, and recognition of the UAW as the sole bargaining agency in GM plants. Sloan absolutely refused on this last point, saying that "no union or labor dictator would dominate General Motors plants." Governor Frank Murphy of Michigan, a key figure in the labor disputes of 1937, tried to keep negotiations moving forward despite Sloan's intransigence. He arranged meetings between Knudsen, Donaldson Brown, and John Thomas Smith of GM and Homer Martin, Wyndham Mortimer, and John Brophy of the UAW, himself acting as mediator and neutral party. These talks didn't work out very well, and the strike dragged on.

The pot was stirred up by an organization called the Flint Alliance, which claimed to be representing some thirty thousand nonstriking workers forced out of their jobs by the strikers; the Flint Alliance claimed that all these workers wanted was to go back to work. Considerable animosity, with threats of violence, grew up between the strikers and the alliance, which was transparently GM-organized and -supported.

Things came to a head on the bitterly cold night of January 11, when company guards tried to prevent union members from bringing an evening meal to the strikers inside Fisher Body Plant no. 2. The company turned the heat off inside the factory, and the police, in collusion with the guards, sealed off the building's entrances. When union men seized the main gate, the security guards, as if in a prearranged manner, barricaded themselves in the ladies' room and called the police, who "conveniently" arrived on the double, formed a line, and fired tear gas, furnished by GM, into the factory. At first the workers scattered, but then the wind changed and blew the gas back onto the police, who retreated in confusion. The workers trained a fire hose on them, and battered them with two-pound door hinges. Physically distressed and humiliated, the police regrouped out of the range of the workers and attacked again, only to be repulsed once more by a hail of hinges, stove bolts, and bottles. There was another retreat, but this time some of the enraged officers fired indiscriminately at the workers at the gate; fourteen were injured and fell. But the union members were prevailing. They spoke to the newspapers, derisively referring to the police action as the "Battle of the Running Bulls."

The next day, Governor Murphy called out the National Guard, and twelve hundred troops surrounded the plant by 3 P.M., aided and abetted by the Flint police and strikebreakers armed with pokers, clubs, and crowbars. January 12 was a freezing day, and on into the night men's tempers were inflamed both inside and outside of the plant. It was a desperately serious moment. Murphy was ready to send in the National Guard but hesitated at the thought of the mayhem and bloodshed that would surely result. Furthemore, this ambitious and rising politician, widely perceived as a friend of labor, did not want such an incident on his conscience and record. "Bloody Murphy" was the last thing this possible presidential contender wanted for a moniker. Murphy decided to ask John L. Lewis what he would do if he sent in the troops.

Manchester describes Lewis's reply: "You want my answer sir? I shall personally enter GM plant number two, I shall order the men to disregard your order, to stand fast. I shall walk up to the largest window in the plant, open it, divest myself of my outer raiment, remove my shirt and bare my bosom. Then, when you order your troops to fire, mine will be the first breast that your bullets will strike. And as my body falls from the window to the ground, you will listen to the voice of your grandfather, as he whispers in your ear, 'Frank, are you sure you are doing the right thing?' Murphy hesitated; his grandfather had been hanged after an Irish uprising." A weary Murphy finally tore up the National Guard's orders. This action broke the back of the strike.

Despite attempted intervention by Roosevelt and Frances Perkins, the strike continued for a while. With Gallup polls clearly showing the public in support of GM, union leaders, with their backs to the wall, cleverly and surreptitiously engineered the seizure of GM's most important plant, Chevrolet no. 4 in Flint. The next day, February 3, Judge Paul V. Gadola issued an injunction against the union's plant seizure, threatening prison terms for union leaders and a $15 million fine. Once again a hesitant and tormented Murphy refused to send in the National Guard, despite many entreaties to do so.

In the end, nobody stood with GM in its crisis. The UAW's strike techniques had brought GM to a standstill, and Lewis's leadership was powerful and effective. He made sure there were only token demonstrations at rival concerns, including Ford, Nash, Chrysler, and Packard, which encouraged those companies' sharp competitive instincts; they stepped up production and did everything possible to make a profit at GM's expense. Even Pierre S. du Pont, who lost $2.5 million when GM halved its dividend, sent word to GM's top management that principles were all right in their place but one shouldn't lose one's head adhering to them. When Murphy joined the bandwagon and caved in too, that was the end. Finally, after forty-four days of strife, Knudsen agreed to confer with the union. When the strikers heard this, they square danced wildly in the frozen yards outside the factory.

By February 11 an agreement was reached among Knudsen, Martin, and Murphy. GM agreed to recognize the UAW as a bargaining agent for its members, though not an exclusive one. It also agreed not to prevent further organizing by the union, nor to retaliate in any way against the strikers. GM wouldn't negotiate with any other group claiming to represent GM workers (read the Flint Alliance) in seventeen of its plants for six months, and would bargain on other issues starting on February 16. Meanwhile, the strikers would evacuate the plants and return to work, pending the outcome of negotiations.

This was a great triumph for the UAW. The magnitude of its victory can be understood by reflecting on the fact that no more than 2,000 sit-downers had prevented 44,000 other GM laborers from working and idled 110,000 more in sixty plants throughout the country. Approximately 280,000 cars, worth $175 million, were not built, and $25 million in wages were lost. Still, in a titanic clash of wills, the UAW had clearly won for the workers what the Wagner Act had provided for union recognition and the right to collective bargaining. Psychologically, too, they gained a big advantage. They had shown they could hold the Flint plants for six weeks and emerge from the dispute with their position substantially improved. This was a great stimulus for recruiting, and gave an enormous impetus to further organizing. Even before the settlement Homer Martin had announced that workers at Graham, Nash, Studebaker, and Willys were fully organized, and that Chrysler, Packard, and Hudson managements were "fair" to the union, that is, they were not trying to prevent it from organizing. In the case of Chrysler, though, that statement would turn out to be somewhat disingenuous on his part.

What the UAW was emboldened to do next was strike Chrysler. After examining what went on in this affair, it seems that both sides knew exactly what was going to happen and exactly what the outcome would be. The union used Chrysler to set up GM during its strike, clearly giving it some advantages and signaling what would be expected when its time on the hot seat came. Walter Chrysler took what was thrown his way, and made it his business to understand every signal he was given. So despite plant seizures, mass rallies, demonstrations, and elaborate negotiations, in a certain sense both sides knew pretty well how things would end before the Chrysler strike began. Some of the participants even commented on this. But perhaps the zeitgeist of early 1937 demanded that the battle had to be fought, and so it was.

The sticking point in all of this was whether the UAW could get to be the exclusive bargaining agent for all the workers in the Chrysler plants. This was the one point that Walter Chrysler, like Sloan and Ford, did not want to concede under any circumstances. Chrysler was ever watchful on the issue. As early as September 13, 1934, he tried to talk UAW officials from withdrawing from the Roosevelt Settlement of March 25th, over the Houde case settlement, which provided for both collective bargaining and majority representation. At the time of the GM strike he maintained close contact with that company, eager to learn every detail of the bargaining process. He was considered something of a labor expert, and GM was happy to have him sit in on many of its strategy meetings, frequently accompanied by Nicholas Kelley. Some of the meetings took place in the New York apartment of Chrysler's close personal friend Alfred P. Sloan. While it cannot be proved that Chrysler was influenced by what he learned, it is certainly sure that he had an insider's view of what was going on.

Labor leader Henry Kraus writes that the UAW thought relations with Chrysler were more enlightened than elsewhere in the auto industry and took pains to publicize the fact, to the obvious detriment of GM. The UAW singled out Chrysler for engaging in meaningful collective bargaining agreements and treating union members in its plants fairly. John L. Lewis said that GM's policy toward its workers, unlike Chrysler's, was "antagonistic." He also took pains to be sure that any strike-related obstacles to Chrysler production before and during the GM strike were removed. The union strategy was to put the squeeze on GM by encouraging high production by its main competitors during the strike. So the Midland Steel strike that began on November 27, 1936, which prevented Chrysler from getting car frames, was over in a week. Furthermore, Sidney Fine says that Lewis arranged directly with Walter Chrysler to settle the glass strikes at Pittsburgh Plate Glass and Libby-Owens-Ford by the end of January. Chrysler couldn't resist "the temporary lure of rather unrestricted profits at the expense of his GM competition, even though it meant playing the C.I.O. game," according to Fine. And indeed, as GM's production fell by 80 percent during the strike, Chrysler's production, as well as Ford's, zoomed.

In early February Chrysler announced its fourth 10 percent wage increase since 1933, raising the basic wage for men to 75 cents an hour and for women to 65 cents an hour; this was on top of two bonuses the company paid out to its employees in 1936, which brought them an extra 2.5 cents or so an hour. Coming at the very end of the GM strike, Chrysler's move seemed like a calculated coup de grace forcing GM to capitulate to the union's demands as quickly as possible. The Chrysler move meant that the company knew pretty clearly what was in store for it: Only a few days earlier, in representative elections, the UAW had won some 84 out of 109 places on the Chrysler works council (at the Kercheval plant, it was a clean sweep). Like it or not, the union had arrived at Chrysler informally, so the quest for formal recognition couldn't be far off, especially in light of the demands at GM. The GM settlement obviously would be a blueprint for Chrysler's own struggles, so Chrysler figured it might as well help to clear up the mess as soon as possible and see what was on the horizon.

GM had not been the original first choice for a strike at the end of 1936. Adolph Germer, a former United Mine Workers official who became an important CIO organizer, had wanted to strike Chrysler, but it just wasn't practical. Not only did Chrysler actually have better relations with its workers, but the union had invested heavily in promoting that idea. As late as February 27, Homer Martin was singing Walter Chrysler's praises thus in the *New York Times*: "Mr. Martin commended Walter P. Chrysler, automobile manufacturer, for his attitude in the negotiations with labor. 'Chrysler has shown an intelligent attitude toward labor and we expect recognition and a working agreement with him without a struggle. There is a man who has found it profitable to maintain good relations with his men, and there is a spirit of good will in his factories that has never prevailed before,' he said."

Walter Chrysler himself was busy polishing his own apple with labor at the same moment, agreeing to allow his personal memoirs, written with Boyden Sparkes, to be serialized in *Collier's*. Originally to be called *Taking the Lamp Apart*, the book was now called *Life of an American Workman*; this colorful look back at his own life was filled with encomiums to the American workingman, with whom he never failed to identify throughout its pages, as indeed he had throughout his life. He was wary of the the public's reception of his story, however. When he learned that his serialized articles were to be advertised in one sheets in subways, rail stations, and other such places, just at the time of the UAW strike against him, he objected strongly, as Boyden Sparkes recalled, out of fear that workingmen might deface the signs.

" 'I was scared,' he said.

" 'Of what?'

" 'Workingmen! They might go and write on those signs.' Then, seeing I was still bewildered, he made a further effort to explain. That time he succeeded, as if by a lightening flash. 'Like a horse out on the road without blinders, I see too many things,' he said."

One of the things he may have seen was an incident from his own past, for in 1894, at the age of 19, he had participated in the Chicago railway strike of 1894, organized by Eugene Debs and his American Railway Union. It began with minor incidents between strikers and police and escalated into an all-out war that shut down almost all passenger traffic west of Chicago. People were killed and railcars were burned in fierce battles. When Chrysler began labor negotiations in 1937 he told Secretary of Labor Frances Perkins that he had been arrested and thrown into jail for two days during the railway strike. "I know what makes men strike," he told her. "I know all about it." So too, he knew what kinds of expression their anger might take.

By the twenty-forth of February, Chrysler had agreed to collective bargaining with the union. Richard Frankensteen had announced that the UAW would begin substantive talks with the company the following Wednesday, and that it would request to be the exclusive bargaining agent for Chrysler workers, since it claimed to represent the majority of them. Walter Chrysler designated corporate counsel L. L. "Tex" Colbert and DeSoto vice president and general manager Herman L. Weckler to speak for the company.

Whatever others from the UAW may have said about the Chrysler Corporation, Richard Frankensteen was not very kindly disposed toward it. On January 27, 1937, he testified before the LaFollette Committee investigating labor espionage that two undercover operatives of the Corporations Auxiliary Company, working for its biggest client, the Chrysler Corporation, spent the enormous sum of $1,152 entertaining him to find out labor secrets. The ruse was that young John C. Andrews, posing as a Chrysler employee, befriended Frankensteen, and while on a lakeside vacation introduced him to his "uncle," A. J. Bath, posing as "a retired play producer worth a million dollars," who happily spent money like water on the two young men while trying to pry labor secrets out of Frankensteen. During the proceedings, Frankensteen turned to Herman L. Weckler and said, "I think men of the type of Mr. Weckler and K. T. Keller [who was on the administrative council of the Metal Trades Association, another spy organization] are worse than a dope peddler who sells narcotics to addicts. They go on and pretend to be decent citizens and hire men for spy jobs—the lowest criminals in the world. Weckler and Keller say they are decent citizens. I say they are not."

Frankensteen would be one of the major union figures involved in the Chrysler strike. The others would be Homer Martin, Adolph Germer, and lawyers Maurice Sugar and Lee Pressman.

When it came, the strike turned out to be something of a surprise. In the first place, the workers themselves seemed reluctant to strike Chrysler, and in the second, the union officials thought negotiations would end in an agreement, which was the usual way with the company. But the strike issue was the UAW's right to exclusive representation of Chrysler workers, a point on which the company was intransigent. Eventually representatives of the various locals grew restive and wanted a strike at Dodge Main.

On March 8 they got their wish, and in a period of just ten minutes the enormous plant, with its twenty-five thousand workers, was shut down. Many of the workers stayed in the plant, but were asked to leave by the union, which wanted just eighteen hundred to remain, to make the feeding and housing problem manageable. The others either picketed or dug up money and supplies to help the sit-downers. The strike moved quickly to other plants, including Kercheval, Jefferson, and DeSoto. Entertainment was provided to keep the workers' spirits high. At DeSoto, their paper, *Sit Downers*, bannered the motto, "We'll be here til hell freezes over, and then we'll skate on the ice." Women's Auxiliary members wrote new pro-striker lyrics to such popular ditties of the day as "Pennies From Heaven" and "Goody, Goody." The latter, by S. Deutsch of District 33, featured lines like,

> So they're down in your plant too,
> They'll be sure to see it through,
> And the women are behind them,
> Now how do you do?
> So, you lie awake, just singin' the blues all night,
> Goody, Goody,
> Cause this union gang's a barrel of dynamite

In all, some eight thousand men were occupying eight plants, and preventing sixty thousand others from going to work. Chrysler attempted to start a back-to-work rally at the union hall, but it was a huge flop. There were big demonstrations at the Kercheval and Jefferson plants, with thousands of picketers. A caravan of some three hundred cars toured all the Chrysler plants, with workers leaning out of the windows, yelling and screaming and waving banners in a show of solidarity with the sit downers.

Walter Chrysler and all his minions protested loudly and long over the illegal seizure of private property by his workers, and he had vast support both among the public and in the press. "Oh Michigan!" the *New York Times* editorialized. "Isn't that uneasy place between the lakes the place where all the trouble that affects the nation starts?"

For sit-down strikes were sweeping the country; hundreds popped up all over, and not just in the automobile business. Department stores, hotels, restaurants, cigar factories, and many other types of firms were seized and crippled. At one dance, the stag line sat down and protested for more dances when the orchestra played, "Good Night, Irene"; wet Nurses in Chicago sat down for more money per ounce of milk, and in New York, a movie projectionist infuriated moviegoers when he stopped the film and complained that he was underpaid.

It all made the public very uneasy. This was still a conservative nation, which had a clear notion it wanted to maintain of the sanctity of private property. For the American people, the seizure of private property and the specter of Communism behind it was a nightmare they never wanted to face. *Newsweek* "sensed a threat against every man's right to keep what he owns, and against the court's power to protect that right." From New York, an executive of the First Machinery Corporation wrote Governor Murphy, "The insurrection against constituted authority is no longer a local concern within the confines of your State. It threatens the safety and security of private property everywhere in our land."

Murphy had been the great conciliator in the GM strike, of course, and was fulsomely praised in the press and by President Roosevelt (who, a few years later, appointed him to the Supreme Court) for his efforts. But the Chrysler strike was a little different, for very personal reasons.

Though he came from humble circumstances, Frank Murphy rose very high in the world from the time of his youth. A real Handsome Harry bachelor about town, he was happily pursued by a boatload of admiring Hesters, Annettes, Violas, Adeles, and Sues as a "fascinator" with a "gorgeous body" and a great capacity for "friendly love in diverse directions." The same charm that attracted the girls made him a well liked and admired friend, and a natural politician. He became Judge Murphy in the 1920s, then the Mayor of Detroit, and finally Governor Murphy, riding into office on the coattails of Roosevelt's sweeping victory over Alf Landon in November of 1936. Along the way, he made some key friendships. One of them was with Byron Foy, with whom he attended university and shared an apartment from 1919 to 1923, when Foy married Walter Chrysler's eldest daughter, Thelma. Murphy was best man at the wedding, and later godfather to their daughter Joan. Thereafter he became very friendly with the Walter Chryslers as well as the Foys, traveling to Europe with them and staying with them in New York.

Walter Chrysler allowed Murphy to invest in a family syndicate in 1924, which paid him a $17,000 profit by the time it was disbanded in April 1925. Foy continued to give him "inside tips" on Chrysler stock, and Walter Chrysler invested Murphy's money in Chrysler securities at "opportune moments." At one point in 1928 he made Murphy a $6,200 profit on a $30,000 investment in just a few days.

Though Murphy never took a proffered job as corporate counsel for the Chrysler Corporation at a high salary in 1928, he did accept a substantial retainer from the corporation for his legal services the following year. Since a Recorder's Court judge was forbidden by statute from engaging in private practice, Murphy was in clear violation of the law. This sorry episode in his career meant that Walter Chrysler and the Chrysler Corporation had good reason to believe he would be friendly to them during the Chrysler strike. But realpolitik, and what seems to have been a genuine sympathy for the plight of the workingmen who elected him, meant that Murphy would have to bring a sense of fairness on all sides to his role as labor mediator, no matter whose toes he stepped on.

Nicholas Kelley went to court to get an injunction against the strikers in mid-March. It was handed down by Circuit Judge Allan Campbell in Detroit, who was somewhat fearful of doing so. If he issued it, and the company went into negotiations with the union and didn't pursue the matter, Campbell would wind up with egg on his face. But he handed it down, and the company insisted on plant evacuation as the first step in its negotiations. By the judge's decree of Monday, March 15, the workers would have to evacuate all the plants within forty-eight hours. Governor Murphy, after consultation with his legal advisers, issued a statement which read in part, "It ought not to be necessary for either public or private agencies to use force. But the agencies of government, both executive and judicial, are bound to take proper steps to see that public authority is preserved and rights of private property are respected. Neither party to any dispute can afford to take a position that is in defiance of the law."

The injunction didn't do any good. Union leaders told the membership to stay put, and besides, the workers themselves would not be budged. After Judge Campbell's order was handed down, one of the strikers said, "Even if Martin and Frankensteen had told us to leave we wouldn't do it. We're going to stay right here."

Things got a little tight on the sixteenth, the afternoon before the injunction was to take effect. Three of the leaders of the local got scared and went to the counsel for the UAW, Maurice Sugar, and asked what to do. After consulting with Martin and Frankensteen, who were in Cleveland, he got them to return to Detroit and make the rounds of the occupied plants, urging the sit-downers to sit tight, exactly as the Flint workers had in the GM strike. They did just that.

Murphy called for a conference on March 17 to establish a board to settle the strike. Maurice Sugar wrote him a letter on the twentieth explaining that no union representatives had attended because they believed that only collective bargaining, not boards, worked. In rebuttal to Murphy's charges that the UAW's actions were "disorderly and unlawful," Sugar listed the workers' grievances against the company about wages, working conditions, industrial spies, and more.

One of the items on the list was that Walter Chrysler was "unconcernedly vacationing in Florida," ignoring union complaints and paying "$1,000 (more than many of us earn in a year) for a case of champagne." (A few days later, in a speech by Homer Martin, this figure would balloon to an even more ludicrous $6,500. It was true that Chrysler lived high on the hog, however. When Kelley, attending one of the GM labor conferences at Alfred P. Sloan's apartment, noted in amazement that Sloan had gold-plated fixtures in his bathroom, Walter Chrysler replied, "Oh hell, there's gold plumbing in my apartment." He had come a long, long way, in distance and life, from the $100 worth of broken-down furniture that fell apart in Childress thirty-odd years before.)

After reminding Murphy that it was labor that elected him, despite management's warnings if it did, Sugar left him with two choices: "You can use your influence to see that our grievances are adjusted. Or you can use the state's troops to try to force us out. The first way will lead to industrial peace and the elimination for the causes for strikes. The second way will lead to bloodshed and violence and more strikes. We are resolved to protect our rights to our jobs with our lives. The choice is flatly up to you."

The Chrysler Corporation, waving the injunction, became more and more indignant at the state of affairs, as did Governor Murphy, and the workers became ever more defiant. Fearing a repeat of the mess at the Fisher Plants no. 1 and no. 2, the Detroit police tried a diversionary tactic to make the Chrysler workers quail. On March 19, after having evicted workers at six shoe stores, a food products concern, and the Newton Packing Company, the police moved in on about two hundred female sit-downers at the Bernard Schwartz Company cigar plant. Three hundred policeman evicted these kicking, screaming, biting, hair-pulling, mold-wielding women from the factory, while nearby forty mounted policemen fought against five hundred sympathizers armed with stone-centered snowballs.

The UAW got the point, and to prevent the same tactics from erupting at the Chrysler plants, the union decided to call for a massive support rally in Detroit on March 23. At first it couldn't get a permit from the city. The union had requested that the rally take place on the steps of City Hall on Woodward Avenue, but Mayor Frank Couzens would have none of it. The union was afraid it might be walking into a police attack if it demonstrated without a permit. Adolph Germer warned, "It's going to be a perfect setup for another Haymarket Square Massacre!"

But the union had given the mayor a face saver, suggesting an alternative location in Cadillac Square, which was agreed upon—not easily, though, as the city's Common Council objected that the demonstration would produce a massive traffic jam. An angry UAW vice president, Ed Hall, gave the defiant rejoinder, "We don't give a good whoop in hell about the permit; we'll be there anyhow." A compromise was worked out, by which the union agreed to hold a peaceful and orderly rally at 5:45 P.M., with a police presence for directing traffic and preventing "outside interference." Downtown offices and stores also complied with police requests to send their employees home at 4 P.M.

The demonstrators were mobilized by hundreds of thousands of leaflets announcing the event. Henry Kraus also printed a special two-page edition of his *United Automobile Worker* with a statement from Homer Martin under a banner proclaiming, "WE HAVE JUST BEGUN TO FIGHT!"

Estimates of how many people showed up varied widely. George Addes, national treasurer of the UAW, estimated that 250,000 attended; fifty-five years later, Henry Kraus called it 100,000 or more, mostly Chrysler workers who were not sitting in or members of other UAW locals. But Fred W. Frahm, Detroit's Superintendent of police, estimated the crowd at 60,000. Reporters, who knew the standing capacity of the square to be 30,000, estimated that there were some 35,000 to 40,000. To those on the spot, many of the people in attendance seemed to be of the curious-bystander variety. It seems that many of the workers in the area, let out at four o'clock, simply hung around to see what was going on, and were joined by other curiosity seekers who lived nearby.

The rally was extremely orderly, due to a "carnival atmosphere," according to the *Detroit Free Press*. Thousands of ebullient demonstrators, banners flying, poured into the square for the rally, which began, of course, with "The Star-Spangled Banner." As the strains of the piece swelled upward, Frankensteen and Martin stood at attention, lips moving in their sternly set features, hands on hearts. Henry Kraus recalled: "I was surprised to see George Edwards at the microphone, as the strong voice hardly sounded like his. His face was taut with earnestness, and it was only later that I learned how scared he was. When the meeting started, Frankensteen had asked him to lead the crowd in singing the national anthem. Edwards stalled until Frankensteen became angry. "Go ahead and start singing!" he muttered. "Goddamn it," Edwards blurted out desperately, "I don't remember the words!" But he had no choice. Frankensteen pushed him up to the microphone and somehow the forgotten words came back."

Some rabble-rousing rhetoric was heard. Frank Martel, president of the Detroit and Wayne County Federation of Labor, bellowed, "From this time on the constitutional rights of this community are going to be respected in City Hall, the police station and the courts, or we'll turn them wrong side up." Most speakers were far more tempered. Homer Martin said, "The automobile workers of this city have suffered from insecurity and from low wages while their employers, such as Walter P. Chrysler, were paying $6,500 for a case of champagne. We have suffered and we have given our lives needlessly, and we are no longer going to do it.

"Those of us who have seen sit down strikes know why the employers don't like them. I'll tell you why. It's because they're effective. They're successful, that's the reason why."

The overall peaceful nature of the demonstration burst the public's anticipatory fears of this event, and the people's worry over civil disorder stemming from labor disputes began to calm down. The police ended their raids on sit-downs, in part to head off a threatened UAW general strike in Detroit, in part to pave the way for the much-desired evacuation of the Chrysler plants. The results of the rally were all good.

But still no settlement came, and there were a lot of anxieties. Frances Perkins pressed Kelley for some resolution to the situation, sure that John L. Lewis would have some idea of what to do. But when asked what she thought that was, she really hadn't a clue. Kelley reports that Lewis was worried, too. He was afraid of a $10 million penalty that the court had threatened to levy against the union, and Kelley wanted Lewis to be responsible for the penalty as well. Chrysler's Detroit lawyers worried about that. "Suppose Lewis has nothing to do with it, and sues on the grounds that we're libelling him?" they asked Kelley. He replied, "I'd pay a hundred thousand any day for Lewis to say he had nothing to do with this strike." They joined Lewis in on the fine, to turn the screws.

Murphy had already figured a way out of the stalemate. On Thursday, March 18, he decided to ask Walter Chrysler and John L. Lewis to a meeting he would arrange to settle the strike. He called Lewis in New York, who said he was interested. By the time Lewis departed for the conference, Murphy had warned him by telegram that writs had been issued and given to the Wayne County sheriff to enforce evacuation of the Chrysler plants. Lewis replied, "Your message suggests that I confer under duress. Nevertheless and notwithstanding, I agree to be present."

Walter Chrysler formally accepted Murphy's invitation on Tuesday afternoon, March 23. In so doing, he issued a stern letter to the governor in which he outlined the company's position. The salient points were that: "The court order against the strikers is not a proper subject for negotiation between the management and Lewis"; "We will not enter any trade to get the men out of the plants"; and "Chrysler representatives cannot agree to any arrangement which will force employees against their will into any organization of labor. The corporation cannot recognize any organization as exclusive bargaining agency and be a party to the use of force and coercion against the company's own workers."

It was arranged that the parley would begin in the state capital, Lansing, on March 24 at 11 A.M. Lewis entrained in Washington, Chrysler in New York, and both arrived in Detroit the next day. From there, they were whisked away to Lansing by automobile.

At last there would be some movement. A week before, Adolph Germer had written John Brophy: "We have discussed the American Revolution, the French Revolution, the Paris Commune, the Civil War, the World War. We've been in Europe, Africa, South America, and all over the United States, and so far as the strike is concerned, we are as near together as when you left (at the outset of the strike)." Nicholas Kelley later noted that that the unions were happy to talk about abstractions, but bogged down whenever you got around to specifics. In any case, nothing at all had happened until Lewis and Chrysler showed up on the scene.

A lot was accomplished on that first day. In addition to Martin, Frankensteen, UAW vice presidents Wyndham Mortimer and Ed Hall, and his counsel Lee Pressman, Lewis had a score of other union officials with him. Chrysler showed up with a phalanx of executives, lawyers, and others—so many, in fact, that they took up a whole floor in one wing of the Olds Hotel in Lansing, where everyone stayed. Chief among them were K. T. Keller, B. E. Hutchinson, lawyers Nicholas Kelley and Tex Colbert, and public relations man T. J. Ross. Lewis referred to them as "Chrysler's House of Lords." To many, it appeared that Walter Chrysler relied heavily on them, but in reality, he manipulated everybody in a masterly fashion. As Kelley said, in the end, "The thing was between Lewis and Chrysler."

Murphy was tickled pink to have the two men there. At the very beginning, things didn't look too promising, as Chrysler refused to shake hands with Lewis, referring to him as "that bastard." But the patented Murphy charm effected a big change in the atmosphere. "Soon after we were there, Murphy came around, smiling, very much pleased," recalled Kelley. "He said he had the two mastodons sitting beside each other in a lounge in his office."

Kelley and Lewis went at each other from the start that first morning, causing quite a ruckus. Kelley said Lewis was being "very bitchy" to him, and Kelley on his part was taunting Lewis in any way he could even resorting to remarks about how much he admired his bushy eyebrows. Kelley was attempting to make him say something about whether or not he had something to do with the strike, because no matter what he said, he would be in an untenable position. Kelley had a man outside the room with papers for a damage suit, and if Lewis admitted he was part of the strike, Kelley would have been able to serve those papers on him. Finally, after watching him roar up and down for some time, Chrysler turned to Kelley and said, "Aw, Nick, go and sit down."

After that was over, they began negotiating to get the men out of the plants. Chrysler had made it crystal clear that he wouldn't do any negotiating on a contract as long as the men still held his plants, so the first order of business was to get them out. The rest of the day was consumed with talk about how to do it. After eight hours, an agreement was reached and announced by Governor Murphy.

The UAW agreed to evacuate the plants, and Chrysler agreed not to operate them or remove any dies or machinery until the negotiations with the union on its demand for exclusive bargaining rights was settled. These terms were absolutely identical to those Lewis had rejected during the GM strike, but he accepted them now. The mood of the country had changed considerably since the GM strike, and Murphy showed Lewis he meant business by obtaining the presence of the adjutant general of the State of Michigan, the commissioner of the Michigan State Police, and Colonel Joseph Lewis in his office.

Other good news came with this agreement. With payroll clerks now able to get into the occupied administration building, some $2 million in wages, formerly unavailable because management couldn't get to the payroll records, could now be distributed. Furthermore, executives, plant officials and their staffs, office help, plant police, maintenance men, and engineering department employees could now go back to work in the freed-up plants.

Murphy made a big show of it when he announced the agreement to the press. In a break with tradition, he placed Lewis on his right and Chrysler on his left. When asked about this, Murphy, ever the politician, said "the position at the right hand of government is one that has [too] long been enjoyed by great power, wealth and influence." Lewis had lost out here, and Murphy was clearly doing anything he could to make him look good publicly. One observer said Chrysler was "piqued" by this arrangement, and "clearly looked sick." But the photo in the *Detroit Free Press* the following morning shows a positively jolly-looking Walter Chrysler facing the camera. And why not? The great legal logjam preventing the negotiations from moving forward had been broken. President Roosevelt called to congratulate Murphy on all this good news.

Making and announcing the agreement was the easy part. Getting the workers to leave the plants was the hard part. Lewis and his contingent departed from the meeting and boarded a bus in Lansing immediately after the late-night announcement to return to union headquarters in Detroit. Frankensteen and Martin careened over icy roads by car from Lansing, stopping at various plants along the way. They didn't reach the strike center, the Dodge Main plant, until one in the morning. They had the most trouble there and at Jefferson. At Dodge Main, many of the workers were furious. One angry striker said, "We might just as well not have sat down at all. We've been sold out." Another shouted, "If the General Motors men could hold out for forty-four days, we must be a bunch of rabbits to be giving up after thirty-one!" Much as these two leaders were excoriated, even worse words were yelled about Lewis. Frankensteen tried to calm the men by telling them that Murphy was one of the closest allies the UAW had in government, and that he could be trusted to make sure that the terms of the agreement would be observed. "But the men were not rational," he said. "They were all keyed up by the rumors floating around that the court orders had been issued on the injunction writ and that the police were mobilizing to smash the picket lines after the evacuation." It took quite a bit of doing to convince them to leave the plant, which they did the following day at 2 P.M. At Jefferson the situation was equally difficult, with a settlement coming only after a long debate over a personal plea from the Governor. DeSoto only went along when it heard that the Dodge Main sit-downers had left the plant the following day.

By 6 P.M. on the twenty-sixth, the evacuation of all the plants was completed. The first one to be emptied out was Dodge Main. At the head of the column of evacuees, a color guard paraded through the gate, followed by Homer Martin and other smiling, confident-looking union officials. A band played stirringly as the strikers marched out. The thousands who waited in the snow and freezing cold to show their respect to them as they left bared their heads as the American flag passed by. It was a very moving scene. Even the *Detroit Free Press*, normally no friend of Murphy's, called the truce "a triumph for good sense and good order."

Negotiations continued on for several days, as scheduled, with Murphy riding herd on the disputants. Perhaps remembering what had happened to Judge Black in the GM strike, Murphy quietly sold 1,200 shares of Chrysler stock he had bought on February 9, the day after the Chrysler strike began. He had hoped to ride it out and make a tidy profit when it rebounded after the strike was finished, but political prudence told him to just take his $6,000 loss and be done with it.

Eleven hours of negotiating on the twenty-sixth ended with Chrysler holding firm to his refusal to give the UAW sole bargaining rights for his workers. After an exhausted Murphy retired to his hotel, a doctor was summoned; visibly drawn and tense, the governor said he couldn't relax. The doctor told him he wasn't sick, but that he must give up working sixteen-hour days if he didn't want to ruin his health. It must be remembered that the GM and Chrysler strikes had taken up most of his time and energy since his election just four and a half months before. He hadn't even had time to set up his administration.

Onward they all plowed through the weekend, with some levity provided by the deliverance of "kiddiegrams," of mysterious origin, to the major participants. All were delivered in official Western Union envelopes by uniformed messengers. Lewis laughed heartily when he received one from "Franklin and Eleanor" pleading, "Make mother and dad happy by being a good little boy." "John L. Lewis" sent one to Murphy, encouraging him to "Please get well and come over to my house and play." Chrysler smiled broadly when "Governor Murphy" wired him, "When you are naughty and scolded you always feel sad. Be good and sweet and make us all glad."

What was it like inside? Well, for all the pulling and hauling, it was better than might be thought. For one thing, Chrysler and Lewis developed a grudging respect for one another rather quickly, and this turned into an actual liking, which didn't hurt matters at all. "Chrysler wasn't very belligerent to Lewis," said Kelley. "They got along very much all right. Chrysler was as charming as he knew how to be with Lewis, in a way. When Lewis was monologuing, he was both interesting and agreeable, an attractive man. He could however, be very, very ugly. And here is a curious part of the man. Part of the time during the negotiations he would go and sit in the corner in an arm chair with his face turned to the wall, chewing a cigar or smoking. He would stay that way for an hour or more."

The two men had to overcome their mutual suspicions of one another. For Chrysler, it was the specter of Communism in Lewis's background. In the 1920s he had routed all kinds of "Reds" from the United Mine Workers, the mother union whence Lewis derived his power. But it was no secret that in the thirties Lewis was associating with the many Communists, some quite important, who were members of his unions. Once Chrysler said to him point blank, "Mr. Lewis, I do not worry about dealing with you; but it is the Communists in these unions that worry me a great deal." Lewis's biographers, Melvin Dubovsky and Warren Van Tyne, said that part of the man's genius was that he appeared to be all things to all people on this issue, because he couldn't imagine anybody taking over influence in his union, including the Communists. So after many reassurances from Lewis he came to seem to Walter Chrysler to be a bulwark against bolshevism.

For his part, at the start of negotiations on the twenty-fourth, Lewis had to be sure he wasn't the victim of some gigantic stock manipulation. He was afraid Chrysler might have gone into the strike to cause the company's stock to fall and allow people to buy it on the cheap, but Chrysler assured him there was nothing in it. Kelley recalled, "I don't know how they got into this part of the conversation, but Lewis was calling him Chrysler and Chrysler was calling him John. Lewis said, 'Chrysler, you've got all my clothes. I'll have to go home in a barrel.'

"I didn't know that that was the first time they had talked together. I could see a light coming into Chrysler's eye. He said, 'John, I haven't got your clothes. You've got my clothes, and you'll throw them into the East

River. You've got my plants—fifty million dollars!' Lewis couldn't answer that."

While the big shots were doing all right with one another, their under- lings were not, and had to be handled. Lee Pressman said Hutchinson said no to everything, and members of the UAW strike committee wanted to hold out for the union's maximum demands, seemingly heedless of the fact that the union was running out of cash and that many of the membership were facing foreclosure on their homes and repossession of their cars.

Chrysler knew what he was up against with Lewis and had his fun with the hotheads who counseled intransigence. Kelley said: "These people of his were saying a lot of things to him, showing their loyalty, but he didn't think it made much sense. Every once in a while on some subject he would send them in to talk with Lewis. Every one of them came out with his feathers all ruffled. They had gotten the worse of it. I think it would just make him laugh. These fellows had been, in a way, talking big, so he tried this on them to see what they could do with Lewis."

One of these people was K. T. Keller, whom Lewis considered a lackey of the financial backers of the corporation and one of the men responsible for the spy system in its plants. Kraus recalled: "In one joust between the two men, Keller made the mistake of being sarcastic with Lewis. 'You know, Mr. Keller,' the latter growled, 'you've got only one goddamned thing on me and that's a few lousy dollars.' Keller tried a comeback, assuring Lewis that he was not afraid of 'your bushy eyebrows.' 'Mr. Keller,' Lewis snapped, 'I've watched you wriggle and swiggle all this time and if I were responsible for hiring stool pigeons the way the newspapers say you've been doing, I'd wriggle and swiggle too.'" Game, set, match.

Chrysler was exceptionally perspicacious about another matter. During the whole of the negotiations, he insisted on keeping all his men together at the hotel. No one was allowed out, nor could they speak to the press unless he was present. He wanted to be sure there were no problematic leaks.

As for poor put-upon Murphy, he did a good job of shepherding things along, but even he got a little testy at times. When Kelley told him one of his suggestions might be divisive, he snapped back, "Do you realize you're talking to the governor of Michigan?" "That was a kind of crazy view he had from time to time," Kelley said.

After the weekend, Chrysler and Kelley returned to New York to digest what had happened and try to forge a solution. By Saturday, they were back in Lansing, ready for a meeting the governor had convened for the following day, Easter Sunday, at 10 A.M. Chrysler was pleasantly surprised by a dem- onstration of support from a hundred or so of his nonunion employees. "We're with you, Skipper!" they called out as he entered the State Capitol. Yelled others, "The best skipper in the world" and "If any boss ever treated his men right, Chrysler did!" Chrysler replied with a "Thank you" and a broad smile. (Whether this demonstration was genuine or a PR stunt dreamed up by T. J. Ross is a matter of some debate.) Meanwhile, Lewis was picked up by his union people in Jackson, and driven to Lansing in a large Chrysler sedan. The two men conferred privately for several hours, greatly encouraging the governor. "A more intelligent exchange of appeals is being made by both Chrysler and Lewis," he remarked. "They take a greater responsibility toward the state and the country."

Easter morning, as the conferees listened to Lewis amusingly describe the trouble he was having with AFL laborers who were fixing up his new house in Alexandria, Virginia, they heard some music and looked out the window. There was a huge motorcade of some two thousand strikers who had come 90 miles from Detroit to demonstrate their solidarity. Kelley recalled: "We all went out on the little stone balconies outside the windows. Chrysler was off to my right. I was standing beside Lewis; we were practically touching shoulders. It was a very moving thing to see these people getting out of their cars and marching along. They had a little band [actually, it was seventy pieces]. I think that Chrysler was really much more popular with them than was Lewis. They were demonstrating for a settlement of the strike so that they could get back to work. They would call up to Chrysler, call him Walter, and say, 'Give us what we want.' He was waving and smiling." At one pont he said to R. J. Thomas, president of one of the Chrysler locals, "These people don't look like Communists to me."

The Free Press reported that the cheers of the crowd were bestowed equally on Lewis, Chrysler, and Murphy. "Chrysler entered the spirit of a United Automobile Workers' demonstration, stood on the balcony of the State Capitol, smiled broadly and waved to his striking employees. They responded with laughter and cheers, some pointing to banners with these inscriptions: 'Will Chrysler lead again with human rights?' 'We're sitting tight—our cause is right!' and 'We're with you, Mr. Chrysler, if you're with us.'" Best of all was one that said, "Three little words, then I'll love you"; the three little words of course, were "sole collective bargaining."

Lewis addressed the crowd in his usual stentorian tones, thanking them for their support and reassuring them that their representatives were working hard on their behalf. Kelley remarked, "I had the feeling—I don't know how I had it, but it was one of the strongest feelings I've ever had in my life—that Lewis was very much moved by the scene, seeing all these people." It certainly was a grand motivator to all involved in trying to bring an end to the strike.

Kelley had made up four different sets of settlement terms, and wanted to push for the one that was best for the company. Everybody sitting around the negotiating table on Saturday night laughed at this. Murphy looked at the papers and handed them to Lee Pressman, who dismissed them and handed them back.

The following day Kelley said to Chrysler, "Let's give them to Lewis." But one of the government mediators, a former railroad man, said that would just make Lewis mad. A worried Chrysler was uncertain. Kelley urged him on. "We've been fooling around for a long time and nothing has been accomplished," he said. "Let's see what he'll do if he gets really mad." Somewhat against his better judgment, Chrysler agreed. Kelley thereupon gave the papers to Lewis, who put them in his briefcase and left. And that was that for the day.

Everyone seemed to think the strike would be settled on Tuesday. Kelley thought the news reporters had some sort of sixth sense about this. The *Detroit News* noted on April 6, "It was apparent when Walter P. Chrysler brought eight key men from Detroit—production chiefs of the various divisions of Chrysler—that an agreement was in the offing. They arrived Sunday night."

Actually, the reporters could smell politics in the air. There were to be elections on Monday, and Republican leaders did not want voters to go to the polls with news of a strike settlement engineered by Murphy, a Democrat, ringing in their ears. So in fact everyone in the know was *sure* the strike would be settled on Tuesday.

Astonishingly, Lewis accepted the exact terms Kelley handed to him on Sunday. Kelley thought that perhaps the union was sobered by the fact that the company, once it got its plants back, had given orders to cool off the buildings, drain the pipes, and put the machinery in white lead to preserve it.

But still, acceptance or no, there was that delay before it was finalized. In the *Detroit News*, "One authority remarked, by way of ilustration, that if some of the conferees had said tweedle-dee instead of tweedle-dum, the strike would have ended." The *Detroit News* noted that, as opposed to the GM negotiations, "in the Chrysler conference the representatives of both sides have always consulted other larger boards of strategy before making decisions." Often agreements were done, then upset in conferences. At one point Lewis was so frustrated that he turned to Chrysler and said, "Here you've got a million dollars worth of brains with you and they can't even write a simple paragraph!" He thought part of the problem was that Chrysler was engaged in some sort of struggle with his Wall Street backers, though there doesn't seem to be much reason to think this. Even Chrysler got annoyed with his own side at one point, when the union came to Kelley and asked him about something and he replied, "I don't know. I'll have to ask my client here."

The settlement was almost identical to the one signed with GM, except that there was to be no letter from Chrysler, like the one from Knudsen, saying both sides would come back to Murphy to settle any later problems that might come up; this settlement was it, and that was that. Lewis also insisted that the agreement be "without prejudice," and that the $10 million lawsuit he feared would be withdrawn.

Under terms of the agreement, Chrysler agreed that it would "not aid, promote or finance any labor group or organization which purports to engage in collective bargaining or make an agreement with any such group or organization for the purpose of undermining the union." The company also agreed to rehire strikers as soon as possible and to consent to the dismissal of Campbell's injunction. For its part, the UAW agreed to end the strike and not to engage in another sit-down strike or work stoppage for the life of the agreement, which went through March 31, 1938. It also promised not to force company employees to join the union, or to solicit new members on company property or company time.

It was also widely thought that Walter Chrysler had given John L. Lewis private assurances that the corporation would consider the UAW the de facto representative of all Chrysler plant workers. Thus, though the agreement was thought to be something of a defeat for the UAW, in a sense it did quite well. As R. J. Thomas put it, "We were just building a union and we were in no position to hold out for too long a period for an item like sole collective bargaining."

The announcement of the settlement came right on schedule on April 6. Photographs of Chrysler and Lewis shaking hands appeared in every newspaper the following day, in addition to official ones of Murphy standing between Lewis, still on his right, with Chrysler on his left. As the three men walked separately from the conference room, hundreds of UAW workers lining the corridor in front of it gave them lusty cheers.

Chrysler expressed his pleasure with the settlement, and called Governor Murphy "tireless, patient, and resourceful in his efforts to reconcile different points of view. I have no hesitancy in saying he has done a great job." Privately he assured Murphy that he had meant every word. He also said that he had enjoyed getting to know Lewis, and later remarked that he was the most intelligent man he had ever met.

Lewis addressed twenty-five thousand of his workers at a mass meeting in the Coliseum at the State Fair Grounds in Detroit the following night. First he told the multitudes that he wished "we had more Frank Murphys as governors of our several states," and after more words of praise for him from Frankensteen, the audience rose to its feet and gave the governor an ovation that lasted several minutes. Then Lewis addressed the central situation: "And lo and behold it came to pass that in March and April of 1937 that our good friend Mr. Walter Chrysler changed his mind. Mr. Walter Chrysler has never changed his mind before, and it was hard and it took a month, but last night he changed his mind, and I know he did because I was there and I saw him put his John Hancock, and I will say this for Mr. Chrysler with all respect: I think he was glad in his own heart that you created an opportunity for him to change his mind. And I think he means to carry out this agreement to the letter and in the spirit of the agreement I have confidence in Mr. Chrysler and in his corporation. He is a man of rugged personality, but when he makes an agreement and gives his word, I have confidence that he will carry it out."

Great cheering and applause followed his oration, and it was a good thing, because the UAW needed every bit of good feeling it could muster to sell this contract to the workers. Before it was signed, several of the locals involved sent messages to the union negotiators that they should continue to hold out for exclusive representation, and they weren't too happy that this did not take place.

Frankensteen boasted that though it was the first contract that Chrysler had ever signed, the union had nevertheless gotten things that it had taken the miners forty-five years to obtain. However, when he entered the local hall at Dodge Main, where certain less-than-strict seniority provisions of the new contract particularly rankled, he walked into a hornet's nest of disapproval. Here is the event, as he describes it in Henry Kraus's *Heroes of an Unwritten Story*: "I had never entered the Dodge local hall when they hadn't cheered me," he said. "But this time their booing was tremendous, and it started below as I began mounting the steps. It became deafening when I came into the hall and I walked down toward the front feeling as if I was on my death march. It continued as I stood facing them.

"Then suddenly a story I had read by Anatole France that I hadn't thought about in years came to my mind and I started by telling them about it. The story was about an old labor leader who had done his best to serve his people. But on one single occasion he took the unpopular side of a certain question, the correct side, and was defeated. A group who had been plotting to get him rode him out of town and taunted him on the way. 'Well, we got you, didn't we?' But the old man replied: 'No, whether I live or die it will be with a clear conscience. But you yourselves can never have that feeling again.'

"Therefore," Frankensteen concluded, "I want to say to you tonight that whether you accept or reject the contract is your prerogative. But I believe in my position so sincerely that if the contract is rejected I will consider it a rejection of myself and my leadership and I will resign." It brought the house down, he ended, "and they voted for acceptance almost unanimously and without discussion."

A personal triumph for Frankensteen, then, but fifteen months later he admitted to Kraus that the agreement had been frankly "bad" for the union. Indeed, it would come back to haunt everyone involved with it in an even longer, and more bitter, strike against Chrysler in the fall of 1939.

The decision came just under the wire for all parties. Chrysler, like other manufacturers, had been balky over the subject of union representation because it had hopes that the Wagner Act would be declared unconstitutional by the Supreme Court. But in a sweeping five-to-four decision on April 12, 1937, the Court upheld the act in the famous *NLRB v. Jones & Laughlin* case. The company had claimed that since its plants were all in the state of Pennsylvania, it was only involved in intrastate commerce, but the Court denied that claim, since the company bought and sold outside of Pennsylvania. If the UAW had been armed with this decision, they might well have been emboldened to hold out for exclusive representation in the Chrysler plants, and the strike might have gone on for quite some time.

But on the other side, this union, like many others, was seeing more and more that the sit-down strike was more trouble than it was worth, legally and otherwise, and began backing away from the tactic. When Ford workers wanted to sit down at Ford's Kansas City plant, UAW vice president Ed Hall persuaded the workers to call it off. After 78 sitdowns in Detroit and 170 nationwide in March, there were only 15 in the city and 52 nationwide in April. In the month of December 1937 the number of sit-downs had dwindled to only five in the entire country. By the time the sitdown strike was definitively declared illegal sometime later, nobody even noticed, because sit-downs were considered completely passé.

There was another reason why it was good for the UAW that it made its stand when it did. That was because by the end of 1937 the country had fallen into a deep recession, and the only labor issue that would matter for the next year was how many workers would be laid off, and for how long. The cost of labor had gone up, and commodity prices had risen sharply. Even though car manufacturers tried to keep their prices down, there was only so much they could do, and the prices of their 1938 models rose sharply. Unfortunately, though some workers' wages in the country had gone up considerably, many others' did not, and there was still a considerable amount of unemployment; farmers, then enduring a year of horrendous floods after the dust bowl of the mid-thirties, were desperately dependent on the government just for survival. It was an atmosphere in which the consumer simply couldn't afford higher-priced cars, and he wasn't buying. Sales for the 1938 model year turned out to be little more than 2 million cars, just about half of the 1937 total.

Other companies, like Packard, Willys, and Hudson, made their accommodations with the UAW during the first half of 1937, but Henry Ford was obdurate. When four men, including Walter Reuther and Richard Frankensteen, tried to distribute UAW pamphlets at the gates of Ford on May 26, 1937, they were brutally beaten by the hired thugs of Harry Bennett's Ford Service Department in what became known as the "Battle of the Overpass." More than two dozen beatings of union organizers took place at Ford in the next few months. The old man was absolutely determined not to have anything to do with the union, and Harry Bennett's strong-arm tactics were his way of making that completely clear.

Unbelievably, this amazing fact of the period is recorded by Robert Lacey: "Professor David Lewis has demonstrated the remarkably consistent endorsement Ford received in these years from public opinion surveys: one poll conducted by the Curtis Publishing Company in May, 1937, the very month of the Battle of the Overpass, showed that 59.1% of Americans believed that the Ford Motor Company treated its labor force better than any other company. The second ranked company, Bell Telephone, received only 14.1%, and General Motors, who had recognized the UAW three months earlier, got only 6.3%. The legend of the Five Dollar day died hard."

It took until June 18, 1941, for the Ford Motor Company to finally recognize the UAW. Old Henry still wouldn't have done it, but his wife, Clara, fed up with the whole union business, told her husband she would leave him unless he recognized the UAW. Overnight, going from one pole to the other, Henry Ford gave the union the most generous contract it ever had. "Never underestimate the power of a woman," he said.

As for Chrysler, it was destined to go through another, much longer strike in the autumn of 1939, one lasting for fifty-four days. This one began because of a dispute over a speedup on the line and devolved upon the issue of whether or not workers should have anything to say about so basic a management issue as the speed of the work. The resolution of this strike was unclear, but one provision of the settlement was that a four-man arbitration board was appointed to settle future disputes. In addition, a three-cent-an-hour raise was granted across the board. Sixty thousand Chrysler workers had been idled by the strike, and ninety thousand others at its parts suppliers were out of work as well. The company lost $102 million in production, and the workers lost $15 million in wages.

As Steve Jeffreys points out, the long-lasting aspect of these Chrysler labor disputes was that management's fight to keep the outside union from the company's plants led to the strikes that caused the company's unionization. Furthermore, "at Chrysler, top management's 'approval' of unionism took the form of an almost willful disregard of what took place on the shop floor, accompanied by a highly combative attitude toward what it saw as external interference from a hostile union. The outcome was that Chrysler fought losing battles in 1937 and 1939 against the UAW, that led to shopfloor militants in its plants being legitimized to a particularly enduring form of shopfloor unionism." In the end, Chrysler became the most strike-torn of the Big Three from 1937 until 1958.

But these were other people's problems, not Walter Chrysler's. The 1937 strike was his last hurrah, the final time he would be a prominent player in a major event on the national scene. He had shown that he still possessed the legendary human and executive powers for which he was renowned, and he had served the company which bore his name proudly and well. It was a fitting valediction for the great man.

⊡ 29 ⊡

How He Lived; Summing Up

The chandelier has fallen from the sky.
Before Sunset
Gerhardt Hauptman

Shooting Star! A memory now . . .
The Milk Train Doesn't Stop Here Anymore
Tennessee Williams

During all the business upheavals of the 1930s Walter Chrysler culti-
vated a personal life too. Like the ancient Romans, who relaxed famously and luxuriously between paroxysms of political and military strife,
Walter Chrysler had a parallel life of beauty, stimulation, and plain old-
fashioned rip roaring fun during these years. He could turn from business
to pleasure on a dime, and got the most out of everything he did in both
realms. Boredom was not in his lexicon.

Since he was a boy, Walter Chrysler had had a great love of hunting,
particularly of waterfowl. In 1929, still in the process of digesting Dodge
Brothers and reconfiguring the now mighty Chrysler Corporation, and while
his glorious new Manhattan skyscraper was abuilding, he decided to buy
some property on the eastern shore of Maryland at Cambridge, by the banks
of the serene Choptank River. John J. Raskob had told him that this area
was a birdhunter's paradise, and after a little investigation, he decided to
put together his own special sportsman's retreat there. He bought a large
piece of property from a man named Cecil Gabler, then added on the adjacent Wilson and Leighton farms when they too became available in the
Depression (Leighton went broke in the wholesale grocery business).

He chose the location he wanted for his house, and then moved Mr.
Gabler's house to it from its old location on a different part of the property.
It wasn't easy to do, as the building was a good size. It was rolled along in
two sections by a team of horses slowly pulling it over huge logs, which
was a very painstaking process indeed. One family remembered seeing the
enormous special logs used for this and other purposes floated up the

The Chrysler family visits the set of the film *San Francisco*, being filmed on the MGM lot in Culver City, CA, 1935. Seated, from left, Thelma Foy, Walter Chrysler, Della Chrysler, Clark Gable, and Byron Foy. Standing behind them are Chester Morris, Jack Chrysler, and Bernice Garbisch. (*Courtesy Frank B. Rhodes*)

Choptank on a barge. Miraculously, the house made the move without any damage to it whatsoever.

Once it was reassembled, Chrysler built it anew. He added a bedroom wing and a kitchen wing on either side of the main house, and did up the main rooms in the style of a hunting lodge. The great room, for instance, had wooden walls and doors surmounted by brick panels and a barrel-vaulted ceiling, from which depended an enormous wagon-wheel chandelier. There were plenty of comfortable green- and rose-colored chairs and sturdy spindle-legged tables placed throughout the room. Atop the mantle of the stone fireplace was a beautiful red clock surrounded by animal figurines, and on the walls were huge stuffed fish, English hunting prints, photos of the very young Walt and Della, and copies of the Chrysler and Breymann family crests. The dining room too was all wood; old pewter and china were highlighted in coved openings in the walls.

The most celebrated room in the house was the barroom, panelled in Georgia pine, and featuring a false wall behind the mahogany-topped bar. At the touch of a button, the whole thing would swing open like a garage door and reveal a bar loaded with glasses and any kind of liquor you could imagine; this arrangement was not just a source of amusement but a necessary ruse, because Prohibition was still the law of the land. A steer head hung over the mantel of the fireplace, and heads of stuffed bulls adorned the other walls, along with a large selection of guns, including Mr. Chrysler's punt gun. A red piano was always at the ready to provide the sounds of merriment. One pure source of amusement in the bar was a large moose head, rigged up to pipes in the basement. At a mechanical command from Mr. Chrysler, it would follow you about with its eyes, and smoke would pour forth from its nostrils, which generally astonished first-time visitors and sent them into gales of laughter. Den and gun rooms were next to the bar, forming a little "man's man" suite, where many a glass was raised and many a tall hunting tale was told.

Poignantly, in the large wine cellar beneath the house, there is still a bottle of Walter Chrysler's own applejack, labelled with his name. Also surviving is a huge papier mâché mask of a green-hatted Walter Chrysler, showing him with a huge smile and a long red-tipped nose. Once upon a time there were other masks too, which Chrysler had musicians wear during big jolly parties at Pokety.

The house was surrounded by lovely gardens, including one devoted to an extraordinary selection of roses. Black walnut trees, huge magnolias, some 600 crepe myrtles, an incredible boxwood hedge labyrinth, and a 300-year-old poplar also adorned the grounds nearby, and greenhouses supplied a magnificent array of fresh flowers whenever the family was in residence.

Mr. Chrysler further beautified the property by constructing a two-mile-long low seawall of local Cambridge tapestry brick, which also was used for a walkway around the gardens. He built a five-acre lagoon on the property too, which was entered through a long, serpentine waterway crossed by a brick bridge near the river. This charming extension of the river was stocked for fishing with carp, catfish, and, of course, Maryland crab.

Tennis courts and a pool (with cabanas and a stone barbecue) provided plenty of opportunity for outdoor excercise and fun. Corn, barley, soybeans, and other crops were grown on hundreds of acres of land on the property, and sheep, chickens, and horses (Rob Roy, Floating Power, and a pony named Della V were among Mr. Chrysler's favorites) were also raised there.

Walter Chrysler gave a great deal of sorely needed employment to the locals in Cambridge, a great boon during the Depression. At times there were thirty or forty men working on the grounds alone. One day in early 1932, he and a young employee, Earl Pritchett, drove into town and noticed a number of men just standing around. When Chrysler asked why, they said it was because there was no work. Without revealing who he was, he said to go up to the Chrysler place, and that they would find work there. When they protested that it wouldn't work out, he told them that they should try it, because he knew someone up there who was sure to give them a job. They went, and got work moving bricks around. Only one lasted more than a day, and he too quit because he didn't like that kind of work. But Chrysler tried to give employment in those dark days, even if it was just of the make work variety, and he was respected by the locals for it.

Fixing up the property went on for most of a decade, and many men were established in business because of it. Charles E. Brohawn was his general contractor, and he and his sons did very well from this work. According to Mrs. Emeline Jones, wife of Jimmy Jones who worked on the property, Mr. Chrysler even set up one of the sons, Lee Brohawn, in business as a Chrysler dealer. Other locals in the building trades, like Charles and Buzzy Potter, also made out well on this project, and used it as a base to become leading businessmen in the area. Add this sort of generosity to a down-to-earth, unassuming manner, and you have in Walter Chrysler a man who was beloved in the community, and still is, to this day.

He called his hideaway Pokety Lodge, reflecting his purpose in buying it. A great deal of both hunting and relaxing were done there, and by all accounts, a very good time was had by all. He would come down from New York by train, in his own special Pullman car that would arrive at a station near Cambridge. This sort of rail accommodation, once fairly common among the very rich, was becoming rarer in the hard times of the 1930s. It certainly was a far cry from the days when he relied on his raiload pass to hitch a ride in coach to wherever he was going. Once arrived, there was plenty of good hunting in the duck blind to the right of the house and in the marshes along the banks of the river. Chrysler had a fine collection of duck decoys, and personally created several that are still admired today.

When hunting was over, there were plenty of "shooters" and laughs in the bar. Chrysler was very much prone to practical jokes of all sorts. There were whoopee cushions in the sofas and plastic bed bugs sprinkled on bedroom pillows, and of course there was that oogling, smoking moosehead. One time he invited a party of friends down for some duck hunting and assured them it would be perfectly o.k. for them to go hunting without licenses. After they went out with their guns, he told the game warden, who promptly found them and fined them.

According to his granddaughter, Joan French, there was a particularly bibulous evening involving some business associates that ended in a sort of slapstick almost tragedy. Chrysler sent the men out on a possum hunt in the pitch black night equipped only with flashlights and paper bags. However, "He neglected to tell them that he had imported a bear from a local circus or zoo, which he had chained to a tree in the woods. One of the men came upon it, and it scared him so that he ran all the way back to the house where he promptly had a heart attack—and lived!"

"The other story which I have heard is that he loved to play poker and

The Chrysler Pavilion at the Century of Progress World's Fair exhibition, Chicago, 1933–34. (*Courtesy DaimlerChrysler Corporate Historical Collection*)

one night bet the Chrysler Building. I guess he won, but I always wonder *what* he won."

Frank Rhodes, Sr., the first husband of Chrysler's granddaughter Gwynne Garbisch, said he had heard many such tales of boyish pranks and highjinks, both at Pokety and elsewhere, from William Reid, Mr. Chrysler's longtime, faithful Scottish butler. "The old man was a swinger," said Rhodes. "He liked a stiff drink and a high time, and he had a lot of fun." Reid saw it all, and stuck by Mr. Chrysler through thick and thin. (It must be remembered that it was Reid who took the rap in Hawaii in 1928 when Mr. Chrysler's luggage was discovered to be loaded with liquor.) "He loved Walter Chrysler, because the old guy was a real, down to earth, no-nonsense human being. Nothing high hat or phony about him."

As far as the game warden was concerned, Chrysler himself ran afowl of him in 1936. He and twenty-five others, including William T. Pritchett, Pokety's estate superintendent, were charged with many violations of the Federal Migratory Game Laws, in an incident that occurred on December 6, 1935. In particular, Mr. Chrysler was charged with hunting wild fowl without a federal stamp on his license, shooting over a baited area, using a gun which had not been plugged to use less than four shells at a loading, and killing ten wild ducks illegally. Each charge could have carried a max-

Walter Chrysler seated in the one-millionth car produced by the Chrysler Corporation in 1936. Standing to his left are K. T. Keller, Fred Zeder, and B. E. Hutchinson, December 15, 1936. (*Courtesy DaimlerChrysler Corporate Historical Collection*)

imum penalty of six months in jail and a $500 fine. On October 28, 1936, both he and Pritchett paid fines of $11, and that was it. Mr. Chrysler was reported to have been plenty riled up against E. Lee Le Compte, the Maryland game warden, over the incident, but he never stepped over the line again.

Ironically, the previous summer Mr. Chrysler had joined a group of thirty-two other nationally prominent sportsmen to create the American Wild Life Institute to assist government and private conservation agencies in protecting wildlife and restoring its natural habitat wherever possible. Chrysler was chairman of the board of the group, and Powell Crosley, Jr., creator of the Crosley compact car after World War II, was chairman of the executive committee. Alvin Macauley, the president of Packard, was one of the members, as was Edward Tinker, the man who had provided the financing to put the first Chrysler car into production in 1924. The group was formed because they were "fed up with the random, loose, and ofttimes politically controlled conservation and restoration methods of professional game savers. . . . Our aim is to restore the environment necessary to natural breeding and nesting. There has been an enormous waste of natural area, by deforestation, over grazing, erosion, and by the reduction in natural

Walter Chrysler standing next to his Chrysler Imperial sedan in the garden of his Great Neck home, 1937. (*Courtesy Frank B. Rhodes*)

water levels in efforts to reclaim land for unneeded agricultural purposes . . . . . . We know those politicians who spend 85% of their appropriations for wardens and warden cars, and they can expect little help from us. They probably won't like us much either. We're out to improve conditions for ducks, you see, and ducks can't vote." And without game wardens, they have a tough time protecting themselves from unlicensed duck hunters too.

One of the very best friends he made in Maryland was Colonel Albanus Phillips, the owner of Castlehaven, a nearby estate; he was the principal in the Phillips Packing Company, which packaged private-label soups and did well at it, until it failed trying to compete with Campbell's Soups after World War II. Phillips, a portly, jocund man, was also an avid hunter of fowl, and he and Chrysler were boon hunting companions. There are photos from the mid-30s taken at the exclusive Bishop's Head Gunning Club of the two smiling men, joined by Grayson Winterbottom, standing by the open doors of Mr. Chrysler's Airflow Imperial sedan. The men are surrounded by hunting dogs, guns, and the results of a very successful goose shoot.

In 1935 Chrysler and Phillips were involved in a friendly bet that had a fabulous result, known as Tomato Justice. It seems that in 1934 soupmaker Phillips had bet a dinner that Chrysler could not grow 1,000 tons of tomatoes on one acre of ground at Pokety during that year. As it turned out,

King George VI and Queen Mary riding in one of two 1939 Chrysler Imperial Parade cars specially constructed for their visit to Canada and the United States, 1939. (*Courtesy DaimlerChrysler Corporate Historical Collection*)

all Chrysler raised was 905 tons, and so the dinner was on him. Hence the name, Tomato Justice. Invitations showing the two men in their hunting gear by that Airflow car at Maryland went out to seventy-eight men (and men only). They were for a sumptuous dinner that would take place at the Waldorf Astoria on April 18, 1935, at precisely 7:05 P.M. Guests included Henry Luce, James A. Farley, Jules S. Bache, Harry F. Sinclair, Charles M. Schwab, prominent socialite Lucius Boomer, Albert Rathbone and John Drye from Chrysler's law firm, K. T. Keller and B. E. Hutchinson from Chrysler,

Walter Chrysler and soup magnate Colonel Albanus Phillips hunting at Pokety Farms, Maryland, 1935. Chrysler's Custom Imperial Airflow CW is behind them. (*Courtesy Frank B. Rhodes*)

Jack Chrysler, and Byron Foy. Walter Chrysler and Albanus Phillips sat next to each other, each flanked by their namesake sons.

Walter Chrysler's good friend Oscar of the Waldorf set a splendid, oval-shaped table, adorned with magnificent floral and greenery arrangements, and a train as the centerpiece. This was the menu:

First Course: Oxtail Soup; Cheese Straws; Celery and Olives; Almonds and Pecans; accompanied by a dry Amontillado Sherry.

Second Course: Diamondback Terrapin, Baltimore Style; Applejack Sherbet; accompanied by Pommery & Greno Champagne, 1926.

Third Course: Breast of Pheasant en Voliere, Toutes les Sauces; Cold Fresh Asparagus, sauce Vinaigrette; accompanied by Chateau Mouton Rothschild, 1924.

Fourth Course: Turban of Vanilla Ice Cream with Tiny Strawberries, Mignardise.

1855 Brandy; Liqueurs; Demi Tasse.

Mr. Chrysler certainly knew how to be a gracious loser.

While at Pokety, he was able to enjoy river cruising on the latest in his long string of yachts, the *Zowie*, for which he had built a handsome boat house on the river. Unfortunately, on September 14, 1934, an explosion and fire destroyed the 42-foot yacht, the boat house, two small power boats, a canoe, and duck-hunting equipment. The blast occurred when caretaker William Pritchett and another employee, Grafton Wheatley, were preparing to take Mr. Chrysler and a party of guests on a fishing trip later that day. Both men were thrown from the boat, but fortunately neither was injured. The cause of the explosion was never determined, but it was believed to be gasoline leaking out when the engine was started up. Everything that burned was a total loss, to the tune of some $20,000. But what a stroke of good luck for Mr. Chrysler that he wasn't there when it happened. (Oddly enough, almost the same thing happened to K. T. Keller when his 83-foot yacht, the *Robark*, exploded and burned completely in a boathouse in Trenton, Michigan, some three years later.)

Shortly after the purchase of Pokety Lodge another milestone event took place in the lives of the Chrysler family. This was the marriage of Walter and Della's younger daughter, Bernice, to Edgar William Garbisch. Bernice was an attractive, dark-haired, dark-eyed girl with a very sympathetic face and something of the mysterious Mona Lisa smile of her mother. Though not a striking beauty like her older sister Thelma, she was nevertheless a very handsome woman with a quiet, ladylike demeanor. She also dressed very conservatively and well. Though she was never on the ten-best-dressed lists like Thelma, she was admired and respected for her quiet good taste. Bernice was graduated from Ely Court in Greenwich, Connecticut, and made her debut into society at a supper dance at the Ritz Carlton Hotel in December, 1926.

A family film of a 1928 vacation in Palm Beach titled *In The Good Old B.C. Days (Before Crash)* shows her merrily exercising with the rest of the family on the sand, serenaded by a three-piece band from the hotel. Later she poses in a chic, light-colored two-piece peau-de-soie outfit before a title that identifies her as "Miss Glamour of 1928."

That same year she, Della, Jack, and Walter Junior went on an exciting round-the-world trip with several friends. It was quite an exotic affair, memorialized in another family film called *Westward Bound to the Far East—Flashes of 1928 Round the World Jaunt*. Snippets of aquatic events and spectacular native dances in Hawaii are followed by visions of beautiful geishas in Tokyo, the Kamakura Buddha which so inspired Kipling, the temple of 1,000 Lanterns, and tame deer roaming the misty grounds of the religious shrine at Naru, near Osaka. The family views inland walled cities teeming with all sorts unusual ethnic groups on the Chinese mainland, and colonies of people living on junks in Shanghai. All smile and wave at the party, gazing at them with intense curiosity.

In Egypt the Chryslers ride camels to the pyramids and the Sphinx in what looks like great splendor. Wherever they go, they are treated like potentates, and clearly are the only westerners around. This was all long before the days of mass tourism, when most people could only learn of such places and people in the pages of the *National Geographic*.

One interesting note is that a Chrysler Imperial Phaeton was constantly at their beck and call, no matter how remote the spot to which they traveled.

But there was more to life than parties and travel. Bernice also immersed herself in art studies after graduation, even spending time in Paris to further her knowledge. In her early twenties she set herself on a lifelong path as a great art collector, amassing some 3,000 American paintings and numerous examples of American folk art by 1930. She was later joined in this consuming passion by her husband.

Edgar William Garbisch was born to Henry Christian and Sophia Carolina Garbisch in LaPorte, Indiana, on April 7, 1899. He was graduated from Washington and Jefferson College in Washington, Pennsylvania with a B.A. degree in 1921. During World War I he served as a private with the Student Army Training Corps, and was honorably discharged on December 15, 1918. He entered West Point in July, 1921, after winning an appointment from Pennsylvania Congressman Guy Edward Campbell.

There he had a distinguished career, earning nationwide fame as one of the greatest football players Army ever had. In the 1922 Army–Navy game Cadet Garbisch's 47-yard place-kick field goal from a yard inside the sideline decided Army's 17–14 victory, and in the 1924 Army–Navy game, his four drop-kick field goals, one from the 46 yard line, accounted for all the points in Army's 12–0 victory. He was chosen All-American center in 1922, 1923, and 1924, and participated, mostly as captain, in the first All East–All West football game, played in San Francisco on Christmas day, 1925, for the benefit of the Shriner's Hospital for Crippled Children. For his amazing football career at West Point, he was elected to the Football Hall of Fame in 1954.

But football wasn't all. Garbisch won tennis championships all four years at West Point, and after graduation played in all the major invitation tournaments, competing with some of the world's greatest players, including Bill Tilden, Jean Borotra, Brian Norton, Gerald Patterson, and George Lott. During his plebe year at West Point he sang in the choir, and taught Sunday school to officers' sons for three years. During his final year he was ranked third Cadet Captain and commanded the 1st Battalion of the Corps of Cadets. He graduated 17th in his class of 245 in June, 1925, and was commissioned a 2nd Lieutenant in the Army Corps of Engineers. After a posting at Fort Humphreys in Virginia, he resigned from the service in December, 1925, though later he would return for active duty during World War II, rising to the rank of full Colonel.

A great athlete, a fine scholar, and dashingly handsome to boot, Ed Garbisch was any girl's romantic dream, and shortly after meeting Bernice Chrysler, the two fell madly in love. Theirs would turn into one of the great romantic marriages, as Bernice and Edgar became inseparable lovers for half a century, parted in the end by death and death alone.

Their engagement was announced in late October of 1929, just at the moment the crash was falling down on everyone's head; indeed, both stories hit the papers at the same time. Della sailed over to Paris with her on the *Berengaria* to pick out a trousseau the following month. On New Year's eve, a special dinner dance was given in the couple's honor.

The wedding took place at St. Bartholemew's Church on Park Avenue on Saturday, January 4, 1930, at 4:30 P.M. The Reverend M. George Thompson of Greenwich, Connecticut, officiated, and Walter Chrysler gave the bride away. She wore a princess gown of heavy white satin, with a seed pearl embroidered motif in front and back from the neck to a low "v" below the waist. A long circular train hung from slightly below the waist. Her tulle veil was fastened with a coronet of twisted pearls, and she carried a sheaf of calla lilies. Thelma was her matron of honor, dressed in a white velvet gown, cut like Bernice's, with a shorter train and a small white velvet tricorn hat with small ostrich plumes. She carried American Beauty roses. Miss Elizabeth Stout, the maid of honor, and eight other attendants were dressed similarly to Thelma.

The groom's brother, Norbert S. Garbisch, was the best man, and among the eleven ushers were Byron Foy, Walter Chrysler, Jr., and Jack Chrysler.

A dinner reception was given at Sherry's, just across the street from Walter Chrysler's apartment at Park Avenue and 48th Street. From there, the couple was taken by motorcycle escort to the Barclay Hotel, on West 48th Street. The following day, they were given a luncheon at the Oyster Bar, and from there they entrained to Florida for their honeymoon, with a side trip to Nassau for shark fishing. Upon their return on February 15, they set up residence in their new home at 520 East 86th Street, by the East River.

Edgar Garbisch's business career began when he took a job as a laborer in the factory of the Postum Cereal Company at Battle Creek, Michigan, in 1926. He quickly became a salesman, sales manager, and insititution sales manager for the company's successor firm, Postum Company, Inc., in 1927 and 1928. Then he was appointed manager of sales and vice-president of Post Products Company, Inc., in 1929, becoming a manager of sales of its successor, General Foods, in 1930. From there it was a year on Wall Street at Winthrop Mitchell and Company, followed by a decade in the paper business, first as president of Cellulose Products Corporation until 1935, and then president, director, and chairman of the board of Tish, Inc. There were also forays into advertising at J. Sterling Getchell and Ruthrauff and Ryan, until the war began in 1942. He was, in short, peripatetic in his business career.

Frank Rhodes Senior says that Walter Chrysler did not have a high regard for him. Chrysler thought he was a lightweight, which was why he never was appointed to the Board of Directors of the Chrysler Corporation, which galled Garbisch to no end, especially inasmuch as Chrysler's other son-in-law, Byron Foy, was both a vice president and board member of the firm. But Foy was a successful auto man from way back, and that was a big difference.

One could tell that the servants at Pokety were not too crazy about him either. Some, like Emeline Jones, would purse their lips and say he was "very particular," and others would come right out and say he was a martinet who would blow up and fire people on a moment's notice if he didn't have his way. But he did share Bernice's love of art and helped her to select and acquire what turned out to be one of the country's greatest assemblages of American art. And he loved her dearly for fifty years, which is more important than anything else.

The couple had two children quickly after their marriage. Gwynne Chrysler Garbisch (now McDevitt) was born in New York City on May 28, 1931, and Edgar William Garbisch, Jr., was born there also on October 3, 1932. (By this time Thelma too had given birth to a second child, Cynthia, born on September 25, 1930.)

But there were other family issues on Walter Chrysler's mind just then. A bizarre story emerged in Topeka, Kansas, in late May of 1931. Richard A. Swallow, a member of the editorial staff of a local newspaper, Fred S. Clark of Manhattan, Kansas, and Ralph Ulrich, alias Ralph Chrysler, were arrested for trying to extort $40,000 from Walter Chrysler. Gordon Ross, Chrysler's personal representative, lodged a complaint against the three after Walter Chrysler received a letter from Ulrich in which their demands were outlined. County Attorney Glenn Logan said the letter threatened that unless the money was paid, a local news bureau would send a release to 409 newspapers dealing with an alleged family relationship between Ulrich and Henry Chrysler, Walter's father, dead some fifteen years. According to locals in Ellis, this had to do with rumors that Henry Chrysler had been a bigamist, with a second family in Salina. Despite the fact that Chrysler's quick action put an end to this caper, the rumor never completely died down, and it is still spoken of as possibly true in Kansas.

A sad note was the death of Walter's older brother, Ed, on March 3, 1932, at his home in La Jolla, California. Like Walt, he had served as a machinist in a variety of railroad shops in Kansas, later becoming a master mechanic on several roads. He followed his brother into the automobile business, where he eventually became the manager of a GM truck plant in Michigan. But ill health forced his retirement, and he lived out his days in an attractive bungalow overlooking the Pacific at La Jolla with his wife, the former May Easterbrook, and daughter Ruth, who married and became Ruth Strickler. Services were held at Glendale, where his sister Irene lived, and interment was at Forest Lawn. Ed Chrysler was 60 years old.

Later in the decade, Mr. Chrysler's beautiful niece, Edna Breymann, a talented soprano with a promising career, who took the stage name Breymann in honor of her grandmother's maiden name, died from cancer at a heartbreakingly young age. She was just at the point of establishing a notable career, and her mother Irene and the rest of the family were devastated by her death.

❧   ❧   ❧

The early '30s were dark times, and for most people and companies the struggle to survive was a grim one. On the 4th of July in 1930, it was announced that all salaried employees at Chrysler would take a 10 percent cut in pay. In a public statement, the company said, after noting the retrenchment necessitated by the Depression, "Labor has already contributed substantially, through reduced working hours, and it was felt to be only fair that salaried employees should also bear some of the burden. The reduction applies uniformly to all salaried employees from Mr. Chrysler down." On February 24, 1932, Chrysler wrote to Owen Skelton of a decision announced at the previous night's board meeting to cut all salaries up to $2,000 per annum by 5%, and all those above that level by 10%.

One of the most famous stories about Walter Chrysler in this regard came a few years later. After the Airflow turned into a big-time flop, he called a meeting of his vice presidents. This is how what went on is described in *The Road is Yours*:

" 'We'd better cut expenses,' Walter Chrysler said, 'or there won't be much of a company left. We ought to shoot for a 30% reduction. It may be hard, but we've got to do it.'

"The engineering department said that with business falling off, engineering work should be doubled to stimulate demand. The sales department said it should launch some special studies. Keller said that tools and machinery needed going over to 'get in shape for another round.'

"Chrysler listened patiently for a couple of hours, then turned to Hutchinson.

" 'Haven't we a book that lists salaries and personnel?'

" 'Yes', said Hutchinson. 'Everybody from president to office boy is in it.'

" 'Let's see it,' said Chrysler.

"When the book arrived, he rifled its pages and held it up. 'Well,' he said, 'that's about one third. Suppose we lay off everybody from here down?'

" 'Oh, Mr. Chrysler,' the chorus wailed, 'don't you think that's a hell of a way to cut expenses?'

" 'Sure!', he said. 'But you fellows haven't suggested anything else, and you will admit my way will work, won't you?'

" 'He gave us the night to think the thing over,' Keller related, 'and I will say that next day an excellent job was done.' " When something of importance needed to be done for the company, Walter Chrysler had no qualms about taking the initiative.

Nor did he try to evade responsibility for difficulties either. On the subject of the Airflow failure, Frank Rhodes, Sr. recalled Edgar Garbisch speaking of a meeting he was invited to attend in which Chrysler and his top executives hashed out the reasons for this financial debacle. After Walter Chrysler watched them all fall on their swords and make excuses, he turned to them and said, "It's nice of you to make excuses, but I'm the captain of this ship and it's my fault. But let's not sit around making excuses, let's forget it. Let's go on, and get back on track." Such a statement at such a moment is what leadership is all about.

But Airflow or no, the company was doing well. Led by the ever-increasing sales of that "Amazing Plymouth," both dollar- and unit-volume skyrocketed from 1933 on, and profits soared. The Plymouth increased its sales by 80,000 in 1935 to 382,000, with sales reaching the 500,000 level in 1936. But it wasn't Plymouth alone that was fueling the company's sales increases. Dodge sales jumped from 90,000 in 1934 to 178,000 in 1935 and 248,000 in 1936, after bottoming out at a dismal 28,000 in 1932. Though hampered by the failure of the Airflow, Chrysler production went from the 35,000 range in 1934 and 1935 to 60,000 in 1936 and over 107,000 in 1937. Even stepchild DeSoto, which saw its sales slip to just 14,000 in 1934 when it fully relied on the disastrous Airflow, tripled production to 43,000 by 1936, and practically doubled it again in 1937 to 82,000, after the conventionally styled Airstream model became its mainstay. As for profits, they almost quadrupled from $9,534,000 in 1934 to $34,975,000 in 1935, and then rose again to over $62,000,000 in 1936. That was more than double Chrysler's best year of the 1920s, 1928, when it made $30,991,000.

Milestones for the Chrysler Corporation were reached and recognized during this period too. The one millionth Plymouth car was made in 1934, just six years after its debut on the market. As Jim Benjaminson points out, "Plymouth had done in just six years what Chevrolet had taken nine years and Ford twelve years to do!" The actual car, a four-door sedan, came off the line on August 9, 1934, and was celebrated at a ceremony attended by K. T. Keller, B. E. Hutchinson, Dan Eddins, a Plymouth vice president who would succeed Hutchinson as president in 1935, Plymouth sales manager Harry G. Moock, and of course, a beaming Walter Chrysler, who now saw his master plan for the corporation vindicated in the low-priced Plymouth's soaring sales.

The car was sold to Mrs. Ethel Miller of Turlock, California, who had bought the very first Plymouth, a Deluxe Coupe, in 1928. When she heard that Plymouth number one million was to be built, she wired Walter Chrysler and asked if she could be allowed to buy it. He agreed, and offered to fly her out to pick it up, but she declined, preferring instead to stay in Turlock for the annual Melon Festival. The car was shipped to Chicago, where it was put on display at the Chrysler exhibit at the World's Fair. Mrs. Miller drove to Chicago in her '28, and when she arrived, her old car was exchanged for the new one and put on display in its stead. Mrs. Miller got a promise from Mr. Chrysler to reserve the two-millionth Plymouth for her also, a car whose construction was not projected until 1938. She got it two years early, when the two-millionth Plymouth, a 1937 sedan, rolled off the line in the fall of 1936, shortly after the 1937 model year introduction. This time Mrs. Miller drove to Detroit for the festivities. Nobody knows whether she asked for, or got, the three-millionth Plymouth.

There were more celebrations of this nature too. On December 15, 1936, Walter P. Chrysler attached an o.k. tag to the one-millionth car built by the corporation that year (a Plymouth of course), and the following year, seven weeks earlier in the calendar, he did the same thing. On the 1936 occasion he said, "20 years ago it took the production of 300 companies to make a million cars and trucks in one year." Now it was done by just one company, and not the largest one either.

Somewhat less publicized, but also significant, was the three-millionth Dodge, which came off the line in late March of 1935, just a little more than twenty years after the first one was produced. That car, like the very first, was driven off the line by Guy Ameel, who was still employed by Dodge. Sadly, the Dodge Brothers themselves were long gone, but what they built had survived and prospered, despite a number of years of caretaker management, mismanagement, and Depression. Though not as spectacular as the Plymouth achievement, the Dodge milestone was a very proud one indeed for the corporation, especially when one considers that all Walter Chrysler really wanted out of Dodge Brothers was its plant. For by this time Dodge was a major profit center of the Chrysler Corporation, a position it maintains to this day.

In 1933, Chrysler had outproduced the Ford Motor Company domestically for the first time, and after it repeated this accomplishment in 1936, it remained the number-two producer in the industry for the next fifteen years. To this day, this is an astounding achievement. The man who started too late had defied all odds and raised his company to the second position in the world in just about a decade. No wonder *Fortune* magazine called its December 30, 1933, issue, devoted completely to Chrysler, *A Century of Progress in Ten Years*. It seemed like nothing less.

He always gave full measure of credit to the men who worked with him to achieve his goal, but two of them have been somewhat undersung. The first was Owen Skelton, one of the Three Musketeers of Zeder-Skelton-Breer.

"He was a quiet, steady guy, without a lot of enthusiasm," as Fred Zeder recalled him. "Skelt's job was to take care of engineering problems after they showed up. He was terrific at what he did, and essential to the success of the team. But the public doesn't know him as well because there wasn't as much publicity put out on him. After all, you don't want to publicize, when something goes wrong, how wonderful he was to fix it."

The other was Ray Dietrich, one of the great designers of beautiful bodies for the grand marques of the Classic Era, who then went to Chrysler and provided designs for its mass produced cars that turned them into industry sales leaders until the late 1940s. His time at Chrysler was a stormy one, but that did not prevent him from giving the company exactly what it wanted and needed for its cars.

Dietrich's conection to Chrysler began with a letter of April 14, 1932, to Fred Zeder. It is very moving. In it he reminds Zeder that he wanted to discuss working at Chrysler some months before, when under contract to Graham. He didn't, because Ray Graham was so pleased with his work that he offered him a six-month renewal to begin work on a rear engine job, with the promise of a permanent position after that. "Well, you know what has happened," he says. "The banks refuse to extend any more money or time to the Graham Brothers, and all work must stop, leaving myself and many others out in the cold." He then begs Zeder for a job, pleading, "I am sure if you will give me a chance I will prove my worth a hundred fold in a short while, for the time is here where design and appearance govern your field against other manufacturers." He ends, poignantly, with "Please answer this right away. I am ready to start tomorrow for I am in need of something to do."

Zeder answered six days later that he was cutting his staff, but would get in touch with him "just as soon as anything presents itself." On July 14, 1932, Zeder wrote to John North Willys, commending Dietrich's talents to him in an attempt to help him get a job in those terrible times. "My only interest is simply a desire to give Mr. Dietrich what assistance I can to make a contact," he said. A reply from Mr. Willys's secretary four days later was not encouraging, as so many other designers, though lesser ones, had applied already.

But Ray Dietrich did go to work for Chrysler later in 1932, or perhaps more correctly, he went to work for *Walter* Chrysler. In an interview with Richard M. Langworth, Ray Dietrich recalled: "I first met Mr. Chrysler at the New York Automobile salon in 1926 or 1927. He came up to me and said, 'I've gone through your exhibit. Will you come with me and tell me about your work?' That's how we met. WPC, to my way of thinking, was a gentleman all the way through, though a hard task master. He knew what he was doing and how he was going to do it, but he had to fight with his engineers, as well as the public at times.

"Zeder and Skelton were always talking about 'service' for cars—how much 'service' you'd get from this and that. Chrysler used to say, 'It reminds me of when I was a kid and my father used to say, "take that cow down and get it serviced." They never let me in the barnyard, but one day I peeked in, and now when I hear the word 'service' I know somebody's getting just that.' "

In an article Dietrich wrote for the members of the Classic Car Club, Dietrich recalled his hiring by Walter Chrysler in late 1932. "The New York Athletic Club was still an excellent place to feel the pulse of business, and one day while lunching there alone, and wondering about my next move, a well modulated familiar voice asked over my shoulder, 'May I sit with you?' I turned to see Walter Chrysler, grim faced as were all businessmen just then. He talked with me awhile, and finally reached the point of suggesting my association with the Chrysler organization. He warned there would be little money at present, but assured me of sky high opportunities when the economic situation resumed more normal balance. My great respect and admiration for this industrial giant with the fine ethical business methods made the offer look desirable at any price. So it was not long after our talk that I joined the Chrysler Corporation."

A look at Walter Senior's personal business ethics can be found in a letter he wrote to Carl Breer concerning an aspect of the Air Temp situation on November 13, 1934. It concerned Chrysler's prospective employment of a Mr. French, a key employee of the Carrier air conditioning company. He writes, "I had a talk with Mr. J. I. Lyle today, who is the head of their business, and I asked him point blank about Mr. French and what would happen to their organization if they lost him. The poor old fellow was scared to death and said it would absolutely ruin the Carrier Company if they lost that man, and, naturally, I told him that we would not approach him in any way, shape or form. . . . . . .Mr. Lyle is a very honorable fellow and if Mr. French means so much to their organization, which I am sure he does, I think it would be wrong for us to approach him, and we will have to look elsewhere." No wonder he was so highly respected in the business community.

To Langworth Dietrich said: "There was a dynamite in WP's step, his walk, his smile and his piercing blue eyes. He never doubted what you would say to him, but he was always trying to get more out of you. The best times I remember were when he would spend mornings in the little design studio, discussing our clay models. It was always a matter of decoration: too much to put on, too little to take off. He would sit in my office and talk, with nobody around to second guess him, and he'd talk about design, I think just to get away from the pressures of the engineering people. About half past eleven he'd say, 'How about having a frankfurter and a bottle of beer?' and we'd go out for lunch. He was that kind of man."

Early on, Dietrich was put in charge of all exterior design departments, clay modeling, surface development, and truck design. Oliver Clark moved up the corporate ladder to become executive body engineer, and Dietrich was now chief stylist, with a staff of four working on exteriors and four working on interiors (Fred Selje was in charge of interior styling). It sounded impressive, but the reality was that he had to work through Charles G. Walker's clay modeling studio to get to Clark and finally management. Various executives also felt free to come into the design studio and change things on a whim, without any consulatation with Dietrich, which made matters even more frustrating. Sometimes too, when Mr. Chrysler wanted things speeded up, he had to produce prototypes and die models directly from clay models, without the usual drafts. When he became concerned about the lack of skilled draftsmen in an ever-expanding drafting department, he got to organize a four-year course in body design at the Chrysler Institute of Engineering, training hundreds of men, which became one of the most satisfying experiences of his life.

Naturally, since Dietrich was a personal hire of Walter Chrysler's, rather than a corporate one, there was trouble with other higher ups at Chrysler, particularly, and ironically, with Fred Zeder. Dietrich felt Zeder resented his relationship with Walter Chrysler, and Dietrich made no bones about his contempt for the Airflow body design, which was engineer driven and kept out of his hands. This incensed Zeder, who, according to his son, felt he had "a great sense of design, symmetry and beauty."

In any case Walter Chrysler had made Dietrich responsible for all body design at Chrysler, and despite the problems and restrictions under which he worked, he did his job. A crash program in body styling in 1934 brought the Airstreams, which did very well, to market for the 1935 model year. At the same time he modified the radical Airflows to resemble these Airstreams as best he could, to try to take the curse off them.

Under Dietrich, Chrysler Corporation body styles of the mid- to late '30s seemed almost interchangeable among the various lines. Slab sided with curvy fenders, they were stodgy, utterly conventional, and quite successful in the marketplace. Only with a new body shell in 1939 did things start to look up, as the cars got vee'd windshields, tapered roof and trunk lines, and pointed ship's prow front ends topped by vertical stainless steel moldings. Headlights were moved farther out and neatly faired into the fenders, and tail lights were flush mounted into the crease lines of the rear fenders. Even the Plymouth, which made do with its 1937 body shell, was cleverly restyled into a handsome vehicle that conformed to the corporation's new body image.

But it was with the designs for 1940 that Dietrich set the tone for the Chrysler bodies that would be used until 1949. Rounder and more aero-dynamic, they had shorter rear decks fully integrated with the rear fenders and, on the sides, running boards had disappeared on many models. The front ends were far more integrated, with fenders, headlights, and hoods fully unified in the modern manner for the first time. Ostensibly, these cars were the work of head designer Robert Cadwallader, because Dietrich had been fired before they came out. In reality though, the company had to bring him back to complete the work. It should be noted, however, that Carl Breer said in his memoirs that a heated argument among himself, Fred Zeder, and Oliver Clark over the clay model of the 1940 Dodge led to the creation of the raised horizon line of the front fenders on the 1940 models, which in turn led to the compound curves of the front and rear ends of these cars.

Dietrich's special status with Walter Chrysler meant that he was never fully accepted into the company, a situation that came to a head in the spring of 1938. One Saturday morning, as Dietrich sat in his office scheduling work for his men for the coming week, Walter Chrysler walked in and asked if there was anything he was supposed to see. "I told him I'd show him what he *wasn't* supposed to see," said Dietrich. However, all the drawings and one-third scale models were locked up in drawers, and Dietrich had no keys, as they were kept by Fred Zeder. Chrysler asked for a hammer and broke the locks. "We went through tons of models," and he was pleased with the designs. However, he was furious that he wasn't supposed to see them. When Zeder and some other officials came in later, he castigated them for not being there earlier. This certainly did not make blood any better between Zeder and Dietrich.

But there was another issue between the two men that ultimately led to the parting of the ways between Dietrich and the Chrysler Corporation. Even in that 1932 letter Dietrich alluded to the fact that Zeder may have heard of some of his behavioral problems. Quite simply, he drank during business hours, something which was anathema to Fred Zeder. Even Dietrich admitted it. "In those days I liked a bottle of beer or a highball with my lunch, and one day, after lunch, Zeder called me into his office. He accused me of being drunk. The next day, in front of Mr. Chrysler, I walked up to him, saluted and said, 'Sir, First mate reporting sober.' 'He really gave it to you that time, didn't he Fred?' said Chrysler."

The end came over a similar incident, not long after the episode of Walter Chrysler's viewing the 'secret' modeling studies. Fred Zeder, Jr., relates: "Dad told me Dietrich used to go out and have two or three martinis at lunch, and one thing he couldn't stand was being drunk on the job; you could drink martinis at lunch, as long as you didn't get drunk. One day Dietrich had his two or three martinis at lunch, came into dad's office and got quite vocal about something. Dad fired him on the spot. He told him to clear out his desk and get the hell out of there, because he didn't want somebody drinking on the job." Walter Chrysler had become incapacitated just two weeks after the styling incident (on that day, Dietrich had remarked, "You don't look well, Mr. Chrysler. Why don't you take it easy?") As soon as he was no longer in the picture, Dietrich was gone. Of Zeder and the other powers that be at Chrysler (though notably not K. T. Keller), Dietrich said simply, "They were in and I was out."

❧   ❧   ❧

Research continued apace at the corporation, and continued to yield profitable results. A discontent with the cooling system in the Chrysler Building led Walter Chrysler, Jr. to become interested in air conditioning, both for industry and the home. After some two years of research, Chrysler's Airtemp models were made available to the public in the summer of 1934. Walter P. Chrysler, Jr. was the head of this division, and first showed his models to the public at the Chrysler building on July 16,1934. By July 28th, in a letter to Hutchinson, he says he has been overwhelmed by the public response. "At the time of writing this letter we have had over 400 bonafide inquiries for distributorship throughout the country, where previously we very frankly felt we would be very fortunate if we could get fifty people throughout the country to take on the distribution of these products at the end of a year's period. There is no question in my mind or in Mr. Jefferson's mind or in Dad's mind that this air conditioning is liable to go far beyond anything we had any conception of."

Unfortunately, at the beginning there were considerble difficulties with the models, particularly the self contained units, and there was some question as to whether they could be brought through into production on schedule. In fact, though many problems ensued, they were ironed out and Airtemp became an important profit center at Chrysler.

As for Walter Chrysler, Jr., his "founding" of the air conditioning division seems to have been more nominal than anything else; it was really his father's project. He ran it for a while, but only as a proxy for others in the corporation, most especially his father. This may have been a way of placating the old man, whom he had rather publicly embarrassed on the subject of his life's ambitions two years before.

The Chrysler Building may have been built as an occupation for him, and he may well have started out there cleaning rooms in the basement, but that couldn't have lasted long, because the building opened in May of 1930, and he was back in school at summer's end. He was always on the building's board until the family sold it in 1953, but nobody seems to have any great recollection of him having much to do with the running of it, especially in later years. He would make his mark in the world, but it was to be outside the realms of business and real estate.

In June of 1931, after completing his junior year at Dartmouth at the age of 23, young Walter announced the founding of his own publishing company, Cheshire House, which was intended to publish only recognized classics on special paper with strikingly original illustrations. (Previously, while at Dartmouth, he and a senior named Nelson Rockefeller started a magazine called *Five Arts*.) These books were to be sold by subscription on a monthly basis, at the cost of $10 each, an extraordinary sum in those days. He told the *Times* he was so interested in it that he might not return to school to get his degree. The offices of Cheshire House were on the fifty-seventh floor of the Chrysler Building, and Walter Senior served on the board. Walter Junior had no compunction about contacting his father's business associates to sell them the $120 annual subscriptions that were pretty hard to unload in that dark Depression time.

The following year Walter Junior opened an art gallery, also called Cheshire, on the ground floor of the Chrysler Building. It was devoted to modern art, and its first exhibit featured the work of Spanish artist Alejandro de Canedo, a member of the "international group," which was an outgrowth of the pre-Raphaelites, and claimed as adherents the Dutchmen Konijnenburg and Toroop, the Belgian Ensor, and Austria's Gustav Klimt.

By November of 1932, he announced that his publishing business, which had 1,200 subscribers, including a post office clerk in Vermont with an income of $60 a month, was breaking even. This was despite a loss of $38,000 on a translation of Dante's *Inferno* by Henry Francis Cary, which had seven illustrations by William Blake. He further said he was entering the trade publishing field, with a novel called *Anonymous Footsteps* by John M. O'Connor, a friend from Dartmouth.

But he and his father had a big falling out over one of the things he intended to publish. Walter had hired a detective and a novelist to work on a book about a sensational rape and murder case in Hawaii that was then making big headlines. The advance sale on the book was mounting on prepublication rumors, and Walter made a movie deal in Hollywood on it. But when his father heard about it, he blew up. "If it's the last thing I do in my life," he told his son, "I'm going to see to it that this book is not published." And so he did. Walter Junior couldn't buck him. After all, this was his father, a member of his board, and one of the most powerful men in the country. Forty-five years later, his son remembered, "I was never so hurt in all my life. I couldn't compete with that kind of power." But imagine how Walter Senior felt when he saw his namesake son quoted in the *New York Times* saying that he believed he was much better fitted for publishing "than say, the automobile business."

No matter what he said, however, by the next year his father had him in his enterprises, working at Airtemp.

◆ ◆ ◆

On June 13, 1934, Walter Chrysler, Sr. was elected a director of the New York Central Railroad, a position for which he was immensely qualified, considering his extensive railroad background. To accept this position, he resigned his directorships of the Erie and Ann Arbor roads, and also left the board of the Chicago, Milwaukee, St. Paul, and Pacific. The following May 22, he was elected to the board. Lucky New York Central, for when Carl Breer, noticing the difference between a ride on the smooth sailing DC 3 airplane and the terribly-bumpy-by-comparison Santa Fe Super Chief, suggested to Walter Chrysler that the center of percussion research done on the Airflow might bear fruit in the passenger railroad business, his boss was all ears.

He had proved his point by writing two letters to Mr. Chrysler, one on the plane and one on the Super Chief. The difference was immediately apparent. Quick as a flash, he put Breer in touch with Paul Kieffer, the engineer in charge of New York Central's Rolling Stock Division. The two men put together a laboratory in which they were to spend millions over the next several years, demonstrating the play of many forces that came to bear on the riding quality of standard railroad equipment of the time. Eventually they came up with patents that greatly increased the comfort of railroad passengers and made a fortune for both the Chrysler Corporation and the New York Central Railroad.

Within the corporation too important new things were being developed in the research labs. Such items as Superfinish, a new process which gave ultra smooth surfaces to such items as bearings and springs, and Fluid Drive, a fluid coupling which, when joined to a semi-clutchless transmission provided the basis for a sturdy semi-automatic transmission that would serve the company for fifteen years, made their debut in the mid- to late 1930s. Both were the result of years of painstaking research, as corporate records show. Any competitor's product was purchased, torn down, and examined. Any inventor's gadget that seemed promising was tested and given a fair shake. If it was deemed worthwhile, it was bought and its lessons utilized. Zeder, Skelton, and Breer continued at the top of their game, with the enthusiastic interest, and supervision, of Walter Chrysler. Voluminous intra-company correspondence shows that he was on top of everything. If it was promising, he followed it up; if it was good, he praised it; if something was wrong, he wanted to know why. Pronto.

❖   ❖   ❖

The success of the corporation was perhaps best illustrated by its exhibit at the Century of Progress World's Fair in Chicago in 1933 and 1934. Six prominent architects and architectural firms were invited to submit designs for the Chrysler Corporation's Fair Building in March of 1932, with the winner, Holabird & Root, announced on April 13th of that year.

The $500,000 building was an Art Moderne affair, colored white with black and yellow trim. It featured four 125-foot pylons, laid out so as to form a Greek cross. The interior of these pylons was painted lavender, with the east and west ones featuring continuous diagonal flutes for their entire widths. At night they were illuminated by more than 1 million candle power of high intensity lights, forming a stunning picture indeed. Leading up to the entrance of the building was a 325-foot reflecting pool, bordered by hedges, shrubs, flowers, and decorative metal trees. The seven acres of grounds on which the building was situated featured a quarter-mile track with ramps, inclines, and curves to simulate ordinary driving conditions. Barney Oldfield and his "Hell Drivers" performed there six times daily, and tens of thousands of visitors had the opportunity to ride the track in the Plymouth, Dodge, DeSoto, or Chrysler of their choice. Airflow cars were rolled over several times a day to show the strength of their all-steel bodies, and braking demonstrations on slick pavements were also done.

A drop forge hammer turned out Plymouth steering knuckles at the rate of one a minute, and inside the building there were 68,000 square feet of exhibition space. Special niches, designed by Count Alexis de Sakhnoffsky, were devoted to displays on the Airflow car, Floating Power, Hydraulic Brakes, and the All-Steel Body. Other items of interest were a miniature steel plant producing alloy steel and a Chrysler battery frozen in a cake of ice that was connected to a starting motor which drove a reduction gear that hoisted a Plymouth sedan four feet in three minutes. A 280-seat motion picture theater offered continuous free shows of shorts like "World's Fair" and "Fashion By Function" to fairgoers.

In addition to the basic monies, some $250,000 was spent to freshen up the exhibit between 1933 and 1934. It was money well spent, for millions of people saw the company's displays in the two years they were shown, and gave the firm invaluable feedback on its products during that time.

"Time is the greatest distance between two places," says Tennessee Williams in *The Glass Menagerie*. At the Columbian Exhibition World's Fair of 1893, Walter Chrysler was just another ticketholder in the crowd, gawking at the marvels on display. Forty years later, he was the proprietor of the biggest exhibit of all at the Century of Progress World's Fair in Chicago. A world away, in time and life.

In the spring of 1935, flush with prosperity and its future continually brightening, the Chrysler Corporation announced that on May 1, 1935, it would retire the remainder of the six-percent gold bonds it had sold in 1928 to acquire Dodge Brothers, a sum amounting to $30,150,500. This was a full five years early. The retirement was to be accomplished by assuming $25 million in notes, payable at the rate of $5 million a year over five years. The balance, plus a premium, was to be paid directly from corporate funds. "The new arrangements will effect a savings of approximately $1,200,000 a year, after the first year, which is the equivalent of 28 cents a share on the common stock outstanding," said Walter Chrysler, "providing for an orderly liquidation of a debt which would have had to be met in full at the maturity of the debentures in 1940. This annual retirement amounts to substantially less than half of the corporation's annual amortization and depreciation charges in recent years, and thus does not constitute any material drain upon the corporation's cash resources." By September 20th of that year, Chrysler paid off another $5 million of the notes, saving the company an additional $140,000 per year in interest.

❖   ❖   ❖

By 1935 the Depression was over. With his factories humming, a crackerjack staff in place, and profits and sales piling up after recovering from the Airflow debacle, Walter Chrysler saw at last the opportunity to do something he had been trying to do since 1919: retire. Well, not completely. But he resigned the presidency of the Chrysler Corporation on July 22, 1935, retaining his position as chairman of the board and chief executive officer. He announced that K. T. Keller would become the corporation's new president. Chrysler had been grooming him for this position since he joined the company in 1926, and finally felt the moment for him to take over the reins had arrived. In his announcement, Chrysler said of Keller, "As vice president and general manager of Chrysler Corporation and president of the Dodge division, K. T. Keller has been responsible for the production of all Chrysler Motors lines, from the purchase of raw materials to the finished automobile. His exceptional manufacturing ability, his thorough knowledge of men, materials and machines, his sense of organization and his compehensive understanding of the operations of the automobile business are widely recognized not only in our company but throughout the industry."

At the same time as he elevated Keller, he raised several other staff members to new positions. B. E. Hutchinson became chairman of the finance committee, H. A. Davies was made treasurer, and Fred Zeder was named vice chairman of the board. Chrysler continued, "Under these three men and their associates in the management group, notably J. E. Fields, head of the Chrysler division, Byron C. Foy, head of DeSoto, W. Ledyard Mitchell, in charge of exports, and A. C. Downey, Dodge trucks, this business has assumed its progressive character. They have designed and built our cars and trucks, financed our operations and marketed our products." He ended his statement reassuringly: "I shall, of course, continue as the directing head of the business."

So now it was done, and as he had promised for many years, he stepped aside and let his hand-picked, tried and tested associates take over the running of his company. Perhaps the Chrysler Corporation was not his company in quite the same sense that Ford was Henry Ford's, but in the Emersonian sense that any corporation is but the elongated shadow of a single man, it surely was his. From the beginning, he organized and directed it in the fullest meaning of these words. Even now, he was turning it over precisely as he wished to do, to those men who he felt had earned the right to run it. At sixty years of age Walter Chrysler believed he had assembled the right team of men to whom he could entrust his extraordinary industrial legacy. Of course, he would still be there for them as much as they needed him to be, as he had promised, but in his own mind he was sure that would be but rarely. For the first time in over forty years, he could truly think of himself as free, as only someone finally separated from a lifetime of heavy diurnal reponsibilities could be.

Over the next few years he brought new young blood to the board of the Chrysler Corporation. In December of 1936 Juan T. Trippe, the thirty-six-year-old founder of Pan American Airways, joined the board, as did Nicholas Kelley, the twenty-eight-year-old Walter P. Chrysler, Jr. and thirty-year-old James Cox Brady, Jr. the following year. Moreover, the board's mature strength was reinforced by the election of Owen Skelton and Carl Breer, also in 1937.

In a certain sense it was fitting that Chrysler should be pulling back at this time, as most of the pioneer figures in the auto industry were either dead or soon would be, or they were retiring from active participation in their businesses. The Dodge Brothers, Walter E. Flanders, Elwood G. Haynes, and the Studebaker Brothers were long gone, and Henry M. Leland, Ray A. Graham, Albert R. Erskine, Hugh Chalmers, Jonathan Dixon Maxwell, David Dunbar Buick, James Ward Packard, Alexander Winton, and Harry C. Stutz had all given up the ghost in the last few years. The years 1935 and 1936 would see the deaths of John North Willys, Howard D. Chapin, and André Citroën. William C. Durant was out of the auto business by 1933, as was Errett Lobban Cord by 1937. Ransom E. Olds retired from Reo in 1936, leaving Henry Ford and Charles Nash the only pioneers besides Chrysler still running their businesses.

Some of these people, such as Buick and Charles E. Duryea (who was to die in 1939), fell into penury; Graham and Erskine, overburdened by the Depression, committed suicide; Willys and Chapin died from illnesses exacerbated by worry and overwork. Others, including Winton and Flanders, made out quite well. Cord went on to make a vast fortune in California real estate. Very few did as well as Walter Chrysler in the automobile business, however, and only Henry Ford and the Dodges did better.

In this list a very special mention must be made, as always, of William C. Durant. Henry Ford may have made more out of the automobile business than anyone else, but no one flew higher than Durant. Before his problems at GM in 1920, he was worth an estimated $100 million (some said $120 million). After recovering and starting Durant Motors, he became one of Wall Street's top plungers in the 1920s.

But when things broke in the autumn of 1929, they broke with a vengeance, and Durant simply did not have the psychological makeup to save himself. His biographer Bernard A. Weisberger shrewdly puts it: "In 1929 he could have closed out his market activities and retired comfortably, as he might have done in 1921 with what was left to him. But that was an inconceivable choice. William Durant believed, like Gatsby, like an entire American generation, in the orgiastic future, the green light, the morning toward which one ran with arms ever outstretched in expectation. To live only for the existing moment was, for him, to confront vacancy. . . . .It threatened not only his paper wealth but his illusions, indispensable to the survival of a positive thinker and a gambler."

Foreseeing a crisis, he had actually gotten out of the market in the summer of 1929, but ever the optimist, he plunged back in after the crash, buying heavily on margin in the belief that stocks were then at bargain levels. Durant kept investing throughout 1930, but as the unthinkable happened, and his stocks kept sinking in value, his brokers were gradually selling him out. Increasingly desperate, he borrowed 187,000 shares of GM from his devoted wife Catherine, who was never to see them again. By the end of 1932, his prestigious Wall Street law firm, Satterlee and Canfield, gobbled up all of his $116,431 tax refund due on several years from the 1920s, saying he owed them $300,000 for their work, due to the fact that they had actually saved him $1.75 million in interest and penalties. When he asked the firm to give him $31,000 cash and a $109,000 note in return for a larger fee, Herbert L. Satterlee himself replied, "I trust that upon further reflection you will realize that our firm has made all the concession that can reasonably be asked of it."

On November 24, 1933, the Interurban Realty Company of Newark placed a $10,000 bid in a foreclosure proceeding on the $15 million Willys plant in Elizabeth, New Jersey, that Durant had bought at auction just 11 years before; in other words, things had become inestimably bleak. In that year, he had a gross income of $9,478, which dropped to less than half that in 1935. On February 8,1936, when he walked into Federal District court in New York to declare bankruptcy, he listed $914,000 in debts, mostly consisting of judgements granted to landlords and brokers. He listed as assets the $250 worth of clothes he had on his back. Everything else was in his wife's name, and that too was disappearing fast. By September of 1938, Raymere, his mansion in Deal, New Jersey, and the entirety of its lavish contents, were auctioned off for $111,778, all of which went to creditors; In 1937, the furnishings alone had been appraised at over $300,000.

But he kept on, leasing an old Durant showroom in Asbury Park, New Jersey, in September, 1936, to various concessionaires who opened a food market and lunchroom. As Weisberger relates, "On the eve of the grand opening, Durant had turned up to provide instructions to the employees on how to keep the surroundings spotless, as he always desired them. A newspaper photographer was present, and had an inspiration. Would Mr. Durant pose while demonstrating the best way to wash a dish? Mr. Durant was pleased to oblige, and readers the next day were presented with the picture of a man who had once been worth fifty to one hundred million dollars, a cloth in one hand, a saucer in the other, apparently reduced to the sub basement of the employment market.

"Follow up stories soon dispelled the idea that Durant was a kitchen worker, but replaced it with the equally inaccurate conception that he was comfortably situated and enjoyed an adequate income from properties that had escaped the net of bankruptcy proceedings, or been restored to him after his discharge from them." It wasn't so then, nor was it to be for the rest of his life. His income was about $500 a month, but his expenses were never less than $1,700. And then there were his "business projects." There were rental houses in Deal, an attempt to sell grain futures through a seat on the Chcago Board of Trade, a spark plug venture and a bowling alley and luncheonette in Flint, and finally a cinnabar mine in Goldfield, Nevada. All lost money.

How did he pay for all this? His personal expenses were taken care of partly by his wife, who sold all she had to keep him afloat, and partly by his daughter Margery and his grandchildren, who helped out as time went on. But the big money came from some of the great associates of former days. Charles Stewart Mott lent him $30,000 in 1936, and he borrowed $20,000 from Alfred P. Sloan shortly thereafter; these loans were a euphemism, as neither man expected to be paid back. When he needed steady nursing care by the spring of 1944, Sloan solicited Mott, Sam McLaughlin, and John Thomas Smith to provide $2,500 a quarter on a rotating basis to "change the closing years of Mr. Durant's life from onc of anxiety to one of reasonable comfort." He shared the sentiments of McLaughlin, who wrote to Smith, "I am sure that Alfred, Stewart, you and I will never regret having done this little thing for our dearly beloved old friend."

Mr. Mott himself, in an interview with Richard Scharchberg in 1972, recalled that he, Sloan, Walter Chrysler, Charlie Nash, and Dr. Edwin Campbell, Durant's son-in-law, clubbed together to give Durant three to five thousand a year to keep him going in the late thirties. "We had a debt of gratitude and honor to pay him for what he had done," he said. "Without Durant, none of us would be here today."

There seems to be evidence that Chrysler may well have done more than anyone else. Durant's faithful longtime secretary, Aristo Scrobogna, said that among other things, Chrysler gave Durant $50,000 to explore the potential of discovering oil in Oklahoma and several other western states; this scheme too didn't work out, but Chrysler knew how important it was for him to have a project with "potential." Durant once described Chrysler as "the finest character and the greatest all around man whom I have ever known." The original draft of Durant's still-unpublished memoirs was dedicated to "Walter Chrysler, The Best Friend I Ever Had, who came to my assistance at the time of my real need, and to whom I am at this time greatly indebted." Chrysler declined the honor of this dedication for his own reasons, but a letter to Durant from S. E. Neiller on January 8,1940, contained the following: "Mr. Morrison, Mr. Chrysler's secretary, phoned last week and asked me to tell you that he had read the booklet you sent [autobiography] to Mr. C., and he cried."

❧   ❧   ❧

We have seen before how much money Walter Chrysler had earned in the car business through the Buick, Willys, and Maxwell days, but what kind of money had he been making running the Chrysler Corporation? In his own hand, he wrote of a salary of $180,000 per annum, plus those all important stock options, for running Maxwell in 1922 and 1923. In 1924 he received a salary of $100,000, plus a bonus of $139,633. Beyond that, the *Federal Trade Commission Report on the Motor Vehicle Industry*, submitted to Congress on June 5, 1939, is enlightening. Under the rubric "Walter P. Chrysler employment contract" we learn that his contract with the Chrysler Corporation, entered into when it acquired the assets of the Maxwell Corporation, extended to May 31, 1927.

After this time a new agreement took effect, "providing that he was to have general charge and control of all the business and affairs of the corporation, subject only to the supervision of the board of directors, and to perform one or more of the offices of chairman of the board, president, director, member of the executive committee, member of the finance committee, etc." The new agreement, effective June 1, 1927, paid him $8,033.33 a month, expenses for maintaining an office and staff in New York City, and through December 31, 1927, "5% of the net profits of the corporation, including all its subsidiary and controlled companies after deduction of interest, taxes, depreciation, and an amount sufficient to pay $8 per share on the preferred stock of the corporation from time to time outstanding, not exceeding 200,000 shares thereof."

Were he to give notice to the corporation not less than 30 days before January 1, 1928, he could replace the previously outlined terms for the period after December 31, 1927. The new terms would pay him $12,500 a month for the balance of the contract, plus New York office and staff, and 10% of the profits of the corporation, subject to the above-outlined conditions, plus "an amount sufficient to pay $3 per share on the common stock of the corporation from time to time outstanding, not exceeding 2,700,000 thereof." Walter Chrysler gave such notice on November 29, 1927, and the new terms remained in effect until October 1, 1933.

On that date, a new contract was executed, paying him a salary of $16,666.66 per month, subject to general salary reductions by the corporation, which he had previously shared with everyone else on a voluntary basis during the worst of the Depression, and in addition, his office and staff expenses in New York. This new contract was to remain in effect until either party gave due notice of termination, or until the death of Mr. Chrysler.

Pursuant to the profit division features of the previous contract, the company accrued the following amounts to be paid to Mr. Chrysler:

1927..	$ 907,211
1928	$2,466,941
1929	$1,550,000
1933..	$ 370,000
Total..................................	$5,294,152

Of course, no profit sharing was paid out for the years 1930, 1931, and 1932, due to the fact that the company was either losing money or barely scraping by during that time. The total profit of the Chrysler Corporation during that period was in the neighborhood of $88 million, so Walter Chrysler, in addition to his salary and expenses, was paid about 6 percent of what his leadership had earned.

Outside of the corporation, he made a lot of money too. He sat on the boards of various companies, in addition to the New York Central and other railroads previously mentioned. They changed from time to time, but mainly they were: Chase Securities Corporation (through July 1, 1931); General Foods Corporation; Madison Square Garden Corporation; Brady Security and Realty Corporation; Commercial Credit Company; Thompson-Starrett Company; the Automobile Manufacturers Association; and, of course, the W. P. Chrysler Building Corporation.

The Commercial Credit association was to become painful, for the Chrysler Corporation had formed a special relationship with it in 1934 to finance its automobiles, buying stock in Commercial Credit and cutting out other companies from taking notes on its cars. Ford and GM were doing the same thing, and after a protracted government investigation, anti-trust charges were brought against all of them, which resulted in a 1938 consent decree with Ford and Chrysler preventing them from forcing their customers to use their finance companies. GM went to trial on this issue in 1939 and basically lost, though it didn't agree to signing a consent decree with the government until 1952.

An article about another of Mr. Chrysler's directorships appeared at a most inopportune and embarrassing moment on February 13, 1937, right before his own workers went on a company-wide strike over wages, general working conditions and union representation. A *New York Times* article stated that counsel for the Securities and Exchange Commission had found that Mr. Chrysler had received $1,000 for each hour he had attended directors' meetings of the United States and Foreign Securities Corporation, because he only attended one of the 28 meetings held since he joined the board. Directors were paid $5,000 per annum, an amount characterized as "not much for the services they render" by Clarence Dillon, who sponsored and was a director of the investment trust. Asked about Chrysler, he laughingly replied, "That's fair compensation—even for Chrysler." He justified the amounts paid to the directors by citing the profits their good management had made, both for this trust, begun by Dillon, Read, in 1924, and another, the United States and International Securities Trust, which the firm had founded in 1928. "By making comparisons with the leading stock averages, Mr. Dillon asserted that the performance of the two trusts had been from 357 percent to 262 percent better than the performance of the averages cited," the article said. True though this may have been, it didn't make Mr. Chrysler look good when his workers were clamoring for 75 cents an hour.

He continued to make money throughout the twenties and thirties by churning around in the stock market. Arnold Bernhard, the founder of Value Line Investment Survey, recalled that when he worked as a clerk for Jesse Livermore, the infamous "King of the Bears," in 1928, Walter Chrysler once handed Livermore $1 million to invest. "After the money had doubled in three weeks, Mr. Chrysler took his money and departed, remarking that the stock market was too speculative for his tastes," Bernhard said. In actuality, it was anything but, as evidence of his participation in various stock market pools indicated. In fact he acknowledged hitting heavy seas in the market in late 1929 along with everyone else, though he said his wife did much better, bailing out ahead of time. However, even at his most adventurous, Walter Chrysler was something of a piker compared to true plungers like Billy Durant.

Chrysler's insider stock market status, as we have noted, can certainly be seen by the names he was involved with in his trading. The Bradys, Durant, Sloan, Raskob, Bache, and many others were top players, and they were all people with whom he had been intimately involved in his auto business dealings over many years. He was as "in with the in crowd" as you could get. At one point, in 1932, it got him into a certain amount of hot water.

In the summer of 1928, after Chrysler acquired Dodge Brothers, its stock became a Wall Street darling, appreciating almost 20 percent in a short period of time. The following year, he got involved in forming a stock pool trading in Chrysler stock with an old crony of the Bradys, William F. Kenny. Bill Kenny, the son of a Brooklyn fireman, was a big burly Irishman who was able to do a lot of dirty hands work for the Bradys in their New York construction projects, due to his roughneck pals and political contacts. Before long he was doing very well, and eventually he was invited into the Bradys's financial pools, where he soon became vastly wealthy. It was said that he spent $50 million of his own money in an attempt to elect Al Smith President of the United States in 1928; of course, that figure was wildly inflated, but whatever the true amount, he surely spent a great deal.

Chrysler was in these same pools, and in October, 1929, he conferred with Jules Bache and Waddill Catchings of Goldman, Sachs about attracting other subscribers into a pool formed to trade common stock of the Chrysler Corporation. On October 16th, the Bache and E. F. Hutton brokerage firms were appointed managers of the syndicate, and they later claimed that Kenny agreed orally to take a ten percent share in it on that same date. Between then and July 16,1930, when the syndicate was terminated, some $1,596,113 was lost by 22 investors, and on January 25, 1932, Hutton and Bache sued Kenny for $159,611, which represented the 10 percent they said he was liable for. Kenny's defense in May was that the agreement was illegal insofar as it required the brokers to conduct fictitious transactions constituting so-called "wash sales," forbidden by New York State law, and also contrary to public policy and unenforceable.

The case dragged out for some time, and though Walter Chrysler was not implicated in any wrongdoing, his manipulation of his own stock at the time of the crash did not look good. This was even more so since his intimations of trouble in early 1929 had caused him to cancel a lot of supply orders, leading to disappointed salesmen spreading adverse rumors about the financial health of the company, making it vulnerable to bear operators on Wall Street. Six years later, the SEC investigated rumors that someone, possibly involved with E. F. Hutton, was trying to create a technical corner in Chrysler common stock. It made more than one Wall Streeter wonder what Walter Chrysler was up to behind the scenes, and led to persistent rumors that culminated in John L. Lewis asking him point blank if he was using the strike of 1937 as an opportunity to make money by temporarily depressing the price of his company's stock. Of course he loudly demurred, and Lewis believed him.

To really understand how well Walter Chrysler did however, you have to look beyond the man himself to his immediate family. In the papers of Nicholas Kelley at the New York Public Library, there is a printed sheet under a phrase in Mr. Kelley's handwriting which says, "From Mr. Davis, August 21, 1936." The top states the amount of (presumedly) Chrysler Corporation stock each of Walter Chrysler's four children owned outright.

Each had about $164,000 in stock bought at $100 a share, $168,920 bought at $103 a share, and $155,800 bought at $95 a share. Beneath that was a list of shares "Owned by W. P. Chrysler, D. R. McLain and B. C. Foy, Trustees for" Della and the four children. At $100, Della owned $241,000 worth, Jack $127,000, Walter Junior, $126,500, Thelma $125,500, and Bernice $125,000. At $103, it was Della, $248,230, and the children, between $128,750 and $130,810. At $95, Della had $228,950, and the children between $118,750 and $120,650. The grand total was $4,173,490. Since none of the women worked, and neither of the boys had made much in their two to four years of gainful employment, the accumulation of this stock had to be the result of Walter Chrysler's manipulations. This is even more impressive when you realize that when he set up trusts for his family in 1919 and 1920 with the money he made at GM, he stipulated that none of it could ever be used as an investment in his own enterprises. Then too, one cannot forget the Chrysler Building, which he built and ran for his children. Having cost some $15 million to build, it eventually netted them $18 million when they sold it in 1953. (Interestingly, some of the family members today say they have never received a satisfactory explanation of what happened to the money after the building's sale. There seem to be no reliable records, and it appears that at least some of the money may have mysteriously vanished.)

Oddly, Joan French notes that she "never remembered packaged gifts at my grandfather's at Christmas—the four children would line up in his apartment and he would pass out envelopes with checks. By all accounts however, he was a very generous man." Indeed he was. He must simply have realized that by his children's stage of life nothing says it like cash.

Like some 200 other executives, Walter Chrysler gave away a considerable amount of money before the end of 1935, to avoid the heavy new inheritance and gift taxes Roosevelt proposed levying on June 28th of that year. In fact, his gift of some 40,000 shares of Chrysler stock, worth some $3.8 million, was second only to John D. Rockefeller, Jr.'s gift of 2,100,000 shares of Socony Vacuum, worth some $27,300,000. The stringent new regulations took effect on January 1, 1936. In May of 1937 he found himself petitioning the Board of Tax Appeals for a deficiency of $27,382 on his 1935 taxes, owing to what he said was an erroneous valuation the IRS Commissioner had placed on insurance policies and those 40,000 shares of Chrysler stock he gave away in that year. (In 1931, Walter Chrysler was said to be the most insured man in the world, with some $12 million worth of policies on his life, and clearly the new tax law made it worthwhile for him to divest some of them.)

❧   ❧   ❧

As hard as he worked during the early 1930s there were nevertheless a great many social occasions and entertainments of various kinds which he attended. He was seen at many sporting events, especially prize fights, and both his wife and daughters were seen ringside with him at the Baer-Schmeling World Heavyweight Championship bout in 1933. Della and he attended the grand opening of Radio City Music Hall in 1932, and were occasionally seen together at Broadway shows, concerts, and the Metropolitan Opera. There were lots of parties too, such as a fancy dress affair they attended with the very social Lucius Boomers in 1932, and the Beaux Arts Ball in 1933, at which they accompanied Oscar of the Waldorf and his wife. They frequently joined the Alfred P. Sloans and guests aboard their yacht, the *Rene*, on Long Island Sound, and reciprocated the favor often on their own yachts, and at their home at King's Point.

One amusing anecdote about the Long Island mansion came from that time. It seems Mr. Chrysler had ordered an ice maker for his parties, but complained that the 156-cube icemaker provided by Brunswick-Balke-Collender was inadequate. "Parties are big out here, and so are the highballs," he said. Brunswick replaced the original machine with two larger ones run by a Frigidaire compressor that could turn out 436 cubes at once. A very unhappy Mr. Chrysler called Brunswick and asked in indignant tones: "Did you understand my name correctly? This is Walter P. *Chrysler*." Thoroughly confused, the man at Brunswick stammered that he understood, and then he and his colleagues spent a couple of hours scratching their heads trying to figure out what he meant. Finally they realized that General Motors made the Frigidaire compressor, and immediately changed the job specifications to designate a Kelvinator compressor, which suited Mr. Chrysler just fine, since Kelvinator hadn't yet merged with Nash, and anyway, he was invested in it.

Granddaughters Joan French and Cynthia Rupp have memories of life at King's Point when they were little girls. Cynthia recalled the marble veranda, stained glass windows, and the music room, almost hidden behind one of the tapestries. "I remember my grandmother with her beautiful white hair, always wearing a red sweater. As a special treat, she let me go through the jewelry box in her bedroom, trying things on to play dress up." Joan often thinks of her grandfather's thoughtfulness. "One summer, when I was four or five, I was visiting Great Neck because my parents were on a trip to Europe. This particular afternoon I was hiding behind a tall gothic tapestry couch listening to my grandparents talk about me. I had told my grandfather that all my friends at school had brown oxfords, while I still had to wear white mary janes. He told my grandmother to go out and buy me the oxfords—how I loved him for that! It *is* interesting though that I remember almost nothing of my grandmother."

The Chryslers traveled a lot too, frequently sailing to Bermuda aboard the *Monarch* and the *Queen of Bermuda*, and to Europe on a variety of ships like the *Berengaria, Bremen,* and *Leviathan.* Aristo Scrobogna said Durant told him that when he met up with the Chryslers in Paris in the early thirties, famed hostess Elsa Maxwell was promoting the family in Europe. No doubt this was in part accountable for the engagements with royalty and aristocracy to be found in Mr. Chrysler's European appointment book.

The couple enjoyed trips to French Lick, Indiana, and frequented the Greenbriar at White Sulphur Springs also. Of course there was Pokety Farms for boating, hunting, and other forms of relaxation, and every winter Walter and Della spent considerable time in Palm Beach, hobnobbing with the crème de la crème of society, artists, businessmen, and the like.

Sometimes Chrysler attended special dinners for salesmen and dealers in New York, Detroit, and Chicago, and occasionally went on trips with them too. K. T. Keller had an amusing memory of one such jaunt. "I remember back in 1938, when all the Chrysler dealers and the top executives of the corporation went on a cruise of the Great Lakes. This Friday night we were just nearing Mackinac, and I was in the midst of a crap game where I was ahead about $10,000. We were docking in two hours, and Walter Chrysler came up and whispered to me in a joking way, 'What the hell are you trying to do, K. T.? We have all these dealers with us, and you're taking all their money. Take my advice and start losing. These guys will be talking about this for the next few years unless they start winning.' I took Walter's advice and let the dealers win their money back. After all, can you imagine what the reactions would have been among the other automotive companies?"

Honors came to Walter Chrysler in these years too. He was decorated by Leopold III, King of the Belgians, who made him an Officer of the Order of the Crown and a Member of the Belgian League of Honor.

At the first commencement of the Chrysler Institute of Engineering on July 12, 1933, Walter Chrysler was given that institution's first-ever Doctorate of Engineering, conferred by its trustees, Zeder, the president, Skelton and Breer, vice presidents, and John J. Eaton, secretary treasurer. B. E. Hutchinson and F. Paul Anderson, Dean of the University of Kentucky were the principal speakers of the occasion, at which 14 masters and 21 undergraduate degrees were also conferred. *The Detroit News* later recalled the scene as Mr. Chrysler listened to the words of his citation read aloud. "As usual, the words that W. P. heard from the scroll were fulsome as all such citations are; but they were all true. As they were read off, the lump in the Chrysler throat became too big for his composure. When he stepped forward to receive the scroll his face was wet and streaming. He could not speak."

On June 20, 1936, he wore a black academic gown with scarlet facings as the University of Michigan conferred the same honor on him, citing him for having "dealt sympathetically and effectively with the complex problem of labor," and for his "courageous policy of engineering research and plant improvement during a period of diminishing returns." The fol-

Walter Chrysler receives a doctoral degree from Fred Zeder on July 12, 1933 during the first commencement exercises of the Chrysler Institute of Engineering. (*Courtesy DaimlerChrysler Corporate Historical Collection*)

lowing year Kansas Wesleyan University made him a Doctor of Mechanical Engineering.

During this period he personally gave two $5,000 four-year scholarships to the colleges of their choice to Frank Churchill and George Ward, outstanding students in the undergraduate division of the Chrysler Institute. On the other end of the spectrum, corporate records show that around the same time, "out of Walter Chrysler's belief 'That no man should lose his job because of age,'" the Chrysler Corporation began its Old Age Department. When men entered this department, they were privileged to work as many hours or days a week as they wished. The company worked things out by having regular departments do some of the same work as these men, so that the jobs would always be turned out. Men in this department ranged from their sixties to their eighties, and K. T. Keller, who was very proud of this innovation, boasted that Chrysler never dismissed anyone because of old age, and noted that a couple of men in their nineties were still on the payroll. "The problem of growing old is definitely one requiring thoughtful solution," he said at Chrysler Day at the New York World's Fair of 1939.

"Naturally industrious workers do not retire easily. At Chrysler, there's always a place for old workers whenever they come." After Mr. Chrysler had passed on, a corporate scribe added, "The old boys have had the experience, they are excellent mechanics and the quality of their work is of the best. To them, Walter Chrysler still lives."

❖   ❖   ❖

One of the ways in which he lived in the thirties, and actually for many years before, was as a party boy. There was a lot of booze around, and plenty of women too. A TV movie of the seventies depicted a Walter Chrysler frolicking with party girls in a hotel suite before coming downstairs to address a business meeting, and that wasn't too far from the truth. Having gotten wind of something, a gaggle of reporters once mobbed him at a train station in New York as he arrived from an overnight trip. Notebooks out and flashbulbs popping, they asked him if it was true he had a girl in his sleeping compartment during the trip. He categorically denied that this was so. As he walked away, and got safely out of the reporters' hearing range, he told a very close associate: "Actually, I had two." A famous businessman once obliquely lectured him on the advantages of locking the front door to one's office on certain occasions, while simultaneously unlocking the rear one. Lee Shubert and Florenz Ziegfeld were not the only men who had "five o'clock girls" paying cocktail hour visits to their offices in those days.

But showgirls on the make, happy to provide a good time in exchange for something shiny from Cartier's or something silky from Bonwit's, or regular good-time girls willing to do the same thing for plain old-fashioned cash, were one thing. But Grande Horizontale Peggy Hopkins Joyce was something else entirely. Simply put, in the late 1920s Walter Chrysler fell madly, passionately, head over heels in love with her. She was quite a fascinator, and he was but one in a long, long line of admirers.

The word "golddigger" was coined by a Hearst flack to describe her after an interview in which she described her "sparkling" philosophy of life. She was born Peggy Upton in rural Virginia in 1893, and at age fifteen she hopped a train to Denver with a vaudeville cyclist and fifty cents in her pocket. On that very train she met the first of her six husbands, Everett Archer, and within 24 hours she became both his wife and the daughter-in-law of the "Borax King." Not surprisingly, the Borax King nixed the marriage, and sent her packing with some cash. Her parents used the money to ship her off to boarding school in Washington, where she spent a year acquiring some polish, and eventually, her second hubby, Sherburne Philbrick Hopkins, son of a well-known and rich Washington attorney. He loaded her with gifts, including her very first diamond ring, later to be joined by many brothers and sisters.

Bored, bored, bored, she was spotted by Fanny Brice, who convinced

Ziegfeld to glorify her as a showgirl in the 1917 *Follies*. By 1918, she was a star in his *Miss 1918* revue, and later Lee Shubert starred her in the legitimate theater in the appropriately named *It Pays to Flirt* and *Sleepless Night*. When she was on the road in Chicago in another Ziegfeld revue in 1920, she met hubby no. 3, lumber tycoon J. Stanley Joyce. He also went gaga over her, spending $1.2 million on her in a single week on such items as a $350,000 pearl necklace, despite the fact that she locked herself in the bathroom on their wedding night and wouldn't come out until he slipped a $500,000 check under the door. Later on, when he had the temerity to object to her carrying on with vastly wealthy Frenchman Henri Letellier, she smashed a champagne bottle over his head. End of marriage, in the dissolution of which she collected another $2 million.

Earl Carroll made her a sensation, robed in chinchilla, in the *Vanities of 1923*, and all of New York, and in the papers, the nation, went wild over her. Millionaires vied desperately for her favors and, as David Grafton put it, "Since the demand for Peggy far exceeded the supply, the bidding started high." The diamonds piled up.

Hubby no. 4 was Count Gosta Morner, a handsome, but alas penniless, Swedish nobleman who lasted two months, and no. 5, in the summer of 1932, was British engineer Anthony Easton. ("All I want is to marry and have babies. At heart I'm a simple girl," she said as she embarked for England. Phooey. Onetime lover Charlie Chaplin, in his autobiography, far more accurately described her as a "bright, immoral and intriguing blonde who left her simple, rural home in Virginia with one single, fierce ambition—to become a millionairess by the time she was 30.")

In between husbands, and sometimes during, she managed to sandwich in a collection of lovers ranging from Lord David Northesk and Prince Lubomirski to Jack Oakie. She had a brief Hollywood career (*International House*, with W. C. Fields, Rudy Vallee, and Burns & Allen), appeared in more Broadway soufflés (Heywood Hale Broun called her acting "hugely inadequate," though he liked her ermine coat), and wrote books (*Transatlantic Wife* and *Men, Marriage and Me*). She also wrote widely syndicated articles ("Men—My Quest for Happiness," "How to Get Your Man," etc.), in which world-shaking issues were discussed, like how to keep a man from killing himself when you turn him down (one unfortunate Argentine lover did just that), whether you should leave your husband if he bores you, and the importance of good skin. One of her deathless comments was, "No girl wants to see a man when she first wakes up, even if he is her husband. A husband should be kept for evenings, like the theater."

Cole Porter wrote no fewer than five songs in which she was mentioned between 1928 and 1950. "Which," from *Paris* in 1928, wondered, "Should I make one man my choice and regard divorce as treason, or should I, like Peggy Joyce, get a new one every season?" "They Couldn't Compare to You," from *Out of This World* in 1950, opined, "I was even amused and abused by Peggy Joyce."

The November, 1954, edition of *Confidential Magazine* featured a smiling picture of Peggy Hopkins Joyce decked out in evening dress and jewels next to another of a broadly beaming Walter Chrysler in white tie; both merrily clutch glasses of champagne in their hands. These photos were taken in the early thirties, when their affair was in full flower. He gave her some $2 million worth of jewelry, including an astonishing 134-karat diamond strung on a necklace of mere 5-karat baguettes. It was said to have cost $500,000, and the gossip columns referred to it as "Peggy's skating rink." He ensconsed two secretaries in her townhouse, ostensibly to work for her, though they reported to him. He even hired a bodyguard to watch over her.

One morning, probably in 1930, Walt awakened her at the townhouse and ordered her to look outside. Parked in front were not one but two Isotta-Fraschinis, worth some $45,000, that he was bestowing on her as yet another gift. One was a magnificent berline town car, the very one used as Gloria Swanson's chariot in the film *Sunset Boulevard* 20 years later. The other was a canary yellow roadster with silver trimmings, glamorously appointed with black patent leather (!) upholstery. Peggy said Walt was so crazy about her that he didn't think his own Chrysler Imperials were good enough for her (though apparently they were good enough for Della and the four children).

He was simply reckless then, exposing Della and the family to shame and ridicule by conducting the affair so publicly. It was said that he was even considering divorcing his wife to marry Peggy. One famous executive with whom he was very friendly went out to see him on Long Island, and loudly admonished him to come to his senses, pointing out that he was wrecking a wonderful home, and foolishly giving up a wonderful wife, even risking losing his children. Whether he did take hold of himself, or it was just a matter of Peggy slogging on to the next outpost on the Great Highway of Love, the affair did end, and he returned to the bosom of his family (though there were still probably a number of casual diversions).

Wine, women, and song. All three were part of a good time for Walter Chrysler. Music came first. He started with the tuba and cornet, but he could sit down and play the piano or just about anything else and add to the jollity of an occasion. Then there was always the appreciation of a pretty girl, and sometimes a lot more than that. As to liquor, in the fashion of the day, he consumed large quantities of it. In fact he was probably what today would be known as a functioning alcoholic. There might be a whoopee time on Saturday night, and more than a few shooters on the yacht on Sunday, but he always showed up ready to work bright and early on Monday morning.

There was an aspect of his relationship to alcohol that was very interesting, for one who drank so much: he supported Prohibition until 1930. A letter from John J. Raskob to him on September 27, 1928, confirms this (Raskob had resigned from General Motors to run "wet" candidate Governor Alfred E. Smith's campaign for President of the United States): "Everything seems fair in politics as well as love and war, so I am having a lot of fun taking a crack at you and Alfred (Sloan) every now and then about denying the workingman his glass of beer, with your lockers filled with vintage champagnes, rare old wines and selected brands of old whiskeys, liqueurs, etc. However, I am not mentioning any names, because sometime I might want to borrow some money from you, and you might remember too much. Anyway, I love you and nothing else much matters, so God bless you and good luck."

Prohibition was not much of a populist or popular notion, and, in any case, it was far more honored in the breach than in the observance by Walter Chrysler as much as anyone else, particularly after 1923. And therein lay the problem. For those who brought you the pleasures of liquor during Prohibition also brought you crime. Everybody wanted booze, especially the well-to-do like Chrysler, and new kinds of criminals called bootleggers were happy to supply it. These were often the children of immigrants, like the Italian Black Hand, eager to make lucrative contact with the upper crust. There were black gangs and Polish gangs, and in Detroit two Jewish ones, the Sugar House Gang and the Purple Gang, the latter of which became the dominant one in the area. Since Canadian officials refused to cooperate with American authorities in this matter, booze flowed freely across the Detroit River from Windsor, Ontario, in boats over the water in summer, in cars over the ice in winter, and through the Windsor-Detroit tunnel which, when it opened in November, 1930, quickly became known as "the funnel."

The $2 billion distillery industry was idled, tax revenues were lost, and thousands of people were poisoned and killed by bad hooch while murderers and thieves prospered; Al Capone alone was estimated to have an annual income of $60 million. (Sotto voce, more "legitimate" fortunes, like those of the Kennedys of Boston, were also made from liquor during this period.)

Gangland killings abounded; Al Capone's 1929 Saint Valentine's Day Massacre of the O'Banion brothers and other members of Buggs Moran's gang in Chicago, for instance, came about when Moran hijacked a shipment of Old Log Cabin from the Purple Gang. By the early '30s, criminals began robbing banks and kidnapping too, and the country was in the grip of a crime wave.

It is interesting to note that Henry Ford was and remained opposed to alcohol, despite the ironic fact that the crimes it spawned all were motorized crimes. Without the motor car, none of them could have occurred.

By 1932, Walter Chrysler had fully realized the dangers of Prohibition, and done an about face. On February 23, 1932, he wrote to Pierre S. du Pont: "Up to a couple of years ago, I was rather favorable to the Prohibition Amendment. Since then however, I have been very seriously concerned over its effects in spreading a disregard for law and order. I have personally come to feel that the whole question of the security of property is, in a measure, bound up with an intelligent handling of the prohibition problem.

"I have given consideration strictly to the question and have come to the conclusion that it is a subject to which business interests must give most serious thought.

"Accordingly, I am inviting a group of business men to meet with me for dinner at the Cloud Club in the Chrysler Building on Thursday, March 3rd, at 7:30 o'clock, and hope very much that I may include you as one of my guests on that occasion, and have the benefit of your counsel."

What this and other similar meetings led to was that on October 9th of that year, Walter Chrysler became general chairman of a committee to raise $175,000 toward a national fund to support candidates for Congress who were for "immediate prohibition reform." This was done under the auspices of the Crusaders, Inc. "To my mind," he said, "it is clear that Prohibition is an utter failure and is doomed. But we must seal that doom as quickly as possible. Many persons believe that Prohibition has already been defeated. I wish that were true, as do most of us, I am sure. But with the right kind of Congress and sufficient active interest among the serious citizenship, I feel that we can hasten the sad story to a reasonably early conclusion. The great fight against Prohibition is beginning now. There has grown up an enormous majority sentiment that demands a change, and this has been crystallized by the Depression."

Not only Chrysler and du Pont, but other former stalwart supporters of Prohibition like S. S. Kresge and John D. Rockefeller, Jr. got on the anti-Prohibition bandwagon. The Democrats had been anti-Prohibition in the 1928 elections, but both parties were in 1932. In February of 1932, both houses of Congress proposed an amendment to the Constitution, the 21st, repealing Prohibition, the 18th. On December 5, 1933, when Utah became the 36th state to ratify it, repeal was at last achieved. (Though many benefits came to the citizenry from this action, it is worth noting that this was the only time an amendment to the Constitution was ever repealed, creating in many minds a precedent which might one day become dangerous.)

Two days later Walter Chrysler resigned from the Crusaders. "It was this purpose only which enlisted my interest and contributions," he said. "I want to congratulate you."

Despite his original interest in Prohibition, it should be emphasized that
Chrysler was in no sense a man of rigid moralistic principles, like, say, John
D. Rockefeller, Sr. In religion, he was Episcopalian, attending church for all
the great occasions in life. Though a believer, he was not an overly observant Christian, unlike Della, to whom religion meant a great deal. He was
a friend to many members of the clergy, Protestant and Catholic alike, however, and he was very helpful in responding to their needs.

In politics he was a Republican, though in 1932 he deserted that standard to support Franklin D. Roosevelt, believing that he was just the right
sort of man to lift the country from its torpor. But as he dealt with him
face to face in the auto labor troubles that began in the autumn of 1933,
he became disillusioned, believing that Roosevelt did not at heart have a
thoroughgoing respect for the sanctity of private property. He negotiated
with Roosevelt of course when it was needful, and attended White House
luncheons to discuss everything from industrial policy to the cotton trade.
But his respect and liking for the man was gone, particularly when he saw
that he was not willing to intervene in the auto strikes of 1937. "In a way,
Roosevelt broke his heart," said Frank B. Rhodes, Sr.

❧   ❧   ❧

On April 29, 1938, Walter Chrysler Junior got married to a very pretty
young socialite named Marguerite Sykes, known as Peggy to her friends,
who had made her debut into society in 1932 at a Ritz-Carlton dinner
dance. She was the daughter of Mr. and Mrs. Walter H. Sykes, of New
York and Long Island, and had been educated at the Nightingale-Bamford
School in New York and the Ethel Walker School in Simsbury, Connecticut, from which she was graduated. They were wed in the chapel at St.
Bartholemew's Church in New York City, as Bernice and Edgar had been
in 1930. The groom was in a morning suit, and the bride wore a gown of
white satin with puffed sleeves at the shoulders and a high split collar.
She carried a huge spray of lilies of the valley trailing long ribbons, and
on her head she wore a tiara-type flower crown from which a diaphanous
veil cascaded. Walter Senior and Della were snapped entering the church,
he smiling in his formal clothes and she in a smart light-colored dress
and off-center disk-shaped flower hat with a short veil. They didn't know
it at the time, but this was to be the last event they would ever attend together in public.

Ten days later, someone took a snapshot of Walt and Della on the lawn
at King's Point. They are in casual clothes, holding golf clubs. He has his
arm around her, holding her close, and they both have warm, sunny smiles
on their faces. Despite all their problems, it was the love of their lifetime
together that shone through now. It was the last photo ever taken of them
together.

Walter and Della Chrysler relaxing outside their home, May 9, 1938. This was the last photo taken of them together. (*Courtesy Frank B. Rhodes*)

On Thursday night, May 26, 1938, Walter Chrysler suffered a stroke at his home at King's Point on Long Island. Though he was only sixty-three, all the years of too much work and too much play, without enough respite, had finally caught up with him. He had been looking tired lately, and associates had suggested that he go on a little vacation and rest up a bit. The health of an executive would be much better monitored today, with doctors warning about too much stress and high living, but back then, it was just considered normal for a hard-driving executive to do everything to the fullest, especially if he was almost never sick.

Reports the following day said that Chrysler became ill in the evening, and the following day at noon he was admitted to the Leroy Sanitarium at 40 East Sixty-first Street in Manhattan. His physician, Dr. Arthur F. Chase, said, "He had a circulatory attack, and we were fearful of complications. There is a danger of pneumonia, and he needs a complete rest. His condition, however, is improving satisfactorily." Three days later, it was reported that he was "doing as well as could be expected, and resting comfortably."

He improved steadily, and after a few weeks, he returned to King's Point for continued recuperation.

There tragedy awaited him. At 2 A.M. on the morning of August 8, 1938, Della Chrysler had a cerebral hemorrhage. She had not been well since the autumn of 1937, when she suffered complications following an operation to remove her appendix, even though she seemed to improve during the winter and spring. Walter's stroke, so unexpected, had been very hard on her. On Sunday night, August 7, she complained of a headache after dinner, excused herself, and retired early. Walter heard her moaning shortly after two and found her unconscious. He summoned household members, who called the Alert Fire Company of Great Neck, which began treatments with an inhalator shortly before three. The truck that answered the call was the very one Walt had given to the Alert eleven years before.

Later in the morning, Della was placed in an iron lung that had been rushed by ambulance from New York. In those days, the iron lung was a brand-new, experimental piece of equipment, and there were only a few in the entire country, so this was a very big deal. Dr. Chase was notified at Lake Placid, and immediately flew to Roosevelt Field on Long Island, taking charge of the case as soon as he arrived at 1 P.M. But in the end nothing availed, and Della died at 7 P.M.

Thelma and Walter Junior had dined with her the previous night, and were there through the whole ordeal. Bernice was summoned and came to the house right away, and Jack, who was in Omaha, chartered a plane as soon as he heard and arrived in the early evening, so all her children were with her when she died.

The funeral was held at 11 A.M. on Wednesday, August 10, in the very same chapel at St. Bartholemew's on Park Avenue where both Bernice and Walter Junior had been married. Several hundred friends and business associates of Walter's attended, and hundreds more sent floral tributes.

The Reverends Francis Hopkinson Craighill, Jr., and Lynde E. May, Jr., officiated. According to the *Times* account, "Following the opening sentences of the Episcopal service read by the Rev. Mr. Craighill, the choir sang the 23rd Psalm. Mr. Craighill then read the lesson from the eighth chaper of the Epistle to the Romans, after which the hymn "Fight the Good Fight" was sung by the choir. The prayers of the burial service were recited by the Rev. Mr. May, during which the choir sang, "I Heard a Voice from Heaven" and "Seven-Fold Amen." The recessional "Hark, Hark, My Soul" concluded the service. Keller, Hutchinson, Fields, Mitchell, Zeder and many others represented the corporation, and staff members of the Chrysler Building Corporation were present also. Mr. and Mrs. E. F. Hutton and Oscar of the Waldorf were among the mourners, and Nicholas Kelley and Lucius Boomer were among the ushers."

Walter Chrysler himself was not present, because he was too ill to go through the ordeal. After the services, a hearse took Della to Sleepy Hollow Cemetery, where she was entombed in the family vault.

Everyone was shocked by this turn of events, and the children were laid low. But no one was as devastated as Walter Senior. He had told everyone that he never would have been able to build the life he did if she had not been there for him to rely on every step of the way. Through it all, she had loved him no matter what, ever since they had been childhood sweethearts in Ellis over fifty years before. That she was suddenly gone in his time of terrible illness was almost inconceivable to him.

In the autumn he went down to Pokety Lodge to recuperate and recovered a bit, returning there after Christmas with the family. In reality, he was pretty much incapacitated, though great care was taken to make sure this was known only to those close to the family. For a while he could still get around a bit and greet old friends. When one associate inquired about his love life, Chrysler smiled and said, "The doctor says I shouldn't rattle my nuts so much anymore."

But mostly he was very sad, and those around him said the light seemed to go out of him after Della died. He would spend long hours at King's Point in his wheelchair, just staring out at the water. Gradually his health deteriorated into a very precarious state.

Aristo Scrobogna brought Billy Durant out to King's Point to see Walter Chrysler one more time in 1940. "Mr. Durant was shocked at the appearance of Mr. Chrysler, that he had deteriorated so badly," Scrobogna said. "I never saw Mr. Durant so shocked as when he came from Mr. Chrysler's bedroom."

By the winter of 1940, it was clear to all that the end would not be far off. In the papers of Nicholas Kelley at the New York Public Library, there is a February 28, 1940, letter to Walter Chrysler, Jr., from Chrysler's publicist, T. J. Ross, in which he outlines plans for the coming funeral. Copies of these plans were to be sent to the other children, as well as to Nicholas Kelley and Harry C. Davis, so that the arrangements could be agreed on as soon as possible.

The letter was written subsequent to a meeting the day before in which plans discussed over the previous three weeks were hashed out. An ironclad strategy for the nurses and other household members to inform Ross and Kelley of Mr. Chrysler's demise was set up. Ross also made it clear to one and all that he was to handle the public dissemination of all information about the death and funeral, as well as all messages of condolence, including important statements made by major figures. He had a list of major questions to be dealt with in the death announcement, such as the location of family members, and whether or not Mr. Chrysler was conscious or said any last words. The family were asked to decide at that time all details of the funeral, such as where it would be held, who the undertaker, minister, and honorary pallbearers would be, whether the interment would be public or private, and even what cars would be available to take people to the cemetery. Clearly, from this document it was felt the end might come at any time, and everyone was asked to cooperate to make sure that nothing would be left to chance when the moment arrived.

It arrived at last on August 18, 1940. On the 15th he had suffered another stroke. Malcolm Neilson, a member of the Alert Fire Company now in his nineties recalled a summons to the Chrysler home on that day. "The fire chief and six or seven others of us raced over to the mansion in the Chrysler fire truck to give him oxygen. One crew went upstairs to his room, and the rest of us remained below. His daughters and sons were there, and pretty broken up. One of the boys said, 'Pop is in pretty bad shape.' Very quickly they brought in extra oxygen and a portable iron lung. We got him through that day, but he didn't last long."

The end came at 6:50 P.M. on Sunday, August 18, 1940. He had been unconscious for twenty-four hours preceding his death, which was caused by a cerebral hemorrhage. His four children and his sister, Irene, had kept vigil by his bedside, and were with him at the end, as were his three physicians, Dr. Chase, William Von Stein, and Edgar E. Stewart.

Reports said he had been up and about until Thursday, but that was just window dressing for the papers. In reality he was put into his wheelchair for a while each day, and that was all. As his lawyer announced in a Supreme Court action ten days before his death, he had recently been in critical condition. There really wasn't much left of him by the time he died.

Newspapers throughout the world reported his demise and editorialized the man and his accomplishments at great length in hundreds of articles. Tributes from automotive industry and even labor union leaders poured in, as did comments from civic leaders from all the places he had lived in, from Oelwein, Trinidad, and Childress to Salt Lake City, Denver, and Flint. Frank W. Roche in *Automobile Topics* said it simply: "The great business he founded, the world renowned building that bears his name—these and many others will stand as material monuments of his accomplishments. But greater than all these is the spiritual fact that Walter Chrysler was enthroned in the hearts of more friends in widely separated walks of life than almost any man of his time. And to whatever valhalla of the spirit he has been translated, countless good wishes acompany him. He truly left the world a better place than he found it."

The funeral took place on Wednesday, August 20th at 11:00 P.M., once again at St. Bartholemew's. Prior to that event a private service for the family and members of Mr. Chrysler's household staff was held at his King's Point

Thelma Foy and Walter Chrysler, Jr. leave St. Bartholomew's Church on Park Avenue after their father's funeral on August 20, 1940. (*Courtesy Frank B. Rhodes*)

home. It was led by Dr. M. C. McKechnie, rector of All Saints Church in Great Neck. Just before it began at 8:30, the Great Neck Fire Department solemnly paraded before the residence.

One thousand five hundred people attended the services in New York. The church was packed, and police were present to keep the throngs outside orderly. Services were conducted by the Reverend Dr. Frederic Underwood, and a vested sixty-voice choir was accompanied by Dr. David MacKay Williams on the great organ of the church. Just before the family entered, Dr. Williams softly played Victor Herbert's "Ah, Sweet Mystery of Life." The family (the men were dressed in morning clothes, the women in black dresses with mourning veils) including the grandchildren, and top executives of the Chrysler Corporation occupied a special reserved section of pews, along with members of the 29 and Question Clubs, with which Mr. Chrysler had stong ties. (The Question Club was an organization of automobile executives which he had founded; their floral piece of red and white carnations in the form of a question was displayed on the altar, as was the

Walter Chrysler's casket is carried past the honorary pallbearers at his funeral on August 20, 1940. (*Courtesy Frank B. Rhodes*)

29 Club's huge standing spray of delphiniums and asters in the form of a 29; the latter club was formed by Mr. Chrysler and his closest friends some years before. There were some 650 other floral tributes, including individual ones from each of the UAW-CIO memberships at the Chrysler Corporation plants.)

Mr. Chrysler reposed in a huge bronze casket banked with red roses, his favorite flower, just inside the chancel; draped over it was a blanket of ferns on which rested a cross of smilax. At each end was a huge cross of Easter lilies, gifts from his sons-in-law and grandchildren. Twenty members of the Question Club attended in a body, each wearing a white carnation which was placed in the casket, according to the Club's custom.

The service began with the choir singing "Ten Thousand Times Ten Thousand," which was followed by a recitation of "I am the resurrection and the life" from the New Testament. The Twenty-Third Psalm was sung, after which Dr. Underwood read the lesson from the Fourteenth Chapter of St. John, beginning, "Jesus said, 'let not our heart be troubled.'" The hymn, "Fight the Good Fight" was sung before additional words from the reverend, after which the choir sang the anthem "I Heard a Voice from Heaven."

After the Apostle's Creed and the Lord's Prayer were spoken by the congregation, the minister spoke, in lieu of a formal eulogy. "We thank Thee, O God, for all the goodness and courage which have passed from the life of thy servant, Walter Percy Chrysler, into the lives of others, and have left the world richer for his presence," Dr. Underwood said. "We thank Thee for the genius and inspiration of his leadership and accomplishment, and that through his life, work gained new dignity."

The hymn "Faith of Our Fathers" preceeded the benediction, and "Hark' Hark, My Soul" followed, as the minister preceeded the casket, followed by forty-nine honorary pallbearers, down the main aisle of the church. They included some of the most illustrious men in American business, from Alfred P. Sloan, K. T. Keller, Jules S. Bache, and Fred J. and Lawrence P. Fisher to Juan T. Trippe and James Cox Brady, Jr.

Among the many luminaries present in addition to these men were former Postmaster-General James A. Farley, Frank Murphy, by now Associate Justice of the United States Supreme Court, Eugene Grace, president of Bethlehem Steel, J. W. Frazer, president of Willys-Overland, Major Edward Bowes, Prince Serge Obolensky, Oscar of the Waldorf, Harley Earl, and Bernard Gimbel.

About 75 family members and close friends then proceeded to Sleepy Hollow Cemetery in Tarrytown, New York, where the family had built a Greek mausoleum after Della's death two years before. There Dr. Underwood recited a brief committal service as the coffin was placed inside the mausoleum.

Walt and Della's final resting place is an impressive work of classical architecture, flanked by aged boxwood and symmetrical pine. It sits on a beautifully landscaped 31,840-square-foot plot; far away, through a long vista, one can glimpse the Hudson. The building's dimensions are 34 feet long by 32 feet wide, and 17 feet high. The steel frame of the building, which is in the shape of a Greek temple, is clad in white Vermont granite. Porticos at the front and back each have four 10-foot-high fluted Doric columns, topped by two-foot-square capitals, cut solid to the shafts.

One enters the mausoleum through an impressively simple seven-foot high bronze door designed by Gorham. The interior, which contains twenty-two catacombs, is finished in Alabama cream and Tennessee pink marble two inches thick. The floor is of American black granite. Four art glass windows in bronze frames, one on each side and two at the back, provide light to the interior. They were taken from the library and music room at King's Point, and each is protected from the outside by one-inch-thick bullet-proof glass. It was a simple and serene spot for Walter and Della to lie side by side in eternity.

On the morning of Mr. Chrysler's funeral, at 10:00 o'clock, a fifteen-minute period of silence was observed in all departments of all plants and offices of the Chrysler Corporation to pay tribute to him.

Eight days later, after issuing a proclamation in his honor, the board of

The Chrysler family mausoleum in Tarrytown, New York, where both Walter and Della Chrysler are buried. (*Courtesy Frank B. Rhodes*)

directors abolished the position of Chairman of the Board, making president K. T. Keller the chief executive officer of the Chrysler Corporation.

❦   ❦   ❦

Almost immediately thereafter Walter's sister Irene Harvey began gathering photographs and information to make a documentary about his life. J. E. Fields from the Chrysler Corporation and many people in each of the towns in which Walter Chrysler lived mobilized forces to provide her with the material she needed. She also hired a crew to go out and film many of the places in which he lived and worked as a young man. The resultant silent short movie, with subtitles, was called *Out of the West*, and gave a good first-hand sense of his background and early life.

The end of the film showed each of the Chrysler plants, comparing its square footage when he came to the Maxwell-Chalmers in 1921 to its square footage in 1940, adding on the 18 new plants added from 1925 to 1940, including Dodge Main, acquired in 1928, the Lynch Road Plymouth plant erected in 1929, and the DeSoto plant built in 1933. In 1940, there were 1,441 acres in plants, which totalled up 17,891,737 square feet in area. This was an increase of 1,253 acres equalling 15,270,461 square feet during Walter Chrysler's time. In addition, in 1940 there were 8 parts depots, 56 regular service offices, 45 regular sales offices, 10,000 domestic dealers serving 6,000 communities, and overseas, there were 3,800 dealers in 100 countries. The Chrysler Corporation built 8 million cars and trucks between 1925 and 1940, employed 80,000 workers at its peak, and paid over $1 billion in wages. More than 300,000 families depended on the Chrysler Corporation for their livelihood.

The last title said, "An institution is the reflection of the people who guide it."—Walter P. Chrysler.

On May 21, 22, and 23, 1941, the Parke-Bernet galleries in New York conducted sales of Della's effects from the home at King's Point. To read the prices realized would make anyone in the present day weep, but it was a different world then. "The Madonna in Glory," by Anthony Van Dyck, yielded $1,350 and "The Holy Family," by Bastiano Mainardi, brought $650. A Kirman Millefleurs carpet, one of more than a score of magnificent rugs, sold for $675. There was a circa 1690 Gobelins tapestry of this description in the sale: "A 3 fold screen composed of a wide center panel and two narrow panels of late 17th century Gobelins tapestry magnificently woven in reds, blues, yellows and tans, with ducal escutcheons, medallions, continuous landscape vignettes, marital and amatory trophies, etc. Bordered with crimson velvet and lined with crimson damask. Height 7 feet, width 6 feet, 2 inches." It sold for $725.

The top price in the sale was paid for a 11'1" by 12'10" circa 1525 Tournai late gothic tapestry portraying the Old Testament scene of Saul offering his daughter Michal to David (from I Samuel 18). The description was thus: "In the foreground, seated upon a canopied throne of Gothic crimson damask is the bearded king surrounded by attendants, receiving the kneeling Michal, the train of whose long gown is held by waiting maids; behind the throne are spearmen, a councillor, and advancing, the figure of David with his harp and, farther off, in the long middle distance, is seen a shepherd with his flock. At right, a glimpse of rolling country with castles, and in the sky above, Cupid shooting his darts toward the couple. Chocolate brown border with a continuous mass of flowers, fruit, grapes and leafage in naturalistic colors. The tapestry shows some careful restoration, as usual, but is otherwise in excellent condition and exhibits lively coloring." This astonishing piece fetched $2,000.

All told, there were 560 items offered for sale. The first day's proceeds were reported as $30,041, and penciled in the official Parke-Bernet catalog for the event were listed amounts of $21,517 for the second and $25,100 for the third. These may not have been final figures however, as the first day, with the least precious items, did much better than its $17,475 estimate, and Parke-Bernet had estimated the second and third at $34,255 and $41,955, respectivlely.

On January 10, 1942, it was announced that the U.S. Government would acquire the King's Point estate to turn it into a facility to train U.S. Merchant Marine officers. To this day it is the U.S. Merchant Marine Academy.

❧   ❧   ❧

Walter Chrysler's will, dated August 30, 1935, was filed for probate with Surrogate Leone D. Howell on August 27, 1940, in Mineola, Long Island. It originally had provided for a $200,000 annual income for Della, but since she had died and her will specified her children as her heirs, the residual estate was to be divided equally among the four children. Two-thirds of these monies were left outright, with the balance in individual trusts over which they had power of appointment in their wills; were they not to exercise that power, the remaining third would be divided among the surviving siblings.

The *New York Herald Tribune* reported "The will established an unusual method for distributing Mr. Chrysler's personal effects—clothing, jewelry, silver, china, furniture, automobiles, objects of art, etc.—among the children. They are to decide who has first, second, third and fourth choice, and in that order each is to select something he wants. Then the child who had second choice is to have first choice, the third is to have second and the fourth third choice in selecting other objects. The rotation is to continue until all personal effects are disposed of."

A total of $89,500 worth of specific bequests were made, including $25,000 to his sister Irene and $10,000 each to his sister-in-law, Mae Chrysler, and his niece, Ruth Strickler, in addition to Guy Nonenmacher, Dick R. McLain, and Harry C. Davis. Eleven others, mostly domestic employees, received smaller bequests, including $2,000 to his butler William Reid, $1,000 to Inez B. Hooper, his longtime Detroit secretary, and $1,000 to William Pritchett, who worked for him at Pokety. There were no philanthropic or charitable bequests.

Walter Junior, Jack, Nicholas Kelley, and John W. Drye, Jr., another lawyer from Larkin, Rathbone and Perry, were named as executors and trustees, with the wish that his sons would follow the lawyers' advice. Each lawyer got $12,500, in addition to the usual administrative and other legal fees. Byron Foy and Edgar Garbisch were the backups to the two sons, should they be unwilling or unable to exercise their duties.

On March 29, 1941, it was published that the transfer tax on Della's estate revealed its value to be $1,350,670, gross, with a net value of $1,247,956. The New York State inheritance tax was $81,136.50

On December 9, 1944, it was revealed that Walter Chrysler left a gross estate of $9,844,394, with a net value of $8,854,761. His stocks and bonds were listed at $5,510,379, including 74,462 shares of Chrysler Corporation stock valued at $5,161,147, and 10,458 shares of Madison Square Garden

Corporation, valued at $100,592. Mortgages, notes, cash, and insurance were appraised at $3,861,877, transfers totalled $408,460, and realty was valued at $500. One of his obituaries, in the *Amsterdam Evening Recorder*, noted that in 1937, the Chrysler Corporation had paid the premiums on $2,891,611 worth of insurance on his life, though it is not clear whether the corporation or his children benefitted from those policies, and if it was the children, whether those amounts were included in the estate or not. In any event, it is clear that since 1920, Walter Chrysler had funnelled a great deal of money to each of his children, whether in cash or in trusts, and that each was independently wealthy quite apart from parental inheritances.

Thelma Foy lived on for another 17 years. She was a patron of many philanthropic organizations, from the Henry Street Visiting Nurses Association and the New York Infirmary for Women and Children to the American Red Cross and the Metropolitan Opera Association. But mainly she was a socialite, known for the fabulous parties she and her husband gave at their New York home, filled with 18th-century French antiques and French Impressionist masterpieces. Members of the Social Register, along with artists, actors, and politicians, flocked to their home to enjoy the beautiful surroundings, the fabulous food and drink, and one another's company. Thelma was constantly on the lists of the Ten Best Dressed Women in the country, and now in the 1990s, she has become known again for her amazing collection of original Dior outfits (her daughter, Cynthia Rupp, noted that she also had an interest in the work of other designers, such as Balenciaga). For much of the century couture clothing was admired, but not really taken very seriously in the realm of art. But now it is recognized as a form of soft scupture, and women like Thelma Foy are considered prescient in their taste for it.

Personally, many have characterized her as a very nervous woman, and apparently she could be a holy terror in dealing with fashion designers, jewelry houses, and decorators. "Mother had her clothes fitted endlessly," said her daughter, Joan French. "She had an uncanny knack of knowing whether anything was even a sixteenth of an inch off, whether it was clothing, pictures, molding or curtains." There was also a no-nonsense side to her. "She was up early, would rather read an interesting book than go out to a social lunch, and washed her own hair" said Mrs. Rupp.

"She was high strung and flamboyant, and not at all easy," Frank Rhodes Senior recalled. Though some found her a haughty woman who could easily snub people when out and about, "actually she was very nearsighted and often just didn't recognize people, which left them with the mistaken impression that she was cutting them," said Mrs. French. On the other hand, Russell Nype, Ethel Merman's Tony Award-winning leading man in *Call Me Madam* recalled, "As a hostess, she was known throughout New York for her beauty, graciousness and charm. Invitations to the Foy's were highly prized."

Thelma entered Memorial Sloan Kettering Hospital in New York on May 20, 1957, suffering from leukemia, and never recovered. She died there on Tuesday, August 20th. Her spirit was indomitable, however—she was making plans for the fall social season from her hospital bed, and dressmakers made daily visits to her right up to the end. She was 55.

Byron Foy, who had served as a Lieutenant Colonel in the Army Air Corps during World War II, remarried in 1961, to Virginia Payne Reynolds. He had headed DeSoto until 1942, and returned there briefly after the War. In 1946, he became board chairman of the Jack and Heintz Precision Industries of Cleveland, an aircraft components manufacturer, and through the years had many other financial and business involvements. He died after a brief illness at his home in Southampton, New York, on June 28, 1970 at the age of 77.

Jack Chrysler's story was a sad one. Extremely handsome and full of life in his youth, he never seemed to find his way. He attended the Roxbury School in Connecticut, and when he was finished there his father gave him $700 for a round-the-world trip, with instructions that he had to manage on that and no more. When he returned, he had just $8 left, but he had done what he was asked to do, and both men were proud of the fact. (In 1934, Walter Chrysler said, "My wife and I were careful our children didn't have too much money to spend, that they would be made to realize the value of a dollar.") At the age of 22, he was reported to be anxious to go into his father's business, and Walter seemed happy with the fact that he apprenticed as a machinist in one of his Detroit factories. It doesn't seem to have worked out though, for there is no more mention of his work in the engineering side of Chrysler, though he became a company vice president in 1938. (The previous year he had become vice president of the W. P. Chrysler Building Corporation.) During the war he would serve as an officer in the Navy.

On November 26, 1941, he married the former Edith Helen Backus, daughter of Frederick C. and Helen C. (Fichtel) Backus, in New York City. Edith was a very beautiful model, but an exteremely difficult woman, and the marriage was a stormy one. Two children were born, Helen, on February 2, 1944, and Jack Junior, on May 31, 1946. After the War he became a director of several corporations, including the Chrysler Corporation in 1956. He also became a member of the New York Stock Exchange in 1955, and of the American Stock Exchange the following year. Fred Zeder, Jr. and he were partners in a venture capital company called Chrysler-Zeder, Inc., which had offices in the Chrysler Building. More than a score of clubs could count him as a member, and he was a trustee for several schools, hospitals, and philanthropic organizations.

A busy life indeed, but he was not a happy man. Everyone liked him, but they felt sorry for him because of the trials he suffered in his marriage. It ate at him incessantly. He also had a weight problem, and was in and out of the Le Roy Hospital in New York, constantly making attempts to slim down. Frank Rhodes, Sr., saw him at the Cloud Club the day before he died, and commented on how well he looked. "I've been on my weight thing," he replied. The next afternoon, November 7, 1958, he died of a heart attack at the Le Roy Hospital, at the age of 46. His wife Edith remarried, to a man named Carr, and rather amusingly became Edith Chrysler Carr. Unfortunately, she eventually developed a debilitating illness, and died after a long seige.

The year after Jack's death, his son, with Uncle Walter by his side, pulled a whistle lanyard, and a huge shovel moved forward and scooped out three tons of earth, as bulldozers and trucks moved forward cutting a path for the new $100 million Chrysler Expressway in Detroit. Three years later at another ceremony, young Jack used a tool from Walter Chrysler's toolbox to cut the ribbon on the finished highway.

Bernice and the Colonel enjoyed a long and happy union. During World War II she became a Red Cross Nurses' Aid, logging over 3,000 hours of service, later performing similar work at New York Hospital, and of course the Colonel had a distinguished wartime service record too. After the War, he was involved with both the grocery and coal businesses. Both Garbisches belonged to an endless number of clubs and philanthropic organizations.

In 1941, they became the owners of Pokety Lodge, being the successful bidders among the four children in a sealed bid sale of the property. When the War was over, they began a decade-long renovation of it, transforming Walter Chrysler's homey, country lodge into Pokety Farms, a grand country seat of true elegance. The couple stocked it with their outstanding collections of American furniture and paintings, American and European brass and wrought iron fixtures, and European and Chinese porcelains of the 17th, 18th, and early 19th centuries. Their New York apartment was similarly well appointed.

Frank Rhodes, Sr. remembers Bernice as a very nice woman, smart as a whip where business was concerned, and very proud of her father. "Every day at 5 o'clock she made martinis, and she could mix great ones, filling them to the top without ever spilling a drop. She always drank Heublein's Wilshire gin, which was their economy label, saying it was as good as anything made, and why pay premium prices? I remember her sitting and playing solitaire by the hour too, waiting for the Colonel, who never seemed to come home on time, to her great annoyance."

They both died on the same sad day in mid-December, 1979. The Colonel died at Pokety after a long illness, and Bernice, overcome by grief, died in a hospital in nearby Cambridge that night. He was 80 and she, 73.

The following May, Sotheby Parke Bernet sold off their belongings in a series of auctions in New York and at Pokety Farms. It was the second largest private estate sale in U.S. history, up to that time. It was at the Pokety sale that Frank Rhodes, Jr. picked up Chrysler family memorabilia left for the trashman, loaded it into a truck, and drove away with it in order to preserve it.

The Chrysler child who made the biggest impact on the world was Walter Junior. From boyhood to the end, he was an avid and eclectic collector of art. From Picasso to Meissen, if it interested him, he bought it. Polly Lieb, a New York decorator, once remembered him walking into a New York antiques shop, and seeing a particular china cup he liked. "He just examined it and said he'd take it, without even asking the price. Of course he overpaid, but that didn't seem to matter to him." In fact, he was usually quite shrewd about such matters, and built up several amazing collections for little money, mainly because he started out quite early, before the market for art exploded. He bought his first painting, a small Renoir, for $350 out of schoolboy savings when he was 14. Over the next 55 years, he estimated that some 25,000 art works had passed through his hands.

According to Bob Lipper, "He was a canny buyer, detecting trends and purchasing cheap against them: small canvasses when large were prized, large canvasses when small were favored, Impressionists and moderns before they became fashionable. In the 1930's, for example, he bought a Picasso from Gertrude Stein for $450; 'That was my smartness to buy it then,' he said." In the late 1930s, he began loaning out some of his collection to various art museums, and by early January of 1941, the Richmond, Virginia, Museum displayed some 341 of his works, the oldest being an African rock picture.

Poor Marguerite Sykes did not know what she was getting into when she married Walter, and by October of 1939, she had taken up residence in Reno, where she obtained a divorce decree on December 4th of that year, on the grounds of cruelty. The problem was that he was homosexual, plain and simple. It is hard in 2000 to know why he wanted to marry, but in 1938, there was enormous social pressure on gay men to marry and give the appearance of living a "normal" life. In any case, this marriage certainly was an unhappy one for both of these young people.

After a brief time as an executive at the commerce Department, Walter joined the Navy as a Lieutenant, J. G., on April 10, 1942. He was stationed at Norfolk for a while, then later was transferred to Key West, Florida. In a highly unusual move, considering it was wartime, he abruptly resigned his commission on December 5, 1944. Years later, Walter said it was due to ill health, alluding to a recurrence of his ulcer problems. But Nelson Macy, Jr., a Connecticut socialite who was also a Navy Lieutenant, and who knew both Walter and Bernice slightly, said it was common knowledge in the Navy that he had resigned because of a homosexual scandal in Key West.

Confidential Magazine in 1955 claimed that Walter Junior had given notorious parties for young sailors at his off-base private home in Key West, as he had done years before for undergraduates during his time at Dartmouth. After an investigation of several months by the Office of Naval Intelligence, he was confronted by a representative of Secretary of the Navy James Forrestal and resigned his commission. Forrestal, a former president of Dillon, Reed, had all records of this case delivered to his office, after which they disappeared. Even his medical records disappeared from the Naval Records Center at Garden City, New York.

It certainly was amazing how quickly he remarried after his resignation. He had met Jean Esther Outland, daughter of Mr. and Mrs. Grover Cleveland Outland, at a party one night at Virginia Beach's Cavalier Hotel. On January 14, 1945, he married her in a quiet ceremony at the Freemason Street Baptist Church in Norfolk. The marriage lasted until her death in 1980. "She was a very nice woman, who had to put up with a lot," said Frank Rhodes, Sr. "But she wanted that Chrysler name, and so she did what she had to do."

In 1941, Walter bought an enormous eighteenth-century estate in North Wales, Virginia, near Warrenton. The 3,200-acre Fairfax Estate was started in 1718, on a 1716 British Crown grant to Lady Culpepper. The house had 40 rooms, including 11 master bedroms, 10 master baths, a ballroom, trophy, hunt and breakfast rooms, a kitchen designed to serve 200, 13 staff rooms, and a number of storage and serving rooms. There were fireplaces in all but one of the bedrooms. The gardens contained both American and English boxwoods, and were perhaps the finest in the country. There were also farm buildings, stables, a horse training track, a lake, a golf course, and a private air strip. The price was $175,000, and for another $1,500, Walter got the artwork in the place, which nobody appreciated. A few years later, he auctioned it off for $50,000. Over the years, Walter poured somewhere between $6 and $7.5 million into the property.

The *New York Times* story on the purchase of the property appeared in the sports section, identifying Walter Chrysler as a "Racing Man." He was described as "a comparative newcomer to American racing who now owns about 50 broodmares." In reality, the farm was operated as a tax shelter, so periodically he changed the nature of its operation from racing farm to breeding farm to poultry farm. In 1957, the IRS changed the laws and plugged up tax shelter loopholes, so Walter put it up for sale in December of that year for $1 million. It finally sold to Victor Oursinger, the Washington "rooming house millionaire," in the fall of 1961, for $700,000. He divided it up for resale into 10-acre plots which he was sure would go because of the location of the property in "Kennedy" horse country.

Interestingly, after he bought it, he found a secret room containing 2,000 bottles of pre-1918 vintage wines, rare cognacs, old bourbons, and Maryland ryes. Walter never knew about it, and a ruling from the attorneys in the sale gave the entire cache to Oursinger, who was a teetotaler. He gave it all away at a party for friends from Washington and Warrenton.

When Walter wasn't buying paintings, or sailing on his yacht, or seeing after his horse farm in those years, he was producing plays on Broadway. In 1952, he put on the stark Jesuit drama, *The Strong Are Lonely*, set in South America in the seventeenth century. Stuart Vaughan, later famous as the first Artistic Director of the New York Shakespeare Festival and a founder of the regional theater movement in the U.S., was an actor in that production. He recalled that the set required a Velasquez painting for the walls. "Instead of having one copied, Mr. Chrysler simply brought in a genuine Velasquez of his own and hung it on the wall, to the amazement of all and sundry." The following year, Walter co-produced Tennessee Williams's much-admired surrealistic play *Camino Real* on Broadway. Neither play succeeded, but each was at least a succès d'estime.

His brother Jack's death in 1958 really affected him. He saw Jack's as a wasted life, and was determined, at the age of 49, to attempt to give his life real meaning. Accordingly, he bought the Center Methodist Church in Provincetown, on Cape Cod, for $40,000, and converted it into the beautiful little Chrysler Museum, which he paid for in part by selling 29 Impressionist paintings in London for $613,256. What he once said about art applied equally to this project: "You don't steal for it, but you beg, you borrow . . ."

He did nicely in Provincetown, and encouraged artists like Mark Rothko to open studios in town, and others to open galleries there. In all, the museum did much to enhance the town's reputation as a haven for artists.

Things went well for him until an exhibition of his works entitled "The Controversial Century: 1850–1950" opened in Ottawa in October, 1962. A page-one article in the *New York Times*, and a *Life* magazine article called "A Colossal Collection of Fakes" charged that he was an indiscriminate collector whose collection was marred by a large number of forgeries and fakes. He kept silent, except to say that he was "satisfied with all the pictures." Years later, in Bob Lipper's article, he said he was the victim of a " 'witch hunt,' a find-a-scapegoat publicity ploy spawned by the then newly formed Art Dealers Association of America." Nevertheless, the scandal cast a pall over Walter Chrysler's collection which lasted for the rest of his life.

Now that has lifted. Originally, former *New York Times* art critic Hilton Kramer "had the impression that Chrysler was the kind of collector who had bought some good things and some bad things, and that the quality was on a hit or miss basis." Eventually however, once he actually saw the collection, he "realized that the quality is by and large very high."

But Walter's ornery personality, combined with his lateness in paying bills and his reputation for backing young artists against the wall by insisting they sell to him cheaply and in quantity, eventually led Provincetown to have a belly full of him. When he demanded tax abatements and the construction of a new parking lot, they just said no, and to the great relief of the local citizenry, he packed up and went to Norfolk. After protracted negotiations, an agreement was signed on August 26, 1970, in which he agreed to bring his collection to Norfolk, in return for which the 1926 Norfolk Museum of Fine Arts and Sciences would be renamed the Chrysler Museum, and the new 2,500-seat theater being constructed nearby would be named Chrysler Hall.

With his usual high handedness, Walter made many demands that often upset other museum board members and city officials, and through the years there was a lot of pulling and hauling that went on between him and everybody else. As Hartney Arthur, a theatrical agent and general man of the theater who had many dealings with Walter Chrysler, said, "He was arrogant as only the very rich can be arrogant. He thought he could buy anything, and of course 90 percent of the time he could." But in the end, everybody benefited, as the museum gradually became nationally known and respected, and finally was gifted with the many Chrysler pieces originally just "on loan from the Walter P. Chrysler collection."

He lived on for another nine years after his wife's demise, dying of cancer in 1989 at the age of 79.

❧   ❧   ❧

So that is it, the story of Walter P. Chrysler, from the chalky plains of Kansas to the granite mausoleum in Tarrytown. The Chrysler Corporation, which has really reinvented itself into several different corportions over the last seventy-five years, survives and flourishes as an enormous success in the 1990s. As of November 17, 1998, it joined up with Daimler-Benz to become DaimlerChrysler, the world's fourth-largest automobile manufacturer. The Chrysler Building, as beautiful as ever, and more appreciated than ever, has been purchased by Tishman Speyer, which promises a glorious renaissance for it in the public presses. And of course the Chrysler family goes on, through such colorful figures as Jack Chrysler, Jr., with his airpower and ranches and art collection, and Frank B. Rhodes, Jr., with the beautiful work of his hands, creating masterpieces of American furniture that may endure through the centuries.

But we cannot let Walter Chrysler go without the words of the people who understood the meaning of his life best.

James C. Zeder, Fred Zeder's brother, said this in a letter to Bernice Garbisch in 1941: "It is unfortunate that all the world could not know Mr.

Chrysler personally. The terrific impact that he had upon his associates as a man and as a friend was demonstrated by the fine self esteem that his men derived from their association with him. Question any of them as to his employment and instead of merely designating the corporation, that person would proudly answer that he worked for Walter Chrysler."

David A. Wallace, the head of the Chrysler Division for the last few years of Walter Chrysler's life, said this of him when he died: "Like all truly great men, he was simple, direct and unpretentious. He was always anxious to give jobs to relatives or friends of his old friends, and he never forgot a friend, no matter how long a time had elapsed since they had met. If those that he asked me to place could hold on to a job, well and good. If they couldn't, I know that he helped them out of his private means. His hand was always in his pocket for a friend and he didn't bother to find out whether the case was particularly meritorious.

"The minute anyone got in trouble through no fault of his own, he was all sympathy. I remember one time seeing him burst into tears when he heard a sad story about one of his old workmen having a very sick wife. The big boss of a great corporation and a plain workman in overalls stood with their arms around each other and cried unashamedly.

"Walter Chrysler was above all else a true leader of men. He got things out of his organization through love and respect, not through fear."

Fred Zeder, in his lecture to the Newcomen Society on March 21, 1947, said this: "Mr. Chrysler's love for men was so genuine and so unselfish that instinctively they loved him in return.

"I well recall one incident in the early days of the Corporation when discouragement had hit us full force. We were in trouble, serious trouble; everything was going wrong, and we didn't know which way to turn. News of the difficulty had reached Mr. Chrysler in New York, and when the inevitable long distance phone call came through I was half sick as I reached for the receiver. I knew I was going to catch hades. But to my surprise it wasn't hell but: 'Hello there, Fred; just thought I'd call you up. I got lonesome for the sound of your voice.' Now, mind you, he had been in Detroit just two days before. Lonesome, my eye, he knew I was wrestling with a tough problem and he wanted to share my burden with me. He told me not to worry too much, the answers to those tough problems come, but they take a little time.

"After that telephone call I was buoyed up, fired with the enthusiasm that would whip any problem. Well now, what wouldn't you do for a man like that? No wonder his men respected him. He was the same way with all of them, and out of this mutual regard grew the power which welded the Chrysler Corporation into a unified entity."

Charles Stewart Mott, in his great age, said this to Richard Scharchberg in 1972: "Walter Chrysler was one of the world's greatest manufacturers and one of the world's best men. He could tell people what to do, and then do it himself."

But it was Edward D. Kennedy, writing in 1914, who gave the best assessment of the meaning of Walter Chrysler's life: "If automobile history were divided into two parts, a pre-1920 section and a post-1920 section, Chrysler's name would be as noteworthy in the second half of the auto story as Ford's name was in the first. Indeed, Chrysler was the only man in auto history (and one of the very few men in industrial history as a whole) who was able to make outstanding progress against the trend of the times.

"The Chrysler Corporation was organized much too late to have a reasonable chance of success. The Chrysler car itself was priced at well over $1,000 just when the $1,000 automobile was wearing out its welcome. The Dodge, at the time Chrysler bought it, was almost universally regarded as a white elephant. The Plymouth, when it came out in 1928, was merely one more addition to a crowded price class. Put the whole business together, add the Depression, and you should come out with a catastrophe. You did come out with a catastrophe in the case of every other auto company except General Motors and Ford. And though Ford never lived on his past in the sense of having nothing to offer in the present, there were times when he was leaning upon wealth previously accumulated to bring him through crises currently arisen.

"But Chrysler made an opportunity out of what might have been a disaster. By making a much better Plymouth at a much lower price, he came out of the Depression in much better condition than he had entered it. And in 1936 the Chrysler Corporation made three times as much money as it had made in 1929.

"Chrysler is a demonstration of the fact that economic events cannot be interpreted entirely in terms of economics: that the personal equation is sometimes not merely an important but a determining factor. Generally speaking, the times make the man; there are many big shots of the nineteen-twenties who are not even echoes today. But in Chrysler's case, the times were against the man and the man was superior to them. Chrysler was the last great individual constructive force in the automobile industry; offhand, one cannot think of a contemporary in any industry who can be compared with him. He never spent much time or got much publicity baiting the New Deal or battling the C.I.O., but he really was an American wayfarer who got along very nicely in the American way. To be sure, little can be said for a system which requires a Chrysler to operate it successfully, but if there were more individualists like Chrysler, the decrepit state of individualism would not be so obviously apparent."

Perhaps the best person to speak of Walter Chrysler's outlook on business and life is Mr. Chrysler himself. He said this in *Achievements by Leaders in*

World Affairs in 1928: "I don't believe there is such a thing as the secret of success. There are certain elements of success, to be sure. But those elements are known, and given the combination of all of them, you will have success.

"The first element is ability. Every man has a certain amount of ability. Some men have more than others. Some have ability and haven't discovered it. Others have ability and don't use it. But we must have, to start with, a certain amount of ability.

"Next we must have what I like to think of as capacity. I mean by that the means to develop, to grow. As a man's ability increases, his ability for work and concentration, for example, becomes greater.

"Next we must have energy. It matters not whether a man has ability and capacity if he lacks energy. A man must be industrious, and given ability, capacity and energy he can make a good start.

"And finally, he must have opportunity. A man may have ability and capacity and energy, but if he lacks the opportunity he may not get far. Some men can't recognize opportunity when they see it. Others go where the opportunities are the greatest. Others create their opportunities. But given the combination of the four elements we have success. . . .

"There are elements which lift ordinary success to the heights of brilliant success. Some men are idea-resourceful . . . some men are particularly enterprising . . . some men are genuinely enthusiastic and are lifted above the heads of others because of intelligent enthusiasm. . . .

"I really envy the young man of today. Never were the opportunities greater. Never were the rewards as large. . . . It all depends upon how hard a man is willing to work to achieve success.

"Be courageous and hopeful and enterprising. March on and achieve. The world will reward you, and when this old world of ours compensates for accomplishments of genuine merit, it invariably proves to be a generous world."

For a valediction, we call upon the Reverend J. Bradford Pengelly, one of a long line of clergymen bouyed up and encouraged by the example of Walter Chrysler. We return to the snowy night of January 22, 1920, when Mr. Chrysler was given a testimonial farewell dinner by the combined membership of the Kiwanis, the Rotary, and the Exchange Clubs of Flint at the Flint Country Club. The Reverend Pengelly was a last-minute substitute for an ailing John North Willys as principal speaker, and this, in part, is what he said:

"I am always pleased to give an appreciation of Walter Chrysler. I call him "The Big Chief." He is a big man in every way, . . . a great force for fellowship, unity and progress. . . . And through it all he remains a human being, unaffected and friendly.

"Chrysler is not like a sphinx, big, but cold and hard. He is warm hearted and likes the men whose cooperation has helped to make his success and his name. He realizes very well that without the friendship and cooperation of these men he could not be what he is, and therefore he is grateful. Mr. Chrysler is not a big, arrogant egotist, sitting in his elegant office and thinking that the whole success of the concern depends on him, that all the glory is his. He asks others to share the responsibility, but his is quite willing to share the glory. That is the spirit of a big man, a man around whom others can gather, and in whose life they can find a common meeting place. Mr. Chrysler thinks in terms of fellowship, he feels in terms of friendship and acts in terms of grateful service.

"He has found a great work. He has done it in a great way. He has made great friends. He loves his work and he loves his co-workers. Henry Van Dyke expresses the spirit of our friend, the spirit we all recognize and to which we pay tribute, for it is so characteristic of Chrysler:

This is my work; my blessing, not my doom;
Of all who live, I am the one by whom
This work can best be done in the right way.

"In those greater lines of a mightier mind we desire to express our good wishes that you may go on realizing greater things and finding that deep, inner joy which comes to a man from high ideals faithfully followed, and from tasks well done. We greet you with the words of Kipling. I quote the entire poem because it would lessen its unity and grandeur to give only a few lines. Here is *Envoi:*

When earth's last picture is painted and the tubes are twisted and
    dried
When the oldest colors have faded, and the youngest critic has died,
We shall rest, and, faith, we shall need it—lie down for an eon or two
Till the Master of All Good Workmen shall put us to work anew.

And those that were good shall be happy; they shall sit in a golden
    chair;
They shall splash at a ten-league canvas with brushes of comets' hair;
They shall find real saints to draw from—Magdalene, Peter and Paul;
They shall work for an age at a sitting and never be tired at all!

And only the Master shall praise us, and only the Master shall blame;
And no one shall work for money, and no one shall work for fame,

But each for the joy of the working, and each, in his separate star,
Shall draw the Thing as he sees It for the God of Things as They Are!

"Chief: You are a "Good Workman"; you have "real ideas to draw from"; you have not worked for money or fame alone, but for man, and "for the joy of working." I hope that "The God of Things as They Are" will still more abundantly prosper you, your family and your work.

"Walter, old boy, here is God-speed to you and all of your enterprises."

Acknowledgments

I must first thank Walter Chrysler's descendants, who were so helpful in the preparation of this book. Frank B. Rhodes, Jr., gave a great deal of his time and attention, and shared many family materials. Jack Chrysler, Jr. was similarly generous, and through his permissions allowed this book to be much richer in Walter Chrysler's own observations than it otherwise would have been. Gwynne Chrysler McDevitt, Joan French, Cynthia Rupp, Frank B. Rhodes, Jack Chrysler III, and Christopher Rupp were also most helpful. I must also acknowledge the hospitality and encouragement of Holly Rhodes, former wife of Frank B. Rhodes, Jr.

C. Fred Breer and Fred M. Zeder offered irreplaceable insights and information on the relationships of their respective fathers, Carl Breer and Fred Zeder, with Walter Chrysler. Their wives, Madge Breer and Martha Zeder, were unflagging in their gracious hospitality.

Professor Louis Bergeron of the Ecole des Hautes Etudes en Science Sociales in Paris kindly introduced me to his colleague Patrick Fridenson whose recommendations proved extraordinarily pertinent to this project. One was that I speak with James P. Womack of MIT, who suggested that I get in touch with Robert Lutz, then president of the Chrysler Corporation. He made it possible for me to make a most valuable contact with the Chrysler Historical Foundation. My heroine there was Barbara Fronczak, its director, who over a period of five years did everything within her power to give me access to information. Her colleagues Bruce Thomas, Brandt Rosenbusch, and her assistant, Art Ponder, were also of great help.

Professor Richard P. Scharchburg of the General Motors Institute Historical Collection provided insight into Chrysler's relationship with William C. Durant and his time at Buick. His assistant Bruce W. Watson was a model of gracious assistance.

Ron Grantz, then head of the National Automotive History Collection at the Detroit Public Library, helped me plumb the depths of that invaluable resource. The Flint Public Library was also most useful, as were the Walter P. Reuther Library in Detroit (Labor Research), the Historical Collections of the Bridgeport (CT) Public Library (Locomobile), and the Hagley Museum and Library (Pierre S. du Pont). Michael Leininger, a librarian at MIT, aided greatly in understanding the material available on the Chrysler Building. Columbia University's Butler Library and Avery Architecture Library were also extremely helpful in this area. The New York Public Library provided exemplary assistance in researching all elements of Walter Chrysler's history. Dr. Mary C. Henderson offered important guidance concerning New York City library resources in the areas of engineering and old periodicals. The Engineering Societies Library in New York was also very useful. Karen Laughlin, Reference Librarian of the Iowa State Historical Society, gave me all my Iowa information. Jerry Brown and Mary Jo Goldsmith of Waupaca, Wisconsin, Public Library worked hard to bring needed materials to that small town, in which this book was written.

Mrs. Anne Hedge, former curator of the Walter P. Chrysler Boyhood Home in Ellis, Kansas, opened up both the town and its nineteenth-century history to me, particularly the histories of the Chrysler and Forker families as they unfolded in Ellis. She also furnished my introduction to the Chrysler family, and extended the best sort of Midwestern hospitality on many occasions. The Ellis librarian, Lois Gashler, painstakingly combed through the town's nineteenth- and early twentieth-century newspaper archives on my behalf. Local historian Eileen Langley also aided me with her keen insights and supplied me with informative antique publications about the citizens of Ellis, the most important of which was compiled by Kitty Dale, the first curator of the Boyhood Home.

In Trinidad, Colorado, Judge Dean C. Mabry supplied me with the history of every rock, building, and person in town in Walter Chrysler's day. He also led me to Mary Frances Wells, who offered me valuable insights into the Bennett family, with whom Mr. Chrysler was so close. Cosette Henritze, editor of the *Trinidad Chronicle News*, also gave her assistance.

Arnold Penner made the connection that enabled me to tour the Chrysler Building from basement to spire. William A. Bassett, Jr., the building's General Manager, and his staff, including John T. Welch and Robert F. Biccochi, were extremely solicitous and informative.

Many automotive historians were openedhanded and forthcoming in sharing materials and giving guidance as to how and where more could be found. Among them were: Jeffrey I. Godshall, Anthony J. Yanick, Lawrence R. Gustin, Jean Maddern Pitrone, James M. Laux, Don Bunn, Jim Benjaminson of the Plymouth Owners Club, Menno Duerksen of *Cars & Parts* magazine, Tom Tjaarda, Dick Bowman of the W.P.C. Club, David R. Askey of the Airflow Club of America, and Richard H. Stout, Tim Kuser, and Stuart R. Blond of the Packard Club.

Additional acknowledgment must be given to: Sam Vaughan, then of Random House, who was responsible for the inclusion of the chapters on the early history of the automobile and mass production; Alfred D. Chandler; Scot Keller; Aristo Scrobogna; Dr. C.R. Haller; Constance Rosenblum; Everett Bell; Aline Hale; Harvey Folks Zimand; Catherine Smith; railroad historians Hol Wagner, Jr., Robert W. Richardson, Donald E. Vaughn, Thomas T. Taber, and W. Allan Waugh; Augie Mastrogiusseppe of the Denver Public Library; Irene Writer of the Childress, Texas, County Heritage Museum; Marie France Pochna; Walter H. Annenberg; Deirdre Egan; Jean Richards; H. Chrysler Hilliker; Stuart Vaughan; John A. Gunnell and Kenneth Buttolph of Krause Publications; Greg Fauth; David McDaniel; Thomas Behring Automotive Museum; Leslie B. Keno of Sotheby's; Dorothy (Mrs. Henry) Kraus; Richie Banaciski and Malcolm Neilsen of the Great Neck Fire Department; Nancy and Ben Chester; Weldon Ferguson; Earl Pritchett; Jerome Mowbray; and Polly Lieb.

I will always be grateful to Steven Englund for starting me on my career as a writer. He also introduced me to Don Congdon, who became my agent on this book.

Don Congdon is the real hero of this volume. He signed me up after reading my previous work and guided my proposal with meticulous attention to its structure. He then set about finding me the right publisher the old-fashioned way, one letter, one meeting, one phone call at a time. Truly, without him this present volume would not exist.

Herbert J. Addison, my editor at Oxford, has been a model of support and understanding. When the book took years longer to write than originally expected, he inquired as to its progress and offered his assistance, but he never pressured me or made me feel uncomfortable in any way. It was an ideal relationship.

Tom O'Brien, an independent editor whom I have come to trust and admire through the years, provided a third eye on the final manuscript that was of great value in many areas, both large and small.

Lastly, I want to thank the late Lucille Lortel, my employer for twenty years at the White Barn Theatre in Westport, Connecticut. In artistic and intellectual matters she was a shining beacon. Vision, commitment, and hard work were her principles in good times and bad, whether there was worldly success or not. For her, the work was what made it all worthwhile. For me, she is a lifetime guide.

Sources

Sources for Chapter 1

Cheyenne Autumn, by Mari Sandoz. Hastings House Publishers, New York, 1953.
Trails of the Smoky Hill, by Wayne C. Lee and Howard C. Raynesford. The Caxton Printers, Ltd., Caldwell, ID, 1980.

Sources for Chapter 3

Cheyenne Autumn, by Mari Sandoz. Hastings House Publishers, New York, 1953.
Trails of the Smoky Hill, by Wayne C. Lee and Howard C. Raynesford. The Caxton Printers, Ltd., Caldwell, ID, 1980.
The Old West: The Pioneers, text by Huston Horn. Time-Life Books, Alexandria, VA, 1974.
The Old West: The Soldiers, text by David Nevin. Time-Life Books, Alexandria, VA, 1974.
"Kansas," by Arthur Kapper. *Britannica,* 14th ed., 1932, v. 13.

Sources for Chapter 4

Trails of the Smoky Hill, by Wayne C. Lee and Howard C. Raynesford. The Caxton Printers, Ltd., Caldwell, ID, 1980.
The Railroaders: The Old West, text by Keith Wheeler. Time-Life Books, New York, 1973.

Sources for Chapter 5

Echoes and Etchings of Early Ellis, by Kitty Dale. Big Mountain Press, Denver, CO, 1964.
Profiles III of Ellis, Kansas, by Maxine Bradbury.
Early Ellis History, by Jessie Bell Omerod.
Gunfighters of Ellis County, by James D. Drees. *The Hays Daily News,* Hays, KS, 1992.
Trails of the Smoky Hill, by Wayne C. Lee and Howard C. Raynesford. The Caxton Printers, Ltd., Caldwell, ID, 1980.

Sources for Chapter 6

Life of an American Workman, by Walter P. Chrysler, in collaboration with Boyden Sparkes. Curtis Publishing Company, New York, 1937; Dodd, Mead & Company, New York, 1950.
Taking the Lamp Apart, unpublished manuscript version of above.
The Ellis Review, Ellis, Kansas, August 25, 1955.
Etchings and Echoes of Early Ellis, by Kitty Dale. Big Mountain Press, Denver, CO, 1964.

Sources for Chapter 7

Life of an American Workman, by Walter P. Chrysler, in collaboration with Boyden Sparkes. Curtis
     Publishing Company, New York, 1937; Dodd, Mead & Company, New York, 1950.
Taking the Lamp Apart, unpublished manuscript version of above.
The Ellis Review, Ellis, KS, August 25, 1955.

Sources for Chapter 8

Life of an American Workman, by Walter P. Chrysler, in collaboration with Boyden Sparkes. Curtis
     Publishing Company, New York, 1937; Dodd, Mead & Company, New York, 1950.
Taking the Lamp Apart, unpublished manuscript version of above.
Union Pacific: the Birth of a Railroad, by Maury Klein. Doubleday, New York, 1990.
Colorado Railroad Annual No. 15. Published and distributed by the Colorado Railroad Museum,
     1981.

Sources for Chapter 9

Life of an American Workman, by Walter P. Chrysler, in collaboration with Boyden Sparkes. Curtis
     Publishing Company, New York, 1937; Dodd, Mead & Company, New York, 1950.
The Ellis Review, Ellis, KS, August 25, 1955.
"The Battle of the Giants," by George W. Sutton, Jr. *Motor World*, January 1928.

Sources for Chapter 10

Life of an American Workman, by Walter P. Chrysler, in collaboration with Boyden Sparkes. Curtis
     Publishing Company, New York, 1937; Dodd, Mead & Company, New York, 1950.
Taking the Lamp Apart, unpublished manuscript version of above.

Sources for Chapter 11

Items in this chapter come from interviews conducted by the author with Judge Dean C. Mabry
     and with Mary Frances Wells, granddaughter of Harlo U. Bennett.
Life of an American Workman, by Walter P. Chrysler, in collaboration with Boyden Sparkes. Curtis
     Publishing Company, New York, 1937; Dodd, Mead & Company, New York, 1950.
Taking the Lamp Apart, unpublished manuscript version of above.
Past and Present of Fayette County Iowa, volume II. B. F. Bowen & Company, Indianapolis, IN,
     1910.
Letter from Everett G. Bell to Vincent Curcio, November 6, 1994.

Sources for Chapter 12

Life of an American Workman, by Walter P. Chrysler, in collaboration with Boyden Sparkes. Curtis
     Publishing Company, New York, 1937; Dodd, Mead & Company, New York, 1950.
Taking the Lamp Apart, unpublished manuscript version of above.
Annual Report, Fort Worth & Denver City Railroad, 1901.
The Denver Times, April 1, 1902.
The Denver Times, October 11, 1902.
The Dallas Morning News, August 19, 1940.

Sources for Chapter 13

Life of an American Workman, by Walter P. Chrysler, in collaboration with Boyden Sparkes. Curtis
     Publishing Company, New York, 1937; Dodd, Mead & Company, New York, 1950.
Taking the Lamp Apart, unpublished manuscript version of above.

History of Linn County Iowa, by Luther A. Brewer and Barthenius L. Wick. The Pioneer Publishing Company, Chicago, 1911.

Past and Present of Fayette County Iowa, vol. II. B. F. Bowen & Company, Indianapolis, IN, 1910.

The History of Linn County, Iowa. Western Historical Company, Chicago, 1878.

Annals of Iowa, vol. XVI, no. 3. Des Moines, 1928.

The National Cyclopaedia of American Biography.

Obituary of C. D. Van Vechten. *Cedar Rapids Gazette*, January 5, 1926.

The Telegraph-Herald's Abridged History of the State of Iowa and Directory of Fayette County, 1906–7.

The Cedar Rapids Evening Gazette, February 1, 1905.

"Watch the Terminals, Not the Way Stations—Chrysler," by O. D. Forster. *Forbes*, February 1, 1925.

"Chrysler Tells How He Did It," by B. C. Forbes. *Forbes*, January 1, 1929.

Sources for Chapter *14*

Some material from this chapter, as in the last two, comes from papers in the possession of Frank Rhodes and Jack Chrysler, and from a Pittsburgh newspaper article that seems to be dated Sunday, October 13 (?), 1929.

Life of an American Workman, by Walter P. Chrysler, in collaboration with Boyden Sparkes. Curtis Publishing Company, New York, 1937; Dodd, Mead & Company, New York, 1950.

Taking, the Lamp Apart, unpublished manuscript version of above.

"Watch the Terminals, Not the Way Stations—Chrysler," by O. D. Foster. *Forbes*, February 1, 1925.

James Jackson Storrow, Son of New England, by Henry Greenleaf Pearson. Thomas Todd Company, Boston, MA, 1932.

The Reminiscences of Nicholas Kelley. Oral Research History Office, Columbia University, 1952–1953.

Sources for Chapter *15*

Carriages Without Horses: J. Frank Duryea and the Birth of the American Automobile Industry, by Richard P. Scharchburg. Society of Automotive Engineers, Warrendale, PA, 1993.

The Buick: A Complete History, by Terry B. Dunham and Lawrence R. Gustin. Automobile Quarterly, Kutztown, PA, 1992.

Birth of a Giant, by Richard Crabb. Chilton Book Company, Philadelphia, 1969.

The Branding of America, by Ronald Hambleton. Yankee Books, Dublin, NH, 1987.

The American Automobile, by John B. Rae. University of Chicago Press, Chicago, 1965.

The Automobile Industry: The Coming of Age of Capitalism's Favorite Child, by Edward D. Kennedy. Reynal & Hitchcock, New York, 1941.

The Turning Wheel: The Story of General Motors Through Twenty-Five Years, 1908–1933, by Arthur Pound. Doubleday, Doran & Company, Garden City, NY, 1934.

The Automobile in America, by Stephen W. Sears. American Heritage Publishing Company, New York, 1977.

Who Me? Forty Years of Automobile History, by Chris Sinsabaugh. Arnold Powers, Inc., Detroit, 1940.

The Road Is Yours, by Reginald M. Cleveland and S. T. Williamson. The Greystone Press, New York, 1951.

Men, Money and Motors, by Theodore F. MacManus and Norman Beasley. Harper & Row, New York and London, 1929.

The Power to Go, by Merrill Denison. Doubleday & Company, Garden City, NY, 1956.

"Half Hour History: Gasoline 1900–1940," by Jerry Heasley. *Special Interest Autos*, August 1982.

"F. E. & F. O. Stanley: The Challenge from Steam," by John F. Katz. *Automobile Quarterly*, vol. XXV, no. 1, first quarter 1987.

Automobiles of America, 3rd rev. ed., by Automobile Manufacturers Association, Inc. Wayne State University Press, Detroit, 1970.

Standard Catalog of American Cars, 1805–1942, 2nd ed., by Beverly Rae Kimes and Henry Austin Clark, Jr. Krause Publications, Iola, WI, 1989.

The Dream Maker: William C. Durant, Founder of General Motors, by Bernard A. Weisberger. Little, Brown & Company, Boston and Toronto, 1979.

Ford: The Men and the Machine, by Robert Lacey. Little, Brown & Company, Boston and Toronto, 1986.

The Image of America, by R. L. Bruckelberger. Viking Press, New York, 1989.

Sources for Chapter 16

From the American System to Mass Production, 1800–1932, by David A. Hounshell. The Johns Hopkins University Press, Baltimore, MD, 1984.

Ford: The Men and the Machine, by Robert Lacey. Little, Brown & Company, Boston, 1986.

The American Automobile: A Brief History, by John B. Rae. University of Chicago Press, Chicago, 1965.

The Road Is Yours, by Reginald M. Cleveland and S. T. Williamson. The Greystone Press, New York, 1951.

The Birth of a Giant, by Richard Crabb. Chilton Book Company, Philadelphia, 1969.

The Public Image of Henry Ford, by David L. Lewis. Wayne State University Press, Detroit, 1976.

My 40 Years with Ford, by Charles E. Sorensen, with Samuel T. Williamson. W. W. Norton & Company, Inc., New York, 1956.

The Machine that Changed the World, by James P. Womack. Rawson Associates, New York, 1990.

My Years with General Motors, by Alfred P. Sloan. Doubleday, New York, 1963.

Standard Catalog of American Cars, 1805–1942, by Beverly Rae Kimes and Henry Austin Clark, Jr. Krause Publications, Iola, WI, 1989.

Who, Me? Forty Years of Automobile History, by Chris Sinsabaugh. Arnold Powers, Inc., Detroit, 1940.

The Automobile in America, by Stephen W. Sears. Simon & Schuster, New York, 1977.

The Power to Go, by Merrill Denison. Doubleday & Company, Garden City, NY, 1956.

Sources for Chapter 17

Life of an American Workman, by Walter P. Chrysler, in collaboration with Boyden Sparkes. Curtis Publishing Company, New York, 1937; Dodd, Mead & Company, New York, 1950.

Taking the Lamp Apart, unpublished manuscript version of above.

The Buick: A Complete History, by Terry B. Dunham and Lawrence R. Gustin. Automobile Quarterly, Kutztown, PA, 1992.

The Dream Maker, by Bernard A. Weisberger. Little, Brown & Company, Boston, 1979.

An Industrial History of Flint, by Frank M. Rodolph. The Flint Journal, Flint, MI, 1949.

Standard Catalog of American Cars, 1805–1942, 2nd ed., by Beverly Rae Kimes and Henry Austin Clark, Jr. Krause Publications, Iola, WI, 1989.

Standard Catalog of Buick, edited by Mary Sieber and Ken Buttolph. Krause Publications, Iola, WI, 1991.

Adventures of a White Collar Man, by Alfred P. Sloan, Jr. with Boyden Sparkes. Doubleday, Doran, New York, 1941.

Birth of a Giant, by Richard Crabb. Chilton Book Company, Philadelphia, 1969.

Master of Precision: Henry M. Leland, by Mrs. Wilfred C. Leland, with Minnie Dubbs Millbrook. Wayne State University Press, Detroit, 1966.

The Plungers and the Peacocks, by Dana L. Thomas. Putnam, New York, 1967.

The Turning Wheel: The Story of General Motors Through Twenty-Five Years, 1908–1933, by Arthur Pound. Doubleday, Doran, Garden City, NY, 1934.

American Technology and the British Vehicle Industry, by Wayne Lewchuk. Cambridge University Press, London, 1987.

"Chrysler May Head General Motors in Great Battle with Ford," by Mars Covington. *The Wall Street Indicator,* September 21, 1927.

"Body by Fisher: The Closed Car Revolution," by Roger B. White. *Automobile Quarterly,* vol. XXIX. no. 1, fourth quarter, 1991.

"Paint Complaint," by Fred B. Shaw. *Chrysler Motors Magazine*, October 1936.

"Chrysler Punches In," by W. A. P. John. *Motor Magazine*, May 1923.

"Co-Operation in the Buick Plant." *The Automobile*, December 25, 1913.

"First and Last Stages in the Building of Buick Motors." *The Automobile*, December 9, 1915.

"Explosion in Brass and Aluminum Foundry at Buick." *The Horseless Age*, vol. XXXI, no. 4.

"Bull Moose Gazes into Buick Factory." *Auto Topics*, October 19, 1912.

"Walter P. Chrysler Resigns as Vice President of General Motors." *Flint Saturday Night*, November 8, 1918.

"Walter P. Chrysler Guest of Honor." *Flint Saturday Night*, January 24, 1920.

Walter P. Chrysler obituary. *The Flint Journal*, October 19, 1940.

Resume of Family and Short Life History; Highlights of My Days at Buick and Peerless Motor Company, by Frederick G. Hoelzle. G.M.I. Alumni Foundation's Collection of Industrial History, Flint, MI.

Walter P. Chrysler article, by Paul H. Krol. *Algemeen Dagblad*, Christmas 1977 issue, Arts en Auto section; from the files of DaimlerChrysler Corporate Historical Collection.

"The Foundry Behind the Automobile." *The Iron Trade Review*, May 24, 1917.

"Ten Great Years With 'Boss' Kettering," by Louis Ruthenburg. *Ward's Auto World*, 1969.

Memoirs of William C. Durant. G.M.I. Alumni Foundation's Collection of Industrial History, Flint, MI.

Memoirs of Herbert R. Lewis (recorded). Library of Michigan State University, East Lansing.

The Buick Bulletin, vol. I, no. 13, December 1913, pp. 4–5; vol. III, no. 10, October 1915, pp. 6–7; vol. IV, no. 2, February 1916, p. 6; vol. IV, no. 4, April 1916, p. 14; vol. IV, no. 9, September 1916, pp. 6–7, 13; vol. IV, no. 10, October 1916, pp. 6–7, 12–13; vol. IV, no. 12, December 1916, pp. 6–7; vol. V, no. 8, August 1917, pp. 6–7; vol. VI, no. 1, January 1918, pp. 6–7; vol. VI, no. 3, March 1918, pp. 6–7; vol. VII, no. 9, September 1917, p. 5; vol. VII, no. 11, November 1918, pp. 6–7; vol. VII, no. 12, December 1919, pp. 6–7; vol. VII, no. 1, January 1920, pp. 6–7.

Sources for Chapter *18*

Life of an American Workman, by Walter P. Chrysler, in collaboration with Boyden Sparkes. Curtis Publishing Company, New York, 1937; Dodd, Mead & Company, New York, 1950.

Taking the Lamp Apart, unpublished manuscript version of above.

Standard Catalog of American Cars, 1805–1942, 2nd ed., by Beverly Rae Kimes and Henry Austin Clark, Jr. Krause Publications, Iola, WI, 1989.

The Turning Wheel; The Story of General Motors Through Twenty-Five Years, 1908–1933, by Arthur Pound. Doubleday, Doran, Garden City, NY, 1934.

The Three Engineers, by Carl Breer. Manuscript, DaimlerChrysler Corporate Historical Collection, published in part as *The Birth of the Chrysler Corporation and Its Engineering Legacy*, by Carl Breer, edited by Anthony A. Yannick. SAE International, Warrendale, PA, 1995.

Origin of Chrysler Corporation and the First Chrysler Car, by Owen Skelton. Manuscript, DaimlerChrysler Corporate Historical Collection.

Memoirs of Tobe Couture. Manuscript, DaimlerChrysler Corporate Historical Collection.

Audio tape of Tobe Couture retirement dinner, November 1956. DaimlerChrysler Corporate Historical Collection.

"The More People You Can Direct—the More You Are Worth." *The American Magazine*, August 1920.

"Zeder-Skelton-Breer Engineering," by Richard P. Scharchburg. *The Encyclopedia of American Biography*.

The Reminiscences of Nicholas Kelley. Oral History Research Office, Columbia University, 1952–1953.

"The Walter P. Chrysler Story, Parts I–V," by Menno Duerksen. *Cars & Parts Magazine*.

"Studebaker: One Can Do a Lot of Remembering in South Bend," by Maurice D. Hendry. *Automobile Quarterly*, vol. X, no. 3, third quarter 1972.

"John North Willys: His Magnetism, His Millions, His Motor Cars," by Beverly Rae Kimes. *Automobile Quarterly*, vol. VII, no. 3, third quarter 1979.

"Human Nature Must Guide Industry Toward Success." *The Willys News*, Toledo, OH, vol. II, no. 35, Friday, June 25, 1920.

"Willys Sales to Lead Field." *Detroit Free Press*, January 6, 1920.
"Chrysler Production to Start in Spring." *Automotive Industries*, December 9, 1920, p. 1191.
"Earl Resigns from Willys-Overland." *Automotive Industries*, December 9, 1920, p. 1193.
"Extension on Claims Sought for Willys." *Automotive Industries*, February 17, 1921, p. 427.
New York Times, September 29, 1920, p. 22, col. 2.
New York Times, November 11, 1920, p. 21, col. 4.
New York Times, March 20, 1921, sect. II, p. 13, col. 2.
New York Times, March 30, 1921, p. 5, col. 2.
New York Times, April 30, 1921, p. 18, col. 4.
New York Times, May 22, 1921, p. 14, col. 4.
New York Times, July 28, 1921, p. 21, col. 3.
New York Times, August 3, 1921, p. 19, col. 2.

Sources for Chapter 19

Life of an American Workman, by Walter P. Chrysler, in collaboration with Boyden Sparkes. Curtis Publishing Company, New York, 1937; Dodd, Mead & Company, New York, 1950.
Taking the Lamp Apart, unpublished manuscript version of above.
Standard Catalog of American Cars, 1805–1942, 2nd ed., by Beverly Rae Kimes and Henry Austin Clark, Jr. Krause Publications, Iola, WI, 1989.
The Three Engineers, by Carl Breer. Manuscript, DaimlerChrysler Corporate Historical Collection, published in part as *The Birth of the Chrysler Corporation and Its Engineering Legacy*, by Carl Breer, edited by Anthony A. Yannick. SAE International, Warrendale, PA, 1995.
Origin of Chrysler Corporation and the First Chrysler Car, by Owen Skelton. Manuscript, DaimlerChrysler Corporate Historical Collection.
Memoirs of Tobe Couture. Manuscript, DaimlerChrysler Corporate Historical Collection.
Audio tape of Tobe Couture retirement dinner, November 1956. DaimlerChrysler Corporate Historical Collection.
The Reminiscences of Nicholas Kelley. Oral History Research Office, Columbia University, 1952–53.
The Automobile Industry: The Coming of Age of Capitalism's Favorite Child, by Edward D. Kennedy. Reynal & Hitchcock, New York, 1941.
The Dream Maker: William C. Durant, Founder of General Motors, by Berrnard A. Weisberger. Little, Brown & Company, Boston and Toronto, 1979.
Men, Money and Motors, by Theodore A. MacManus and Norman Beasley. Harper & Row, New York, 1929.
Motor Memories, a Saga of Whirling Gears, by Eugene W. Lewis. Alved Publications, Detroit, 1947.
Going for Broke: The Chrysler Story, by Michael Moritz and Barrett Seaman. Doubleday & Co., Inc., Garden City, NY, 1977.
"Maxwell Motor Cars," by Richard Bowman. *WPC News*, vol. XXVI, no. 7, March 1995.
"In Search of the Chrysler Model 'A': Interview with the First Chrysler Mechanic," by Roy Moore. *WPC News*, vol. VII, no. 1, September 1975.
"Chrysler Tells How He Did It," by B. C. Forbes. *Forbes*, January 1, 1929.
"Zeder-Skelton-Breer Engineering," by Richard P. Scharchburg. *The Encyclopedia of American Business History and Biography*.
"Walter Percy Chrysler," by Richard P. Scharchburg. *The Encyclopedia of American Business History and Biography*.
"The Walter P. Chrysler Story, Parts I–V," by Menno Duerksen. *Cars & Parts Magazine*.
"90 and Counting," by Lanny Knutsen. *The Plymouth Bulletin*, vol. 35, no. 5, July–August 1994.
"Durant's Bid Gets Elizabeth Plant" and "Maxwell Had Plans for Chrysler Six," *Automotive Industries*, June 15, 1922, pp. 1344, 1351.
"The Chrysler Family Tree Has Many Roots," by Christy Borth. *Ward's Quarterly*, winter 1965.
"Complete Refinancing of Maxwell-Chalmers." *Automotive Industries*, September 30, 1920.
"New Maxwell Models About Ready for Production." *Automotive Industries*, October 29, 1921.
"History of Maxwell Organization." Manuscript, National Automotive History Collection, Detroit Public Library.

"A Challenge to the Champions," by Christy Borth. *Ward's Quarterly*, winter 1965.
"Chrysler of Maxwell-Chalmers," by W. A. P. John. *Motor*, September 1923.
"Chrysler Punches In," by W. A. P. John. *Everybody's Magazine*, September 1925.
New York Times, August 18, 1920, p. 18, col. 6.
New York Times, September 25, 1920, p. 18, col. 6
New York Times, September 27, 1920, p. 23, col. 3.
New York Times, September 29, 1920, p. 22, col. 2.
New York Times, September 30, 1920, p. 9, col. 4.
New York Times, November 10, 1920, p. 9, cols. 6–8.
New York Times, January 12, 1921, p. 27, col. 2.
New York Times, January 14, 1921, p. 18, col. 2.
New York Times, May 21, 1921, p. 19, col. 3.
New York Times, August 21, 1921, sect. VIII, p. 8, col. 1.
New York Times, October 27, 1921, p. 30, col. 4.
New York Times, February 16, 1922, p. 17, col. 2.
New York Times, March 10, 1922, p. 15, col. 4.
New York Times, March 21, 1922, p. 19, col. 5.
New York Times, March 29, 1922, p. 24, col. 6.
New York Times, April 29, 1922, p. 24, col. 2.
New York Times, June 4, 1922, sect. I, p. 17, col. 2.
New York Times, June 10, 1922, p. 18, col. 5.
New York Times, September 15, 1922, p. 29, col. 2.
New York Times, December 8, 1922, p. 28, col. 3.
New York Times, November 28, 1923, p. 24, col. 2.
New York Times, November 29, 1923, p. 32, col. 4.
New York Times, December 6, 1923, p. 30, col. 5.

Sources for Chapter *20*

Life of An American Workman, by Walter P. Chrysler, in collaboration with Boyden Sparkes. Curtis Publishing Company, New York, 1937; Dodd, Mead & Company, New York, 1950.
Taking the Lamp Apart, unpublished manuscript version of above.
Who, Me? Forty Years of Automobile History, by Chris Sinsabaugh. Arnold Powers, Inc., Detroit, 1940.
"The Chrysler Six—America's First Modern Automobile," by Mark Howell. *Antique Automobile*, vol. XXXVI, no. 1, January–February 1972.
"A Challenge to the Champions," by Christy Borth. *Ward's Quarterly*, winter 1965.
"Chrysler Tells How He Did It," by B. C. Forbes. *Forbes*, January 1, 1929.
Standard Catalog of American Cars, 2nd ed., by Beverly Rae Kimes and Henry Austin Clark, Jr. Krause Publications, Iola, WI, 1989.
Birth of a Giant, by Richard Crabb. Chilton Book Company, Philadelphia, 1969.
The Buick—A Complete History, by Terry B. Dunham and Lawrence R. Gustin. Automobile Quarterly, Kutztown, PA, 1992.
"What Is Ahead for the Automobile Industry?" by Walter P. Chrysler. *The Annalist*, October 22, 1923.
Memoirs of Tobe Couture. Manuscript, DaimlerChrysler Corporate Historical Collection.
Audio tape of Tobe Couture retirement dinner, November 1956. DaimlerChrysler Corporate Historical Collection.
"The Walter P. Chrysler Story, Parts I–V," by Menno Duerksen. *Cars & Parts Magazine*.
Letter from Michael J. Kollins to Glenn E. White, vice president, Chrysler Corporation, November 19, 1966. DaimlerChrysler Corporate Historical Collection.
Informational pamphlet, United States Merchant Marine Academy.
Chrysler advertisements, *Saturday Evening Post*, December 8 and December 29, 1923.
"Chrysler." *Fortune*, August 1935.
Automobile Topics, January 5, 1924.
Automobile Topics, January 12, 1924.
New York Times, January 6, 1924, section IX, p. 16.

"Built Like a Bridge." *Auto Topics*, December 30, 1933.
"The Chrysler Sales Corporation—A Romance of Industry." *Auto Topics*, December 30, 1933.
"Plymouth's Record in 1933 Brightest Spot on Industrial Horizon." *Auto Topics*, December 30, 1933.

Sources for Chapter *21*

Life of an American Workman, by Walter P. Chrysler, in collaboration with Boyden Sparkes. Curtis Publishing Company, New York, 1937; Dodd, Mead & Company, New York, 1950.
Taking the Lamp Apart, unpublished manuscript version of above.
Men, Money and Motors, by Theodore F. MacManus and Norman Beasley. Harper & Row, New York, 1929.
Motor Memories, a Saga of Whirling Gears, by Eugene W. Lewis. Alved Publications, Detroit, 1947.
Standard Catalog of American Cars, 1805–1942, 2nd ed., by Beverly Rae Kimes and Henry Austin Clark, Jr. Krause Publications, Iola, WI, 1989.
Standard Catalog of Chrysler, 1924–1990, by John Lee. Krause Publications, Iola, WI, 1990.
The Reminiscences of Nicholas Kelley. Oral Research History Office, Columbia University, 1952–1953.
The Three Engineers, by Carl Breer. Manuscript, DaimlerChrysler Corporate Historical Collection, published in part as *The Birth of the Chrysler Corporation and Its Engineering Legacy*, by Carl Breer, edited by Anthony A. Yannick. SAE Publications, Warrendale, PA, 1995.
Chrysler in Competition, by Ray Jones and Martin Swig. *Automobilia*, San Francisco, 1997.
Leadership, a Message to America, by Fred M. Zeder. A tribute to Walter P. Chrysler delivered at a dinner of the Newcomen Society of England, Mayflower Hotel, Washington, D.C., March 21, 1947; pub. by Princeton University Press, 1947.
"90 and Counting." *The Plymouth Bulletin*, v. XXXV, no. 5, July–August 1994.
"Racing with Chrysler," by Celeste Pestlin. *WPC News*, vol. XVIII, December 1986.
"Maxwell Motor Cars," by Richard Bowman. *WPC News*, vol. XXVI, no. 7, March 1995.
"Chrysler, The Early Years," by Cullen Thomas. *Automobile Quarterly*, vol. I, no. 1, summer 1967.
"The Chrysler Story, Part 1," by Menno Duerksen. *Cars & Parts*.
"Free Wheeling," by Menno Duerksen. *Cars & Parts*, July 1968.
Auto Topics, December 6, 1923.
"Byron C. Foy Is Power Behind DeSoto." *Auto Topics*, December 30, 1933.
"Chrysler Sees Prices and Business Steady." *Automotive Industries*, January 20, 1924.
N.A.C.C. General Bulletin G-854, for Annual Statistical Review of Automotive Industry, 1923.
N.A.C.C. General Bulletin G-948, for Annual Statistical Review of Automotive Industry, 1924.
Maxwell Motor Company and Subsidiaries Annual Report, Year Ending December 31, 1923.
Maxwell Motor Company and Subsidiaries Annual Report, Year Ending December 31, 1924.
New York Times, September 24, 1923.
New York Times, December 4, 1923.
New York Times, April 17, 1925.
New York Times, April 21, 1925.
New York Times, May 27, 1925.
New York Times, May 29, 1925.
New York Times, June 3, 1925.
New York Times, June 4, 1925.
New York Times, June 5, 1925.
New York Times, June 7, 1925.
New York Times, June 9, 1925.
New York Times, June 25, 1925.
New York Times, July 5, 1925.
New York Times, July 7, 1925.
New York Times, July 15, 1925.
New York Times, July 18, 1925.
New York Times, July 29, 1925.

New York Times, October 25, 1925.
New York Times, November 19, 1925.
New York Times, June 24, 1926.
New York Times, September 4, 1925.
New York Times, October 26, 1925.

Sources for Chapter 22

Ford: the Men and the Machine, by Robert Lacey. Little, Brown & Company, Boston and Toronto, 1986.
My Years with General Motors, by Alfred P. Sloan. Doubleday, New York, 1963.
My Life and Work, by Henry Ford, with Samuel Crowther. Doubleday, Garden City, NY, 1923.
Harley Earl and the Dream Machine, by Stephen Bayley. Alfred A. Knopf, New York, 1983.
The Legend of Chris Craft, by Jeffrey R. Rodengen. White Stuff Syndicate, Inc., Fort Lauderdale, FL, 1988.
The American Automobile: A Brief History, by John B. Rae. University of Chicago Press, Chicago, 1965.
The Automobile Industry: the Coming of Age of Capitalism's Favorite Child, by Edward D. Kennedy. Reynal & Hitchcock, New York, 1941.
The Three Engineers, by Carl Breer. Manuscript, DaimlerChrysler Corporate Historical Collection, published in part as The Birth of the Chrysler Corporation and Its Engineering Legacy, by Carl Breer, edited by Anthony A. Yannick. Society of Automotive Engineers, Warrendale, PA, 1995.
The Public Image of Henry Ford: An American Folk Hero and His Company, by David L. Lewis. Wayne State University Press, Detroit, 1976.
Standard Catalog of Cadillac, 1903–1990, edited by Mary Sieber and Ken Buttolph. Krause Publications, Iola, WI, 1995.
The Power to Go, by Merrill Denison. Doubleday & Co., Garden City, NY, 1956.
Men, Money and Motors, by Theodore F. MacManus and Norman Beasley. Harper & Row, New York and London, 1929.
"Harley Earl's California Years, 1893–1927," by Michael Lamm. Automobile Quarterly, vol. XX, no. 1, first quarter 1982.
"LaSalle Led G. M. Styling for Years," by Robert C. Ackerson. The Standard Catalog of Cadillac, 1903–1990, edited by Mary Sieber and Ken Buttolph. Krause Publications, Iola, WI, 1995.
"A Challenge to the Champions," by Christy Borth. Ward's Quarterly, winter 1965.
"Amplex, a Rapidly Growing Division of Chrysler Corporation." Auto Topics, December 30, 1933.
History of the Great Neck Alert Fire Company. Great Neck, NY, 1990.
"It Was All Push and No Pull for W. P. Chrysler." Detroit Free Press, April 6, 1919.
Ellis Review, March 25, 1924.
New York Times, March 1, 1926.
Boston Transcript, March 1, 1926.
The Sportsman, August 1926.
Auto Topics, December 11, 1926.
New York Times, January 9, 1927, sect. IX.
Auto Topics, December 10, 1927.
S.A.E. Journal, vol. XXIV, no. 2, February 1929.
The Iron Age, March 21, 1929.
Denver Post, August 19, 1940.
Letter, staff of Walter P. Chrysler to John North Willys, December 1, 1922.
Interview, Malcolm Neilson, Richie Banaciski, Thomas Jennings, Leon Motchkavitz, Great Neck Alert Fire Company, March 23, 1994.

Sources for Chapter 23

Life of an American Workman, by Walter P. Chrysler, in collaboration with Boyden Sparkes. Curtis Publishing Company, New York, 1937; Dodd, Mead & Company, New York, 1950.

Taking the Lamp Apart, unpublished manuscript version of above.

Poems, Plays and Essays of Oliver T. Goldsmith. Thomas J. Crowell & Co., New York, 1890.

Kaiser-Frazer: The Last Onslaught of Detroit, by Richard Langworth. *Automobile Quarterly*, Kutztown, PA, trade dist. by E. P. Dutton, New York, 1975.

Going for Broke: The Chrysler Story, by Michael Moritz and Barrett Seaman. Doubleday & Company, Garden City, NY, 1977.

The Dodges, by Jean Maddern Pitrone. Icarus, South Bend, IN, 1981.

Dodge Pickup Buyer's Guide, by Don Bunn. Motorbooks International, Osceola, WI, 1994.

The Dodge Story, by Thomas A. McPherson. Crestline, Glen Ellyn, IL, 1975.

Plymouth 1946–1959, by Jim Benjaminson. Motorbooks International, Osceola, WI. 1994; also, unpublished manuscript of first part of same.

Standard Catalog of American Cars, by Beverly Rae Kimes and Henry Austin Clark, Jr. Krause Publications, Iola, WI, 1989.

Motor Memories, a Saga of Whirling Gears, by Eugene W. Lewis. Alved Publications, Detroit, 1947.

The Automobile Industry: The Coming of Age of Capitalism's Favorite Child, by Edward D. Kennedy. Reynal & Hitchcock, New York, 1941.

The Reminiscences of Nicholas Kelley. Oral Research History Office, Columbia University, 1952–1953.

Birth of a Giant, by Richard Crabb. Chilton Book Company, Philadelphia, PA, 1969.

Chrysler in Competition, by Ray Jones and Martin Swig. Automobilia, San Francisco, 1997.

The Power to Go, by Merrill Denison. Doubleday & Co., Garden City, NY, 1956.

"The Chrysler-Dodge Merger as an Indication of Automobile Development," by Ralph C. Epstein. *The Annalist*, June 6, 1928.

"How Henry Ford Gets Phenomenally Low Manufacturing Costs," by J. Younger. *Manufacturing Industries*, vol. XV, no. 1, January 1928.

"Efficiency Without Volume." *Iron Age*, vol. CXXI, no. 2, May 17, 1928.

The Literary Digest, June 16, 1928.

"Chrysler Tells How He Did It," by B. C. Forbes. *Forbes Magazine*, January 1, 1929.

"Keller of Chrysler Motors," by B. C. Forbes. *Forbes Magazine*, September 1, 1939, and October 1, 1939.

"The Brothers Dodge," by Stan Grayson. *Automobile Quarterly* vol. XVII, no. 1, first quarter 1979.

"Chrysler, The Early Years," by Cullen Thomas. *Automobile Quarterly*, vol. I, no. 1, summer 1967.

Chrysler Tonic, vol. II, no. 3, January 1, 1950.

"What's in a Name?" by C. T. Schaefer. *Motor Life Magazine*, October 1926.

"The Dodge Brothers," by L. M. Wallace. *WPC News*, vol. VIII, no. 5, January 1977.

"1929–42 DeSoto: Excess Baggage," by Arch Brown. *Collectible Automobile*, August 1990.

"Plymouth: The Beginning, 1928–1931," by Richard Bowman. *WPC News*, vol. XIX, no. 6, February 1988.

"1929 Plymouth QU," by Sherwood Kahlenberg. *WPC News*, vol. XII, August 1981.

"The Plymouth Story, Part I: The Four Cylinder Era," by Arch Brown. *Cars & Parts*, June 1994.

"Chrysler's Finest: The Official Classic Imperials, Part I," by Warren H. Erb. *WPC News*, vol. XXVII, no. 6, February 1996.

"1928: The Year All Went Well," by Sherwood Kahlenberg. *WPC News*, vol. X, June 1979.

"Eighty Days from Factory Foundation to Finished Construction." *Machinery*, May, 1929.

"Highlights of Chrysler Accomplishments for 1928." *Chrysler Motoring*, 1929.

"F. J. Haynes Retires from Dodge Brothers." *Automobile Topics*, August 11, 1928.

Automobile Topics, August 14, 1926.

Automobile Topics, July 16, 1926.

Automobile Topics, August 14, 1928.

Automobile Topics, December 20, 1933.

Advertisement, *Saturday Evening Post*, July 7, 1928.

Speech by K. T. Keller at tenth anniversary dinner of Automobile Old Timers, Inc., October 18, 1949.

Speech by K. T. Keller at Minneapolis Chamber of Commerce Public Affairs Luncheon, June 28, 1950.

Interview with Eugene Weiss, February 25, 1995.

Letter from Joel R. Miller to Vincent Curcio, February 8, 1993.

Letter from Jean Maddern Pitrone to Vincent Curcio, April 9, 1992.

"Take Advantage of an Opportunity to Learn the Systems of Big Men—Machines Work Alike, but Not Men," by Ray Priest. *Detroit Sunday Times*, December 9, 1928.

Detroit News, May 30, 1928.

Detroit Times, May 29, 1946.

Detroit News, September 23, 1958.

"Touch of Genius Saved Tottering Dodge Empire," by David C. Smith. *Detroit Free Press*, April 18, 1966.

New York Times, April 12, 1927.

New York Times, August 17, 1927.

New York Times, January 8, 1928.

New York Times, May 30, 1928.

New York Times, June 1, 1928.

New York Times, June 6, 1928.

New York Times, June 8, 1928.

New York Times, June 16, 1928.

New York Times, June 26, 1928.

New York Times, June 27, 1928.

New York Times, July 8, 1928.

New York Times, July 18, 1928.

New York Times, July 27, 1928.

New York Times, July 28, 1928.

New York Times, July 29, 1928.

New York Times, July 31, 1928.

New York Times, August 3, 1928.

New York Times, August 4, 1928.

New York Times, August 11, 1928.

New York Times, August 23, 1928.

New York Times, September 8, 1928.

New York Times, September 23, 1928.

New York Times, October 12, 1928.

New York Times, October 17, 1928.

Sources for Chapter 24

Life of an American Workman, by Walter P. Chrysler, in collaboration with Boyden Sparkes. Curtis Publishing Company, New York, 1937; Dodd, Mead & Company, New York, 1950.

Taking the Lamp Apart, unpublished manuscript version of above.

"77 Stories, The Secret Life of a Skyscraper," by David Michaelis. *Manhattan, Inc.*, June 1986.

"The Chrysler Building as I See It," by Kenneth M. Murchison. *The American Architect*, vol. LIII, no. 4, September 1930.

"The Chrysler Building, New York, William Van Alen, Architect," by Eugene Clute. *The Architectural Forum*, October 1930.

"The Structure and Metal Work of the Chrysler Building," by William Van Alen. *The Architectural Forum*, vol. LIII, no. 4, October 1930.

"Manhattan's Mightiest Minaret," by F. D. McHugh. *Scientific American*, vol. CXLII, April 1930.

The Reminiscences of Nicholas Kelley. Oral History Research Office, Columbia University, 1952–1953.

"Draftsmanship and Architecture, V, as Exemplified in the Work of William Van Alen," by Francis S. Swales. *Pencil Points*, vol. X, no. 8, August 1929.

"Chrysler's Pretty Bauble," by Douglas Haskell. *The Nation*, vol. 131, no. 3407, October 22, 1931.

77 Stories, the Chrysler Building, "The World's Tallest Building," complied and published by John
      B. Reynolds, New York, 1930.
The Chrysler Building. Chrysler Tower Corporation, New York, 1930.
"Flights of Fanciful Steel," by David D. Levine. *Dichotomy,* spring 1988.
"Is Carelessness on Your Payroll?" by Walter P. Chrysler. *Building Age,* vol. LII2, no. 3, March
      1930.
"The Perfect Space; The Chrysler Building Lobby, New York," by Paul Goldberger. *Travel &
      Leisure,* June 1989.
"Chrysler," by Cervin Robinson. *Architect,* May–June 1974.
Delirious New York, by Rem Koolhaas. Oxford University Press, New York, 1978.
Skyscraper Style: Art Deco New York, by Cervin Robinson and Rosemarie Bletter. Oxford Univer-
      sity Press, New York, 1975.
"The Chrysler Building," by Dan Klein. *Connoisseur,* April 1978.
The Frozen Fountain, by Claude Bragdon. Books for Libraries Press, New York, 1970, reprint of
      1924 edition.
"The Chrysler Building: Art Deco Magnificence," by Charlie Kaplan.
Letter-brochure, The 67th Floor Holding Corporation, The Cloud Club, Inc., 1930.
"Worldly Cities of Iron and Angles," by Herbert Muschamp. *New York Times,* March 27, 1994.
"New York Skyscrapers as Ancient Temples," by Michael Frank. *New York Times,* July 11, 1997.
"Scalloped Dreams, a Hotelier's Fantasy," by Tracie Rozhan. *New York Times,* July 24, 1997.
New York Times, October 4, 1928.
New York Times, October 13, 1928.
New York Times, October 17, 1928.
New York Times, March 10, 1931.
New York Times, April 23, 1929.
New York Times, April 29, 1929.
New York Times, November 24, 1929.
New York Times, December 2, 1929.
New York Times, December 15, 1929.
New York Times, May 28, 1930.
New York Times, June 15, 1930.
New York Times, June 18, 1930.
New York Times, August 2, 1930.
New York Times, August 11, 1930.
New York Times, October 22, 1930.
New York Times, October 25, 1930.
New York Times, January 2, 1931.
New York Times, February 8, 1931.
New York Times, August 1, 1931.
New York Times, August 22, 1931.
New York Times, November 24, 1932.
New York Times, July 20, 1933.
New York Times, January 28, 1934.
New York Times, April 15, 1936.
New York Times, May 2, 1936.
New York Times, March 4, 1937.

Sources for Chapter 25

Life of an American Workman, by Walter P. Chrysler, in collaboration with Boyden Sparkes. Curtis
      Publishing Company, New York, 1937; Dodd, Mead & Company, New York, 1950.
Taking the Lamp Apart, unpublished manuscript version of above.
The Plungers and the Peacocks, by Dana L. Thomas. G. P. Putnam & Sons, New York, 1967.
The Dream Maker: William C. Durant, Founder of General Motors, by Bernard A. Weisberger. Little,
      Brown & Company, Boston and Toronto, 1979.

Ford: The Men and the Machine, by Robert Lacey. Little, Brown & Company, Boston and Toronto, 1986.

The Automobile Industry: The Coming of Age of Capitalism's Favorite Child, by Edward D. Kennedy. Reynal & Hitchcock, New York, 1941.

The Mirror of Wall Street, by Anonymous. G. P. Putnam & Sons, New York, 1933.

"What Is Ahead for the Automobile Industry," by Walter P. Chrysler. *The Annalist,* October 22, 1923.

"Tendencies in the Automobile Industry," by Walter P. Chrysler. *The Bankers Magazine,* July 1924.

The Bankers Magazine, July 1924.

"Parking and the Motor Industry," by Walter P. Chrysler. *Nation's Business,* November 1926.

"Think of Your Business in Terms of Just One Customer," by Walter P. Chrysler. *Printers' Ink,* April 28, 1927.

"There Is Plenty of Good Business for Those Who Have Confidence," by Walter P. Chrysler. *Printers' Ink Monthly,* January 1928.

"Saturation? No—Replacement," by Walter P. Chrysler, as told to E. S. Mackay. *Business,* August 1927.

"Chrysler Tells How He Did It," by B. C. Forbes. *Forbes,* January 1, 1929.

"Here Comes Prosperity," by Walter P. Chrysler. *The Dragon,* August 1929.

Interview with Walter P. Chrysler, 1926. DaimlerChrysler Corporate Historical Collection.

Interview with Malcolm Neilson, March 23, 1994.

The Good Old Days of 1928, Chrysler family film. Collection of Frank B. Rhodes, Jr.

In the Good Old B.C. Days (Before Crash), Chrysler family film. Collection of Frank B. Rhodes, Jr.

Turn Back the Calendar, Chrysler family film. Collection of Frank B. Rhodes, Jr.

Handwritten list by Walter P. Chrysler of jobs and salaries, 1916–1924. Collection of Frank B. Rhodes, Jr.

The Engineering Profession, by Herbert C. Hoover. Reprint flyer from Rockwell Standard Corporation.

Chrysler Family History. Privately printed, 1959.

Auction catalog, property of the Estate of Mrs. Della V. Chrysler (Mrs. Walter P. Chrysler), May 21, 22, 23, 1941, Parke-Bernet Galleries, Inc.

"Walter Chrysler: A Search for Self, a Stab at Immortality," by Bob Lipper. *The Virginian-Pilot (Lighthouse),* July 3, 1977.

"A Good Week for the Dow," by Vartanig G. Vartan. *New York Times,* 1970s.

New York Times, January 6, 1924.

New York Times, August 7, 1925.

New York Times, October 25, 1925.

New York Times, January 10, 1926.

New York Times, April 2, 1926.

New York Times, May 14, 1926.

New York Times, May 15, 1926.

New York Times, June 12, 1926.

New York Times, January 9, 1927.

New York Times, January 29, 1927.

New York Times, February 13, 1927.

New York Times, October 2, 1927.

New York Times, November 2, 1927.

New York Times, February 12, 1928.

New York Times, April 4, 1928.

New York Times, January 2, 1929.

New York Times, January 25, 1929.

New York Times, February 15, 1929.

New York Times, April 26, 1929.

New York Times, June 28, 1929.

New York Times, October 27, 1929.

New York Times, October 29, 1929.

New York Times, November 22, 1929.
New York Times, December 18, 1929.
New York Times, January 5, 1930.
New York Times, November 10, 1930.

Sources for Chapter 26

The Classic Car, by Beverly Rae Kimes. Classic Car Club of America, 1990.
Conspicuous Production: Automobiles and Elites in Detroit, 1899–1933, by Donald Finley Davis.
     Temple University Press, Philadelphia, PA, 1988.
The Banking Crisis of 1933, by Susan Estabrook Kennedy. Lexington University Press, Lexington,
     KY, 1973.
Ford: The Men and the Machine, by Robert Lacey. Little, Brown & Company, Boston and Toronto,
     1986.
The Olympian Car, by Richard Burns Carson. Alfred A. Knopf, New York, 1976.
My Forty Years with Ford, by Charles E. Sorensen, with Samuel T. Williamson. W. W. Norton &
     Co., Inc., New York, 1956.
Plymouth, 1946–1959, including unpublished early Plymouth section, by Jim Benjaminson.
     Motorbooks International, Osceola, WI, 1994.
The Story of Superfinish, by Arthur M. Swigert, Jr. Lynn Publishing Company, Detroit, 1940.
The Glory and the Dream, by William Manchester. Little, Brown & Company, Boston and Toronto,
     1972.
Management and Managed: 50 Years of Crisis at Chrysler, by Steven Jeffreys. Cambridge University
     Press, New York, 1986.
The Complete Encyclopedia of the American Automobile, by Karl Ludvigsen and David Burgess
     Wise. Chartwell Books, Secaucus, NJ.
Chrysler Corporation: The Story of an American Company. Department of Public Relations, Chrys-
     ler Corporation, 1955.
Standard Catalog of American Cars, 2nd ed., edited by Beverly Rae Kimes and Henry Austin
     Clark, Jr. Krause Publications, Iola, WI, 1989.
The Automobile Industry: The Coming of Age of Capitalism's Favorite Child, by Edward D. Kennedy.
     Reynal & Hitchcock, New York, 1941.
The One Hundred Greatest Advertisements, by Julian Watkins. Moore Publishing Company, New
     York, 1949.
Advertising and Selling, by J. V. Tarleton.
The Reminiscences of Nicholas Kelley. Oral History Research Office, Columbia University, 1952–
     1953.
"I Like to Build Things," by Stephen Fox. *Invention and Technology*, summer 1999.
"The Last Years of Auburn," by Karl S. Zahm. *Collectible Automobile*, June 1984.
"In the Face of Adversity: The Cars of 1932," by John A. Conde. *Collectible Automobile*, October
     1996.
"1930 Hupmobile Model C," by Bob Stevens. *Cars & Parts*, December 1996.
"Hupmobile in the Thirties: A New Car for a New Age," by Karl S. Zahm. *Collectible Automobile*,
     December 1989.
"1932–35 Graham: A Blue Ribbon for the Blue Streak," by Jeffrey I. Godshall. *Collectible Au-
     tomobile*, April 1993.
"Like a Blue Streak: 1933 Graham." *Special Interest Autos*, December 1972–January 1973.
"Undeserving of Defeat: The 1932 DeSoto Model SC," by Mike Mueller. *Automobile Quarterly*,
     vol. XXXI, no. 1, fall 1992.
"Chrysler." *Car Life*, January 1967.
"A Challenge to the Champions," by Christy Borth. *Ward's Quarterly*, winter 1965.
"The Career and Creations of Alan H. Leamy," by Dan Burger. *Automobile Quarterly*, vol. XX,
     no. 2, second quarter, 1982.
"1931 Chrysler 6," by Michael Zamm. *Special Interest Autos*, no. 40, May–July 1977.
"There Are No Automobiles." *Fortune*, October 1930.
"The New Chrysler 6." *WPC News*, vol. XXVII, no. 3, November 1995.

"1932 Plymouth PB," by Phil Goldberg. *WPC News* vol. XIX, no. 7, November 1988.

"The Plymouth Story: Part I, The Four Cylinder Era, 1928–1932," by Arch Brown. *Cars & Parts*, June 1994.

"The Plymouth Story: Part II, The Early Six Cylinder Era, 1933–1939," by Arch Brown. *Cars & Parts*, July 1994.

"Plymouth, The Years of Triumph," by Jeffrey I. Godshall. *Automobile Quarterly*, vol. XXIII, no. 2, second quarter, 1985.

"The 1933 Plymouth," by K. C. Eberhard. *WPC News*, vol. IX, no. 6, February 1978.

"Chrysler, The Early Years," by Cullen Thomas. *Automobile Quarterly*, vol. VI. no. 1, summer 1967.

"A Century of Progress in Ten Years." *Automobile Topics*, December 30, 1933.

"Fame and the Chrysler Car," by Chuck Jensen. *WPC News*, vol. XXVI, no. 11, July 1995.

"Classic Chrysler: 1932 Custom Imperial," by Arch Brown and Bud Juneau. *Special Interest Autos*, no. 105, June 1988.

"Chrysler's Finest: The Officially Classic Imperials, Part I," by Warren H. Erb. *WPC News*, vol. XXVII, no. 6, February 1996.

"Imperial: Chrysler's Flagship," by Jeffrey I. Godshall. *Automobile Quarterly*, vol. XXI, no. 2, second quarter, 1983.

Chrysler Corporation Annual Report, March 3, 1933.

Letter from Fred Zeder, Jr. to Vincent Curcio, May 4, 1992.

Letter from Walter P. Chrysler, Sr. to Nicholas Kelley, September 9, 1931.

Automotive Industries, October 29, 1932.

Automobile Topics, November 12, 1932.

Automotive Industries, May 5, 1934.

Automotive News, February 4, 1933, pp. 138–142.

Detroit Free Press, July 10, 1932.

Detroit Free Press, August 16, 1933.

"Help of Employees Benefit a Complete Social Agency," by William C. Richards. *Detroit Free Press*, February 18, 1934.

New York Times, July, 3, 1930.

New York Times, January 6, 1931.

New York Times, January 11, 1931.

New York Times, June 16, 1931.

New York Times, January 14, 1932.

New York Times, January 15, 1932.

Sources for Chapter 27

The Three Engineers, by Carl Breer. Manuscript, DaimlerChrysler Corporate Historical Collection, published in part as *The Birth of the Chrysler Corporation and Its Engineering Legacy*, by Carl Breer, edited by Anthony A. Yannick. SAE International, Warrendale, PA, 1995.

Standard Catalog of American Cars, 1805–1942, 2nd ed., by Beverly Rae Kimes and Henry Austin Clark, Jr. Krause Publications, Iola, WI 1989.

"The Slippery Shapes of Paul Jaray," by Jerry Sloniger. *Automobile Quarterly*, vol. XIII, no. 3, 1975.

"Research Is the Spearhead of Chrysler Engineering," by Niran Bates Pope. *Auto Topics*, December 30, 1933.

The Automobile Age, by James J. Flink. MIT Press, Cambridge, MA, 1988.

The Art of American Car Design, by C. Edson Armi.

Make 'Em Shout Hooray! by Richard H. Stout. Vantage Press, New York, 1993.

Tatra, by I. Margolius and J. G. Henry. S.A.E. Publications, 1990.

100 Ans d'Automobile Française, 1884–1984. Editions S.O.S.D., 1984.

The Automobile: The First Century, by David Burgess Wise, William Boddy, and Brian Laban. Greenwich House, New York, 1983.

The Oxford Companion to American Theater, edited by Gerald Boardman. Oxford University Press, New York and Oxford, 1992.

Chrome Dreams: Auto Styling Since 1893, by Paul Carroll Wilson. Chilton Book Company, Radnor, PA, 1976.

"Streamlining," in *Compton's Picturebook Encyclopedia*. F. E. Compton & Co., Chicago, IL, 1953.

"Automobile Aerodynamics, Form and Fashion," by Karl Ludvigsen. *Automobile Quarterly*, vol. VI, no. 2, fall 1967.

"The Path of Least Resistance," by James J. Flink. *Invention and Technology*, fall 1989.

Bulletin, Museum of Modern Art, New York, December 1942.

"Half of a Streamlined Body of Revolution Called Ideal Aerodynamic Form for Cars." *Automotive Industries*, vol. LXX, no. 25, June 23, 1934.

"How the Airflows Were Designed." *Automotive Industries*, vol. LXX, no. 25, June 23, 1934.

"Summer of '34," by Ross MacLean. *Airflow Newsletter*, vol. XXXI, no. 6, June 1992.

"The History of the Airflow Car," by Howard S. Irwin. *The Scientific American*, August 1977.

"The Evolution of the All-Steel Body and Its Part in Airflow Design," by Oliver H. Clark. *Auto Topics*, December 30, 1933.

"Chrysler Employs New Methods in Making Airflow Cars," by Banham Finney. *The Iron Age*, November 1, 1934.

"C. W. Memories," by C. Fred Breer. *The Classic Car*, June 1984.

"Magnificent Turkey," by Michael Lamm. *Special Interest Autos*, April–May 1973.

"Substance over Style: The Keller Era," by John Matrin. *Automobile Quarterly*, vol. XXXII, no. 4, April 1994.

"Hupmobile in the Thirties: A New Car for a New Age," by Karl S. Zahm. *Collectible Automobile*, December 1989.

"Of Reo Royales and Flying Clouds," by Karl S. Zahm. *Collectible Automobile*, May 1985.

"1933 Reo Royale," by Walter F. Robertson Jr. *Special Interest Autos*, January–February 1978.

"1932–1935 Graham: A Blue Ribbon for the Blue Streak," by Jeffery I. Godshall. *Collectible Automobile*, April 1993.

"Airflow Prototypes." *Special Interest Autos*, April–May 1973.

"Pierce-Arrow in the Thirties," by Karl S. Zahm. *Collectible Automobile*, March 1985.

"The 1934 DeSoto Airflow," by Wilbur Jeanes. *Car & Driver*, September 1985.

"Volkswagen Nine Lives Later," by Dan R. Post. *Horizon House*, California, 1966.

"The Star and the Laurel," by Beverly Rae Kimes. *Mercedes-Benz of North America*, Montvale, NJ, 1986.

"Chicken or Egg?" *Autocar*, June 19, 1953.

"1934–1937 Chrysler/DeSoto Airflow: Future Shock," by Karl S. Zahm. *Collectible Automobile*, January 1986.

"Historians May Lead Us, but Are They Right?" by Darwyn Lumley. *Car Classics*, October 1978.

"An Airflow in Toyota's Future, and in Peugeot's Too," by David Duricy, Jr. *Special Interest Autos*, October 1989.

"Detroit News Letter." *Sports Cars Illustrated*, April 1960.

"History of the Beetle: Part Two." *Volkswagen Parts & Advice*, no. 2, 1993.

"Profile: Tom Tjaarda," by Pete Coltrin. *Road & Track*, September 1977.

"I Remember My Father," by Tom Tjaarda. *Special Interest Autos*, April–May 1972.

"Tatra: The Czech Marque of Innovation," by Hans Otto Meyer-Spelbrink. *Collectible Automobile*, October 1997.

"The Stream-Line Carriage Body—Jaray's System; Being a Popular Account of Its Origins, Applications and Advantages," by Charles Frey. Stream-Line Carriage Body Company, 25 Stocker Street, Zurich.

Chrysler News, Airflow Extra, vol. I, no. 1.

"The Present Status of Automobile Aerodynamics in Automobile Engineering and Development," by William D. Bowman. Presented at the AAIA symposium on the aerodynamics of sports and competition vehicles, Los Angeles, California, April 20, 1968.

"Story of the Airflow Cars (1934–1937)." Engineering Office, Chrysler Corporation, October 1963.

"Retail Salesman's Service Bulletin no. 13; The Ross Roy Service; August 1, 1934." *The Airflow Newsletter*, vol. XXXI, no. 7, July 1992.

Automotive Industries, July 27, 1935.

Interview with Fred Zeder, Jr. and C. Fred Breer, Palm Springs, California, November 12, 1993.

Letter to Vincent Curcio from Fred Zeder, Jr., April 4, 1992.

Letter to Carl Breer from Walter Chrysler, August 18, 1931; C. C. Recordak microfilm #72.

Letter to Carl Breer from Jack Whitaker, June 20, 1934; C. C. Recordak microfilm #92.

Letter to Carl Breer from Jack Whitaker, July 2, 1934; C. C. Recordak microfilm #92.

Letter to Walter Chrysler from Charles W. Berg, August 25, 1934.

Letter to J. W. Frazer from Charles W. Berg, August 25, 1934; C. C. Recordax microfilm #92.

Letter to Fred Zeder from Walter Chrysler, August 28, 1934; C. C. Recordak microfilm #92.

Letter to Walter Chrysler from Carl Breer, August 31, 1934; C. C. Recordak microfilm #92.

Letter to Charles Simon from Carl Breer, October 26, 1934; C. C. Recordak microfilm #92.

Letter to B. E. Hutchinson from Lowell H. Brown, March 15, 1933; C. C. Recordak microfilm #87.

Letter to O. R. Skelton from Lowell H. Brown, March 15, 1933; C. C. Recordak microfilm #87.

Intercompany correspondence to Fred Zeder from Carl Breer, August 22, 1934; C. C. Recordak microfilm #92.

Intercompany correspondence to Carl Breer from Charles Simon, October, 22, 1934; C. C. Recordak microfilm #92.

Sources for Chapter 28

Life of an American Workman, by Walter P. Chrysler, in collaboration with Boyden Sparkes. Curtis Publishing Company, New York, 1937; Dodd, Mead & Company, New York, 1950.

Management and Managed: 50 Years of Crisis at Chrysler, by Steve Jeffreys. Cambridge University Press, Cambridge, 1986.

The Visible Hand: The Managerial Revolution in American Business, by Alfred D. Chandler. The Belknap Press of Harvard University Press, Cambridge, MA, 1977.

The Concept of the Corporation, by Peter F. Drucker. John Day Company, 1946.

The Glory and the Dream, by William Manchester. Little, Brown & Company, Boston and Toronto, 1972.

Frank Murphy: The Depression Years, by Sidney Fine. University of Illinois Press, Urbana and Chicago, 1979.

The American Automobile: A Brief History, by John B. Rae. University of Chicago Press, Chicago, 1965.

Ford: Decline and Rebirth, by Allan Nevins and Frank Ernest Hill. Charles Scribner and Sons, 1962.

The Automobile Under the Blue Eagle, by Sidney Fine. University of Michigan Press, Ann Arbor, 1953.

Chrome Colossus, by Ed Cray. McGraw Hill, New York, 1980.

Walter Reuther and the Rise of the Auto Workers, by John Barnard. Little, Brown & Company, Boston and Toronto, 1976.

Sit Down, by Sidney Fine. University of Michigan Press, Ann Arbor, 1969.

Heroes of an Untold Story, by Henry Kraus. University of Illinois Press, Urbana and Chicago.

John L. Lewis, by Melvyn Dubovsky and Warren Van Tyne. New York Times Books, New York, 1977.

The Many and the Few, by Henry Kraus. University of Illinois Press, Urbana and Chicago, 1988.

Ford: The Men and the Machine, by Robert Lacey. Little, Brown & Company, Boston and Toronto, 1986.

The Automobile Industry: The Coming of Age of Capitalism's Favorite Child, by Edward D. Kennedy. Reynal & Hitchcock, New York, 1941.

The Reminiscences of Nicholas Kelley. Oral Research History Office, Columbia University, 1952–1953.

"The Hammer Man," by Victor Shipway. *Chrysler Motors Magazine,* vol. I, no. 3, 1934.

"1931 Chrysler 6," by Michael S. Lamm. *Special Interest Autos,* no. 40, May–July 1977.

"The Men Who Make Chrysler Motors." Pamphlet, Chrysler Corporation.

Chrysler Motors Magazine, vol. I, no. 1, June 1934.

"Depression Nudges State into Lead on Unemployment Benefits," by Dennis McCann. *Milwaukee Journal-Sentinel*, March 12, 1998.

Obituary, Mario Savio; *New York Times*, November 8, 1996.

New York Times, January 27, 1937.

New York Times, February 28, 1937.

Detroit Free Press, March 16, 1937.

Detroit Free Press, March 24, 1937.

Detroit Free Press, March 25, 1937.

Detroit Free Press, March 26, 1937.

Detroit Free Press, March 29, 1937.

Detroit Free Press, April 4, 1937.

Detroit Free Press, April 5, 1937.

Detroit Free Press, April 6, 1937.

Detroit Free Press, April 7, 1937.

Detroit News, April 6, 1937.

Sources for Chapter 29

The Road Is Yours, by Reginald M. Cleveland and S. T. Williamson. The Greystone Press, New York, 1951.

The Dream Maker: William C. Durant, the Founder of General Motors, by Bernard H. Weisberger. Little, Brown & Company, Boston and Toronto, 1979.

Achievements by Leaders in World Affairs. American Educational Press, 1928.

Ford: The Men and the Machine, by Robert Lacey. Little, Brown & Company, Boston and Toronto, 1986.

My Years with General Motors, by Alfred P. Sloan. Doubleday, New York, 1983.

Chrysler Family History. Privately printed, 1959.

The Automobile Industry: The Coming of Age of Capitalism's Favorite Child, by Edward D. Kennedy. Reynal & Hitchcock, New York, 1941.

The Plungers and the Peacocks, by Dana L. Thomas. G. P. Putnam & Sons, New York, 1967.

Standard Catalog of American Cars, 1805–1942, 2nd ed., by Beverly Rae Kimes and Henry Austin Clark, Jr. Krause Publications, Iola, WI, 1989.

Plymouth, 1946–1959, by Jim Benjaminson. Motorbooks International, Osceola, WI, 1994.

The Mirrors of Wall Street, by Anonymous. G. P. Putnam & Sons, New York, 1933.

"1939 Chrysler Corporation Cars: Kissing Cousins," by Jim Benjaminson. *Collectible Automobile*, vol. X, no. 5, February 1994.

"1940–48 Chrysler: Pride of the K. T. Keller Years," by Tim Howler. *Collectible Automobile*, vol. X, no. 4, June 1993.

"I Like to Build Things," by Stephen Fox. *Invention & Technology*, summer 1999.

"General Motors and Chrysler," by Loring Dana, Jr. *The Magazine of Wall Street*, September 8, 1928.

Ward's Quarterly, winter 1965.

"The Dietrich Story, Part I," by Raymond H. Dietrich. *The Classic Car*.

"Ray Dietrich on Chrysler's Leadership," an interview with Richard M. Langworth.

"Ray Dietrich's Prolific Pen Helped Put the Class in Classic Car Bodies," Part II, by R. Perry Zavitz. *Best of Old Cars*, vol. V.

"Walter Chrysler: A Search for Self, a Stab at Immortality," by Bob Lipper. *The Virginian-Pilot (Lighthouse)*, July 3, 1977.

"The Strange Case of Walter Chrysler, Jr." *Confidential Magazine*, July 1955.

"Start Losing, K. T.," by Ronald J. Roberts. *Detroit Magazine*, April 4, 1971.

"Peggy Joyce's Big Switch," by J. Stanley Frew. *Confidential Magazine*, November 1954.

"Peggy Hopkins Joyce, Inc.," by David Grafton. *Forbes 400*, October 23, 1989.

"Golddigger," book proposal by Constance Rosenblum, May 1997.

"Leadership, a Message to America," lecture to the Newcomen Society by Fred M. Zeder, March 21, 1947.

"Walter P. Chrysler: The Man," speech given at a banquet in honor of Walter P. Chrysler by the Rev. J. Bradford Pengelly, rector, St. Paul's Parish, Flint, MI, at Flint Country Club, Flint, MI, January 22, 1920.

"Chrysler Enjoys 'Kick' in Sons' Hard Work," by James L. Kilgallen. *International News Service*, July 18, 1934.

"M. S. Rukuyser Tells Chrysler's Human Side in Review of Career." *New York Journal-American*, August 19, 1940.

Property of the Estate of Mrs. Della V. Chrysler (Mrs. Walter P. Chrysler), May 21, 22, 23, 1941. Parke-Bernet Galleries, Inc.

"The Prohibition Era." *Encyclopedia Britannica*, 1978.

Papers of Nicholas Kelley, New York Public Library.

C. C. Recordak microfilm #85, #88, #92; Chrysler Historical Foundation.

Federal Trade Commission Report on the Motor Vehicle Industry, June 5, 1939.

Letter to W. C. Durant from S. E. Neiller, January 8, 1940.

Letter to W. P. Chrysler from John J. Raskob, September 27, 1928.

Letter to Pierre S. du Pont from W. P. Chrysler, March 31, 1932.

Letter to Walter P. Chrysler, Jr. from T. J. Ross, February 28, 1940.

Letter to Bernice Garbisch from James C. Zeder, March 20, 1941.

Letter to Vincent Curcio from Joan French, February 22, 1999.

Interview with Cynthia Rupp, February 10, 1999.

Interviews with Earl Pritchett, Frank B. Rhodes, Sr., Frank B. Rhodes, Jr., Wendy Rhodes, Emeline Jones, Ben and Nancy Chester, Charles Worthington Stevens, Arthur Wheatley, John Lewis, and Jerome Mowbray, October 7, 1993.

Interview with Fred Zeder, Jr., November 12, 1993.

Interview with Charles Stewart Mott (Richard Scharchberg, interlocutor), June 7, 1972.

Interview with Aristo Scrobogna, March 12, 1994.

Out of the West, Part I, film produced by Irene Chrysler Harvey. Collection of Frank B. Rhodes, Jr.

Out of the West, Part II, film produced by Irene Chrysler Harvey. Collection of Frank B. Rhodes, Jr.

A House Party at Pokety, Chrysler family film. Collection of Frank B. Rhodes, Jr.

Our House at Great Neck, Summer, 1940, Garbisch family film. Collection of Frank B. Rhodes, Jr.

Through the Years, 1935, Garbisch family film. Collection of Frank B. Rhodes, Jr.

The Good Old Days, B.C. (Before Crash), Chrysler family film. Collection of Frank B. Rhodes, Jr.

Westward Bound to the Far East—Flashes of 1928, Chrysler family film. Collection of Frank B. Rhodes, Jr.

Round the World Jaunt, Chrysler family film. Collection of Frank B. Rhodes, Jr.

Turn Back the Calendar, October, 1929, Chrysler family film. Collection of Frank B. Rhodes, Jr.

Fortune, February 1937.

Chrysler Motors Magazine, July 1937.

Automotive Industries, September 2, 1934.

Automobile Topics, July 15, 1933.

Automobile Topics, August 26, 1940.

Detroit Free Press, March 4, 1932.

Detroit Free Press, June 20, 1936.

Detroit Free Press, May 8, 1938.

Detroit Free Press, May 29, 1938.

Detroit Free Press, August 19, 1940.

Detroit Free Press, August 20, 1940.

Detroit Free Press, August 21, 1940.

Detroit Free Press, August 25, 1957.

Detroit Free Press, March 9, 1962.

Detroit Times, July 3, 1960.

Detroit News, February 5, 1936.

Detroit News, August 25, 1940.

Detroit News, August 25, 1957.

Detroit News, June 29, 1970.

New York Herald Tribune, August 5, 1938.

New York Herald Tribune, August 19, 1940.

New York Herald Tribune, August 22, 1940.

New York Herald Tribune, August 28, 1940.

Mancato (Minn.) *Free Press,* August 22, 1940.

Amsterdam Evening Recorder, August 20, 1940.

New York Journal American, August 21, 1940.

New York Sun, August 27, 1940.

New York Times, January 5, 1930.

New York Times, July 3, 1930.

New York Times, May 31, 1931.

New York Times, June 1, 1931.

New York Times, June 10, 1931.

New York Times, January 26, 1932.

New York Times, March 8, 1932.

New York Times, April 19, 1932.

New York Times, May 20, 1932.

New York Times, October 9, 1932.

New York Times, November 24, 1932.

New York Times, November 25, 1933.

New York Times, December 8, 1933.

New York Times, September 15, 1934.

New York Times, February 15, 1935.

New York Times, March 15, 1935.

New York Times, August 16, 1935.

New York Times, August 22, 1935.

New York Times, October 16, 1936.

New York Times, October 29, 1936.

New York Times, February 13, 1937.

New York Times, March 2, 1937.

New York Times, May 29, 1938.

New York Times, August 11, 1938.

New York Times, December 5, 1938.

New York Times, June 21, 1939.

New York Times, December 5, 1939.

New York Times, December 29, 1940.

New York Times, March 31, 1941.

New York Times, May 23, 1941.

New York Times, January 11, 1942.

New York Times, December 10, 1944.

Index